Prehistoric Intertidal Archaeology in the Welsh Severn Estuary

Martin Bell, Astrid Caseldine and Heike Neumann

with a CD prepared by
Barbara Taylor and Heike Neumann

and major contributions by
J R L Allen, S J Allen, J Barrett, K Barrow, R N E Barton,
R Brunning, N Cameron, M G Canti, R Coard, J Crowther,
G M Cruise, S J Dobinson, P Q Dresser, J Foster,
Y Hamilakis, J Hillam, C Ingrem, J James, S Johnson,
R Macphail, S McGrail, R Morgan, P Osborne, J Parkhouse,
M P Richards, S Rippon, J Schelvis, R Schulting, D Smith,
B Taylor, D Upton, and A Woodward

D1437932

CBA Research Report 120
Council for British Archaeology
2000

Published 2000 by the Council for British Archaeology
Bowes Morrell House, 111 Walmgate, York YO1 9WA

British Library Cataloguing in Publication Data
A catalogue record for this book is available from the British Library

ISSN 0141 7819

ISBN 1 872414 11 7

Typeset by Archetype IT Ltd, Cheltenham, UK and Camplong d'Aude, France
web site http://www.archetype-it.com

Printed by York Publishing Services

This book is published with the aid of a grant from
Cadw: Welsh Historic Monuments

Front cover: Goldcliff: Rectangular Building 1 emerging from the retreating tide in August 1991 (Photo: M Bell)

Back cover: Goldcliff: Excavating a wall of rectangular Building 6 (Photo: L Boulton)

Contents

CHAPTER 1: INTRODUCTION TO THE SEVERN ESTUARY AND ITS ARCHAEOLOGY
by Martin Bell 1

CHAPTER 2: GOLDCLIFF ISLAND: GEOLOGICAL AND SEDIMENTOLOGICAL BACKGROUND
by J R L Allen 12

CHAPTER 3: INTRODUCTION TO THE HOLOCENE SEDIMENTARY SEQUENCE
by Martin Bell with John James and Heike Neumann 19

List of figures

List of tables

List of CD contents

Chapter 1   Introduction to the Severn Estuary and its archaeology

1.1   A memorandum describing the discoveries at Goldcliff on 31 October 1990, *by Bob Trett, Newport Museum*

1.2   A memorandum concerning a visit to Goldcliff on 2 November 1990, *by John Coles*

Chapter 2   No material on CD
Chapter 3   No material on CD

Chapter 4   The Goldcliff late Mesolithic site

4.1–4.2   The late Mesolithic assemblage, *by N Barton*

4.1   Goldcliff Mesolithic site (Contexts 1200, 1201, and 1202) classification of lithic finds, *by N Barton*

4.2   Goldcliff Mesolithic site: core types, *by N Barton*

4.3–4.7   Fish and bird remains, *by C Ingrem*

4.3   Fish species represented in sieved samples, *by C Ingrem*

4.4   Fish and bird species represented in hand collected material, *by C Ingrem*

4.5   Fish from samples according to species and element, *by C Ingrem*

4.6   Fish from hand collection according to species and element, *by C Ingrem*

4.7   Fish species representation according to sample, *by C Ingrem*

4.8–4.15   Micromorphological tabular data and plates from Mesolithic contexts, *by R I Macphail and G Cruise*

4.8   Key to soil micromorphology. This outlines the types of microfabric, structure, anthropic inclusion, clay, organic materials, and pedofeatures, *by R I Macphail and G Cruise*

4.9   Soil micromorphological features, *by R I Macphail and G Cruise.* The occurrence and abundance of microfabrics (M1–6b), structures (S1–5), anthropogenic inclusions (AI1–4), clay, organic materials (O1–5), and pedofeatures (P1–8) as defined on CD 4.8

4.10   Soil micromorphological plate Sample 2056, coarse wood charcoal (AI1) at base of massive grey estuarine clay (M1a), at junction with Mesolithic soil; note iron staining. Plane polarised light (PPL), frame length is 5.5cm, *by R I Macphail and G Cruise*

4.11   Micromorphological plate Sample 2056 as CD 4.10, crossed polarised light (XPL); note medium interference colours, *by R I Macphail and G Cruise*

4.12   Micromorphological plate Sample 2056; compact, reddish-brown burned loamy Mesolithic soil containing abundant charcoal (M2). PPL, frame length is 5.5cm, *by R I Macphail and G Cruise*

4.13   Micromorphological plate Sample 2056 as CD 4.12, XPL; note very low interference colours, *by R I Macphail and G Cruise*

4.14   Micromorphological plate Sample 2056; burned bone (AI2) within Mesolithic soil. Plane polarised light (PPL), frame length is 5.5cm, *by R I Macphail and G Cruise*

4.15   Micromorphological plate Sample 2056; XPL; bone has lost its birefringence, *by R I Macphail and G Cruise*

4.16–4.18   Phosphate and magnetic susceptibility studies, *by J Crowther*

4.16   Samples taken (1993 excavation) on a 0.5m grid from silty clay containing charcoal and bone (Context 1202) at the Mesolithic site, *by J Crowther*

4.17   Samples taken (1994 excavation) on a 0.5m grid from silty clay containing charcoal and bone (Context 1202) at the Mesolithic site, *by J Crowther*

4.18   Phosphate-P concentrations in bone samples from the Mesolithic and Iron Age sequences, *by J Crowther*

4.19–4.20   Charcoal from the Mesolithic site, *by A Caseldine and S Johnson*

4.19   Charcoal from the Mesolithic site, *by A Caseldine and S Johnson*

4.20   Table of charcoal from the Mesolithic site and Goldcliff East, *by S Johnson*

Chapter 5   Skull deposition at Goldcliff and in the Severn Estuary

5.1   (a) Craniometrics (mm) of the Newport crania, (b) Cranial and facial indices of the Newport crania. Accompanies report, *by R Schulting (data from Cowley 1961)*

5.2   Stable isotope results for human bone collagen from the Severn Estuary, *by R Schulting and M Richards*

Chapter 12 Wood and woodworking at Goldcliff *c* 400–1 BC
by R Brunning, S Johnson and R Morgan

Chapter 15 Other environmental evidence from Goldcliff
by R I Macphail and G Cruise

Chapter 16   The intertidal peat survey *by Heike Neumann*

Chapter 17   No material on CD

Summary

Wetland prehistoric sites dating between 5500 Cal BC and 200 Cal BC have been investigated in the intertidal zone of the Severn Estuary in Wales. A major sequence of peats and clays outcrops on the foreshore. Detailed survey and excavation has taken place on 3km of shore at Goldcliff. Here Mesolithic activity c 5500 Cal BC was concentrated on a palaeosol at the edge of a former bedrock island. Charcoal was widely distributed on the soil and there were areas of lithic debitage, small numbers of tools and bone. Seasonal winter hunting is suggested, especially of deer and pig with fishing particularly for eel. Extensive deer footprints on many sites in the estuary attest to the ecological richness of the coastal zone in this period and human footprints c 3km away point to fishing and hunting expeditions from this, or other, settlements.

Burning and temporary clearance episodes are attested by pollen and charcoal layers during various episodes between 5500 and 1800 Cal BC. Until about 1500 Cal BC peat development was extensive but there was limited evidence of prehistoric activity on the wetland. Sometime between 1450 and 550 Cal BC two human crania were deposited near the edge of the former Goldcliff island beside a small post structure, evidence elsewhere in the estuary also points to ritual deposition of human skulls between the Neolithic and the Iron Age. Innundation of the bog began around 1400 Cal BC. A small palaeochannel in clay postdating the peat was crossed by a short trackway which included two planks from a sewn boat the oaks for which, dendrochronology shows, were cut after 1170 BC.

A subsequent marine regression in the mid 1st millennium BC was associated with development of reedswamp and fen woodland fringing a raised bog which had escaped earlier innundation. The main concentration of prehistoric activity was associated with this mid-1st millennium BC peat. On the peat surface were rectangular buildings of average size 7m by 5m with rounded corners. In three cases some flooring survived, but hearths were absent and artefacts few. Building 1 had evidence of plank subdivisions. Environmental evidence, particularly beetles and mites, indicates that the building housed animals and there were many cattle footprints around two of the buildings. Dendrochronology shows that the wood for Building 6 was mostly cut in April / May 273 BC. Most of the Goldcliff buildings, trackways and other wood structures on the same peat outcrops have similar radiocarbon date ranges in the period 400–100 Cal BC. Eighteen trackways, mostly of brushwood, were investigated, some running between, or from, buildings, others crossing reedswamp, probably towards stream channels. The main activity seems to have been seasonal grazing of cattle in the coastal wetland; the presence of neonatal animals, tree ring evidence, seed heads of reeds and evidence of flooding between activity episodes indicates a concentration of activity between April and September. Wood for trackways was mainly winter cut demonstrating that some activities probably took place at other times of year. Diverse environmental sources, including pollen, plant macrofossils, beetles and diatoms shows that activity largely took place when the peat surface was experiencing the initial stages of a marine transgression which led to the demise of the bog in the 3rd century BC.

The Goldcliff evidence is put in a wider context by a survey of 25km of intertidal coast between Cardiff and the Second Severn Crossing. Peat outcrops, palaeochannels and other features in this intertidal area have been mapped using air photographs and the area has been fieldwalked to locate previous discoveries and new sites. Evidence of activity, usually associated with the surface of peat outcrops, becomes extensive from the middle Bronze Age. On three sites there are roundhouses of c 1400–900 Cal BC, that building type is typical of dry land structures of the last two millennia BC. At Redwick there are four rectangular structures dating between 1510–930 Cal BC. Thus the tradition of rectangular structures here, and at Goldcliff, lasted a millennium, and the type of structure we see here is otherwise unattested in British prehistory, although with parallels in mainland Europe. Short lengths of trackway cross minor palaeochannels in the peat surface. Many palaeochannels have post structures, three of which are radiocarbon dated between c 1400–400 Cal BC. At Cold Harbour Pill 2 a line of small posts ending in a circular woven basket was probably a fishing structure.

At Goldcliff and the other sites the specialised use of a great coastal bog from c 1500–c 250 Cal BC has been documented. On each of the main sites the activity seems to be concentrated during the early stages of marine transgressive phases highlighting the association between activity and coastal influences. Limited material cultural evidence on all sites points to temporary, perhaps seasonal, activity on the wetland mainly associated with cattle grazing. The role of fishing remains equivocal because, although there are many wood structures which could be fish traps, fish bones have not yet been found in post-Mesolithic contexts.

A new wetland perspective has been added to the later prehistory of Wales. It may relate to seasonal exploitation from dryland sites, however, there are also contrasts between the material culture of dryland and wetlands such as the rectangular structures and the largely aceramic nature of some wetland sites. The results demonstrate the complex and locally variable nature of later Holocene coastal sedimentary sequences, the contribution which archaeology can make to dating these sequences and the relationship between human activity and episodic environmental change. The text is supported by a CD containing the survey map base and associated databases and images.

Sommaire

Des sites préhistoriques des zones humides datant d'entre 5500 Cal avant J.-C. et 200 Cal avant J.-C. ont été étudiés dans la zone intercotidale de l'estuaire de la rivière Severn au Pays de Galles. Une importante séquence d'affleurements de tourbe et d'argile sur l'estran. Un levé détaillé et des fouilles furent effectués sur 3 km de rivage à Goldcliff. Ici, l'activité mésolithique d'environ 5500 Cal avant J.-C était concentrée sur un paléosol au bord d'une ancienne île du socle. Le charbon de bois était largement répandu sur le sol et il y avait des zones de débitage de pierre, des outils et os en petits nombres. La chasse hivernale saisonnière est suggérée, particulièrement du cerf et du cochon, et la pêche, en particulier pour l'anguille. De nombreuses empreintes de cerf sur de nombreux sites dans l'estuaire témoignent de la richesse écologique de la zone côtière à cette époque et des empreintes humaines à environ 3 km indiquent des expéditions de chasse et de pêche en provenance de ce peuplement au d'autres peuplements.

Des couches de pollen et de charbon de bois durant divers épisodes entre 5500 et 1800 Cal avant J.-C. témoignent d'épisodes de déblaiements temporaires et de brûlis. Jusqu'à environ 1500 Cal avant J.-C., le développement de la tourbe fut considérable mais il n'y avait que peu d'indices d'activité préhistorique dans la zone humide. Entre 1450 et 550 Cal avant J.-C., deux crânes humains furent déposés près du bord de l'ancienne île de Goldcliff à côté d'une petite structure en poteaux, des indices ailleurs dans l'estuaire indiquent également un dépôt rituel de crânes humains entre le Néolithique et l'Age de Fer. L'inondation du marécage commença à peu près en 1400 Cal avant J.-C. Un petit paléocanal en argile datant d'après la tourbe était traversé par une courte piste qui comprenait deux planches d'un bateau assemblé sans clous, dont les chênes avaient été coupés, comme l'indique la dendrochronologie, après 1170 avant J.-C..

Une régression marine fit suite au milieu du premier millénaire avant J.-C. et était associée au développement du marais de roseaux et des bois de marécage bordant une tourbière surélevée qui avait échappé à la dernière inondation. La principale concentration d'activité préhistorique était associée à cette tourbe du milieu du premier millénaire avant J.-C.. Il y avait des bâtiments rectangulaires sur la surface de la tourbe, de 7m x 5m en moyenne, avec des angles arrondis. Dans trois cas, il restait une partie du sol, mais il n'y avait pas de foyers et peu d'objets façonnés. Le bâtiment 1 contenait des indices de subdivisions en planches. Des indices liés à l'environnement, en particulier des hannetons et des mites, indiquent que le bâtiment abritait des animaux et il y avait de nombreuses empreintes de bétail autour de deux des bâtiments. La dendrochronologie indique que le bois pour le bâtiment 6 avait été coupé principalement en avril/mai 273 avant J.-C.. La plupart des bâtiments de Goldcliff, pistes et autres structures en bois sur les mêmes affleurements de tourbe avaient des plages similaires de datation au radiocarbone, dans la période de 400 à 100 Cal avant J.-C.. Dix-huit pistes, pour la plupart en brindilles, ont été étudiées; certaines allaient entre les bâtiments ou d'un bâtiment à un autre, d'autres traversaient le marais de roseaux, probablement vers des lits de cours d'eau. Le pâturage saisonnier du bétail dans les zones humides côtières semble avoir été l'activité principale ; la présence d'animaux nouveau-nés, les indices des cercles des arbres, les péricarpes de roseaux et les indices d'inondations entre épisodes d'activité indiquent une concentration de l'activité entre avril et septembre. Le bois pour les pistes avait principalement été coupé en hiver, indiquant que certaines activités avaient probablement lieu à d'autres saisons de l'année. Diverses sources liées à l'environnement, y compris le pollen, les macrofossiles de plantes, les hannetons et les diatomées, indiquent que l'activité eut lieu pour la plupart lorsque la surface de la tourbe fut soumise aux premières phases d'une transgression marine, laquelle aboutit à la disparition du marécage au troisième siècle avant J.-C..

Les indices de Goldcliff se situent dans un contexte plus large par un levé de 25km de littoral intercotidal entre Cardiff et le Second Severn Passage. Les photographies aériennes ont permis de dresser la carte des affleurements de tourbe, des paléocanaux et autres caractéristiques dans cette zone intercotidale et toute la zone a été arpentée afin de localiser les découvertes déjà faites et de nouveaux sites. Des indices d'activité, normalement liés à la surface des affleurements de tourbe, se multiplient considérablement à partir du milieu de l'âge de bronze. Sur trois sites, il y a des maisons rondes datant d'environ 1400 à 900 Cal avant J.-C., ce type de bâtiment est typique des structures sur terre sèche des deux derniers millénaires avant J.-C.. A Redwick, il y a quatre structures rectangulaires datant d'entre 1510 et 930 Cal avant J.-C.. Donc, la tradition des structures rectangulaires ici et à Goldcliff a duré un millénaire et il n'existe pas d'autres indices du type de structure que nous voyons ici dans la préhistoire britannique, bien qu'il y ait des parallèles en Europe continentale. De courtes longueurs de piste traversent de petits paléocanaux dans la surface de la tourbe. De nombreux paléocanaux ont des structures en poteaux dont trois ont une date au radiocarbone d'environ 1400 à 400 Cal avant J.-C. A Cold Harbour Pill 2, une rangée de petits poteaux se terminant en panier tissé circulaire était probablement une structure de pêche.

A Goldcliff et dans les autres sites, l'utilisation spécialisée d'un grand marécage côtier datant environ de 1500 à 250 Cal avant J.-C. a été documentée. Sur chacun des sites principaux, l'activité semble être concentrée pendant les premières phases de la transgression marine, soulignant les liens entre l'activité et les influences côtières. Des indices culturels matériels limités sur tous les sites indiquent une activité temporaire, peut-être saisonnière, dans les zones humides, principalement associée avec le pâturage du bétail. Le rôle de la pêche reste équivoque parce que, bien qu'il existe de nombreuses structures en bois qui pourraient être des genres de nasses, on n'a pas encore découvert d'arêtes de poisson dans des contextes post-mésolithiques.

Une nouvelle perspective sur les zones humides a été ajoutée à la fin de la préhistoire au Pays de Galles. Elle peut se rapporter à l'exploitation saisonnière des sites des zones sèches mais il y a également des contrastes entre la culture matérielle des zones sèches et des zones humides, comme les structures rectangulaires et la nature largement sans céramique de certains sites dans les zones humides. Les résultats démontrent la nature complexe et localement variable des séquences de sédiments côtiers de la fin de l'Holocène, la contribution que peut faire l'archéologie à la datation de ces séquences et les rapports entre l'activité humaine et les changements épisodiques dans l'environnement. Le texte est accompagné d'un CD avec la carte du levé ainsi que les bases de données et images qui s'y rapportent.

Zusammenfassung

Funde aus einem prähistorischen Moor im Gezeitenübergangsgebiet der Severn Mündung in Wales wurden auf den Zeitraum 5500–200 v.Chr. datiert. Bei Ebbe wird hier ein ausgedehnter Komplex aus Torf und Schlicklagen freigelegt. Mesolithische Funde von ca. 5500 v. Chr konzentrierten sich hauptsächlich auf einen Paläoboden am Rande einer Insel aus resistentem Gestein. Holzkohle und Feuersteindebitagen sind weitverbreitet und es wurden kleinere Funde von Werkzeugen und Knochen gemacht. Diese Überreste weisen wahrscheinlich auf Winterjagt hin, insbesondere auf Rotwild, Wildschwein und der Fischfang auf Aale. Die häufig vorkommenden prähistorischen Wildspuren bezeugen den ökologischen Reichtum der Küstenlandschaft aus dieser Zeit und menschliche Fusspuren in ca. 3 km Entfernung lassen uns vermuten dass Fisch- und Jagtausflüge von dieser oder anderen Siedlungen ausgingen.

Kurzzeitige Episoden der Brandrodung sind durch Pollenanalyse und Holzkohleüberreste in den Zeitraum 5500–1800 v. Chr. einzuordnen. Bis ca. 1800 v. Chr. war aktive Torfbildung weitverbreitet, es fanden such jedoch wenige Hinweise auf prähistorische menschliche Aktivität. Zwischen 1450 und 550 v. Chr. wurden zwei Schädelreste neben einer Holzpfostenstruktur am Rande der früheren Insel Goldcliff deponiert. An anderen Stellen der Severn Mündung gibt es ebenfalls Indikatoren für eine rituelle Hinterlegung von Schädelüberresten aus dem Neolithikum bis zur Eisenzeit.

Ab ca. 1400 v. Chr. begann die langsame Überflutung des Torfmoores durch den steigenden Meeresspiegel. Ein kleiner, mit Schlick gefüllter Entwässerungsbach wurde durch einen kurzen Bohlenweg überbrückt, der aus den wiederverwerteten Planken eines Nahtbootes konstruiert wurde. Dendrochronologische Untersuchungen haben ergeben, dass diese Planken nach dem Jahre 1170 v. Chr. gefällt wurden.

Der darauffolgende Meeresspiegelrückgang Mitte des ersten Jahrtausends v. Chr. ging mit der Entwicklung von Schilfmoor und Bruchwald einher, der sich am Rande des vom Meerespiegelanstieg verschont gebliebenen Hochmoores bildete. Mit diesem Meerespiegelrückgang begann die intensive prähistorische Nutzung des Moores. Auf dem, durch die Gezeiten freigelegten Torf aus dieser Zeit wurden acht rechteckige Hausumrisse von 7 m Länge und 5 m Breite mit abgerundeten Ecken entdeckt. In dreien dieser Hausumrisse war der Holzfussboden noch intakt, Feuerstellen fehlten allerdings und Begleitfunde waren spärlich. Im Gebäude 1 waren interne Abtrennungen durch Holzwände zu erkennen.

Archäozoologische Untersuchungen, insbesondere von Käfern und Milben deuten auf eine Stallnutzung der Gebäude hin, diese Interpretation wird durch Hufabdrücke von Rindern um zwei der Gebäude weiter gefestigt. Dendrochronologische Untersuchungen haben erwiesen dass das Bauholz für Gebäude 6 hauptsächlich im April/Mai 273 v. Chr. geschlagen wurde. Die meisten der Gebäude, Bohlenwege und diversen Holzstrukturen derselben Torflage haben eine ähnliche C14-Altersbestimmung von 400–100 v. Chr.. Achtzehn Bohlenwege, die meisten aus Reisiglagen konstruiert, wurden untersucht, sie verbinden Gebäude oder gehen von Gebäuden aus, andere überqueren Schilfmoor oder führen an Bäche heran. Die Haupttätigkeit scheint die saisonbedingte Nutzung von Weideflächen im Küstenfeuchtgebiet zu sein; die Präsenz von neonatalen Nutztieren, Jahresringen, Rohrsamen, und Hinweise auf zwischenzeitliche Überflutungsepisoden deuten auf eine Nutzung zwischen April und September hin. Das Holz für die Bohlenwege wurde hauptsächlich im Winter geschlagen, es waren also nicht alle Aktivitäten auf den Sommer beschränkt. Mit diversen archäobotanischen und archäozoologischen Methoden (zum Beispiel Pollenanalyse, botanische Untersuchung von Pflanzenresten, Analyse von Käfern und Diatomen) wurde gezeigt, dass die menschlichen Aktivitäten hauptsächlich dann stattfanden, als die Torfoberfläche durch die ersten Stadien des Meeresspiegelanstieg überflutet wurde. Diese Transgression führte schliesslich im dritten Jahrhundert v. Chr. zu dem Verfall des Hochmoores.

Die Studie über Goldcliff wird durch eine Begutachtung der Gezeitenübergangszone über eine Länge von 25 km, zwischen Cardiff und der Zweiten Severn Brücke, in einen weiteren geographischen und archäologischen Zusammenhang gebracht. Die durch die Ebbe freigelegten Torfschichten, Entwässerungsrinnen und Holzstrukturen wurden kartiert und vermessen, zum Teil mit Hilfe von Luftbildaufnahmen. Das gesamte Gebiet wurde durchlaufen um sowie bekannte Funde als auch Neuentdeckungen zu

beschreiben und kartieren. Diese Studie hat gezeigt, dass die menschliche Nutzung des Hochmoores mit der mittleren Bronzezeit begann. An drei Stellen wurden Rundhäuser auf 1400–900 v. Chr. datiert, ein Haustyp der auf dem Festland für die letzen zwei Jahrtausende v. Chr. typisch ist. Bei Redwick wurden vier rechteckige Hausstrukturen auf 1510–930 v. Chr datiert. Die Tradition der rechteckigen Hausstrukturen ist damit auf über ein Jahrtausend dokumentiert, eine Hausform die in der Britischen Vorgeschichte bisher unbekannt ist und deren parallelen nur auf dem Europäischen Festland zu finden sind. Kurze Bohlenwege überqueren seichte Entwässerungsrinnen die das Moor durchziehen. In vielen dieser Wasserrinnen sind Holzstrukturen erhalten, drei davon sind auf 1400–400 v. Chr. datiert. An der Fundstelle Cold Harbour Pill 2 war eine Reihe von Rundhölzern mit einem Korbgewebe verbunden, vermutlich ein Gerät zum Fischfang.

Die spezialisierte Nutzung dieses ausgedehnten Küstenhochmoors ist durch Goldcliff und die anderen Fundstellen für den Zeitraum von 1500–250 v. Chr. dokumentiert. Die Belege an den Hauptfundstellen deuten darauf hin, dass sich die Nutzung im Anfangsstadium der Meerestransgression intensiviert; der Zusammenhang zwischen Küstendynamik und menschlicher Nutzung wird dadurch hervorgehoben. Die Fundarmut in der Nähe der Holzstrukturen deutet auf vorübergehende oder jahreszeitlich bedingte Nutzung des Feuchtgebietes, hauptsächlich im Zusammenhang mit Viehhaltung. Die Rolle des Fischfangs bleibt bisher unbestimmt, es gibt zwar viele Holzstrukturen die als Reusen interpretiert werden können, aber bisher gibt es noch keine Funde von Fischknochen nach dem Mesolithikum.

Durch die intensive und multidisziplinare Untersuchung dieses Küstenmoores ist eine neue Perspektive in der spätprähistorischen Geschichte von Wales eröffnet worden. Zwar geht die jahreszeitlich bedingte Nutzung dieses Gebietes von Siedlungen auf dem Festland aus, es gibt jedoch wichtige Unterschiede im Fundmaterial die das Feuchtgebiet von dem Festland abgrenzen. Die Resultate dieser Studie veranschaulichen die Komplexität und lokale Variabilität der Spätholozänen Sedimentabfolge und den Beitrag den die Archäologie macht, indem sie diese Abfolgen datiert und die Beziehung zwischen menschlicher Nutzung und episodischen Umweltveränderungen veranschaulicht.

Der Text ist durch eine CD ergänzt die Karten, eine Datenbank und Bilder enthält.

Crynodeb

Ar y llain rhwng llanw a thrai (y gylchfa rynglanwol) yn aber afon Hafren yng Nghymru, archwiliwyd sawl safle tir gwlyb o'r cyfnod cyn hanes, yn dyddio rhwng 5500 Cal CC a 200 Cal CC. Yn brigo i'r wyneb ar flaen traeth, mae dilyniant sylweddol o fawndiroedd a chleiau. Am 3km hyd lan y môr yn Allteuryn, bu archwilio a chloddio manwl. Yma, yr oedd gweithgarwch Mesolithig oddeutu 5500 Cal CC wedi ei ganoli ar baleodir o gwmpas ymylon cynynys greigwely. Ar y tir, yr oedd sercol ar wasgar yn helaeth, a naddion cerrig, niferoedd bychain o arfau, ac esgyrn mewn sawl man. Awgrymir hela tymhorol yn ystod y gaeaf, yn enwedig hela ceirw a moch, a physgota, yn arbennig am lysywod. Mae olion helaeth traed ceirw ar lawer safle yn yr aber yn brawf o gyfoeth ecolegol y gylchfa arfordirol yn ystod y cyfnod hwn, a dengys olion traed dynol oddeutu 3km i ffwrdd bod teithiau hela a physgota wedi cychwyn o'r aneddiad hwn, neu aneddiadau eraill.

Mae haenau paill a sercol yn profi bod cyfnodau ysbeidiol o losgi a chlirio tir dros dro wedi digwydd yn ystod amryw gyfnodau ysbeidiol rhwng 5500 ac 1800 Cal CC. Tan oddeutu 1500 Cal CC yr oedd cryn ddatblygu ar y mawn ond tystiolaeth gyfyngedig a gafwyd o weithgaredd cyn hanes ar y tiroedd gwlyb. Rywbryd rhwng 1450 a 550 Cal CC, cafodd dwy benglog ddynol eu dyddodi yn agos at gyrion cynynys Allteuryn wrth ochr adeiladaeth bychan o bren, ac mae tystiolaeth o fannau eraill yn yr aber hefyd yn dangos bod dyddodi defodol wedi digwydd i benglogau dynol rhwng Oes Newydd y Cerrig a'r Oes Haearn. Dechreuodd y dŵr orlifo'r gors oddeutu 1400 Cal CC. Mewn clai a oedd yn ôl-ddyddio'r mawn, yr oedd paleosianel fechan, gyda sarn fer drosti a oedd yn cynnwys dwy astell o gwch gwniedig, ac yr oedd dendrocronoleg yn dangos bod y coed derw ar gyfer y llong wedi eu torri ar ôl 1170 CC.

Yr oedd ymgilio diweddarach y môr yng nghanol y mileniwm 1af CC yn gysylltiedig â datblygiad corsydd cawn a choetir corsiog, o gwmpas ymylon cyforgors a oedd wedi goroesi'r gorlifiad cynt. Yr oedd y prif weithgaredd cyn hanes yn gysylltiedig â'r mawn hwn a oedd yn dyddio o ganol y mileniwm 1af CC. Ar wyneb y mawn yr oedd adeiladau hirsgwar o faint canolig 7m wrth 5m, gyda chorneli crynion iddynt. Mewn tri achos yr oedd peth o'r llawr yn aros, ond nid oedd aelwydydd yno a phrin oedd yr arteffactau. Yn Adeilad 1 yr oedd yna dystiolaeth o ymrannu estyll. Dynoda'r dystiolaeth amgylcheddol, yn enwedig chwilod a gwiddon, bod anifeiliaid wedi byw yn yr adeilad, ac yr oedd llawer o olion traed gwartheg o gwmpas dau o'r adeiladau. Mae dendrocronoleg yn dangos bod y pren ar gyfer Adeilad 6 wedi ei dorri gan mwyaf ym misoedd Ebrill / Mai 273 CC. Yn achos y rhan fwyaf o adeiladau Allteuryn, y

sarnau, ac adeiladaethau pren eraill ar yr un tir mawn sy'n brigo i'r wyneb, pur debyg yw'r amrywiad yn eu dyddio radio carbon, sef rhwng 400– 100 Cal CC. Archwiliwyd deunaw o sarnau, o goed bychain gan mwyaf, a oedd yn rhedeg rhwng, neu o, adeiladau, gyda rhai eraill ohonynt yn croesi corsydd cawn, tuag at sianeli nentydd yn ôl pob tebyg. Ymddengys mai'r prif weithgaredd fyddai pori gwartheg yn dymhorol ar diroedd gwlyb yr arfordir; mae presenoldeb anfeiliaid newydd-anedig, tystiolaeth cylchoedd coeden, hadlestri pennau cawn, a thystiolaeth o lifogydd rhwng cyfnodau o weithgaredd yn dynodi bod y rhan fwyaf o'r gweithgarwch yn digwydd rhwng misoedd Ebrill a Medi. Ran fynychaf, torrwyd pren y sarnau yn y gaeaf, sy'n dangos bod rhai gweithgareddau'n digwydd ar adegau eraill o'r flwyddyn yn ôl pob tebyg. Mae amryw byd o ffynonellau amgylcheddol, gan gynnwys paill, macroffosilau planhigion, chwilod a diatomau, yn dangos bod gweithgaredd yn digwydd gan mwyaf pan oedd wyneb mawnog y tir yn mynd trwy gyfnodau cynnar gorlifiad y môr, a arweiniodd at dranc y gors yn ystod y 3edd ganrif CC.

Caiff tystiolaeth Allteuryn ei gosod mewn cyd-destun ehangach trwy gyfrwng arolwg a wnaed o 25km o'r arfordir rhynglanwol rhwng Caerdydd ac Ail Groesfan Afon Hafren. Mapiwyd mannau lle yr oedd mawn yn brigo i'r wyneb, paleosianelau, a nodweddion eraill yn yr ardal rynglanwol hon gan ddefnyddio ffotograffau a dynnwyd o'r awyr, a cherddwyd dros yr ardal gan weithwyr maes er mwyn dod o hyd i ddarganfyddiadau blaenorol a safleoedd newydd. Mae tystiolaeth o weithgaredd, yn gysylltiedig fel rheol â thir lle mae'r mawn yn brigo i'r wyneb, yn tyfu'n fwyfwy helaeth o ganol yr Oes Efydd ymlaen. Ar dair safle, mae tai crynion o tua 1400– 900 Cal CC, ac mae'r math hwn o adeilad yn nodweddiadol o adeiladaethau tir sych yn dyddio o'r ddau fileniwm olaf CC. Yn Redwick, mae pedwar adeilad hirsgwar yn dyddio o'r cyfnod rhwng 1510–930 Cal CC. Felly, yr oedd traddodiad yr adeiladau hirsgwar a gafwyd yma, ac yn Allteuryn, wedi para am fileniwm; ac nid oes unrhyw dystiolaeth arall ar gael o'r cyfnod cyn hanes ym Mhrydain o'r math o adeilad a welwn yma, er bod pethau cyffelyb ar gyfandir Ewrop. Mae sarnau byrion yn croesi paleosianeli bychain i mewn yn y mawn, yn agos at yr wyneb. Mae gan lawer o'r paleosianelau adeiladaethau o byst, gyda thri ohonynt â dyddiad radio-carbon oddeutu 1400–400 Cal CC. Wrth ymyl Caer Harbwr Oer 2, mae'n bur debyg mai teclyn pysgota oedd y llinell o byst bychain yn diweddu mewn basged gron wedi ei phlethu.

Yn Allteuryn ac ar y safleoedd eraill, mae'r defnydd arbennig a wnaed o gors fawr ar yr arfordir rhwng tua 1500– a thua 250 Cal CC wedi ei gofnodi. Ar bob un o'r prif safleoedd, ymddengys mai yn ystod cyfnodau cynnar gorlifiad y môr y byddai'r gweithgaredd mwyaf diwyd, gan danlinellu'r cysylltiad rhwng gweithgaredd a dylanwad glan y môr. Ar yr holl safleoedd, mae tystiolaeth gyfyngedig sy'n berthnasol i ddiwylliant yn arwydd o weithgaredd dros dro ar y tir gwlyb, yn dibynnu ar y tymor efallai, ac yn bennaf gysylltiedig â phori gwartheg. Mae swyddogaeth pysgota yn para'n ansicr oherwydd, er bod nifer o adeiladaethau pren a allai fod wedi cael eu defnyddio i ddal pysgod, nid oes unrhyw esgyrn pysgod wedi eu darganfod yn y cyd-destunau ôl-Fesolithig.

Ychwanegwyd gwedd tir gwlyb newydd i'r cyfnod cyn hanes diweddar yng Nghymru. Gall fod yn gysylltiedig ag elwa tymhorol o safleoedd tir sych, ond ceir gwthgyferbyniadau hefyd rhwng diwylliant materol y tir sych a'r tir gwlyb, megis yr adeiladaethau hirsgwar a natur rhai o'r safleoedd tir gwlyb, sydd heb grochenwaith ar y cyfan. Mae'r canlyniadau'n dangos natur gymhleth dilyniannau gwaddodol y cyfnod Holosen mwy diweddar ar hyd yr arfordir, ynghyd â'u hamrywiaeth yn lleol, yn ogystal â'r cyfraniad y gall archeoleg ei wneud i ddyddio'r dilyniannau hyn, a'r berthynas rhwng gweithgaredd dynol a newid ysbeidiol yn yr amgylchedd. Mae Cryno-Ddisg ar gael gyda'r testun, yn cynnwys map sylfaen yr arolwg, a databasau a delweddau cysylltiedig.

Preface: the report and CD

This is a report on prehistoric intertidal sites exposed by coastal erosion in the Welsh Severn Estuary from 1990–8. Chapter 1 introduces the project in the context of the history of work in the area. Chapters 2–15 are concerned with the detailed investigation of Mesolithic to Iron Age sites at Goldcliff from 1990–4 and extensive palaeoenvironmental studies of those sites. Goldcliff is then placed in a wider context by the Board of Celtic Studies intertidal survey of the Welsh Severn Estuary outlined in Chapter 16, that work mostly took place from 1995–8. Chapter 17 is a synthesis of evidence from both Goldcliff and the intertidal survey.

The published text is supported by a CD which is supplied with every copy. We are aware that not every reader will be able, or wish, to use the CD. Our intention is that the text can be read and understood without reference to the CD, which contains additional information supporting and extending the text. The CD is not an electronic version of the published text. The text provides the necessary explanation and context for the blocks of data available on the CD. The CD index contains the following sections: people (specialists and team members); maps; tables; documents; graphics; data supplementing specific chapters of the published report.

The core of the CD is a digital map base for the intertidal part of the Welsh Severn Estuary (a partial version of the maps is printed in Appendix 1) and supporting databases of sites and radiocarbon dates (Goldcliff dates only are printed in Appendix 2). The CD also contains 80 colour photographs which supplement the 34 black and white photographs in the printed report. An additional element of the CD is short profiles of the authors who have contributed to the publication, our view being that it may be helpful to the reader to know the background from which contributors have approached their work.

A further section of the CD contains 174 separate entries which provide supporting information to chapters of the printed report. There are c 80 tables on the CD (in addition to 31 in the printed text). Specialist readers are likely to need to consult the CD to obtain information on plant or beetle taxa and their ecology. There are also more complete pollen diagrams (those in the printed text are selected taxa). The CD also needs to be consulted for details of the stratigraphy of the pollen monoliths and zonation of pollen diagrams. The CD contains numerical information about bones and wood and illustrations of an additional 52 pieces of wood.

A full list of material on the CD which supplements the text is in the printed CD contents list. These entries are referred to in the text as CD 1.1 etc, that example being Chapter 1: first CD entry. To have published all this information in the conventional way would have taken two volumes and much greater post excavation resources than we had. To have published entirely using new technology would have restricted access and excluded many of those interested in intertidal archaeology. That subject has relied particularly on the commitment and local knowledge of non-professional archaeologists. The publication strategy we have adopted is a compromise which attempts to explore new ways of publishing archaeological work and we hope will meet the requirements of a range of readers. We hope also to have demonstrated the archaeological potential of the intertidal zone and to encourage those working in other areas to explore an aspect of coastal heritage which until recently has been surprisingly neglected.

Instructions for the operation of the CD *by Barbara Taylor*

Minimum systems requirements

- Hardware – minimum 386 processor with 4MB RAM or equivalent
- Double speed CD-ROM drive
- Ideal screen resolution – 1024 × 768 (minimum screen resolution – 800 × 600)
- 24 bit colour monitor
- Minimum Operating System – Windows 3.1 or equivalent
- Image enabled browser (see below)

Background

The concept behind the CD is that of a 'storyboard' which determines the overall structure, design and layout of thepresentation; the organisation of the data into main sections of related information, and the development of hierarchies that link the information together from a home page to the various topics. The framework is based on a hierarchical structure of data (similar to a family tree) and there are several ways to access information; a logical sequential route throughout the entire database; shorter pathways through each particular entity; or via loops which link attributes between and within sections. A thematic approach was decided upon, with the broad aims of simplicity and consistency in title, logo and link button layout to enable users to access information confidently. After the framework and navigation systems were created, all the data, whether text, graphics or tabular, were converted into html files.

Browsers

HTML stands for HyperText Markup Language and works differently from the standard WYSIWYG (What you see is what you get) format that is used in, for instance, Microsoft Word. In order to retrieve, display and read the files written in this language, you will need to have access to a Web browser. There is a wide array of browsers available for most platforms (Mac, Windows etc). Most machines now include one or other of these programs, or they can be downloaded either freeware or shareware from the Net. Popular ones include Netscape Navigator or MS Internet Explorer. The main function of a browser is to take the information from a particular file and to format and display it for your system. Please note that different browsers may format and display the same file differently, depending on the capabilities of that system and the default options for the browser itself. However, it must be stressed that whilst presentation and layout may therefore alter slightly, the data themselves are constant.

PIAWSE folder

All the files for the CD are held in the folder named PIAWSE (Prehistoric Intertidal Archaeology in the Welsh Severn Estuary). To access them, firstly, load and open the CD. You should now have access to a file labelled **startup.htm**. Opening this file acts as a shortcut route to reading the files in the logical sequence in which they were created. First time readers of the CD, in particular, are advised to follow this method and then proceed as below. (An alternative method would be to open the PIAWSE folder and open the index.htm file contained herein).

Links and hotspots

The sections are related through **link buttons**; **live links** (special key words) or areas called **hotspots**. The following is an explanation of how to navigate using the **link buttons** which are located at the head and foot of each page:

- Back – goes to the previous page in a section, or the last page of the section before
- Home – goes to the main index or title page
- Index – covers the section index relating to the relevant data
- Next – goes forward to the next page in a section, or the first page of the section following

Conversely, the back and forward buttons on your browser take you to the last page you were viewing, (and to the next page), regardless of its level in the hierarchy.

Use this method if you wish to read the CD sequentially. One exception is the Home Page, which does not contain these link buttons. You will therefore have to follow the live link method described below. The text of the **live links** is differentiated by a different colour. When the mouse is placed over such a link, the pointer will change to a hand and can be operated by clicking on it. Live links are to be found on most pages containing text and can be followed in a more abstract, or 'loop', fashion. In some cases, this will only take you to a certain level and then you are advised to follow the link button method as above.

Live links are also on the pages containing the map data and can be used in the same way as on pages containing primarily text. Also, within each map, are live areas known as **hotspots**. As with live links, the mouse pointer changes to a hand and the area can be activated by again clicking on it. It may take you to an enlargement of the area or to a graphic relating to it. Again, this route may take you to a certain level only and if you wish to proceed further, then you are advised to follow the link button method as above.

Home page

The **index.htm** file takes you to the Home Page. The data are subdivided into 10 main indices under the following headings:

- people – short profiles of the specialists and team members
- maps – includes digitally produced maps and plans. The basemap is the definitive database for the project and the other data sets are related to it. This shows the whole of the Welsh Severn Estuary but because of the scale, it is impossible to read the data. To overcome this, the basemap has been subdivided to allow an enlarged view of a particular area. You can either go to the table at the bottom of the map to view the area you require, or you can achieve the same effect by clicking on the many 'hotspots' within the map.
- tables – data in tabular format (c 80). Including lists of sites and radiocarbon dates. These are either supplementary to the printed report, or else provide complete tables.
- documents – entries which provide supporting information to the Monograph
- graphic images – graphics include 80 colour photographs and freehand drawings of, for instance, wood illustrations. (Digital plans are in the map section).
- Goldcliff and intertidal survey – this section is dedicated to the Goldcliff and other intertidal survey material supplementing specific chapters in the printed text, commencing at CD 1.1 right through to 16.13. Under this section are 3 subdivisions; the monograph headings (for ease of comparison); a full listing of the Goldcliff CD material itemised by entry no and heading and a unique Goldcliff alphabetical listing.
- alphabetical index – for all the material on the CD
- table of contents – each file is listed in a left hand frame with its data being correspondingly shown on the right
- bibliography (for CD only)
- system overview – for the more technically minded, an information management structure of the files and their relationships has been included

Acknowledgements

This report is dedicated to Derek Upton who discovered many of the sites described here. We are grateful to Derek for generously sharing his discoveries and for his help and companionship in the field.

The Goldcliff Project was largely funded by Cadw: Welsh Historic Monuments. We are grateful to Rick Turner for much help and encouragement as the Ancient Monuments Inspector responsible for work in the Severn Estuary. Other funding for work at Goldcliff came from the National Museums and Galleries of Wales, Newport Museum, the University of Wales, Lampeter and the European Social Fund.

For permission to work at Goldcliff we are grateful to the Crown Estate Commissioners and Mr Martin Hazell. For permission to work at Redwick we are grateful to Sir Richard Hanbury-Tennison. Many other landowners also granted permission or access at various stages of the work and are thanked for their help.

The Goldcliff project has benefited greatly from its advisors Professor John Allen FRS and Professor John Coles FBA and we are grateful to both, and to Rick Turner, for their rapidly produced comments on an earlier draft of this monograph which were most helpful in preparing a revised text. We were not able to make every change they suggested but their advice has helped us to produce a briefer and more focused report.

Bob Trett, Kate Hunter and Newport Museum are thanked for their support of the project, particularly the provision of a wood store and work space in Newport. Jonathan Parkhouse carried out the initial work for Glamorgan–Gwent Archaeological Trust, establishing the date and importance of the site; we are grateful to him and the Trust for help in bringing the report to publication.

Those who carried special responsibilities in the field were as follows: Steve Allen (1992–4); Peter Bewers (1993–4); Lesley Boulton (1994); Richard Brunning (1991); Kath Buxton (1991–3); Ray Caple (1993–4); Kath Dowse (1992); Nicky Evans (1994); Jennifer Foster (1991–4); Jan Grove (1991, 1994); Ian Halfpenny (1994); Katherine Henry (1992–3); Hazel Riley (1991–3); Jenni Heathcote (1991); John James (1991–4); Su Johnson (1992–4); Gareth Longden (1993–4); Geoff Morris (1991); Susan Ripper (1991–4); Andrea Selly (1991–4); Robin Taylor-Wilson (1992–4); Bill Timmins (1991–4); Cressida Whitton (1994). Catering for the team was in the capable hands of Moira Woods (1991) and Ben Lowe and Jeanette Ward (1992–4).

An important contribution was made by teams from the Wetland Archaeology Training Scheme financed by the European Social Fund and organised by University College Dublin and Exeter University.

That team played a key role in recording the wood structures revealed by the storm of 1992. Dr Caroline Earwood and Professor Barry Raftery facilitated involvement by the Dublin team.

Others involved in the fieldwork were:

1991: C Ambrose; A Edwards; G Fincham; D Ingram; N Ledwith; A Macintyre; N Smith; T Smith; L Stephens; M Stephens; M Prescott; L Probert; G Sinclair; M Vaughan-Brown; J Ward.
1992: C Cross; M Grute; R Haslam; N Hawksley; B Hensman; K Hodgson; E Jefcoate; B Mosley; J Murphy; J Rawson; J Sharpe; M Stewart; Z Taylor; K Venus; J White; N Wigfield; E Yorath.
Dublin team: C Jordan; E O'Donovan; J Taafe; M McAlinney; O Brierly; J Whitaker; J Hickey; M Deevy.
1993: E Clarke; D Davies; J Dobson; T Eatock-Taylor; J Gidlow; G Glover; M Grute; G Hall; B Hensman; S Holman; A Howells; S Jackson; R Nixon; D Stansfield; P Wilson.
Dublin team: S Cafferkey; J Corlett; E Byrnes; G Morris; A-M Murphy; G Plunkett; C Trace; K Stephens.
1994: C Anderson; J Beresford; I Clews; C Cross; K Cuthell; D Druce; H Dyer; S Foster; J Gidlow; D Guest; I Halfpenny; A Heck; T Herron; M Iversen; S Kemp; T Kluge; J Moore; W Morgan; J Murphy; D Platt; S Taylor; M Tomozawa; A Wallace; P Wilson; N Wigfield.

The local community at Goldcliff and Witson made us most welcome each summer. Mr Martin Hazell is particularly thanked for granting access and help. The Community Hall at Witson was an ideal base and campsite for this project and we are grateful to the local community who made this possible, particularly Mrs Jill Jones and Mrs Bev Williams. We are also grateful for the accommodation and access provided by Gerald and Hilary Walters.

The project has benefited greatly from the involvement of many dedicated and talented individuals who made specialist contributions; they are listed on the title page. These specialists have stuck with the project and delivered reports despite the fact that funding was often very limited.

Particular assistance has been provided at the post-excavation stage by Ms Nicky Evans (1991–4); and Mrs Barbara Taylor (1994–9). Barbara is particularly acknowledged for her key role in developing the digital map and plan base, which was originally established by Heike Neumann. Barbara has prepared the CD for publication, involving a workload very substantially greater than that for which we were able to secure funding. We are also grateful to Peter Griffiths for his help with the CD. Other major post excavation contributions have been made by Steve Allen; Richard Brunning; Kate Barrow; Dr Jennifer Foster; Mrs Barbara Garfi; John James and Mrs Su Johnson. We are grateful to the late Dr Barbara Noddle for undertaking initial work on the animal bones. Wood conservation has been undertaken by Philip Parkes at University of Wales, Cardiff. Dr P Q Dresser provided many of the radiocarbon dates. Collaboration with the Oxford AMS Laboratory on dating programmes on human skulls and Mesolithic samples is also acknowledged. Martin Bell also acknowledges the help and forebearance of his daughters Eleanor and Sarah.

The Board of Celtic Studies of the University of Wales played a key part in funding the intertidal survey carried out by Heike Neumann. Without the establishment of a digital map base and databases the Goldcliff project could not have been brought to completion and it would not have been possible to place the results from Goldcliff in a wider setting. A contribution towards the fieldwork costs of the intertidal project was also made by Cadw. The Board of Celtic Studies project was monitored by an advisory committee chaired by Dr S Aldhouse-Green comprising Professor J Allen, Professor J Evans, Dr Heike Neumann and Dr M Bell. We are also grateful to the Board of Celtic Studies and particularly the chairman Professor Geraint H Jenkins for encouragement.

The intertidal survey was mainly conducted by Heike Neumann and Derek Upton with help from Ian Halfpenny. For the recording of key areas larger teams assisted for short periods and those who helped are as follows:

1995: I Clews; J Gidlow; J James; G Longden; J Murphy; P Woodham; T Woodham.
1996: D Anderson; I Clews; K Edwards; N Evans; I Halfpenny; D Lewis; J Murphy; H Neumann; E Sacre.
1997: S Allen; I Clews; J James; H Neumann; H Riley; B Taylor.
1998: S Allen; I Clews; C McOwen; M Redding; E Sacre.

The writer and the project have benefited greatly from those who have introduced him to the wetland archaeology of other areas particularly Professors John and Bryony Coles (WARP); Dr Helmet Schlichtherle and Dr Bodo Diekmann and colleagues in Landesdenkmalamt Baden-Wurttemberg; Professor L Louwe Kooijmans and Professor W Groenman-van-Waateringe and colleagues in the Netherlands; Professor Barry Raftery and Aiden O'Sullivan in Ireland and many colleagues in Denmark. With fellow members of the Severn Estuary Levels Research Committee it has been exciting exploring a new and developing area of archaeology. Many members have contributed in a variety of ways in addition to those mentioned elsewhere, the interest and collaboration of Dr Stephen Rippon, Nigel Nayling and Martin Locock should be particularly mentioned. Collaboration with Professor M J C Walker on pollen studies in the Severn Estuary has also contributed to the wider picture.

M Bell did much of the fieldwork for this project whilst based at the University of Wales, Lampeter and is grateful for the facilities provided by that institution where Astrid Caseldine is still based. In 1997 M Bell moved to the Archaeology Department at Reading University which is thanked for providing a light year of teaching which made it possible to complete this report. Reading University also provided drawings and many other facilities. Astrid Caseldine is particularly thanked for the additional administrative responsibility she has carried since M Bell's departure to Reading.

For permission to reproduce images in this monograph we are grateful to the Royal Society of London and Professor J R L Allen (Fig 3.1); The Royal Commission on the Ancient and Historical Monuments of Wales (Fig 1.2); and Aerofilms Ltd (Fig 16.4). Editorial work at the CBA has been done by Mrs Barbara Morris and Ms Kate Sleight to whom we are most grateful for their care and help.

For those involved this project was something of an intertidal voyage of discovery. Often conditions were difficult, we were beset (and helped) by storms, frequently dwarfed by the size of the task in relation to the availability of resources and most of the time the landfall of completion seemed a very distant prospect. That much was, in the end, achieved is testimony to the positive spirit and collective efforts of those acknowledged above.

Martin Bell

1 Introduction to the Severn Estuary and its archaeology *by M Bell*

1.1 Introduction

Occasional storms sweep away the mud from the Severn Estuary foreshore and at low tide reveal a succession of remarkable prehistoric landscapes. This report is about a waterlogged prehistoric landscape at Goldcliff in South Wales and a wider survey of the prehistoric intertidal archaeology of the Welsh Severn Estuary as a whole.

At low tide, during periods of reduced mud cover, you can walk for kilometres along a narrow exposed transect of prehistoric landscape represented by peat shelves exposed in the intertidal zone. Such a walk passes through former swamp, fen woodland and bog. One encounters individual trees, stream and river channels, the footprints of animals and people. There are the waterlogged remains of prehistoric roundhouses and rectangular buildings. Wood trackways provide evidence of patterns of prehistoric communication. In stream channels are arrangements of wooden posts which probably represent the remains of fishing structures. No encounter with a prehistoric landscape could, at times, be more vivid.

The archaeology consists, not of the traditional pottery, metalwork and postholes, but largely of waterlogged wood structures preserved within sediments, particularly peats. They also preserve a wide range of palaeoenvironmental evidence, particularly pollen, plant macrofossils and insects. The sediment sequence which is exposed on the foreshore is one of the most complete Holocene records in Britain. The area is unique in northwest Europe in terms of the scale of Holocene exposures (John Allen personal communication). That affords special opportunities for investigation of the relationship between prehistoric ways of life and environmental changes within a highly dynamic environment. This monograph concentrates on the parts of that sequence between 7000 BP and the Roman conquest.

Severn Estuary discoveries are adding a new dimension to the archaeology of Wales and western Britain. The types of site, and the range of activities and artefacts are very different from those on neighbouring dryland. The Bronze Age roundhouses we find on the intertidal peats may be familiar from dryland contexts, but rectangular buildings of the Bronze and Iron Ages, and many of the other wooden structures, probably reflect specifically wetland activities. This highlights the richness and diversity of the wetland archaeological resource, which, over the last 30 years, archaeologists have increasingly come to appreciate (Coles and Coles 1989).

The Severn Estuary Levels were, until the mid-1980s, almost totally unknown to archaeologists. Maps showing the distribution of Welsh archaeological sites published in 1980 contain no hint of what has subsequently emerged (Taylor 1980). That this situation has changed so dramatically is largely due to the activities of one person, Derek Upton, by profession a skilled steelworker from Llanwern, who, through a lifetime's intimate knowledge of the estuary, came to appreciate the significance of the things he observed and has shared his knowledge and enthusiasm unstintingly with many archaeologists and scientists. Upton found most of the sites reported here and has been closely involved in their subsequent study. He has demonstrated, probably more clearly than anybody else in recent decades, the enduring contribution of the amateur in modern archaeology. This volume is dedicated to Derek Upton and we are pleased that on 18 April 1998 he was awarded an honorary MA of the University of Wales in recognition of his contribution to Welsh archaeology and natural history (SELRC 1998).

1.2. Geographical context of the Severn Estuary and Goldcliff

The geography and environmental processes of our study area are dominated by the inlet of the Bristol Channel and the Severn Estuary at its head (Fig 1.1). The Bristol Channel narrows rapidly to the east and at the entrance to the Severn Estuary between Brean Down and Lavernock Point, Cardiff it is 17km wide. The mouth of the Rumney (or Rhymney) River just east of Cardiff is the western limit of our survey area. At Goldcliff, the principal site considered here, the channel is 9.2km wide and by the Second Severn Crossing, the eastern limit of our survey area, it has narrowed to 3.4km. The estuary continues to narrow to the northeast, reaching its tidal limit near Gloucester. Upstream, the River Severn and its many tributaries drain a substantial area of the English Midlands, Welsh Marches, and the eastern flank of the Cambrian Mountains.

The comparatively straight, embanked, and clearly defined shore of the Severn Estuary, as we see it today, differs from what existed earlier in the Holocene. Shaded areas on Figure 1.1 show areas of peats and clays, which were subject to marine influence of fluctuating extents during the Holocene. On the English side a dune system forms the coast between Sand Point and the Parrett Estuary; behind

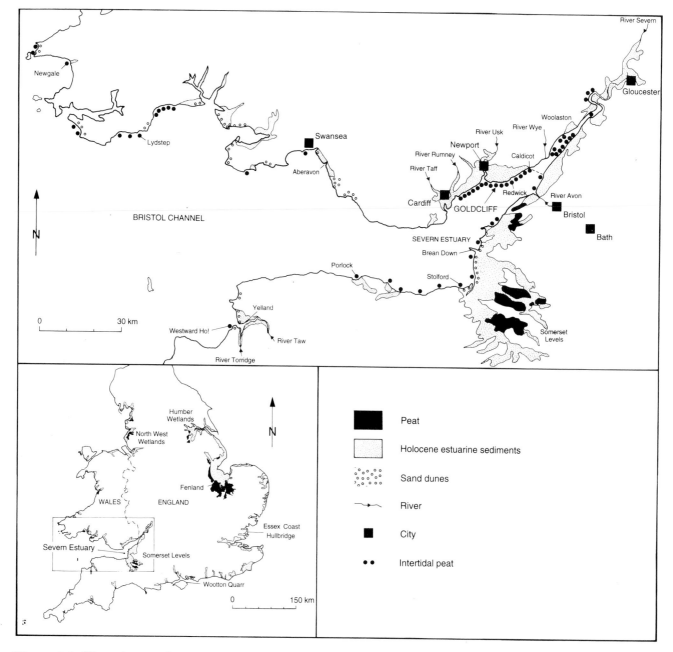

Figure 1.1 The submerged peats, coastal bogs, and sand dunes of the Severn Estuary showing key archaeological and palaeoenvironmental sites

this are reclaimed clay levels with peats inland. On the Welsh side there is no substantial dune or shingle bar. Here, Holocene sediments have been cut into by later Holocene marine erosion creating a series of low cliffs, of which the upper part is now partly masked by seawalls. The two main areas of coastal levels, the Wentlooge Levels to the west of the Usk, and the Caldicot Levels to its east, are clay lands. Together they form the Gwent Levels, an area 42km × 5.5km. The surface clays conceal a complex alternating sequence of peats and clays exposed by erosion in the intertidal area and in deep excavations into the reclaimed levels. The clays represent phases when marine influence extended further inland than it does today, the peats periods of reduced marine influence, when terrestrial plant communities extended further seaward than they do today. Several

periods of peat development occurred between 6500 and 3000 radiocarbon years BP and for much of that time there existed on the Welsh side a vast peat bog mirroring the better known and more intensively studied examples on the English side in the Somerset Levels. The Welsh bog is almost entirely buried and hidden below later marine clays.

This great estuary has the second highest tidal range in the world, 14.8m at Avonmouth. Thus, at low tide a very wide intertidal area is exposed. In the Welsh estuary as a whole this is mostly about 1km wide at mean low water but much wider at low water spring tides. In the Bedwin Sands area the mean low water intertidal area reaches a width of 5.8km. Before reclamation it is probable that, during periods of greatest marine influence, the intertidal area would in many areas have been 4–6km wide, a vast landscape offering a diversity of zoned resources reflecting the frequency of marine inundation.

Within the estuary there are islands, Flat Holm and Steep Holm at its mouth and the tiny Denny Island off Avonmouth. Prior to Holocene sedimentation and reclamation, and at times of greatest marine influence, there would have been other islands rising from the periodically inundated coastal wetland. On the English side are Brean Down, Worlebury, Sand Point, and Aust. On the Welsh side we know of only one former bedrock island at Goldcliff, but others could be buried within the Holocene sequence. In Chapter 2, John Allen considers the geomorphological evidence for the formerly greater extent of the Goldcliff Island. The island margins are partly buried by Holocene sediments and the archaeological sites at Goldcliff, which form the core of this monograph (Chapters 3–15) extend from the edge of this island for 1.5km to the west and are associated with intertidal peat shelves (Fig 1.2). A wider survey of the intertidal archaeology, mostly exposed on peat shelves between Cardiff and the Second Severn Crossing, is reported in Chapter 16.

1.3 Early archaeological and palaeoenvironmental research in the Severn Estuary and Bristol Channel

Archaeological discoveries in the Welsh Severn Estuary are very recent, but intertidal archaeology can claim a far longer pedigree in the Bristol Channel area. In AD 1170 Giraldus Cambrensis (c 1191, 1908 edn) observed a submerged forest at Newgale, Pembrokeshire. Such sites excited the curiosity and speculation of many writers during the formative period of geology and archaeology in the 18th and 19th centuries when finds began to be made at Westward Ho! (Risdon 1811), where subsequent work has produced a Mesolithic midden, (Balaam et al 1987), nearby Yelland with its intertidal prehistoric stone row (Rogers 1946), and Porlock where Boyd-Dawkins (1870) discovered flints in a submerged forest.

From 1885 flintwork was being found below, and within, the submerged forests of Pembrokeshire and in this area many discoveries were reported by Leach between 1909 and 1951 (eg Leach 1918); more recently this Mesolithic evidence from Pembrokeshire has been reviewed and put in an environmental context by Lewis (1992). The first hint of the coastal zone's potential for the finding of wooden artefacts was a Neolithic polished stone axe in a birchwood handle from coastal peats at Aberavon, Glamorgan (Savory 1980a, 212).

A 19th and very early 20th century boom period for shipping in the Bristol Channel led to the digging of deep docks which enhanced understanding of the Holocene sediment sequences and revealed buried archaeology. The expansion of Newport Dock, for instance, revealed the remains of a boat, which we now know is early medieval (Morgan 1878, Hutchinson 1984), and a human skull and other bones. Other skulls were reported from the making of docks at Aberavon and Avonmouth, and these skull finds are reviewed in Chapter 5. The making of Barry Docks revealed part of a flint axe and two possible bone needles in the uppermost peat (Wheeler 1925, 279).

The 18th to early 20th century discoveries from the submerged forests, and the later spate of dock constructions, provided the foundation of a national survey Submerged forests (Reid 1913). Apart from Leach's long-term work in Pembrokeshire, the intertidal zone received little archaeological attention in the first 80 years of the 20th century. Palaeoenvironmental interest was limited and focused mainly on the submerged forests as sources of evidence for vegetation history (eg Godwin 1943), coastal change (North 1955), and changing sea levels (Hawkins 1971 and 1973).

1.4 Wetland projects and intertidal archaeology

During the 19th century discoveries began to be made in the Somerset Levels; the Abbot's Way in 1834 was followed by the Lake Village discoveries of Bulleid and Gray which began in 1893 and continued until 1956. This archaeological activity was complemented by Godwin's work on vegetation history (eg Godwin 1960). Excavations were resumed under John and Bryony Coles from the mid-1970s and this developed into the English Heritage Somerset Levels Project, which ran from 1973 until c 1989 and was the first of a series of major English Heritage wetland archaeology projects. Then followed projects in the Fenland (1981–88), the North West Wetlands (1990–98) and the Humber Wetlands (1992–2000). Each project has been concerned substantially with Holocene sedimentary sequences which were the result of coastal and sea level change, but none has concentrated much on the intertidal zone. The potential of this zone has long been apparent from the previously noted discoveries in the Bristol Channel, finds on the Essex coast (Warren et al 1936), and Bronze Age boat finds from the 1930s on the Humber at Ferriby (Wright 1990). The first detailed demonstration of the intertidal zone's potential for prehistoric research was by Wilkinson and Murphy (1995) on the Essex coast and subsequently by work in the Severn Estuary, summarised here, and the north coast of the Isle of Wight (Tomalin et al forthcoming). Growing awareness of the archaeological potential of the coastal zone has developed in parallel with concern about coastal management and the possible effect of a range of development pressures, including sea defence upgrading. In response to these concerns English Heritage commissioned a literature and SMR based survey of the archaeology of England's coasts (Fulford et al 1997). A rather different survey was commissioned in Wales involv-

4

e→
d→
c→
b→
a

*Figure 1.2   Goldcliff: showing the former island and intertidal area with outcropping peat exposures (a)
Goldcliff bedrock 'island' with recent fish traps extending seaward in the foreground, (b) Mesolithic site, (c)
boat plank site, (d) Buildings 1–3 area, (e) Goldcliff West. Photograph by Chris Musson, Crown copyright
Royal Commission on the Ancient and Historic Monuments of Wales*

ing the creation of regional inventories of coastal sites which involved some field examination (Yates 1995); the last of the regional inventories was completed in 1998 and concerns the area covered by this volume (Locock 1998c).

1.5 Intertidal and wetland archaeology in the Severn Estuary

Recent finds at Goldcliff were prefigured in 1878 by the finding of the inscribed Roman Goldcliff Stone on the foreshore eroded from a cliff and reported by Octavius Morgan (1882), a polymathic local antiquary (Dictionary of Welsh Biography 1940). Almost a century later came a pioneering paper by Locke (1971) which draws on borehole evidence to demonstrate a clay–peat–clay sequence below the reclaimed levels, linking the peat exposures with submerged forests in the intertidal zone. Locke summarises what was then known of the archaeology. In the 1950s and 1960s finds of Roman pottery had been reported on the foreshore at Cold Harbour Pill in 1950 (Nash-Williams 1951), and at Magor (Boon 1967), as well as on the seawall at Goldcliff in 1961 (Boon 1961) and below the reclaimed levels at Uskmouth power station in 1959 (Barnett 1961). At this stage the stratigraphic context of these finds remained unclear. Boon (1967, 126) discussed the Magor finds and reviewed the evidence as a whole (Boon 1980), hypothesising the existence of Romano-British drainage and a seawall.

The first prehistoric find from the Welsh intertidal area seems to have been a barbed-and-tanged arrowhead picked up on the beach of West Pill (Savory 1954). In 1979 Upton made his first discoveries. A Bronze Age spearhead at Portland Grounds and a wooden roundhouse at Chapeltump were the first of a steady stream of finds reported to the National Museum of Wales and Newport Museum, a stream which has now continued for 19 years.

During the 1980s the sedimentological studies of Professor John Allen led to the identification of an estuary-wide Holocene sedimentary sequence (Allen 1987a, Allen and Rae 1987) which is introduced in Chapters 2 and 3. Allen's work developed an increasing archaeological emphasis in order to refine the chronology of the sequence. Fieldwork at Rumney Great Wharf showed that extensive evidence of Romano-British activity and drainage ditches was stratified in the upper part of the Holocene sediments (Allen and Fulford 1986, Fulford et al 1994).

A key factor at this time was the conjunction between Upton's discoveries on the intertidal peats and Allen's sedimentary sequence which provided an overall chronology and showed that the peats were prehistoric. Growing awareness of the significance of these archaeological finds and concern about the possible effects on them of a proposed Severn Tidal Barrage led, in 1985, to the formation of the Severn Estuary Levels Research Committee (SELRC). Its objective was to coordinate the activities of the many

organisations and individuals which had an interest in the archaeology of the estuary. The committee seeks to encourage research by constituent organisations, and individuals, and provides a forum for the discussion of results and research problems. Since 1990 the committee has published an annual report which presents ongoing research (SELRC 1990–98).

In 1986 Alasdair Whittle carried out limited excavations on three sites discovered by Upton at Chapeltump, Cold Harbour and a palaeochannel at Magor Pill (Whittle 1989). Green (1989) concurrently prepared a synthesis of the individual prehistoric artefact finds from the intertidal area.

Proposals for the Severn Barrage led to a wide-ranging environmental impact assessment in 1988, which included an archaeological survey. This provided an opportunity for some limited fieldwork and a synthesis of what was known at that time. A summary of the results was included in the multidisciplinary environmental assessment (Severn Tidal Power Group 1989). The full report on the Welsh side of the Estuary (Whittle and Green 1988) was not published, although the important sites are covered in Whittle (1989), Green (1989), and a later report on Mesolithic footprints (Aldhouse-Green et al 1992). In the event, plans for the Severn Barrage were put into abeyance for economic reasons, but development pressures of other kinds proliferated. A barrage across Cardiff Bay led to a need for amelioration measures: a large nature reserve as Alternative Bird Feeding Grounds. For this purpose an area at Rumney was considered and assessed in terms of archaeological implications (Parkhouse and Parry 1990). Subsequently, that site was abandoned in favour of a far larger reserve on a coastal strip between Goldcliff and Uskmouth. Here archaeological work in advance of the making of the reserve continues at the time of writing.

Discovery of a Bronze Age site in the clay levels of the Nedern Valley at Caldicot in 1987 led to a programme of excavation of a complex of wooden structures, some dendrochronologically dated, and fragments of boats (Nayling and Caseldine 1997). Construction of a new bridge, the Second Severn Crossing and its approach roads, was preceded by archaeological work on the Levels behind the seawall on the English side (Barnes 1993) and on the Welsh side by archaeological assessment, both on the reclaimed levels (Parkhouse 1991b, Ferris and Dingwall 1992) and by work in the intertidal zone, where there was important evidence of medieval fish traps (Godbold and Turner 1993, 1994). Archaeological assessment of a site for industrial development on the reclaimed clay levels at Barland's Farm produced evidence of a Romano-British site and a well preserved boat (Nayling et al 1994). Another boat, this time of medieval date and dendrochronologically dated to AD 1240, was found by Upton in the intertidal zone at Magor Pill in 1994 (Nayling 1998). In 1990 Stephen Rippon embarked on a long-term study of settlement patterns, reclamation and drainage of the Levels on both the English and Welsh sides from the Romano-British period to the present (Rippon 1993 and 1997). That study included a detailed analysis of the clay levels landscape behind the seawall on the Welsh side; it, thus, complements the present study by providing an account of landscape evolution in the post-prehistoric period (Rippon 1996a).

In terms of palaeoenvironmental research, particularly influential are the many papers by John Allen on the sedimentary sequence. Realisation of the area's potential for other forms of palaeoenvironmental analysis took longer. Caseldine's (1990, fig 11) survey of *Environmental archaeology in Wales* shows a distribution of pollen sites which is overwhelmingly inland and upland. There were just three sites in the estuary: Hyde's (1936) study of peats at East Moors Cardiff, work by Blackford (1990) on peats from the Alternative Bird Feeding Ground site at Rumney, and the work of Smith and Morgan (1989) at Goldcliff. Now the situation is very different, with twenty new pollen diagrams from Goldcliff (Chapter 13), other long Mesolithic to Bronze Age diagrams from the Second Severn Crossing at Vurlong Reen and Barland's Farm (Walker *et al* 1998), and shorter diagrams from five other sites.

Thus, although the Welsh Severn Estuary was a virtual blank on archaeological maps until the mid-1980s, there has been a tremendous increase in finds since. In terms of published results work has been particularly productive in relation to settlement patterns, reclamation, drainage, fishing, and boat transport of the Romano-British to medieval periods. Important work on prehistoric sites had been done, on the inland levels at Caldicot (Nayling and Caseldine 1997), and, on a relatively modest scale, in the intertidal zone by Whittle (1989), Green (1989), Aldhouse-Green *et al* (1992), Trett and Parry (1986), and Allen (Allen 1996a and b, Allen and Rippon 1997). The work reported here was designed to build on what they had achieved and provide a synthesis and palaeoenvironmental context for the prehistoric period.

1.6 Development of work at Goldcliff

Figure 1.3 shows the location of the main sites investigated and the pattern of fieldwork from 1987 to 1997. Following the formation of the SELRC, Professor Alan Smith, a noted pioneer of palaeobotany (see Chambers 1993), then of the Botany Department, University of Wales, Cardiff, embarked on a detailed pollen study of an intertidal peat sequence. This was 'as a baseline for a research programme on the archaeology and environmental history of the Severn Estuary' (Smith and Morgan 1989, 145). The site was at Goldcliff, 800m east of the bedrock former island. It was selected because it had a good peat sequence. None of the prehistoric archaeology which we report here had, at that stage, been found. It cannot have been foreseen how

appropriate the choice of site would be, and what a valuable foundation it would provide for our work.

In 1987 Derek Upton and Bob Trett discovered charcoal and flint flakes below intertidal peat on the west edge of the bedrock former island. Newport Museum mounted a short recording exercise on this site in April 1989 under the supervision of Malcolm Lillie. A grid was laid out, the peat edge was planned and sections were drawn, demonstrating the flints came from a charcoal layer below the peat, a site which has proved to be Mesolithic (Chapter 4).

Monitoring of this site continued and one visit by Upton, Trett and others on 31 October 1990 followed a major storm (CD 1.1). It was observed that the mud had been swept away and peat surfaces were visible between the former Goldcliff Island and Goldcliff Pill. On the peat shelf above the Mesolithic site there was a human skull (Chapter 5).

As the party walked to the west along the peat shelf they began to find trackways formed of aligned roundwood held in places by pegs. There were other more enigmatic alignments of verticals (Chapter 10). Their most significant discovery came as they approached Goldcliff Pill, where roundwood verticals formed the outlines of rectangular Buildings 1 and 2 (Chapter 7). Greatly to the credit of those involved in the discovery that day, they at once appreciated the significance of the site and contemplated a prehistoric date, given its relatively low position within the tidal range, and knowing what they did of the previously investigated roundhouse at Chapeltump. Trett at once sought advice from Professor John Coles who, with others, visited the site the following day, confirmed its importance and urged a programme of recording (CD 1.2). One week of work followed, directed by Jonathan Parkhouse for the Glamorgan–Gwent Archaeological Trust, and another week in December, by the end of which, in anticipation of the effects of winter storms, the buildings had been planned and recorded, but excavation had been limited (Parkhouse 1991a).

Further archaeological work was undoubtedly needed the following summer. It was agreed that this would be done as a training excavation for the University of Wales, Lampeter by the writer with Jonathan Parkhouse. Professors Coles and Allen acted in an advisory capacity. The work was funded mainly by Cadw: Welsh Historic Monuments, through the good offices of Rick Turner, who has contributed throughout to the development of a strategy for the site. Additional support came from University of Wales, Lampeter, the National Museum of Wales and Newport Museum. Work took place over 4 weeks in August and early September 1991 with a team of about a dozen experienced wetland archaeologists and 30 students. This involved complete excavation and lifting of rectangular Buildings 1 and 2. In addition, a basic plan was made of nearby rectangular Building 3, a double post row (970), and of a number of trackways to the east.

The 1991 season had confirmed earlier indications that the two buildings were part of a larger site, all

7

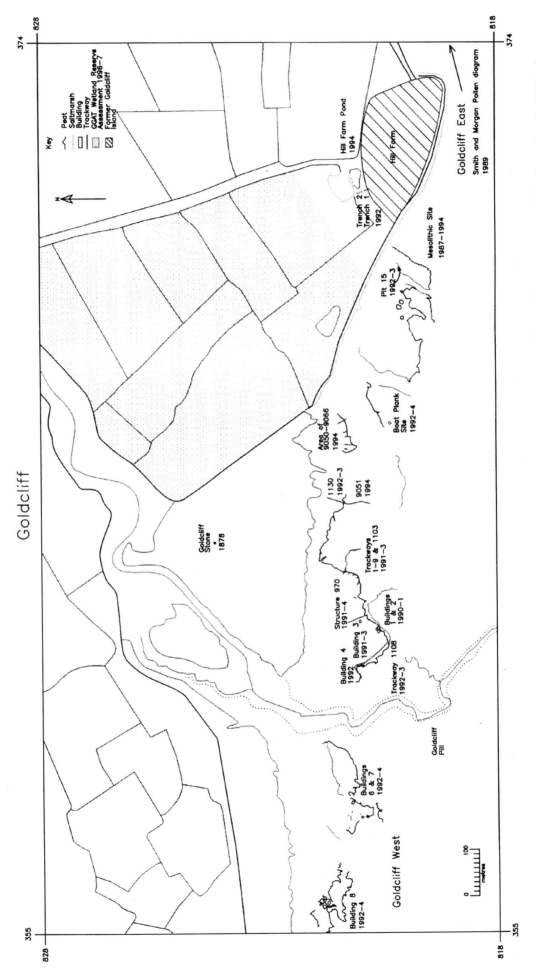

Figure 1.3 Goldcliff: showing the main sites investigated, and the pattern of discoveries and fieldwork from 1987 to 1994. Drawing by B Taylor

equally vulnerable to erosion. Cadw, with the support of the other funders, readily agreed to one further season in 1992 (Bell 1992), which had the objective of planning the rest of the later prehistoric site, but only doing limited strategic excavation. During this season, excavation funded by Newport Museum took place on the Mesolithic site. Two trenches were also dug behind the seawall at the edge of Goldcliff Island. These had the objective of looking at the wetland–dryland interface, in the hope that it would be possible to relate human activity on the island to the wetland sedimentary sequence. These dryland trenches were also intended to provide a place for aspects of student training away from the, often difficult, working conditions of the intertidal area. In the event that proved a pious hope because the season was wet and stormy, so at times this trench was almost as muddy as the intertidal area!

Stormy conditions had more beneficial effects which altered the course of the project. On 25 August, Upton noticed that there was a good exposure of peat west of Goldcliff Pill and went to have a look, discovering three more rectangular buildings (6–8) on the peat surface. A preliminary photographic record was made on 29 August. The following morning the team arrived at site to find waves breaking over the seawall (Fig 1.4). The storm removed mud from the whole survey area and exposed peat surfaces and many prehistoric structures which had not previously been seen, including

a structure with reused boat planks which proved to be Bronze Age (Chapter 6), several trackways (Chapter 10), and a fine exposure of the newly found site at Goldcliff West. As a result of all these new discoveries, the 10 days which remained of that season were a period of phrenetic activity to make a basic record of all the newly discovered sites. That was achieved, thanks to the dedication of the team, whose energy was concentrated on planning the new finds; there was no time for excavation, or even for sampling of the new sites.

This work had more than doubled the area of the site and the number of separate findspots. Accordingly, two further seasons of work took place in 1993 (Bell 1993) and 1994 (Bell 1995) in order to make a full record of all these discoveries. During both seasons further excavations took place on the Mesolithic site. In 1993 an environmental sampling pit near the edge of the former island revealed a human skull near the spot where Upton and Trett had found another skull in 1990 (Chapter 5). The 1993 season saw more detailed investigation of several trackways, a further look at the stratigraphic setting of the previously excavated Building 2 and, at Goldcliff West, excavation of one corner of Building 6 and part of a palaeochannel around it which had produced artefacts. East of the former Goldcliff Island the embayment, which we called Goldcliff East, was also surveyed. This was the location of the original Smith and Morgan (1989) pollen study and it was important

Figure 1.4 A storm on 30 August 1992 overtopping the seawall beside the Mesolithic site at Goldcliff. This storm dramatically increased the number of known prehistoric sites. Photograph by M Bell

that our study was linked as closely as possible with that detailed and well-dated sequence. Some evidence of Mesolithic activity was found at Goldcliff East but the survey did not reveal evidence of the concentrated later prehistoric activity previously encountered west of the former island.

The 1994 season saw more concentrated work at Goldcliff West, where Building 6 was totally excavated for possible display in the National Museum of Wales, and excavation took place in the surrounding palaeochannel. What remained of Building 8 was also excavated. Between the site where the boat planks had been found in 1992 and Trackway 1130 there was an area which had never been examined; this was planned and two further trackways and other structures (9050–9066) were found.

1.7 Discovery of a Romano-British landscape at Goldcliff

The 1878 discovery of the Romano-British inscribed Goldcliff Stone suggested the possibility of Roman finds. Almost to the end of fieldwork such evidence was very limited: one unstratified penannular brooch, a few sherds from the intertidal area and the top of the seawall. Just as that final season was being completed, Martin Hazell, who owns Hill Farm at Goldcliff, began work on a large extension to a pond behind the seawall on the edge of the former island and 200m inland from the Mesolithic site. With Mr Hazell's permission, the team maintained an informal watching brief on this work, which extended to within 6m of the 1992 island edge trench. For the first week of this work, when the top 0.5m were being removed, it was sterile. Then at a depth of 0.7–0.8m Roman pottery began to be found. By this time it was the end of the excavation season, the team had departed for the last time, and Roman pottery was turning up in considerable quantity. The writer remained and, with the help of his family, recorded the sections revealed, returning over the next 2 weeks whenever other commitments allowed to record further discoveries, including two Roman ditches and traces of a ground surface at a depth of 0.8m (Bell 1995). Discoveries in this pond are included in this volume where they are relevant to an understanding of the overall stratigraphic sequence. The evidence for Romano-British activity is briefly noted in Chapter 3, but not presented in detail, because the theme of this monograph is prehistoric. Furthermore, there is much continuing work on the buried landscapes of this reclaimed area by the Glamorgan–Gwent Archaeological Trust (Locock 1997, 1998a–d). This arises from the plans to dig large, shallow lagoons as part of the proposed Gwent Levels Wetland Reserve. It was clearly necessary to establish whether the lagoons would impinge on the buried prehistoric site and the Romano-British ditches and land surface which had been discovered during digging of the pond in 1994.

1.8 Board of Celtic Studies intertidal peat survey

When work ended on the intertidal area at Goldcliff in 1994 it had produced probably the greatest concentration of intertidal archaeological finds round the British coast. As a result of repeated observation and the effects of storms, the sites expanded numerically, and in area. The question then arose: how did the 3km investigated in detail at Goldcliff compare with the evidence from the Welsh Severn Estuary as a whole? Many sites had been discovered by Upton and a few had already been the subject of small-scale excavation. The sites which were recorded were outnumbered by many more, of which no written records existed, and which had not been located on a map. It was considered essential that this situation be addressed so that the work at Goldcliff could be appreciated within a wider archaeological context and, more particularly, because development pressures had continued to grow and, as archaeologists, we needed to be armed with a much more complete record of a threatened resource. Development pressures included plans for coastal defence upgrading and, most alarmingly, proposals for an international airport covering 8km of the intertidal area including Goldcliff and many of the other known and unrecorded sites (Bell 1995).

In 1995 the Board of Celtic Studies of the University of Wales supported the writer's proposal for an intertidal survey. The project was to last for 1 year, later extended by 4 months. Funds were available for a Research Assistant and Dr Heike Neumann was appointed. The aim was to create a computer database and map base of all the known prehistoric sites in the estuary and to walk the intertidal area to record known sites and locate others. This survey benefited very greatly from the active help and encouragement of Derek Upton. Cadw also helped with the cost of an assistant (Ian Halfpenny) for the field work period and with the costs of a number of short field periods involving more people in recording specific sites. Neumann left for a new job at the end of 1996; she continued to be involved in the completion of the project in her own time and further development work was done on the map base by Barbara Taylor, with some funding from Cadw and the Board of Celtic Studies. The results of this intertidal survey are presented in Chapter 16. It involved the production of a map base for the whole Welsh Estuary, including Goldcliff, which is presented in Appendix I.

1.9 Intertidal working conditions

In much of the intertidal area, the Quaternary sediment sequence is for most of the time obscured by a mobile covering of mud and sand of variable thickness. A major storm (Fig 1.4), or persistent high winds up the estuary from the southwest, mobilises the mud and exposes Quaternary sediments and archaeology. Mud thickness also varies through the spring–neap tidal cycle and is often less around the spring tides. In the Estuary it is seldom necessary to excavate for new finds; the sea does the excavation, but the secret is to be on hand at the right time to record what is exposed.

All archaeological work must be done within a tidal window. When low tide is around midday, then that gives about 6 hours working time. At the other extreme, when low tide falls in early morning and evening, then there may be two shorter working periods at the beginning and end of the day in summer, but in the shorter days of winter there may be no opportunity to work. Recording was made difficult by the mud, the demands of the situation varying greatly. Under conditions of little mud and good weather it was possible to achieve a great deal very quickly. Under muddy conditions and rain or cold, productivity can be severely limited.

Field technique has to adapt to working in 6 hour shifts. Between shifts, sites are covered by between c 3–7m of sea and variable amounts of mud are deposited. The strategy is to clean what can be recorded at each tide. Generally speaking, it has been found desirable to limit excavation as much as possible and to concentrate on recording what the sea exposes. This leads to the development of an additive picture where sites gradually emerge as a result of successive exposures over several years. Consequently, one formulates a series of plans showing different stages in the exposure of a site, varying extents of mud cover, and often very different scales depending on what was exposed on a specific occasion. It was in order to deal with these varied plans that Neumann developed a computer map base using Autocad and GIS software. This has the additional advantage that, once developed, it can be constantly added to when new discoveries are made.

The main objective was to get everything which was exposed on a plan. Three buildings were totally excavated at Goldcliff. In relation to the other structures, the aim was to supplement the plans where possible by small-scale strategic excavation and sampling for dating and environmental analysis. In the intertidal peat survey the emphasis was almost wholly on planning with very limited excavation, mostly to obtain samples for radiocarbon dating.

1.10 Radiocarbon dating and dendrochronology

Radiocarbon dating was an essential component of the development of this project. We began with a series of wood structures on peat. Those which did not have horizontal components stratified in the peat, and were not sealed by clay, could have been of any date from the period of the peat to the present day. In fact, we fully expected that some of the structures we dated would turn out to be recent, perhaps relating to fishing. What actually happened was that all 21 of the Goldcliff dates on wooden

structures were prehistoric, demonstrating the richness of the archaeological resource and encouraging its more detailed investigation. The Goldcliff project has a total of 63 radiocarbon dates, mostly on structural wood and peat. That programme is complemented by the series of 22 dates from Smith and Morgan's (1989) work at Goldcliff East. The project's chronological precision is greatly enhanced by 51 dendrochronological dates from five structures. Our policy has been to mark the location of each piece of dated wood or peat on the relevant plan or section.

Radiocarbon years are not the same as calendar years for reasons which are explained in Bowman (1990) or any recent standard text on archaeological dating. Calibration curves have been worked out using the radiocarbon dates of wood of known dendrochronological age. Thus, for each radiocarbon dated sample there are two dates: the original date issued by the laboratory, which we quote in the form of radiocarbon years BP, and the calibrated date which we quote as years Cal BC/AD. The calibration curves used for our dates are those in Stuiver and Kra (1986) and they have been calibrated using the OxCal v2.18 computer programme.

In those parts of the text where the primary evidence is being outlined, on the plans and sections and in the environmental Chapters 13–15, we use the original uncalibrated date. In the discussion and synthesis sections, in which broader comparisons are being made, including those with dendrochronological dates, we use the calibrated ranges. Linking the two together is the radiocarbon table in Appendix II which provides a full list of dates and calibrated ranges. In the intertidal survey (Chapter 16), in which we are dealing with a combination of data presentation and synthesis, we quote uncalibrated dates followed by the calibrated range.

1.11 Project philosophy

Hodder (1989) has been critical that archaeologists are slow to relate changes in the theoretical perspectives of the subject to the practice of excavation. He advocates (Hodder 1999) a more self-reflexive approach to evidence and its interpretation which he is evolving through the current field project at Çatal Hüyük, Turkey (Hodder 1997). It is appropriate to comment on how we have approached these issues in the context of this project.

The stochastic processes (ie those involving random variables) affecting site exposure mean that the archaeology of the Severn Estuary is necessarily in a state of constant change; erosion reveals fresh sites, depending on the occurrence of storms and the presence of a knowledgeable observer to make a record. Archaeological investigation in this type of context is a necessarily interdisciplinary activity, the result of team collaboration. Our objective has been to structure the project, and this report, in a way which takes account of these circumstances.

Rather than putting forward a single definitive

interpretation, we have tried, in so far as space allows, to identify a range of multiple working hypotheses which are then evaluated against the evidence. This has the advantage that the reader is aware of which possibilities have been considered, why some are favoured and others regarded as less likely. The hope is that this will bring the key problems into focus and make it easier for them to be addressed by new work. A multiple working hypothesis approach is a logical one for an interdisciplinary team. Each member has a distinctive viewpoint reflecting specialist expertise, background and preconceptions. Varied background should encourage the development of a diversity of hypotheses and should help to avoid the preconceptions of one individual unduly dominating the agenda.

The philosophy which we have tried to implement is that every hypothesis, however unlikely, has an equal right to appear on the agenda. Thereafter, it depends entirely how they fare in a critical dialogue with the evidence derived from a range of sources. One great strength of waterlogged contexts, such as those of the estuary, is the multiplicity of different datasets against which the evidence can be examined. One way in which this was achieved was two seminars, in September 1997 and March 1998, when most members of the project team met to discuss the integration of sources of evidence. The project also benefited from the fact that many of the specialists had been involved to some extent with the excavation. In situations where no single favoured interpretation has emerged we have tried to avoid a lowest common denominator compromise in the belief that it is better to identify the differences of evidence and hypothesis clearly and, thus, to suggest profitable topics for future research. Such an approach was adopted with the report on another waterlogged context, the Bronze Age Wilsford Shaft, in which very contrasting conclusions were drawn from the environmental and archaeological evidence (Ashbee *et al* 1989). That approach acknowledges that in a multidisciplinary project a plurality of voices should have an equal opportunity to be heard. It similarly acknowledges that an excavation report should not aim to be a definitive statement so much as an interim report on ongoing dialogue with the evidence, a statement of what those involved believe they found and on what basis certain conclusions were reached.

1.12 Compact disc and project database

The Board of Celtic Studies survey stage of this project involved the setting up of an Autocad map base linked to databases of sites. As a supplement to the published volume these computer databases are presented on CD. This has been prepared by Taylor based on the computer database previously prepared by Neumann. The computer version of the geographic information is more complete and versatile than the extracts presented as figures in the printed volume. Maps and plans can be consulted on a wide range of spatial scales, and selected layers of information can be compared. The map base can also be linked to text on individual sites and to plans and photographs of sites. On the CD we also include supplementary plans and photographs which there was not room to include within the published volume. We have also put nearly all the tables on the CD. In doing so our aim has been to include the basic information in the text but detailed evidence to support and substantiate these points will often be contained on the CD. Entries on the CD in support of points in the text are referenced in the form: CD 1.1 (Chapter 1, Entry 1). There are instructions on how to use the CD in the preface.

The approach of monograph publication and supporting CD has been adopted because we felt it was the most effective way of making the range of results widely available from this project. We have endeavoured to structure our material so that the monograph can be read totally independently of the CD because we are aware that many of those interested will not have access to new technology. We are concerned that no reader should be disenfranchised for this reason so we will, on request to the author, provide a print-out of what is on the CD at as low a cost as we can arrange.

1.13 Intertidal safety warning

Remarkable archaeological discoveries from the intertidal zone are presented in this monograph and we hope it will lead to continued vigilance, scientific investigation and discoveries. The estuary is an environment of many dangers, the tide comes in rapidly and can encircle and cut off the unwary. Deep mud is widespread and quicksand occurs. There are pits and hollows in which people could become stuck. It follows that the intertidal area should not be visited by the inexperienced without a knowledgeable guide. Great care should also be taken not to damage or disturb archaeological sites, particularly wooden structures which can be extremely fragile. The Estuary is also an area of Special Scientific Interest on account of its birdlife and natural history, so particular care needs to be taken to avoid disturbance, especially to nesting birds, and the Countryside Council for Wales should be consulted about any proposed visits. Any archaeological discoveries which are made should be recorded as carefully as possible at the time of discovery so that they can be located on the maps published in this volume (Appendix I). New finds should be reported to the National Museum of Wales, Newport Museum, the Glamorgan–Gwent Archaeological Trust, or the writers.

2 Goldcliff Island: geological and sedimentological background *by J R L Allen*

2.1 Introduction

The outcrop of Holocene estuarine alluvium that forms the Severn Estuary Levels owes its intricate shape to the complicated relief of the bedrock surface beneath. That surface, broadly a 'valley within a valley', was created over the recent past by glacial, marine, periglacial, and fluvial processes, driven by Quaternary climatic instability (Steers 1946, Anderson 1968 and 1974, Williams 1968, Gilbertson and Hawkins 1978, Allen 1987b). It is dissected by buried river valleys and bounded by degraded sea cliffs; at many places bedrock ridges, hills, and knolls rise above the surface of the alluvium from the floor of the outer valley. One of the more isolated of these knolls lies at Goldcliff, far out on the coast of the Caldicot Level (British Geological Survey Sheets 250 and 264, Rippon 1996a). Such an 'island' can furnish resources normally restricted to the dry mainland, and is a natural landmark and focus of human activity in the wider setting of a coastal wetland.

Geologists had long valued the cliff exposure known as Gold Cliff (in the wider Parish of Goldcliff) for the section it afforded in late Triassic–early Jurassic beds (Richardson 1905), but it was not until 1991 that well-exposed Pleistocene raised beach and head were recognised (by this author) as circumscribing the island, beneath the archaeologically rich Holocene alluvium in the district.

2.2 Pre-Pleistocene

At Gold Cliff (Fig 2.1a) the rocks dip extremely gently in a direction a little east of north. The only beds now visible are the uppermost Red Marl (Trias), represented by red, concretionary mudstones, and the lowermost Lower Lias (Jurassic), of interbedded grey limestones and shales. The former appear on a planar, wave-cut platform (Reynolds 1906) which ranges southeastward from roughly mid-tide level at the foot of the armoured seawall to the low-water line about 800m away. The mudstones also occur, but concealed by the Holocene and Pleistocene, between Goldcliff Pill and Gold Cliff and are likely to be widespread at depth in the district. Pits on the top of Gold Cliff reveal the Lower Lias. Formerly, until the cliff was permanently encased in stone and brick, the Tea Green Marl (1.7m) and the Rhaetic (5.6m) were exposed (Richardson 1905, Welch and Trotter 1961). The Rhaetic beds are especially variable, consisting chiefly of various limestones interbedded with black, grey, and yellow fossiliferous shales.

2.3 Pleistocene

General

The knoll of Gold Cliff is all that remains of a once much larger bedrock 'island' roughly coincident with the present outcrop of the Triassic–Jurassic beds on the surviving island and wave-cut platform. Encircling the oval island were variable, outward-dipping, shelly beach deposits (raised beach), presumed to have been banked against a low rock cliff. Because they became calcite-cemented, these beds partly survived erosion and remain exposed. On the more level, buried rock surface further from the island, the beach deposits appear to grade laterally into locally shelly sands and gravels of probable shoreface origin. Largely burying the raised beach, and in places concealing the shoreface deposits, there is a younger, extremely variable, and locally fossiliferous head.

Raised beach

As exposed intertidally (Fig 2.1a), the deposit is nowhere thicker than 3–4m, resting sharply and erosively on a slightly uneven surface of variable dip cut across the Red Marl. It consists chiefly of well-cemented, shelly pebble–cobble conglomerates, conglomeratic sandstones, and sandstones, with some poorly to uncemented sands and gravels. The basal beds are invariably conglomerates, mainly of cobble-grade fragments of local materials. Upward these become thinner bedded and finer grained, and increasingly interbedded with wedges and lenses of pebbly sandstone, sandstone, and lightly cemented to loose sand. The latter predominate in the transition into the overlying head. In the concealed ground between Gold Cliff and Goldcliff Pill (Fig 2.1b), where the rockhead lies at *c* –7.5m Ordnance Datum (OD), the equivalent of the raised beach is an apparently continuous, level series of locally cemented sands and gravels 0.5–4.25m thick. At one place these are shelly.

To the southwest and south of Hill Farm, the raised beach is exposed as a low, curving rib and a stack of almost level-bedded, pebble–cobble conglomerates with lenticular, very fine–fine grained, well-sorted quartz sandstones which rest on an uneven surface of Red Marl that steps down to the southwest (Fig 2.1a). The coarser deposits are a jumble of ill-rounded blocks and plates of red mudstone and various limestones set in shelly sandstone; no far-

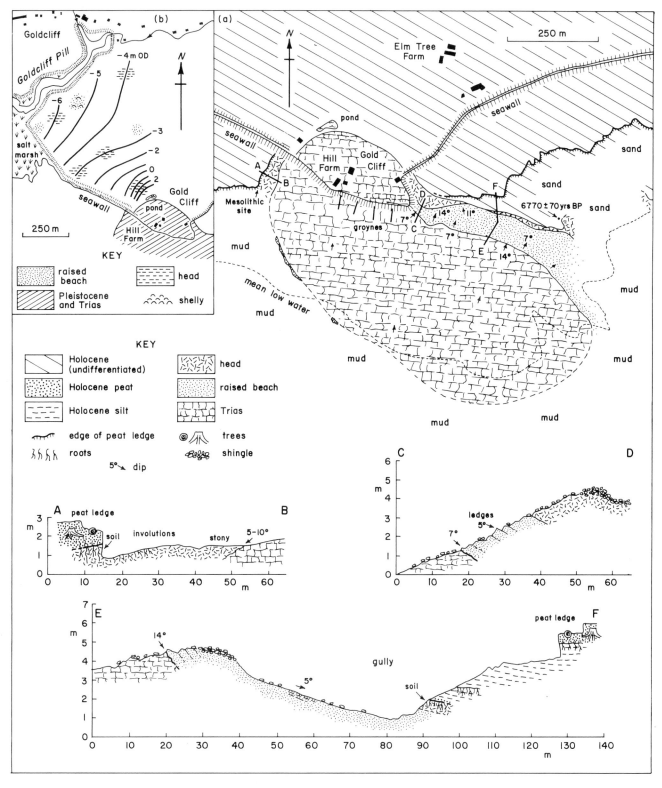

Figure 2.1 Geology of the Gold Cliff 'island' (a) Geological map (evidence accessible in 1991–92), (b) Contours on and composition of the sub-Holocene surface between Gold Cliff and Goldcliff Pill

travelled gravelly components were recognised. Bedding surfaces in the sandstones chiefly reveal symmetrical wave ripples and linguoid current ripples. Occasional beds are parallel laminated. The raised beach is overlapped toward the seawall

to the north where the head rests directly on the Trias.

The raised beach chiefly outcrops as a bold, debris-covered ridge that curves away from the cliff for some 600m to the east-southeast (Fig 2.1a).

Figure 2.2 Raised beach. Northeastward dipping basal bed resting on Trias southeast of Gold Cliff. Spade 0.94m tall

Figure 2.4 Raised beach. Cemented sandstone southeast of Gold Cliff. Lens cap for scale

Showing consistent northeasterly dips of 2–26°, the beds are exposed as ribs and ledges at many places on both sides of the ridge and along its crest (Fig 2.2). The uneven surface of the Red Marl on which they rest displays similar dips. The lowermost deposits are pebble–cobble conglomerates of ill-rounded mudstone and limestone blocks and plates with occasional, well-rounded pebbles of quartzite and vein-quartz but no far-travelled igneous debris (Fig 2.3). These quickly grade up into shelly, very fine to medium grained, well-sorted quartz sandstones and lenses of pebble conglomerate, interleaved with sheets of loose sand. Characteristically, the surfaces of the cemented sandstone layers display irregular ribs that run with the dip (Fig 2.4); some of the sand is cemented into partly fused and even discrete fingerlike masses. Parallel lamination with parting lineation is more common in these sandstones than current and wave ripples. The uppermost 1–2m of the raised beach deposit, widely exposed on the floor of the deep gully to the northeast of the ridge, consist mainly of yellowish, lightly cemented, well-laminated shelly sandstone. It appears to be from a level

in these deposits that Haslett (1997) recorded an extensive foraminiferal assemblage.

Sand-sized and larger fragments of molluscan shells abound in the raised beach deposits. Whole shells were collected from cemented deposits on the rib to the southwest of Hill Farm and from two places on the main ridge. The three assemblages are similar and combine to give the species count in Table 2.1.

Heavy mineralogy of the raised beach

The sandstones include laminae darkened by heavy minerals. A sample (A, very fine–fine grained) from the rib southwest of Hill Farm, and another (B, fine–medium grained) from the main ridge, was disaggregated in cold, dilute hydrochloric acid, washed and dried, and the heavy minerals separated

Table 2.1 Mollusca from the raised beach at Gold Cliff

Mollusc species	No.
Astarte sulcata (da Costa)	1
Gibbula (?)*G. umbilicalis* (da Costa)	1
Macoma balthica (L.)	220
Mytilus edulis L.	1
Spisula elliptica (Brown)	1
Buccinum undatum L.	8
Littorina littoralis (L.)	5
L. littorea (L.)	2
Nucella lapillus (L.)	16
Total	255

The identifications follow Tebble (1966), McMillan (1968) and Beedham (1972).

Figure 2.3 Raised beach. Detail of basal bed resting on Trias. Spade 0.94m tall

Table 2.2 Heavy minerals present in Ipswichian sand-grade deposits

Mineral	Sample (%)					
	A	**B**	**C**	**D**	**E**	**F**
Zircon	26.2	14.2	26.2	35.3	14.7	12.8
Tourmaline	9.0	10.9	5.2	6.2	9.0	12.3
Rutile	4.2	1.0	2.8	7.3	3.5	2.4
Garnet	32.2	31.3	43.4	35.2	16.6	11.9
Staurolite	3.1	4.1	2.6	1.1	9.1	6.2
Kyanite	0.8	1.4	0.4	1.6	1.0	0.9
Andalusite					0.2	0.4
Hornblende (green)	10.7	16.3	7.5	5.2	33.9	36.8
Hornblende (brown)	1.4	1.7	0.7	0.5	0.5	1.6
Pyroxene	2.3	5.4	2.6	1.3	1.3	2.6
Epidote	3.3	0.6	3.7	1.9	4.3	3.1
Chlorite	0.6	5.8	1.3	0.2	0.5	2.6
Fluorite				0.2	0.2	0.2
Monazite		0.4		0.6	0.6	0.2
Titanite	0.3	1.2	1.3	1.3	2.1	3.3
Sillimanite	0.6	2.5	1.5	1.0	1.1	1.2
Spinel	0.3	1.9	0.2	1.3	1.0	0.4
Dumortierite	0.5	0.6	0.2	0.2	0.2	
Zoisite	4.5	0.8	0.4			1.2
Topaz	0.2					
Corundum					0.3	
Total	100.2	100.1	100.0	100.4	100.1	100.1
Total grains	646	486	465	634	625	578

A and B, raised beach, Gold Cliff; C, cemented sandstone in head, Gold Cliff; D, Bed 8, Swallow Cliff; E, Burtle Beds, Huntspill; F, Burtle Beds, Pawlett.

Figure 2.5 Head. Subvertical fabric in densely packed head, crest of ridge southeast of Gold Cliff. View looking down onto the surface. Lens cap for scale

little to the north of west at 5–10°. The lowermost 2m consists of very abundant, angular blocks and plates of mudstone and limestone set in a compact, structureless red silt. Some limestone blocks are very irregular and show deep solution pits. Upward the head becomes sandier and the blocks fewer and smaller; the latter are accompanied by irregular plates and fingers of calcite-cemented sandstone similar to the sandstones in the raised beach to the south and east. Locally, the matrix is grey or yellow, and a green colouration appears toward the very top. A few dispersed teeth, identified by Annie Grant (University of Leicester) as *Bos* sp., were recovered from the upper, sandy head.

The head is less well-exposed and generally much thinner along the ridge to the east-southeast of Gold Cliff. It is best seen immediately east of the seawall at the cliff, but was traced in test-pits along the deep gully further to the east. Grey and yellow colours are more conspicuous, and limestone and mudstone blocks and plates generally less plentiful than in the exposure to the southwest of Hill Farm.

At both places the head widely displays involutions (Vandenberghe 1988). Typically, these in plan are oval to irregular zones in which the platier debris, including delicate fragmentary sheets and fingers of cemented sandstone, is arranged subvertically parallel to the margins (Fig 2.5). Locally, this fabric can be traced over linear zones, but these could not be shown to contribute to polygonal patterns and need not be ice-wedge casts. Mineralogically, a sample of cemented sandstone clasts (C, very fine–fine grained) from the involutions affecting the upper head resembles sandstones in the raised beach (Table 2.2).

off in tetrabromoethane. The mineral assemblages are similar and dominated by euhedral and angular–subangular grains, chiefly of regional metamorphic origin (Table 2.2). In particular, the amphibole and pyroxene grains are fresh-looking.

Head

The head (Harris 1987) occurs as a discontinuous blanket that shrouds the raised beach deposit (Fig 2.1a, b). At depth between Gold Cliff and Goldcliff Pill, the head is up to 2.5m in thickness immediately beneath the Holocene, but is lacking in a number of places, at which the alluvium directly overlies the shoreface deposits. It is exposed intertidally at two places.

Southwest of Hill Farm the head is 4–5m thick and directly overlies the Red Marl, the base dipping a

Dating and corrrelation

The molluscan assemblage implies a later Pleistocene date for the raised beach and, in the predominance of *M. balthica*, closely resembles the modern molluscan fauna of the Severn Estuary (eg Boyden and Little 1973, Boyden *et al* 1977, Shackley 1981). Attribution of the deposit to an interglacial episode within the later Pleistocene may, therefore, be suggested.

Measurements by Dr G A Sykes and Professor D Q Bowen (University of Wales, Cardiff) of the amino acid ratios in seventeen selected shells show that the raised beach can be assigned to the Ipswichian interglacial (Oxygen Isotope Sub-stage 5e). The D-alle/L-Ile ratios obtained were:

Littorina littoralis	0.087 ± 0.067 ($n = 3$)
Nucella lapillus	0.095 ± 0.009 ($n = 8$)
Macoma balthica	0.150 ± 0.009 ($n = 6$)

The ratio for *Macoma* is reported as leaving little room for doubt about a 5e age; the ratios for *Littorina* and *Nucella* are on the low side for the sub-stage, but can be matched elsewhere in Ipswichian deposits eg Portland Bill (Bowen *et al* 1985). It is possible, given the low ratio for *Littorina*, that the Gold Cliff beach

belongs to the later of the two Ipswichian high-stands (Bowen 1994).

The Ipswichian raised beach at Gold Cliff has many correlatives on the north side of the Bristol Channel–Severn Estuary (Fig 2.6). At Llanwern 4km away to the north, on the inland margin of the Caldicot Level, *Macoma*-dominated sandy gravels of 5e age lie concealed between the Holocene and the Trias (Andrews *et al* 1984). A borehole in the same context at Bishton nearby revealed in the same position 4.6m of shelly sands with lumps of Triassic and Rhaetic–Jurassic rocks toward the base (Locke 1971). Even closer, at Whitson, Locke (1971) records 3m of coarse deposits beneath the Holocene. A similar sequence occurs on the coast of the Caldicot Level at Magor Pill to the northeast, where about 2m of gravel capped by (?)head succeeds the Trias but underlies the Holocene. The bedrock surface exposed intertidally here reveals definite ice-wedge casts (Allen and Rippon 1997). At Caldicot the Holocene is underlain by sands and gravel capped by a head

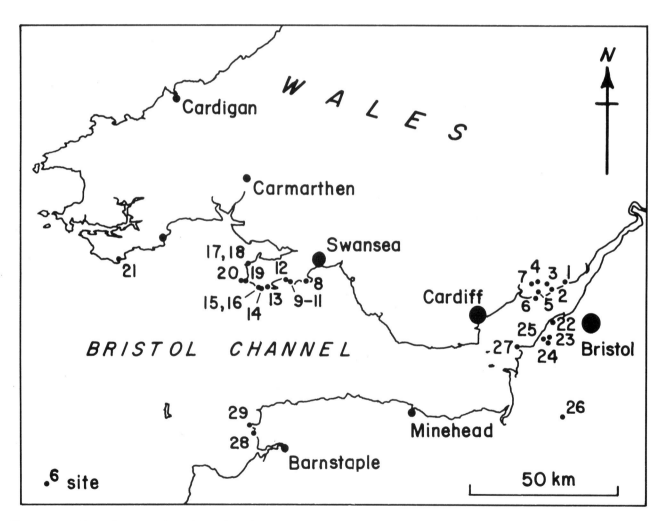

Figure 2.6 Distribution of confirmed and probable Ipswichian raised beach and estuarine deposits in the Bristol Channel–Severn Estuary. 1-Caldicot, 2-Magor Pill, 3-Llandevenny, 4-Bishton, 5-Whitson, 6-Gold Cliff, 7-Llanwern, 8-Langland Bay, 9-Hunt's Bay East, 10-Hunt's Bay West, 11-Overton Mere, 15-Overton West, 16-Overton Cliff, 17 and 20-Worms Head, 18-Broughton Bay, 19-Rhossili, 21-Broadhaven, 22-Vale of Gordano, 23-Kennpier, 24-New Blind Yeo Drain, 25-Kenn Church, 26-Burtle Beds (Greylake), 27-Swallow Cliff, 28-Saunton, 29-Baggy Point

affected by periglacial processes (Bell *et al* 1990, Dingwall and Ferris 1993). Borings at Llandevenny, between Caldicot and Bishton, proved sands and gravels with a littoral–estuarine fauna including *M. balthica* and *Buccinum* situated between Triassic mudstones and a variable head (GGAT 1994). The coarse deposits at Bishton, Whitson, Magor Pill, Caldicot and Llandevenny are so far attributable to the Ipswichian only on general grounds, but to the west of the Caldicot Level, and especially along the limestone cliffs of the Gower Peninsula, reliably-dated Ipswichian raised beaches abound (Bowen *et al* 1985).

The Ipswichian is also well-represented on the southern margins of the Bristol Channel–Severn Estuary (Fig 2.6). Attributable to the stage on general grounds are gravels and sands with *Macoma* and *Buccinum* beneath a head on the edge of the Vale of Gordano (ApSimon and Donovan 1956). On the open coast at Swallow Cliff, Middlehope, a pebble–cobble beach deposit rich in *Macoma* is of Ipswichian age (Gilbertson and Hawkins 1977, Andrews *et al* 1979, Briggs *et al* 1991). Around Kenn, in the North Somerset Levels, abundantly fossiliferous, estuarine sands and silts date to Sub-stage 5e (Gilbertson and Hawkins 1978, Andrews *et al* 1984). The most widespread estuarine deposits dated to the Ipswichian are, however, the Burtle Beds outcropping from near the coast to far inland in the Somerset Levels (Bulleid and Jackson 1937 and 1941, Green and Welch 1965, Kidson 1970 and 1971, Kidson *et al* 1978 and 1981, Andrews *et al* 1979, Hunt and Clark 1983, Whitaker and Green 1983, Edmonds and Williams 1985). These comprise richly fossiliferous, quartzose, bioclastic limestones with bands of silt clasts and other pebbles; there is no underlying clay unit of Burtle age (Hawkins and Kellaway 1973). The rip-up clasts and varied sedimentary structures in the bioclastic sands – channelling, cross-bedding, parallel laminations, various ripple marks – together with the outcrop shapes, recall the shifting mid-tide sand shoals of the modern Severn Estuary. A rich foraminiferal assemblage is present (Kidson *et al* 1978), on the basis of which Haslett (1997) referred the Gold Cliff beds to the Ipswichian. Around the fall-line of the rivers that fed the Burtle estuaries there are cemented, fluvial gravels of Ipswichian age (Hunt *et al* 1984). The westernmost raised beaches dated to the stage are at Baggy Point and Saunton (Bowen *et al* 1985).

Since they would all appear to have formed in the same tidal seaway, the mobile, sand-grade components of the Ipswichian deposits may be expected to display compositionally a family resemblance. In Table 2.2 the Gold Cliff samples are compared mineralogically to a very fine–fine grained sand (D) from Bed 8 at Swallow Cliff (Gilbertson and Hawkins 1977) and to the insoluble extract (coarse silt–very fine sand) from very fine grained bioclastic rocks in the Burtle Beds at Huntspill (E, British National Grid Reference ST 308463) and Pawlett (F, ST 238438) near the coast of the Somerset Levels. All six samples display broadly the same, regional-

metamorphic signature, but the roles of garnet and hornblende are reversed between Huntspill–Pawlett and Gold Cliff–Swallow Cliff, and there is a similar sharp difference in the garnet–staurolite and hornblende–pyroxene ratios. The sub-beach aeolian silts at Swallow Cliff have quite different heavy-mineral characteristics (Briggs *et al* 1991), and there is likewise little similarity with modern, beach-derived dune sands of the area (Stuart 1924).

The presence in the head of *Bos* sp. and of periglacial structures suggests a latest Pleistocene (Devensian) age (Stuart 1982, Gilbertson and Hawkins 1978). Similar materials with frost structures, locally associated with, or replaced by, aeolian deposits, occur widely on the bedrock slopes marginal to the Severn Estuary Levels (Greenly 1922, Palmer 1934, Welch and Trotter 1961, Green and Welch 1965, Gilbertson and Hawkins 1978 and 1983, Whitaker and Green 1983, Kellaway and Welch 1993). They may conceal other Ipswichian raised beach deposits. Ice-wedge casts and other periglacial features are widely preserved on the bedrock surface in the Severn Estuary (Allen 1987b, Harris 1989, Allen and Rippon 1997).

2.4 The Holocene in relation to the Pleistocene

The Holocene peats and estuarine silts (Wentlooge Formation) lap on to gentle–moderate slopes, underlain by head and raised beach deposits, that skirt the island (Fig 2.1a, b). On each flank the contact is underlain by a silty–sandy, slightly pebbly soil with a prominent bleached horizon which merges up into organic-rich material. Southwest of Gold Cliff the latter partly overlies a lenticular occupation deposit of late-Mesolithic date (Chapter 4). Succeeding it is a thin wedge of estuarine silt and the mid-Holocene main peat (Chapters 5 and 13); the roots of trees present in the woodland facies developed within the latter extend locally down into the head, where their channels are preserved within stout, moderately inclined to upright siderite concretions. There is no obvious occupation deposit at the contact to the southeast of Gold Cliff, but the soil exposed along and at the end of the gully yields flint and chert flakes. At the far end, at about –3.7m OD, a thin basal peat directly overlies the soil. A young oak in the peat gave a conventional radiocarbon age of 6770 ± 70 BP (Beta-60761). Above lies 3–4m of estuarine silt with root beds, in turn overlain by the main peat (Fig 2.1a, Section E–F). Smith and Morgan (1989) dated the latter some 600m to the east to between 5950 (base) and 3130 (top) radiocarbon years BP.

An auger transect from the pond on the northern slopes of the island (Fig 3.6) clearly reveals the crucial role of differential sediment compaction above an uneven rockhead in shaping the present and buried topography, and the stratigraphy, of the Severn Estuary Levels (Allen 1997b and forthcoming c). Here the main peat is a basal peat. On the transect and beyond,

18

the top descends by almost 4m as the bed passes out into silts above the deeper-lying but more level rockhead a few hundred metres from the sloping side of the island. Haslett *et al* (1998a) describe a parallel situation from the Axe Valley in the Somerset Levels. A thick basal peat overlying a sloping rockhead has a top of uniform radiocarbon age but which descends by 2.1m within 70m out across the slope. These effects undermine the validity of the peat-based sea level curves so far suggested for the area, but provide a solution to the problem of the low altitude (*c* 1m OD) of the Goldcliff later Iron Age buildings, at a place where the diachronous top of the main peat (Bell and Neumann 1997) may be at its youngest.

2.5 The evolution of Goldcliff Island

The Ipswichian sea level in the inner Bristol Channel–Severn Estuary lay at about the same altitude as today. At least as far to the northeast as the Magor area, the coasts were gravelly or sandy and, therefore, were probably wave-dominated. Goldcliff Island, standing off in the Ipswichian sea like Steep Holm, Flatholm, and Denny Island today, was encircled by a beach and shoreface deposit which may have built up most extensively on its sheltered, northeastern side. There is no sign, either in the Ipswichian sediments or the known faunas, of high intertidal mudflats and salt marshes that would denote a tide-dominated shore. It must be supposed that these environments, if developed in the Ipswichian, lay further up the Severn Vale than the Magor area. Salt marshes and mudflats may, however, have formed around the heads of the subordinate estuaries of the Parrett and Brue that branched off toward the southeast, since mud clasts are common in the Burtle Beds, which appear to have formed largely as tidal sand shoals.

No doubt many sources contributed sediment to the Ipswichian sea, but much sand came from glacial and related deposits of northern origin that underwent reworking (Table 2.2). Pre-Ipswichian ((?)Oxygen Isotope Stage 16) ice, penetrating eastward along the Bristol Channel (Gilbertson and Hawkins 1978), may have introduced some of the parent material. Hydraulic sorting (Barrie 1980a, b, and 1981), rather than multiple sources, may explain the differences between Gold Cliff–Swallow Cliff and Huntspill–Pawlett.

At some time during the Devensian cold period, periglacial processes acting on the local bedrock created a substantial apron of head around Goldcliff Island. By this time, the beach gravels and sands beneath had locally acquired a strong calcite cement, probably introduced by meteoric waters that leached lime from either the Rhaetic–Liassic rocks or from shells in the deposit itself. Knight (1998) attributed a similar style of cementation in Irish outwash deposits to melting permafrost. The presence in the head – a gravity-emplaced deposit – of cemented sand mineralogically identical to that in the raised beach (Table 2.2) suggests that either the beach ranged to higher altitudes than its present outcrop

or that the island had a partial cover of wind-blown sand. If the latter is correct, the head, in comparison with the Somerset sequence (Gilbertson and Hawkins 1978), might be latest Devensian.

Sea level rise during the Holocene created space in which some 10–15m of coastal marsh deposits could accumulate to form the Severn Estuary Levels. These deposits lapped on to the flanks of Goldcliff Island, diminishing it as a feature, and created a landmark isolated in a sea of marsh. When and how was this hill, some 900m long by 300m across, reduced to the knoll and extensive intertidal rock platform visible today (Fig 2.1a)?

Marine erosion during the sea level rise drove back the shoreline of the Severn Estuary Levels in much of the area, as witness the widespread intertidal peats and submerged forests (Allen 1990b and 1992) and the many inland-repositioned seabanks (Allen and Fulford 1986, 1992 and 1996, Allen and Rippon 1997). Goldcliff Island was not exempted from this process. The oval wave-cut platform seen today has a generally lower altitude than the adjoining late-Mesolithic occupation and is also overlooked by the mid-Holocene main peat (Fig 2.1a, b). Moreover, the Mesolithic occupation (Chapter 4) stands off the modern, stabilised cliff by some 75m. The island could, therefore, have been largely destroyed since late-Mesolithic times; the horizontal retreat amounts to about 300m, assuming a cliff with the same general orientation as the modern one facing southwest and the greatest fetch of waves.

Its removal over such a short period is not implausible in terms of local rates of horizontal cliff retreat (Mackintosh 1868, Williams and Davies 1987 and 1989, Davies and Williams 1991). Lias cliffs erode on average at 0.06–0.08 m/year, giving a required period of 3750–5000 years. A common rate for cliffs of Triassic–Rhaetic beds similar to those which predominate at Gold Cliff is 0.2m/year, yielding a figure of 1500 years. An even shorter period of 650–730 years is possible, since retreat rates for such cliffs as high as 0.41m/year and 0.46m/year are quoted. Erosion continues today at Gold Cliff, but only over the wave-cut platform (cliff now encased), which is descending at about 0.01m/year, judging from the four concrete groynes (Fig 2.1a) built in 1955 (Colin Green personal communication 1993) with bases proud of the surface (1991) by an average of 0.37m. It is not surprising that the prior of Goldcliff was writing in 1424 (Williams 1964) of the marine threat to the priory walls and the partial destruction of the parish church. During the Mesolithic, and probably also the Iron Age, Goldcliff Island was a major landscape feature and a potentially important natural resource.

Acknowledgements

I am very grateful to Professor D Q Bowen and Dr G A Sykes for the provision of amino-acid dates, to Annie Grant for animal identifications, and to Colin Green for information about the Gold Cliff groynes.

3 Introduction to the Holocene sedimentary sequence
by M Bell with contributions by J James and H Neumann

3.1 Introduction

This chapter introduces the sedimentary sequence containing intertidal archaeological sites. It begins with a brief outline of sea level change, followed by a review of the general sediment sequence from the estuary as a whole, then focuses on a more detailed analysis of the Goldcliff sequence.

3.2 Sea level change
Heike Neumann and Martin Bell

The Holocene sequence has accumulated in the context of an underlying upward trend of sea level as documented in the successive sea level curves for the Bristol Channel region published by Hawkins (1971 and 1973), Kidson and Heyworth (1973), Heyworth and Kidson (1982), Scaife and Long (1995), and Jennings *et al* (1998). The curves have been constructed as age/altitude plots based largely on widely distributed radiocarbon dated samples of peat for which their present altitude is known in relation to OD. The most recent curve of Jennings *et al* (1998) provides a total of 49 sea level index points, including eleven dates from Smith and Morgan's (1989) pollen profile at Goldcliff East. This indicates a rapid early Holocene (c 9000 Uncal years BP) rate of sea level rise of 16mm/year, decreasing to 8.5mm/year by c 6600 Uncal years BP. It is in this period that the bulk of the sediment underlying the intertidal peats was deposited. As discussed in Allen (1990a), minerogenic mudflats pertain when the magnitude of sea level rise is sufficiently high to continue to supply sediment to a growing mudflat or saltmarsh, which was the case during the rapid early Holocene sea level rise. The basal clays and silts were becoming finer-grained and laminations more pronounced towards the top of this formation (Allen 1997a) which suggests a slowing down of the rate of sea level rise as the marsh was inundated by progressively fewer tides and for shorter periods at a time.

There was a further deceleration in sea level rise by 6100–5700 Uncal years BP to between 2.7 mm/year and 2.1mm/year. This deceleration coincides with the onset of reed and fen wood peat formation. According to Allen (1990a), peat formation commences when minerogenic supply ceases and will continue if organogenic accretion levels are roughly equal, or exceed, the magnitudes of the sea level rise and compaction. Around 5200 Uncal years BP sea level rise was further reduced to <1mm/year. There is evidence for raised bog developing at

Goldcliff at around 4900 Uncal BP which suggests that the continued growth of a fully freshwater ombrotrophic (rain-fed) mire was independent of sea level.

Within the overall rising sea level trend of the Holocene, there is evidence of fluctuations in relative sea level, with periods of reduced marine influence, or negative tendency, marked by peat formation, alternating with periods of increased marine influence, or positive tendency marked by the deposition of minerogenic sediments (Long and Roberts 1997). These fluctuations have been variously interpreted in terms of reductions in the overall rate of sea level rise (van de Plassche 1982), or as rises and falls of sea level relating to secular climate change (eg Tooley 1978 and 1985). Modelling by Allen (1997c, d) shows that the observed sedimentary changes can be produced by sea level fluctuations which, in the Thames and Fenland area, are in the order of 0.1–1m.

Locally, the formation and breaching of sand and shingle bars can also give rise to regressive and transgressive sequences. Such bars exist on the English side of the Severn Estuary, but there is no evidence for their existence on the Welsh side. We should, nonetheless, consider whether other factors relating to erosion of bog margins and the effects of stormy episodes could have exerted a significant influence on the sequence. On the human timescales, with which archaeology is concerned, specific events are of particular interest in terms of the human perception of coastal environmental change (Bell 1997). Secular trends such as sea level rise will often have been made up of a number of individually perceptible inundation events. Given the high quality of the intertidal archaeological record, it may be possible to relate events to specific responses, or coping strategies, by human communities.

3.3 Introduction to the sedimentary sequence
Heike Neumann

An estuary-wide sedimentary sequence has been defined by the works of Allen (1987a, 1990c), Allen and Rae (1987) and Allen and Rippon (1997). These outline the effects of natural estuarine sedimentary processes during the Holocene, the use of archaeological, radiocarbon, and chemostratigraphical evidence in dating those sequences, and the effects of human agency, particularly drainage and reclama-

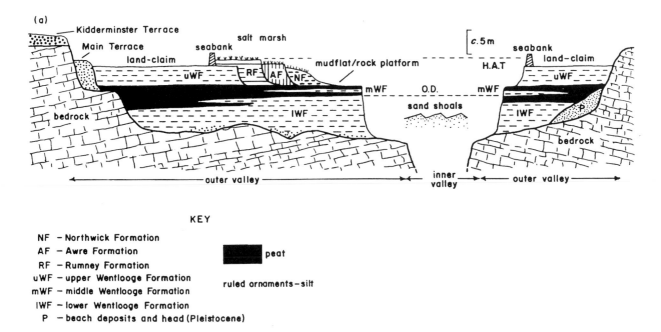

Figure 3.1 Severn Estuary: General sedimentary sequence (from Allen 1997a, fig 17)

tion. The generalised sequence is illustrated in Figure 3.1.

The Holocene sediments are exposed as a series of step-like layers of alternating grey estuarine clay/silts and peats. These can be seen at low tide, in plan, where later erosion has removed younger layers to expose whole areas of former mudflats or bog, and in section, where marine erosion has carved out clay/peat cliffs. The marine clay and peat complex which contains the archaeology has been called the Wentlooge Formation (Allen and Rae 1987) and is informally sub-divided into the lower, middle and upper Wentlooge Formations.

Rapidly rising sea levels of 16–8.5mm/year during the first millennia of the Holocene (Jennings *et al* 1998, 175) resulted in deposition of estuarine clays and silts of the lower Wentlooge Formation which are often strongly laminated. Occasionally thin peats, sometimes with tree roots, are exposed, as at Sudbrook dated 6660 ± 80 BP (Beta-79886, Scaife 1995, 77) and Goldcliff dated 6770 ± 70 BP (Beta-60761, Chapter 2). Deposition of the lower Wentlooge Formation took place from the early Holocene until around 6000 BP (Bell and Neumann 1997, table 1) when sea level rise decelerated to <1m/year (Jennings *et al* 1998, 196). Pollen and foraminifera analysis at Rumney and Uskmouth has shown that the environment of deposition was open mud flats with local formation of saltmarshes (Aldhouse-Green *et al* 1992, 29, Green 1989, 192).

The middle Wentlooge Formation is characterised by a number of episodes of peat formation intercalated with estuarine silts and clays. The Formation was laid down between *c* 6000 and 2500 BP (Allen 1997a, 502, chapter 19). The terrestrial peatbog

extended seawards at varying rates of expansion and retreat during the period. Uninterrupted sequences of peat are located towards the inner margins of the estuary and towards bedrock islands. Where marine influence was greater, peat formation was interrupted by temporary marine transgressions which formed layers of estuarine sediments intercalated within the peat. During low tide these intercalated peats are visible as a series of distinct peat shelves, in particular near the mouths of rivers, such as at Uskmouth, Peterstone and Magor. These lower peat shelves are usually thin and dominated by reed peats, although they can develop into alder carr. Where the peat is thickest the typical sequence comprises reed swamp → alder carr → willow carr → raised bog (Walker *et al* 1998). Within this succession there are occasional reversions and woodland invasions of raised bog, which can probably be related to factors such as the changing extent of marine influence and desiccation. At the closing stages of the bog the upper part of the middle Wentlooge Formation is again characterised by intercalated peat with estuarine silt and organic silt.

A widespread marine transgression led to the demise of peat forming terrestrial bog and renewed deposition of up to 4.5m of marine silts and clays, the upper Wentlooge Formation. On the surface of this at Rumney there is a complex of drainage ditches, which are dated to the Romano-British period and indicate drainage and embankment at that time, which has continued, uninterrupted by major estuarine sedimentation to this day, so much so that the basic plan of Romano-British drainage ditches is fossilised within the present landscape (Allen and Fulford 1986, Fulford *et al* 1994, Rippon 1996a).

Romano-British drainage is widely attested in other parts of the levels but in most other areas there was a return to estuarine sedimentation in the post-Roman period (Rippon 1997); and these deposits are considered to be part of the upper Wentlooge Formation.

The medieval and post-medieval periods were characterised by episodes of erosion and deposition, of which the earliest deposit is the Rumney Formation (Allen 1987), which rests unconformably on the Wentlooge Formation. It is coarser than the Wentlooge sediments and contains occasional bands of sand, which may relate to particular storms. The discovery of 13th- and 14th-century pottery at the sharp contact between the Rumney Formation and Wentlooge Formation, as well as historical evidence, suggests an early-14th century date for the onset of deposition, but elsewhere the basal deposits are late-17th century (Allen 1987a).

In many locations the Rumney Formation is superseded by the Awre and Northwick Formations. The Awre Formation is thought to have been deposited in the late-19th century and the Northwick Formation began to form in the 'second or third quarter of the 20th century' (Allen 1997a, 502, Allen and Rae 1987, 194).

3.4 The prehistoric sequence at Goldcliff
Martin Bell

This project provides an opportunity to test and develop the general model outlined for the prehistoric Wentlooge part of this sequence in a context where, because of the archaeology, we have many radiocarbon and dendrochronological dates. Evidence of the stratigraphic sequence at Goldcliff is based on four main sources:

(i) surface foreshore exposures of sediments (eg peats and clays), best exposed after storms, and mapped when the opportunity arose (eg Fig 3.2);
(ii) small-scale excavation;
(iii) auger holes, of which the project put down 68, mostly to a depth of 3–5m. These were put down entirely by hand, using either a Jarrett gouge auger for the silts and clays and Eylenkamp Riverside auger with a 0.1m diameter bucket, the latter employed particularly on the margins of the former island where drier clays and more stony sediments were encountered. In general, auger holes were put down at the rate of about one per 6 hour shift but some deeper, or more difficult holes, occupied a longer period. Holes were individually logged and described on the spot using a proforma. Some samples were taken of key horizons but none of these has been the subject of laboratory analysis. Diagrams of auger hole stratigraphy and descriptions are based on the records kept in the field by John James who supervised the auger survey throughout;
(iv) longer cores were put down at seven spots (201–207) behind the seawall by Cardiff Bay Development Corporation (CBDC). These were up to 14m long and enable us to show how the deposits on the foreshore extend inland below the seawall. Much further coring and excavation behind the seawall was subsequently carried out by CBDC and the Glamorgan–Gwent Archaeological Trust (GGAT) during an environmental assessment of plans to create bird feeding lagoons for the Gwent Levels Nature Reserve (1997 and 1998d). This work continues at the time of writing and will be published elsewhere.

The distribution of auger holes and cores is shown in Figure 3.2. Each hole is numbered, and the numbers also appear on more detailed plans of individual areas of the site in subsequent chapters. This chapter aims to show how the individual sites investigated link together as part of an overall sediment sequence; for a more detailed picture of the sequence at individual sites, the relevant parts of Chapters 4–10 should be consulted. Three master transects are as follows (Fig 3.2):

Transect A Intertidal transect linking together most of the sites studied from Goldcliff Island in the east to the limits of the Goldcliff West site (Figs 3.3–3.4)
Transect B At right angles to the seawall, from the reclaimed levels to the intertidal Iron Age site of Building 2 (Fig 3.5)
Transect C A transect from the former Goldcliff Island to the west, entirely on reclaimed levels inland of the seawall (Fig 3.6).

Fig 3.8 is a simplified isometric interpretation of how the three master transects link together.

3.5 Transect A: the intertidal area from Goldcliff Island to Goldcliff West (Figs 3.3–3.4)

At the east end of the transect, shown in detail in Figure 3.3, at the island edge, is a wave cut platform of Triassic mudstone. This is overlain by various layers of head of which one outcrop c 38m × 9m has been investigated because there were many bones stratified on its surface. This was a silty clay (Context 1120) with 5–30% rounded Lias stones mostly 40–80mm in diameter, many fractured, probably by frost shattering in situ. The surface of this deposit had fissures (20–50mm wide) containing Lias stones which may represent involutions or ice wedge casts (Chapter 2.3); these are present elsewhere on the floor of the estuary (Allen 1987b). Unstratified on the surface of this outcrop were two loose blocks of cemented sandstone (c 0.7m × 0.5m × 0.19m) which are probably derived from the last interglacial beach (Chapter 2). This deposit is interpreted as a

22

Goldcliff

Auger Transects

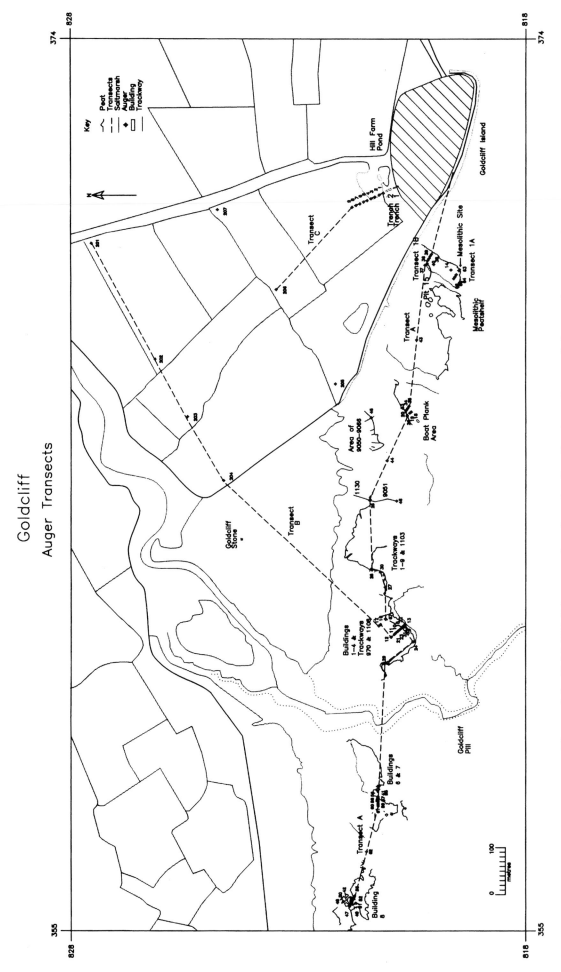

Figure 3.2 Goldcliff: Diagram showing the distribution of auger holes and transects in
relation to the peat shelves and the main archaeological sites. Drawing by B Taylor

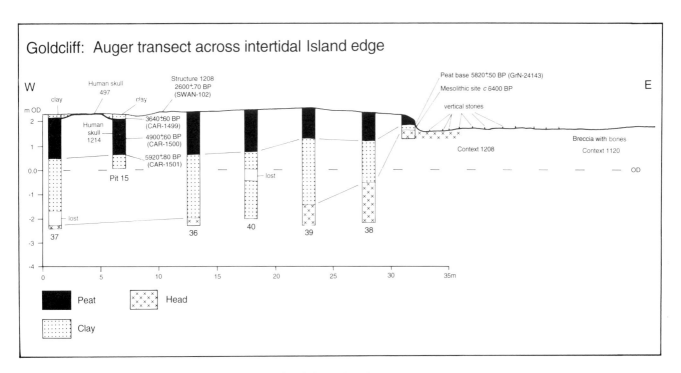

Figure 3.3   Goldcliff: Auger transect A from Goldcliff Island to Pit 15. A detail of the island edge area at the east end of Figure 3.4. Dates at right for peat base and Mesolithic site are projected from the latter 60m south. Drawing by S J Allen

Pleistocene head; it contains abundant bovid remains which will be reported elsewhere by Coard. There is no evidence of human involvement in the death of these animals, or the accumulation of the bones.

Overlying the head was sandy grey clay (Context 1208) in which roughly polygonal areas of diameter 1–1.5m were delimited by pitched flat stones, probably representing truncated periglacial involutions in head. The transect shows the basal head dipping to the west, away from the island; above the head is charcoal corresponding to the Mesolithic site dated *c* 6400 BP which has been excavated 70m south of the transect (Chapter 4). In that area the Mesolithic horizon of charcoal, lithics and bone is overlain by 0.7m of estuarine clay, a deposit which is very thin and disrupted by later tree growth at the peat shelf edge on the transect. The peat thickens to the west reaching 1.4m in Pit 15, where peat inception is dated 5920 ± 80 BP (CAR-1501), and the highest surviving peat to 3640 ± 60 BP (CAR-1499), although there is evidence of an erosive hiatus at the top. Pit 15 is the main environmental sequence spanning this period, as outlined in Chapters 13 and 14. Chapter 5 presents evidence for the deposition of human skulls in the upper part of the peat.

The continuation of the transect for 1.5km to the site of Goldcliff West is shown at a smaller scale in Figure 3.4. Short transects of auger holes were put down to investigate the detailed stratigraphic context of individual sites: the Bronze Age boat planks, Buildings 2, 6, and 8. On Transect C each is shown as a single representative auger hole. Individual auger holes were put down where other structures

were investigated, and three holes were put down in the gaps between sites. Even so, there are gaps up to *c* 150m wide which makes it difficult to establish the location of some palaeochannels.

The auger holes and the sites associated with them were linked together by a levelled transect running along the line shown in Figure 3.2 from the island to the edge of Goldcliff Pill. A few auger holes (eg Hole 45) were projected onto this transect from further north, where the sequence is less eroded and, consequently, the tops of the holes are at a higher level. Other holes (eg 46) were projected from more eroded surfaces to the south and are below the level of the transect. The profile of Goldcliff Pill has not been levelled, and is entirely schematic. West of the Pill the transect was also not levelled, so the known heights of the auger holes have been linked to give a crude idea of the topography of the transect surface. Above the transect a narrow strip summarises the sequence of sediment types exposed along the foreshore in order to show how the surface exposures and vertical sequences relate.

West of Goldcliff Island auger survey reached a maximum depth of –4.8m OD at Hole 24. The basal deposits, which correlate with the lower Wentlooge Formation, were silty clays with an increasing proportion of sand towards the base. The four deepest holes (43, 15, 24, and 41) have *Phragmites* peat some 0.1m thick, this lay at between –2.2m and –3.7m OD. Above that peat was between 1.1m and 2.7m of silty clay and then the thickest peat horizon, which we have already noted in the Pit 15 area. This dips for some 500m west of the former island then levels off at just above OD. Further west the peat top

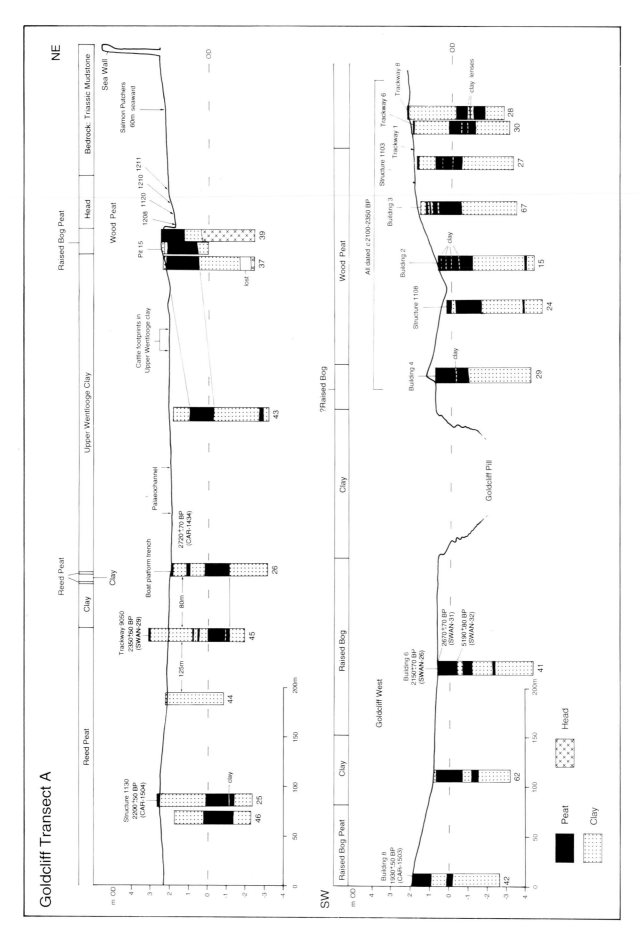

Figure 3.4 Goldcliff: Auger transect A from the former Goldcliff Island west to Building 8. For structures between Building 4 and Trackway 8, only the range of central dates is given. For full details of these and other dates see Appendix II. See Figure 3.3 for a detail of the island edge at the east end and radiocarbon dates from Pit 15. Drawing by S J Allen

and bottom still fluctuates in relation to OD, probably reflecting undulating basement topography (Allen forthcoming c).

East of Goldcliff Pill this peat is c 1.3m thick. It tends to be more woody towards the base with raised bog peat in its upper part, although wood was recorded at various points within the sequence. Within the peat variable numbers of thin clay lenses were recorded, some up to 0.1m thick, but most c 10mm. They are thought to represent events when the bog surface was subject to marine flooding.

Auger Hole 44 failed to produce any peat. It was, unfortunately, only 3m deep but the peat had been encountered by this depth in all other holes. That implies the existence of a major palaeochannel in this area, where the peat edges (Fig 3.2) have a north-east–southwest trend which is likely to reflect the direction of a channel.

East of Goldcliff Pill the surface of the peat is dated 3640 ± 60 BP (CAR-1499) in Pit 15, where there is evidence of some truncation. In the area of Building 2 it is dated 2580 ± 70 BP (CAR-1438). Overlying the peat is clay which reaches a maximum thickness of 3m in the area of later Trackway 9050. To the west this clay thins and in the area of the later Buildings 2 and 3 there are two clay bands separated by peat. It is probable that the flooding episode represented by the deposition of minerogenic sediment between Hole 24 and Goldcliff Island relates to a palaeochannel in the area of Hole 44, where the underlying peat was absent. The main evidence for this is that the band of clay in question is thickest on either side of Hole 44. This hole was not sealed by the thin Iron Age peat which is present to its north but it is thought unlikely that the putative channel is post-Iron Age. There was no indication of a palaeochannel edge cutting the peat here, and none of the tilted blocks, which are a feature of palaeochannel edges elsewhere (Allen and Rippon 1997, fig 16). It is, accordingly, suggested that the features described are most likely to represent the position of a palaeochannel of the later Bronze Age.

Within the clay in question there were two distinct thin bands of *Phragmites* peat. These outcropped in the intertidal area as two sinuous lines about 9m apart. Between the two a wooden structure exposed on the foreshore included two planks reused from a sewn boat. The structure is dated 2720 ± 70 BP (CAR-1434) and by dendrochronology to post-1017 BC, thus, clearly Bronze Age and significantly earlier than any of the other waterlogged wooden structures at Goldcliff, as is consistent with the stratigraphic sequence of Transect A. A detailed auger transect (Chapter 6) showed that, contrary to expectation, the thin peat bands did not represent the two edges of a palaeochannel. They were two separate bands 0.8m apart dipping to the west. The boat plank structure corresponded to a small palaeochannel within the marine transgressive phase between these two peats.

Above the two reed peat bands was further clay and then another peat, the most prominent exposed in this part of the intertidal zone. Between Holes 25 and 30 this was a reed peat which gave way to a wood peat between Holes 27 and 24. It was on this peat that the richest concentrations of archaeology occurred: many trackways on the reed peat and Buildings 1–3 and some trackways on the wood peat. The base of the peat is dated 2360 ± 70 BP (SWAN–136) and the archaeology, which is mostly on its surface, has many dates clustering around 2200 BP which are broadly confirmed by dendrochronological determinations on three structures.

Clays from the Bronze Age marine incursion were not present west of Hole 24. In Hole 29, and to the west, there had been continuous peat growth from the Neolithic to the middle Iron Age. It was on this thick peat that Building 4 was erected 2140 ± 60 BP (CAR-1435); that is contemporary with the development of wood and reed peat to its east on which the other structures are situated.

Particularly noteworthy is a close similarity between the sequence at Building 4, just east of the major current channel of Goldcliff Pill, and the sequence west of the Pill. This similarity strongly suggests that the present position of the Pill is post Iron Age and it has cut through the earlier bog. On both sides we see the same thick peat. West of the Pill that peat is divided into upper and lower units by a clay band which thickens to the west up to 0.7m. This is likely to correlate with the clay band in Hole 29 east of the Pill. This clay may relate to flooding associated with a palaeochannel or embayment to the west. A radiocarbon date from the base of the peat above this clay indicates that this flooding episode came to an end around 5190 ± 80 BP (SWAN-32).

Once peat formation had restarted west of Goldcliff Pill it continued without interruption of minerogenic bands until the period when Buildings 6, 7, and 8 were constructed on peat hummocks in the Iron Age. The date for the surface of the peat within Building 6 is 2760 ± 70 BP (SWAN-31), but it is clear that the peat surface on the top of this hummock has been truncated. Building 6, which sits on that surface was, according to dendrochronological evidence, made of wood cut in 273 BC, by which time the environmental evidence shows that the peat at the hummock edge was subject to periodic marine inundation, which was the precursor of the upper Wentlooge marine transgression. Previous inundations, which had occurred since the Mesolithic, had all affected only part of the area; this one was widespread.

3.6 Transect B: north to south across the seawall

Figure 3.5 shows the sedimentary sequence roughly at right angles to the seawall, demonstrating how peats and clays exposed on the foreshore extend inland below the seawall. It is, thus, a specific case of the generalised sequence presented in Figure 3.1. The south, intertidal, end of this transect is at Building 2 (Hole 15). At the base is a thin horizontal reed peat, at −4m OD. The main middle Wentlooge

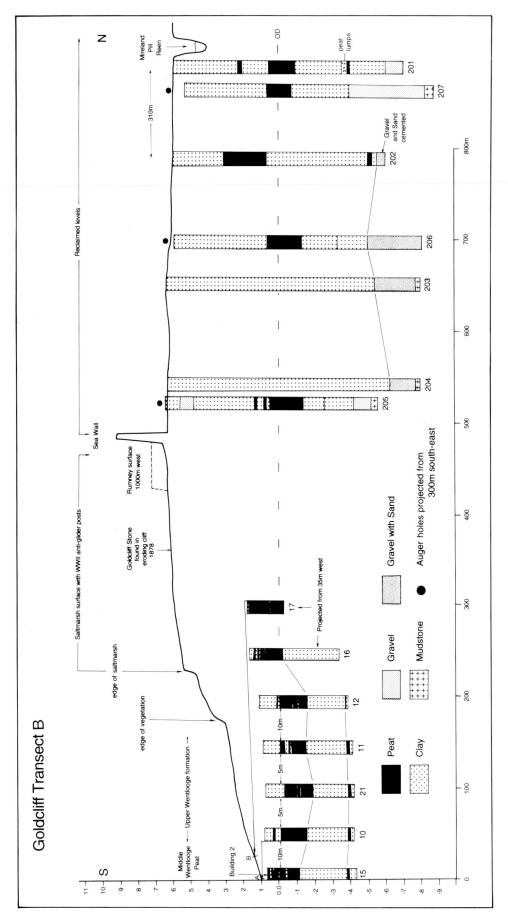

Figure 3.5 Goldcliff: Auger transect B at right angles to the present seawall from the reclaimed area to Building 2. Holes 15–17 are an expanded version of the area A–B. Drawing by S J Allen

peat, conversely, has a fluctuating base level. Thin marine clay inundation episodes are seen within the peat in most cores. The upper part of the peat shows the alternating peat clay sequence, which was a feature of the area round Buildings 1 and 2. It is evident that this area was subject to more episodes of marine inundation than any other part of the site prior to the construction of Iron Age buildings and trackways. This is likely to reflect the proximity of a palaeochannel which has not been located and may have lain to seaward. A possible channel candidate was identified north of Building 3 where two low peat ridges projected through the overlying upper Wentlooge clay (Fig 7.2). It was thought that these had formed over levées at the edges of a channel. Holes 16 and 17 were put down between the peat bands and show continuous thick peat. Therefore, if we are correct in interpreting the peat ridges as representing a channel, then that topography would seem to have been inherited from a pre-Neolithic surface, thus highlighting the complex and ancient genealogy of some of the channel-like features exposed on the foreshore (Allen forthcoming c).

Behind the seawall, four of the seven long cores put down by the CBDC (1993) reached mudstone bedrock, at between –5m and –8m. Covering this was gravel and sand identified as a Pleistocene deposit in Chapter 2. Lower Wentlooge clays vary considerably in thickness between 2.9m and 5.7m. The middle Wentlooge peat reaches its maximum thickness of 2.5m in Hole 202. Hole 205 shows two, and Hole 201 one, thin peats, above the main middle Wentlooge peat which can probably be correlated, in the intertidal area, with the peat bands on which Buildings 1–3 and many of the trackways sit.

Two cores (203 and 204) lack the middle Wentlooge peat, which presumably has been removed by a channel sometime between the middle Bronze Age and the present. Since both holes are within 100–150m of the present Goldcliff Pill, the peat could have been removed by an earlier meander of that channel.

Seaward of the seawall is grazed saltmarsh where we can document extensive coastal change in the last 120 years. In 1878 there was an eroding cliff 100m seaward of the seawall where the Goldcliff Stone was found (Morgan 1882). Nineteenth-century maps show the cliff continuing to erode back, eventually isolating the surviving fragment of the Rumney surface which is at the edge of Goldcliff Pill 100m west of Transect C, its surface about 1m above the surface of the reclaimed levels. Subsequently, extensive silt deposition occurred, burying the former cliff and findspot of the stone and creating the present saltmarsh. On the surface of this are many substantial wooden posts which, we understand, are anti-glider posts emplaced during World War II. Thus the present saltmarsh was in place by 1939–45, although it has been subject to continuing deposition. Today the sea is once again eroding the edge of the saltmarsh as its stepped profile to the south demonstrates.

3.7 Transect C: west of Goldcliff Island behind the seawall

This auger transect was northwest of the former island behind the seawall (Fig 3.2). Two trenches were dug across the island edge deposits in 1992 and much further stratigraphic information was obtained when a pond was made in 1994.

Hill Farm Trenches 1 and 2 (Fig 3.6)

These trenches were excavated to examine the sedimentary sequence at the island edge in the hope that interstratification of, for instance, alluvium-edge colluvial deposits (Bell 1981) might enable us to correlate patterns of activity on the island with the wetland sediment sequence. This was partly successful in the earlier part of the sequence, but later levels had been cut away by a post-medieval pond. At the base of Trench 2 head was located in small soundings; it was overlain by lower Wentlooge clay, then by a stabilisation surface, within which were two distinct charcoal layers separated by marine clay. These charcoal horizons were associated with burnt clay, a scatter of flints and bone, and some poorly preserved waterlogged roots. This was shown by the later pond excavation to be the feather edge of peat which thickens to the west. The lower of the charcoal horizons has a radiocarbon date of 3670 ± 60 BP (CAR-1505). Neither charcoal horizon can, therefore, be contemporary with the Mesolithic charcoal layer on the foreshore. Remarkably, however, the date is exactly the same as a date for a *Tilia* decline and farming at Smith and Morgan's (1989, fig 3) pollen diagram at Goldcliff East. There is good evidence, therefore, of clearance on the island itself during the middle Bronze Age. In Trench 2 the charcoal layers were overlain by marine clay. At a point corresponding to this junction, cleaning of the surface revealed a number of cattle footprints, demonstrating that animals were present on the island edge at this time.

The auger transect and Hill Farm Pond

In 1992–94 the line of Trenches 1 and 2 was extended 135m to the west by auger holes 1–9 (Fig 3.6). Borehole 206 extends the sequence 200m further west. Much additional information was obtained in 1994 when the pond was made. Figure 3.7 shows a detail of the south side of the pond, with the main sedimentary units numbered from the base.

Unit 1 Head: This dips from 5m OD in Trench 2 to 3.1m at the south edge of the pond and 1.8m at the north edge. This probably corresponds to the head underlying the Mesolithic site in the intertidal area. In Hole 206 the basal deposit was described as gravel at –5m OD, overlain by clay with some gravel.

Unit 2 Grey clay: Only briefly exposed in one area and not subject to any analytical investigation, therefore, of uncertain origin. The field interpretation

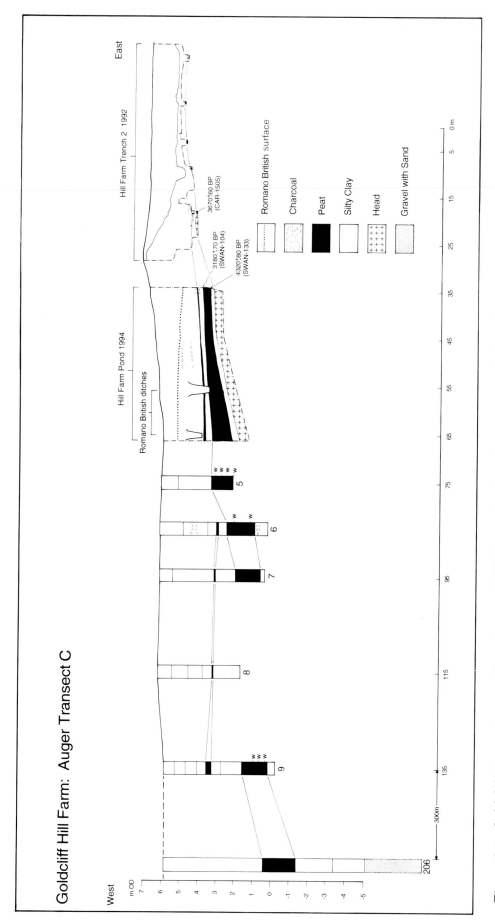

Figure 3.6 Goldcliff: Auger transect C northwest of Hill Farm, showing the sections from Trench 2 and Hill Farm Pond. Drawing by S J Allen

Goldcliff Hill Farm Pond 1994

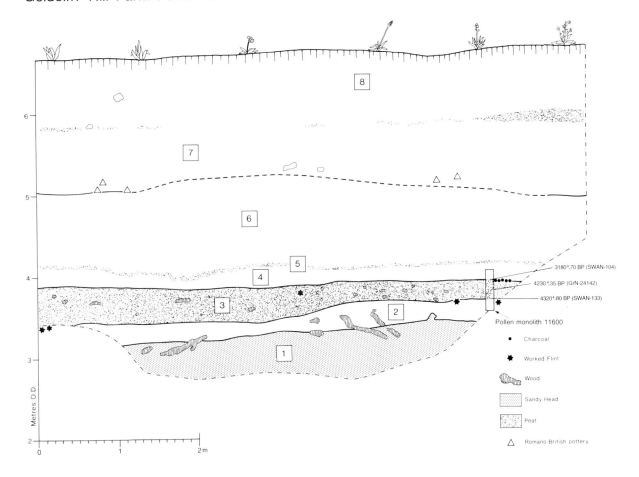

Figure 3.7 Goldcliff: Section of the sediments revealed in Hill Farm Pond. Drawing by B Garfi

was that it was estuarine, but on the basis of a constant thickness to the west (Fig 3.6). John Allen (personal communication) suggests it may have been weathered head. Thicker, probably unrelated, clays to the west had charcoal in their upper part in Hole 6 and, in Hole 206, reached a maximum thickness below the peat of 3.7m.

Unit 3 Wood peat: Up to 0.40m thick. Trees growing on this unit are probably responsible for roots in the underlying two units. In nearby Section 11702 (not illustrated) there was a marked charcoal layer at the base of the peat. The peat base in Monolith 11600 is dated 4320 ± 80 BP (SWAN-133) and a pollen sequence from that monolith is discussed in Chapter 13. A second charcoal layer is present on top of this peat and is dated 3180 ± 70 BP (SWAN-104). Four flint flakes were found at the base of the peat and, thus, represent the only archaeological evidence we have for late-Neolithic activity. One worked flint occurred in the upper part of the peat and thus relates to Bronze Age activity.

The thin peat encountered in the pond thickens rapidly to the west where, in Hole 206, it reaches 1.75m. Its base drops from 4m OD to –1.3m OD in

Hole 206. The surface of the layer drops correspondingly; the reasons for this westward dip are discussed in the conclusions.

Unit 4 Marine clay: 0.2m thick (Fig 3.7), thickening to 1.7m in Hole 9 (Fig 3.6).

Unit 5 Peaty clay band: 20m–50mm thick at c 4.1m OD on Figure 3.7; this thickened to a distinct peat 0.15m thick to the north (Fig. 3.6). To the north in Holes 6–9 the peat was at between 3m and 3.5m OD. Given its relationship to the main peat, this can probably be correlated with the intertidal peat shelf on which the main concentration of Iron Age Buildings and trackways was found. The nearest intertidal outcrop of that peat at Trackway 9050 (Fig 3.2) was at 3m OD.

Unit 6 Estuarine clay: 1m thick. Correlated with the upper Wentlooge clay. In Hole 2 charcoal occurred at c 1.5m and in Hole 6 at 2m. These might point to later Iron Age burning episodes on the island. However, in view of what is said below about Romano-British activity, the possibility must also be considered that the charcoal derives from the fills of features cut from a higher level.

Unit 6a Stabilisation horizon: An indistinct and

discontinuous buried soil which contained Romano-British sherds. In Figure 3.7 this occurs at 5m OD but, averaged over the pond area as a whole, the surface producing Romano-British material was at 5.29m OD. Two Romano-British ditches were identified in the temporary sections for the pond, and are shown schematically in Figure 3.6; detailed sections have been published elsewhere (Bell 1995, fig 63). The edges of Ditch 11537 were traced no higher than 4.7m OD, but they did not relate to a definable old ground surface. Ditch 11520 had been cut from a surface which was discontinuously observed at 4.8m OD. A large collection of Romano-British pottery from the pond has so far only been subject to preliminary examination (Brennan 1995). It is mostly 2nd–4th century, with some material that could be 1st century. Most of this material is unstratified, but there is a small collection from the ditches and old land surfaces. The Romano-British evidence from this pond will be published in greater detail elsewhere.

Unit 7 Estuarine clay: Of average thickness 0.77m. It was very noticeable that, during the first few days of pond excavation when this layer was being excavated, no Romano-British finds were made, then as the top of Unit 6a was reached, pottery became abundant. Thus Unit 7 is a sterile blanket of estuarine clay which buries the ditched landscape. Unit 7a (Fig 3.8) comprised clay with desiccated peat; this might represent a localised feature such as a ditch. The overlying Unit 8 on this section is estuarine clay, partly perhaps deposited from the making of an earlier pond.

3.8 Goldcliff East

During 1993 the embayment east of Goldcliff Island, which we have called Goldcliff East, was surveyed by Ray Caple (Appendix I, Map 16). This survey was done because, within the embayment, there had been a previous coring survey and two very well dated pollen diagrams by Smith and Morgan (1989), to which it was important to relate our own work. It was also desirable to establish whether the abundant archaeology west of the island extended to its east, which it did not.

On the west of the embayment is the interglacial beach described in Chapter 2, overlain by a lower peat at c –3.7m OD. At its base are charcoal and some flint flakes. John Allen has obtained a radiocarbon date of 6770 ± 70 BP (Beta-60761) for one of the oak trees on this peat surface, which is thereby shown to be contemporary with the earliest evidence of Mesolithic activity west of the island, although at a much lower level. This lower peat can be confidently linked to that which occurs in the deeper holes in Transects A and B west of the island.

The peat is overlain by clay and then by the main middle Wentlooge peat shelf where, 0.55km east of the island, Smith and Morgan put down two auger transects. The base of the peat was at c OD, here

again it rises towards the former island. At the eastern end the bog surface is at about 1.6m OD but at the eastern end the upper part of the sequence has been eroded. The chronology for this sequence is provided by a series of 21 radiocarbon dates which are of great value for comparison with our own series west of the former island. Peat inception was dated 5950 ± 80 BP (CAR-659) and ended 3130 ± 70 BP (CAR-645). The total thickness of peat is 1.58m, broadly comparable with the transects west of the island.

During the 1993 and 1994 seasons the surface of the peat shelf at Goldcliff East was occasionally relatively mud free and was examined for archaeology; however, all that was found were three alignments of stakes which are thought to be relatively recent fish traps. Given the great wealth of archaeology west of the former island it is notable that there was no clear evidence of post Mesolithic activity at Goldcliff East. The absence of occupation can partly be explained because here peat ceased forming in the middle Bronze Age. There is no evidence here for the upper peat on which the Iron Age archaeology was located west of the island. It is possible, however, that peat has been eroded away, since there is evidence for an upper peat in the Redwick area further east (Chapter 16).

3.9 Discussion of the sequence

This chapter has shown that within the tripartite model of lower, middle, and upper Wentlooge with which we began (Fig 3.1) there is considerable stratigraphic complexity, particularly within the middle Wentlooge peat/silt complex. Figure 3.8 is an attempt to simplify the sequence outlined and to show how the three transects link together. Correlation of the various sites has been facilitated by radiocarbon and dendrochronological dating.

We have noted the pronounced dip of the main peat away from the former island which is largely a result of autocompaction (Allen forthcoming c). The Holocene sequence thickens rapidly to the west, reaching a maximum thickness of 11m in Hole 206. Where the sequence is thickest, away from the island, compaction will have had a much greater effect. It would seem to be a reasonable proposition to assume that during the Bronze Age the peat surface was, in broad terms, level; it may even have risen to the west, given that the upper part of the peat is mainly raised bog, and this tends to adopt a domed profile (eg Godwin 1981). Since we know that in the pond the top of the peat is dated 3180 ± 70 BP and is at 4.25m OD, it may be reasonable to suggest that to the west the peat surface once lay at that level, or above. This would imply a peat which was at least 5.5m thick, now compressed to a thickness of 1.8m thick, ie one third of its original thickness.

Given that compression is considered to be the chief factor responsible for the dip of the main peat away from the island, it is noteworthy that the upper

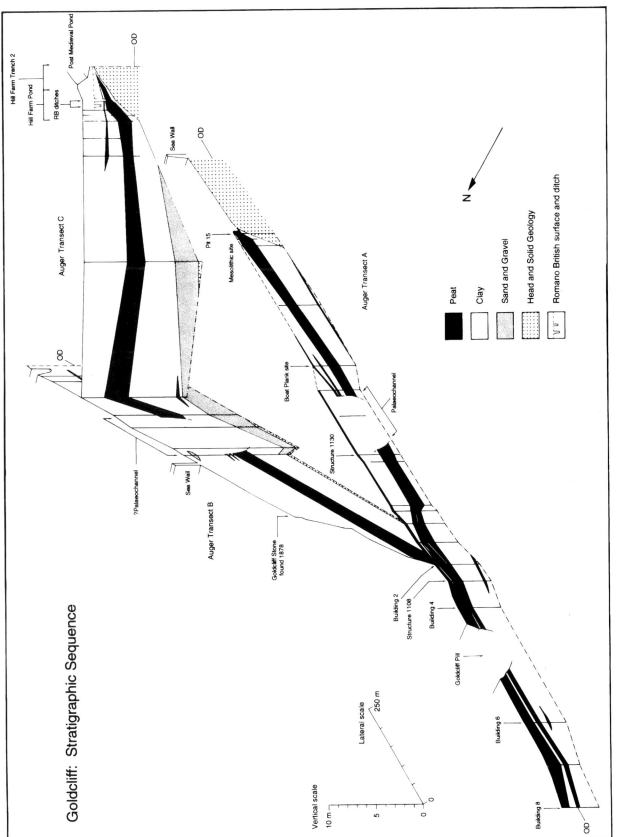

Goldcliff: Stratigraphic Sequence

Hill Farm Trench 2

Hill Farm Pond

RB ditches

Post Medieval Pond

OD

Auger Transect C

Sea Wall

OD

Pit 15

Mesolithic site

Auger Transect A

Peat

Clay

Sand and Gravel

Head and Solid Geology

Romano British surface and ditch

N

OD

?Palaeochannel

Sea Wall

Auger Transect B

Boat Plank site

Palaeochannel

Goldcliff Stone found 1878

Structure 1130

Building 2

Structure 1108

Building 4

Goldcliff Pill

Building 6

Building 8

OD

Vertical scale

10 m

5

0

Lateral scale

250 m

0

Figure 3.8 Goldcliff: Interpretative isometric drawing showing the relationships between the sediment sequences in Transects A, B, and C. Drawing by S J Allen

peat Unit 5 is, in Transect C, roughly horizontal. The implication of this is that the significant compression of the underlying peat occurred rapidly after the drowning of the bog and before c 2400 BP. However, it should also be recorded that in Transect A in the intertidal area the Iron Age peat does dip significantly to the west (Fig 3.4). Such height differences may reflect concealed basement valleys as demonstrated by Allen (forthcoming c). In this specific case the differences may be of more local origin, reflecting the decreasing thickness of the Bronze Age clay lens within the peat. Clay lenses within the middle Wentlooge appear to be a significant factor creating topographic contrasts. It has been suggested that the number and extent of these clays relates to the proximity of palaeochannels. The greatest number is around Buildings 1 and 2. There are two particularly thick clay layers within the middle Wentlooge: near the top of the main peat between Holes 25 and 24 and in the lower part of the main peat at Goldcliff West. These, presumably, relate to marine incursion up palaeochannels, the amount of sediment deposition being greatest close to the channel and decreasing with distance from the water body (Allen 1996c, 16).

Where thick clay lenses were deposited within the peat and, thus, for a period, relatively uncompactable clay was being laid down instead of highly compactable peat, the effect of subsequent compaction would be to create a higher surface above the area of clay deposition. This is the phenomenon which in the Fenland gives rise to roddens (Godwin 1938, Hall and Coles 1994, 19, Allen forthcoming c). It probably explains why, in some parts of the site, the Iron Age surface was at a notably higher level. Examples are the area of Trackway 1130, where the Iron Age surface was at 2.6m OD and 2.4m of clay had been

deposited within the middle Wentlooge, and at Building 8, where the surface was at 1.8m OD and 0.75m of clay had been deposited within the middle Wentlooge. Between these there is the area of Buildings 1 and 2 where the surface was at c 0.6m and Hole 24, where it was at 0.23m OD. It should be emphasised that, although these surfaces are at very different OD heights, the field evidence shows they form a single surface and the radiocarbon evidence demonstrates that without doubt they are contemporary. Differential post-depositional autocompaction is the factor responsible for the differences we see today.

In the Transect B across the seawall (Fig 3.5) the upper Wentlooge Formation has an average thickness of 4.5m. Evidence from Hill Farm Pond (Bell 1995) shows a surface and associated ditches at a depth of c 0.8m below the levels behind the seawall. Thus, it can be suggested that up to 3.65m of sediment was deposited at Goldcliff between the 3rd century BC and the phase of Romano-British activity represented in the pond. A high rate of sedimentation at that time may reflect higher sea level, enhanced by the effects of autocompaction, which modelling by Allen (forthcoming c) shows leads to much higher sedimentation in the period following peat/silt transitions. Once this substantial thickness of sediment had been laid down, the extent of Romano-British drainage and activity on both sides of the estuary (Rippon 1997a) points to a pronounced regressive phase, which in places led to more or less permanent reclamation, as at Rumney Great Wharf (Allen and Fulford 1986). More widely in the estuary, as at Goldcliff (Bell 1995), and many sites on the English side (Rippon 1997), there is evidence for renewed estuarine sedimentation during the post-Roman period.

4 The Goldcliff late-Mesolithic site, 5400–4000 Cal BC

by M Bell with J R L Allen, R N E Barton, R Coard, J Crowther, G M Cruise, C Ingrem, and R Macphail

4.1 Introduction

Nineteenth-century discoveries of flint artefacts below intertidal peats in the Bristol Channel and Pembrokeshire provided the earliest evidence for intertidal archaeology in this region (Chapter 1). Such contexts manifestly relate to human activity at a time of lower sea level. As sources of evidence for the Mesolithic they are of particular importance, being well stratified and suitable for the preservation of environmental evidence, including bone.

Opportunities to investigate the coastal Mesolithic have been limited by inaccessibility of sites for excavation because of sea level rise. A storm in 1983, which removed the sand cover from the Westward Ho!, Devon Mesolithic midden, provided the opportunity for a brief field investigation and more detailed programme of analytical work (Balaam *et al* 1987). Pollen analysis of Pembrokeshire sites where Mesolithic flints occurred below intertidal peats was also carried out by Lewis (1992). The discovery of a Mesolithic intertidal site at Goldcliff provided the opportunity for a more detailed investigation of a class of site which is well represented in western Britain but, because of the logistical difficulties involved, has not received the attention it deserves.

The Mesolithic site was found in 1987 by Derek Upton and Bob Trett and represented the first evidence for prehistoric intertidal archaeology at Goldcliff. They observed a layer of charcoal with flint flakes below the peat shelf on the western flanks of the former Goldcliff Island (Parkhouse 1991a, 14). They, and others, collected lithics and bone which are housed in Newport Museum and have been made available to us for study. In April 1989 Newport Museum commissioned Malcolm Lillie to carry out further recording at the site. He laid out a grid of pegs on the peat shelf at 10m intervals which has survived for a decade and has been the basis of our own work and subsequent monitoring of erosion. Lillie also made a map of the peat edge at a scale of 1:100, recorded the position of 34 numbered pieces of worked lithic and two pieces of bone on that plan and drew the section of 89m of irregular exposed peat shelf. The careful record made by Lillie has been invaluable in establishing the character of the site, its stratigraphic sequence and as a source of baseline data against which we have been able to monitor subsequent erosion by resurveying the peat edge each year between 1991 and 1995. Newport Museum subsequently obtained a radiocarbon date 6430 ± 80 BP (GU-2759) on charcoal from the site.

Even before the regular monitoring it was apparent that erosion was rapid. Clay which underlay the peat shelf was subject to undercutting, producing peat overhangs which, from time to time, broke off forming peat rafts in the deeper channel to the east. Accordingly, when work began on the later prehistoric complex at Goldcliff it was decided that a limited excavation on the Mesolithic should form part of this project. Work on the Mesolithic site was, however, relatively small-scale, not through any failure to recognise the importance of the site, but as a consequence of mounting pressure to record the many later prehistoric sites.

4.2 Excavation method

Excavations on the Mesolithic site took place for a month each summer between 1992 and 1994. It was done by students under the supervision of W M Timmins, with G Longden in 1994. Each year an area along the eroding peat face was excavated: 12m^2 in 1992, 16m^2 in 1993, 8m^2 in 1994, plus 18m^2 in Trench 50, at right angles to the exposed face (Figs 4.1–4.2). The peat surface was planned prior to excavation. Excavation then proceeded through the peat and underlying estuarine clay, generally without finding anything. Below the clay the finds were concentrated in a band of charcoal. This surface was generally excavated one or more metre squares at a time. This had the disadvantage that it was only occasionally possible to view cleaned surfaces of more than 2m^2 or 3m^2 in plan. However, the approach was dictated by the twice daily tidal inundations, the muddy conditions, and the need to minimise trampling on areas prior to excavation. The lower levels of the site, particularly in Trench 50, proved especially difficult to excavate because of mud.

Each artefact was three dimensionally recorded using the simple method developed for the study of colluvial stratigraphy (Bell 1983) and subsequently employed in work on the Brean Down settlement sequence (Bell 1990). Finds were placed in a series of pre-numbered tubs or bags. Garden tags with the same number were attached with a nail to the findspot. At appropriate intervals during, and at the end of each tidal shift, the coordinates of each piece were recorded. The horizontal coordinates were recorded using the grid originally established by Lillie and each piece was also levelled to OD.

34

Figure 4.1 Goldcliff: Mesolithic site section with the charcoal layer marked by an arrow. Scale 2m (horizontal), 1m (vertical). In the background is the cliff edge and buildings on the former Goldcliff Island and below the cliff on the right the salmon putcher racks which are still in use. Photograph by L Boulton

4.3 Stratigraphic sequence

The excavation and survey around the Mesolithic site showed that the site formed a single horizon within a sequence of sediments dipping west from the former Goldcliff Island. The Quaternary setting has already been outlined in Chapters 2 and 3. The sequence at the Mesolithic site is shown on Figures 4.3–4.4 as follows, from the earliest deposits to the latest:

Context 1242
Head of brownish grey sandy clay with numerous small pebbles of quartz and flint.

Context 1204
Sandy clay with some small stones. This is the lowest layer encountered in the Mesolithic site and is considered to be head.

Context 1203
Clay, which in the lower parts of the site underlay the Mesolithic charcoal horizon.

Context 1202
Clay with much charcoal also containing lithic artefacts and bones producing a clear and largely continuous occupation horizon of average thickness 80mm. At the northern, landward end of the peat-shelf on Lillie's section the layer is at 2m OD. It dips

at about 2° to the south where it is at 0.1m OD. There is also a dip to the west of 3.5°. The layer is inclined to be more patchy at the southern end. On Figure 4.4, 1.3m north of Section d, there are pockets of clay at the base of this layer, one 50mm wide and 40mm deep, the other 80mm wide and deep. Between these are lenses of clay in the underlying sandy clay. With hindsight it is suggested that these features may represent animal footprints, but this was not recognised at the time of excavation. A sharp boundary between this and the overlying clay (Fig 4.3) suggests there has been only slight erosion and reworking at this junction (see below for micromorphology report).

Context 1201
Estuarine clay, which at the southern end of the section is 0.7m thick, thins northward down to 0.05m at the north end of the excavated area; further north in the section drawn by Lillie, clay disappears as a distinct and continuous layer. North of this the occupation layer of charcoal and clay occurs at the base of the overlying peat and the junctions between these layers are much disrupted by rooting activity associated with the peat.

Context 1200
Peat; this was between 0.05m and 0.2m thick at the edge of the peatshelf, but the auger survey and Pit 15 (Fig 3.3) showed that it thickened very rapidly to the west. The lower part of the peat is woody, with

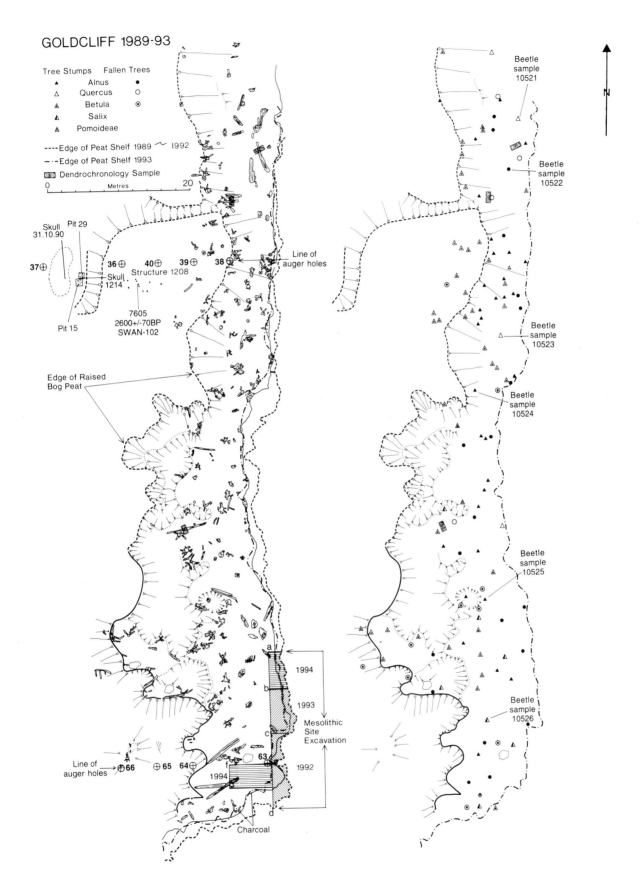

Figure 4.2 Goldcliff: Plan of the peat shelf overlying the Mesolithic site showing the locations of the Mesolithic excavation trenches, Pit 15, Strucure 1208, and the distribution of tree types in the submerged forest which dates to the later Mesolithic and Neolithic period. Drawing by K Buxton and B Garfi

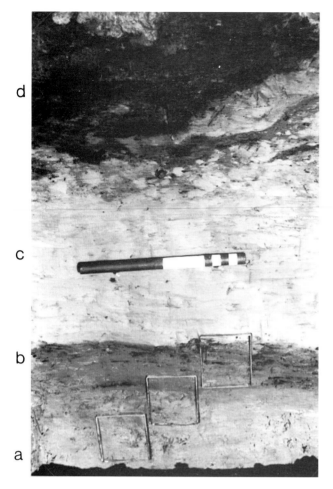

Figure 4.3 Goldcliff: Section of the Mesolithic site showing (a) underlying head (1204), (b) Mesolithic charcoal layer (1202), (c) estuarine clay (1201), (d) peat (1200). Photograph shows the locations of sediment micromorphology samples from bottom 2058, 2057, and 2056. Scale 0.4m. Photograph by M Bell

many tree stumps, with roots penetrating the underlying estuarine clay, some as far as the charcoal layer. The involuted junction between the peat and the clay includes depressions in which lenses of, probably redeposited, clay occur within peat. These can almost certainly be interpreted as tree-throw phenomena in which the uprooted tree bowl carries with it sediment from the underlying horizon, which then weathers off to create a lens of inverted stratigraphy. Such patterns, in a somewhat different guise, are familiar to excavators of many terrestrial sites (Kooi 1974). Their occurrence here, together with other evidence for the effects of rooting activity, has implications for the amount of mixing which may have occurred as a result of tree-throw and root growth within fen wood peats and, thus, the extent to which these peats may preserve a detailed vegetational record.

Within this peat a single flint flake was located and some charcoal also occurs. In Trench 50 there were fragments of charcoal at the very base of the peat. Within the wood peat at a higher level one willow stump had a scatter of charcoal around it. These finds indicate very limited human activity during the early

stages of peat inception which in Pit 15 is dated 5920 ± 80BP (Car-1501), thus, also within the Mesolithic.

Features on the Mesolithic surface 1202

On the Mesolithic surface, represented by a scatter of charcoal, some features were recorded as shown in Figure 4.5. When the charcoal layer had been removed in Trench 50, a circle 0.15m in diameter of clay and charcoal was observed (Context 1241). When sectioned this turned out to be 0.40m deep, with a pointed base; it may be a post cast. Beside this was a roughly circular area 0.9m in diameter with a marked concentration of charcoal with some burnt clay; this may mark the position of a hearth. The 1993 excavation 7m to the northeast produced a second concentration of charcoal, and 2m from this was a particularly large piece of charcoal 0.44m × 0.30m.

4.4 Artefact distributions and environmental sampling

The total number of artefacts three dimensionally recorded over the three seasons excavation was 1650, although a large number of these were pieces of flint debitage and fragments of unidentifiable bone. The artefacts were highly concentrated in the charcoal band, with only small numbers occurring within 50–100mm above or below that band. Apart from this, one bone was found in the overlying clay (1201) and, as already noted, a single flint and some charcoal in the peat (1200) above this. For a distribution plot in vertical section see Bell 1995, fig 60a.

Figures 4.5–4.6 show that charcoal, flints, and bone show distinct nucleations. Although the area of plotted artefacts is not extensive, the clear impression is of patches of increased density which it is thought are most economically explained in terms of human activity. There is no sign of linear bands of charcoal along the contour, which is the pattern anticipated if the major formative processes had been those of reworking along the strandline. Bones and charcoal show particular nucleations, and in the same areas, which could hint at the cooking and processing of food, since there are significant numbers of burnt bones (Fig 4.6). There is a pronounced tendency for the density of finds to reduce to the southwest away from the edge of the former island, so we may have reached the edge of the site in that direction.

Sieving was, unfortunately, limited by the logistical demands of the project as a whole. With hindsight, it is particularly regretted that more resources were not put into overcoming these problems as they produced both plant macrofossils and fish bones. In the event, one sample was taken from most 1m squares for sieving. It was only possible to sieve some of these in the laboratory.

A phosphate sample was also taken from each quadrant of each 1m square. Pollen work was

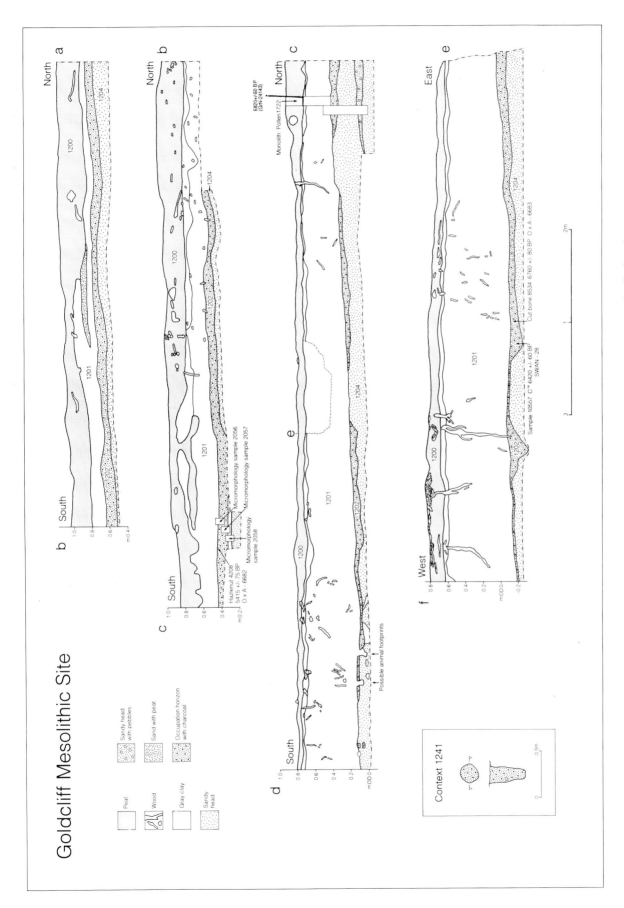

Figure 4.4 Goldcliff: Sections of the Mesolithic site. Drawing by B Garfi

concentrated on Monolith 1722 from the main section (Fig 4.4) and this short Mesolithic sequence overlaps with the much longer sequence from nearby Pit 15, the context of which is outlined in Chapter 5. Three micromorphological samples were taken from one area across the charcoal band, as shown in Figure 4.3, in order to investigate the character of this horizon and the formation processes responsible.

4.5 Raw materials
J R L Allen

Introduction

A limited range of geological raw materials (flint, chert, tuff, and quartzite) was exploited by humans at Goldcliff, of which flint greatly outweighed the rest. The flint worked took the form of subangular to subrounded pebbles and small cobbles that represented individual small nodules, broken small nodules, and fragments devoid of traces of cortex naturally broken from nodules. Almost all surviving natural surfaces reveal clear signs of water wear. Any surviving cortex is smoothed and locally abraded, and naturally broken surfaces show a degree of polish. The edges and corners of many lumps are slightly rounded and percussion-marked; in a few cases, typically the rounder clasts, these fractures apparently covered the entire surface. Most of the flint is opaque and dark grey–black, with occasional grey mottles, but a few such flakes are translucent at thin edges. A moderate amount of flint is pale–mid grey; a very little is a translucent honey yellow–pale brown. Some flint flakes became burnt, and now show a delicate surface crazing. A few of these remained red–brown, but most were afterwards pedologically bleached to pale grey.

The chert utilised also occurred as water-worn pebbles and small cobbles which seem to have been rather better rounded than the lumps of flint. It is mainly black, breaking with a rough to coarsely hackly surface. Traces of fossils and other detrital components abound, and suggestions of lamination are evident in some cases.

Tough, dark-coloured, siliceous tuffs were also worked at Goldcliff. These vary in hand-specimen from intensely black, very fine grained tuffs that flake with a smooth, satiny fracture, through dark grey silty tuffs, to mid grey varieties dominated by sand-sized components that afford rougher breaks. Most appear structureless but a faint centimetre-scale banding ranging to a more obvious millimetre-scale lamination is evident in some examples. Occasional flakes show veins or patches of crystalline quartz, but no cleavage was seen. The tuffs appear to have occurred as larger cobbles than was typical of the flint and chert. These were water-worn and mainly subangular, with smoothed surfaces and, in some instances, percussion-marked corners and edges. No evidence of wind-polishing was seen. Thin-sections cut from four flakes and the two axe/adzes show the rocks to be heavily recrystallised, quartzo-feldspathic, and pyritous. The finer-grained examples show scattered, aligned feldspar laths, clay/mineral aggregates of uncertain origin, and very occasional, large, tabular plagioclase crystals in a fine-textured, chloritic groundmass rich in iron ores and pyrite. Present in the coarser rocks are recrystallised glass sherds, fragments of trachytic lavas, and occasional crystals of plagioclase and quartz.

Quartzite is extremely rare but was put to a wider

Table 4.1 Goldcliff Mesolithic site, surface assemblages and Hill Farm: total artefact counts

	Goldcliff Mesolithic site 1990–92 excavations	Mesolithic surface material 1987–94	Goldcliff Hill Farm 1992 excavation
Flakes	409	167	17
Blades/bladelets	11	5	5
Chips	28	0	1
Cores	36	43	3
Core shatter	45	19	0
Core rejuvenation	20	7	1
Unidentified	63	28	6
Non-flaked stone	6	6	0
Retouched tools			
Microliths	3	+	1
End-scrapers	2	1	+
Retouched flakes	10	2	1
Axes/adzes	+	2	+
Natural	439	74	+
Total	633	280	35

Totals exclude natural pebbles. + denotes absence, or where data are unrecorded. For further information on the composition of the assemblage in terms of numbers of complete, broken, burnt, part-cortical and fully cortical pieces see CD 4.1; for core types see CD 4.2.

range of uses than the other rocks. The collections include small, well-rounded cobbles of pale-grey, medium–coarse grained, slightly micaceous, quartzitic quartz sandstone that are deeply penetrated overall by polygonal thermal contraction cracks. Signs of flaking are restricted to (i) a single, well-rounded pebble of tough, very fine grained, greyish-green quartzite, and (ii) a tough, medium grained, pink quartzite.

Mesolithic site

The main collection of stratified lithic material was from the excavations of 1992–94. There are 30 worked items of chert (4.8% of artefact assemblage), 28 of tuff (4.5%), one flaked pebble of greyish-green quartzite, one thermally-fractured cobble of quartzitic quartz sandstone, and three other fragments of quartzitic quartz sandstone (one exploited as a hammerstone). The small amount of unstratified material linked to the site also includes items in tuff and chert.

Newport Collection

The Newport Museum and Art Gallery Collection, assembled from 1987, is made up of stratified worked material from the main Mesolithic site, unstratified worked material linked to that site, and unstratified worked material from the general area. In total, the assemblage includes seven items of tuff (including two axe/adzes from Porton and Goldcliff East), 22 of chert, and fragments from at least two thermally fractured cobbles of quartzitic quartz sandstone. The larger axe/adze was made from a homogeneous, very fine grained tuff, the smaller from a slightly coarser and faintly banded lithology.

In combination with the other unstratified material, the unstratified element (excluding the axe/adzes) in the Newport collection gives the impression of consisting on the whole of larger items, including substantial cores, than the stratified lithics from the excavation. This may indicate that the focus of Mesolithic activity had already been lost through erosion by the time the site was discovered, although to some extent it could also reflect sampling bias or water-sorting on the pocket beaches from which most of the material was probably collected. The unstratified assemblage is likely to have become sequestered as the result of the erosion of a much larger area than is represented by the peat-ledge excavation.

Hill Farm

The worked material in this small, stratified assemblage from several contexts differs lithologically from that at the Mesolithic site on the foreshore below. The same opaque, mainly dark grey–black flint is represented, but there is no definite chert, and no tuff was

seen. The main newcomer is a translucent, honey yellow–pale brown flint (five items) that lacks a Mesolithic counterpart. Also present is a single, irregular flake struck from a well-rounded cobble of pink quartzite.

Provenance of raw materials

Whereas it is impossible to point with certainty to the ultimate sources of the lithic materials described, there can be little doubt that all of the components could have been procured relatively locally from the marine and fluvial gravels of the inner Bristol Channel–Severn Estuary and immediate surroundings. The clasts recorded from Goldcliff show clear signs of water transport in river or tidal currents or on the strand, but the generally modest degree of percussion marking rules out their collection from beaches on exposed coasts.

Small quantities of pebble–cobble flint, especially opaque, grey–black types, occur in many of the Pleistocene terrace gravels of the lower Severn and Severn Estuary (Wills 1938, Gilbertson and Hawkins 1978, Hey 1991) and are widely distributed in the contemporary as well as older marine gravels of the estuary and inner Bristol Channel. Chert, much of it derived from the Carboniferous Limestone, occurs in the marine gravels of the southern and eastern bank and in inland fluvial gravels. The water-worn cobbles of tuff could also have been procured by carefully searching comparatively local gravels. Gravel patches on the modern foreshore between Redwick and Magor Pill, for example, include occasional cobbles of dark grey to black tuffs similar to those at the Mesolithic site. An ultimate source in Welsh Ordovician rocks, but not exposed in an intensely deformed area, seems possible.

The distinctive, honey yellow flint at Hill Farm has no known source, but closely resembles the translucent–opaque material exclusively used in the Bronze Age at Oldbury Power Station further up the estuary (Hume 1992).

The thermally-fractured cobbles of quartzite closely resemble local fluvial materials (Squirrell and Downing 1969, Waters and Lawrence 1987), exploited again in Bronze Age and Roman times on the nearby Wentlooge Level (Allen 1996b, Fulford *et al* 1994). They probably originate in the Upper Carboniferous of the South Wales Coalfield.

4.6 The late-Mesolithic assemblages
Nicholas Barton

Introduction

This analysis is based principally on the examination of in situ finds recorded in the 1992–94 excavations. To avoid any ambiguity of interpretation this collection was treated separately from Mesolithic material recovered from the surface between 1987 and 1994, even though some of it was recorded either on, or near, the site itself. In retrospect, however, it seems clear that there is very little difference between any of the Mesolithic finds, either in the surface collections, or in the excavated assemblage. This high degree of internal consistency is also shared by a third much smaller collection of artefacts from 1992 excavations at the inland locality of Hill Farm. The total number of artefacts recorded in the collections is shown in Table 4.1. Classification of the assemblages is based on standard typological and technological criteria developed for the British Mesolithic (Clark 1934, Jacobi 1979, Berridge and Roberts 1986, Barton 1992).

Virtually all of the 633 lithic artefacts recovered in the excavated assemblage come from a single horizon (Context 1202). Only six of those finds examined are from the overlying estuarine clay (Context 1201) and two are from the upper fen peat (Context 1200).

Flakes

The overwhelming majority of artefacts (409/633) are flakes, defined as waste pieces whose length is less than twice their width. Many of them can be described as being laminar in shape, ie elongate rather than broad. The flakes are predominantly of flint, although a small number are in tuff (27) and chert (18). At Goldcliff the flakes are generally fairly short and small, rarely exceeding 30mm in length. Over 50% of the flakes are broken. Many of the breakages recorded are simple flexional snaps. The presence of these and a few examples of longitudinal *siret* fractures (cf Inizan *et al* 1992, 98) is consistent with straightforward manufacturing accidents and implies that knapping occurred on site.

Measurement of a representative sample of 54 complete flakes gave mean length–breadth–thickness dimensions of $(22.5 \pm 0.96) \times (16.4 \pm 0.91) \times (3.85 \pm 0.24)$mm. There is little difference between the dimensions of the flint flakes and flakes in other raw materials. The tuff flakes are superficially slightly thicker at the proximal ends. This may be partly due to the greater intractability of the rock which would require striking further back from the core edge. Overall, however, the maximum dimensions are otherwise virtually identical.

In addition to these characteristics, a high proportion of flakes reveal either partly or wholly corticated surfaces (308/409). Given the nature and small size of the cobble raw materials, this is not in itself surprising, but it does provide added confirmation that primary flaking took place on-site and not elsewhere. The quantity of lithic waste, which includes tested cobbles, implies that there was no obvious shortage in the availability of suitable materials for manufacture.

The spatial distribution of flakes (Fig 4.6f) reveals a general scatter of material across the whole site with a slightly higher concentration in the central part of the excavation. Relatively few burnt artefacts

were recorded (70/409) but it is noticeable that these form two distinct clusters that overlap in their distribution with burnt bone and charred hazelnut shells (Fig 4.6i).

Not found in the excavated assemblage, but consistent with the collections as a whole, were three *pièces esquillées*, including one from the surface of the Mesolithic site found by Upton (Fig 4.7: 70045). These artefacts, sometimes also known as 'scaled flakes' or *outils écailles* (Breuil 1932, Jacobi 1980, 177), are most likely the product of bipolar knapping technique. They can result when a cobble is rested on an anvil and the ensuing blow detaches tiny flakes from both ends of the same piece (Barton 1992, 264). Alternatively, if such objects were used as wedges for cracking or splitting bone, hammering and other contact might cause identical splintering (Tixier 1963). Jacobi (1980, 178) has suggested that the occurrence of such artefacts might be chronologically linked to the very end of the Mesolithic.

Blades/bladelets

Conventionally, blades have a length to width ratio of 2:1. Bladelets are related forms but have a narrower width of 12mm or under. Both these types, normally very common components in the Mesolithic, only form a miniscule proportion of the total assemblage. Just eleven examples are known, of which nine are bladelets.

At Goldcliff the manufacture of blades and bladelets was clearly a subsidiary activity to that of flake production. The same careful abrasion observed on some of the flake butts is also seen on the bladelets, suggesting a clear continuity in technique and probably implying that the bladelets were incidental by-products of the flake making process. Blades and bladelets are equally scarce in the surface collection. There is no suggestion that the low representation of these forms is related to selective winnowing by humans in the Mesolithic, or due to biases in excavation technique.

Chips

These are defined as tiny flakes <10mm long. Also known collectively as 'microdebitage', these items are often the truest indicators of on-site knapping and the in situ nature of deposits. At Goldcliff the excavated assemblage only contains 25 chips, a much smaller quantity than would be predicted either on the basis of experimental flint knapping or from the presence of the bigger debitage. To exclude any possibility of unintentional retrieval biases in the original excavations, a number of environmental samples was inspected for the presence of chips and very small flint debris. As these had been sieved to 250µm they provided a fine-grained method of testing whether significant amounts of small debitage had been overlooked or lost during excavation.

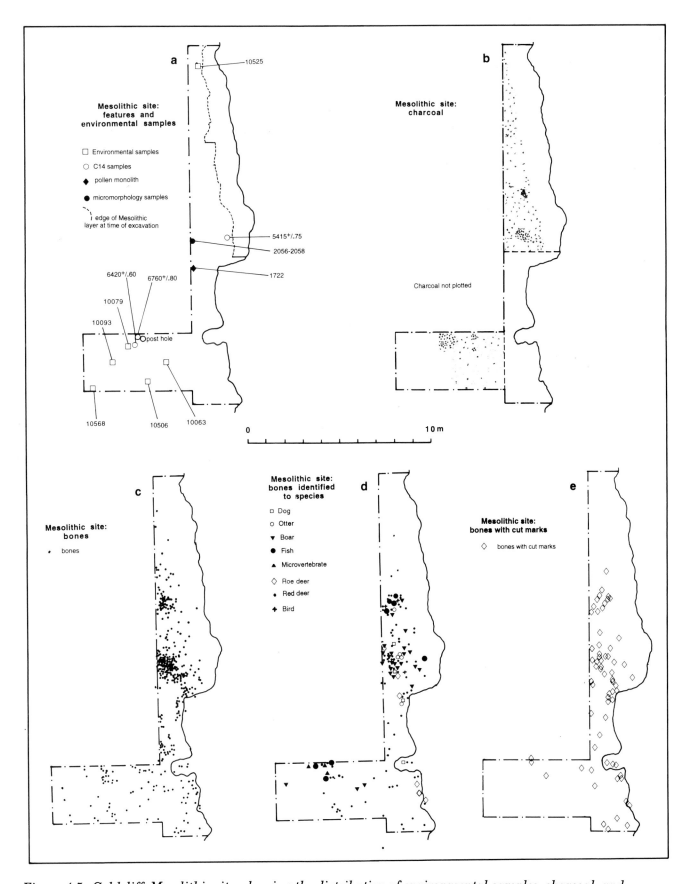

Figure 4.5 Goldcliff: Mesolithic site, showing the distribution of environmental samples, charcoal, and bones. Drawing by J Foster

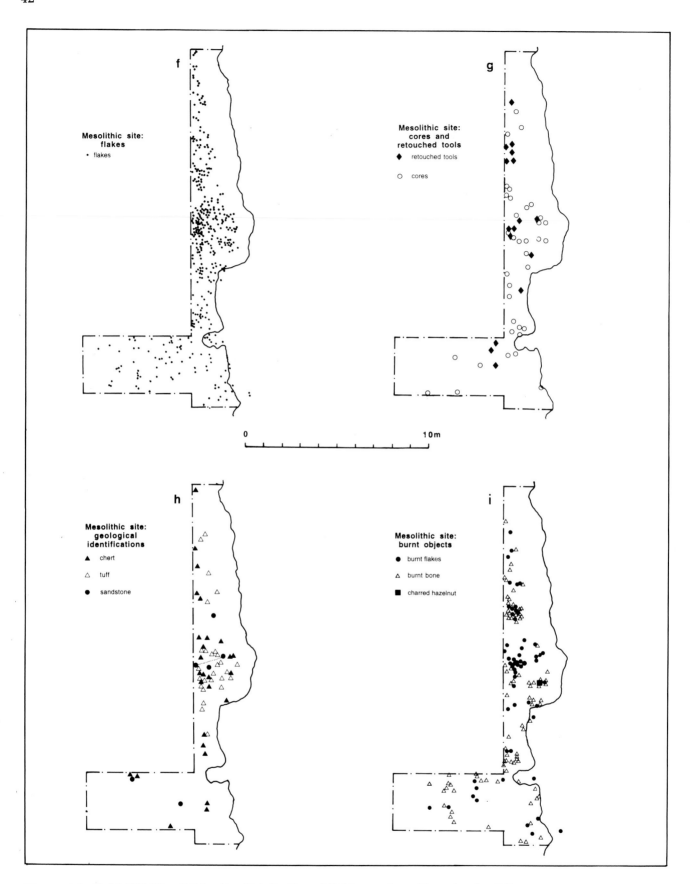

Figure 4.6 Goldcliff: Mesolithic site, distribution of lithic artefacts. Drawing by J Foster

Results revealed only a minimal presence of struck debris (three chips from ten environmental subsamples) thus confirming the appropriateness of the excavation methods.

Cores

Most, if not all, of the cores in the excavated sample are on small water-rounded cobbles. Except for two chert examples, they are all of flint and, significantly, there are no cores in tuff. The heaviest core weighs 115g and the lightest has a weight of 1g, giving an average figure of 23g and providing an idea of the very small size of raw material. Of the 36 examples examined, the most common categories are single platform (16) and multiple platform (11) types. The single platform cores include five examples characterised by only one flake removal and it is clear in these and a limited number of other cases with two or three removals that these were rejects, abandoned after testing. Despite the presence of single as well as opposed platform cores with laminar flake scars (Fig 4.7: 4423, 8008), there are no examples that can be described as classic blade or bladelet types. Amongst the multiple platform types are five disc cores (Fig 4.7:8120). There is only one core on a flake.

Evidence of burning is limited to two cores. Both burnt examples (4745, 4928) were found on the periphery of one of the combustion zones near the central part of the excavation (Fig 4.5). Other than this there is no evident clustering in the distribution of cores which are scattered across most of the site (Fig 4.6g).

Classified separately from the cores are 45 pieces of 'core shatter', defined as fragments of cores too badly broken to identify more precisely. Since only five are burnt, it seems likely that the majority of breakages occurred as a result of knapping accidents. The patterns of fracture indicate that common causes of breaks were hidden flaws and natural fault planes within the rock.

The cores from the surface collection hardly vary from those in the excavated assemblage, the only exception being the three *pièces esquillées*, mentioned above, which can probably be considered as variants of bipolar cores.

Rejuvenation flakes

There are twenty artefacts which can be identified as the by-products of core rejuvenation. Eight of them are core tablets, flakes typically associated with correcting faulty flaking angles and/or removing damaged platforms on cores (Barton 1992, 264–265). There are five *flancs de nucleus* or flakes which have removed all or part of the core's flaking surface. These result either deliberately from the action of rejuvenating the front of the core or accidentally, as when the blow is not struck close enough to the edge of the platform (Barton 1992, 267). Only four of the

seven crested pieces are unidirectionally flaked and typical of the debitage associated with repairing the flaking face. The remaining three display bifacial flaking and are similar to *éclats debordants* (Boëda 1993, 397) which are associated with discoidal core technology. An alternative explanation, certainly possible in the case of one of the crested flakes in tuff, is that it is a broken edge of an axe/adze roughout.

Unidentifiable waste

In this category there are 66 irregular fragments of struck flint either too broken or too small to classify in any of the other existing categories. Over half of them (36/66) are burnt.

Non-flaked stone artefacts

Six non-flaked stone artefacts were recovered in the main assemblage. They are all of a quartzitic sandstone and must have been humanly introduced to the site. Two of them are fragments of rounded cobbles with signs of battering on part of their circumference. They appear to be parts of broken hammerstones. Of the remainder, three are very similar fragments of what might be a sandstone 'rubber' (cf Barton 1992, fig 5.29). Two of these pieces (4901 and 6431) can be shown to refit. Such items are often oblong-shaped cobbles with flat upper and lower sides and have well-developed damage or polish at the extremities. Sandstone rubbers are well known in the Mesolithic where they have sometimes been interpreted as arrowshaft smoothers or tools for stretching skins (Barton 1992, 238). The refitting pieces were found in fairly close proximity (Fig 4.6h), which suggests that the object might have been broken in use.

The surface collection contains six other items in this category. Three fragments of quartzitic sandstone were found on the surface of the main site itself. Two of them could be refitted to form the corner or end of broken cobble (Fig 4.7:87.487). The combined fragment is sub-rectangular in shape with a rounded edge and two flattish surfaces. The upper one of these surfaces has a noticeably dished or concave appearance where it has been worn or ground smooth. The type of wear is consistent with its use as a mortar or for grinding. There are three other stray finds all from near the site. Two of the three pieces are burnt. They might originally have belonged to a larger block but the edges are too badly eroded and they cannot now be conjoined.

Retouched tools

There are fifteen retouched tools comprising three microliths, two end-scrapers and ten retouched flakes. The microliths include one small broken

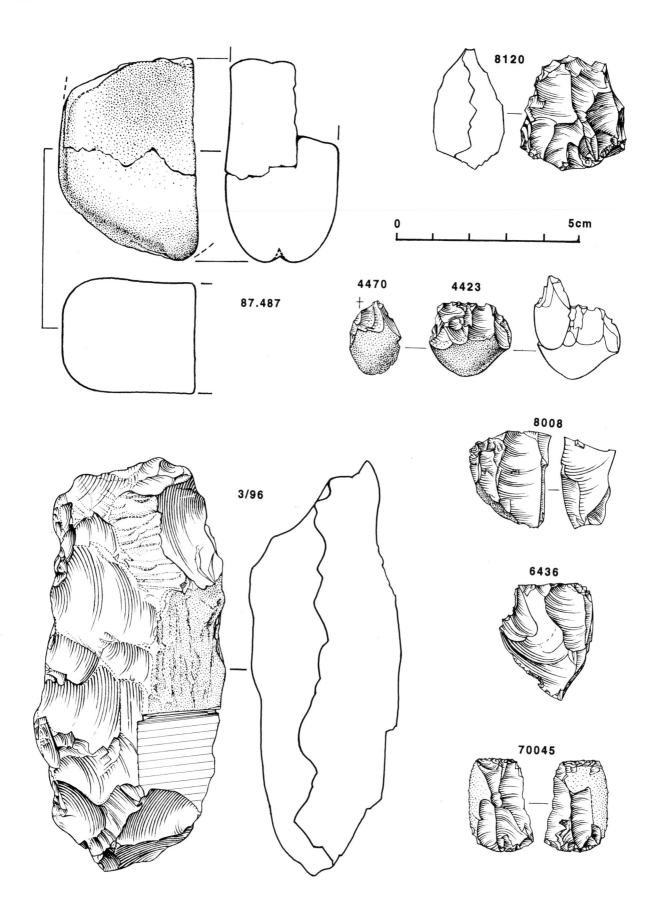

Figure 4.7 Goldcliff: Mesolithic site: Quartzitic sandstone grindstone (87.487), disc core (1201/8120), single platform core (1202/4423) with refitting flake (1202/4470), single platform cores (1200/8008 and 1202/6436), pièce esquillée (GC92/70045), Goldcliff East axe/adze (3/96). Scale 1:1. Drawing by H Martingell

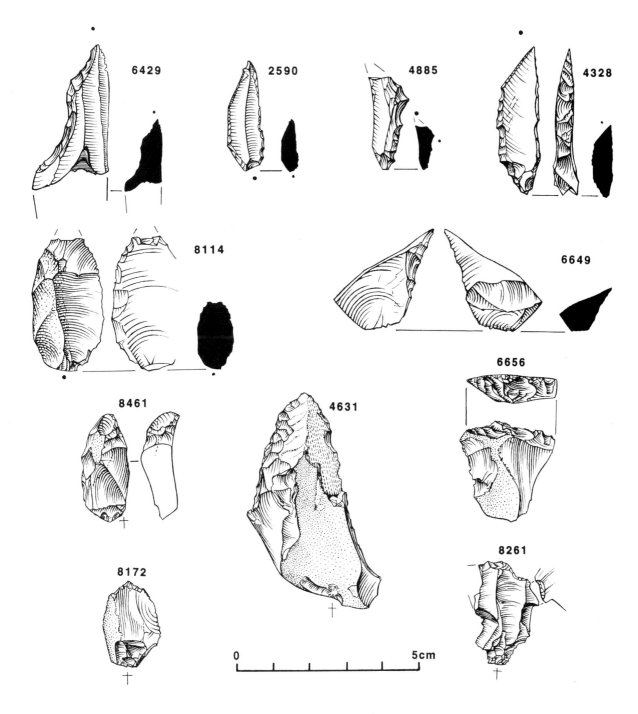

Figure 4.8 Goldcliff: Mesolithic site: Broken microlith tip (1202/6429), scalene triangle (1202/4885), bilaterally backed microlith (1202/4328), retouched flake with inverse retouch (1202/8114), retouched becs (1202/8461 and 8172), bifacially retouched flake fragment (1202/6649), retouched tuff flake (1202/4631), scraper/straight truncation (1202/6656), end-scraper (1201/8261). Goldcliff Hill Farm: Bilaterally backed microlith (1401.2590). Note: Silhouettes of artefacts indicate actual size. Solid dot denotes point of percussion. Scale 1:1. Drawing by H Martingell

scalene (Fig 4.8:4885), one bilaterally 'backed' form (Fig 4.8:4328) and a broken tip (Fig 4.8:6429). Despite being such a restricted collection of microliths, all three tools are forms typical of the later Mesolithic (Clark 1934, Jacobi 1976). The two broken specimens are also both burnt, making further observations difficult, but is, nevertheless, possible

to see that 4885 was made on a broad flake, with the point of percussion originating on one of its longer sides. The bilaterally 'backed' form is retouched on all of its sides and could, therefore, be described as a class 'D6' rhomboid (cf Clark 1934, 58 and 155). Perhaps significantly, it too is made on a flake rather than a bladelet and there is no evidence for the microburin technique. In terms of their distribution, the two broken microliths are located close together within the largest concentration of burnt artefacts and bones, whilst the unburnt, complete specimen occurs to the south, just outside this cluster. It is conceivable that the two burnt microliths were parts of projectiles lodged in one of the dismembered animal carcasses.

One typical end-scraper can be identified in the excavated collection (Fig 4.8:8261). The tool, which is burnt and broken, is recorded as coming from Context 1201, above the main artefact horizon. But since just a few centimetres separate it from the rest of the Mesolithic assemblage it is unlikely to represent a different phase of site activity (Bell personal communication). A second retouched piece recovered from the main artefact horizon may be an atypical scraper (Fig 4.8:6656). However, it is made on a thick flake with a straight retouched edge. The retouch is abrupt, rather than semi-abrupt and scars making up the 'scraper edge' are quite large. In profile, the scraper front is not curved or hooked but forms virtually a right-angle with the ventral surface. There are no signs of heavy edge-wear or damage scars along the leading edge. In traditional terms it falls within the definition of both a scraper and a flake core. It is unburnt.

Apart from formal categories of tools, ten retouched flakes were recovered which vary a great deal in terms of shape and the extent and form of the retouch. Two examples (Fig 4.8:8461 and 8172) have fine marginal retouch at their distal ends which in both cases converge to form a pointed stub or *bec*. These may have been used for piercing or boring, although there are no signs of wear on the projecting tips. Another of the retouched flakes is made of tuff (Fig 4.8:4631) and comes from the same general part of the site as the rest of the volcanic artefacts. All of these tools can be precisely matched in other late Mesolithic assemblages in south and western Britain (Berridge and Roberts 1986, Jacobi and Tebbutt 1981). The sole exception is a broken proximal flake fragment, with direct, abrupt retouch on one edge and flat, invasive flaking on the ventral surface (Fig 4.8:6649). It is reminiscent of the early stages of making a pressure-flaked bifacial tool. Under other circumstances it might be mistaken for a broken 'Neolithic' leaf shaped arrowhead. However, there is no evidence to suggest that the artefact is intrusive; it is well-stratified and comes from within a small cluster of other Mesolithic retouched flakes near the northern end of the excavation. Small bifacial points known as *feuilles de gui* (Bohmers 1956, 36) are known from late Mesolithic contexts in the Netherlands but none has so far been identified from Britain (Jacobi 1976, 80).

In addition to the tools in the site assemblage, only three other small retouched artefacts and two core tools have been identified in the surface collections. They comprise one end-scraper from the foreshore near the Mesolithic site and two miscellaneous retouched flakes.

Axes/adzes

The surface assemblage includes two axe/adzes, both of tuff. Theoretically these types are distinguishable by their cross-sectional form, which in adzes tends to be D-shaped and in axes more biconvex (Berridge and Roberts 1986, 19). In practice, however, as in the case with these examples, such differences are often rather subtle and, in the absence of direct information on hafting position or other functionally related data, they can be difficult to tell apart. For this reason the more neutral term axe/adze is used here instead. Both types are more easily separated from picks which terminate in a tapering point and have triangular or asymmetrical cross-sections (Palmer 1977, 25–26).

Neither of the axe/adzes comes from the main site itself. The first (Fig 4.9) was found by Upton in 1995 lying unstratified on the surface in the same area as the lowest peat at Porton, approximately National Grid Reference ST 39158243, 2.3km east of the site (Appendix I, Map 17). The object is matt black in colour and has maximum length, width and thickness measurements of 208mm × 82mm × 43mm. The artefact is in sharp condition, its edges are very fresh and there is no evidence of rounding or subsequent damage. Due to its freshness and complete shape it is possible to suggest that the axe/adze was abandoned as a roughout rather than as a finished form. Such an interpretation is based partly on the relatively large amount of unmodified cortical surface exterior as well as the presence of deep flake scars on both of the main faces. There is no evidence of secondary flaking or thinning and the tool displays none of the characteristic transverse re-sharpening removals noted on tranchet axes (Wymer 1977, xii). In itself, of course, this does not automatically exclude active use, but from the thickness of both ends it is unlikely they were sharp enough for most functional purposes, except perhaps digging. The small area of unflaked surface left on the tool reveals that it was made from a large, heavily rounded cobble.

The second axe/adze (Fig 4.7:3/96) was also found by Upton, but at a different location at Goldcliff East, 1.2km to the east of the main site, in 1996 (Appendix I, Map 16). The object has maximum measurements of 109mm × 51mm × 39mm, so is considerably smaller than the first tool. It too is matt black in colour, but unlike the other axe/adze, the *arêtes* between the scars are heavily rolled and there are barnacle-like attachments on its surface. Bifacial flaking covers most of the surfaces except in two places where the original, slightly green-stained and smooth, exterior of the rock is exposed. The negative flake scars include not only deep primary removals but also evidence of invasive, curved flake scars typical of axe thinning. The edges of the tool are much more regular than in the first example, and at one end it appears that attempts had been made to resharpen the cutting-edge by detaching several flakes. The tool may have been heavily used, but it

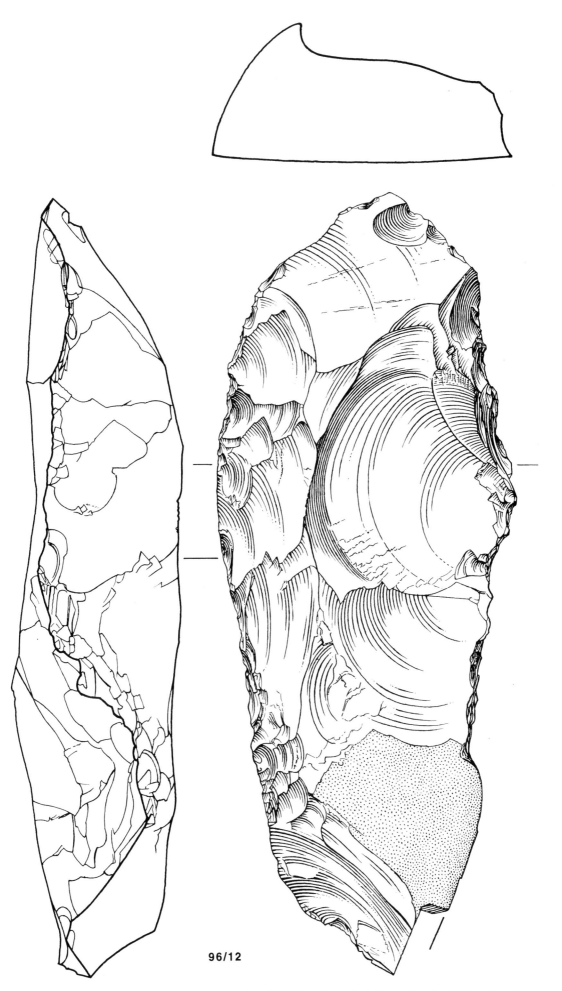

96/12

Figure 4.9 Porton: Mesolithic axe/adze (96/12). Scale 1:1. Drawing by H Martingell

is difficult to be certain, given the post-depositional alteration caused by water-rolling.

Although no other complete axe/adzes have yet been found, evidence that they were definitely being manufactured nearby comes from a snapped end of a tool identified in the surface collection (70062). It comes from 20m east of the Mesolithic site and is typical of an 'end-shock' form of breakage which often occurs accidentally during biface manufacture.

By-products of tool manufacture

Amongst the 27 tuff flakes from the main site is one which might be an axe thinning flake (4581). Its distinguishing features include a slightly thinner and more curved profile, and it ends in a feathered termination. However, in the absence of other positive indicators (eg special butt preparation, the remains of bifacial flaking) it is not possible to be more definite. Attempts to refit this flake, or any of the other tuff flakes, to the axe/adzes which are of the same material, proved futile. However, conjoins were possible between individual tuff flakes (4614–4959 and 4269–4276). The former, which is a dorso–ventral refit, demonstrates beyond doubt that tuff was flaked on site, an opinion also supported by the distribution of these artefacts which form a distinct cluster in the area of one of the combustion zones (Fig 4.6h). Given the absence of cores in tuff or typical core rejuvenation flakes, it is likely that the flakes represent the initial 'roughing out' stages of axe/adze reduction. The fact that many of the flakes are large and corticated is certainly consistent with this view. The presence of relatively few flakes may best be explained by the high utility value of such artefacts. It has already been noted that one flake tool in this material has been recorded (Fig 4.8:4631).

There are no obvious examples of other tool by-products such as scraper retouch chips. Noticeably absent too, in either the site or the surface collections, are any examples of microburins, the typical by-products of microlith manufacture (Barton 1992, 269). Given the type of flake blanks for microliths, it is unlikely that they were made using the microburin technique.

Goldcliff Hill Farm

A small assemblage of 35 artefacts was also examined from the excavations at Hill Farm (Table 4.1). The majority of pieces are flakes (17) and there are five blades/bladelets. Amongst the debitage are also a single *flanc de nucleus* and two cores (one multi-platform, the other two-platform) indistinguishable from others found in the main Goldcliff Mesolithic assemblage. There are two tools; one is an undiagnostic flake, the other a small geometric bilaterally 'backed' microlith (Fig 4.8:2590), similar in some respects to a short lanceolate (cf Jacobi 1984, fig 4.15).

The finds come from a variety of contexts so it is most unlikely that they all derive from one period of activity. Perhaps significantly, the microlith, the *flanc de nucleus*, the two cores, and a bladelet were all from the same context (1041), which underlies the prehistoric palaeosol with charcoal layers at the site (Fig 3.6). These items are all of late Mesolithic type and are consistent with the finds already described for the main coastal locations.

Also amongst the flakes are included five examples in an unusual 'honey brown flint' which does not have parallels in any of the other Mesolithic collections. Two of them come from the same context as the microlith while the others are from the topsoil, Context 1074, and unknown, respectively.

Summary

Observations of the artefacts in the excavated and surface samples make it clear that they should be regarded as coming from closely related assemblages of demonstrably late-Mesolithic type. Further confidence in this assertion is provided by the presence of narrow geometric microlith types which are known to occur in the British Mesolithic record between about 8500 BP and 5500 BP (Switsur and Jacobi 1975). One other relevant observation worth making in relation to this timescale is the preponderance of flakes over blade or bladelet debitage. Although there is good evidence that the size and shape of the raw materials (small cobbles) were clearly influential factors, laminar flake production is a recurrent feature observed at the younger end of the late-Mesolithic record (Pitts and Jacobi 1979, also see Hemingway in Jacobi and Tebbutt 1981). It may, therefore, be another useful chronological indicator.

4.7 Large mammal bone assemblage
Ros Coard

The large mammal assemblage consists of two collections, one excavated from Context 1202 and the other, collected prior to the excavations, is housed at Newport Museum. The context of the Newport Museum material is uncertain but is possibly a mixed one. Although the provenance of all of the Newport Museum material cannot be fully established, it, nevertheless, has an interesting contribution to make to the interpretation of the excavated material.

In addition to the normal objectives of faunal analysis, specific research questions were central to the work on the Goldcliff assemblage. Formation processes were of particular concern, whether the site had been disturbed by marine inundation and represented little more than a hydraulic jumble or whether the site was undisturbed and in situ. Also of special interest was any evidence of seasonality, the duration of occupation, and the hunting and procurement strategies employed.

The faunal patterning at Goldcliff is largely attributable to human activity. Although there may be some background scatter of micro-faunas, the macrofauna shows clear evidence of human activity in the form of butchery marks, cut-marks, breakage patterns, skeletal part representation, and evidence of burnt bones. The spatial distribution of the bones would suggest specific localities being used to process different animal species. The condition of the bone is generally good. The surface texture is well preserved, with the majority of the bones showing little post-depositional deterioration. Had the site been habitually inundated by marine activity or modification by carnivores, poorer surface detail might have been expected. The bone is, however, fragmented, with a large proportion of very small fragments, which accounts for the high number of unidentifiable bones.

Goldcliff 1202 Mesolithic assemblage

The assemblage excavated from Context 1202 consists of 1000 bones in total, of which 423 have specimen numbers. A total of 861 bones are indeterminate to species, but 326 can be identified to anatomical part, while 139 are identifiable to species, *Cervus elaphus* (red deer), *Sus scrofa* (wild pig), *Canis lupus* (wolf), *Capreolus capreolus* (roe deer), and *Lutra lutra* (otter). In addition, small quantities of bird bones (coot and possibly mallard), fish, and rodents are present. The number of individual specimens present (NISP), relative percentage, and minimum number of individuals (MNI) for these species are listed in Table 4.2. Figure 4.10a shows the relative percentage of the indeterminate to determinate bones. Figure 4.10b shows the relative percentage of the identified bones. Red deer (*n* = 87, 63%) and wild pig (*n* = 27, 20%) are the most numerically dominant species. They also represent the most frequently occurring number of individuals. The remaining large mammals are represented by fewer bones and could all be attributed to a single individual.

The 1202 canid material is provisionally identified as *Canis lupus* L. (wolf). Most of the 1202 material is

Table 4.2 Goldcliff 1202 list of species

Species present		NISP	NISP (%)	MNI
Cervus elephas	(Red deer)	87	63	4
Sus scrofa	(Pig)	27	20	3
Lutra lutra	(Otter)	7	5	1
Capreolus capreolus	(Roe deer)	4	3	1
Canis lupus	(Wolf)	4	3	?
Aves	(Bird)	3	2	–
Microvertebrates		3	2	–
Fish		2	1	–

NISP is number of individual specimens; MNI is minimum numbers of individuals, with relative percentages for all species.

post-cranial, and some of it juvenile and/or fragmented. The size of the bone appears small, compared with modern captive wolf, but this could be explained by the Goldcliff examples being juvenile or even female. Exact taxonomic identification has been hampered by the lack of good measurable bone and with most discussion being based on cranial morphology and adult individuals (Benecke 1987, Degerbol 1961). Unlike the other large mammals at Goldcliff, there is little taphonomic evidence to link the canids directly with the human activity. The canid material shows no signs of being butchered (fracture patterns), cut-marked or burnt.

The skeletal part representation for the main species show a marked difference (see Fig 4.10c, d). The red deer are represented by a similar minimum number of individuals as the wild pig, four and three, respectively, but are represented by a greater NISP and by a wider range of body parts. More bones of the axial skeleton are present, including a scapula, some vertebrae, and a sacrum. In particular, what is striking about the red deer is the number of major limb bones that are present compared with the pig. The pig is represented by one front limb and two lower back limbs, with only five major limb bones in total, compared with around ten limbs and 30 major limb bones and fragments for the red deer. The similarity in the MNI indicates that perhaps one of several things is happening; either that there is a survivorship problem, in that fewer pig bones survive compared with those of red deer, or that the Mesolithic hunters were utilising the carcasses of these two species in different ways. The different survival rates of bone are well known and documented (Brain 1967, Shipman 1981). However, this patterning is unlikely to be due to different survival rates as the most robust bones, such as teeth and mandibles, are the most likely to survive regardless of the species, and there is differential survival of these bones across these two species. Equally, adult and juvenile bones represent both species, so it is not a case of adult of one species compared with juvenile of another. The limb bones, including the metapodials, podials and phalanges, are the most frequently occurring bones for the red deer. The dentition, mandible, maxilla, and isolated teeth, are less well represented. This is in contrast to the pig, where the skull, mandible, maxilla and teeth are much more prominent. This again suggests different utilisation of the carcasses by the Mesolithic hunters.

The taphonomic processes that are evident on the bones indicate that humans were primarily responsible for the accumulation of the assemblage. The bones show evidence of butchery, both in the diagnostic breakage patterns and by cut-marks. About 38 (2%) of the bones are cut-marked. They are present on a wide range of species including the red deer, pig, roe deer, and otter as well as some indeterminate bones. All of these species have cut-marks that are consistent with filleting, with marks present on the mid-shaft or on the shaft just below the articular ends (Binford 1981, Trolle-Lassen 1987 and 1990).

50

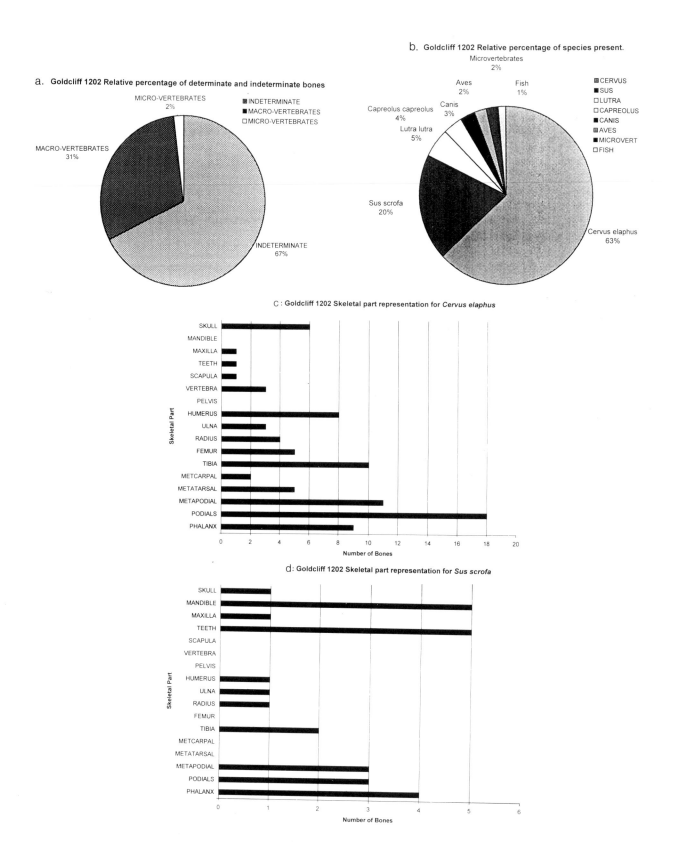

Figure 4.10   Goldcliff: Animal bones, proportions of animal species and skeletal parts representation of deer and pig

The red deer and roe deer are the only species that have marks consistent with skinning activity, with marks appearing on a phalanx of the red deer and astragalus of the roe deer (Binford 1981, Trolle-Lassen 1987 and 1990). Some of the marks present on the red deer, such as those on the metapodia and distal tibia, are more ambiguous and could be consistent with scraping, skinning or dismemberment (Trolle-Lassen 1990).

The fracture patterns suggest that some of the long bones have been split by twisting them and many of the identifiable long bones show green fractures; most common is longitudinal fracturing ($n = 26$). Again, these patterns can be seen across most of the species, including the red deer, roe deer, and pig. This can be interpreted as part of the butchery process for marrow extraction (Binford 1981). An interesting pattern emerged with the red deer metapodials; many had been fractured longitudinally, with the distal epiphyses and condyles showing evidence of being split. From the taphonomic indicators it looks as if the metapodials were held inverted and a cleaver like tool used to split them longitudinally. As yet, the only cleaver type tools capable of performing such a task are the axe/adzes found 1km and 2.3km east of the site (Figs 4.7 and 4.9). The axe/adze would need to be fairly thin in order to get between the two condyles, unless an indirect percussion method were adopted; if so, some of the lithic artefacts at the site may have been entirely suitable.

Very few of the bones show evidence of interference by carnivores. Only eight bones showed clear evidence of being gnawed or punctured by carnivore teeth. Whether this was part of the site formation process while the Mesolithic hunters were there, or something that happened once the site was abandoned, is unclear at this stage. Either scenario is possible. Further, but more ambiguous, evidence of carnivore activity can be seen in the number of bones that have been spirally fractured ($n = 18$). This can be interpreted as a product of either carnivore or human activity, and as such is not clearly diagnostic (Binford 1981, Shipman 1981, Haynes 1983). Both longitudinally split and spirally fractured bone show evidence of having been burnt, and at least one spirally fractured bone has been gnawed.

Further evidence of human activity comes from the burnt bones ($n = 156$, 13%). Interestingly the burning seems to have been confined to only a few species: the red deer bones, some indeterminate bones, and a single bird bone (possibly a Mallard) and fish bones (see below). The assumption is that the burning was part of a cooking procedure and was done for consumption purposes.

The burning also supports the idea of the different species being used for different purposes. The red deer were butchered and burnt at the site, whereas other species, pig, otter, and roe deer, were butchered at the site but not cooked there. These bones show no evidence of having been burnt. The otter could have been utilised as a source of food or fur. The burnt bird and fish bones, if done intentionally, could indicate that they were processed at the site and could have either been eaten there, or at least some carried off for later consumption.

Different utilisation of the carcasses suggests that the Mesolithic hunters carried out specific tasks. The number of surviving red deer bones, predominance of limb bones compared with dentition, evidence of butchery and burning, all suggests the carcasses were processed and, by inference, eaten and discarded at the site. This does not preclude some of the carcass being carried away. In contrast, the pig bones suggest that the presence of butchery to the bones but lack of burning, and the anatomical representation and paucity of limb bones, indicate that the Mesolithic hunters processed the carcasses but took the limb bones away, leaving mainly the low utility skull and dentition behind.

Spatial distribution

The spatial distribution of the bones indicates that the different species were processed in specific locales. The scatterplot distributions (Figs 4.5–4.6) clearly show that some of the species cluster in a small area, c 1m², with only one or two isolated bones falling outside of this distribution. This can be most clearly seen with the micro-vertebrates, the otter, the roe deer, and the wolf. The pig bones have a more general distribution, but still form a restricted distribution pattern. The only species that does not appear to be spatially restricted is the red deer. They show little patterning, with a more general spread across the site.

Post-depositional disturbance

The spatial distribution showing clusters of bones associated mainly with one species also indicates that there has been little post occupation disturbance. Had the site been habitually inundated by marine activity, a distinct possibility given its location, a more mixed spatial distribution would have been expected. Although the taphonomic effect of bone in estuarine environments is not well documented, let alone understood, it is unlikely that such species specific sorting would occur. It is more likely that bones would be sorted according to their hydraulic potential than to their taxa (Voorhies 1969, Coard and Dennell 1995). This gives strong and demonstrable evidence that the site does not represent a hydraulic jumble but is relatively undisturbed and can be regarded as in situ.

Seasonality

Establishing the season, or seasons, when a site was occupied are central research questions in establishing the settlement systems of Mesolithic populations. Establishing the relationship of inland and coastal areas is central to such studies and is often inferred rather than established in fact. The Goldcliff Mesolithic site is rare. There are few Mesolithic sites where such studies are possible. The evidence is not, however, without problems. Establishing the season of death of any animal depends on accurately knowing the birthing season of animals and assuming uniformitarian principles. Establishing the age of death has been initially undertaken based on tooth eruption, tooth wear, and bone fusion rates. A more detailed and accurate estimate of the season of occupation may be established with the study of the fish or bird remains and incremental growth patterns of animal teeth. The red deer and pig bones and teeth were studied and provided similar but not necessarily conclusive evidence.

Only four pig mandibles were available to establish eruption and wear rates; three of these were juveniles and the other a mature individual. Three to four teeth were present in the juvenile mandibles, the first molar and deciduous premolars. As Rowley-Conwy (1993) indicates, knowing the eruption rates (and fusion rates) for modern counterparts is essential in establishing season of death. It is difficult in this particular case because there are no extant wild pig populations in Britain today. Silver (1969) cites dental ageing for a historically recent population, along with modern domestic populations. Research indicates that the permanent fourth premolar erupts around 12 months (Silver 1969, Bull and Payne 1982). The lack of erupted fourth premolars suggests that the Goldcliff pigs died before their first year but after 6–7 months, as the first molars are fully erupted (Silver 1969). If an early spring birthing season is correct for wild pig populations, Rowley-Conwy (1993) suggests 1 April, then this would indicate a winter–spring occupation at the site. The fusion data for the pig long bones lends some limited support to this interpretation (Silver 1969, Bull and Payne 1982). From the six bones that lend themselves to fusion analysis, the lack of fusion for the distal humerus would suggest slaughter at less than 1 year, the proximal radius, which is fused, does so around 1 year. The unfused tibia and metapodials suggest slaughter at less than 2 years, and, as such, are not particularly helpful. This data would again suggest slaughter at less than, or around, 1 year but before 2 years.

Little progress has been made in attempting to assess the season of death for the red deer. The surviving mandible is that of a fully mature adult with wear on all cusps of the M3 and M2 and, as such, is not diagnostic. The wear stage is estimated to be around Lowe's Stage 7 (Lowe 1967). The surviving antlers are fragmented, consisting mainly of tine points or broken tines. There is one burr but, again, this is fragmented and not readily diagnostic. There is a wide range of unfused juvenile post-cranial material, but part of the problem is that these fusion rates are imperfectly understood and are not documented to the same degree as those of the more common domestic species. Other than placing these individuals into age categories (juvenile, sub-adult,

adult etc), little corroborating evidence can be gained from the red deer post-cranial material.

The fauna does give some indication of the surrounding habitat. Although large mammals can be very versatile and adaptable in the range of habitats that they occupy, the indications here are of species preferring either deciduous woodland (pig, roe deer), or transitional woodland edge zones (red deer). Canids are even more versatile, occupying areas ranging from open environments to heavily wooded ones. Otter and fish reflect the adjacent estuarine/riverine environment.

Newport Museum collection

The material from Newport Museum is a collection of animal bones from a variety of contexts, some of which are more clearly contexted than others. This material has been identified and described by Barbara Noddle in an unpublished report and we are grateful to her for making information available. The bones from Newport Museum are either from stratified areas of the Mesolithic charcoal layer or are from Goldcliff 'Meso' West. There is one bone from Goldcliff Intertidal, which is a fully mature red deer antler and is virtually complete, with the exception of a single broken tine on the crown of the antler. The Goldcliff 'Meso' West material is a mixed assemblage, with material from unstratified contexts or eroding out of known contexts. This assemblage also contains species not seen in the excavated assemblage and, as such, should perhaps be viewed as mixed and not form part of the wider discussion of the Mesolithic sample as a whole. The material from the charcoal layer is, however, consistent with the Goldcliff 1202 assemblage. There is a similar range of species; indeed the opposite side to the otter scapula is present in this collection. Also present are red deer, wild pig and wolf. Not only is the range of species similar, but there are similar taphonomic indicators, the colouring and preservation of the bone is similar, as is the evidence for burning, butchery, and fracturing patterns the same. Even the distinctive splitting of the metapodial condyles is present.

There is one exception to the apparently contexted Newport Museum material: a canid mandible which was labelled as 'eroding out of charcoal band' and was similar in appearance and staining to the Mesolithic assemblage. This has been AMS dated with the result: 2685 ± 45BP (OxA-6461). It shows that the Newport assemblage does include some material from later contexts and the canid is further discussed in Chapter 5 in relation to possible ritual deposition at the wetland edge in the late Bronze Age.

Conclusion

The faunal evidence suggests that a group of Mesolithic hunters occupied the site for a short duration and for specific activities. Mesolithic hunters targeted a range of mammals from different age ranges and utilised the carcasses in specific ways. Most of the species show cut-marks taken as evidence of butchery, but not all were then burnt, eaten, and discarded at the site. Some, eg the pig, show that major meat bearing parts of the body were carried away and none of the bone was burnt, although there is evidence of them being processed at the site. In contrast, the red deer were fully utilised at the site, although this does not preclude parts of the carcasses also being carried away. Some animals may have been targeted for fur or skin as well as for food. Taphonomic indicators suggest that post-occupation disturbance in the form of carnivores or marine activity was minimal. The site represents a rare opportunity to study a seasonal coastal occupation site and, as such, has much to contribute to the wider discussion of Mesolithic seasonal settlement systems in Britain.

4.8 Fish, bird and small mammal remains
Claire Ingrem

Introduction

The remains of fish, bird, and small mammals were recovered from samples from the Mesolithic charcoal layer (1202). Considerable numbers of small fish remains (mainly vertebra) were retrieved from sieved samples using 250µm–2mm mesh. These were analysed with the aim of providing information on the origin and nature of the fish remains, the season at which they were deposited, and the local environment or (if anthropogenic in nature) the environments exploited.

Methods

The fish remains were identified to species and anatomical element, where possible, using a low power (×10) binocular microscope, the unpublished manuscript of Lepiksaar (1981), comparative material from the Faunal Remains Unit (FRU), University of Southampton, and the private collection belonging to Alison Locker. Measurements were not taken due to the extremely small and fragile nature of the samples, but comparisons were made with skeletons of known length in order to gain some idea of size. The bird and small mammal remains were also identified to species and anatomical element using the FRU reference material for comparison.

Data

The vertebrate remains were meticulously picked out by Kate Barrow from the samples taken for the study of plant remains (1516 bones). Over half (812 bones) of this material was identifiable to species (Table CD 4.3), and almost all of it was derived from fish; less than 1% was identified as small mammal whilst bird was absent. Most of the identified remains (811 bones) came from just three samples taken from a single metre grid square (CD 4.7). In addition, 30 fragments were recovered from hand collection (Table CD 4.4), of which only three fish bones were identifiable to species level.

4.8.1 Fish

Species and body part representation

Five species were identified, the following percentages of these in the sieved samples being: eel (*Anguilla anguilla*) 56%, smelt (*Osmeridae*) 8%, goby (*Gobiidae*) 29%, three-spined stickleback (*Gasterosteus aculeatus*) 6%, and flatfish 1%. The goby could only be identified to family, although there are ten possible species in the North Atlantic (Muus and Dahlstrom 1964). Similarly, there are numerous possible flatfish, although plaice (*Pleuronectes platessa*) and flounder (*Platichthys flesus*) are the most likely, being commonly found in shallow coastal waters. More than half of the identifiable fish remains are eel, while goby is also well represented, constituting almost a third of the total identifiable bones. Smelt and stickleback are present in significant numbers and flatfish represented by a few bones.

More than three quarters of the total identified fish bones were caudal vertebrae, whilst the second most abundant element was precaudal vertebrae (Table CD 4.5–4.6), probably a reflection of their robust and identifiable nature. However, head parts of the eel were present and consisted of several dentaries, hyomandibulars, operculars, and suboperculars, in addition to one articular. Dentaries and operculars of smelt and goby were also present, as was an articular from both goby and stickleback, and a flatfish premaxilla. The presence of head parts from all the species indicates that they were initially present on the site as whole fish.

Size

All of the fish bones were derived from small specimens; in particular, the goby vertebra were not visible as anatomical elements with the naked eye. The largest fish recovered were the eel; the majority were estimated at between c 150mm and c 290mm in length, a significant proportion were approximately 290mm, and a few were larger (Fig 4.11). The gobies were all smaller than the reference specimen, which was 70mm in length; the smelt were similar in size to the reference specimen which was 87mm in length, although some were slightly smaller. The smallest fish were the sticklebacks, the largest of which were estimated at about 45mm. The few flatfish that were

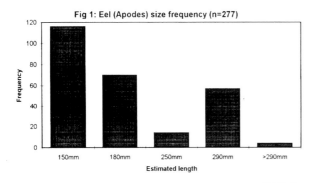

Fig 1: Eel (Apodes) size frequency (n=277)

*Figure 4.11 Goldcliff: Diagram of eel (*Anguilla anguilla*) size frequency from Mesolithic site, n = 227*

present ranged between 130mm and 199mm in length. The small size of the fish makes it likely that they were introduced whole.

Bone modifications

A considerable number of the fish remains showed signs of burning. A total of 105 bones from the sieved samples had been burnt; the majority were black and a few were calcined. No butchery was noted. However, this is not unusual, especially considering the small size of the fish material which would not have required cutting or chopping. The fish remains were generally well preserved, with no visible evidence of distortion, which might suggest that they had passed through the gut (Wheeler and Jones 1989). None of the bird bones displayed evidence of having been either butchered or gnawed.

Environment

All of the species identified are commonly found in coastal and estuarine habitats. The eel is also often found in pools in the intertidal zone (Wheeler 1969). Smelt are rarely found far from the shore, some spending all their lives in large estuaries and, during the summer, the young are often found in the intertidal zone (Wheeler 1969). Sticklebacks have a wide distribution, being found in freshwater, around the coasts in estuarine conditions, and on the shore (Wheeler 1969). Gobies are generally found in large numbers in shallow coastal waters, although a few species occur in freshwater (Muus and Dahlstrom 1964).

Seasonality

The life cycles and distribution of both eel and smelt is dependent on age and season. In addition, the size of fish increases with age, the majority of growth taking place in the summer months. These two factors combined, therefore, have the potential to

provide some indication of the season in which the Goldcliff fish died.

Comparisons of eel from Goldcliff with the reference material indicate that the majority of eels were between 150mm and 290mm in length; a few were larger. According to Wheeler (1969), elvers have usually reached about 70mm when they begin their ascent of rivers or take to life in the littoral zone. They arrive in January or February and remain for a number of years. When they have reached at least 410mm in length they begin the return migration. The growth of young eels is dependent upon temperature and food supply. However, in the second winter they are 170–190mm long, while adults are in the range 290–1000mm (Muus and Dahlstrom, 1964). The size range of the eels from Goldcliff suggests that they had entered the estuarine/freshwater stage of the life cycle. Almost threequarters are between 150mm and 180mm, the size range expected for fish which have reached, or almost reached, their second winter. A significant number were about 290mm in length (Fig 4.11). It is possible that eels would have attained this size by their third winter, thus indicating a seasonal catch.

Adult smelt congregate around river mouths in winter ready to spawn in estuarine water in early spring. In summer, adult smelt return to the sea, whilst the young remain in the estuary. By the end of the first summer they have reached 50–70mm, and become sexually mature at an age of 3–4 years and a length of 150–180mm. The smelt from Goldcliff were approximately 87mm maximum, which suggests that they had survived past their first summer, and probably into the winter months.

Seasonality evidence based on the size of both the eel and smelt, therefore, appears to indicate autumn–winter occupation, thus, supporting the evidence from the mammals (above).

4.8.2 Bird from Mesolithic contexts

Two bird bones fragments were recovered from the hand collected material, an ulna and a carpometacarpus, considered unidentifiable to species, but possibly from mallard (*Anas platyrhynchos*). Mallard are found in estuarine and coastal habitats.

4.8.3 Rodents

The identified remains of small mammals were a probable mouse (*Apodemus* sp.) upper incisor and a possible vole (*Arvicola* sp.) lower incisor.

4.8.4 Discussion

The present habitats of the fishes identified are estuarine and coastal waters (Muus and Dahlstrom 1964) and they are all species which are found close to the shore in shallow water. Gobies are coastal fish, but the other species can be found in both saline and brackish water.

How they came to be incorporated in the occupation deposit is uncertain. It is interesting that virtually all of the identified remains came from one area; the deposit is, therefore, the result of either a single event or the build up of material from the repetition of the same event occurring in one location. It is possible that this occurred by natural means; the fish might have become stranded after a particularly high tide. Fish bones are found in otter spraints, but the lack of damage from gastric acids makes this origin unlikely. They are also found in bird pellets. At Westward Ho!, Devon three possible goby vertebrae from a Mesolithic midden were interpreted as the remains of a predator's meal (Levitan and Locker 1987).

The occupation context from which the fish remains were recovered, the fact that most were from a hearth area, and that a large proportion was burnt, makes it highly likely that they represent food remains. The rarity of fish larger than 300mm is unusual; however, it is possible that any larger fish may have been preserved as dried or smoked fish for consumption during periods when food was more scarce.

The evidence from contemporary Scandinavian coastal Mesolithic settlements provides additional support for an anthropogenic origin. At Ertebølle, a coastal shell mound in Jutland, Denmark dated to c 3900–3250 BC (Bahn 1992) eel, stickleback, and goby were also amongst the fish identified (Enghoff 1986). It was argued that the remains of these small fish had not been washed ashore from the sea, nor were they the remains of gull pellets. At Skateholm, Scania many of the graves contained small fish remains (up to 200mm). These were interpreted partly as preserved stomach contents, and partly as food offerings in the form of a stew made from eel, roach, stickleback, and rudd (Jonsson 1986 and 1988). The food crust inside a vessel from Tybrind Vig, West Funen contained several fish remains, including an opercular bone from a 200mm gadid (Andersen and Malmros 1984). Thus, the exploitation of small fish from shallow coastal waters appears to have been common practice in the Scandinavian Mesolithic.

If Mesolithic people were exploiting these small, inshore fish for food, then it is likely that they were caught in fish traps, perhaps baskets, located in shallow water similar to that found at Vedbaek (Enghoff 1983) where the remains of a plaited fish trap were found. Alternatively, fish stranded in shallow pools when the tide went out would have been easy to catch even without the use of nets. Of course, it is possible that these small fish represent rubbish discarded when the traps were emptied but it is more plausible that this potential food resource would have been utilised. As Enghoff (1986) reminds us, 'small fish form an important and constant food source for many people', even today.

Acknowledgements

I am grateful to Alison Locker for her help and assistance with the identification of these bones and to Dale Serjeantson for her helpful suggestions and comments.

4.9 Soil micromorphology on the Mesolithic site
Richard Macphail and Gill Cruise

Introduction and methods

Three samples were examined from the Mesolithic soil; all were Kubiena samples. The tins were sent to Stirling University, where they were impregnated with a crystic resin mixture and manufactured into thin sections (Murphy 1986). The soil micromorphological study was carried out employing plane polarised light (PPL), crossed polarised light (XPL), oblique incident light (OIL), and ultra violet light (UVL), at magnifications ranging from × 1 to × 400. Descriptions follow Bullock et al (1985) and the approaches to archaeological soils and sediments as developed by Courty et al (1989). Microfabrics, structure, anthropogenic inclusions, organic materials, and pedofeatures were counted for each contextual/layer (Table CD 4.9), according to principles discussed with the Working Group on Archaeological Soil Micromorphology and as employed and tested at the Overton Down Experimental Earthwork and numerous archaeological sites (eg Crowther et al 1996; Acott et al 1997; Macphail and Cruise in press). They are reported on the basis of frequency and abundance scales (Bullock et al 1985).

Results

Soil micromorphological analysis from the site as a whole (including the Iron Age samples, Chapter 15) identified six main microfabric types (M1a–M6b) (see key to soil micromorphology CD 4.8), four anthropogenic inclusions (AI1–4), clay (estuarine silt and clay), five organic materials (O1–5), and eight pedofeatures (P1–8). The three samples (2056–2058) represent a sequence through the estuarine clay (Context 1201) above the Mesolithic occupation horizon (Context 1202) and into the subsoil below (Context 1204), as shown in Figures 4.3–4.4. The frequency and abundance of the microfabric features is outlined in CD 4.9. The Mesolithic soil is sealed by laminated and massive structured estuarine silts and clays (M1a) that are mainly grey in colour, except for brown areas of iron staining (P5). The sediment contains occasional to many diatoms and phytoliths and has been affected by rooting and pyrite formation. At the sharp junction with the Mesolithic loamy soil, large (>20mm) fragments of wood charcoal are embedded across both contexts. A piece of charcoal sitting on the Mesolithic soil boundary, but within the estuarine clay, is illustrated (CD 4.10 and 4.11).

The Mesolithic soil differs from the overlying estuarine clay by being a poorly sorted loam, with common silt, frequent medium, and few fine sand, with very few quartzite gravel. The fine soil is composed of common, large (5–25 mm) pieces of dark reddish brown soil in a similar matrix (M2). The reddish soil is compact and dark brown and orange brown under OIL. It contains charcoal fragments and very abundant fine charred and amorphous organic matter. This soil material dominates the uppermost 20–30 mm of the soil (CD 4.12 and 4.13). It has an irregular, burrowed boundary with the underlying, mainly greyish-brown dominated soil (M3). Ferruginised burrows and associated <500µm size organo-mineral excrements occur throughout the sampled profile. Of further interest are the presence of charred, coarse (10mm), woody roots (O2) and many burned bones (CD 4.13–4.15) in the uppermost 25mm of the Mesolithic soil, and a 10mm size flint flake at 190mm depth at the base of the burrowed soil (M3). The underlying subsoil (M4) is grey, with only occasional organic matter. A number of pedofeatures occur. Occasional micropans occur in the reddish soil, while down profile many voids are infilled with dusty clay and silt (P1). In grey areas, these textural features are grey, whereas in the brown areas these features are brown.

Discussion

The reddish soil fragments can be identified as burned and compacted soil. These occur alongside coarse and fine wood charcoal and burned bone and, with the burned soil, are indicative of a hearth. Much of the humic soil, which occurs down to 190mm also contains much charcoal. A flint flake occurred at the base of this burrowed soil. Textural features within the burned and, hence, fossilised Mesolithic soil are indicative of disturbance, such as by trampling. The charring of woody roots is evidence of the Mesolithic fire(s)/hearth being essentially in situ.

Studies of archaeological analogues (eg burned mounds, alluvially buried burned tree hollows, estuarine clay buried soils, and occupation surfaces) indicate that the Goldcliff Mesolithic occupation was followed by a short-lived period of biological activity, mixing soil, artefacts and charcoal throughout a topsoil that now has a thickness of some 190mm (eg Macphail and Goldberg 1990, Lewis *et al* 1992, Macphail 1994). At Three Ways Wharf, Uxbridge a relic biologically worked soil with Mesolithic flints was preserved by iron and manganese impregnation (Lewis *et al* 1992, fig 22.3). The effects of such biological mixing can also be assessed from the flint

scatter and refitting patterns of the artefacts (Fig 4.6). The ferruginisation of organic remains in the soil is one consequence of the soil becoming waterlogged (Bouma *et al* 1990), with consequent localised drifting of light remains such as wood charcoal occurring as the site became inundated. As at the Stumble, Essex, very little disturbance of the site itself is envisaged, as it became buried by estuarine silts (Macphail 1994). The lack of disturbance is exemplified by the very coarse wood charcoal being present across the boundary of the Mesolithic soil and the estuarine clay at Goldcliff, with coarse charcoal also being present within the clay. The last is evidence of very gentle sedimentation.

On the other hand, fine soil material was dramatically affected by increasing site wetness and inundation. The soil became generally leached of iron (reduced conditions) and fine soil slaked under the influence of Na^{++} ions (Duchaufour 1982). Much of this fine soil is now present as microlaminated dusty clay void coatings and infillings throughout the Mesolithic profile. These textural features are unrelated to any history of clay translocation as found in forest soils (argillic brown earths), as discussed with the SEESOIL group (Macphail 1994). Some silty inwash features are the direct result of estuarine clay being washed directly into the Mesolithic soil profile. Such soil transformations are typical of drowned palaeosols (Wright 1992). Just as at the Blackwater Estuary, Essex, the Mesolithic soil at Goldcliff was transformed into a Saline (Alluvial) Gley Soil, with attendant features such as mottling and pyrite formation (Miedema *et al* 1974, Avery 1990).

The present thickness of the Mesolithic soil is probably not representative of its original depth, because of such factors as loss of structure and void space, and diminished organic matter content. Instead of its original biological structure of crumbs and blocks, it now has a massive structure. Data from the Overton Down Experimental Earthwork imply that the Goldcliff soil profile may have been reduced by some 40% in thickness (Crowther *et al* 1996). Context 1202, therefore, represents the remains of a probably thicker topsoil A1h horizon, while underlying Context 1204 is the subsoil B horizon. This last mainly differs by being very little burrowed and containing much less organic matter. It may be speculated that the original soil was a groundwater gley.

Conclusions

The uppermost part of the 'Mesolithic soil' contains fragments of burned soil, which are assumed to be relics of the Mesolithic campfire(s) that also produced coarse wood charcoal and burned bone. There is some evidence that a fire was built on a humic and trampled topsoil. The fireplace may subsequently have become broken up by biological activity. Increasing site wetness and gentle site inundation by estuarine silts had two main effects on the Mesolithic soil:-

(i) on flooding, saline water saturating the upper soil slaked the fine soil component, and this caused the elutriation of the soil except for the strongly coherent burned soil, with the result that fines form coatings in voids down-profile;

(ii) on inundation, which is likely to have been very gentle, and just sufficient to pick up coarse charcoal present on the soil surface and move it locally. For example, there are large fragments of charcoal embedded across the estuarine/Mesolithic soil boundary. Heavier materials such as the burned bone were not moved.

Acknowledgements

The authors acknowledge funding support by Lampeter University and wish to thank Nick Barton, Martin Bell, Astrid Caseldine, and John Crowther for their collaboration and discussion. Marie-Agnès Courty and Paul Goldberg are thanked for their discussion of the thin sections.

4.10 Phosphate and magnetic susceptibility studies
John Crowther

A general background to the objectives of these studies and the problems of their application in waterlogged contexts is given in Chapter 15.

Samples ($n = 109$) were taken on a 0.5m grid across parts of the surface of the charcoal-rich layer (CD 4.16 and 4.17). The sediments are minerogenic (loss-on-ignition (LOI) mostly <4.0%), and their relatively high sand content (28.9–36.4%) confirms that they are derived, at least in part, from the underlying head deposit. Phosphate-P concentrations are mostly quite low. More than half are <0.400mg g^{-1}, and this is taken as being indicative of natural background concentrations. There are, however, very clear signs of localised phosphate enrichment (Fig 4.12), with four samples exceeding 2.00mg g^{-1} (maximum, 3.46mg g^{-1}). Interestingly, there is a highly significant rank correlation ($r_s = 0.843$, p <0.001) between phosphate-P and LOI. Since there is no clear evidence of an individual

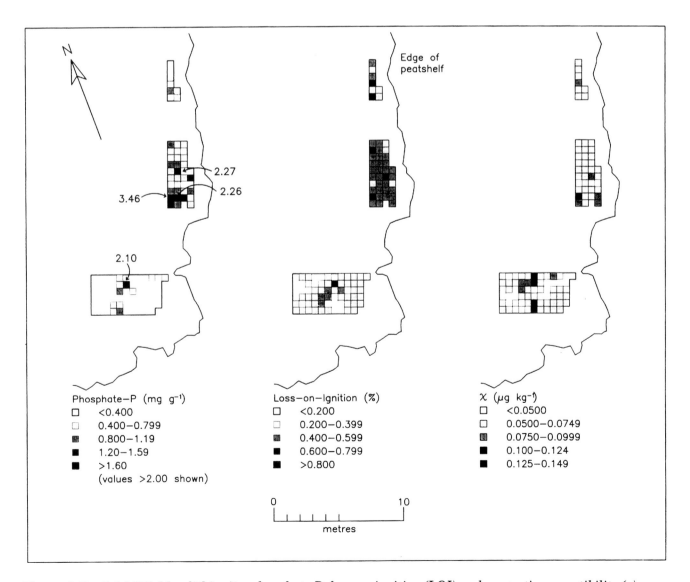

Figure 4.12 Goldcliff: Mesolithic site, phosphate-P, loss-on-ignition (LOI) and magnetic susceptibility (χ)

occupation horizon within this layer, which might have been particularly organic and phosphate-rich, the observed variations in LOI (Fig 4.12) and phosphate seem unlikely to have been influenced to any significant extent by sample depth (see discussion in Crowther 1997). It may be assumed, therefore, that the phosphate data truly reflect the pattern of phosphate input, and this appears to be very closely related to the distribution of visible bone remains (Fig 4.5c). This suggests that the elevated concentrations are largely attributable to bone-derived phosphate (phosphate-P concentrations in bone samples from the Mesolithic site were in the range 76.5–113mg g^{-1}; CD 4.18), either as fine bone fragments or in a mineralised form, rather than more general enrichment, as might be associated with more diffuse forms of human activity and/or with the development of a topsoil horizon. The presence of fine fragments of undecomposed bone could also be a contributory factor in the relationship between LOI and phosphate. It should be noted, however, that LOI and phosphate will also be augmented by charcoal and plant material (eg roots penetrating through overlying sediments).

As anticipated, the χ and χ_{max} values are very low, the maxima being 0.141 and 2.17μm^3 kg^{-1}, respectively. Unfortunately, χ_{max} exhibits quite a high degree of variability (coefficient of variation, 34.8%) compared with χ(27.1%), which is presumably attributable to variations in parent material and differential gleying. Least squares regression analysis on 40 samples for which χ_{max} was determined showed that little of the variability in χ (r^2 = 0.132, ie 13.2% explained variance) is directly attributable to variations in fractional conversion. In these circumstances some of the peaks in the χ survey (Fig 4.12) are caused by a high potential susceptibility rather than enhancement through burning (Crowther and Barker 1995). It is uncertain, therefore, whether the poor correspondence between the χ survey and the distribution of charcoal (Fig 4.5b) genuinely reflects an absence of in situ burning in some of the locations where high concentrations of charcoal were recorded, or is simply due to the effects of gleying.

4.11 Mesolithic site conclusions
Nicholas Barton and Martin Bell

Context and extent of Mesolithic activity

In the Mesolithic, the excavated area was essentially dryland, a soil developed on head at the island edge. The situation is, thus, comparable to the lithic scatters of the Essex Coast, such as the Stumble, which are on now submerged former old land surfaces (Wilkinson and Murphy 1995). Several of the intertidal Mesolithic flint scatters of the Bristol Channel are similarly situated on head, often overlain by peat (Lewis 1992). At Goldcliff the site was later buried, first by estuarine clay, then by the development of peat. A peat band with charcoal at

Goldcliff East is contemporary with the excavated site and from this it is clear that waterlogged strata contemporary with the site exist, but at a lower level around the fringes of the former island.

Evidence of Mesolithic activity is concentrated on the fringes of the former bedrock island. The discovery of a microlith with other flints in Hill Farm Trench 2 indicates that the lithic scatter extends at least 220m north. Small numbers of flints, together with charcoal, occur at Goldcliff East 0.8km from the main Mesolithic site. The island itself is entirely pasture, so there has been no opportunity to establish whether a lithic scatter exists over the island as a whole. Linkage between various areas of Mesolithic activity, suggesting that they were used contemporaneously, is also implied by the presence of axe manufacturing debris and by axe/adzes made of tuff, recovered from different parts of the wetland. The indications are, therefore, of a significant concentration of Mesolithic activity around the edge of the former island. Indeed, rather than thinking of Goldcliff as a 'site' we should perhaps consider it as a continuum of overlapping activity zones dispersed across the contemporary landscape. The artefact scatters represent patches of activity which can be demonstrated to be coexistent, or very closely related in time.

Dating

The radiocarbon dates from Mesolithic contexts and their calibrated ranges are shown on Figure 4.13. The earliest archaeological date is on cut deer bone from the excavation and shows that occupation began around 5600 Cal BC. The three charcoal dates are very close, between 5200 and 5500 Cal BC. Two are from the excavation site, one from the lowest peat at Goldcliff East (0.8km east), where activity is clearly contemporary with the main site. The charred hazelnut date is about 1000 years later; alone this indicates that activity may have continued over an extended timescale until the end of the Mesolithic.

The radiocarbon dates for the main Mesolithic concentration are in close agreement with those recorded for other late Mesolithic 'narrow-bladed' assemblages in western Britain (Jacobi 1980, Berridge and Roberts 1986, David 1990, Roberts 1996). Based on microlith forms and other tool components, parallels for Goldcliff may be sought in the south Welsh sites of Pen-y-Bont, Ogmore, Glamorgan (Jacobi 1980), Gwernvale, Powys (Britnell and Savory 1984), and at various other locations along the Pembrokeshire coast (David 1990). Of the few radiocarbon dates available from these places, the most relevant might be a pair of dates from Site II at the Nab Head, Pembrokeshire, which gave readings on charcoal of 7360 ± 90 BP (OxA-860) from a shallow pit and of 6210 ± 90 BP (OxA-861) on a hearth (David 1990, 250). A date of 6895 ± 80 BP (CAR-118) is also available from within a pit on the pre-construction surface of a Neolithic long cairn at Gwernvale

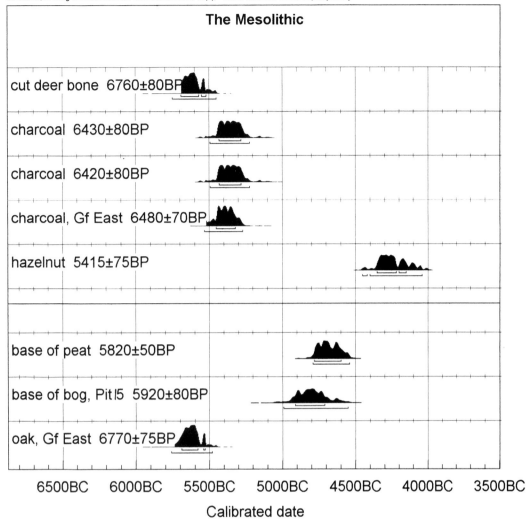

M. Stuiver, A. Long and R.S. Kra eds. 1993 Radiocarbon 35(1); OxCal v2.18 cub r:4 sd:12 prob[chron]

The Mesolithic

cut deer bone 6760±80BP

charcoal 6430±80BP

charcoal 6420±80BP

charcoal, Gf East 6480±70BP

hazelnut 5415±75BP

base of peat 5820±50BP

base of bog, Pit l5 5920±80BP

oak, Gf East 6770±75BP

6500BC   6000BC   5500BC   5000BC   4500BC   4000BC   3500BC

Calibrated date

Figure 4.13 Goldcliff: Radiocarbon dates from archaeological and selected environmental contexts and their calibrated ranges based on the calibration curve of Stuiver, Long, and Kra (1993) and the OxCal programme (v2.18)

(Britnell and Savory 1984, 50). Extrapolating information from these results is difficult, but they appear to correlate well with those on other assemblages in western Britain where dating is available. The most secure of these include a small collection of artefacts with microscalene triangles from Three Holes Cave, Devon which has associated dates on cut-marked red deer of 6330 ± 75 BP (OxA-4491) and 6120 ± 75 BP (OxA-4492) (Roberts 1996, 202). Further analogies are difficult to assess because of the severely restricted size of the Goldcliff tool collection. Broadly contemporary are microliths from the Lydstep pig, Pembrokeshire (see below) and the body of data from Mesolithic coastal locations, which contain either small scalene triangles or microlithic rods in combination with a range of non-microlithic tools such as denticulated scrapers, truncated pieces, burins and awls (Jacobi 1980, 169). A further feature of chronological significance may be the fact that the Goldcliff debitage is dominated by flakes rather than blades or bladelets, an observation which finds parallels in other late Mesolithic industries in southern Britain

(eg High Rocks, Sussex, see Jacobi and Tebbutt 1981, tables II and III).

The environment

Radiocarbon dates for an oak tree and charcoal at Goldcliff East are from peat at about –3.7m OD. Their calibrated ranges (Fig 4.13) are broadly contemporary with three of the four archaeological dates from the excavated site. From this we can deduce that at the time of the first Mesolithic activity MHWST was some 3.5 metres below the lowest part of the excavated site, assuming peat inception at roughly MHWST level. Highest astronomical tides might add another 1m, and storm surges more, but it is unlikely that during the main period of Mesolithic activity the excavated site would have been subject to direct marine influence.

The contemporaneity of the charcoal and cut bone dates with that from the oak tree in the lowest peat at Goldcliff East (Chapter 2) demonstrates that the onset of Mesolithic activity occurs during a marine regressive phase, which can probably be correlated with the thin lowest peat recorded during the auger survey at c –3m OD. A contemporary peat is recorded at Caldicot Pill (Scaife 1995), suggesting that this regressive phase may have been widespread in its effects. Comparing the Goldcliff East oak tree with charcoal dates from the same peat indicates that it formed over a period of at least 300 calendar years, between around 5600 and 5300 Cal BC. That period spans the calibrated ranges of four out of five archaeological dates from the Mesolithic and, thus, suggests that the main occupation was during that marine regressive phase when oak woodland spread out from the island fringe. Much of the rest of the area was covered by reedswamp, interrupted by numerous channels where peat did not form and which were probably subject to marine influence.

Pollen analysis (Chapter 13) provides a detailed picture of the Mesolithic environment from around 4900 Cal BC. Unfortunately, this starts some 400 calendar years later than the main period of Mesolithic activity. Pollen analysis was not done on the peat at –3.7m at Goldcliff East, which is contemporary with the Mesolithic occupation; this is something which would be well worth doing in the future. Pollen and beetle evidence were not preserved through most of the Mesolithic soil horizon because it was only subsequently waterlogged. Waterlogged seeds were also few in this layer and dominated by species such as elder, which are decay resistant. Their presence does, however, indicate that the site became waterlogged within a few decades of the final burial of the charcoal band, thus attesting to rapid sea level rise during this period. The pollen record from the Mesolithic soil is only from its surface, where high Chenopodiaceae values mark the onset of marine influence. The pollen record is, thus, a little later than the charcoal record from the Mesolithic site but they both point to oak woodland with hazel scrub. The growth of hazel may have been encouraged by human activity; we know from the charred hazelnut that this resource was being used.

Because the pollen evidence is later than the charcoal layer, we lack direct evidence for the effect of this burning on the surrounding vegetation. We know that the burning extends over 0.8km round the island edge. We can rule out natural fires because of its strong association with artefact concentrations. This raises the question of whether the burning signifies deliberate Mesolithic use of fire, eg in hunting, to alter the vegetation and create more favourable conditions for the growth of specific plants for human consumption, or to attract wild animals (Mellars 1976). The use of fire, apparently for a combination of these purposes, is increasingly attested at the woodland/moorland edge in the British upland (Simmons 1996) and appears to be a distinctive aspect of the insular later Mesolithic, use of fire being only rarely evidenced in the continental Mesolithic. In a South Wales context such burning is documented at Waun-Fignen-Felen in the Brecon

Beacons (Smith and Cloutman 1988); other possible Welsh evidence is noted by Caseldine (1990, 35).

Simmons (1996) points out that we know little of the effects which Mesolithic communities had in coastal and lowland situations. The charcoal horizon at Goldcliff is, however, paralleled by a similar horizon on the later Mesolithic intertidal site at Westward Ho! (Balaam et al 1987) and by the occurrence of charcoal on a number of the intertidal sites below submerged forest peat in Pembrokeshire studied by Lewis (1992). Northeast of Goldcliff on the edge of the wetland at Vurlong Reen (Walker et al 1998, 75), charcoal and evidence of vegetation change suggest the possibility of human impact in the later Mesolithic, roughly at the time of the Goldcliff hazelnut date. Thus, in the Bristol Channel–Severn Estuary area there is evidence of the use of fire in the coastal woodland edge which parallels that in the uplands. In the specific case of Goldcliff, it seems most unlikely they were burning the island forest to create more open conditions for grazing animals; the island was, at the time, surrounded by an enormous reed swamp within which the resources afforded by this area of oak woodland must have been greatly valued in their own right. More likely, perhaps, is that firing was carried out to favour valued plants such as hazel, or as an aid to hunting the many animals which are likely to have sought out this dry island, particularly during flooding episodes. It is also possible that the charcoal reflects generations of campfires; the distributions of charcoal and burnt artefacts certainly suggest that campfires are responsible for the charcoal within the excavated area. However, the excavated evidence does not suggest many phases of activity over a long period, and the occurrence of extensive charcoal spreads at Westward Ho! and the Pembrokeshire sites does support the idea of larger scale landscape management practices.

Marine inundation occurred sometime between about 5200 Cal BC and the onset of bog formation around 4900 Cal BC. The basal layers of the bog show only minor charcoal peaks and little in the way of vegetation changes that can be clearly attributed to human activity. The charred hazelnut date and the presence of charcoal and two flints at the base of the peat above the Mesolithic site show some human activity, but not of the intensity indicated by the charcoal layer itself. More definite human impact registers about two centuries before the elm decline c 3300 Cal BC.

Significance of the main assemblage and site formation

The artefacts and fauna in the main concentration appear to have suffered no major post-depositional disturbance. The micromorphological evidence points to a gentle inundation sufficient, perhaps, to pick up some charcoal and move it locally. Evidence that the site is undisturbed comes from a number of different sources. First, the animal bones, though not in full articulation, are also not widely separated and show no obvious signs of anatomical sorting by hydraulic or other natural processes (Coard and Dennell 1995). The presence of localised concentrations of fishbones and microfauna, unless trapped in shallow hollows or surface depressions are, likewise, unlikely to have survived major flooding episodes or extensive re-working of the deposits. Indications that objects lying at the surface were soon covered or incorporated into the deposit are also given by examples of refitting artefacts and the close spatial association of the tuff flakes (Fig 4.6). The major exception to this pattern concerns the very low quantities of microdebitage (chips <10mm long) recorded in the excavation. In all, only 25 chips were identified in the entire assemblage, and this is considerably less than would otherwise be anticipated for freshly knapped lithic scatters, where it is usual for small chips to absolutely outnumber all other debitage (Newcomer and Sieveking 1980, Barton and Bergman 1982). Given the presence of debitage from each of the different stages in the *chaîne opératoire* it would seem extremely unlikely that knapping did not take place on site. Whilst no wholly convincing explanation is yet forthcoming to explain this scarcity of small material, we would nevertheless offer three possible solutions: (i) it is due to inadequate sieving, the samples which were sieved happening to be in areas where knapping did not occur, (ii) that natural wind winnowing removed much of the microdebitage, or (iii) that the chips were simply trampled into the softer ground and may, therefore, have been buried deeper than the bulk of the bones and artefacts (cf Gifford-Gonzalez *et al* 1985). Of the three possibilities, the winnowing explanation seems less likely, given the large quantities of charred wood and charcoal fragments also found at the site. However, the fact that some dilation to the artefact scatters did take place, either by natural processes (wind?) or by human interference (scuffage or trampling?), is implied by the horizontal distances of 1m or more between refitting examples of flake waste, and we have noted possible evidence of animal footprints in section. The two concentrations of charcoal (Fig 4.5b) would appear to coincide with separate combustion zones. In the absence of dug structures or hearth stones, it would seem the fires were set in unlined flat hearths.

Season of occupation and interpretation of human activities

The faunal assemblage consists of cut-marked or burnt bones of red deer, roe deer, pig, and otter. Traces of burning are also present on some of the bird and fish bones and, in the case of unburnt material, it is clear these were not the digested remnants of animal scats or regurgita. Information about the season of occupation is available from the bones of fish and pig. Assuming uniform growth rates, the size of eels shows they were caught in winter. Likewise, based on size criterion, the smelt could have been netted during the winter months. A further positive indication of winter (or spring) residence is provided by the ageing of the wild pig mandibles. The only potentially contradictory evidence comes from the presence of charred hazelnuts but, if these had been deliberately parched and stored, they could have been consumed at any time of the year, including winter.

In the Mesolithic the former Goldcliff Island was several times its modern extent (Chapter 2) and would have offered significant opportunities for food procurement. Deciduous oak woodland in the area is likely to have provided suitable habitats for wild pig and red deer populations, whilst the marshland areas of the surrounding shoreline furnished other possibilities for collecting wild plants, fowling, trapping smaller mammals, and trapping fish. This variety of food resources is confirmed by the diversity of species represented in the faunal assemblage.

The interpretation of human activities at Goldcliff is dependent on understanding the nature of the faunal remains and the lithic assemblage. The faunal component has already been discussed in detail but it is worth reiterating that red deer is well-represented by mostly limb bones and extremities at the expense of cranial material and other parts of the axial skeleton. If not simply due to the vagaries of preservation or sampling, it might speak in favour of selective transport of the meatier elements of the carcass to the site for consumption. In contrast, the fact that more parts of the pig skeleton reached the site implies that these animals were probably hunted and killed in the immediate proximity of the main activity area. It may also be relevant that two burnt microliths were recovered within the same concentration as the wild pig bones (Fig 4.5d). That these were parts of broken projectile equipment, transported to the site in the kill, is given added credence by the finding of a pair of microliths in association with the neck vertebrae of a pig from Lydstep Haven, further along the south Welsh coast (Leach 1918, Jacobi 1980, 175). The burnt nature of the microliths at Goldcliff could be explained by the roasting of meat in hot charcoals. The Lydstep pig has been dated 5300 ± 100 BP (OxA-1412, Lewis 1992). It escaped from its hunters and died, presumably of its wounds, in coastal fen woodland. The animal bone evidence shows the reed and fen peat which surrounded Goldcliff Island at the time was a good habitat for wild pigs and especially deer. The situation is reminiscent of Thesiger's (1964) accounts of the Marsh Arabs hunting pigs in the *Phragmites* swamps of Iraq, something which took place particularly when the animals were flushed out by floods.

Deer was the most abundant species represented by animal bones and there is also a very extensive record of their presence, and that of humans and wild cattle (curiously not represented in the bone collection), in the Mesolithic wetland in the form of the footprint evidence presented by Allen (1997b). At

Goldcliff (Appendix I: Maps 14 and 16) he reports red deer footprints 500m to the west of the Mesolithic site, whilst 700m to the east at Goldcliff East he reports deer and ill-preserved human footprints. These are described as below the lowest peat, the base of which has been dated by Smith and Morgan (1989) to 5530 ± 90BP (CAR-657); the footprints are, thus, broadly contemporary with the Mesolithic activity. At Uskmouth, 2.8km to the west, Mesolithic human footprints are sealed by peats dated 6250 ± 80BP (OxA-2627), whilst at Magor human footprints are sealed by peat dated 5720 ± 80BP (OxA-2626) (Aldhouse-Green et al 1992).

As already explained, the Mesolithic activity seems to be concentrated during a marine regressive phase of extensive peat formation. Interestingly, the footprint evidence occurs in minerogenic sediments above and below the lowest peat band. This demonstrates that people were continuing to exploit this landscape during the saltmarsh phase, and little wonder given the abundance of animals which the footprints shows. As the only known area of dryland within 6km, it is highly likely that Goldcliff Island would have been often visited, one of the 'persistent places' of Barton et al 1995. Given these circumstances, it is, thus, perhaps not unreasonable to suppose that some of these lines of human footprints mark the specific daily actions of those people who occupied the Goldcliff Mesolithic site. Their expeditions are likely to have been responsible for deposition of the two axe/adzes and, perhaps, the antler mattock found by Upton near the footprint site at Uskmouth 2.8 km west of the site and dated 6180 ± 80BP (OxA-4574) (Aldhouse-Green et al 1992, Aldhouse-Green and Housley 1993).

The birds of the estuary were also exploited and the fish bones indicate that fishing was an important activity. Some of the fish bones are burnt, and they were mostly from a hearth. This suggests cooking, and possibly drying of fish on the site. It is even possible that the posthole beside the hearth formed part of some sort of drying rack. The fish represented are small, and it is probable that traps were used, perhaps wooden eel weirs, fish fencing, stake supported nets, or wickerwork traps (for references see Pedersen 1995). Various forms of fishing baskets and traps have been observed in minerogenic sediments in the estuary, but so far the earliest dated examples are of late Bronze Age or early Iron Age date (Chapter 16). The axes/adzes may well have been employed in making or mending such equipment. In this respect, it is interesting that flaking of rocks used in axe/adze manufacture is evidenced in the excavated site, whilst the two axes/adzes were found in isolation, presumably discarded, or lost, during maintenance work. It is puzzling that salmon bones were totally absent from the assemblage because there is a working salmon putcher rack (basketwork trap) within 120m of the site (Fig 4.1, Green 1992), and this activity is documented at Goldcliff from the 13th century AD. Ingrem (personal communication) is confident that had salmon bones been present, they would have survived, given their similarity to smelt bones which were present. Adrian Williams (personal communication), who owns the Goldcliff Fishery today, informs us that salmon are likely to have been present at all times of year, but the time of particular plenty would have been associated with the runs of salmon beginning in April and going through to the spawning period in Autumn. Maybe, as the other evidence hints, people were not around at Goldcliff at that time, maybe they did not eat salmon or, given the highly localised distribution of some artefacts and bone classes, perhaps they did catch salmon but they were processed somewhere else.

There is nothing in the species list to suggest an ephemeral kill-site or a permanent residential location occupied over several months. Instead it should be considered whether Goldcliff Island was a transitory hunting and processing camp, with the implication that it was occupied only briefly. This question is, however, necessary to answer with reference to the lithic collection. The homogeneous nature of the lithic assemblage and the relative scarcity of tools would appear to be the strongest evidence against this being a residential site, or home base. The lithic assemblage contains only fifteen retouched tools and ten of these are non-standardised retouched flakes. At the same time, it is clear that it does not fit the description of a kill location either, where isolated groups of microliths are likely to be the only evidence of hunting activity (Jacobi 1980, Barton et al 1995). From the amounts of debitage recovered, it is likely that much of the lithic production was focused upon the manufacture of laminar flakes suitable for making microliths. This type of work could be linked with repairing broken hunting equipment. There is, however, no evidence that any microliths were actually made on site. The absence of typical manufacturing by-products, such as microburins, or broken and unfinished forms, might, therefore, imply that the better flake blanks were cached and transported for later use elsewhere. The only other recognisable tool-forms are end-scrapers. Noticeably missing from the tool inventory are denticulated flakes and scrapers, truncated pieces, burins, awls, 'rubbed end' pieces, and a range of other types which might characterise a site visited a number of times, or occupied over a prolonged period. The lack of evidence for tool production and tool use does not, of course, preclude the possibility of other equipment being deployed for which there is no surviving archaeological record.

Goldcliff Island, thus, appears to have been ideally situated to enable Mesolithic hunter-gatherers to maximise their resources and gain access to a variety of distinctive, closely-spaced habitats viz marshland, estuarine, and mixed oak woodland. Despite this fact, and the abundant evidence of activities in the form of mammal, fish and bird bones, artefacts, and zones of combustion, there is little to indicate the location was occupied for any length of time. For example, the excavation area revealed no structural evidence of dwellings, only an isolated post hole, and there were no stone lined hearths. Furthermore, the total large vertebrate remains represent portions of relatively few individuals of red deer (4) and wild pig (3). Aside from a small number of retouched tools, most of the lithic finds consisted of debitage left behind from knapping pebbles, perhaps from the gravels in the estuary (see Section 4.5). Thus, the accumulated evidence would seem to suggest impermanent settlement of short-term duration. Other occupation sites may, of course, have existed beyond the excavated area. The seasonality studies place the occupation in the winter or early spring.

If this interpretation proves correct, it follows that existing models on the seasonal mobility of late-Mesolithic hunter-gatherers may need to be considerably revised. Up until now, it has been widely accepted that human settlement patterns during the Mesolithic were fairly predictable, and could be envisaged in terms of movements between 'inland home bases' and 'coastal home bases' (Bailey 1978, 42–45, Jacobi 1979, 84–85). According to the model, occupation in either of these locations would depend on the attraction and accessibility of resources. For the southwest of Britain, Jacobi (1979, 84) has proposed that the availability of ungulate meat in the upland interior exerted the strongest influences in the summer months, whereas in the spring, when coastal productivity was at its peak, human groups would have migrated to the estuarine and shore areas, while in winter low-lying inland bases might have been preferred. Against this is a growing body of evidence which suggests that there was much more flexibility in prehistoric hunter-gatherer systems. Woodman (personal communication), for example, now sees evidence for a more complicated resource-based strategy in Ireland in which some late-Mesolithic groups were entirely coastally

situated (eg Ferriter's Cove, Kerry), while others were focused on inland settings or followed the inland–coastal migration pattern (eg Bann Valley sites). It is worth noting that Woodman's 'diversity' model allows for sometimes much higher residential mobility, which in turn would be reflected in the existence of short-term transitory encampments in places where one might have expected base camps. In this respect it could be relevant that, apart from the absence of shell midden material, there are some interesting parallels to be drawn between Goldcliff and the Kerry site. At Ferriter's Cove (Woodman and O'Brien 1993), which occupies a prime location for the exploitation of coastal resources, the absence of any structures, combined with the restricted nature and quantity of faunal and artefactual remains, also indicates only very ephemeral occupation (Woodman and Anderson 1990, 382).

Thus, perhaps, rather than seeking large residential units in the lowland interior, or even on the coast, we should instead expect to find many more sites like Goldcliff: small transitory encampments which may have been occupied for short periods within certain seasons. The larger coastal sites, such as the Nab Head (David 1990) may give a false impression of base camps, since they were examples of 'persistent places' (Barton et al 1995) where people habitually returned. In reality, the latter may represent major palimpsests of material which camouflage a series of transitory events, although it has to be admitted that the greater diversity of tool-types still needs to be adequately explained. Whether this means that movements of peoples in this part of western Britain were focused along the coast (Palmer 1977), or between the coast and inland (Jacobi 1980, Barton et al 1995), can only be judged in the light of fresh evidence. But at the very least, the existence of sites such as Goldcliff, provide a guide as to where our searches should now be intensified.

5 Skull deposition at Goldcliff and in the Severn Estuary *by M Bell with contributions by M Richards and R Schulting*

5.1 Introduction

Possible ritual and symbolic associations of the buried wetland landscape of the Severn are emphasised by the discovery of human skulls and other bones (Fig 5.1). Goldcliff has produced two stratified skulls, the context of which is discussed in this chapter, together with two old finds from Newport Alexandra Docks and Orb Works and an unstratified skull found at Redwick during the present survey. An AMS radiocarbon dating programme was carried out on these skulls and the finds will be reviewed in the context of prehistoric skull deposition elsewhere.

5.2 Bog development at Goldcliff

Chapters 3 and 4 have outlined how, in the later Mesolithic, the predominantly minerogenic sediments of the lower Wentlooge Formation gave way to an extensive peat bog which grew from the late Mesolithic to the middle Bronze Age. Palaeoenvironmental investigation of this bog has concentrated on the edge of the island where the bog overlies the Mesolithic site discussed in Chapter 4. On 31 October 1990, Upton and Trett visited the site following a major storm. The peat shelf had been swept clear of mud and they found fragments of a human cranium (Newport Museum Lab No 497) 'in situ from the surface of the peat shelf in an area of woody peat. A small fragment of cervid cranium was also removed' (CD1.2). Newport Museum holds a photograph showing the human cranium in the peat. With admirable foresight, they recorded the exact position of the skull fragments using the grid of pegs which Lillie had laid down (Fig 4.2) during survey of the Mesolithic site 18 months earlier. In 1998, the cranial fragments were AMS radiocarbon dated with the following result: 2580 ± 35 BP (OxA-7659).

The next recorded event which removed the mud from the peat shelf was the storm on 30 August 1992, after which Buxton prepared a detailed survey of the peat edge and submerged forest and found a rather enigmatic wooden structure (1208) (Fig 4.2). Most of the submerged forest wood was sampled and has been identified to tree type by Johnson (Figure 4.2

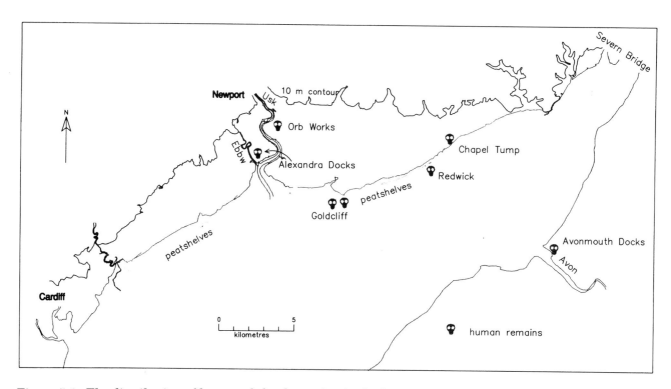

Figure 5.1 The distribution of human skeletal remains in the Severn Estuary wetlands, all skulls except the Chapeltump-2 longbone. Drawing by B Taylor

and Chapter 12). At the edge of the peat shelf the peat is deceptively thin, just 0.1–0.3m, as shown in Figure 4.4. However, as the auger survey discussed in Chapter 3 showed, it thickened rapidly to the west. This is the result of two processes, firstly natural thickening away from the island, secondly the post depositional factor of thinning by oxidation and surface pealing adjacent to the edge of the peat shelf, the part exposed for the longest period. Thus, at the position now occupied by the peat shelf, it is supposed that the peat would originally have been significantly thicker. Adjacent to the edge of the shelf the peat has been eroded down to a wood peat which is at about 0.8m OD. The trees on this peat shelf were mainly alder and birch, with some willow on the southern part and oak and Pomoideae to the north; this latter part may well reflect a somewhat later stage in the vegetation succession where a greater thickness of peat survives. Three of the oaks were sampled for dendrochronology but, unfortunately, they did not date. Beside five of the trees in the submerged forest Smith took samples for beetle analysis, pursuing an interest of the beetle faunas of old woodland (Chapter 14).

Towards the west there is a pronounced rise in the peat surface to about 2.4m OD. The smooth, heterogeneous surface of this higher peat, the lack of wood, and the presence of *Calluna*, *Sphagnum*, and *Eriopherum* show that this is raised bog peat. What has happened here is that, adjacent to the peat edge, erosion has peeled off the overlying raised bog to reveal the submerged forest. The same erosion phenomena affecting a similar sequence is seen at Goldcliff East in the area where Smith and Morgan (1989) worked.

5.3 Environmental sampling Pit 15 and the skull find

In order to investigate the bog sequence, it was decided in 1992 to excavate Pit 15 at a point where the raised bog surface was overlain by the edge of upper Wentlooge clay, in the hope that this would provide the most complete sequence. It turns out that the spot selected for this pit was within 1.5m of the 1990 findspot of the human cranium; however, that was not appreciated at the time because a record of that findspot in Newport Museum was only noticed after the field project had been completed. The pit dug in 1992 was 1m square and it was put down to a depth of 1.6m. The peat, being thicker than expected, was not bottomed but the section was drawn and samples were taken.

During the 1993 season the pit was reopened and enlarged to 2m × 1.7m. During the cleaning back of the section a human cranium was exposed within the peat (Fig 5.2) and in that way the pit took on a significance beyond the environmental sequence which it was originally designed to obtain. Section drawings of two walls of the pit are shown in Figure 5.3 and the sequence will be outlined from the base upwards. The broader context of the stratigraphy outlined is shown in Transect 1A (Fig 3.3).

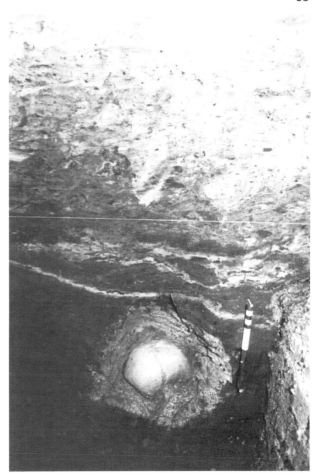

Figure 5.2 Goldcliff: Environmental sampling Pit 15 showing the human cranium in position. Above this is a palaeochannel with a fill of mixed peat and clay. Vertical clay zones probably represent animal footprints in section. Scale length 0.2m

1231
Below 0.13m OD there was a fine sandy clay with fragments of charcoal. This may well relate to Mesolithic burning on the adjacent island. Auger Transect 1A indicates that this layer may be up to 2.8m thick and overlies head.

1230
Clay 0.55m thick. This, together with 1231, comprise the lower Wentlooge Formation.

1229
Organic clay 30mm thick. Reeds are present and this represents the beginning of peat accumulation. Flecks of charcoal up to 3mm in diameter. Charcoal was also noted at the base of the peat in Trench 50 on the Mesolithic site (Chapter 4). This confirms evidence for fire postdating the main phase of Mesolithic activity but still within that period because the bog base is dated 5920 ± 80 BP (CAR-1501).

1228
Woody peat 0.65m thick. This is the peat which corresponds to the submerged forest exposed on the peat shelf 18m to the east (Fig 4.2).

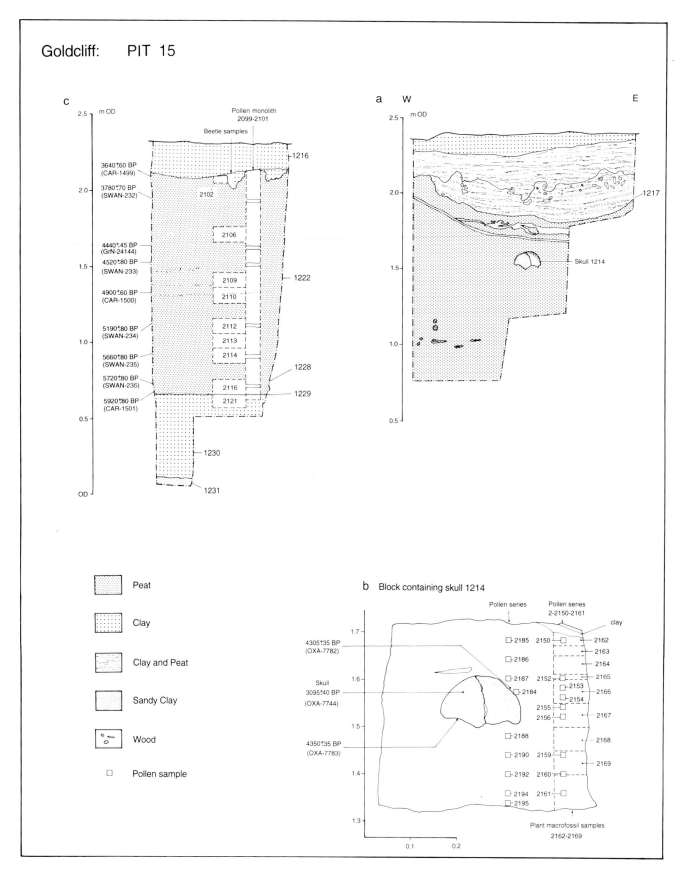

Figure 5.3 Goldcliff: Sections of Environmental Sampling Pit 15 (a) the north wall showing the location of the human skull, (b) the block in which the skull was lifted showing the locations of dated samples and botanical samples, (c) the west wall showing the location of the environmental samples and radiocarbon dates. Drawing by S J Allen

1222

Raised bog peat, 0.80m thick. This started to form as a fibrous and unhumified *Sphagnum* band 50mm thick in 4900 ± 60BP (CAR-1500). The human skull was found in the lower part of the raised bog peat at 1.5m OD.

1217

A palaeochannel cuts the surface of the peat to a depth of *c* 0.1m above the skull. In Figure 5.3a the channel is just over 1.5m wide and 0.55m deep. Its base is marked by a thin layer of pure clay. Above this are layers with varying proportions of peat and clay reflecting erosion of the bog surface and the transition to minerogenic sedimentation as Figure 5.2 shows. A number of small bowl-shaped areas of clay on the same section seem to have been intruded from more clay rich layers above; these are assumed to represent animal footprints.

1216

Clean clay overlies the palaeochannel and the raised bog and this corresponds to the upper Wentlooge clay. The main purpose of this pit was to obtain a sequence of environmental samples (Fig 5.3c). Being very close to the former island, it was hoped that this would link wetland and dryland human activities and vegetation. The pit was also roughly midway between the pollen sequences on the archaeological sites to the west and those of Smith and Morgan (1989), so it would help to link these sequences. Accordingly, a 1.5m monolith column (Samples 2099–2101) was taken for pollen and macrofossil work outlined in Chapter 13. Twelve radiocarbon dates from the monolith and skull peat block (Fig 5.3) provide a chronology for this sequence. Paralleling the pollen column was a series of bulk samples for beetles, of which nine have been analysed (Chapter 14).

5.4 Pit 29

Following discovery of the human cranium in Pit 15 another pit was excavated beside it, in case more of a body awaited discovery, or additional information could be obtained about the context of the find. A 0.5m baulk was left between the two pits and the adjoining 2m square Pit 29. Once the sterile upper Wentlooge clay had been removed, the pit revealed that the head of the palaeochannel (1217), which had been sectioned by Pit 15, lay about 2.1m from the findspot of the skull. The edges of the palaeochannel were clearly defined (Fig 5.4). The cutting of the channel had been followed by deposition of laminated peat and clay, the proportion of eroded peat clasts decreasing upwards. The upper channel edges show pronounced involutions at the clay/peat interface, the clearest of which is arrowed in Figure 5.4. They can confidently be interpreted as animal footprints in section. Similar examples are shown by Allen (1997b, figs 1 and 24).

5.5 Skull excavation and sampling

The skull was lifted in a block of peat 0.50m × 0.40m × 0.3m and removed to the laboratory where the faces of the block were drawn (Figure 5.3b). This exercise, and subsequent excavation, confirmed that the skull lay 0.12m below the clay, representing the base of the palaeochannel. The lighter area surrounding the skull on this photograph simply represents an area of peat which has not been scraped clean to avoid damaging the skull. The skull was clearly within the peat, although small lenses of clay were visible. The final stages of excavation of the skull from the peat block were carried out at the Natural History Museum, London. Here Dr T Molleson arranged for the X-raying of the block to check for the presence of any other hard or soft tissue, which was found not to be present; following this, the remainder of the block was excavated by Gillian Comerford at the Museum. No evidence was found at any stage for soft tissue, or hair, associated with the skull, and given the broken edges of the cranium which were eventually revealed, it is concluded that it reached the bog in a defleshed and broken condition.

A series of pollen samples was taken at 20mm intervals running above and below the skull and a parallel pollen series 0.1m east (Fig 5.3b). Macrofossil samples were also taken from the latter column and around the skull, confirming that it was surrounded by raised bog peat, but with some evidence of marine influence from about the level of the skull (Chapter 13). Mollusc analysis of the upper Wentlooge clay (1216) and the peaty clay fill of the underlying palaeochannel produced only *Hydrobia* sp., confirming an estuarine origin.

Samples for dating were also taken from the peat block as shown on Fig 5.3b:-

Peat above skull:	4305 ± 35BP (OxA-7782)
Bone sample from skull:	3095 ± 40BP (OxA-7744)
Peat below skull:	4350 ± 35BP (OxA-7783)

Comparison of OD heights shows that the peat dates above and below the skull are consistent with the sequence of dates from the Peat Monolith 2099–2101 (Fig 5.3c). However, the skull is some 1300 radiocarbon years younger than the peat in which it was contained. Possible explanations include the deliberate burial of the skull within the peat. A more likely explanation is, perhaps, that the skull was deposited on the peat surface or palaeochannel floor and was trodden into the peat by cattle hooves, the effects of which were very evident at a higher level within the palaeochannel fill (Fig 5.4).

5.6 Structure 1208

On the surface of the raised bog, just east of the skull finds, the storm on 30 August 1992 revealed twelve roundwood verticals projecting slightly from the peat

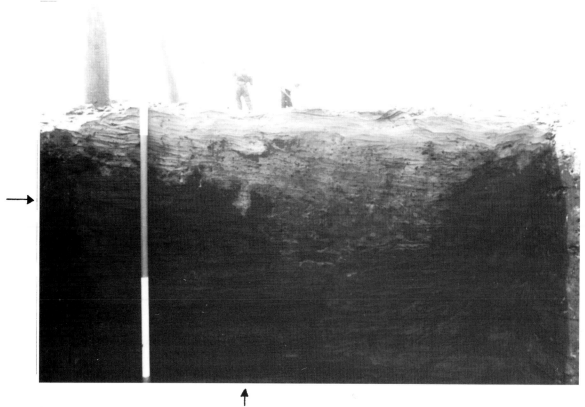

Figure 5.4 Goldcliff: Section of Pit 29 showing the palaeochannel with probable animal footprints, of which the clearest example is arrowed, in the surface of the raised bog

surface (Fig 4.2). The posts occurred in an area 5m × 2m. They do not make a clear pattern, although two rough lines of five posts cross at 55°. A surrounding area of the peat surface 5m × 10m was cleaned to look for associated evidence. The exposed raised bog surface is likely to have been eroded and oxidised, so it is perfectly possible that other parts of this structure have been lost. Some hollows containing clay were recorded, but they formed no pattern and there is no firm evidence that they related to the structure. During 1994 a section was excavated to reveal two roundwood posts. Post 7605 was submitted for radiocarbon dating with the result 2600 ± 70BP (SWAN-102). This date centres on a period within 20 radiocarbon years of the date of the 1990 cranium find 8m away, so they are likely to have been connected.

All twelve posts forming this structure were sampled and identified by Johnson. Remarkably, the structure was made up of six or seven different wood types: alder (2); willow (3); willow/poplar (1); ash (1); birch (3); field maple (1); hawthorn family (1). Morgan looked at the ash roundwood stake which was 33 years old. Its ring width indicated variable growth suggesting the tree grew on drier ground.

5.7 Canid skull

One of the finds which had been made in 1990 and was held in the collection of Newport Museum was a canid jaw which was labelled as 'eroded out of charcoal band' and, therefore, assumed to be Meso-lithic. The jaw was examined initially by Noddle and subsequently by Coard who writes as follows:-

> Part of the right mandible including part of the ascending ramus. A young adult with teeth showing little sign of wear. Examination of the jaw by Barbara Noddle and the writer show that the size and proportion of the tooth row in comparison with the mandible, particularly the carnassials, look shortened and cramped. This led Barbara Noddle to suggest it could be a domestic dog but she was not certain and suggested that the characteristics might relate to its being a female. Another possibility is that this may be a sub-adult in which remodelling of the jaw, to accommodate full adult dentition, is not yet complete, accordingly the wild or domestic status of this canid has not been conclusively established.

In view of the supposed association of this skull with the Mesolithic site, and features indicative of possible domestication, a sample from the skull was AMS dated: 2685±45BP (OxA-6461). This shows the original attribution to the Mesolithic site was incorrect and the find is late Bronze Age, or early Iron Age, but still of interest. The evidence suggests that it comes from somewhere in the area of the Mesolithic site and, thus, it is unlikely to be more than 80m from the two human skulls. What is notable is that the date of one of the skulls centres on a period within a century of the canid, suggesting the possibility of deposition of both human and canid at the island edge at this time.

5.8 The Alexandra Docks skull

In 1910 a human skull was found during an extension of Newport Docks. This massive excavation, well documented in contemporary photographs (Dawson 1995), created the largest single enclosed dock in the world. The earlier making of a timber pond at the dock had revealed the remains of a boat, which with radiocarbon dating, has recently been shown to be early medieval (Hutchinson 1984). The position of the human skull find (ST 317841) was recorded in plans and sections by the Resident Engineer, Mr Couper whose drawings are in Newport Museum and whose records form the contextual basis of an anatomical report by Keith (1911), who also discussed the find in his *Antiquity of Man* (Keith 1925, 59) in a chapter on 'The people of the submerged forest'. The skull is recorded as being below clay and in gravel, about 2m from the base of the gravel at *c* –9m OD. The positions of sixteen animal bones were also recorded and these include a sheep metatarsal from a level below that of the skull. Keith noted reports that some flint artefacts had been found but regrettably, he notes, no record had been kept of these. He suggested a Neolithic date for the skull, on no very precise grounds. Since its discovery, the skull has been in Newport Museum (No D8/74/1) which readily allowed sampling for AMS dating: 3995 ± 45 BP (OxA-7656). Thus, Keith's guess at a Neolithic date is confirmed, and it is seen to relate to the end of that period. Locke (1971) had expressed doubts that the skull came from the gravel, suggesting it may have derived from overlying clay. However, on the underside of the skull iron stained sand adheres to the bone and this does support the idea of its derivation from basal coarser sediments which, in this position, might relate to an earlier course of the Rivers Usk or Ebbw.

5.9 The Orb Works skull

Cowley (1961) reports how, in that year, a human skull was found at the Orb Electrical Steelworks in Newport. It was found at a depth of 10m embedded in clay or 'bungum'. From the depth, and comparison with the Alexandra Docks find, he came to the conclusion it was Neolithic. The discovery of *Bos* and sheep bones is also mentioned but it is not clear whether they were at the same depth. I am grateful to Mr L J Cawley (personal communication), Manager of Metallurgical Products at the Orb Works in 1998, who has been able to clarify the location and circumstances of the discovery. It was made at a time of large-scale development which included 'the excavation of deep pits for the vertical storage of wire loops'. He marks the findspot as ST 32468634. The depth of the find indicates it between *c* –3m and –4m OD. Locke (1971) made the interesting observation that the depth of the skull would correspond with a 'peaty development in a borehole at Stephenson Street', which is some 200m from the findspot

identified by Mr Cawley. Peat at that depth at Uskmouth (Aldhouse-Green *et al* 1992) and Goldcliff (Chapter 4) is Mesolithic. The possibility of the skull being earlier Holocene was one particular reason for wanting to establish its date. In fact the AMS date proved very different: 1925±40BP (OxA-7658). Given that late-Iron Age or Romano-British date it is likely to derive, not, as supposed, from the base of the middle Wentlooge but from a former channel of the River Usk.

5.10 The skull from Redwick

During this project Upton discovered a human skull in an area seaward of the main peat shelf at Redwick in an area where there were a large number of fallen blocks of peat. Although the skull was unstratified, it was considered worth dating because it had been found within 125m of Bronze Age Building 1 at Redwick (Chapter 16). In the event, it proved to be far later, the AMS date was 670 ± 30 BP (OxA-7657). This might, therefore, represent a medieval burial washed out by coastal erosion, or a drowned mariner. Indeed, the Magor Pill boat was wrecked 1.33km from the findspot and, given the dendrochronological date of its construction is AD 1240 (Nayling 1998), its demise is likely to have been quite close in date to this skull. But of course there must have been dozens of other unknown tragedies during the medieval and other periods in the hazardous waters of the estuary.

5.11 Human cranial remains from the Severn Estuary
Rick Schulting

Goldcliff 1214

This specimen consists of a partial calva with most of the frontal and left parietal, together with part of the right parietal. The bone surface is eroded, and peat still adheres to the inner table of the vault. The degree of suture closure, while not a very accurate indicator, suggests that an older individual is represented. Sex is indeterminate as no diagnostic areas are preserved.

Goldcliff 1990 Find 497

A number of separate cranial fragments are represented. Eleven parietal fragments have been reconstructed. A section of open suture is present along one side, indicating that the individual is an adolescent or young adult, in any case certainly younger than Goldcliff 1214. The bone surface is again unevenly eroded. There is also a small portion of frontal bone centred on the anthropometric point glabella which may, or may not, belong to the same individual. The presence of fairly well-developed supraorbital ridges suggests that a male is probably represented. Finally, there is a small, nondescript cranial fragment lacking any further identifying features.

Alexander Dock, Newport

The Alexander Dock specimen consists of a damaged calvarium, also stained dark. The coronal suture is nearly obliterated, indicating a middle or older adult. The right frontal region is damaged, as is the left parietal, and both mastoids have been sliced off, perhaps at the time of discovery. The specimen shows clear male features in its large supraorbital ridges and mastoids and robust occipital region. Nevertheless the overall size of the calvarium is quite small, with the cranial capacity originally reported as 1450cc (Keith 1911); Cowley (1961) later revised this estimate to 1557cc. The Alexander Dock and the Orb Steelworks specimens present very similar dimensions (Table CD 5.1). No cribra orbitalia can be observed on the preserved left orbit.

Orb Steelworks, Newport

This is the most complete specimen of this group of Severn human crania, represented by a nearly complete cranium, stained dark. The right mastoid is damaged, and a number of teeth are missing. The cranium is quite small, but may be tentatively assigned as male, based on the overall shape of the vault and the presence of moderate supraorbital ridges. Craniometrics, as reported by Cowley (1961), are provided in CD Table 5.1. No cribra orbitalia is present. The maxillary dentition includes all six molars as well as the right third premolar. All other teeth have been lost postmortem. The third molars are fully erupted but unworn, suggesting an age in the range 20–25 years. The cusps of the second molars are slightly worn, while those of the first molars are nearly worn flat. Some small spots of dentine may be exposed, but it is difficult to be certain due to adhering material and the black staining of the teeth. Enamel hypoplasia may be present on the premolar, although the staining again makes it difficult to be certain.

Redwick

This specimen consists of an adult calvarium. The obliteration of the central part of the coronal suture and much of the sagittal suture suggests that the individual was of middle–older age. Sex is uncertain but possibly male, based on the relatively robust occipital region, moderate supraorbital ridges, and relatively large mastoid (the left mastoid is damaged, the right complete). It is not possible to comment on the presence or absence of cribra orbitalia due to the erosion of the bone surface in the orbits and the adherence of marine carbonate.

5.12 Stable isotopes from human remains from the Severn Estuary
Michael Richards and Rick Schulting

Introduction

As part of the radiocarbon dating process at the Oxford University Radiocarbon Accelerator Unit (ORAU) the $\delta^{13}C$ and $\delta^{15}N$ values of bone collagen are routinely measured. The human bone samples submitted for dating, therefore, have associated stable isotope values, which are briefly discussed here. Stable isotope analysis of human bone collagen has been routinely applied to archaeological samples since the late 1970s (Chisholm et al 1982 and 1983, DeNiro and Epstein 1978 and 1981, Schoeninger and DeNiro 1984, Schoeninger et al 1983, Sealy and van der Merwe 1985, Vogel and van der Merwe 1977). The current understanding of collagen stable isotope ratios is that they reflect the stable isotope values of the protein consumed by an individual over the last ten or so years of their lives.

The two most important elements for palaeodietary analysis are carbon and nitrogen. The stable carbon ($\delta^{13}C$) value can be used to determine the relative amounts of marine vs terrestrial protein in diets. In areas of the world where C4 plants (eg maize, millet) are common, $\delta^{13}C$ values can also be used to investigate the relative contributions of C3 and C4 plants (or the flesh and milk of animals that consumed those plants). The stable nitrogen ($\delta^{15}N$) value can be used to determine the amounts of plant vs animal protein in past diets. Ideally, the collagen $\delta^{15}N$ values of contemporary herbivores and carnivores from the study area are measured, and then the human values compared with these. If the human values are similar to the herbivores, one concludes that plant food was important in the diet; if they are more similar to the carnivores, then animal flesh and/or milk dominated the protein component of the diet. Unfortunately, it was not possible to measure the collagen $\delta^{15}N$ values of fauna contemporary with any of the humans discussed here. However, there is not a great deal of variation in faunal $\delta^{15}N$ values in Britain, or Northwest Europe in general, in the Holocene (Richards 1998). Therefore, the human $\delta^{15}N$ values are compared with fauna from other British archaeological sites.

The stable isotope data

The collagen isotope values are plotted in Figure 5.5 (data on CD 5.2). The collagen extracted was of good quality, as the C:N ratios are within the recommended range of values for intact collagen (DeNiro 1985). The three oldest samples all show similar isotope values. The low $\delta^{13}C$ values indicate that marine foods did not form a significant part of the diet (<5% of the dietary protein, if any). The $\delta^{15}N$ values of these three individuals are fairly high, which is consistent with a diet high in animal protein

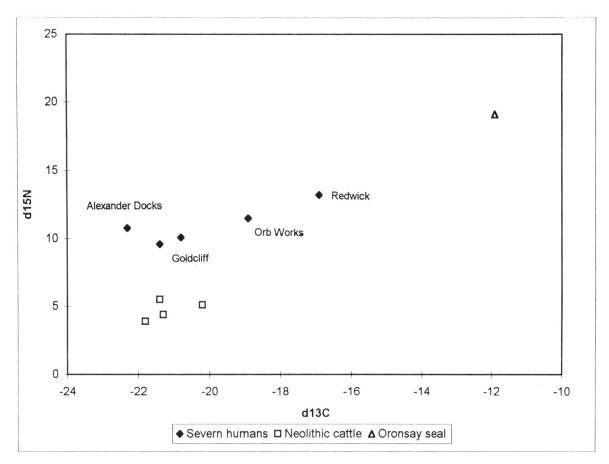

Figure 5.5 Plot of stable carbon and nitrogen isotopes from human skulls in the Severn Estuary compared with Hazleton cattle and Oronsay seals. (Cattle and seal data from Richards 1998)

(meat or milk). Without a range of associated faunal values, the species of animal(s) consumed cannot be identified more specifically. There is also the possibility that freshwater fish had a small influence in the diet, but freshwater or marine fish were certainly not the main dietary protein staple.

The two younger samples do have $\delta^{13}C$ values indicative of marine components in the diet. The Orb Works sample has a $\delta^{13}C$ value and elevated $\delta^{15}N$ value suggesting a diet incorporating 10–15% marine protein. The Redwick sample values indicate that marine foods were much more important in this individual's diet. Assuming $\delta^{13}C$ marine and terrestrial endpoints (100% of the diet) of 12‰ and 20‰, respectively, this individual derived 40–50% of their protein from marine sources. The high $\delta^{15}N$ value confirms the marine origin of the isotopic signal (C4 plants, which could have been available at this time, would result in a far lower value), and furthermore suggests that it did not consist of low trophic level marine foods like shellfish, but more probably involved higher trophic level organisms like marine fish. Estuarine species can have $\delta^{13}C$ values between the two extremes noted above, so that the value for the Redwick individual could be underestimating the amount of estuarine foods in the diet. Unfortunately, it is impossible to address this possibility without measuring contemporary species from the Severn.

Conclusions

This limited stable isotope study has shown that human isotope values in isolation have some limited value for providing information about certain aspects of past human diets. The avoidance of marine foods in the Bronze and Iron Age samples is consistent with a large body of isotopic data from these periods in Britain (Lennon 1996, Richards 1998, Schulting 1998). The indication of significant use of marine foods for the more recent Redwick individual is particularly interesting, and is an unusual find from this period. Further research may show that certain coastal areas of Britain saw elevated use of marine foods at this time.

5.13 Conclusions

Within the intertidal area, Upton and others not uncommonly find unstratified non-cranial human bones. Many may represent eroded burials, or those lost at sea, and we have suggested that this could be the case with the Redwick medieval find. Similar scenarios must have obtained in prehistory and such circumstances might explain the wide spread of dates obtained. However, the Goldcliff evidence cannot be explained in this way, suggesting more interesting practices may be involved. The AMS dating programme highlights the probability of ritual activity on the fringes of the former Goldcliff Island. Dates on the two Goldcliff skulls indicate deposition over a period of around 500 radiocarbon years in the late Bronze Age. A similar date for the canid skull could also relate to ritual deposition in the same period. The date of the 1990 human skull find is within 20 years of that of the wooden structure (1208) just 8m away. This seems unlikely to be a coincidence and the wooden structure and skull deposition are probably connected. The use of six or seven different species for the twelve posts forming the structure suggest that it was not all erected in one go and might strengthen the impression of non-utilitarian activities.

Perhaps the posts carried skulls, which, when they broke, became crushed into the peat nearby. Alternatively, the posts might be all that survive of a crude platform or alignment connected with ritual deposition or, perhaps, some form of platform used for body exposure or skull display. Four of the posts could form a rectangle 3m × 1m, and body exposure has been hypothesised in the Iron Age in connection with rectangular post settings on dryland sites (Ellison and Drewett 1971). Deposition of human skeletal material is widespread in wetland contexts. In the Severn Estuary the later Bronze Age settlement at Chapeltump-2 (Chapter 16) has produced a human femur dated to 1130 ± 70 BC (CAR-956, Trett and Parry 1986), and an enigmatic wooden alignment c 963 BC at Greylake in the Somerset Levels has also produced human skeletal material (Brunning 1998). The most telling evidence comes, however, from the later Iron Age Glastonbury Lake Village where, of the fifteen adult skulls, other human bones, and neonatal burials, seven skulls come from just outside the palisade boundary of the settlement (Coles and Minnitt 1995, fig 8.10).

As at Newport, so too at Avonmouth: the making of docks between 1903 and 1907 led to the discovery of human skulls, some perhaps derived from a post-medieval gibbet, some apparently stratified in Holocene sediments on the edge of Dunball Island (Brett 1996). From this site there is also evidence for the deposition of a Bronze Age rapier. It seems probable that skull deposition also occurred in the major rivers, as at Newport and Avonmouth Docks and another skull found during dock construction at Port Talbot suggest (Wheeler 1925, 280, Keith 1925, 58). Evidence for deposition of defleshed human skulls in rivers is particularly strong in the Thames where four examples have been AMS dated to the middle–late Bronze Age, precisely the period when, between 1300 and 800 BC, weaponry was being deposited in the river (Bradley 1990, Bradley and Gordon 1988). The Avonmouth rapier could be analagous. One of the Thames finds is Neolithic and, together with the Alexandra Docks find, may indicate that the practice of skull deposition goes back to that period.

Deposition of human skulls in wetland contexts is documented beyond Britain. In discussing the un-stratified skull from the Carrigdirty Rocks site on the Shannon Estuary in Ireland, O'Sullivan (1996, 67) notes evidence from a number of Irish sites for deliberate deposition of human skulls, always fragments, beside wetland habitats. In Denmark, Koch (personal communication) has identified 71 finds of skulls in bogs; some are as early as the Neolithic and some were clearly deposited without other parts of the body.

Human remains are also associated with substantial Bronze Age platform structures at Flag Fen (Pryor 1991), Crouch 1, Essex (Wilkinson and Murphy 1995, 132), and Shinewater, East Sussex (Greatorex personal communication). Those finds reinforce an emphasis on 'islands', both geological and culturally created, which could be suggested on the basis of the evidence from Goldcliff (natural) and Glastonbury (artificial crannog). The distinction which seems logical to us between natural geological features and monuments created by human agency cannot necessarily be assumed in the past, as Bradley (1998) has pointed out in the different context of tombs and tors.

The practice of skull deposition may have continued into later Iron Age and Romano-British times. It was in this period that a head was deposited in Lindow Bog, apparently separately from the body to which it belonged (Turner and Scaife 1995). Skulls from the Thames and Walbrook (Bradley and Gordon 1988), and possibly the Orb Works find reported here, also suggest the continuance of skull deposition into these periods.

In reviewing the evidence of Roman activity in the Somerset Levels, Rippon (1997, fig 31) poses the question of the extent to which we interpret this as a ritual landscape. He notes seven certain, or possible, temples on the fringes of the levels. It may be significant that three of these are on islands of bedrock surrounded by former wetland which had been reclaimed in the Roman period. All are within, or adjacent to, Iron Age hillforts. Another former island at Aust has produced a bronze human figure of Iron Age date (Cunliffe 1991, 431, Stead 1984) and the existing island of Steep Holm has produced a carved stone head of supposed late Iron Age, or Romano-British, date (Green 1993), which may also point to ritual associations. On the Welsh side, there is no known concentration of temples, just one major establishment on the Estuary edge at Lydney, dedicated to the Celtic god Nodens; the imagery associated with this god indicates maritime connections (Woodward 1992, 76). Lydney, likewise, was situated within an Iron Age hillfort. The Roman evidence is tantalising because it hints that the Estuary itself, and the islands within it, may have been seen, by native and Roman alike, as of ritual or religious significance. This could be consistent with the evidence presented here for skull deposition in the late Bronze Age and Iron Age. However, the forms of ritual activity associated with the Roman period sites were very different and did not normally involve deposition of human remains, although, interestingly, the temple sites at Cannington, Brean Down, and Henley Wood were reused for burial in the sub-Roman period.

Evidence in this chapter complements the discoveries presented in Chapters 6–10 which mostly relate to activities of apparently utilitarian character. This serves to remind us that utilitarian and symbolic are generally false dichotomies in prehistory. Furthermore, beyond the minutiae of individual sites, prehistoric communities may have perceived the Estuary itself and its flanking wetlands in terms which were far from utilitarian and were charged with symbolism, a perhaps not unnatural reaction to a frequently awe inspiring landscape transformed twice daily by such a dramatic tidal range and so subject to periodic inundations.

The continuity which is suggested from later Bronze Age to the Iron Age, and possibly Romano-British periods, is intriguing because it spans a period marked by very dramatic and widespread environmental changes: changes from late Bronze Age peat bog, to Iron Age saltmarsh, to the reclaimed agricultural landscapes which characterised most of the estuary levels, except the coastal clays south of Brent Knoll, in the Romano-British period. Thus, whilst the particular topographic context of wetlands, and specifically islands, has been suggested as having ritual or symbolic associations, these were certainly not confined to a narrowly defined set of environmental conditions.

6 Boat planks of *c* 1170 BC *by M Bell with R Brunning, S Johnson, S McGrail, and R Morgan*

6.1 The boat plank structure

The storm on the 30 August 1992 swept away the mud, revealing an almost clean clay surface between the peat shelf with Buildings 1–4 and the Mesolithic site. Midway between the two were traces of a small wooden structure. This was in a 10m wide band of clay which lay between two sinuous outcrops of peat which were aligned roughly at right angles to the shore. The character and setting of these is best appreciated from an air photograph taken in 1994 by Chris Musson for the Royal Commission on the Ancient and Historic Monuments of Wales (Fig 1.2).

Of the structure (1124) all that was visible at first were parts of two flat pieces of wood and the ends of six pieces of roundwood, all partly buried in the clay. Six days later, when these were further excavated by Steve Allen and a party of Dublin wetland students, it became clear the two flat pieces of wood had extensive evidence of working (Fig 6.1). There was a raised ridge down the axis of each plank, and the ridge was perforated by mortices. Many small holes occurred down the edges of the planks. As McGrail

explains below, these timbers are likely to be part of a sewn plank boat. Here they were manifestly reused: they had breaks at ends and edges, and Plank 3438 had a hole rather crudely cut through a flat surface, probably to take a peg. No such peg was found in this position, indicating that this plank may have been in its third use at the point of discovery.

The excavation of an area 2.5m square, and the cleaning of a wider surrounding area (Fig 6.2), showed that the planks formed part of a structure which comprised six pieces of roundwood laid parallel with the planks to create a surface 1.4m × 0.8m (Fig 6.3). Two pegs were found in the same area. A scatter of small roundwood and brushwood to the west is mostly parallel to the other timbers and extends the total length to 1.65m. Two of the pieces of roundwood which lay between the two boat planks had been charred and this is particularly noteworthy, given a lack of evidence for charcoal from post-Mesolithic intertidal contexts. There was also more scattered brushwood and roundwood and occasional pegs extending in an arc *c* 1.5m south and east of the main structure.

Figure 6.1 Goldcliff: Excavation of the boat planks of Structure 1124. Photograph by M Bell

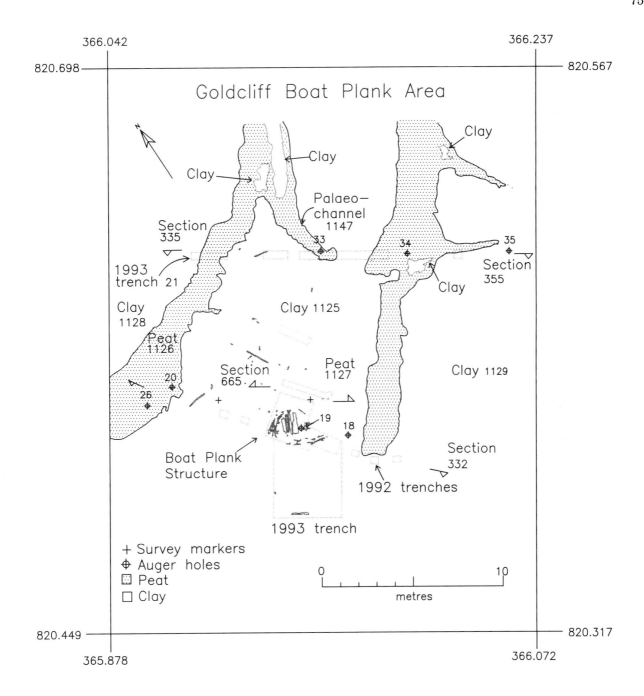

Figure 6.2 Goldcliff: The boat plank site showing peat outcrops, excavation trenches and auger holes. Drawing by B Taylor

During 1992 some small trenches were excavated to east and west to look at the stratigraphic context of the find and try to establish whether this linear structure could be traced in either direction. There was no evidence of an extension beyond the area planned. However, a watch was kept on the area during occasional monitoring visits, and scattered wood was noticed. Accordingly, in 1993 a larger trench 4m × 4m was excavated immediately south of the earlier find; this produced only one unworked horizontal and a peg 3.2m from the main structure. A transect of trenches (21) was also excavated to the north as part of a further investigation of the stratigraphic sequence in the area (see below). During 1994 some additional pieces of wood had

become visible as a result of small-scale marine erosion of the clay surface. Once again the surface was cleaned and planned, revealing 22 additional pieces of wood; ten were vertical, or at an angle, and could be pegs, although only two of these were excavated, establishing that they had worked ends. There were two roundwood horizontals (1.3m × 40mm and 0.76m × 60mm). The remainder were unworked fragments which could equally have been washed from a structure, or have been of natural occurrence. A small trench was excavated 1m north of the boat plank site to produce Section 665 (Fig 6.7) which shows four stakes, one vertical, the others at 45°. In this section the upper clay, in which the boat planks sat, contained pieces of

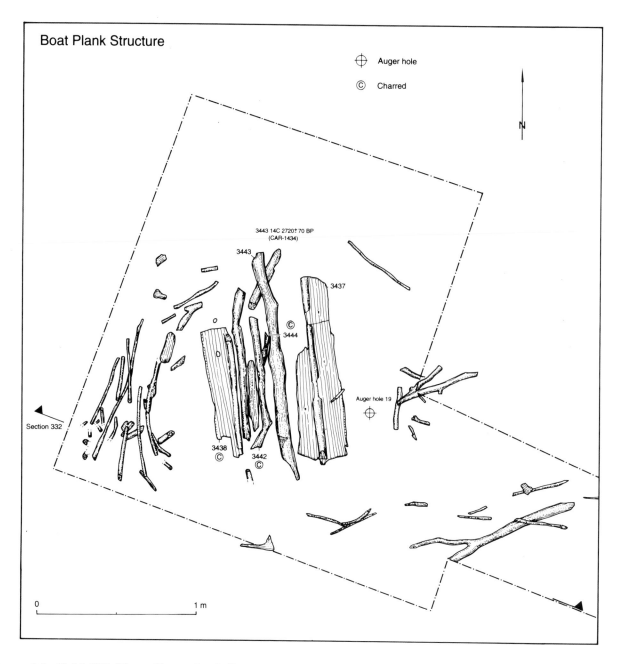

Boat Plank Structure

⊕ Auger hole

© Charred

3443 14C 2720±70 BP
(CAR-1434)

3443

3437

©
3444

3438
©   3442
         ©

Auger hole 19
⊕

Section 332

0   1 m

Figure 6.3   Goldcliff: Plan of boat plank Structure 1124. Scale 1:8. Drawing by S J Allen

peat, indicating some erosion. It may have come from the lower peat, which had an irregular surface, and was patchy. There was little peat at the east end, possibly indicating the position of the inferred palaeochannel, with three of the stakes at its edge. The wood recorded in 1994 made no real pattern, although the pegs indicate a wider zone of activity around the main boat plank find.

When originally discovered, it was uncertain how the two peat bands and clays associated with the boat plank site related to the sedimentary sequence elsewhere in the intertidal area. The three layers appeared to be within the clay below the peat shelf which, to the north and west, was associated with rectangular buildings and trackways and dated to the later 1st millennium BC. However, the large

expanse of clay surface was never clean enough to be confident of this relationship.

Confirmation that this structure was indeed earlier than the Iron Age structures and peat shelf came from a radiocarbon date on a piece of cut roundwood (3443) which formed part of the main structure: 2720 ± 70 BP (CAR-1434). Hillam also succeeded in dendrochronological dating of the two oak boat planks (Chapter 11). This showed the trees were felled after 1017 BC; unfortunately, there was no sapwood, so we do not know how long after that date. Both sources of dating show the structure is Bronze Age, some centuries before the Iron Age discoveries on the main peat shelf. Thus, the clay in which the finds were made corresponds in date to that overlying the raised bog in Pit 15 (Chapters

3 and 5) and underlying the peat shelf with Iron Age structures.

6.2 The boat planks
Sean McGrail

The two plank fragments (3436 and 3438; Figs 6.4 and 6.5), from the platform-like Structure 1124, were converted for their primary use from slow-grown, half-logs of oak (*Quercus* sp). A ridge, 30–50mm wide, was left standing along the centreline, proud of each plank's upper face. Sub-rectangular/elliptical holes, *c* 80mm × 35mm, were cut parallel to the plank faces through these ridges at a spacing of *c* 0.50m, centre to centre. Close to the edges of each plank, where the thickness has been reduced from *c* 25mm to 15–20mm, circular, 8mm diameter, holes were worked at right angles to the plank faces at an average interval of *c* 40mm. A large vertical hole through Plank 3438, rounded in shape and *c* 40mm in diameter, should probably be associated with the secondary use of this plank fragment.

The main woodworking features of these timbers, holes through projecting cleats and smaller holes along plank edges, have parallels in the prehistoric sewn plank boats from North Ferriby and Brigg in the Humber Estuary (Wright 1990, McGrail 1981), from Caldicot in the Severn Estuary (Parry and McGrail 1991, McGrail 1997) and from Dover (Parfitt 1993). The Goldcliff finds have been discussed in the context of Bronze Age boats from Northwest Europe by McGrail (1996, 35).

The cleat ridges on the Goldcliff planks are comparable, in some respects, with those provisionally reported to be on the Dover boat. The holes along the plank edges are very similar in position, size, and spacing to fastening holes on the Brigg 'raft'. This Brigg planking was caulked in the seams with moss held in place by longitudinal laths, and fastened together by two-stranded ropes of willow (*Salix* sp.) 'sewn' diagonally through such holes: the original Goldcliff planks were probably similarly fastened. The Goldcliff fragments have no means of protecting the sewing from abrasion when beaching, so these planks probably came from the sides of the boat rather than the bottom.

6.3 Woodworking on the boat plank site
Richard Brunning

Twenty-nine pieces of wood were lifted from the structure associated with the boat planks, comprising 4 pegs, the 2 boat planks, and 23 other horizontal items. A selection is illustrated in Figure 6.6. The only timber trees represented were two pieces of ash (eg 3493) and one of oak (3488), in addition to the boat planks. These three pieces were all split debris from the working of larger timbers. The other species used for the pegs (examples illustrated) and brushwood,

were mainly birch and alder with smaller numbers of hazel, alder buckthorn, and willow. This, together with the fact that all these pieces, bar one, were quite knotty roundwood, suggests that this material was derived from the waste from tree felling or scrub clearance in the local woodland. The largest piece of brushwood was a large forked willow branch (3490) which still had several side branches intact. The ash and oak fragments suggest that timber preparation may have been taking place nearby. This combination of evidence is similar to the non-structural wood assemblage from Caldicot (Brunning and O'Sullivan 1997).

The foregoing material forms part of a larger assemblage of 47 pieces of wood sampled and identified by Johnson from the area around the boat planks (see CD 6.1). Birch (14 pieces) and alder (13 pieces) again predominate and, in addition to the previously mentioned species, there is lime, buckthorn, and hawthorn, highlighting the great variety of wood types represented in this area. Morgan writes on tree ring studies of the assemblage:

> Forty-three samples were largely birch and alder roundwood (33% each) with small numbers of seven other species. Most birch was 3–5 years old and the alder more varied at 2–11 years (CD 6.2). In size the majority of stems clustered at 15–25mm with a few larger stems of oak, alder, willow and hazel. Most of the wood was winter cut (34 out of 43 samples) and revealed fast and uniform rates of growth suggestive of favourable conditions.

Because of the small size of the excavation, only a small proportion of the wooden items were removed in their entirety. For this reason only ten cut ends were available for study. Simple chisel points predominated, with only the large willow branch and two of the larger pegs having pencil points. The medium facet lengths of 30–53mm and the shallow cutting angles of 15–20° were probably more a product of the relatively small size of roundwood being used than a characteristic of the axes doing the cutting.

The choice of oak heartwood for the two boat planks reflects the qualities of strength, large size, and resistance to rot which timbers of this species display. The lack of any sapwood on either timber could be due to decay at some point in their primary or secondary uses, but it is more likely to have been removed deliberately to avoid including a weaker and less resistant part of the tree at the edge of the planks. Of the other prehistoric sewn boat timbers from Northern Europe, oak heartwood was almost always used for planks. The only exceptions are the Hjortspring vessel from Denmark, which had timbers made of lime (Rieck 1994), and five out of six Brigg 'raft' timbers which also had sapwood (McGrail 1981), as did a single timber from Ferriby 3 (Hillam 1985b, 152–3).

The diameters of the trees used for the Goldcliff planks are unknown because of the lack of sapwood. Plank 3438 was >90 years old while the tree for 3436

Figure 6.4 Goldcliff: Bronze Age boat planks, upper photo plank 3438, lower photograph Plank 3436. Both planks show the replaced sections which were cut for dendrochronological dating. Scale 0.1m. Photography by Rex Morton, Newport Museum and Art Gallery

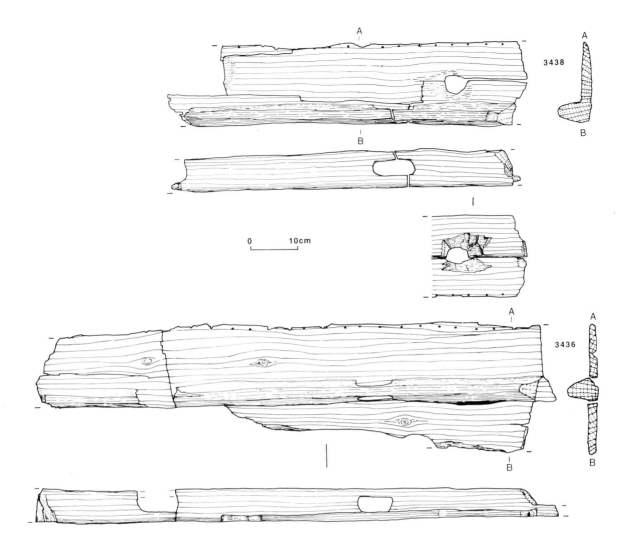

Figure 6.5   Goldcliff: Bronze Age Boat Planks 3438 and 3436. Drawings by S J Allen

was >114 years old (Chapter 11). Both the trees are very slow grown, more so than the Ferriby and Caldicot examples (Hillam 1985b and 1997). The slow growth would have produced lighter, and possibly more buoyant, timbers but the individual tree selection is more likely to have been dominated by what was available of a suitable size. Timber 3436 displays knots from several small side branches, suggesting that a branch-free tree bole of the required size was not available to the boat builders.

The way in which the boat timbers from Goldcliff were fashioned was very similar to that from the other Bronze Age sewn boat finds. Both the planks were made from oak trunks that had been split in half. The flat side resulting from this divide formed the bottom, or outboard, of the planks. The bottom face of 3436 was some distance from the central pith, but this is probably due to a combination of wood being removed during the dressing of the timber, and being lost to later erosion. The cleat ridge on the inboard face was made by axing away the wood on either side of the ridge. This may have been done by cutting notches across the grain and then splitting off the

intervening chunks, but no evidence survives for this process. The planks may also have been finely finished using adzes, but subsequent erosion and decay has removed all fine detail from this original working.

This method of plank production is extremely wasteful of wood, as very little of the original half-split trunk ends up being used in the finished timber. In addition, the timber lacks the integral strength of radially split planks, and will be liable to split along the rays running outwards from the centre of the tree. This occurred on one of the Brigg planks and on many of the Ferriby timbers (McGrail 1985, Wright 1990, 141–2) and also happened at some point around the hole on 3438. Frequent repairs and reassembly may, therefore, have been the norm for such vessels. Such tangentially split timbers will also warp more than radial ones during seasoning. The timbers would have been worked, and probably assembled, in a 'green' state so that the seasoning process may have been slowed by the boat's immersion in the water. Because of the orientation of the cleat ridges, any shrinkage of the timbers would pull the edges of the

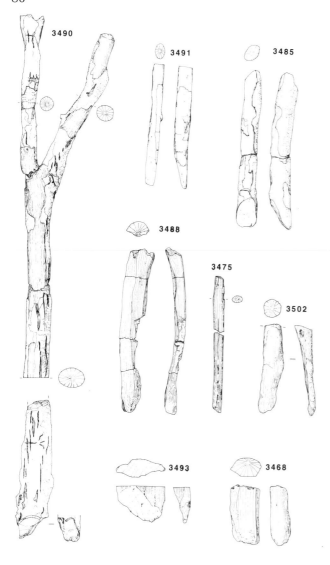

Figure 6.6 Goldcliff: Worked wood from Structure 1124 and surroundings. Scale 1:4 except 3490, 3488, 3475 (1:8). Drawings by S J Allen

planks towards the centre, accentuating the curvature of the hull.

This fairly wasteful process of production was essentially driven by the need to create very long and wide planks which would minimise the joinery involved in the construction of the vessel. Radially split planks would have required a much larger tree to create the same sized timbers, and would have had an inherent weakness along the rays on the bottom of the cleat ridge. Virtually every other sewn boat plank of this period known from Northern Europe was made in the same way as the Goldcliff timbers (McGrail 1981, McGrail 1985, McGrail 1997, Parfitt and Fenwick 1993, Wright 1990). Plank 3436 is typical of the orientation of such planks in that the cleat is running straight out from the centre of the tree. In contrast, 3438 is slightly offset to one side of the trunk, possibly because the parent trunk curved slightly over its length. One of the bottom planks from Ferriby-1 had a similar alignment, possibly for the same reasons (Wright 1990, 61,127).

The cleat holes were probably made with chisels or gouges, while the stitch holes would have required a very fine auger. The later cutting of the cleat ridge ends, and the formation of the hole in 3438, were done with an axe. The hole may have been cut from both sides, with erosion on the top surface masking much of the evidence. The irregular shape of the hole suggests that it was not used as part of a joint, such as a mortice and tenon, but was simply a hole to accommodate a small stake. This conforms to the other known evidence for such features on Bronze Age timbers in Britain and Ireland (eg Orme and Coles 1983, Brunning and O'Sullivan 1997, O'Sullivan 1997).

6.4 Stratigraphic context

The stratigraphic context of this find and the relationship between the blue clay in which it sat, and the two bands of peat on either side (Fig 6.2), were investigated by two transects (Fig 6.7). A transect done in 1992 ran west-northwest to east-southeast through the site and traversed the boat plank excavation trench, six small pits and four auger holes. This showed that the two linear peat outcrops related to two separate bands of reed peat. The upper (1126) was 80mm thick at the most, the lower (1127) 160mm thick. They were separated by 0.74m of clay (1125) within which was the boat plank structure. The bands dipped to the west, the lower at 3°. The result was two bands outcropping as separate parallel shelves. The lower peat shelf is underlain by between 1.7m and 1.2m of clay (1129), below which is a peat (1134) 1.2m thick. That is thought to be the main raised bog peat widely encountered in the intertidal area (Chapter 3). The peat had three clay lenses within it.

The boat plank structure occurred in the clay between the two upper peats at a point where the lower peat appeared to be discontinuous. It was hypothesised, therefore, that a small palaeochannel within the clay may have cut the lower peat at this point. Environmental Monolith 1715 was taken through the sequence at a point where the lower peaty clay (1127) was present; pollen analysis suggested saltmarsh conditions (p226). Adjoining samples of 1125, 1127, and 1129 were taken for mollusc analysis and all contained *Hydrobia*, confirming estuarine influence.

The 1993 Section 355 transect (Fig 6.7) c 8m to the north confirms this sequence. In the middle of the section there is one of the sinuous peaty ridges marking the course of a minor palaeochannel (1147); this is joined to the westerly of the two peat outcrops (Fig 6.2). Below the peat, an earlier channel base cuts the lower peat in a channel 1.35m wide. This might be the hypothetical channel represented in the 1992 section in the position of the boat plank find, but that is uncertain. The convoluted nature of the lower peat surface at the east end is suggestive of animal

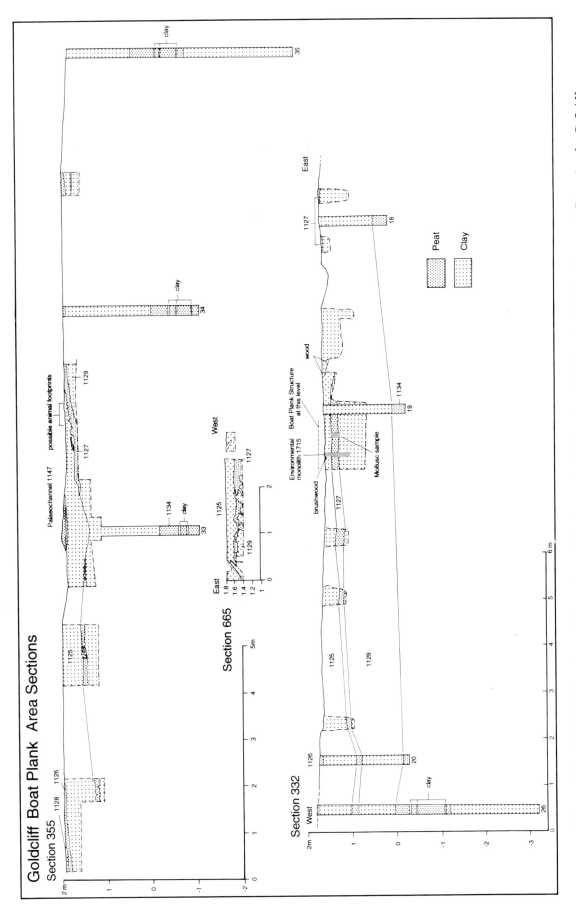

Figure 6.7 Goldcliff: Stratigraphic sections of the boat plank Structure 1124 and adjoining transect. Drawing by S J Allen

footprints on that surface, but this patterning was not examined in plan.

As regards the wider context of the boat plank structure, it lies between two linear strips of peat running seaward (Figs 1.2 and 6.2). Such features have generally been interpreted as marking two edges of a large palaeochannel, just as single strips of peat mark the axes of small palaeochannels at Peterstone (Chapter 16) and elsewhere. In the present instance, detailed investigation shows that the situation is more complex. The two bands have been shown to represent different peats dipping to the west. The orientation of these bands may, nonetheless, reflect that of a palaeochannel, perhaps in the area of Auger Hole 44.

6.5 Discussion of Bronze Age activity

The stratigraphic evidence implies that the Goldcliff boat planks were reused as part of a small structure which lies in a minor palaeochannel within the clay and is most simply interpreted as a short trackway crossing the channel. Association with the minor channel makes less likely the earlier hypothesis of a small platform associated with hunting or fowling activities (Bell 1992, 19). One other possibility which deserves serious consideration is that the structure provided a firm base across a small channel when plank boats were hauled up from a larger palaeo-channel. Two pieces of evidence could support this idea. The boat planks showed evidence of cracking (Fig 6.4), which could be consistent with the passage of significant weight. There is a scatter of brushwood in a semi-circle a little away from the boat planks (Fig 6.3), which could be consistent with deposition around a larger structure, perhaps a boat, which once stood on the planks. If so, the arc suggests it may have been 2–2.5m wide. An area where boats were hauled from the water is a likely place to find discarded planks from repairs, as has been hypothe-sised for the comparable planks in the palaeochannel edge at Caldicot (Nayling and Caseldine 1997). This area of foreshore deserves continued vigilance when mud free conditions obtain, as shown by the boat

discoveries made by Wright (1990) and others on the foreshore at Ferriby over a period of 60 years.

The hypothesis of a landing place is attractive, but the stratigraphic evidence suggests that in the Bronze Age dry land was not close at hand. The archaeology of the platform and its surroundings is consistent with a low level of activity which continued over a period of time, leading to the occurrence of pegs and pieces of wood at different levels within the clay. An occasionally used route-way and/or boat landing place would be consistent with this evidence.

Bronze Age activity at Goldcliff is sparse in comparison with the concentrations of finds from this period noted elsewhere in the intertidal area (Chap-ter 16). Smith and Morgan's (1989) pollen diagram from Goldcliff East provides indications of two clearance episodes during the early and middle Bronze Age c 3700 BP and 3500 BP. The latest peat at Goldcliff East is c 3130 BP and in the area of Pit 15, 3640 BP. Neither sequence extends as late as the boat plank structure. The area of the boat plank site had certainly been inundated before 2720 BP. The boat plank structure is the only one of the prehistoric Goldcliff structures to be contained within marine clay. A discovery which reminds us that the large expanses of clay, which are clean of mud less frequently than the peat shelves, must also be seen as potential sources of archaeological finds.

The boat plank find relates to a period in the late Bronze Age when the raised bog east of Building 4 had been largely overwhelmed by the sea, marine sediments were being laid down, and the bedrock island outcrop at Goldcliff was once again literally an island. We have hypothesised a palaeochannel some-where between Trackway 9050 and Pit 15 where sewn plank boats were being landed and repaired and their planks reused as part of the platform, whether or not directly associated with boat haulage. As regards Goldcliff Island, we have no direct evidence as to how it was being used in the later Bronze Age, although the presence of Structure 1208 and skull deposition nearby (Chapter 5) suggests that boat traffic to the island was not all for purely subsistence and utilitarian purposes.

7 Rectangular structures east of Goldcliff Pill
c 400–100 Cal BC by M Bell with J Parkhouse

7.1 Introduction

The most remarkable aspect of the Goldcliff finds is the discovery of eight rectangular structures on the intertidal peats (Fig 7.1). Of these, five (Buildings 1, 2, 3, 6, and 8) were well preserved and we can be reasonably confident they are the remains of roofed buildings. Two others (Buildings 4 and 7) were partly preserved but shared characteristics with the better preserved structures. One, Structure 5, was only identified at the post-excavation stage. Buildings 6–8 were on the raised bog surface at Goldcliff West, the remaining five east of Goldcliff Pill. Building 4 was on the edge of the former bog and Buildings 1–3 and 5 on wood peat. The buildings east of the Pill (Fig 7.2) are discussed in this chapter. For more detailed discussion of wood and woodworking in these structures and illustrations of selected wood see Chapter 12.

7.2 Planning and excavation of Buildings 1 and 2 in 1990
Jonathan Parkhouse

(See CD 7.1 for a more detailed account)

Walking on the foreshore after a storm on 30 October 1990 Derek Upton and Bob Trett found the first rectangular buildings at Goldcliff. High winds had cleared mud from the peat, revealing rectangles of vertical roundwood posts and traces of flooring within. Nearby were traces of similar structures and several short lengths of possible trackways; the various structures extended for about 200m along the main peat shelf.

The finders at once recognised the importance of their discovery and sought advice from Professor John Coles, who visited the following day and stressed the need to fully record 'a unique site, a rare chance to examine and analyse a prehistoric wooden structure' (CD 1.2). It was agreed that the Glamorgan–Gwent Archaeological Trust (GGAT) would undertake a rapid recording project, with financial assistance from Newport Museum, in the 4 or 5 day window afforded by the tidal cycle and daylight hours.

This was done in the first week of November 1990. It involved planning and describing the two subrectangular structures and recording the position of some of the other structures. Assistance was received from John and Bryony Coles and students from Exeter University. A limited exploration was undertaken of a layer of reeds which appeared to represent flooring overlying horizontal flooring timbers, and a few samples were taken. One objective of this work was to assess the vulnerability of the site, which had been highlighted by the washing away of some flooring timbers within a few days of the site's discovery, despite relatively calm conditions.

Decisions about the site's future required additional information so further limited work, jointly funded by Cadw and the National Museum of Wales, was arranged in the next window of suitable tidal conditions during early December. Its objectives were to determine the length of the vertical timbers and the thickness and coherence of the probable

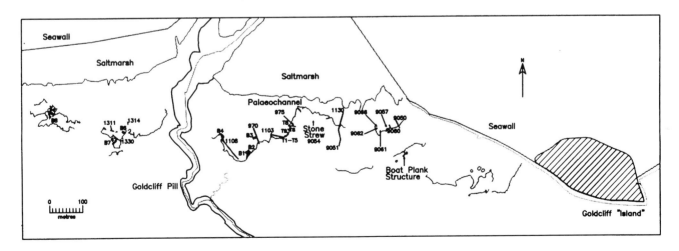

Figure 7.1 Goldcliff: The distribution of rectangular buildings (B1–8), trackways and linear structures. Drawing by B Taylor

83

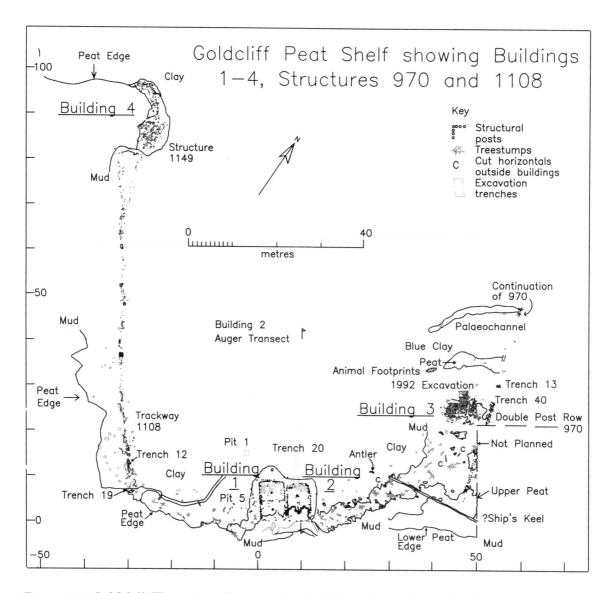

Figure 7.2   Goldcliff: The setting of rectangular Buildings 1–4 and associated structures on the peatshelf. Drawing by B Taylor

flooring, which was also to be sampled. It was also proposed to lift those, mainly horizontal, timbers which were considered to be most vulnerable. The opportunity was also taken to assess the potential of the northwest corner of Building 1 which, as the best preserved part, the National Museum of Wales was interested in conserving. The information gathered (Parkhouse 1991c) was seen as contributing to a longer term strategy which could be implemented under more favourable conditions the following summer.

The two periods of fieldwork in Autumn 1990 were limited by short windows of daylight and suitable tides and by weather which was calm but usually cold. During the work in early November the amount of mobile sediment deposited upon the site with each tide began to increase, reducing the visibility of the structures. This was overcome by using a 1″ (25mm) bore pump to hose the site at the commencement of work. This removed mud without damage to the more fragile surfaces.

The priority in early November had been to produce a plan of Buildings 1 and 2. Building 1 was planned conventionally at 1:20 using a drawing frame; Building 2 was planned using a Zeiss Elta total station theodolite which also picked up key points in Building 1, enabling the two plans to be put together on a best fit basis. The plan was published by Parkhouse (1991a and CD 7.2). Figure 7.3 shows a more detailed plan made in 1991.

This section is largely concerned with those aspects of the buildings, especially possible flooring, which were particularly investigated in 1990. Aspects of the buildings recorded in outline in 1990, but worked on in greater detail in 1991, are covered in the next section.

It was considered that there was a significant risk of damage during the winter to the reed layer which might represent flooring, and it was decided to lift as much as possible. In Building 1 this (Context 901) was scraped clean and then lifted in blocks (0.2m × 0.25m × 20mm or 10mm thick), many of which were sufficiently coherent to be lifted in one piece. Timbers were lifted selectively, concentrating on those which appeared vulnerable, mostly horizontals in Building 2.

Buildings 1 and 2 were situated side by side with a gap of 0.5m. Larger upright posts occurred down the main axis of each building. These were interpreted as the supports for a roof ridge. The north wall of Building 2 was set back from Building 1 by about 0.7m, suggesting that there were two discrete structures rather than parts of a single structure. The buildings were entirely of wood and other organic materials. These, particularly the horizontals, had been exposed for sufficient time to have been worn irregularly by the sea. Seaweed had colonised surfaces, and the buildings must have been exposed, probably on several occasions, prior to discovery.

The structures seemed to be of comparable size, c 8m × 5.6m, but the south wall of Building 2 was not, at this stage, located. The exterior walls consisted of roundwood uprights typically of diameter 0.1m, some smaller. A curious feature, was the bowed nature of the end walls particularly noticeable in the north wall of Building 1 (Fig 7.3). An apparent gap in the middle of this wall was thought to represent an entrance, and it was noted that the possible flooring material spread beyond the limits of the wall line at this point.

The presence of probable wooden flooring in the northern ends of both buildings was of particular interest. This comprised horizontal roundwood laid mainly at right angles to the axis of the building. During 1990, more of this flooring was visible in Building 2 than Building 1. In Building 1, however, was an organic layer consisting of a very high proportion of plant material which appeared either to cover, or replace, the timbers. The upper part of this layer was black and oxidised with strands of plant material lying at various angles. Below this the layer consisted of reeds in a good state of preservation, all lying parallel to the axis of the building. This layer was generally 50–100mm thick. Notes made by Bryony Coles at the time record that individual bundles of reeds lay in slightly varying directions. Occasional squarish woodchips (c 15mm × 30mm) were noted. Above the reeds was a very compacted 'almost polished' layer which in the field was interpreted as possible dung. It was noted that below the top layer were some angled chips of wood mixed with something like chopped straw with no general direction, then a layer described as dungy clay, and another layer of oriented reeds. This description indicates more than one distinct layer of reeds and 'dung-like' material and shows there were woodchips in this material. The regular orientation of the reeds suggested that they were deliberately laid, perhaps as flooring. Occasional lenses of clay were noted within the material, perhaps representing marine inundations. There were also traces of a similar reed layer in Building 2, but it was not so extensive, and the reeds were less distinct.

In several places the reed layer rested directly on top of a series of roundwood logs resting, in turn, on the surface of the peatshelf. In places the horizontals consisted of little more than tubes of bark, although this is probably the result of lateral compression. In the northwest corner of Building 1 horizontals of split timber had been laid diagonally at 45° to the corner (Fig 7.3). In the same corner were traces of a partition of split timber, 0.85m from the north wall, with traces of another partition of split timber and roundwood 0.8m south.

In 1990, a roundwood post (127) from the north wall of Building 1 was excavated and submitted for radiocarbon dating: the date, 2120 ± 90 BP (GU-2912), was the first evidence to suggest that the building was Iron Age. Tool marks on the wood were consistent with the use of an iron axe, but no datable artefacts were found.

Other structures surveyed during the 1990 work included part of another rectangular structure with surviving flooring (Building 3) to the east of Building 2 and part of another (Building 4) with walls but no flooring was noted northwest of Building 1. A double row of posts (970) near Building 3 was planned but there was no opportunity for the recording of a series of trackways noted to the east at the time of the original discovery.

7.3 Excavation of Buildings 1 and 2 in 1991
Martin Bell and Jonathan Parkhouse

The method of excavation was to clean a few square metres of the peat surface at each tide and plan the structures (Figs 7.3–7.4) at a scale of 1:20. The area inside and outside the buildings was divided into 1m squares and excavated. In the early days of the excavation a pump could be used to spray water to clear some of the mud from the slightly raised hummock. However, as excavation progressed, and depressions and irregularities increased, this method was no longer effective and was abandoned in the face of frequent problems with the pump.

As complete a plan as possible of the structures was first prepared. All the wood was then lifted for detailed recording on dry land and so that a selection could be conserved. Trenches were excavated outside the walls so that the wall timbers could be exposed in section. Figure 7.5 shows the lines of illustrated excavated sections. Lengths of 2–3m of wall were exposed at a time so that these could be drawn at a scale of 1:10 and the wood lifted between tides. It should be noted that many of the sections are composites of several drawings; the section lines are not always straight, because of the need to expose and record groups of wood quickly. This can introduce an element of distortion into the relationship between verticals compared with the more precise plans. Comparison with the plan also shows that not every single post is shown on sections, as some lay behind others, whilst some were only found when other posts were being excavated. To reduce the number of published sections, and try to make the overall structures as comprehensible as possible, wood which appeared on other sections, just behind

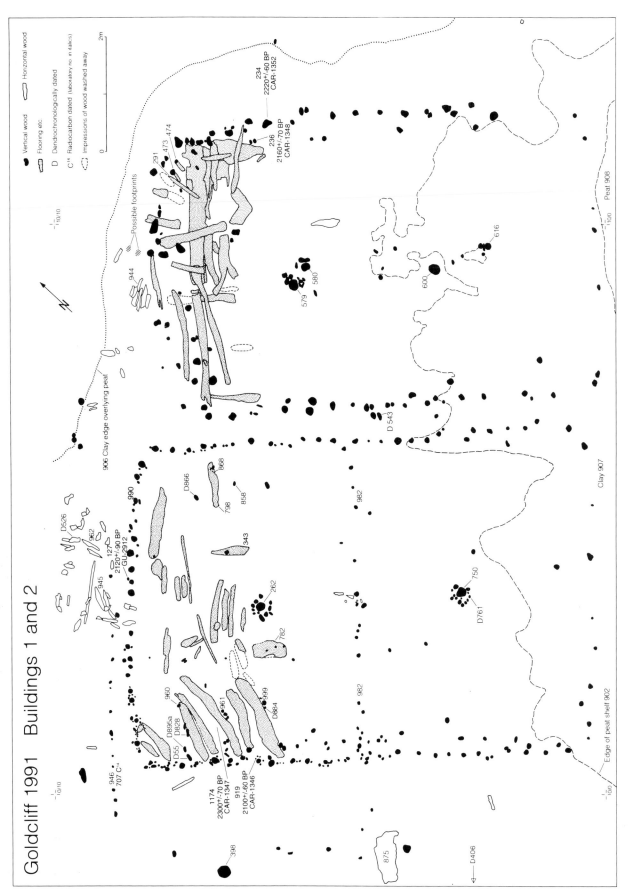

Figure 7.3 Goldcliff: Plan of Buildings 1 and 2 made in 1991. Since this drawing was made, Post 707 has been radiocarbon dated: 2270±50 BP (GrN–24153). Drawing by H Riley and B Garfi

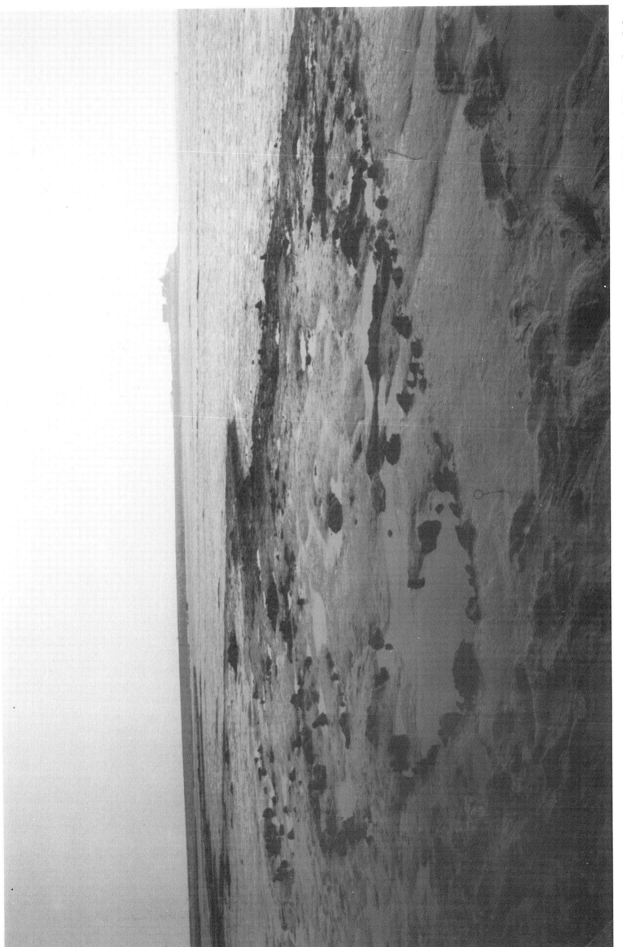

Figure 7.4　Goldcliff: Building 1 in foreground, Building 2 beyond showing the peat shelf and in the distance the former Goldcliff Island. Verticals of the buildings project through the mud cover before the 1991 excavation. Photograph by M Bell

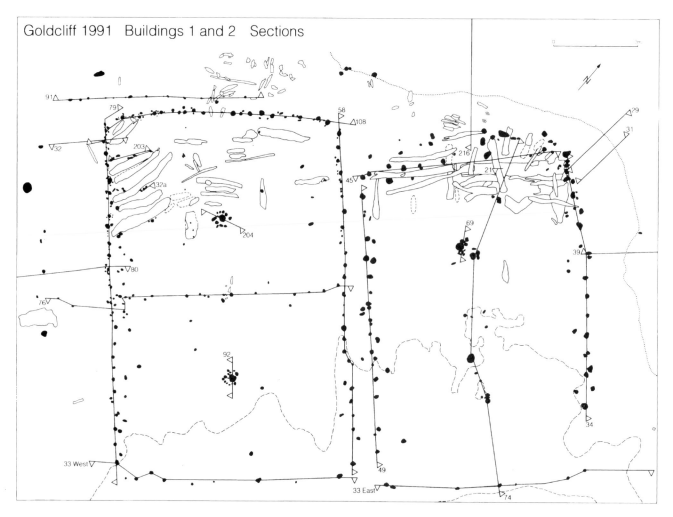

Goldcliff 1991   Buildings 1 and 2   Sections

Figure 7.5   Goldcliff: Buildings 1 and 2 showing the lines of section drawings. Drawing by H Riley and B Garfi

the main sections illustrated, has been projected onto the main sections as broken lines.

Total excavation of these buildings was not easy. There was no time, within the tidal frame, to completely clean whole buildings for photography. It was usually a struggle to complete the excavation, recording, and lifting of the stretch of wall allocated for each day's work. Once the wood had been lifted, each piece had then to be transported 600m across quite thick mud and saltmarsh, mostly using a plastic sledge. The task of excavating and transporting the wood, often in the face of an advancing tide, and sometimes with failing light, was frequently exhausting. These circumstances, and the difficulties of recording in such a muddy environment, mean that the record is not always as full, or consistent, as we would wish. That so much was achieved, with little loss of wood, is a great tribute to the team involved.

7.4 Building 1

The building (Figs 7.3–7.4) measured 8.4m long by 5.6m wide. A narrow entrance 0.6m wide in the middle of the northwest wall, suspected in 1990, was confirmed. The walls were defined by 167 pieces of roundwood. There were many more (97) in the southwest wall than the northeast (32) and northwest (32), with just six forming the southeast wall. The contrasting numbers are attributed to the effects of erosion. The relationship between the posts and the underlying alternating sequence of peats and clays (Fig 7.6) indicates that the southeast wall of the building had been truncated by about 0.4m, and here only the ends of the posts were preserved. Truncation of the southern end of the southwest wall was about 0.2m and the southern end of the east wall about 0.35m. Thus, the building was constructed on a sequence of layers which, when it was exhumed in recent times, was planed off on the southern side, removing the peat and cutting well into the less resistant underlying clay. South of the building underlying peats and clays were exposed in a series of small steps. This planing effect at the edge of the peat shelf is a particularly clear case of a phenomenon which appears to affect the edges of peat shelves in general.

Roundwood elements comprised the walls. They had been driven up to 0.7m into underlying sediments (Fig 7.6). The posts were of markedly different

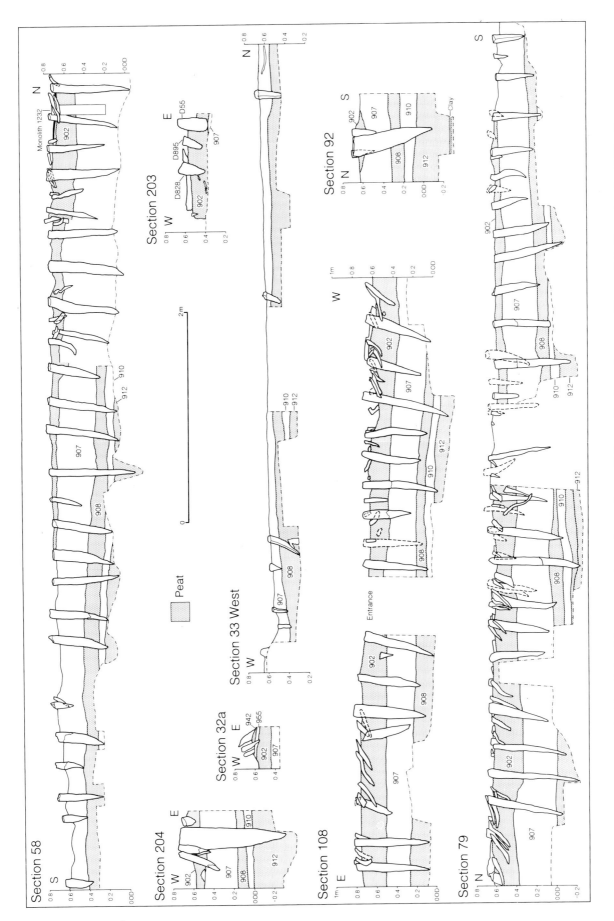

Figure 7.6 Goldcliff: Building 1, sections along the wall lines. For locations see Figure 7.5. Drawing by B Garfi

lengths, some penetrating into an underlying main peat, others ending in clay between this and the fen peat on which the structures lay. In places, as in Section 108 (Fig 7.6), it appears that longer, more substantial posts were used at fairly regular intervals of 1.8–2m. Elsewhere, however, the impression was that wood of different lengths had been selected and driven in until the tops of the walls were level.

Where preservation was good, on the northwest wall and the northern 3m of the northeast and northwest walls between the main structural elements, there were smaller (20–30mm) diagonal roundwoods, each of which had been sharpened by a single axe blow, then inserted diagonally at c 45°, mainly in one consistent direction (Fig 7.6). It is thought that these represent the remains of wattles which would have been woven between the larger vertical roundwood elements to create a basketwork structure. Experimental reconstructions show that this would have been of some strength (Reynolds 1979). The west wall has suggestions of a double wall of posts, with an inner line averaging 0.3m from the main wall consisting of fewer more widely spaced posts, perhaps indicating rebuilding or strengthening.

Much of the weight of the roof appears to have been taken by substantial posts down the centre of the long axis. The north post (262, Fig 7.7) was 0.17m in diameter and 1.09m long. It had been packed in place by fifteen smaller pieces, most roundwood, the equivalent of stone packing found on dryland sites. The south post (750) was 0.19m in diameter and 0.83m long with thirteen pieces of packing. The 1990 drawing by Parkhouse (1991a, fig 4; CD 7.2) suggests that there may originally have been three axial posts. Between those described is a concentration of six pieces of wood, which is suggestive of the packing of a third post which might have been removed.

Subdivisions

Internal posts form three subdivisions (Figs 7.3 and 7.8). The northernmost (960) was of six pieces, three of split oak, which provided important material for dendrochronological dating (Chapter 11). They were only bedded some 0.15m into underlying peat and partitioned an area 0.8m wide. Where fully preserved, this was 1m deep but roundwood elements to the east imply it may originally have been 2m deep. Subdivision 961 was of eight pieces, largely roundwood, which again defined an area 0.7m wide. The southernmost subdivision (999) comprises four or six verticals defining an area 0.7m wide. Other internal posts, particularly those which are of oak (858 and 866), hint at the possibility of further, largely eroded, subdivisions. The building was divided into two equal halves by a line of posts (982) across its middle (Fig 7.3). The possibility is discussed below that these posts are nothing to do with Building 1 and relate to an earlier structure (5) on the site.

Figure 7.7 Goldcliff: Building 1, Axial Post 262. Scale 0.25m. Photograph by J Parkhouse

Interior horizontals and reeds

In the northern third of Building 1 were 29 pieces of horizontal wood (Fig 7.8). These were variable in size, the largest 1.5m × 0.34m, the smallest c 0.4m × 0.1m. It was mostly roundwood, was highly compressed, retained its bark and, with one exception noted below, showed little sign of working. Some pieces could be split debris from woodworking. Preservation was best where roundwood lay diagonal to the northeast corner, forming a surface at c 0.65m OD. Smaller pieces of wood, planned and lifted in 1990, had lain parallel to the northwest wall between the entrance and the northern axial post, and one piece adjoined the east wall. This surface is thought to represent flooring; the rough, largely unmodified, and irregular wood seems less likely to represent collapsed wall or roof timbers. Furthermore, there was no evidence that it had compressed the plank subdivisions, which appeared to have been emplaced after the roundwood.

The only horizontal which showed signs of preparation was a badly preserved alder plank (782) 0.65m × 0.2m which had three oak pegs in holes, one clearly a cut mortise (Fig 12.8); it is the only piece of mortised timber from the buildings. We need to consider whether it is in situ, part of the floor, an internal fitting, or roofing. If it were part of the roof, it could be a ridge timber to which rafters were joined by pegs at intervals of 0.09m and 0.14m. However, successive plans show that the full size of the plank only emerged as excavation of the peat proceeded; it seems, therefore, to have lain at a relatively low level within the peat and is, accordingly, more likely to represent flooring. A possible interpretation is that it represents the end of the internal subdivisions, which would give them a depth of 2m. Just such a mortised beam formed the groundplate of internal subdivisions in an Iron Age building in Assendelver Polder in The Netherlands (Therkorn et al 1984).

Figure 7.8 Goldcliff: Building 1 horizontals and internal sub-divisions from south. In the area of the scale a remaining part of the reed layer can be seen draped across the underlying roundwood. Scale 1m. Photograph by J Parkhouse

Some support for this comes from seven other verticals which are on roughly the same line, ie parallel to the side wall and 1.9m away. We have noted hints of other subdivisions on the east side. If, hypothetically, these mirrored those on the west, perhaps with horizontal 343 representing their end, this would create a central aisle 1.6m wide with the axial post in the middle. This would allow for ten subdivisions in the northern half of Building 1, or twenty subdivisions, if the whole building were divided in this way, but the suggestion is highly speculative. Such subdivisions, interpreted as animal stalls, are commonly found in the Bronze Age and Iron Age rectangular buildings of continental Europe (Therkorn *et al* 1984, Louwe Kooijmans 1993).

The wooden flooring was overlain by the layer of reeds (Fig 7.8) which lay mostly along the axis of the building. Originally, reed covered some 10m^2 at the north end of the Building. It was 10–20mm thick, highly compressed, and could be peeled from the underlying wood flooring like matting. Possible interpretations of the reeds are (i) natural reedbed later than the building, which the environmental evidence in Chapters 13–15 appears to rule out, (ii) collapsed roofing, ruled out because the direction is along, rather than at right angles to the building axis, (iii) byre flooring, which is supported by the environmental evidence.

Entrance and exterior

One 0.6m wide entrance was found in the middle of the north side, flanked by two posts of more than average size (Fig 7.6, Section 108). There was no evidence of a support or pivot for a door itself. A scatter of wood fragments was found at various levels outside the entrance, presumably to stabilise a muddy area. Brunning (Chapter 12) shows that this debris was largely from the working of oak, with some underlying roundwood. Oak was not a major component of the building, but it was used in the subdivisions. The debris may derive from the finishing of these timbers on the spot. The main concentration of woodworking debris (945) was directly in front of the entrance, with another (962) at a slightly higher level and further east. The two phases of wood deposition were separated by a peat band 20mm thick.

Dating

Radiocarbon dates are available as shown on Figure 7.3 for a post (127) at 2120 ± 90 BP (GU-2912), a wattle (919) at 2100 ± 60 BP (CAR-1346), and the reed layer at 2300 ± 70 BP (CAR-1347). Although the last is potentially an earlier date, the reeds overlie the floor timbers, and the environmental evidence (Chapters 13–15) leaves no doubt that the reeds are contemporary with the use of the building. Dendrochronologically dated pieces of wood (Chapter 11) are

mostly from the partitions and interior and give a latest date of 392 BC, but sapwood is missing.

7.5 The possibility of an earlier Structure 5

There is evidence for an earlier structure on the site of Building 1, and at right angles to that building's axis. This was not suspected during the excavation stage but emerged as a result of post excavation work. The structure would comprise two parallel lines of posts (Figs 7.3 and 7.9). One of these lies *c* 0.3m north of the northwest wall of Building 1 (946). This comprises thirteen posts. It was noted in the field that these posts were of such similar character as to leave no doubt that most belonged to one structure. Three posts in this line continue beyond the west wall of Building 1. Another post (835), which could be part of this line but is not shown on the section, lay in front of the entrance to Building 1.

Parallel to this line and 4.6m south is the line of posts which ran across Building 1 (982). As already noted, this could be an internal division within Building 1; it does divide the structure into two equal halves. However, there is evidence that its line continued beyond the southwest wall of Building 1. Thus, the line comprises fifteen posts within the building and possibly four to its west, of which two are shown on Section 76 (Fig 7.9).

The case for associating these two lines as part of an earlier structure is based on the fact that they both continue beyond the west wall of Building 1 and, in both cases, alder buckthorn (*Frangula alnus*) was more commonly used than elsewhere (Fig 12.2). This wood type comprised *c* 47% of Structure 5 and only 6.5% of all the wood from the area of Buildings 1 and 2. No convincing end walls for the hypothetical structure have been identified. To the west, Posts 399a, 601, 602, and 604 might have formed part of a west wall. A possible hint of a northeast wall is the presence of a roundwood vertical (868) below probable flooring (798). No axial posts can be associated with the structure with confidence. A particularly large post to the west (398) might have been an axial, or entrance, post but it was not excavated and it is not exactly mid-way between the suggested two side walls. Given the circumstances of excavation previously outlined, it should not be assumed that every post present will necessarily have been located.

Although the evidence could not be regarded as conclusive, the writer feels there is a high probability that a separate Structure 5 existed on the site, at right angles to Building 1. They overlap and cannot be contemporary: Structure 5 appears to be earlier because, on initial excavation, only Building 1 was obvious. For instance, only four, at most, of the posts forming this structure were shown on the 1990 plan (Parkhouse 1991a, fig 4, CD 7.2). Most posts in both lines only emerged as excavation of the peat proceeded. The impression is that this structure lay at a lower level within the peat. Since the hypothesised

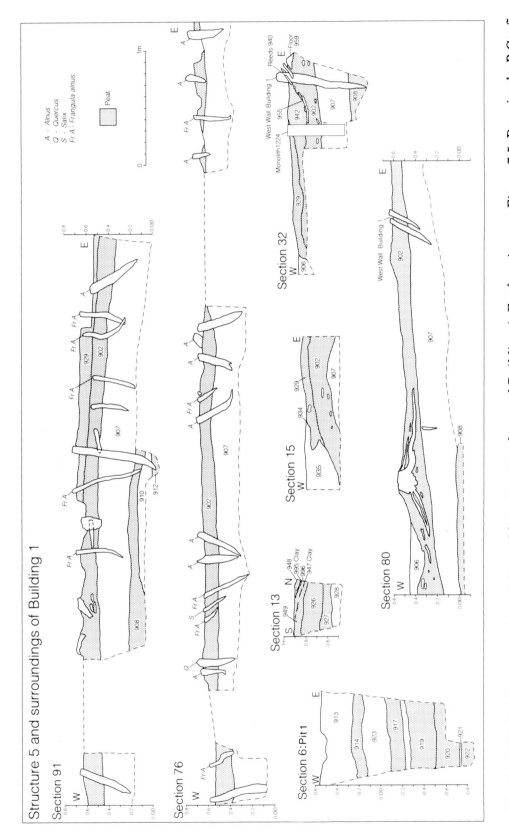

Figure 7.9 Goldcliff: Sections along the wall lines of Structure 5 and around Building 1. For locations see Figure 7.5. Drawing by B Garfi

Structure 5 lacks axial posts, entrance, and flooring, it is far from certain that it was a roofed building; it might easily have been an unroofed pen or enclosure, which the unsuitability of alder buckthorn for structural purposes, the irregular post arrangement, and the angles of several posts, might support. However, we should also consider the possibility that more substantial posts had been removed in prehistory. Given the dimensions, it does seem possible that we are dealing with a less well preserved, or less substantial, example of the same general type as Buildings 1 and 2. Whether a building or a pen, the fact that the posts remain and overlap implies that an interval for the collapse and breaking off of Structure 5 wood separated it from the later construction of Building 1. The interval does not, however, seem to have been long. A radiocarbon date for Post 707 of Structure 5 gave the result 2250 ± 50 BP (GrN-24153), which is close to the Building 1 dates.

7.6 Building 2

This lay parallel to Building 1 and 0.5m to the northeast. It was 7.4m long and 5.2m wide with a 0.92m wide entrance at the northwest end and horizontals at the north end (Fig 7.3). The walls (Fig 7.10) comprised some 89 verticals, mostly roundwood. They were distributed as follows: west wall (28); east wall (28); north wall (26); south wall (7). As with Building 1, the southern wall was eroded down to underlying sediments, so only post bottoms remained. Posts on the east wall averaged about 0.6m long, whereas those on the west wall were 0.4m, probably as the result of greater erosion on the west side. Where the arrangement of posts was at its most regular on the east side, roundwood verticals were at 0.4m intervals.

The walls lacked the diagonal wattling, a distinct feature of the northern part of Building 1. Building 2 had fewer, more widely spaced verticals, and they were often a little larger but not driven in so far. Building 2 may, therefore, have been differently constructed, or the lower part of the walls have been more eroded. In the middle of the west wall and the north wall there appeared to be a double line of posts, 0.2–0.3m apart. Wood identifications (Fig 12.2) show that the inner posts were more varied wood types than the outer alder posts, suggesting different phases, perhaps repairs or rebuilding. Rebuilding would seem to be a real possibility because at the north end there appeared to be two separate walls, one curved, the other relatively straight. Another possibility is that some of the additional posts represent supports for a structure which had started to lean, which might explain why some were at an angle.

The entrance was defined by four substantial posts, the outer two creating an entrance 1.12m wide, the inner two a gap 0.92m wide. As previously suggested, these may represent entrances to successive constructional phases but if, in a later phase, they were all standing, they might have formed a porch-like structure some 0.7m deep, an arrangement comparable with that in roundhouses (Guilbert 1981).

In the north corner of the building (Fig 7.3) there were clear signs that part of the wall had collapsed inwards: vertical roundwoods (473–474) were bent over and had been compressed into the floor, and this may also explain some other timbers at comparable angles with the corner. Since this was the area within the two buildings where prehistoric stratigraphy survived to the greatest height, it seems possible that collapsed walling may elsewhere have been eroded away.

Axial posts were present in two groups. In the north Post 579 was 0.95m long by 0.17m surrounded by eleven pieces of wood packing. At a distance of 0.2m was Post 580 (1.02m × 0.15m) with two pieces of wood packing. In the south was Post 600 (0.62m × 0.18m) without packing and 0.90m away two smaller timbers (616 and 619). Perhaps these paired axial posts reflect the strengthening, or rebuilding, of the structure which has been suggested on the basis of double posts in the walls. The four posts which, it is suggested, supported the roof ridge are not in a straight line, but each pair is offset in a way which may correspond broadly to the distance between the paired wall posts and the possible double wall at the north end. Because all the timbers were in place and encountered at the same stratigraphic level, we cannot be dealing with successive structures, in contrast to the previously described relationship between Building 1 and Structure 5. The likely explanation in the case of Building 2 is strengthening and partial rebuilding.

Horizontals

Horizontal timbers were present in the northern 2m of the building. All 27 recorded were in bad condition, compressed, some little more than squashed tubes of bark containing decayed wood. The largest horizontal was 1.89m × 0.17m, while most were much smaller, some just 0.4m × 0.1m.

The plan made by Parkhouse (1991a, CD 7.2) in 1990 shows horizontals in two distinct directions at right angles. Four timbers run along the building axis and are reasonably regularly spaced with respect to the ridge line. They are overlain by some timbers at right angles. The arrangement is suggestive of collapsed roof timbers. Section 21 (Fig 7.11) drawn in 1991 shows one timber (573) down the building's axis overlying a timber which lay at right angles but, as already noted, this could represent collapsed walling.

Some pieces of the possible roofing described above were lifted in 1990, while others were washed away between then and the 1991 excavation. Most of the horizontals remaining in 1991 appeared to represent flooring; the wood was rough and, although in very bad condition, lacked evidence of working or preparation. One piece retained a branch. Most of this wood was at right angles to the axis of the building. One or two larger pieces ran along the axis, but these

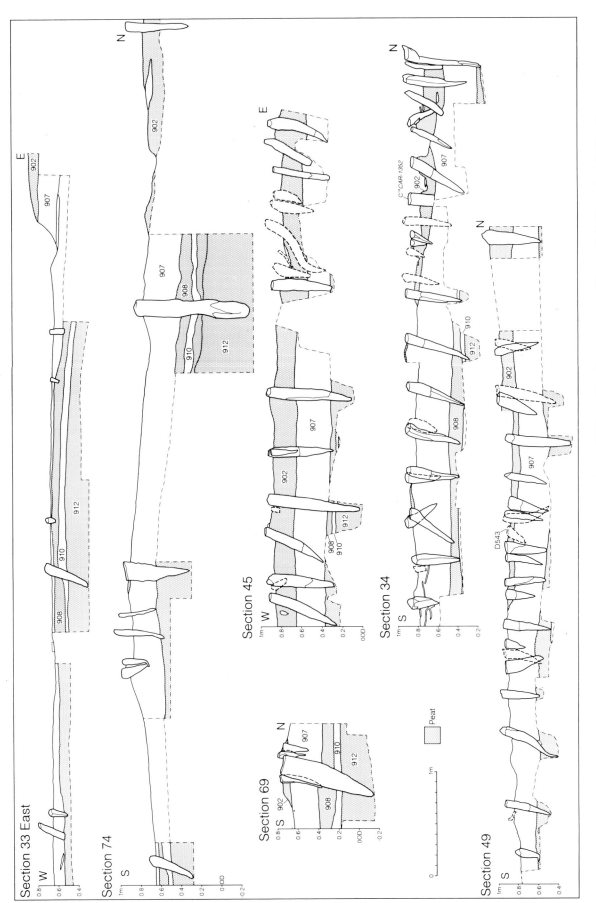

Section 33 East

Section 74

Section 45

Section 69

Section 34

Section 49

Peat

1m

Figure 7.10 Goldcliff: Building 2, sections along the wall lines. For locations see Figure 7.5. Drawing B Garfi

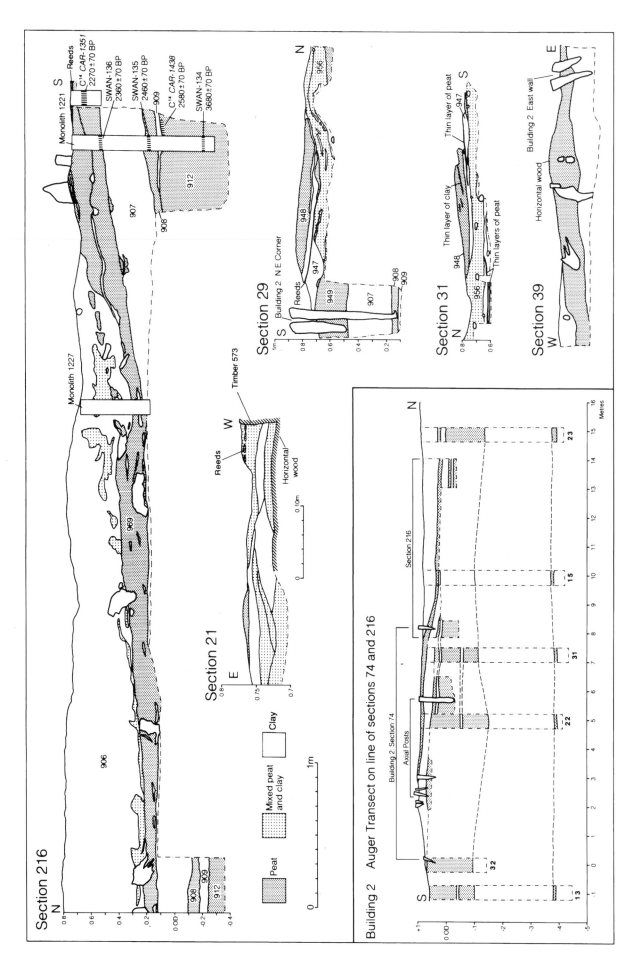

Figure 7.11 Goldcliff: Building 2 sections of the surrounds. Inset, bottom left shows the auger transect across the axis of Building 2. For locations see Figure 7.5. Drawing by B Garfi

underlay and, presumably, provided support for the smaller flooring timbers parallel to the northwest wall. In the light of the 1991 evidence, it seems most likely that the timbers planned in 1990 were part of the floor rather than collapsed roof, mainly because no underlying floor survived on the west side. The horizontals in the north corner of this building had been preserved because they had been compressed into a underlying feature, perhaps a small palaeochannel.

Overlying the horizontal wood was peaty sediment, in places with distinct laminations and lenses of grey clay or peat (Fig 7.11, Section 21). In 1990, c 1.5m² of reed were removed from this area (Fig 7.12) but only small patches remained at the time of the 1991 excavation. The reed layer may originally have extended over Building 2, although Section 21 shows that here it is separated by some 40mm from the horizontal timbers.

Dating

Two posts have been radiocarbon dated as shown on Figure 7.3: Post 236, 2160 ± 70 BP (CAR-1348); Post 234, 2220 ± 60 BP (CAR-1352). In addition, there is one dendrochronologically dated piece (543) with its last ring dated 464 BC, but there was no sapwood.

7.7 Artefacts and environmental samples from Buildings 1 and 2

Large numbers of reed samples were taken from the floors of Buildings 1 and 2. Many were sieved in the laboratory and many of the remainder were pulled apart in the laboratory to look for any artefacts, which were almost entirely lacking. The interiors were clean of artefacts, the exceptions being occasional woodchips and three bones. Figure 7.12 shows the distribution of the bones which were three dimensionally recorded during the excavation; all are outside the entrances of Buildings 1 and 2. The same figure shows the positions of the range of environmental samples which was analysed in order to investigate what activities were associated with these buildings and their environmental setting. Evidence from these samples is presented in Chapters 13–15; suffice it to say here that this evidence indicates that the peat was subject to some, presumably periodic, marine influence at the time that the structures were in use, that the reed layer is byre flooring material, and that cattle were probably housed in Building 1.

7.8 The stratigraphic context of Buildings 1 and 2

The relationship between the structures and the sedimentary sequence was outlined in Chapter 3 and has been elucidated in greater detail by the excavated sections, particularly by Section 216 (Fig 7.11)

running north of Building 2, which provides the key environmental and dating sequence for this part of the site. The same section was extended through the axis of Building 2 by a line of auger holes which provides a sequence to a depth of 5m. A detailed outline of the layers in the Building 1 and 2 area is given in CD 7.3. This section summarises the salient points from latest to earliest:-

(i) The wood peat and buildings were overlain by upper Wentlooge clay (Context 906, 935). Pieces of peat in the clay suggest some erosion at the peat clay interface (Fig 7.11, Section 216);

(ii) In places just outside Building 1 to its north, 0.1–0.2m of peat occurred above worked wood or bone, indicating some peat growth after human activity;

(iii) The upper part of the peat was a complex series of lenses of detrital peat, reeds, woodworking debris, and clay;

(iv) Within the buildings the occupation horizon was defined by the flooring. Building 1 had flooring at 0.6–0.7m OD in the northwest corner and 0.7–0.8m OD in the entrance. Building 2 had flooring at 0.7–0.8m OD in the northeast corner but the horizontals were uneven, with some horizontals at 1m OD. One episode of wood deposition consolidating the entrance to Building 1 was at 0.64–0.7m OD, but there were others above this. The bone scatter north of Buildings 1 and 2 was between 0.58m and 0.79m OD. The artefacts occurred within layers of peat, reeds, wood, and clay. These OD relationships show that activity occurred over a period represented by about 0.2m of peat development, distinct phases of wood chip deposition, in particular, being separated by peat formation or clay deposition. Much of the organic deposition appeared to relate to human activities, the clay to flooding episodes. One clay lens overlay woodworking debris put down to consolidate the entrance to Building 1, but wood chips put down in the entrance to Building 2 were within a clay lens (Fig 7.13). This implies flooding between phases of activity. The reed layer was present in places in the floor area and sometimes extended just beyond the wall line. Sometimes the reeds rested directly on the wood flooring, elsewhere there was a thin lens of clay between;

(v) Below the flooring was wood peat which predated the buildings. Its base is dated 2360 ± 70 BP (SWAN-136). The underlying sequence is clay (907) 0.3m; peat (908) 0.1m; clay (909–911) 0.1m; raised bog (912) up to 2m; silty clays 2.65m; peat at –3.8m OD, and clay of the lower Wentlooge. What this sequence demonstrates is that the buildings were on a part of the site which had seen many changes, from minerogenic sedimentation to peat growth. Such changes were, on a far shorter timescale, also apparent during the period that the buildings were in use.

98

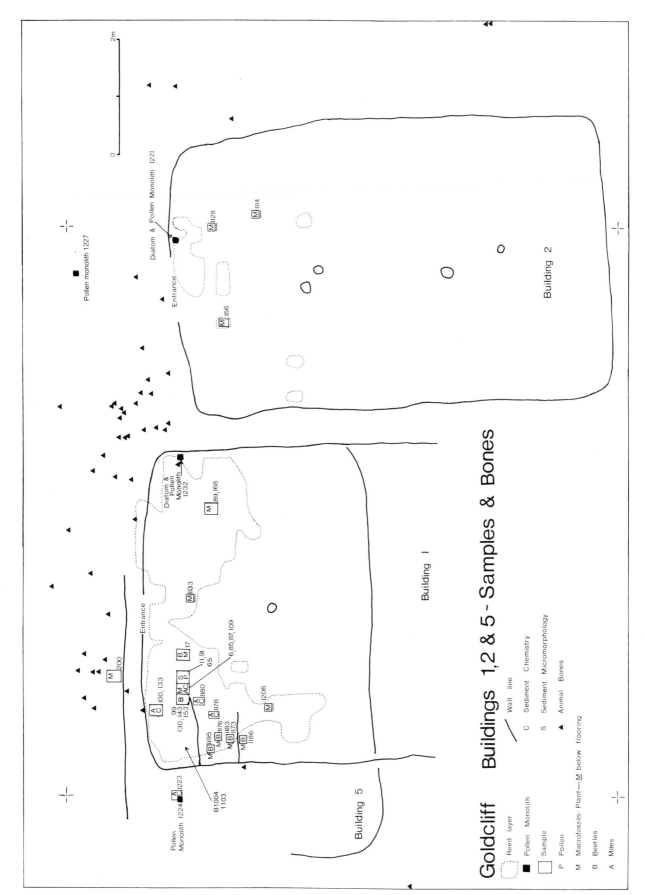

Figure 7.12 Goldcliff: Buildings 1 and 2: distribution of artefacts and environmental samples. Drawing by M Bell

Figure 7.13 Goldcliff: Woodworking debris put down to consolidate the entrance to Building 2 in a layer of grey clay. Scale 0.5m. Photography by J Parkhouse

7.9 Buildings 1 and 2: discussion

The radiocarbon dates of Buildings 1 and 2 are similar but the two buildings may not have been constructed at exactly the same time. Differences in the method of construction have been noted and there were also differences in the types of wood used (Chapter 12). The dendrochronological dates might suggest Building 2 is earlier but without the sapwood that could simply mean that the single piece of oak from Building 2 was split from nearer the centre of the tree. Both buildings were largely constructed of types of wood locally available (Chapter 12). Given Morgan's evidence (p203) that the trees used in Building 1 were not as old as those in Building 2, this might suggest that the latter was constructed later. Some support for this comes from woodworking debris consolidating the entrances, since that in the entrance to Building 2 was stratigraphically later than that in the entrance to Building 1.

Despite the foregoing, the two buildings had parallel walls, indicating that when one was constructed the other is likely to have been still standing. However, that would leave little room for the eaves overlap of the roofs and would also mean that water shed by one roof was likely to be discharged into the other structure. Conceivably, by this time, one was no longer in full use.

The sections clearly show that Buildings 1 and 2 are on a raised hummock of fen wood peat some 0.4–0.5m high. This surface drops away to north-west, northeast, and west. The fen wood peat layer does not vary a great deal in thickness and it is thought that the hummock is inherited from an earlier topographic feature. The auger transect (Fig 7.11) shows that the clay layer (907) which underlies the peat shelf is almost twice as thick below the buildings as to their north. The underlying raised bog peat is up to 2.1m thick below Building 2 and 1.4m thick to its north; thus, this topography apparently relates to much earlier stratigraphic differences.

Detrital peats with a marked greenish colour (Contexts 930 and 942) occurred around Building 1 (Fig 7.9, Section 32) and in places on its floor. In each case the stratigraphic horizon corresponds to that of the flooring and the artefact scatter. In the field it was thought that this material might represent animal dung, an hypothesis supported by environmental analysis in Chapters 13–15. Hints of the presence of animals come from the bones and a few small circular patches of clay (Fig 7.3), some 80mm in diameter, in peat north of Building 2. These were planned and, although not recognised at the time, can retrospectively be identified as probable animal footprints of the type subsequently found around Buildings 6 and 8. Animal footprints can also, probably, be retrospectively identified as the cause of small bowl-shaped depressions in Section 216 (Fig 7.11) at the base of Peat 969 and at the time of a clay deposition phase within 969.

The stratigraphic evidence indicates that Buildings 1 and 2 and their surroundings have been subject to erosion by the sea on at least two, perhaps three, separate occasions. The earliest is the least certain. During deposition of a clay layer within the peat a mixed clay/peat layer was deposited (Fig 7.11, Sections 29 and 31); this indicates erosion of the peat but it might have been very local. The second episode was during the onset of upper Wentlooge clay deposition; peat lumps and wood occur near the base of this layer (Fig 7.11, Section 216) and erosion at this time might have been significant. Finally,

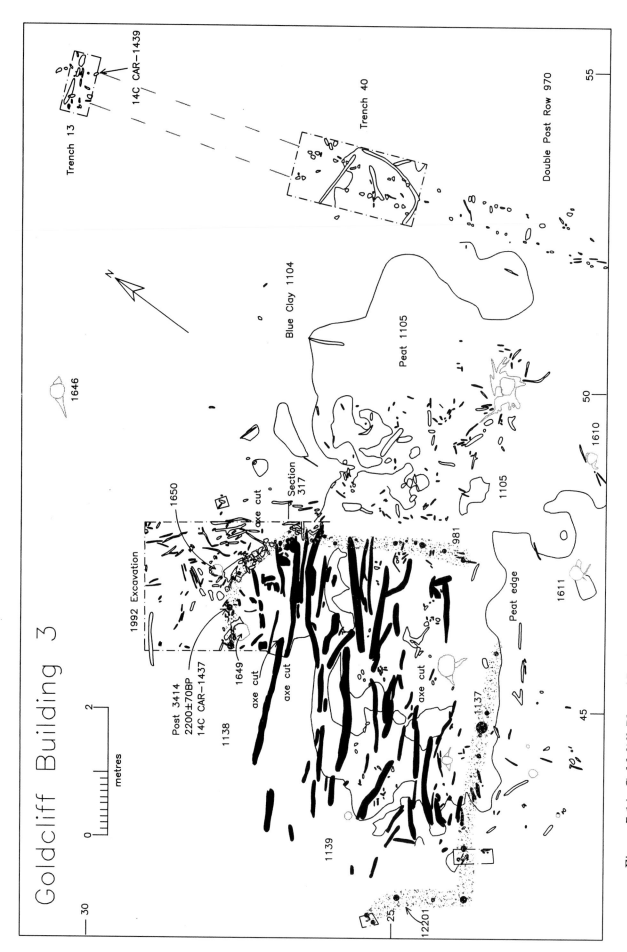

Figure 7.14 Goldcliff: Plan of Building 3 and the adjoining part of double post row (970). The probable outline of Building 3 is marked by grey shading, horizontal flooring is black. Drawing by K Henry and B Taylor

Figure 7.15 Goldcliff: Building 3, floor, the wall line is marked by arrows and some horizontals extend slightly beyond the wall line. Scale 1m

during recent decades there is the exhumation of the building by erosion of the clay cover. We have already noted that during that process the seaward side was severely truncated.

7.10 Building 3

This was 38m north of Building 2 on the same fen wood peat shelf. Its location was planned in 1990 and 1991, with more detailed planning and limited excavation in 1992 (Fig 7.14). Horizontals representing flooring are found on the surface of the peat within the area of the building. In places the peat is covered by patches of grey clay, which also surrounds the building except on its southeast side where the small 'island' of peat joins the main peat shelf. Thus, the building is partly buried by grey clay. Examination in 1992 involved cleaning some 80m², in sections of a size which two people could clean and plan at 1:20 in a single low tide. Some nineteen probable verticals were identified on the basis of size and relationship to lines of other vertical elements. We cannot be sure that all are structural and, without excavation, it is not possible to distinguish structural wood from natural wood in the peat. Most clearly defined is the east wall (981) which comprises fourteen verticals in a slightly bowed line. This wall showed some evidence of larger verticals with small wattles between. The north wall (1138) was represented by some verticals protruding through the clay, which in this area buried the peat. Other verticals

were found beneath the clay during subsequent excavation. A possible south wall (1137) is represented by nine verticals in a line. The west wall (12201) is least well defined, with two possible verticals protruding through grey clay. Small surface excavations around one post in this possible wall and two in the south wall (1137) indicated that verticals that appeared to be structural were in peat below 20mm of grey clay.

Within the area defined by the verticals were twenty horizontals on a surface about 1.45–1.5m OD. This was raised by 50–100mm above the level of the clay which surrounded the peat and horizontals. Five horizontals had ends which had been cut diagonally with an axe, and all the horizontals had a similar orientation which corresponds to the inferred long axis of the building. The horizontals are exposed on the peat surface and, in some cases, there is clay between them. Clay also buries parts of some horizontals. The vertical and horizontal elements appear to define a rectangular area 4.2m × 5.8m. However, this assumes that the limits of the building have been defined in all directions and that is far from certain, particularly in the west.

Excavation was restricted to a trench 2m × 3m, including the supposed north corner of the structure and some 1.2m² (or 5%) of the interior. This was really a keyhole excavation with the limited purpose of establishing whether a building was present, obtaining wood for radiocarbon dating, and a pollen monolith. Six vertical structural elements were recorded, forming a curve which is thought to

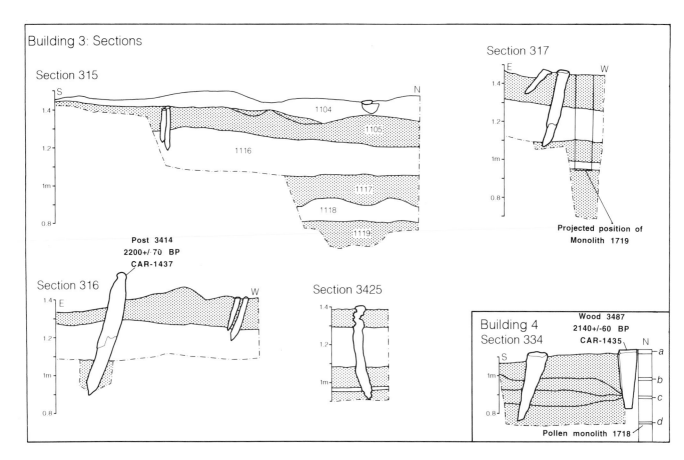

Figure 7.16 Goldcliff: sections of Buildings 3 and 4. Additional radiocarbon dates for the peat below Building 4 are marked on Section 334 by (a)–(d) as follows: (a) 2160 ± 40 BP (GrN–24145), (b) 3000 ± 40 BP (GrN–24146), (c) 3360 ± 40 BP (GrN–24147), (d) 3500 ± 30 BP (GrN–24148). Drawing by B Garfi

represent the north corner. Some (eg 3414, Fig 7.16) are substantial, others more like wattles just 20mm in diameter. The excavation did confirm the corner of the building but it indicated that verticals were less closely spaced and the structure as a whole was much less substantial than Buildings 1 and 2. It demonstrated the existence of some other horizontals sealed by the clay but also showed they did not cover the whole floor area.

Three pieces of substantial roundwood with cut ends occurred between 3.4m and 12m south and 15m southwest of the building within the fen peat. These might derive from in situ working of wood, perhaps cut from the fen woodland, or they could be structural timber eroded or blown from the building.

Stratigraphy

The building was sealed by upper Wentlooge clay. Flooring wood was sealed by the clay and rested on wood peat. The stratigraphy associated with this building lacked the complex lenses of reeds, detrital peats, and clay found in and around Buildings 1 and 2 that might imply activity of lesser intensity and duration. The underlying stratigraphy revealed by the trench and auger hole is as described for the Building 2 area.

Discussion

Dating of this building rests on a single radiocarbon determination from vertical Post 3414 which was 2200 ± 70 BP (CAR-1437), very close to those of other structures on the same peat shelf. It appears to be a structure of the same general type as the other rectangular structures. There are hints of a wattle-work construction, and it appears to share the slightly bowed ends of Buildings 1 and 2. Limited excavation indicates it may have been less substantially constructed. One substantial vertical 0.14m in diameter (1139) midway between the two side walls could be an axial post, but it was buried in the clay and could equally be a tree stump. The horizontals are this building's clearest elements, and are interpreted as flooring. Five horizontals continue between 0.05m and 0.25m east of the wall line (Fig 7.14, south of Section 317); this could indicate the position of an entrance. No artefacts, apart from cut wood and a woodchip, were found during work on the structure. The paucity of artefacts is noteworthy given the survival of floor levels.

7.11 Building 4

First noted in 1990, this building was cleaned and planned in 1992. It was one end of a rectangular

Figure 7.17 Goldcliff: Building 4 from south

structure with one or more post lines to its south (Structure 1149). The structures were located on a crescent *c* 3m wide by 16+ m long, of slightly higher peat (Figs 7.17 and 7.18). This was at *c* 1.2m OD, and most of the time was surrounded by a sea of mud. When the mud cover was reduced, there was a steep erosion face to seaward, the base of which was never seen. To landward the peat was overlain by grey clay. Building 4 consists of three sides of a rectangle from which an enormous bite has been taken by the sea. The structure was 7.3m long and its surviving maximum width 4.6m. There were two rounded corners. It comprised 33 verticals spaced on average 0.19m apart. Of the verticals, twenty are roundwood and thirteen split timber.

Only two posts were excavated (Fig 7.16), those closest to the erosion face. Post 3484 was roundwood 110mm in diameter and 0.37m long, and 3487 was split wood 90m × 50m and 0.30 m long. It has a radiocarbon date of 2140 ± 60 BP (CAR-1435) and is, therefore, broadly contemporary with the nearby Buildings 1–3.

There is possible evidence of an entrance on the northwest side where an interval between posts is 1.3m wide, but there is a hole where a post may have been lost which would give a gap of 0.8m. There are no other intervals of this width. It seems probable that these three sides once formed part of a complete rectangle, forming a structure similar to the other Goldcliff buildings. If the entrance was in the middle of the end wall, as in Buildings 1 and 2, then that would give us a structure 5.8m wide by 7.3m long, with rounded corners comparable with the other

structures and a slightly bowed end similar to Buildings 1 and 2. That reconstruction gives an interior area of 43m², of which 16.5 m² (40%) survived. Axial posts were absent, but if they were positioned comparably with the other structures (ie *c* 2m in from the mid point of the end wall), that would place them in the eroded area.

Only three verticals were found in the interior, one in the north corner and two on the southern side. The absence of any flooring or disturbance associated with activity on the smooth peat surface makes it likely that the floor levels of the building have been planed off by erosion. However, the radiocarbon date for the top of the peat (Fig 7.16) 2160 ± 40 BP (GrN-24145) is very close to that of the building, indicating that very little of the peat surface can have been eroded. Since the steep erosion face to seaward is within 3m of all the surviving wall circuit, what remains could be eroded at any time. Remarkably, however, the peat edge remained largely unchanged between 1992 and 1995. Finds were just two bones.

Information on the stratigraphic context of this building is restricted to the 0.5m deep face cleaned for removal of the two posts (Fig 7.16, Section 334) and the 5m deep auger hole (29), which was 2m south of the building. The building was on reed peat and, as botanical evidence (Chapter 13) shows, the underlying stratigraphy is very different from that of the other structures on the main peat shelf (Chapter 3). There is no sign of the two clay layers and the intervening peats, including the upper fen wood peat which characterised the sequence in the area of Buildings 1–3. Thus, the limits of those inundations

104

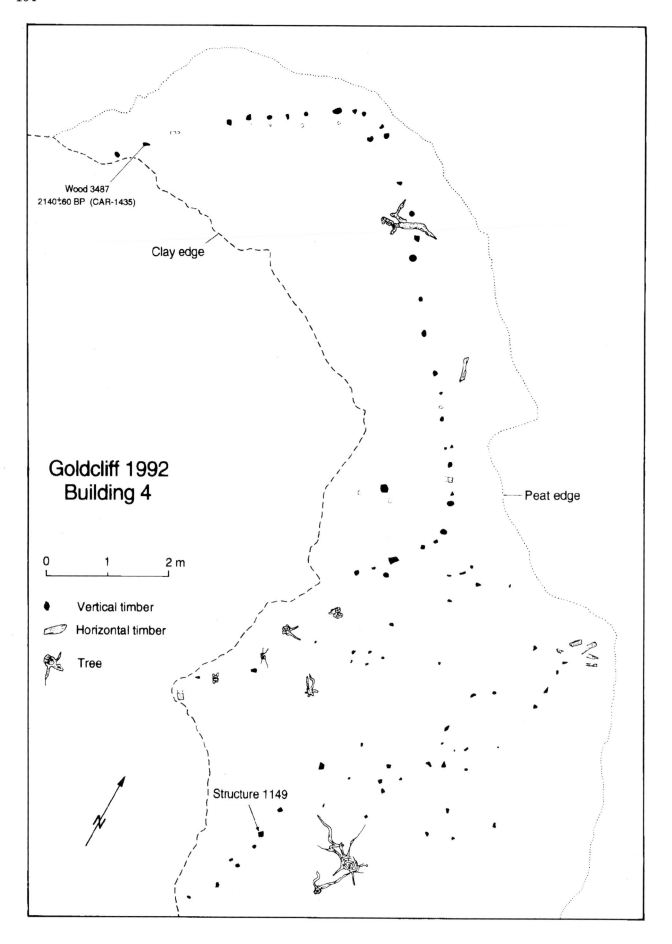

Wood 3487
2140±60 BP (CAR-1435)

Clay edge

Peat edge

Goldcliff 1992
Building 4

0   1   2 m

● Vertical timber

▱ Horizontal timber

Tree

N

Structure 1149

Figure 7.18   Goldcliff: Plan of Building 4 and adjacent linear structure (1149). Drawing by S J Allen

lay between Buildings 1 and 4. The fact that Building 4 is of comparable date with Buildings 1–3 implies that the raised bog to the west continued to grow long after it had been drowned to the east. This is also evident from the Goldcliff West sequence. The later survival of the raised bog surface at Goldcliff West *and* Building 4 shows the major channel of Goldcliff Pill did not at that time run between the two sites.

8 Rectangular structures at Goldcliff west of the Pill, *c* 750 Cal BC–150 Cal AD

by M Bell with J R L Allen, S J Allen, and R Brunning

8.1 Discovery

Derek Upton discovered on 25 August 1992 that the prehistoric site extended west of Goldcliff Pill. Preliminary photographic recording took place on 29 August. The following day a major storm led to many new discoveries, creating considerable recording pressure. Much was achieved between then and the end of the excavation season on 12 September. It was just as well so much recording was done because it turned out to be the only complete record of one of three buildings prior to its destruction. Further recording and excavation at Goldcliff West took place in 1993 and 1994.

Before considering the individual structures, the general topography of the Goldcliff West site will be introduced (Fig 8.1) The peat was covered by hummocks of varying size; the buildings lay on three of the larger hummocks. Buildings 6 and 7 were *c* 220m west of Goldcliff Pill and Building 8 was 200m further west. Between Building 6 and Goldcliff Pill, there were very clearly defined hummocks which were not associated with wooden structures. The hummocks were surrounded by encircling depressions; some channels had clay on their floor, others peat; both were covered with animal footprints. The peat was overlain by clay and, on the rare occasions when this was swept clear of mud, cattle footprints were also observed in this. Northeast of Building 6, a palaeochannel some 3.5m wide curved eastwards. The edges of this were picked out over part of its course by changes in the clay, eg a channel edge or the inclined orientation of bedding. In places strips of peat marked slightly higher areas where peat development had occurred over former levées. This suggested that, although fairly narrow, the palaeochannel had some longevity, although the associated stratigraphic sequence was not investigated.

8.2 The setting of Building 6

This rectangular building was on a low peat hummock with a clay-filled palaeochannel to the north. Figure 8.2 shows the setting soon after discovery, when there was no mud cover. A contour map of the area (Fig 8.3) was prepared in 1993 by levelling on a 0.5m grid. On this the darker shading represents lower areas. The prominent palaeochannel extends for 145° around the building. The palaeochannel was 4.5m wide at the east and tapered to a point in the west. A slighter depression in the surface of the peat continued round the remainder of the circuit. The southeast side of the hummock, the darkly shaded area, had been cut into by the erosion of the peat shelf. A crack extending back from the peat edge to the south of the building, together with erosion scars on the surface of the hummock, show an active erosion threat at the time of excavation. One erosion scar expanded by 2m and removed the south west corner of the building between the 1993 and 1994 field seasons (Fig 8.4).

8.3 The excavation of Building 6
Steven Allen

The building is rectangular, with rounded corners, measuring some 7m × 5m, aligned roughly east–west (Figs 8.4–8.6). It was defined by a wall line surviving as upright wooden posts exposed at the modern peat surface, with two settings of similar posts on the longitudinal axis of the building within the wall line. There were also occasional isolated posts within the building. In 1992 there was only time to make a plan of the building at 1:20. Investigations recommenced in 1993 when the area around the building and the palaeochannel was planned. Following examination of the visible wood of the building, it was decided to excavate a single corner of the structure to examine its form, construction, and the character of the wood, to identify any surviving floor layers and recover samples for dendrochronology. A square around the southeast corner was marked out, planned at 1:10, and the peat outside the building removed to expose the timbers of the wall. These were drawn at 1:10. The timbers were then lifted and excavation continued into the interior of the building. The surviving timbers proved to be around some 0.3m long. The absence of any flooring material or occupation horizons within the building demonstrated that the ground surface on which the structure had been erected had been truncated at some point prior to its discovery.

Since the National Museum of Wales wished to conserve the building for possible display, it was decided to excavate the entire building during the 1994 season. This was supervised by the writer. The method adopted was based on previous experience at the site and the need to work around the tide cycle. A strip was marked out around a convenient length of wall. The peat surface was cleaned, the timbers

107

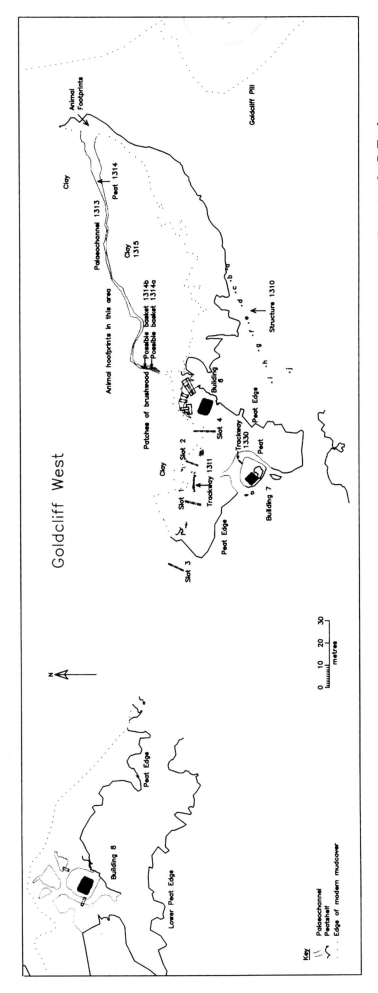

Figure 8.1 Goldcliff West showing the relationships between Buildings 6–8, Trackways 1311 and 1330. Drawing by B Taylor

Figure 8.2 Goldcliff: Building 6, on the right, from west. It is on a low peat hummock with a clay filled palaeochannel to the north. In the foreground is upper Wentlooge clay with animal footprints at the peat/clay interface. Photograph by E Yorath

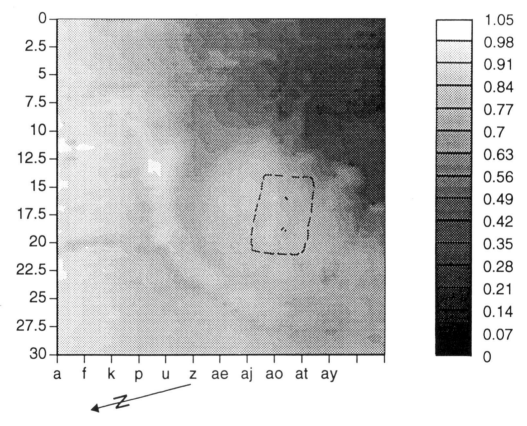

Figure 8.3 Goldcliff: Building 6 contour survey of the surroundings. Darker shading represents the lower areas. Drawing by G Longden

planned at 1:10, and photographed. Peat was then removed from outside the wall line with hand shovels and spatulae, working towards the timbers and below the estimated depth of the wood. A thick baulk of peat was left overnight to hold the wood in position and protect it during the next inundation. When we returned, the trench could be baled without damaging the wood. The baulk could then be peeled away from the wood into the trench, the elevation photo-

graphed, drawn (Fig 8.7), the timbers labelled and lifted, whilst a second team began the adjacent trench/wall section, leaving a baulk of peat between the two trenches. The final stage was to remove the baulk between the trench just completed and the previous trench to recover any wood which might be hidden within it. Work proceeded from the seaward corner of the building (excavated in 1993) to minimise any damage to unexcavated timbers.

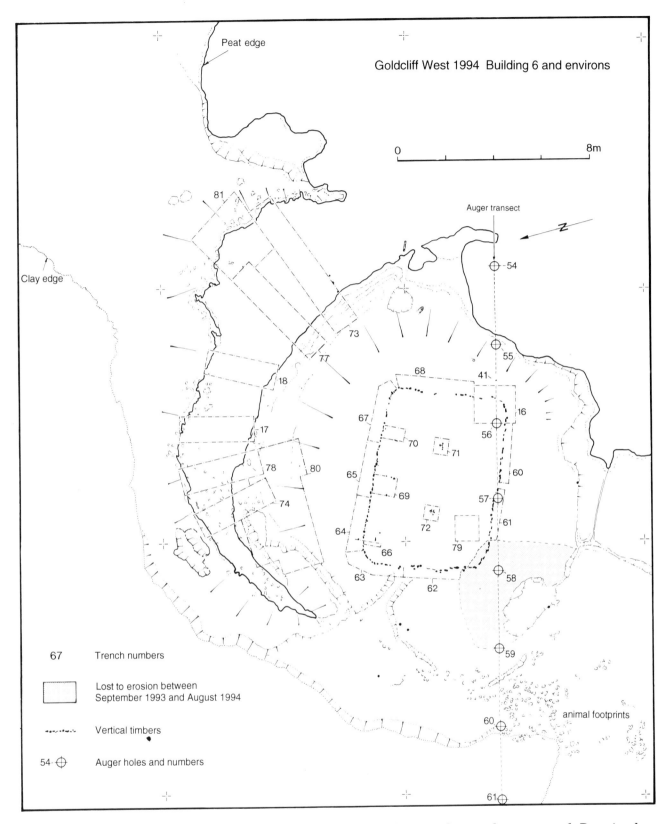

Figure 8.4 Goldcliff: Plan of Building 6 and its surroundings showing the trenches excavated. Drawing by S J Allen

It was discovered that, during the winter, the hitherto undisturbed southwest corner of the building with some twelve timbers had been lost to erosion. It was found, as digging progressed, that the timbers on the northwest corner and north side of the building were much deeper than those elsewhere,

requiring modification of the size of trench excavated to allow a task to be completed within the 6 hours of exposure permitted between tides. Trenches were dug at right angles to the line of the north wall to investigate and recover the remains of possible partitions. Finally, squares were marked out around

Figure 8.5 Goldcliff: Building 6 from west. Photograph by L Boulton

the two axial timber settings, which were excavated by quadrant, drawn, and the timbers lifted. It was soon apparent that the wooden posts were the uppermost surviving ends of vertically set timbers driven into the peat, forming a plan similar to that of previously excavated Buildings 1 and 2. Cleaning and planning of the area of the structure revealed the wall line as a single, near continuous, row of split timbers interspersed at regular intervals (c 0.6–0.8m) with similarly sized roundwood uprights (Figs 8.6–8.8). Excavation confirmed that the only significant gap (of 0.7m) in this wall line was midway along the east side of the structure. Most of the timbers had been driven in with their points terminating around 0.4–0.6m below the modern peat surface, but those at the northwest corner, and for much of the north side, tended to be longer, with their points at 0.7–0.9m below the peat surface.

The two axial groups of posts (Fig 8.6) within the area defined by this wall line were similar in character. Each group comprised a close spaced setting of roundwood points with some split timber. None had been driven more than 0.5m below the modern peat surface and none were more than 0.10m in diameter. There was no trace of any post similar in size to those recovered from the axial settings of Buildings 1 and 2.

The other internal timbers form a pattern reminiscent of the partitions identified in Buildings 1 and 2. The wood here, both roundwood and split, was very shallow and had not penetrated to a depth >0.15m.

It became clear in the course of the excavation that

no floor levels survived within the structure. There was also evidence that an unknown depth of peat had been eroded; some posts were only represented by truncated points, and shallow voids marked the positions of lost posts. Many of the small gaps in the wall line may, therefore, once have been filled with upright timbers which have subsequently been lost, and it may be presumed that the wall of the building was originally a complete palisade broken only by the entranceway.

The surviving, modern, peat surface is not, therefore, the peat surface or floor level which was contemporary with the construction and use of the building. This is confirmed by the fact that the peat surface on top of the hummock in Pit 79 has a radiocarbon date of 2760 ± 70 BP (SWAN-31), some 700 radiocarbon years earlier than the building. Post 7025 of Building 6 is dated 2150 ± 70 BP (SWAN-26), and there is also a precise dendrochronological date of 273 BC (Chapter 11).

Other posts

A small scatter of six small posts were observed between 2m and 4m east of the building on the peaty palaeochannel floor. These might relate to a trackway across the channel. Trackway 1311 leads in this direction, although there was no evidence of brushwood on the channel floor at this point. There was a substantial stake (7137, Fig 12.13) 0.82m long and 0.14m in diameter 3m east of the building and 2m from the palaeochannel. It may not be too fanciful to

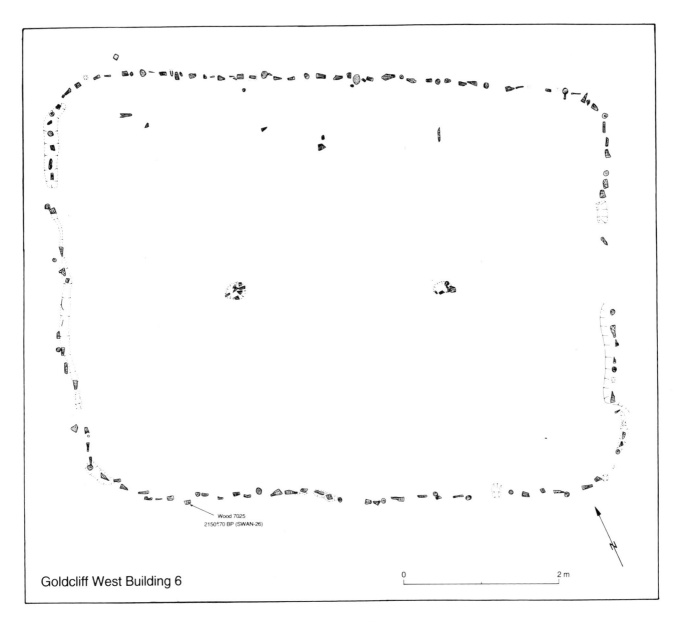

Goldcliff West Building 6

Wood 7025
2150±70 BP (SWAN-26)

0   2 m

N

Figure 8.6   Goldcliff: Plan of Building 6. Drawing by S J Allen

suppose that this might have served as a tethering point for boats or animals.

8.4 The palaeochannel around Building 6

When first observed, the palaeochannel was clear of mud and artefacts were exposed by erosion on its surface; here Upton found the only sherd of stratified prehistoric pottery, a withy tie, and some pieces of worked wood. During the 1993 season, 1m wide Trenches 17 and 18 were excavated across the channel and, likewise, in 1994 Trenches 73, 74, 77, 78 (Figs 8.9 and 8.10). In this way *c* 40% of the channel length was excavated, the objective being to recover artefacts and to establish whether these contexts were contemporary with the use of the building. The method of trench excavation was dictated by the need to work in areas of a size which could be baled between tides, and also the need to obtain sections across the channel.

The palaeochannel has an average depth of 0.65m. The five sections highlight its character as an erosive feature cutting into the peat. Sections of Trenches 17 and 74 show that the base of the channel is a steep sided gully (Figs 8.10 and 8.11). Both sections also show clay extending from the gully north *below* 0.8m of peat. This implies that gullying may have been associated with the development of horizontal fissures within the peat, a feature of the present day erosion of the peats in the area of Building 8. Fracturing of the peat may have occurred as a result of desiccation. The palaeochannel fills were complex, representing a number of distinct episodes of erosion and deposition. The fills were of two main types; the earlier (1320) comprises mixed peat including blocks and pebbles of peat with lenses of pure clay. In some

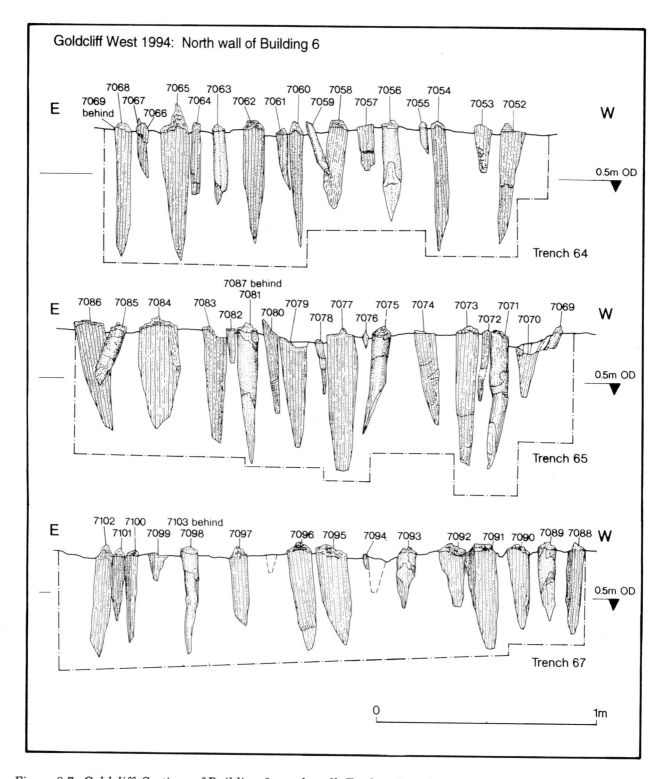

Figure 8.7 Goldcliff: Sections of Building 6, north wall. For location of trenches see Figure 8.4. For sections and photographs of additional lengths of wall see CD 8.1–8.4. Drawing by S J Allen

sections, this sediment occurs in the base of the channel; in Trenches 17 and 74 it occurs as a 'terrace' on the side of the channel cut into by a later gully. These fills clearly relate to a phase when the peat was subject to active erosion. The later channel fill (1303) was grey clay with a few small peat pebbles, artefacts, and other pieces of wood. South of the palaeochannel on the edge of the peat hummock, Trench 78 showed a marked lens of clay 0.13m below the peat surface. This would seem to relate to a flooding episode during the period of peat formation.

8.5 Artefacts and distribution

Artefacts were three-dimensionally recorded. Their distribution is shown in Figures 8.9 and 8.10. In these diagrams symbols mark the main categories of

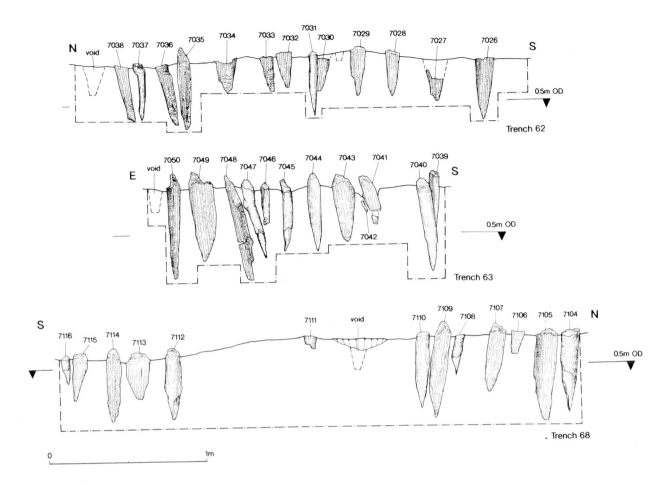

Figure 8.8 Goldcliff: Sections of Building 6 east and west walls. For location of trenches see Figure 8.4. For sections and photographs of additional lengths of wall see CD 8.1–8.4. Drawing by S J Allen

artefact, and objects which are illustrated are numbered. Artefacts found in 1992–93 were within the palaeochannel. However, the excavation in 1994 of Trenches 73 and 74 revealed artefacts in peat on the edge of the hummock and, in retrospect, the excavation strategy should have concentrated more on these deposits. A very limited excavation in 1995 of Trench 80 to an average depth of just 70mm was an attempt at redress, although finds were few.

In the four most easterly trenches (Fig 8.9), finds were concentrated nearest Building 6, their probable source, indicating there was an entrance at its east end. A scatter of woodworking debris within the peat at the edge of the hummock, and in the palaeochannel, indicates that some, at least, of the wood for the building may have been worked on the spot. At the south end of Trench 74 was a marked concentration of *Bos* bones, some apparently articulated (CD 8.5).

The sections (Fig 8.10) show a general scatter of artefacts through the palaeochannel fills. In Trench 74, however, it is noticeable that finds are confined to the top 0.15m. In each section, artefacts were more numerous in the mixed peaty clay (1320) on the south side of the channel and fewer in the upper clay fill (1303). Such a distribution could be interpreted in two ways: (i) the lower fill accumulated during the life of the building when artefacts were dumped or

washed into the channel or (ii) that artefacts in the channel have been largely eroded from the peat hummock. The fact that clay lenses occur within the peat hummock edge south of the channel (Fig 8.10, Section 78) is taken to indicate marine incursion up the palaeochannel around the time of Building 6 activity.

8.6 Pottery
J R L Allen

5000 On the day the site was discovered, Upton found two joining sherds on the clay palaeochannel surface (Fig 8.12). These were the only prehistoric sherds found during the project. The sherds (weighing 6.4g) were uniformly thin (c 4mm) and in a soft, fine-textured black fabric with common to abundant, mainly angular fragments of off-white to pale grey limestone (<1mm). The surfaces of the sherds are thinly but extensively coated in carbonised (?)food residues. Where exposed, the external surface is smooth and burnished but without signs of other decoration. The sherds are possibly from a small jar.

A precise date cannot be offered for the sherds. They clearly fall within Spencer's (1983) group of limestone-tempered pottery. This ware is well-attested at

114

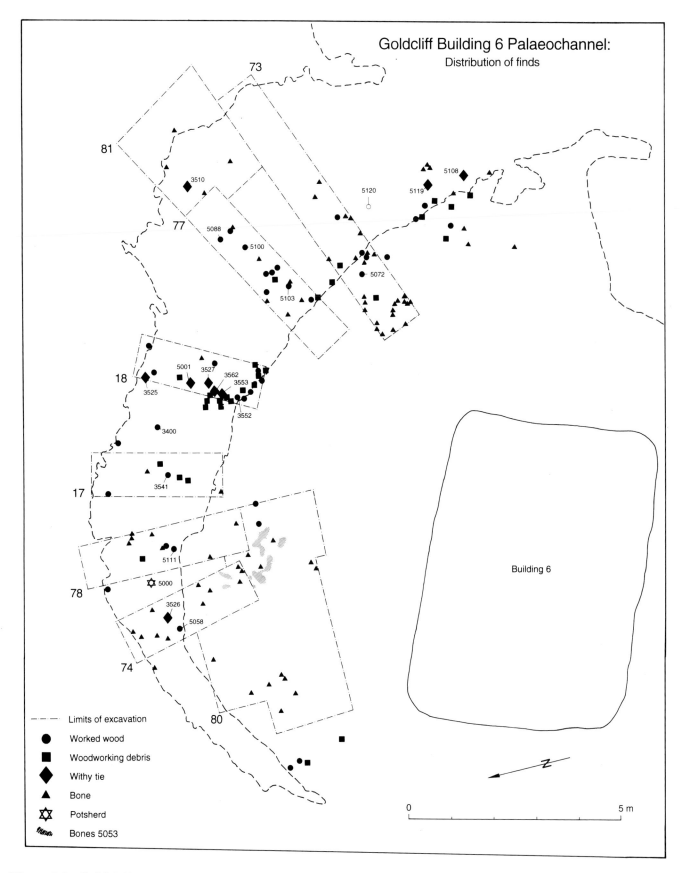

Figure 8.9   Goldcliff: Building 6 palaeochannel showing the excavation trenches and the distribution of finds. Drawing by S J Allen

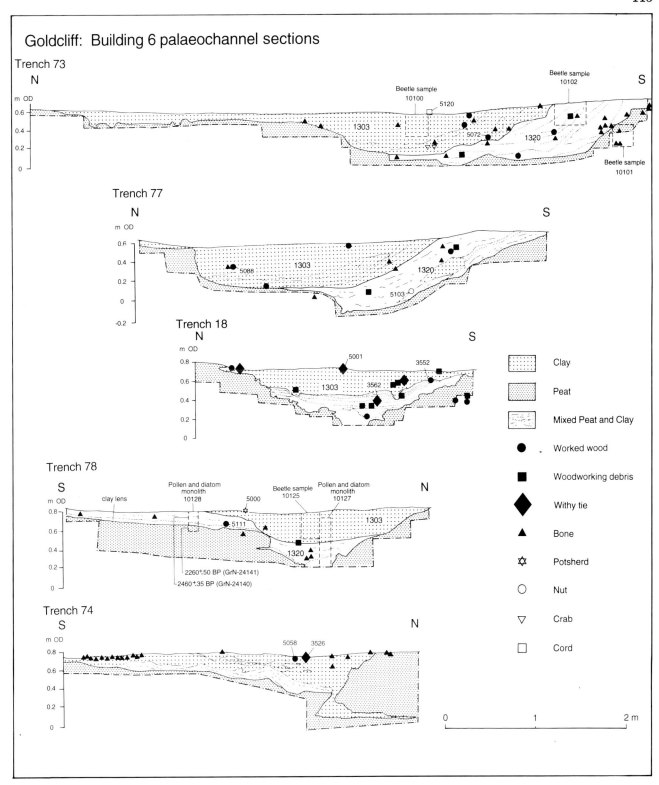

Goldcliff: Building 6 palaeochannel sections

Clay

Peat

Mixed Peat and Clay

● Worked wood

■ Woodworking debris

◆ Withy tie

▲ Bone

✡ Potsherd

○ Nut

▽ Crab

□ Cord

Figure 8.10 Goldcliff: Building 6 palaeochannel sections of Trenches 73, 77, 18, 78, 74, showing the location of samples and the distributions of finds. Drawing by S J Allen

Goldcliff West 1993   Trench 17

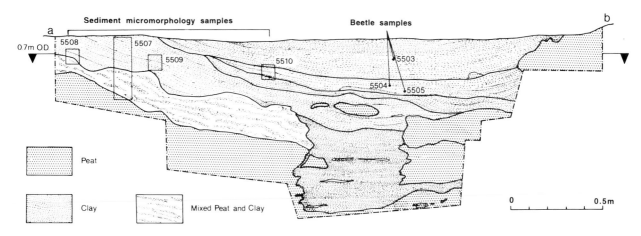

Figure 8.11 Goldcliff: Building 6 palaeochannel section of Trench 17. Drawing by S J Allen

many mid- and late-1st century AD contexts on both sides of the lower Severn and Severn Estuary. One decorated variant–the Goldcliff sherd is too small to be assigned to variants–occurs at a number of pre-Conquest but not more-closely dated sites (eg Llanmelin, Caldicot, Lydney), and the Goldcliff sherd could be of this date. Peacock (1969) does not record a limestone tempered fabric from the Somerset area, but these fabrics are not well known and he restricted himself exclusively to vessels with Glastonbury-style ornament. However, only a small proportion of the wares from eg Glastonbury and Meare are decorated in this style. The Goldcliff sherd is in the general late-Iron Age tradition and a 1st century BC date is possible, as was suggested for the pottery (which includes a single limestone-tempered bead-rimmed jar) from Magor Pill east, also in the fill of a palaeochannel cutting the peat (Whittle 1989, fig 11.7).

8.7 Wood artefacts (Fig 8.12)
Richard Brunning and Martin Bell

Wood containers

3541 Part of the side of an alder container. Survived to height 141mm, by 65mm wide and a thickness of only 7mm. Curvature indicates a diameter of c 0.3m. At its lower edge, a groove (5mm wide, 2mm deep) was formed on the inner face to accommodate a discoidal base plate. The groove was formed by cutting at right angles to the wood at the top edge, and at a much shallower angle at the bottom, so that the bottom edge is less pronounced. Both the side edges were damaged and the top edge was eroded away, so the original size of the piece is unknown, nor is it entirely certain whether the piece is a stave or part of a hollowed two-piece container with an inserted base; both types of prehistoric vessel are

illustrated by Earwood (1993). If a stave, it was shaped from a tangentially split timber. No trace of toolmarks, or vestiges of hoops or ties survived on the outer face, which was slightly damaged during excavation on its lower edge. On the inside face traces of toolmarks survived where the thickness increased around the groove, with impressions left by the cutting blade up to 42mm wide. The traces of toolmarks in the grove itself were far less clear.

5058 Possible alder vessel fragment, from clay palaeochannel fill (1303); 31mm × 28mm × 5mm. No edges were complete, and no traces of toolmarks survived.

5111 Possible alder vessel fragment from clay palaeochannel fill (1303); 55mm × 40mm × 8mm. Edges incomplete, no evidence of toolmarks survived.

5088 Possible fragment of lime wood vessel from clay palaeochannel fill (1303). Broken into two pieces and eroded on its edges; 194mm × 32mm × 6mm. Radial split, no trace of toolmarks survived.

Only 3541 can be regarded as a certain stave or container fragment. Similar pieces come from Bronze Age Caldicot (Brunning and O'Sullivan 1997, 208–9) and Wilsford Shaft (Ashbee et al 1989, 60) and there are several examples of Iron Age date at Glastonbury (Bulleid and Gray 1911, 318–23) and Corlea-1 trackway in Ireland (O'Sullivan 1997, 264). The Goldcliff pieces are unusually thin by comparison with these examples. The tangential alder fragments could all be the remains of staves but the radial lime piece would be a very unusual choice for such a function. Wooden buckets or tubs undoubtedly fulfilled a multiplicity of functions including the haulage of water from a well at Wilsford Shaft. Composite wood vessels of similar type were traditionally used in dairying in Wales and, no doubt, elsewhere until a few generations ago. With cattle, and some neonatal calves present at Goldcliff, a connection with dairying seems a distinct possibility.

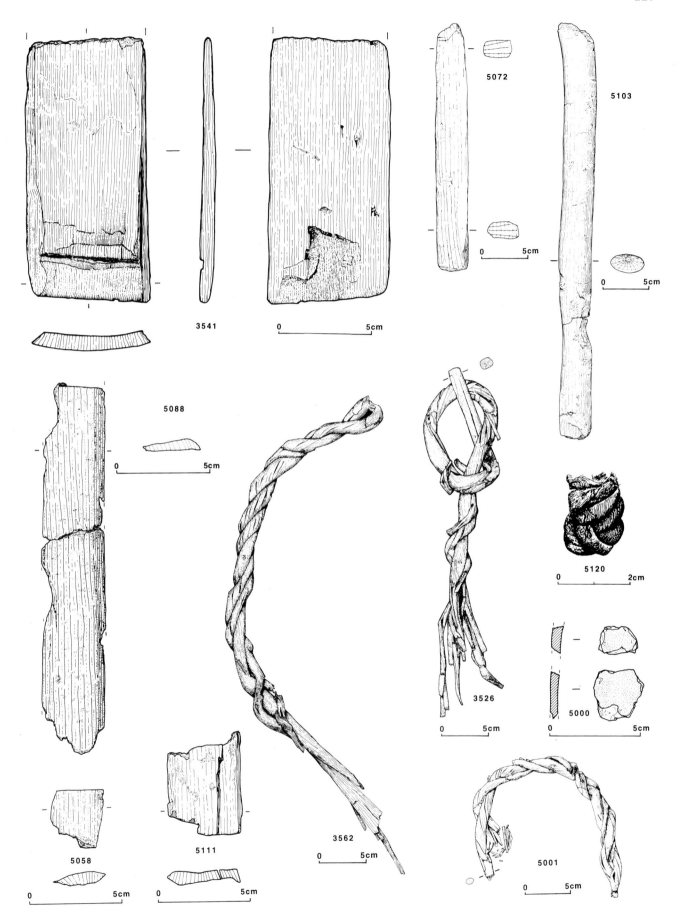

Figure 8.12 Goldcliff West: Worked wood, withy ties, cord (5120) and pot sherd (5000) from the palaeochannel around Building 6. Scale 1:2 (3541, 5088, 5111 and 5058). Scale 1:4 (others). Drawings by S J Allen, except 5120 by H Mason

Possible tool handles

5072 Probable tool handle of oak from peaty clay at palaeochannel edge (1320). Radially split, length 259mm, section roughly rectangular 34mm × 20mm. One end was cut, the other broken so the original length is unknown. Near the complete end was a slightly worn or smoothed area producing a more oval section, which strengthens the impression that this was a tool handle.

5103 Possible tool handle of elm from clay with peat (1320). This piece of roundwood, lacking bark, possible cut at one end, broken at the other. Length 442mm, diameter 35mm, slightly curved with traces of possible toolmarks along its length.

Neither of the possible tool handles can be conclusively proved to have performed such a function. The oak piece is the more likely, because the radial section was commonly used for axe handles up to the present day. Handles of similar form occur at Glastonbury on objects such as billhooks, adzes, gouges, etc (Bulleid and Gray 1917, plate LX). Roundwood handles are known from prehistory, but elm was rarely chosen in contrast to oak which was commonly selected.

Woodworking debris

A total of 26 pieces of wood could, with confidence, be assigned as debris from woodworking, many other fragments were possibly of similar origin. Of these pieces, nineteen were from the palaeochannel fill and eight from the peat between the channel and the building. For additional wood see CD 8.10–11.

Withy ties (Fig 8.12)

5001 A curved withy of hazel, with one fragment of willow. Exposed in 1992 by erosion on the clay surface of the palaeochannel (1303). Made by twisting together three withies of diameters 11mm, 9mm, and 5mm to form a rope of diameter 20mm, formed into a curved shape 145mm across the arc. Bark present on one strand only, both ends eroded.

3562 Withy loop of hazel from clay with peat laminations (1303). It is 617mm long made by bending a single withy, 12mm thick, double to create an oval loop 13mm × 5mm, and then twisting the two strands together. A third strand of diameter 6mm was present 130mm from the looped end, so the withy rope created was originally 3-ply, and 22mm thick; patchy bark remained.

3526 Knotted hazel withy tie from clay fill of the palaeochannel (1303). It is 370mm long with a knot of diameter 85mm. A cut end is neatly trimmed by a single diagonal cut. The main piece of roundwood from which it was made was left in the round and was 15mm in diameter; twisted round this are two pieces of diameters 12mm and 7mm. All retain some bark. Knot end is in good condition, the other end frayed and eroded.

In addition to those illustrated, there were fragmentary examples of six less well preserved withy ties (CD 8.10 and 8.12), of which four have been identified as hazel and two are not identified. All were from the clay channel fill (1303). One piece (5108) was bent round to form a loop and the two strands twisted together; a small, poorly preserved version of 3562.

These withies were made by taking a straight length of hazel averaging 9mm in diameter, probably from a coppice. This was twisted to separate the fibres and make the wood flexible. Hazel is one of the woods traditionally used for withies (Wright 1990, 65), although in recent times on the Severn Levels willow osiers were generally used for this purpose (Upton personal communication), as described more generally by Edlin (1970, 204). In most cases, the withy was twisted with two or three other pieces to create a withy rope which, in three cases, have looped ends. Withies were used in prehistory for many purposes which involved joining things: in the Neolithic tying hurdles at Walton Heath track (Coles and Coles 1986, plate 42); in the Bronze Age at Wilsford Shaft they may have formed the binding for buckets (Ashbee *et al* 1989, 67), and at Ferriby they joined the planks of a sewn boat (Wright 1990, 65). It is also likely that they formed components of fish traps and we report an example in Chapter 16 near probable fishing structures at Peterstone. Fragments were found at Caldicot (Nayling and Caseldine 1997, 215) and Glastonbury (Bulleid and Gray 1911, fig 115). At Goldcliff a withy such as 3562 could have been part of the handle or binding of a bucket but it is likely that many of them joined structural components of the building, perhaps tying rafters to the wall plate or purlins to the rafters (Fig 9.2).

Cord (Fig 8.12)

5120 Tightly knotted cord from peaty clay (1320) on channel surface. It was 23mm × 15mm and the individual strands are 4mm in diameter. It is formed of very fine fibres which have not yet been identified, and the cord as a whole is fine, more like string than the Bronze Age cord from Wilsford Shaft (Ashbee *et al* 1989, 62), or the Neolithic grass rope from the Sweet Track (Coles *et al* 1973, 288). Cord would have served many purposes, including nets for fishing which would have had many such knots. The find, though tiny, emphasises the Estuary's potential for the discovery of nets, textiles etc which are known from the Alpine 'lake villages' (eg Schlichtherle 1990, 124) and Denmark.

8.8 Animal footprints

Evidence of animal footprints was extensive in the peat at the edge of the channel (Fig 8.4), and north of this at the junction between the peat and the overlying blanket of upper Wentlooge clay (Fig 8.2).

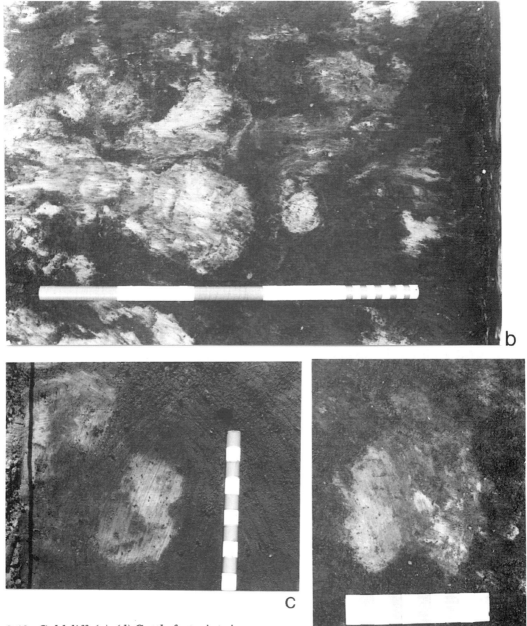

*Figure 8.13 Goldcliff: (a)–(d) Cattle footprints in
Trenches 73 and 81 in the palaeochannel beside Building
6. Photographs by (a) M Bell, (b)–(d) L Boulton*

In some channel sections, such as the north side of Trenches 18 and 73, these appeared as small involution features (Fig 8.10). Excavation of the north end of Trench 73 revealed that the interface between clay and peat was covered with a very clear mottled pattern of clay-filled circular to oval depressions in the peat. Trench 81 was excavated in 1995 to further record this pattern (Fig 8.13). Many were complex shapes created by superimposition and the way the animal had inserted its foot. Recurring features were a distinct curving edge and, opposite this, evidence that the foot was dragged forward (Fig 8.13b). As some of the clearer examples were excavated, the oval patches resolved themselves, firstly, into an indented, heart-shaped oval and then two kidney-shaped ovals. Examples which were excavated were between 70mm and 110mm long and 60mm and 95mm wide. These observations are consistent with cattle footprints (Lawrence and Brown 1967, 130). As Figure 8.13 shows, animals of a range of sizes, and presumably ages, were present. Some of the less distinct footprints might have been sheep or horse, but there was no certain evidence of any species other than cattle, the presence of which is confirmed by the cattle head biting lice present in the palaeochannel (Chapters 14–15). There was also evidence of animal footprints in the exposed clay on the surface of the palaeochannel and, although more eroded, they had similar dimensions and character. Thus, the evidence implies that cattle were present throughout the period when the palaeochannel sediments were accumulating, including the early stages in the deposition of the overlying blanket of upper Wentlooge clay. Cattle footprints are also extensive in a similar context 130m west of the Mesolithic site and many other places within the area of the intertidal survey (Chapter 16). These footprints add to the body of footprint evidence from a range of Holocene contexts within the Severn reviewed by Allen (1997a). Those at Goldcliff would repay more detailed study than was possible in this project. They could provide evidence for a wider range of species, and metrical analysis would contribute to an understanding of the range of ages present within the herd and the size of animals in prehistory.

8.9 Stratigraphic sequence and environmental context

The stratigraphic sequence was investigated by nine auger holes in an east–west line across the building (CD 8.6). This demonstrated that there was no evidence of the Bronze Age marine incursion found east of Goldcliff Pill; the building was on a thick raised bog which formed part of an underlying sequence discussed in Chapter 3. The upper 1.7m of the sequence was investigated by environmental sampling Pit 79 (Fig 8.4). The peat was 1.27m deep, with wood in its lower 0.35m and predominantly raised bog peat above. Sequences of samples were taken for pollen/macrofossils and beetles. These

samples provide an outline environmental sequence for Goldcliff West but this was not subject to analysis at very close intervals because, as radiocarbon dating showed, the top of the peat hummock in Pit 79 is dated 2760 ± 70 BP (SWAN-31), significantly predating Building 6.

The part of the environmental sequence which is missing on top of the peat hummock is, however, preserved in the peat sequence at the palaeochannel edge, where there are two radiocarbon dates (Fig 8.10) of 2460 ± 35 BP (GrN-24140) and 2260 ± 50 BP (GrN-24141), which show that peat formation continued up to the time of the building. The locations of environmental samples for pollen, macrofossils, beetles and micromorphology are shown on sections of the palaeochannels (Figs 8.10 and 8.11) and discussed in Chapters 13–15. The pollen and macrofossil evidence from Monolith 10128 demonstrates that the raised bog was being encroached on by taxa indicative of saltmarsh habitats. There is the clay band, suggestive of marine flooding, in Trench 78 associated with increasing grass and chenopod values. Clay laminations occur within the upper part of the peat and it is within this that woodworking debris and the scatter of semi-articulated bovid bones occurs on the edge of the peat hummock in Trenches 74, 78 and 80. This suggests that construction and use of Building 6 occurred during the final stages in the life of the peat bog at a time when its margins were already subject to periodic deposition of marine clay. Thus, the environmental scenario is similar to that in the better preserved sequence from Buildings 1 and 2. Periodic inundation with some erosion may explain the stratigraphic reversal of the two radiocarbon dates from the hummock edge (Fig 8.10).

We can envisage that after millennia of peat development there existed a topography of hummocks and depressions on the peat surface similar to that at Building 8 and elsewhere at Goldcliff West. Building 6 was apparently constructed on a low hummock surrounded by a natural palaeochannel. Although the incised channel could have originated as a humanly cut drainage feature, there was no evidence that this was the case. Surviving edges were manifestly the products of erosion; the section of Trench 74 was so undercut that it could not have been produced by hand digging.

The evidence indicates that during the early stages of this marine incursion, the encircling depression round the Building 6 hummock began to be incised, probably through headward erosion of a gully. Whether the palaeochannel sediment sequence as a whole relates to the period of building use, or artefacts have been eroded into it later, is not certain. The only potsherd from the site is from the clay channel fill, and for this sherd John Allen suggests a date in the 1st century BC. It is possible, therefore, that the channel fill is a couple of centuries later than the buildings, which produced no pottery. In common with the other Goldcliff structures, Building 6 was not demolished and the timber reused. It was left to decay. Presumably the uprights rotted, broke off and were washed away by the sea, and what ended up in the palaeochannel was only a small part of the original structure.

Botanical and beetle analyses confirmed that the palaeochannel fill was associated with saltmarsh conditions. The fill does contain biota which appear to indicate activity by people and animals in and around the buildings, notably the presence of synanthropic beetles, some indicative of stabling manure. Human fleas and cattle head biting lice hint that the building may have housed both animals and people. It is possible that this evidence was eroded into the channel from occupation horizons on its edge. The many cattle footprints demonstrate the presence of grazing animals during both the early and late phases of palaeochannel sedimentation.

8.10 Building 7

This was 38m southwest of Building 6 on a peat hummock 13.5m × 11m (Fig 8.14, CD 8.7), the seaward edge of which is the eroded edge of the peat shelf. The other three sides are formed by an encircling depression which was part of a wider net-like pattern. On the only occasion when the floor of the depression on the east side was clear of mud, an irregular surface was observed, marked by probable animal footprints. During the cleaning of the peat surface, it was noted that there were clumps of cotton grass, and natural wood fragments were very few. It seemed likely, therefore, that the building had been constructed on the surface of raised bog.

On the southern side of the hummock, erosion has begun to eat into its surface and there are shallow bowl-shaped scars where lenses of peat have been lifted off. In the same area is a hole 0.9m square and 0.65m deep, the sides of which carry the tell-tale fork marks of the bait digger. Erosion appears to have affected about a third of the floor area on the southeast corner of the building, accounting for the fact that there is just one post in that corner. In the northeast corner one small vertical had been eroded between original planning in 1992 and replanning in 1994. There is little doubt that significant parts of the original structure have been lost by erosion prior to its discovery.

The building is rectangular (4.8m × 4.2m) with wall lines marked by thirteen irregularly spaced uprights, of which roughly half were identified in the field as roundwood and half radial splits. Apart from these verticals there is no more precise evidence of the method of wall construction. What makes this convincing as a building is the presence of two substantial axial posts with associated surrounding smaller posts, probably roof supports, similar to the other buildings. The western axial post (7183) was the only wood from this building excavated; it was roundwood of diameter 160mm and surviving length 0.7m. With it were two smaller pieces of roundwood and a piece of split oak. Post 7183 is radiocarbon dated 2380 ± 70 BP (SWAN-27) which means that

this structure is apparently earlier than the other radiocarbon dated structures. The east axial post (7188) is a piece of roundwood of diameter 180mm. Adjacent to this were two pieces of alder roundwood and two pieces of split oak. Some of the smaller timbers associated with the axial posts may be packing, but others were a little distance away and might relate to subdivisions of the building, particularly a split oak east of 7188. Although only one axial post was lifted, each piece of wood has been identified, as reported in Chapter 12.

There is no surviving flooring and, if we are correct in inferring that it was a roofed building of comparable type to the others recorded, then it is likely to have undergone significant erosion. No entrance could be identified, although the orientation of Trackway 1330 (Chapter 10), which crosses the encircling depression, indicates that it might have lain near the northeast corner. A peg and a piece of split wood on the hummock, but on the same line as the brushwood trackway, indicate that it may originally have continued closer to the building.

Building 7 is squarer in plan and smaller than the other buildings. Apart from the structural posts, no artefacts were found, but investigation was largely limited to cleaning and planning. Since there has been little excavation, the only information on the stratigraphic context of this building comes from the cleaning of the sides of the bait digger's pit. The sequence was interpreted as raised bog peat, with very occasional small twigs to 0.6m and, below this, more wood. Some 40m to the south erosion has exposed this lower level within the peat sequence and there are tree stumps on this surface, but none have been identified in this area.

8.11 Building 8

This lies 190m west of the previously described structures. It occupied the largest of the peat hummocks, a raised subrectangular area 15m × 15m, surrounded by encircling depressions (Figs 8.15–8.17). The depression floors were covered in animal hoof prints. The building stood on the southern end of the hummock and was rectangular (7.6m × 5.7m).

Due to the many discoveries made in the last week of August 1992, there was only the opportunity for Taylor-Wilson and a Dublin team of wetland archaeologists to spend just two low tides recording Building 8 and the surrounding palaeochannels. It is fortunate that this was done because, in the event, it is the only record for much of this site.

The building gave the impression of being truncated by erosion. There was no evidence of any flooring level, the posts were somewhat irregularly spaced and some were only small points. The building was delimited by 37 pieces of wood. They include at least five pieces of roundwood of between 80mm and 120mm diameter. Some 21 of the pieces appear to be split timbers, and others were so small

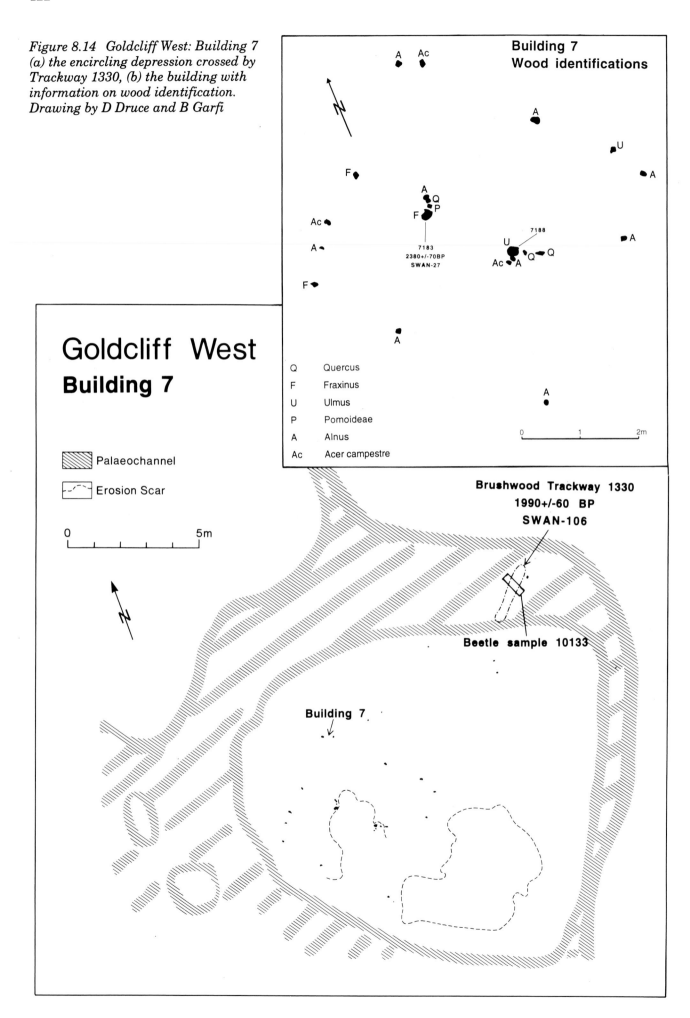

Figure 8.14 Goldcliff West: Building 7 (a) the encircling depression crossed by Trackway 1330, (b) the building with information on wood identification. Drawing by D Druce and B Garfi

Building 7
Wood identifications

Q	Quercus
F	Fraxinus
U	Ulmus
P	Pomoideae
A	Alnus
Ac	Acer campestre

7183
2380+/-70BP
SWAN-27

7188

Goldcliff West
Building 7

Palaeochannel

Erosion Scar

0   5m

Brushwood Trackway 1330
1990+/-60 BP
SWAN-106

Beetle sample 10133

Building 7

Figure 8.15 Goldcliff West: Building 8 on a peat hummock surrounded by an encircling depression, the irregular floor of which is marked by animal footprints. Photograph by E Yorath

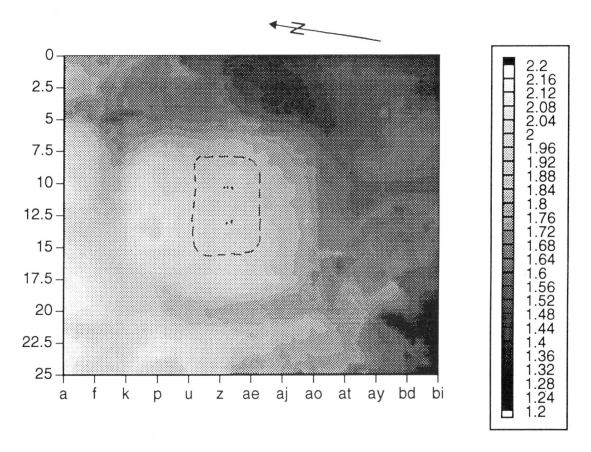

Figure 8.16 Goldcliff West: Building 8 contour plan of the peat hummock and the surrounding encircling depression, the darker shades are lower. Drawing by G Longden

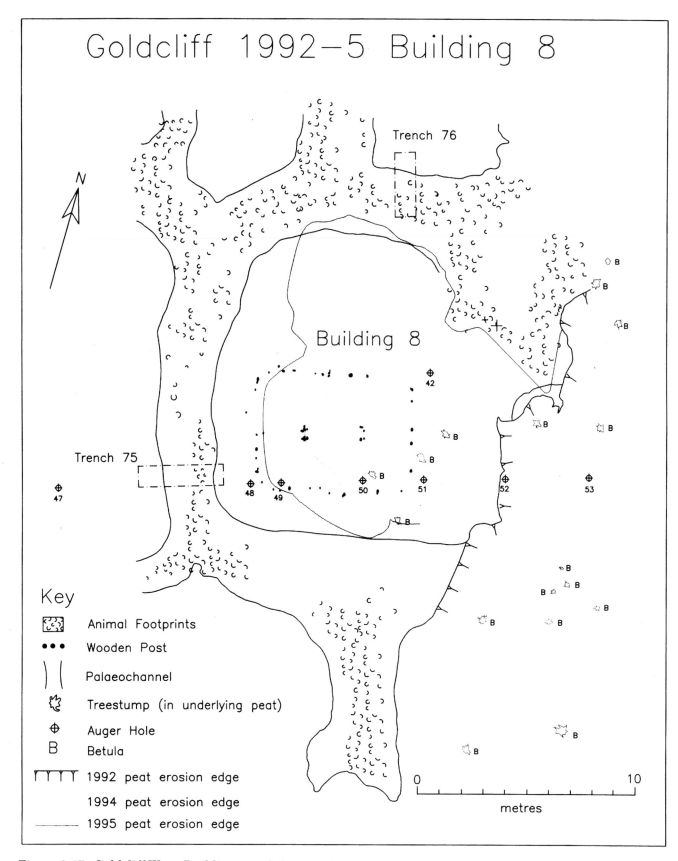

Goldcliff 1992–5 Building 8

N

Trench 76

Building 8

Trench 75

47

48 49

50

51

52

53

42

Key

⬚ Animal Footprints

••• Wooden Post

)(Palaeochannel

🍂 Treestump (in underlying peat)

⊕ Auger Hole

B Betula

⊤⊤⊤⊤ 1992 peat erosion edge

1994 peat erosion edge

········· 1995 peat erosion edge

0   10

metres

Figure 8.17   Goldcliff West: Building 8 and the encircling depression, showing the encroachment of erosion from 1992–94. Drawing by R Taylor-Wilson and B Taylor

or eroded on the surface that their original form is not clear. The general impression is that the building may have been similar to Building 6, a combination of roundwood verticals with split timber planking between. Two pieces of evidence do, however, hint that the original building could have been somewhat different. A few of the posts seem to be paired, and it was recorded in 1992 that some consisted of roundwood circles with a 90° segment removed. Such arrangement could have been designed to hold in place planking, either vertical or horizontal. There was no evidence of such an arrangement in the better preserved Building 6.

Along the north and east walls of the building there was a crack in the surface of the peat which picked out the line of the wall. This is regarded as a post-depositional phenomenon seen in other structures. The crack continues even where the surviving posts are widely spaced, and abrupt changes of direction in the crack are likely to mark the positions of posts at a higher level, which have been eroded away. Similarly, five holes in the peat surface along the line of the north wall probably mark the positions of lost posts. There is no clear indication of an entrance, but at the east end two roundwood posts are symmetrically placed 0.6m apart in the middle of the wall in a similar relationship to the entrance to Buildings 1 and 2. Outside the opposite, west, wall a single oblique post was 0.5m west of the west wall line; it might have had something to do with entrance arrangements.

What makes the small, rather irregularly spaced wall posts more convincing as the remains of a roofed structure are posts down the long axis, which are likely to have supported a roof ridge. Symmetrically positioned down the long axis were two pairs of post

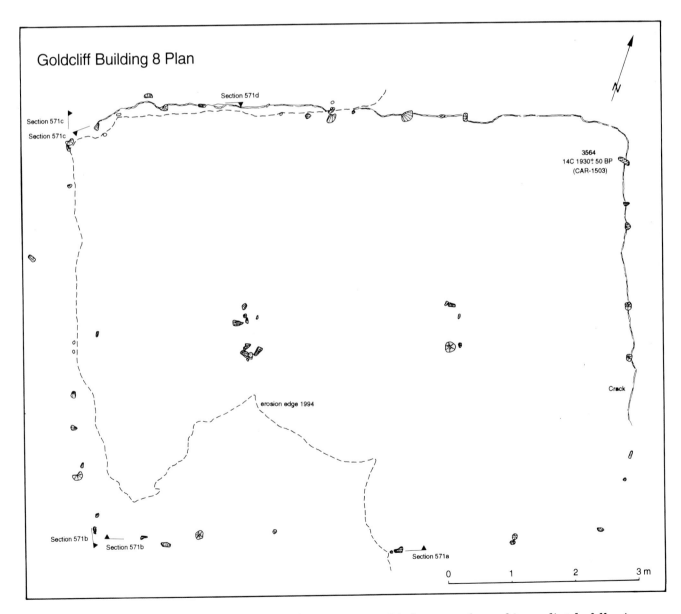

Figure 8.18 Goldcliff West: Building 8 plan. The eastern two thirds are as planned immediately following discovery in 1992. The western third is as excavated in 1994, by which time the remainder of the structure had been lost by erosion. Drawing by R Taylor-Wilson and S J Allen

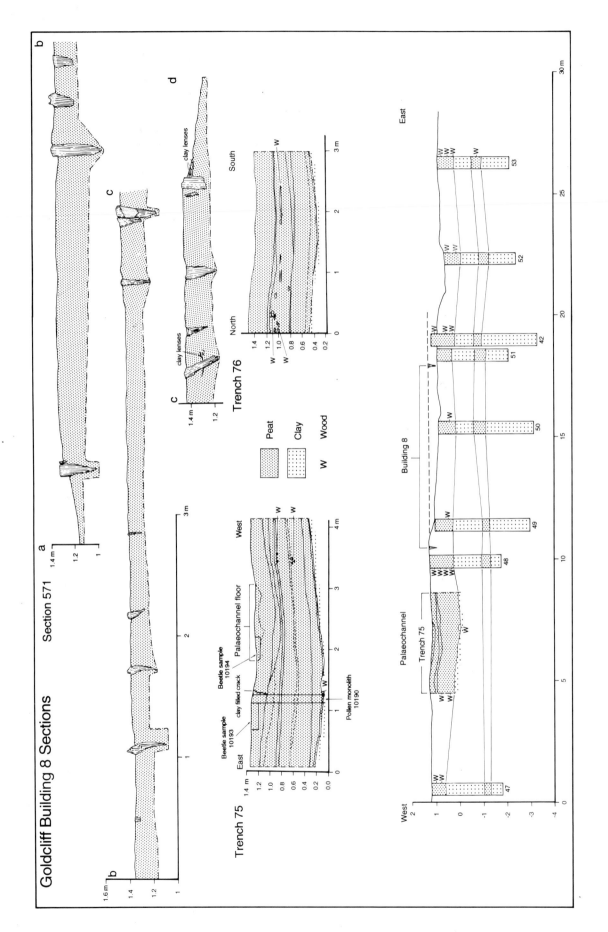

Figure 8.19 Goldcliff West: Sections of Building 8 and the encircling depressions. Drawing by S J Allen

groupings, each 0.3–0.4m apart. Only one had a roundwood vertical 0.14m in diameter. Each had a group of other pieces of split timber like that which formed packing round the axial posts in Buildings 1 and 2. These four groupings are, therefore, interpreted as the remnants of eroded axial posts. Why both are paired is not clear; perhaps this larger building required a more elaborate arrangement of axial posts.

In 1993, a detailed contour survey was done to show the relationship between the building and the encircling depressions (Fig 8.17). The opportunity was also taken to lift a post (3564) at the northeast corner; this was submitted for radiocarbon dating with the result 1930 ± 50 BP (CAR-1503), suggesting that the building could be two to three centuries later than Buildings 1–6.

During the final season of excavation in 1994, the intention was to make a more detailed plan of the building and to remove a small sample of each piece of wood for identification. It was not proposed to excavate the building as a whole because it was regarded as being less vulnerable to erosion than the other structures. Events proved otherwise. In early July 1994, Upton observed that about one third of the building had been eroded away. By the time the excavation season began on 5 August 1994, of the originally recorded structure, about half the original wall line remained. The east end and most of the interior of the building had been cut into by the lifting off of great plates of peat. About half of the original hummock had been obliterated; so altered was the scene that it was difficult to recognise it as the same site.

Plans had, accordingly, to be rethought and it was decided to excavate the eighteen pieces of wood which remained at the west end (Fig 8.18, CD 8.8–8.9). Because erosion had cut into the interior of the building, the method employed was to excavate the peat in the interior, exposing the wall posts in section. The sections highlight the big differences in the size of posts and their spacing, strengthening the view that we are dealing with a rather eroded building. The excavated posts confirmed the building comprised both roundwood and vertical planking. Apart from the structural wood, finds were very few: one bone in the encircling depression 7.6m north of the building and three small pieces of worked wood in the western encircling depression. This contrasted with the concentration of material in the Building 6 palaeochannel, although that was more intensively excavated.

The building sat on a hummock surrounded by encircling depressions as shown by Figure 8.17. The floors of these depressions were covered in irregularities, of which the most well preserved were cattle footprints. The areas in which these occurred are shown by the convention of a C-shaped symbol. The abundance of footprints on the depression floors, and their absence from the hummocks, is interesting. One possibility is that, at the time of formation, the channels were much wetter and, thus, animals made an impression here, but not elsewhere. There is certainly no evidence that animal movement was restricted to the depressions by fences etc. A more probable explanation would seem to be that the tops of the hummock have been planed off by oxidation, erosion etc; this would also account for the apparent truncation of the building itself. The clearest impression of the form of the topography is obtained from the contour survey (Fig 8.16). The lighter areas represent the higher peat hummock, the medium greys the encircling depressions and dark grey–black the areas to the south and southeast which at that time represented the edges of peat erosion.

To further investigate the character of the encircling depressions, two trenches were cut across them in 1994 (Figs 8.17–8.19). Trench 75 was west of Building 8, at right angles to the channel. The section revealed that the floor of the depression contained c 0.14 m of mixed peat and clay, probably cattle trample. The underlying peat was 1.1m thick. The upper 0.4m of this sequence, which appeared to be of raised bog peat, had layers within the peat which dipped along the line of the channel. This was taken to indicate that the topography of the depression was an inherited feature from the time of the raised bog, or earlier. In the lower part of the peat sequence were occasional wood layers, of which the upper may have corresponded to a horizon of small birch stumps revealed when erosion pealed off the raised bog to the southeast (Fig 8.17). At the base of the peat sequence in Trench 75 were two substantial tree trucks of ash and alder. Blue clay underlaid this and on its surface there was a depression about 1m wide. So far as could be established from the trench, the orientation of the depression was oblique to the line of the later depression.

Trench 76 was cut across at right angles to the depression north of Building 8. The section revealed a sequence comparable with Trench 75. Here there was no indication of mixing of clay on the channel floor. There were hints that lower layers within the peat dipped along the line of the channel, and that surface of the underlying blue clay had a shallow depression, although, once again, this did not appear to be on the same alignment as the later depression.

The shaded contour survey suggests that the plan of the encircling depression was rectilinear and that Building 8 sat squarely on the hummock; features which might suggest a ditch. However, the two trenches showed no evidence of a cut feature, whether natural or of human origin. Instead, they indicated that the hummock and encircling depression topography was inherited from an earlier stage in the life of the raised bog. Thus, the evidence suggests opportunistic use of natural topography rather than alteration of the surface to create a suitable context for a building. The sedimentary setting of Building 8 has been discussed in Chapter 3 and was further investigated by a transect of eight auger holes which crossed the hummock from west to east along the line of Trench 75 and the south wall of the building (Fig 8.19). This showed that the underlying sedimentary sequence was similar to that at Building 6.

9 Rectangular buildings of the later 1st millennium BC at Goldcliff: dating, character, and reconstruction *by S J Allen and M Bell*

9.1 Buildings: general discussion
Martin Bell

In all, eight rectangular structures have been identified at Goldcliff. There is a good case that most represent roofed buildings. Buildings 1–3 have evidence of interior flooring while, 1, 2, and 6–8 have axial posts which are highly likely to be roof supports. In Building 4, the area which would have contained axials had been eroded and no definite axials were found in Buildings 3 and 5. Structure 5 is the most tenuous; it could represent either an unroofed pen, or a building from which many of the main structural elements have been removed. Comparison between the buildings needs to take account of the fact that they have been subject to varying degrees of erosion. Buildings 1 and 3 were well preserved; Building 7 particularly badly eroded. Building plans are very similar, rectangular with rounded corners. Entrances are clearly defined in Buildings 1 and 2 and more doubtful examples have been identified in Buildings 3, 4, 6, and 8. All, except perhaps Building 3, are in the middle of a shorter end wall. Despite a similarity of plan, there are striking differences in the method of construction: roundwood verticals with wattlework in Building 1, roundwood verticals in Buildings 2, 3, 5, and 7, a mixture of roundwood and split timber in Building 4, and mainly split timber in Buildings 6 and 8. The two latter buildings are on the raised bog at Goldcliff West and are constructed of a contrasting range of wood types, probably from a dryland source. It is puzzling that such a repertoire of constructional techniques should be used in buildings of similar form, which are not widely separated in terms of date.

9.2 Dating of rectangular buildings at Goldcliff
Martin Bell

The precision of radiocarbon dating in the Iron Age is limited by a very marked plateau in the calibration curve at c 2450 radiocarbon years BP, a problem exacerbated by a later wiggle in the curve around 2200 radiocarbon years BP, which corresponds to the main concentration of dates at Goldcliff (Cunliffe 1991, 591, Stuiver and Becker 1993, 2E–F). Full details of the radiocarbon dates are given in Appendix II. The calibrated date ranges of the Goldcliff buildings are shown on Figure 9.1. This has been prepared using the calibration curve of Stuiver and Kra (1986) and the OxCal computer programme v2.8. It can be seen that Buildings 1–6 have closely comparable, but wide, ranges in the period between 100 and 400 Cal BC. It was argued in Chapter 7 that Structure 5 must have predated Building 1, but both have similar calibrated ranges so the time difference is unlikely to be great. Fortunately, three of these buildings have the additional precision of dendrochronological dates which are fully discussed in Chapter 11. The dendrochronological dates are marked by arrows on Figure 9.1. Most precisely dated is Building 6 which was largely made of oak planks cut in Spring 273 BC with some wood, possibly repairs, cut in 271 BC. These are dates which fall within the two standard deviation calibrated ranges. For Building 1, the three radiocarbon dates together cover a wide spread, but the dendrochronological dates show that the building was constructed after 382 BC, and possibly before 342 BC. Thus, the building relates to the earlier end of the calibrated range for the structure. Building 2 has radiocarbon dates with very similar calibrated ranges, but the dendrochronological date showing construction after 454 BC is about 50 years earlier than the two standard deviation calibrated ranges. Given that the timber lacked sapwood, this might be because it came from the inner part of a larger tree. Thus, whilst the calibrated date ranges of Buildings 1–6 cover much of the Iron Age between about 100 and 400 Cal BC, those for which we have closer dendrochronological dates are tied down more closely to the period between 464 and 271 calendar years BC.

Building 7 has the main probability of its, very wide, date range earlier than that of the other buildings between 800 and 400 Cal BC. Building 8 has a calibrated range between 50 Cal BC and 220 Cal AD and is younger than the two standard deviation ranges of most of the other dates. The implication of this is that rectangular buildings may have continued to be constructed until the end of the Iron Age, or even into the Romano-British period. That, in turn, gives us a surprisingly late date for the inundation of the middle Wentlooge peat at the extreme west of the site. We should not forget, however, that this rests on just one date from Building 8. The Goldcliff West building and trackway dates (Figs 9.1 and 10.21) span the whole of the Iron Age and the beginning of the Roman period, a surprising result given the presence of Trackway 1330 between Buildings 7 and 6 and Trackway 1311

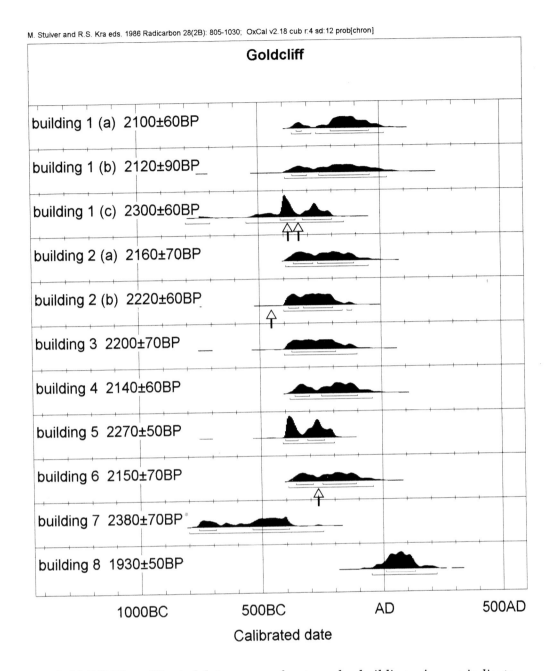

M. Stuiver and R.S. Kra eds. 1986 Radiocarbon 28(2B): 805-1030; OxCal v2.18 cub r:4 sd:12 prob[chron]

Goldcliff

building 1 (a) 2100±60BP

building 1 (b) 2120±90BP

building 1 (c) 2300±60BP

building 2 (a) 2160±70BP

building 2 (b) 2220±60BP

building 3 2200±70BP

building 4 2140±60BP

building 5 2270±50BP

building 6 2150±70BP

building 7 2380±70BP

building 8 1930±50BP

1000BC   500BC   AD   500AD

Calibrated date

Figure 9.1 Goldcliff: The calibrated date ranges of rectangular buildings. Arrows indicate dendrochronological dates for the same structures (see discussion in text). For comparison with trackway dates see Figure 10.21

between Buildings 6 and 8, which were thought to suggest that the three buildings were contemporary. In fact, dating evidence for the trackways reviewed in Chapter 10, and shown in calibrated form on Figure 10.21, confirms the impression from the calibrated building date ranges that activity at Goldcliff West may have extended over a period of centuries, far longer than had been anticipated on the basis of the rather ephemeral field evidence.

As regards the duration of activity in relation to individual buildings, there are marked contrasts. Building 6 seems to have been constructed and repaired over a two year period (273–271 BC), although it could obviously have remained in use for longer. Buildings 3, 4, and 8 showed no evidence of repair, or multiple phases of activity for which there

was much evidence in and around Buildings 1 and 2. Here we have the apparently earlier Structure 5, evidence of replacement of axial and wall post and stratigraphic evidence from around these structures that a number of phases of activity and wood deposition were separated by phases of estuarine flooding and peat growth. There was no comparable cultural stratigraphy in any other part of the site.

9.3 Comparanda for the rectangular buildings
Martin Bell

The Iron Age rectangular buildings at Goldcliff contrast with the roundhouses which overwhelm-

130

ingly dominate the buildings of the Bronze and Iron Ages in both Wales and England. The only close comparisons are with the Bronze Age buildings found 6.4km to the east at Redwick and discussed in Chapter 16. The uniqueness of these two sites raises questions about the origins and character of this structural form.

Structures of rectangular shape, although not of comparable plan, are present in Neolithic England and Wales as, for instance, at Clegyr Boia, Pembrokeshire and Mount Pleasant, Glamorgan (Savory 1980a, fig 5.5). There are a few long rectangular structures in Bronze Age and Iron Age contexts at Down Farm, Cranbourne Chase (Barrett et al 1991 who note other examples), and one of probable Bronze Age date at Barley Croft Farm, Cambridgeshire (Evans and Knight 1996). Square buildings have been claimed in the Marches hillforts, such as Croft Ambrey (Stanford 1974, 123), but most are small four posters, probably granaries. Rectangular buildings have also been hypothesised on the basis of reused wood at Flag Fen (Pryor 1991, fig 81) and there is some evidence of small rectangular structures at Glastonbury; the most complete is 3.5m × 3.3m. However, a recent analysis by Coles and Minnitt (1995) rejects previous ideas that they reflect a rectangular phase predating the roundhouses. A rectangular structure is reported from a wetland crannog context at Barnston in Yorkshire (van de Noort and Davis 1993, 59, Varley 1968). Rectangular structures occur in the Iron Age hillfort/enclosed sites at Danebury (in one case with plank walls (Cunliffe 1993, 71)), South Cadbury (Alcock 1972), and Heathrow (Grimes and Close-Brookes 1993, 312), but each of these is interpreted as a specialised shrine. Woodward (1992) notes that thirteen out of seventeen Iron Age shrines are rectangular. Geographically, the closest examples of prehistoric rectangular structures are within the Crickley Hillfort (Dixon 1994, plate C24) on the Gloucestershire side of the Upper Severn Estuary where a late Bronze Age/early Iron Age phase with rectangular buildings is succeeded by a roundhouse phase, suggesting successive building traditions. The form of the Crickley structures, based on two parallel rows of large posts represents an aisled structure, unlike those in the estuary. At Whitton, 11km west of the estuary in Wales, a late Iron Age and early Romano-British enclosed settlement, mainly of roundhouses, has two structures 7.5m square, delimited by wall trenches which held substantial vertical timbers (Jarrett and Wrathmell 1981, fig 37). They are the closest parallels in plan and building technique to those at Goldcliff 35 km away. It is also interesting that the rectangular buildings at Whitton lacked hearths. The Whitton structures are dated to the Roman phase, and the wall trenches contained individual illustrated sherds of Roman date. Jarrett and Wrathmell (1981) saw them as representing a transitional form from the roundhouses of the Iron Age to the rectangular buildings of the 2nd century Romano-British farmstead.

Rectangular buildings are found extensively on the continent in the Bronze and Iron Ages (eg Horn and Born 1977, 43, Audouze and Büchsenschütz 1991, 56, Louwe Kooijmans 1993, fig 6.10). The continental buildings are, on the whole, longer and mostly of aisled form, but there are examples similar to those in the estuary (eg Waterbolk 1995, 8). Many continental buildings accommodated people at one end and animals at the other. Well-preserved animal stalls are found, as in Goldcliff Building 1, with hints of similar subdivisions in other rectangular structures at Goldcliff and Redwick (Chapter 16). The longhouse accommodating people and animals was the traditional vernacular house form of medieval Wales. It is generally assumed that the rectangular plan derives from Roman influence, but these examples from the estuary, together perhaps with the Witton evidence, may point to earlier origins.

9.4 Reconstruction of rectangular Buildings 6 and 1
Steven Allen

General assumptions and the reconstruction of Building 6

With any reconstruction, certain assumptions are necessary, especially where a building survives only as a ground plan. The primary assumptions made in preparation of the reconstruction drawings are:

(i) Since contemporary floor levels of Building 6 are missing, it is assumed that the surviving wood in the peat reflects the form of the above ground structure. Since the loss of peat cover cannot now be precisely determined, the drawings are based on the surviving plan, as if that were the contemporary ground level;

(ii) The presence of axial post settings indicates that this structure was a roofed building rather than an open stockade.

Accepting (i) and (ii), secondary assumptions can be made. These are:

(iii) The height of the walls is not known, so a sufficient internal clearance is allowed at the meeting of wall and roof structure for human occupants. An arbitrary wall height of 1.5m has been shown for the smaller Building 6, and a height of 1.2m for the larger Building 1;

(iv) The roof pitch allowed is sufficient for rainwater to run off without soaking into the roofing material; 45° is normally considered the minimum for thatch. With a building of this form, the pitch of any roof will be at its steepest when measured from the axial post at right angles to the axis of the building. That same pitch will, however, be reduced when measured from the axial post to the corner of the building. The solution assumed here is to take the roof pitch

31

as measured from the head of the axial post to the corner of the building, and make that pitch the minimum of 45°. Knowing the plan distance from the axial post to the corner of the building, the specified wall height, and the required roof pitch, we can suggest the height of the axial posts of Building 6 was *c* 4.5m, and that for Building 1 was *c* 4.6m;

(v) The joints and timber conversions shown are kept as simple as possible on the understanding that this is almost certainly an underestimate of the skills available, and that a more complex solution might well have been adopted.

It must be stressed at the outset that the only timbers for which dimensions are known are those which were identified during the excavation. The sizes, and indeed the forms, of the timbers shown in the drawings are speculative. We do not know what diameter of poles were used for rafters; whether roundwood poles or squared timbers were employed. Decoration and fittings, though probably present on the original, are omitted, as is any assumption about the precise nature of the activities within. The drawings should, therefore, be seen as minimum solutions to the problem of constructing a building on this plan.

Several visitors to the site have suggested that the buildings were only seasonally occupied, being abandoned each winter. Such a pattern of occupation might not require a substantial roof but only something temporary which might be taken down and put up again the following year. Figure 9.2A is a suggestion of how Building 6 might appear in such form. The walls are the most substantial part of the structure and serve to anchor the edges of a hide canopy used as a temporary roof. This reconstruction suggests that each of the individual timbers in the axial post settings could represent a single season of occupation, with a light post and axial ridge pole used to support a temporary roof. The vertical poles could be cut down at the end of the season, the hide roof folded away and removed, leaving the walls of the structure to stand over winter. A new set of poles and a suitably repaired hide roof might be put up in the following year, with possible repairs to the wall.

One objection to this reconstruction is the relative fragility of the roof cover. Each seam would represent a source of weakness, and it would take a great number of hides to cover this size of building. No fixings for such a cover, to attach it to the roof or walls, have been recovered. The few poles required for this form of roof would not, in themselves, be sufficient to support the vertical poles, and substantial posts would have been needed outside each corner to provide anchors for the necessary guy ropes. No such posts were found.

Increasing the number of rafters to strengthen the roof would require larger individual posts than are present here; increasing the number of rafters and using larger posts would seem to work against the idea of a temporarily covered structure. There is also the question of whether a temporarily occupied structure would really need such substantial walls. If they were used to shelter livestock, a need would arise for more robust walling. If they are viewed as seasonal shelters for humans, these walls are more elaborate than strictly required. Hides hung from the top of a wall plate supported by uprights would appear to be a simpler solution than a continuous wall of timber. Overall, it seems easier to treat the structure as a building with a more permanent timber roof.

Figure 9.2B represents one version of how such a building might have appeared. In this arrangement, the weight of the roof is primarily carried on the walls. The axial wood settings are depicted here as the remains of composite posts, that is a single post made up of a number of separate smaller posts driven into the peat and bound together. These posts support an axial ridge pole. The function of this timber is to add stability to the upper ends of a series of light poles used as rafters. Although a simple tied crossing junction is shown here, it might also be possible for the rafters and/or the ridge pole to be notched or jointed to provide more secure anchoring points.

Dealing with the hipped ends of the roof requires that a horizontal tie is placed between the rafters at each extremity of the side on which the outermost rafters of the ends can be fixed. These, in turn, provide points on which a second horizontal tie can be fastened to support the tops of the remaining rafters of the end of the roof. Such an arrangement provides a near continuous sweep to the roof, with the only changes in pitch being those required by the extension of the roof to cover the corners.

In this arrangement, the axial posts and ridge pole are acting as little more than props for the rafters. They do not support more than a fraction of the weight of the roof. The load is taken, instead, on the walls of the building, which requires a fairly rigid form to the wall. In this case, rigidity is supplied by a squared wall plate. Notches into which the rafters slot are cut into the upper face/outer edge of the timbers. An alternative would be to have the rafters notched to fit over the wall plate, but this would weaken the rafters at the very point where they meet the wall. Again, withy ties might be used to help hold the joint together.

The wall plate is held to the wall by a continuous groove along the lower face of the wall plate. This groove houses the upper ends of the upright timbers, locking them together and distributing the weight of the roof along the entire length of the wall. This method has been used successfully in the reconstruction at Lejre, Denmark of a rectangular building excavated at Oltydsbyen, Denmark, of 2nd century BC date (Ryder 1970).

Although this is perhaps the simplest solution to placing a roof on the excavated building, there are still some problems to be addressed. Firstly, the Oltydsbyen reconstruction, although rectangular, is of an aisled building, with a wider roof span and heavier weight which is supported primarily by aisle

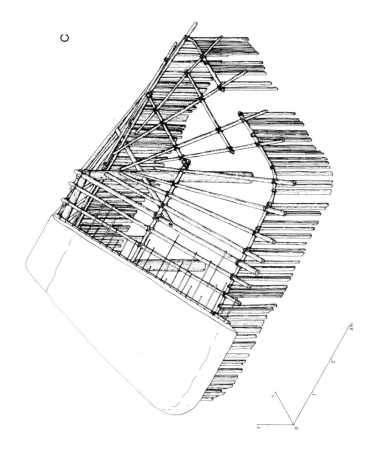

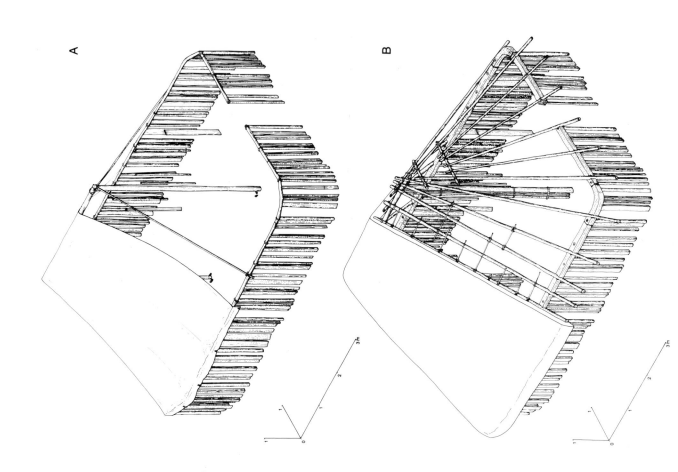

Figure 9.2 Goldcliff: Suggested reconstructions of Building 6, (A) with a hide roof, (B) with a composite axial post and a squared wall plate, (C) large axial posts, a frame of roundwood posts and infill of planks. Drawing by S J Allen

posts and purlins, rather than carried on the walls. The main function of the Lejre wall plate is to tie the tops of the upright split planking of the walls together, not to take the weight of the roof.

A minor objection is that the natural plan for a building with such a wall plate would incorporate sharp, near right angled corners, whilst the corners of Building 6 (and the other Goldcliff buildings) are rounded. A solution to this, as shown in the drawing, would be to assume that those parts of the wall plate fitting over the corners were cut from the junction of a tree trunk with one of the principal branches, much in the way that curved timbers were cut for boat building until recent times (Greenhill and Morrison 1995, 28).

The main problem with the presence of such a wall plate is that it removes any reason for the regularly spaced roundwood uprights in the wall line. With a wall built in this fashion, there is no reason why the wall should not have been made of split upright timber throughout. The drawing indicates a possible function for the uprights by having them pass through holes cut through the wall plate to 'peg' the plate in place on top of the split uprights, but this is hardly essential, and other reasons must be sought for the incorporation of the roundwood uprights.

Figure 9.2C proposes the most plausible reason for the roundwood uprights. In this reconstruction, the roundwood uprights form the vertical elements of a frame, tied at the top by a horizontal wall plate made of roundwood elements. The exact form of the joints between the post and plate are open to speculation (Fig 9.3), the post could be tenoned into a mortise in the plate, the top of the post could be dished or forked to allow the plate to sit on top or, indeed, two roundwood poles could have been used to clasp the top of the roundwood upright. Any version could be further strengthened by withy ties.

This arrangement would form an open frame. The vertically driven split timbers form the infill to this frame. They might also be tied to the wall plate, but this is not essential since the wall is not load bearing. The weight of the roof in this drawing is transferred through the axial posts instead of resting on the top of the wall.

As no individual post stump in the axial settings is large enough to be the main axial post, it is suggested here that the actual axial posts have been lost and that those timbers which do survive are those which wedge the axial post, as in Buildings 1 and 2, or provide a platform on which a shallow set post could rest.

If this is correct, then the following roof arrangement can be suggested (Figs 9.2 and 9.3). The axial posts support a more substantial ridge pole which provides a firmer seating for the rafters. A principal rafter is carried from the end of the ridge pole at right angles to the axis of the building to rest on the wall plate. A horizontal brace is taken from the axial post to the principal rafter halfway along the slope height of the roof. A further horizontal timber or purlin is fastened between the two principal rafters on the same side. This purlin is carried beyond the principal rafters towards each end of the building and linked

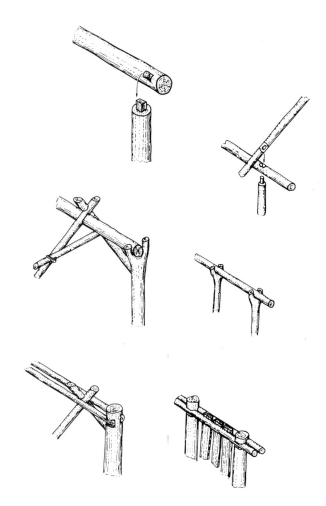

Figure 9.3   Goldcliff: (left) alternative arrangements of axial post-ridge pole-rafters, (right) alternative forms of wall plate. Drawing by S J Allen

by another purlin across the end of the roof. The remaining rafters of the roof are tied to the ridge pole, the wall plate, and to the purlin on which they rest.

This arrangement has the rafters resting on the purlins, which transfer much of the weight of the roof on to the principal rafters, which, in turn, transmit this pressure to the axial posts via the braces. The braces, being held in compression, prevent the roof from collapsing inwards and taking the top of the wall with them. The process is apparently similar to that used in many medieval timber framed buildings, replacing the tie beams and collars of the latter with a brace and axial post. This resemblance, though, is only superficial. Collars and tie beams are held in tension, acting to stop the feet of the rafters sliding outwards under the downwards thrust through the apex of the roof. In the structures under discussion, the apex of the roof is directly supported by the axial posts, putting horizontal braces such as those suggested here in compression.

Possible variations on this arrangement might include altering the angle of the brace to meet the rafter at an angle closer to 90°, and placing further braces directly between the common rafters.

The doorway of Building 6 is a problem. The surviving wood on each side is relatively slender. It would be possible to put a doorway here, composed of larger uprights forming a frame, by assuming that the timbers had been robbed or eroded away. The only problem with this is that the existing gap is only 0.70m wide. Introducing more timbers would narrow this gap further. The best solution would seem to be that the surviving flanking timbers did, indeed, form the door frame, but the frame would not be strong enough to bear the load of any rafters.

It might be suggested that this sort of structure is too sophisticated in appearance for the Iron Age. It should be remembered that at this time, rectangular aisled buildings were being built and used on the continent. Reconstructions based on their ground plans, as at Roskilde, Denmark (Coles 1973, 64) have shown that quite complex structures can be built using very simple carpentry techniques.

Building 1

Many of the above suggestions apply equally to the reconstruction of Building 1 (Fig 9.4). This structure is better preserved than Building 6. Though similar

in plan, there are some important differences. Firstly, Building 1 (5.6m × 8.4m) is larger than Building 6 (7m × 5m), consequently requiring a higher roof. Secondly, its walls consist of roundwood uprights infilled with wattle, which survived in its northwest corner. Thirdly, both axial post settings included a single large post, and finally, part of the flooring was also recovered.

Assuming that the height of the walls is 1.2m, the increased size of the building will require axial posts 4.6m high to achieve a 45° roof slope at each corner. The roof construction is a lighter form of that used on Figure 9.2C of Building 6, and the same principles apply here.

The major differences concern the walls of the structure, which are of upright roundwood posts and interwoven wattle roundwood. It was apparent that a number of the lowest wattle rods had been driven in to the peat before being twisted between the posts. There are also some pairs of posts which might represent repairs to the wall at points of perceived weakness or additional supports for the wall plate as shown on the drawing, but otherwise their exact function remains unknown.

Unlike Building 6, the break in the wall, which is interpreted as an entrance is flanked by substantial

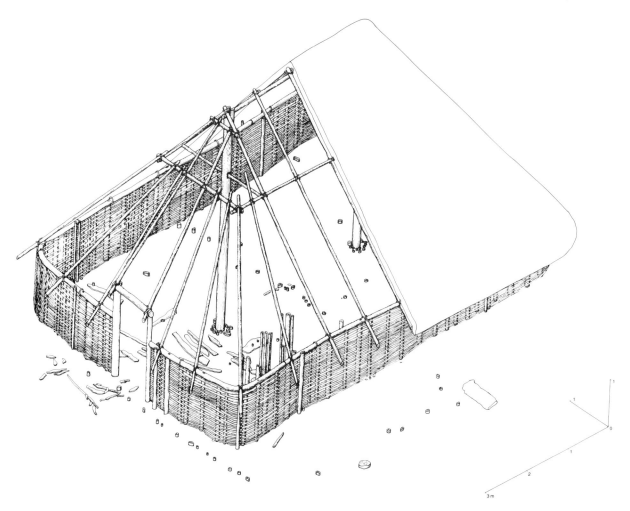

Figure 9.4 Goldcliff: Suggested reconstruction of Building 1 with roundwood and wattlework walls. The drawing also shows the remains of a possibly earlier Structure 5. Drawing by S J Allen

roundwood uprights, which allow a door and frame higher than the wall height to be postulated. That shown here is 1.8m high.

Concluding remarks

Much of the foregoing is speculation, the buildings being unparalleled in Britain, apart from at Redwick (Chapter 16). Although rectangular Iron Age buildings have been excavated on the continent, eg at Ezinge, Drenthe (Harsema 1982) and Assendelver Polders Site Q (Therkorn *et al* 1984), these structures are aisled, with the roof carried on trusses and aisle posts, not axial posts. More importantly, they also stand apart from the general tradition of round house construction, which relies on a concentric circle of inner posts to carry a ring beam to support the rafters, essentially half of a single aisled building bent round into a circle. Ultimately, perhaps the only way to determine the character of these buildings with greater confidence is to attempt a full-size reconstruction.

10 Trackways and other linear structures at Goldcliff
by M Bell

10.1 Introduction

The archaeological interest of the rectangular buildings described in the previous chapters is greatly increased by trackways, which in some cases lead to buildings and also provide clues to wider landscape relationships. In addition to the clearly defined trackways, there are a number of other linear structures, some perhaps eroded trackways, others of uncertain purpose. All are on, or apparently relate to, the peat shelves and, where we have radiocarbon dates, they are of the later 1st millennium BC. The sites (Fig 7.1) are described from Goldcliff Pill east, followed by the site of Goldcliff West. In order to appreciate the relationship between trackways, buildings, and peat shelves, it will be necessary from time to time to refer to area plans in Chapters 7 and 8, as indicated.

10.2 Linear Structure 1108

At the southwest limit of the main peat shelf (Fig 7.2) just east of Goldcliff Pill. At its southern end the structure lies 29m west of Building 1. Possible vertical pegs were noted here in 1991 under muddy conditions. In 1992, twelve verticals visible in rough alignment, were cleaned and followed north (Fig 10.1). The storm on 30 August 1992 showed this structure continued for 83m north to rectangular Building 4. Remaining mud was cleaned and it was drawn to create the greatly reduced plan on Figure 7.2. The structure will be described in terms of distances north from the peat edge near Building 1.

Between the peat edge at 5m north and 11m north, the structure was quite fully exposed: two parallel alignments of vertical–diagonal elements, both roundwood and split timber, c 0.25m apart. Occasional horizontals and brushwood lay along the axis (Fig 10.1). Beyond 11m there was a partial covering of clay, but verticals protruded. Between 11m and 37m it basically comprised two parallel lines of verticals. These formed a wavy line, and in one area at 25m north appeared to curve around a tree stump. The peat was a little higher along the line of the structure, with islands of peat protruding through the clay.

From c 16m to 37m there was a clearly marked double line of verticals. In the northern part of the

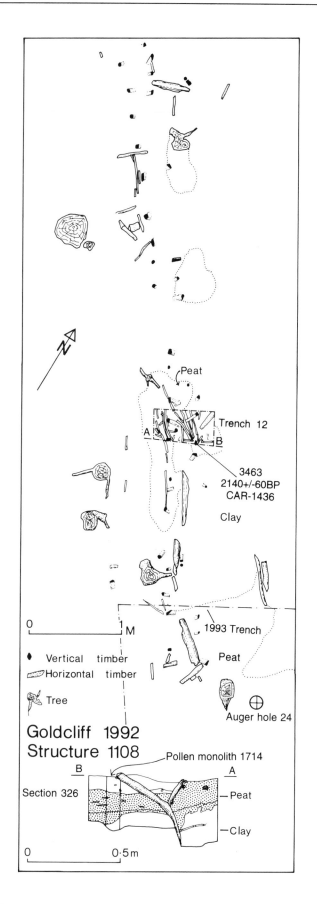

Figure 10.1 Goldcliff: Linear post alignment 1108. Plan of southern end made in 1992. Drawing by K Henry

Figure 10.2 Goldcliff: Linear post alignment 1108, 1992 excavation. Photograph by M Bell

structure there were very few horizontal elements, presumably because these were buried. As far as 49m north, tree stumps protrude from the clay along the line of the track and west to the edge of the peat shelf which is 10m away.

North of c 37m the alignment could still be followed but was patchy. By 65m north the structure was wider, 1.2m between pegs, and at 69m north it appeared to diverge into two branches, both of essentially similar character. One went west of Building 4, the other branch (1149) ran some 2.5m to its south and continued; it has been traced going below the later clay cover.

Having investigated this structure in plan and traced its linear extent to the north, a small excavation was made during 1992 at the southern end, to obtain a radiocarbon sample and pollen monolith (1714). This keyhole excavation 0.7m × 0.3m (Fig 10.1) provided a very clear idea of the structure's character. Timbers, both roundwood and split, had been driven in obliquely from alternate sides to form a 'V-shaped' cradle (Fig 10.2). Between, and just outside, was horizontal roundwood. Some thin pieces appeared to have been woven along the diagonally driven verticals. There were indications of brushwood filling the 'V' and it was thought that the occasional larger timbers may have formed part of a trackway surface.

Further excavation of an area 4m × 2m took place in 1993, 1.7m south. The excavation took place in four 1m strips. Each section was cleaned, overlying sediment excavated and the surface of the structure planned (Fig 10.3a). The horizontals were then lifted, the vertical–diagonal elements replanned (Fig 10.3b) and lifted. The section was drawn after each 1m strip. The 'cradle' consisted of roundwood pegs and less commonly split roundwood. Usually they were pointed with three facets and driven in obliquely. The structure included some quite substantial stakes up to 0.1m in diameter. In places on the east side, wooden planks some 0.1m thick had been driven in obliquely. As before, small roundwood lay within and just outside the 'cradle' formed. This lay alongside the oblique elements and, in places, seemed to have been woven around them. Beetle samples (1730–1732) were taken through the trackway stratigraphy (Fig 10.3).

It was also considered important to establish the character of the structure where it had forked just east of Building 4. Accordingly, in 1993 three small trenches 1m × 0.5m were cut across 1149 (Fig 10.3). These confirmed that it consisted of two lines of verticals. Only in Trench 25 were there horizontals and, even then, very few. These trenches indicated that 1149 just east of Building 4 was of somewhat similar character to 1108.

Stratigraphically the structure is near the surface of the wood peat. In Section 326 (Fig 10.1A, B) the horizontal roundwood elements are mainly within the peat. Sections in Figure 10.3 show a thin layer of clay, or peaty clay, between the peat and overlying brushwood or horizontal elements. That suggests some marine flooding had already occurred by the time when the surface of the structure was made.

138

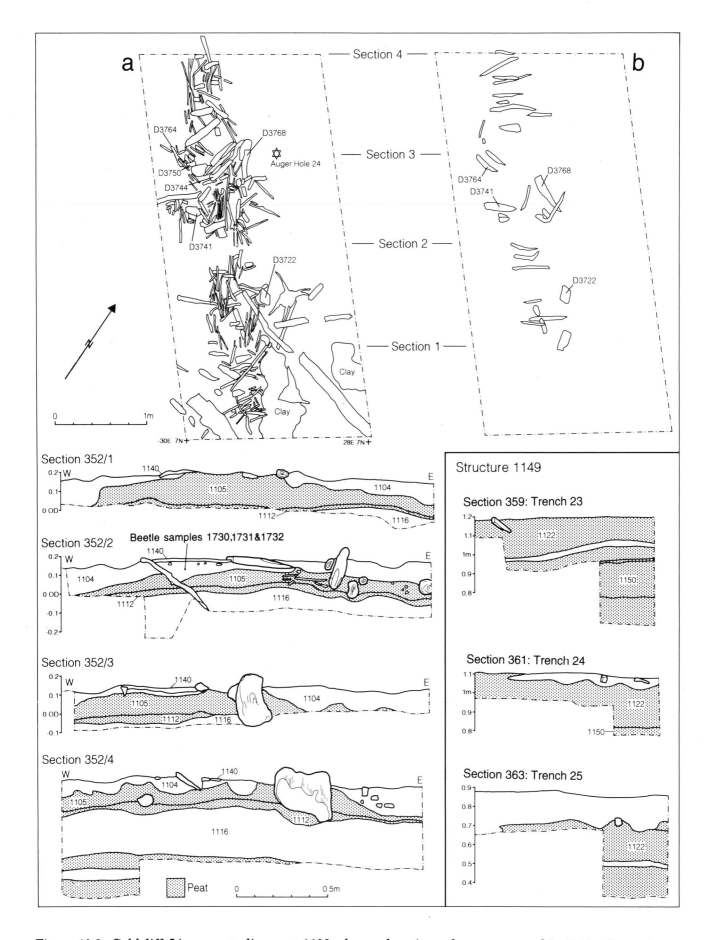

Figure 10.3   Goldcliff: Linear post alignment 1108, plan and sections of area excavated in 1993; also sections of 1149, a possible continuation of 1108 near Building 4. Drawing by B Garfi

This structure of diagonally driven posts is interpreted as a trackway and reconstructed in Figure 10.20C. A trackway of similar type and probable Bronze Age date has been recorded in the Severn Estuary at Coldharbour Pill (Locock 1997); also comparable is a Bronze Age trackway excavated at Beckton, London (Meddens 1996). This group of tracks is, in some ways, reminiscent of the method of construction of the, much more substantial, Neolithic Sweet Track (Coles and Coles 1986). They seem to have been designed to create slightly raised walkways across a partly flooded landscape; Trackway 1108 traversed the interface between wet woodland and reeds (Fig 10.20C). At the northern end the branches diverge round Building 4, which may be contemporary; they have identical radiocarbon dates, that for 1108 being: 2140 ± 60 BP (CAR-1436). Oak timbers have also been dendrochronologically dated; one had some sapwood but no bark edge. Allowing a range for the probable amount of sapwood, this suggests that the wood for this structure was cut between 336 and 318 BC (Chapter 11).

10.3 Double Post Row 970

On the main peat shelf 5m east of Building 3, comprising two lines of small posts about 0.40m apart, the most obvious feature on the peat shelf in the 1990s (Fig 10.4). It was observed in the preliminary survey in 1990, cleaned and planned in 1991 (Fig 10.5). It was 32.1m long, ending at the north at

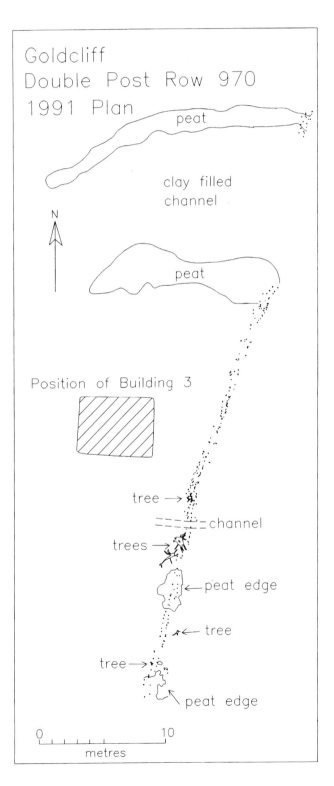

Figure 10.5   Goldcliff: Double post row 970 planned in 1991. Drawing by B Taylor

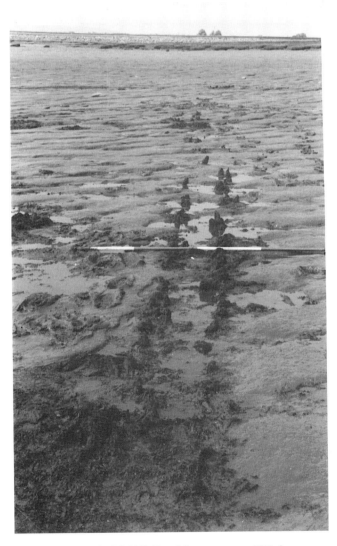

Figure 10.4   Goldcliff: Double post row 970 from south. Photograph by M Bell

a large palaeochannel 11m wide. On the opposite side of this channel its continuation could be traced for 1.6m across a peat ridge, which probably marks the edge of a former palaeochannel, giving an overall length of 48m; beyond this it was not traced under deep mud cover. The 1990 survey identified 250 verticals. It is not straight, but in places seems to have short straight sections which are not precisely aligned (Fig 10.5). Evidence for construction in individual sections gains some support from Johnson's (Chapter 12) evidence of contrasts in the tree types utilised within the sampled area (Chapter 12). The structure also curves by some 0.6m in the area of two prominent tree stumps. The impression in the field was that this was to avoid standing trees.

In 1992 the small 1m × 0.5m Trench 13 was excavated 8m north of Building 3, where the peat surface was largely buried by overlying blue clay (Fig 7.14). This keyhole investigation showed that, in addition to the main vertical elements, there were smaller vertical pieces of roundwood and two horizontals at right angles to the axis of the row. The main features of the section (Fig 10.6) are the prominent verticals, in this case 0.3m apart and with another vertical which only appeared at a lower level. During 1994 a further excavation of this structure (Trench 40) took place 3.5m south of the 1992 trench and close to Building 3 (Fig 7.14). This trench was

2m × 1m, aligned along the axis of the structure, its main purpose to gain a fuller understanding of the structure's character. In the north part of the trench the peat surface was covered by clay. On initial cleaning (Fig 10.6), 28 vertical elements were visible, many others appearing as excavation proceeded; eventually 58 pieces of wood were lifted, many stratified within the peat layer. The main elements were two parallel rows 0.35–0.4m apart; most was split timber. There was a pronounced tendency for the western line to be nearly vertical and for the eastern line to show a dip in a westerly direction. This averaged about 70° to the horizontal. Within the structure were a number of small roundwood pegs 20mm in diameter. Three pegs were found forming a line roughly parallel with the main structure 0.15m east. Three other pegs were beside larger vertical timbers. The pegs have no obvious function in the structure as planned, strengthening the impression that key elements have been lost. Within the peat was one broken horizontal timber 0.3m × 0.15m roughly aligned along the axis. Once all the peat had been removed, and the wood stratified within it lifted, the structure resolved itself into fifteen more substantial timbers (Fig 10.7).

The structure lay in the upper part of the wood peat and its setting is reconstructed in Figure 10.20E. Interpretation has to be based on very limited

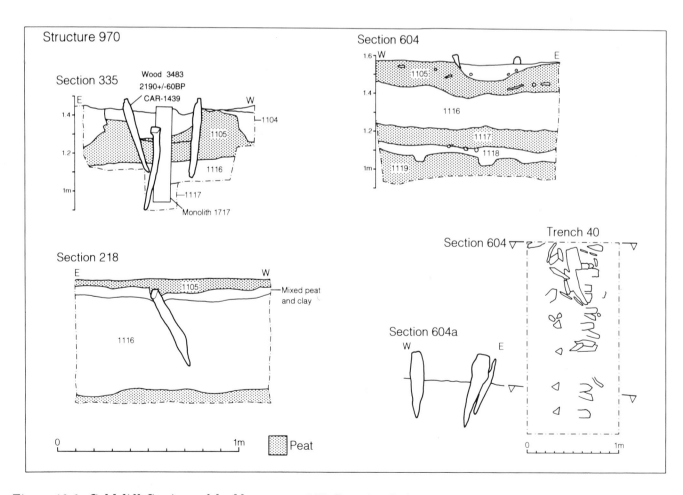

Figure 10.6 Goldcliff: Sections of double post row 970. Drawing B Garfi

Figure 10.7 Goldcliff: Double post row 970, 1994 excavation. Photograph by L Boulton

excavation. It was initially thought that it was a post-prehistoric fish trap (eg Green, C 1992), but the radiocarbon date of 2190 ± 60BP (CAR-1439) is very close to those of the buildings and other structures on the peat shelf, and is now thought most likely to be a trackway of which a plank surface may have been removed or washed away. This could explain the slightly differently aligned segments, and gains some support from compression of the peat between the two rows (Fig 10.6).

10.4 Linear Structure 1103

A linear alignment of posts and pegs first observed in 1992 when it was cleaned, planned, and subject to limited excavation (Figs 10.8 and 10.9). It ran for 10.3m from the peat edge in a curving line. The inland part, which had two parallel post lines, was a slightly raised ridge of peat through the surrounding clay. It ended as two parallel ridges of peat corresponding to the post lines. Some 65 verticals were recorded, but there was much other wood in the area, and excavation showed that the structure was more complex than suggested by the surface exposure. Two trenches were excavated. Trench 1 (1m × 0.4m) was at the inland end of the structure where a single stake projected through the clay. Excavation showed that other posts and pegs were sealed by clay (Fig 10.9). Trench 2 was 1.05m × 1.3m and gave two sections at right angles to the structure (Fig 10.9d, e) and four sections along its axis (Fig 10.9f–i). Trench 2 suggested the possibility of two lines of posts and pegs on the outside holding in place

horizontal lateral timbers (Fig 10.9 f, g). Between these were other verticals and horizontal roundwood 10–20mm in diameter which appeared to have been woven in layers from side to side of the structure.

It is clear that the structure is contemporary with the peat shelf, much of the wood being stratified within the peat. In the area excavated there were 75 pieces of wood, seven times as many pieces as had been visible on the surface; this indicates continued peat growth during, or after, the life of the structure. The presence of wood chips shows some wood was worked on the spot. A radiocarbon date on a vertical peg (3333) of 2160 ± 60 BP (CAR-1440) shows that the structure is close in date to the other structures on the peat shelf. These factors are considered to make unlikely interpretation as a fishing structure. It might have been a compressed wattlework fence, of several phases, near the peat shelf edge. Figure 10.9 shows a single, rather than double line of verticals. This might have served to keep animals from the *Phragmites* swamp to the east. However, this hypothesis does not so easily accommodate the larger roundwood laterals. A trackway is perhaps the most likely hypothesis, given the evidence from Trench 2 and similarity between this and Structure 1108. A possible reconstruction of this structure in its fen wood and reed setting is shown in Figure 10.20F.

10.5 Trackways 1–9

A series of eight trackways occurs where the main peat shelf curves inland towards the saltmarsh (Fig 10.8). Trackways were first observed here by Upton and Trett in November 1990. Preliminary planning of Trackways 1–8 took place in 1991 and limited excavation and planning of individual trackways in 1992–93. Replanning of some trackways in successive years gives an indication of how rapidly these structures are eroding. The stratigraphic sequence in this area is simple. The main peat shelf is underlain by blue clay (1159). The natural fen wood, which is everywhere on the peat shelf to the west, continues as far east as Trackway 1, but east of this the peat is of reed type with virtually no natural wood. The wood which is present is all orientated and forms trackways. The reed peat is presumed to mark a wetter area to the east of the fen woodland. The exposed peat shelf is, in most places, only about 2.5m wide and the trackways have been eroded and lost at the very front of the shelf, but short lengths are preserved a little back from the edge; they then disappear below overlying blue grey clay.

Trackway 1

Up to 10m of this trackway was exposed from time to time when the mud was swept away (Figs 10.10 and 10.11). The trackway consists mainly of brushwood, with some larger roundwood; these form a path

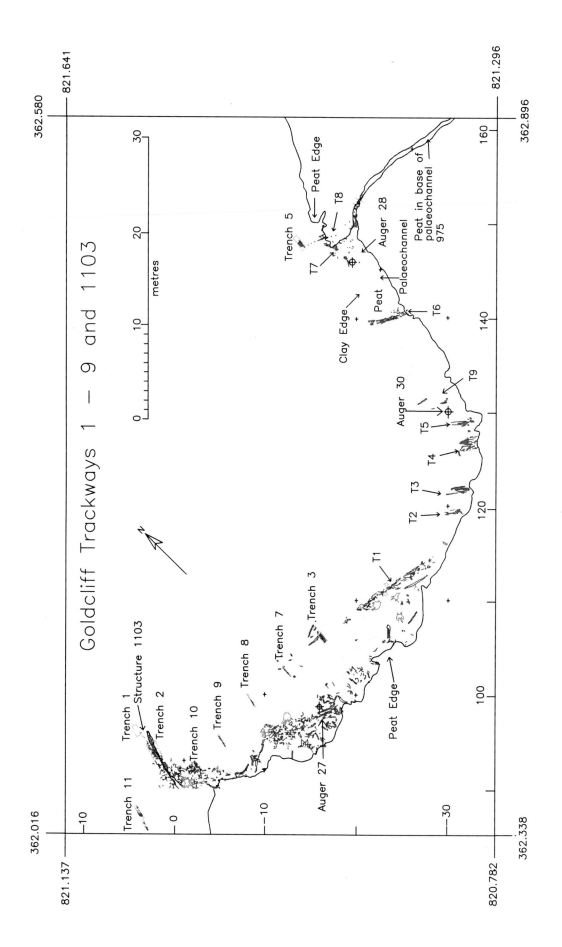

Figure 10.8 Goldcliff: Plan of the peat shelf showing Trackways 1–9 and Structure 1103. Drawing by B Taylor

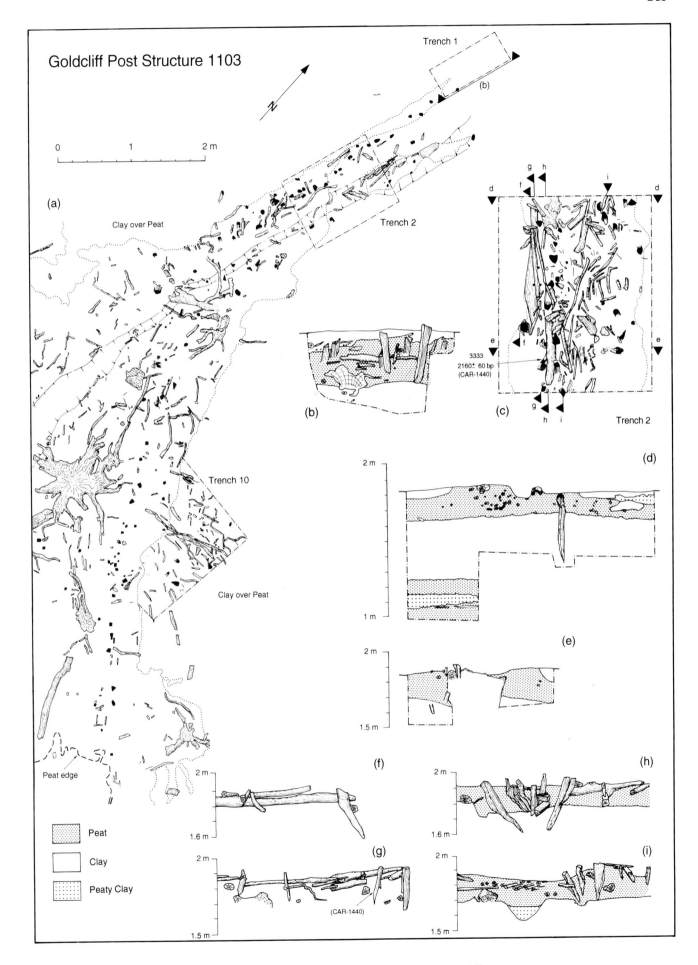

Goldcliff Post Structure 1103

Trench 1

(b)

(a)

Clay over Peat

0   1   2 m

Trench 2

(b)

(c)

3333
2160± 60 bp
(CAR-1440)

g h
f   i
d   d

e   f   e

g
h i   Trench 2

(d)

2 m

1 m

(e)

2 m

1.5 m

Trench 10

Clay over Peat

Peat edge

Peat

Clay

Peaty Clay

(f)

2 m

1.6 m

(g)

2 m

1.5 m

(CAR-1440)

(h)

2 m

1.6 m

(i)

2 m

1.5 m

Figure 10.9 Goldcliff: Structure 1103, plan and sections. Drawing by S J Allen

Figure 10.10 Goldcliff: Trackway 1. Photograph by M Bell

0.4–0.6m wide. In places there are larger pieces of roundwood (0.16m diameter) and pegs along the edges of the track. Peg 953 was 0.53m long and displayed abrupt bends as a result of compression; it was dated 2260 ± 60BP (CAR-1349). At the east end, a substantial piece of roundwood with a peg on both sides was present 0.6m south of the line, suggesting, either that the track was originally wider at this point, or an earlier parallel line had existed to the south. The trackway ran along the edge of the fen woodland at its junction with the reed swamp; its character and setting are reconstructed in Figure 10.20A. There are two substantial tree roots close by and the trackway gave the impression of curving slightly to avoid these. Comparative plans of this track made in 1991 and 1992 showed that in the seaward 2m roughly half the brushwood had been lost but the overall extent of the track was the same. The later plan shows the trackway extending 2.4m further inland, so significant erosion of the overlying clay has occurred, although this might partly be the result of more vigorous cleaning before the second planning.

It was assumed from the surface exposure of this

Figure 10.11 Goldcliff: Trackway 1, plan 1992, and section of Trench 3. Drawing by S J Allen

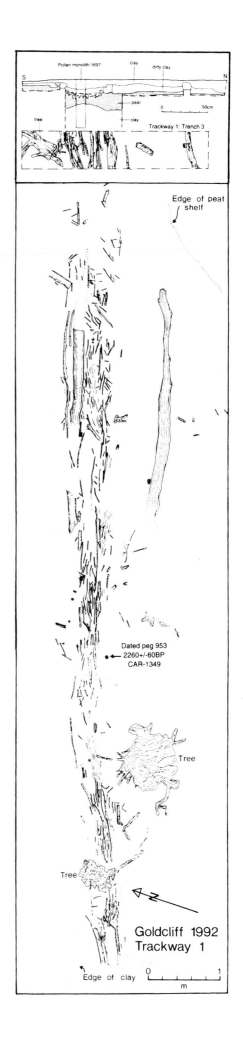

trackway that it ran beneath the overlying clay, but was it a very local feature and what was its character where uneroded? An attempt was made to follow the trackway. At 4m west of the exposure, three substantial pieces of roundwood were on the line of the track projecting through the clay, beside one was a peg. Trench 3 was put down here (Figs 10.8 and 10.11). At 0.15m below clay was the trackway, better preserved and more substantial than where exposed. It was 0.4m wide, in a hollow 80mm deep, and flanked by larger roundwood laterals, outside one of which was a peg. Two pieces of roundwood to the east could represent displaced laterals. The section showed the track surface to be overlain directly by blue clay with some organic inclusions. Pollen Monolith 1695 was taken.

Further key hole Trenches 7–10 were 0.1m wide and followed the track to the west below clay (Fig 10.8). Wood was uncovered and planned but not excavated in this minimally destructive exercise. Trench 10 was where it approached Structure 1103 (Fig 10.9); here some pegs and brushwood came to within 0.4m of 1103. Trackway 1 seemed to fade out against the slightly raised line of 1103 and there was no stratigraphic relationship between the two. Trench 11 was put down to explore the possibility that Trackway 1 continued west of 1103. It revealed two pieces of apparently split timber and one of roundwood, but it remains uncertain whether this is a continuation of the trackway. The stratigraphic context of Trackway 1 on the exposed peat shelf showed evidence in places of peat growth sealing roundwood and brushwood, but in Trench 3 there was no intervening peat growth. Here, and in Trench 7, the grey clay which overlay the track was slightly peaty and the inclusion of peat fragments in this layer in Trench 8 indicates some reworking at the peat clay interface.

Trackway 2

At 4m east of Trackway 1 (Fig 10.8), fragmentary and marked only by aligned brushwood 0.5m wide without pegs or more substantial roundwood. It was originally planned in 1991, when the total exposed length was 2.14m; when replanned in 1993, the fragments of brushwood on the seaward 0.9m had been lost but another 0.4m had been exposed by erosion of the overlying clay. No excavation has been done.

Trackway 3

At 1.6m east of Trackway 2 (Fig 10.8), it comprised two roundwood laterals of diameter 0.60m and 0.8m, 0.55m apart with brushwood between. One peg (954) was excavated in 1991; it was 0.76m long, contorted by peat compression, and dated 2290 ± 60 BP (CAR-1350). When originally planned in 1991, the brushwood extended about 0.3m further seaward compared with replanning in 1993, by which time another 0.4m of one roundwood piece was exposed to landward.

Trackway 4

At 3.8m east of Trackway 3 (Fig 10.8). When first planned in 1991, it comprised two lines of pegs 0.7m apart, with some evidence for larger roundwood at the edges and fragments of brushwood in the centre. One peg (955) was excavated and was 0.25m long. The line of the track was marked by a slight hollowing of the peat surface. The trackway was replanned in 1993 and a 0.5m wide section excavated in Trench 31. This revealed a greater concentration of brushwood and roundwood 1.1m wide and 1.8m long. Larger pieces tended to be on top and aligned along the track, smaller pieces below having a more random orientation. There was a very thin layer of peat (10mm) above the trackway surface. The environmental sequence associated with this trackway was further investigated with three beetle samples (1754, 1748, and 1746, Chapter 14).

Trackway 5

At 1.4m east of Trackway 4 (Fig 10.8), a slight linear hollow containing fragmentary brushwood 0.6m wide, 3.1m long. The most substantial piece of roundwood was 20mm in diameter, there were no pegs. In 1993 Trench 32, 1m long and 0.1m wide was excavated across it to obtain wood for identification.

Trackway 9

At 2.1m east of Trackway 5 (Fig 10.8), it consisted of seven brushwood horizontals on the same orientation, roughly parallel to the neighbouring trackways. A trench excavated across this showed that below the wood there was a depression 80mm deep containing wood fragments.

Trackway 6

At 10.2m east of Trackway 9 (Fig 10.8), it comprised three pieces of roundwood, one (951) 0.11m in diameter with a cut end. There were four pegs and traces of brushwood. The heavier timber may have been laid down because here the trackway crosses minor Palaeochannel 975. Trench 33 (1.2m × 0.5m) was excavated across this trackway in 1993. The section showed a hollow 0.4m wide and 0.1m deep, possibly with wood related to the base of the peat and another hollow on the peat surface, so there is the possibility of more than one trackway level. The environmental sequence associated with the trackway was further investigated by two beetle samples (1757 and 1756, Chapter 14).

Trackway 7

It is far from clear that this is a distinct trackway. It is 9m east of Trackway 6 and 1.5 m west of Trackway 8 (Fig 10.12). When planned in 1991, there were 20 pieces of roundwood defining an irregular area about 0.6m wide. When replanned in 1992, most of these

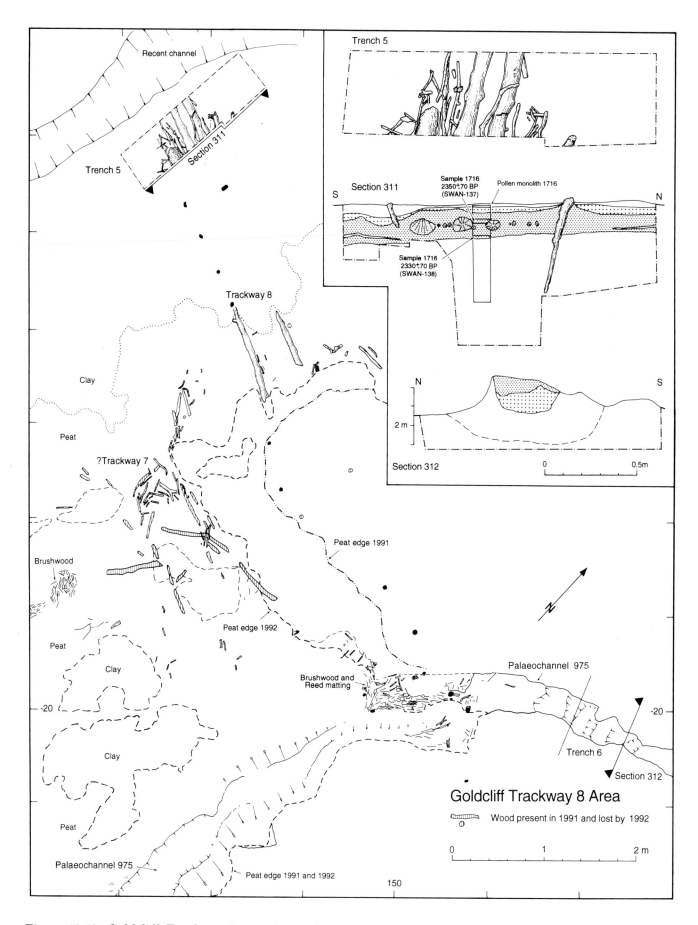

Figure 10.12 Goldcliff: Trackway 8 area plan and sections. Drawing by S J Allen

had gone, but there were 44 pieces of brushwood, mostly small, two with cut ends embedded in the peat surface to the west, but without any overall orientation. Wood from both plans has been combined on Figure 10.12. It might be the remains of a largely eroded trackway or material washed from the adjoining Trackway 8. No excavation was done.

Trackway 8

The most easterly of this group of trackways, 1.5m from the possible Trackway 7. It is at a point where a palaeochannel (975) curves east from the main peat shelf and behind this the peat edge has been eroded in an irregular embayment which cuts right through the trackway (Fig 10.12). Where erosion has cut away the trackway it reveals a double row of pegs 0.6m apart. At the point where the palaeochannel is crossed there is a concentration of pegs and a layer of small brushwood fragments and reeds within the channel. On the peat shelf itself the track is marked by two roundwood laterals 60mm in diameter and 0.35m apart, with traces of brushwood between. These dipped to the west, suggesting the possibility that a palaeochannel was being crossed here. West of this the line of the track can be traced as pegs projecting through overlying clay. In total the trackway can be traced for 6.4m.

In 1992, Trench 5 was excavated across the line of this track, 1.7m west of the peat shelf, where it was overlain by blue clay (Fig 10.12). The trench was 1.7m × 0.5m and the trackway was encountered at a depth of 0.1m. It was flanked by two vertical pegs 0.85m apart which projected through the underlying clay, probably as a result of compression. The main track surface was formed by three pieces of roundwood of diameter *c* 0.1m and between these was brushwood. The section clearly shows that 40mm of peat growth has taken place above the surface of the trackway. Pollen Monolith 1716 was taken through the sediment sequence, including the trackway, to further investigate the environmental sequence. Radiocarbon dates from this monolith show that the base of the peat is dated 2330 ± 70 BP (SWAN-138) and the peat just above the trackway is dated 2350 ± 70 BP (SWAN-137).

Comparative plans of the Trackway 8 area made in 1991 and 1992 show no measurable change to the seaward peat edge; however, the face of the erosion embayment which cuts into the trackway has seen erosion at an average rate of 0.46m in 1 year. The edge of the clay overlying the peat has retreated by an average of 0.3m; eight pegs had been lost and six more revealed.

Stratification of trackways and Structure 1103

There was evidence that peat formation continued during and after the period of linear Structure 1103. The extent of trackway investigation varies; in the case of Trackways 2, 3, 5, 7, and 9 it was insufficient to clarify stratigraphic relationships. Trackway 1 was generally on the very surface of the peat, but there was evidence for peat growth above the track in some trenches. Trackways 4 and 8 had clear evidence of peat growth above the track. The evidence from Trackway 6 is unclear, but it may represent more than one phase.

It is tempting to suggest that this evidence for structures at different levels within the peat could account for contrasting species compositions in the trackways (Chapter 12), if wood was derived from different stages in a succession. The evidence for trackway stratigraphic relationships does suggest some duration to activity in this area and it implies that the concentration of trackways relates to successive attempts to consolidate particular routes.

10.6 Palaeochannel 975/9053

This channel could be traced in a markedly sinuous course for 94m. It runs on the peat shelf parallel with its edge between Trackways 6 and 8 and then curves east away from the edge, where it forms a peaty ridge on the foreshore (Fig 10.8). Trench 6 (Fig 10.12) cut through the channel, showing that the peaty ridge representing the channel line was 0.34m wide and the peat was underlain by peaty clay containing three bones. It was shown to be part of a larger channel in the underlying clay which was 0.84m wide; the peat and clay channel together were 0.34m deep. This feature was interpreted in the field by John Allen as a pre-peat 'shadow channel' (Allen forthcoming c). The channel can be shown to have remained wetter at the peat stage because there were larger trackway timbers where the line of the channel was crossed.

Some 35m east of the peat shelf an area of the channel was cleaned and planned (CD 10.1 and 10.2). In it were three vertical pieces of wood, probably pegs, also twigs and some horizontal roundwood, one piece with a cut end. Worked wood was often found in channels of a wide range of sizes in the intertidal survey (Chapter 16) and, as in this case, its significance is often not clear. East of this minor channel was an area *c* 15m across with a strew of thirteen stones (9054), the largest 1.2m × 0.4m, and four tree trunks, the largest 7m long (CD10.2 and 10.3); there were also some possible pegs. The stones and treetrunks may have accumulated in a palaeochannel which may predate the peat shelf to the west, but this has not been established with certainty.

10.7 Trackways 1130 and 9051

This trackway (Figs 10.13 and 10.14) was revealed by the storm on 30 August 1992. A rapid plan was made a week later, but there was no opportunity for sampling or excavation, which took place in 1993. It lies 145m east of the area of brushwood Trackways

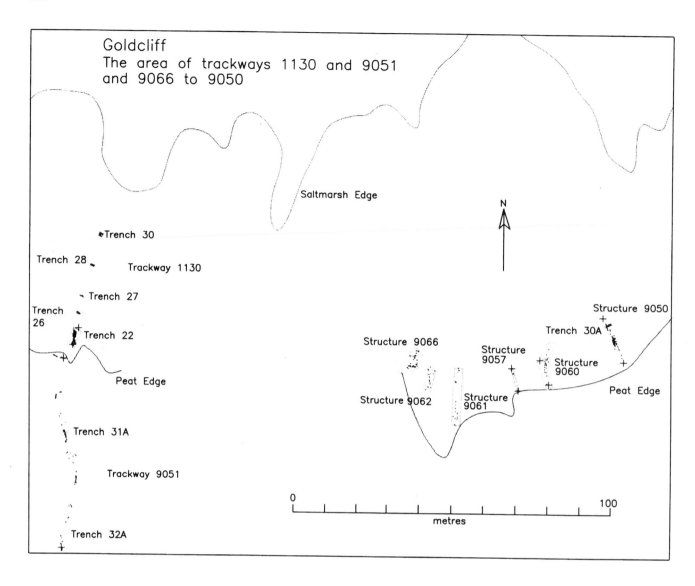

Figure 10.13 Goldcliff: Plan of the area of Trackways 1130, 9051, the group of trackways, and other structures 9066, 9062, 9061, 9057, 9060, and 9050. Drawing by R Caple and B Taylor

1–8, on the same thin (c 50mm) reed peat with no natural wood. As originally exposed the trackway (Figs 10.14 and 10.15) was well-preserved about 4m back from the peat edge. A total of six pegs between the track and the edge indicated it had originally extended to the edge and had subsequently been eroded. Some 3.6m of the track was exposed by erosion and planned in 1992. The trackway was replanned in 1993 and by this time 26% of the wood which had been recorded the previous year had been lost, mostly in the seaward 2m. As a result of erosion, about 0.5m more of the trackway was exposed to landward. It is more substantial than the other Goldcliff trackways, of corduroy construction comprising, mainly, pieces of roundwood laid at right angles to its line, creating a track 0.9m wide with pegs at somewhat irregular intervals. In places there was some brushwood between and below the main timbers. A radiocarbon date for the structure is provided by a *Betula* horizontal 3796: 2200 ± 50 BP (CAR-1504), demonstrating its contemporaneity with the other structures on the main peat shelf.

During 1993 five trenches followed this track below clay to the north (Fig 10.14). In these trenches the trackway horizontals were c 80mm above the main peat layer in mixed peaty clay. In Trench 26 (Fig 10.16) the trackway surface was better preserved than where exposed with a surface of planks and some roundwood. A pollen monolith (1745) and beetle samples (1750–1753) were taken to investigate the sequence. Trench 30 was 30m north of the exposed track, and here it was buried by 1.6m of clay and the trackway surface was disrupted with wood at all angles, perhaps as a result of erosion (Fig 10.14, Bell 1993, fig 30).

The five trenches demonstrate that it is feasible to follow linear structures for 40m across the intertidal area, even, as in the case of Trench 30, where they are deeply buried running inland towards the saltmarsh and seawall. Trackway 1130 is the most substantial of those at Goldcliff, and the trenches confirm observations elsewhere on the site that wooden structures are significantly more substantial and better preserved, where buried, than they

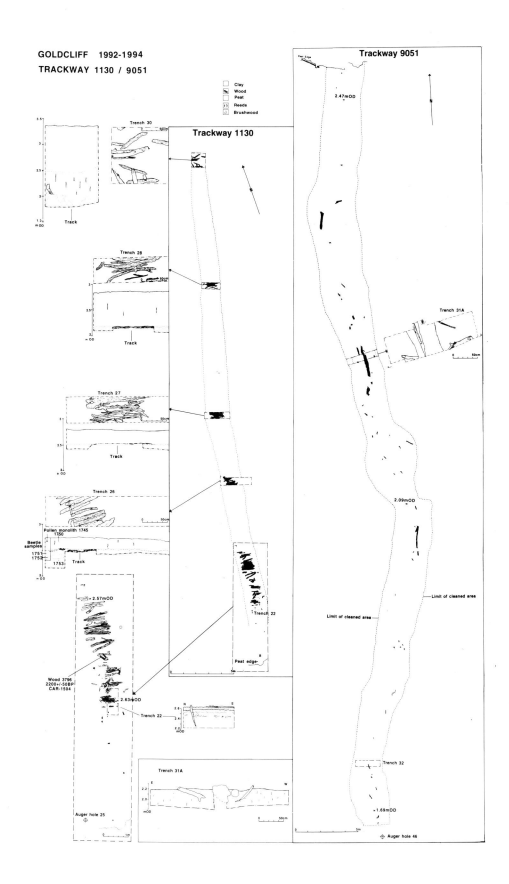

Figure 10.14 Goldcliff: Trackways 1130 and 9051. The two lengths shown join at B with 1130 to the north and 9051 to the south. Larger scale plans and sections are shown of individual trenches, for a more detailed version of parts of this plan see CD 10.4. Drawing by N Evans

Figure 10.15 Goldcliff: Trackway 1130 as cleaned in 1993, view to seaward, below the scale the trackway is buried below overlying clay. Photograph by M Bell

Figure 10.16 Goldcliff: Trackway 1130, Trench 26. Photograph by M Bell

appear on the eroding peat shelf. On the peat shelf the trackway is at 2.6m OD but it drops to the north and is at 2m in Trench 30. This may relate to construction on an originally undulating surface, or, more probably, to the effects of differential compaction of underlying strata. A reconstruction of Trackway 1130 in its reedswamp setting is shown in Figure 10.20D.

During the final season of fieldwork in 1994, the intertidal area around Trackway 1130 was examined in greater detail revealing a scatter of wood, including probable pegs, extending south of the trackway on a similar line (Fig 10.14). Here the reed peat had been eroded away and the wood occurred in underlying clay. Mud was cleaned away in a strip 3–4m wide and 60m long in order to investigate the structure, revealing 57 pieces of wood, including eighteen vertical pieces of roundwood of average diameter 30mm, which are probably pegs. Most of the remaining horizontal pieces were orientated along the line of the structure and these included five tree trunks partly buried in the clay. A possible interpretation of 9051 is as a seaward extension of Trackway 1130, the trackway surface having been eroded away with the reed peat and its line being represented by occasional

pegs and more substantial timbers which were laid down, perhaps, to cross palaeochannels (eg Trench 31A). Wood identifications for the two structures contrast, however (Chapter 12), so 9051 may represent the eroded remains of an earlier trackway along roughly the same line as 1130. Structure 9051 has not been radiocarbon dated.

10.8 Structure 9050

In 1994 the thin reed peat shelf east of Trackway 1130 was clearer of mud than it had been in earlier seasons. This led to the identification of Structures 9050 and 9060 and some more ephemeral structures (Fig 10.13). A trackway (9050) was planned and limited excavation done (Fig 10.17). Seaward of the peat shelf the trackway was represented by a single row of pegs in the underlying clay. The peat shelf in this area was just 1–3m wide and at *c* 3m OD. Here the line of pegs (average diameter 30mm) bounded a strip of brushwood 0.8m wide which, on excavation, was mostly aligned along the track. There were at least three other pegs on its west side and, in places, roundwood laterals at its edge. Trench 30 investigated the structure 4m from the peat face, where it was buried by 0.12m of clay and better preserved. Here the trackway was 0.45m wide, consisting of brushwood and roundwood aligned along the trackway, with more substantial roundwood laterals, and some roundwood underlying these at right angles to the axis. One lateral was held in place by a peg on the outside. The method of construction was, therefore, the same as Trackways 1–9. The section showed that the trackway sat on the surface of the peat which is 0.8m thick. It is directly overlain by clay, with some peaty lenses. Lateral 7433, which was sealed by the clay, was sampled for radiocarbon dating: 2350 ± 60 BP (SWAN-29). It is, therefore, broadly contemporary with the other trackways and most of the rectangular structures.

10.9 Structure 9060

The peat shelf averaged 3m in width at 3.05m OD. The peat was very patchy, with some patches of peat 50–100mm in diameter; these may represent animal footprints, but none was sufficiently distinct for confidence. Cleaning revealed seventeen roundwood pegs which were of average length 0.30m and average diameter 20mm. Most were on the peat shelf, but some projected from the underlying clay to the south, or the overlying clay to the north. The pegs formed two parallel lines 0.4m apart and were traced for 10.5m. Peg 7494, which was sealed by clay (Fig 10.18), was radiocarbon dated, with the result 2320 ± 70 BP (SWAN-30) showing it was contemporary with the other structures on the peat shelf, including the adjacent Trackway 9050. The two lines of pegs may be the eroded or robbed out remains of a similar trackway; both have pegs of mainly alder with some willow (Chapter 12).

10.10 Possible wood structures between 1130 and 9060

Four groupings of pegs were noted in this area. They are somewhat enigmatic in character and none has been dated. They are more fully described and illustrated on CD 10.5 and are briefly noted as follows:

9066 (plan CD 10.6)
A total of 34 small roundwood pieces in an area 4m × 2m. Those of alder made a rough semi-circle which could be the remains of a very light hide or shelter.

9062 (plan CD 10.7)
A total of sixteen pegs and some horizontal fragments in rough alignment, very insubstantial and of uncertain character.

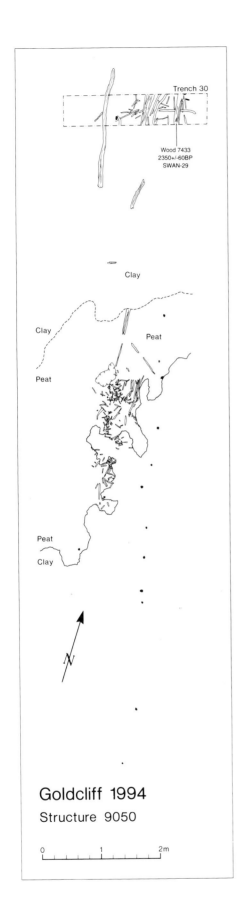

Figure 10.17 Goldcliff: Plan of Trackway 9050. Drawing by J Grove and S J Allen

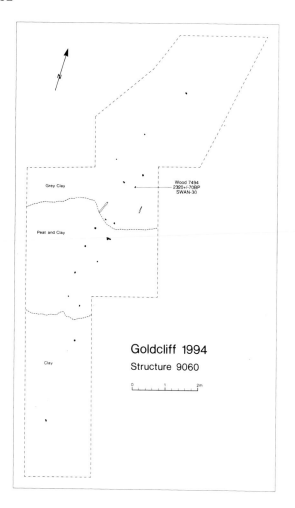

Figure 10.18 Goldcliff: Structure 9060. Drawing J Groves and S J Allen

9061 (plan CD 10.8)
A group of twelve small pegs, four in a line, eight in a rough oval at one end. Such a structure might, perhaps, have formed a hide or part of a trap for birds.

9057 (plan CD 10.9)
A piece of horizontal wood and a peg.

10.11 Trackways and brushwood structures at Goldcliff West

The peat surface at Goldcliff West was raised bog peat with a pattern of rounded hummocks surrounded by encircling depressions. The trackways here were of quite different character, being slight and discontinuous brushwood affairs designed to cross the wet areas of the depressions.

Trackway 1311

A brushwood track west of Building 6 leading in the direction of Building 8. The surface was cleaned and the trackway was traced intermittently over a dis-

tance of 40m. Four separate areas were planned, as shown in Figure 10.19. The eastern end (Fig 10.19b) was 16m west of the entrance to Building 6. Here, crossing a depression 1.8m wide, was an area of brushwood 1.1m long. Some 9m west the track became clearer and rather more continuous over a length of 9m (Fig 10.19c), where the peat surface dipped into quite a wide channel, the floor of which was marked by many animal footprints. A post 0.4m south of the track may have marked the line across this wetter area. Here the trackway was 0.4m wide where it was most clearly defined. In 1995 two small sections were put across this part of the track in order to obtain samples for beetle analysis (Sample 10134) and radiocarbon dating with the result 2140 ± 60 BP (SWAN-105). The sampling exercise showed that there was more brushwood below than on the surface. Another 1.4m of brushwood 0.3m wide with one peg at its edge lay 14.4m west, while 3m further west there was another peg on the same line and another isolated peg 4m to the north. The line of Trackway 1311, as planned, was discontinuous with gaps in which there was no trace of brushwood. In order to investigate whether these gaps were real, or whether the track was buried within the peat, three long slots were cut, 0.15m wide and 0.1m deep. None revealed any trace of brushwood. We must assume, therefore, that the track was probably not originally continuous and was laid down to cope with wet parts of a longer route. A reconstruction of the trackway is shown in Figure 10.20B.

Trackway 1330

When the mud, which normally covers the base of the encircling depression round Building 7, was removed in 1993 a short length of brushwood trackway was observed running in the direction of Building 6. It was traced for only 2.4m and was 0.5m wide on the depression base. However, a peg further north and two others on a similar line 0.6m south imply that the track may once have been longer. In 1995 part of the trackway was cleaned and sampled for beetles (Sample 10133). A sample for radiocarbon dating was 1990 ± 60 BP (SWAN-106). The sampling exercise demonstrated that the brushwood was thicker below the surface.

Brushwood structure in Palaeochannel 1314

North of Building 6 there was a very pronounced palaeochannel (1314) running roughly north–south; this then swung round in a curve to run east–west (Figs 8.1 and 10.19). The centre of the channel was filled with clean grey clay, its sides marked by slight peat ridges. At the edges of the clay there was peaty clay, and in three areas within this patches of brushwood. Two of them are shown in relation to the channel edge on Figure 10.19f and g. Unfortunately, on each occasion when they were exposed, pressure

153

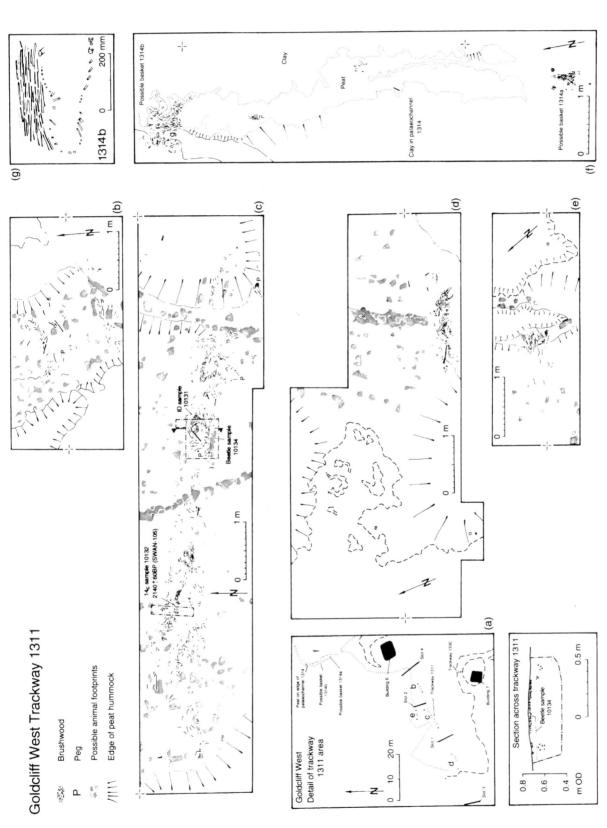

Figure 10.19 Goldcliff West: Linear and brushwood structures. (a) The location of planned structures at Goldcliff West in relation to rectangular buildings, (b) Trackway 1311 east, (c) Trackway 1311 central, (d) Trackway 1311 west, (e) Trackway 1311.5, (f) brushwood areas on the edge of palaeochannel 1314; these may represent the remains of fish baskets, (g) field sketch of Brushwood Area 1314b. Drawing by S J Allen

of work elsewhere on the site meant that there was not the opportunity for detailed recording or excavation. The impression gained in the field was that they are likely to be the remains of squashed and partly eroded fish baskets. Structure 1314a is a V-shaped area of brushwood 0.43m × 0.14m. Although the brushwood runs mostly in one direction, there are suggestions in places of pieces at right angles. Figure 10.19g shows 1314b; it is a, probably somewhat subjective, sketch prepared by the writer on 12 August 1994. This shows a basket-like structure 0.34m long of two sections, one 0.14m wide, the other 0.18m wide. An earlier plan of this area made on 1 September 1993 (Fig 10.19f) shows more brushwood, but not such a clearly defined structure. They resemble the fish and eel baskets which were widely used in the Estuary until recent times (eg Jenkins 1974). Unfortunately, they have not been dated. However, the impression gained in the field was that the palaeochannel, in the edge of which they were found, was part of the topography of the surface of the peat; if so they are probably broadly contemporary with Building 6. A prehistoric date is made more plausible by the circular basketwork structure at Cold Harbour Pill 2, which has been radiocarbon dated to the 1st millennium BC.

10.12 Trackways and other linear structures: conclusions

Types of trackway and environmental setting

In all, nineteen trackways, including the Bronze Age boat plank structure (Chapter 6), have been identified (details on CD 10.10). Of these, Trackway 7 is doubtful, 9051 could be a continuation of 1130, and there is some doubt whether 970, 1103, and 9060 were trackways. Six clearly defined types can be identified and are illustrated in Figure 10.20 in the environmental setting of one example of each type. The environmental information on which this is based is discussed in Chapters 13–15.

Type A

Brushwood with pegged roundwood laterals, the most common type with eight examples (T1, 3, 4, 6, 8, Structure 9050). T9 and T7 are probably of the same type but produced no pegs; 9060 might represent the pegs of an eroded example. Type A is based on Trackway 1 which was at the edge of the alder and willow wood to the left with reeds on the site itself and to the right. By the time of this track there was evidence of some marine influence.

Type B

Brushwood only, four examples (T2, T5, Trackways 1311 and 1330). Type B is based on 1311 at Goldcliff

West. It is situated in an area of raised bog with bog moss, heather, cotton grass, and bog myrtle. The track crosses one of the channels, the floor of which receives some marine influence and has saltmarsh plants. Cattle footprints are abundant along the channel edge.

Type C

Cradle of cross pieces, a single track (1108) which is illustrated. This was constructed at the transition from carr woodland to saltmarsh. The woodland was alder and birch, some cut down, some by this stage probably dying. At its edges were reeds and sedges.

Type D

Corduroy, one track (1130) which is illustrated. It shows the trackway in a reed swamp, with standing water and some marine influence.

Type E

Double post row, one example (970), not certainly a trackway, which is illustrated. It was situated in alder woodland with some willow. Some trees had been cut down and there was woodworking debris on the woodland floor. Reeds grow between the trees.

Type F

Woven track, one example (1103), but not certainly a trackway. It runs through a woodland of alder and willow with reed swamp to the right.

The diversity of trackway types is notable and there is some patterning in terms of environment type. The brushwood tracks of Type A are restricted to areas of reed peat, but reed peat also produced the single example of corduroy track Type D. Purely brushwood Type B occur on both reed peat and the surface of blanket bog. The more complex and enigmatic types C–F occur on the fen wood peat.

Stratigraphic context of trackways

Although most of the archaeology is located on the surface of the peat, this chapter has noted some exceptions to this general pattern. Four main types of stratigraphic context can be identified:

(i) within clay, this applies only to the boat plank Structure 1124 (Chapter 6);
(ii) sealed within peat, six of the linear structures and trackways are in this context (970, 1103, and Trackways 4, 8, 1311, and 1330;
(iii) at peat clay interface, two examples (Trackways 1 and 9050). Seven other examples are

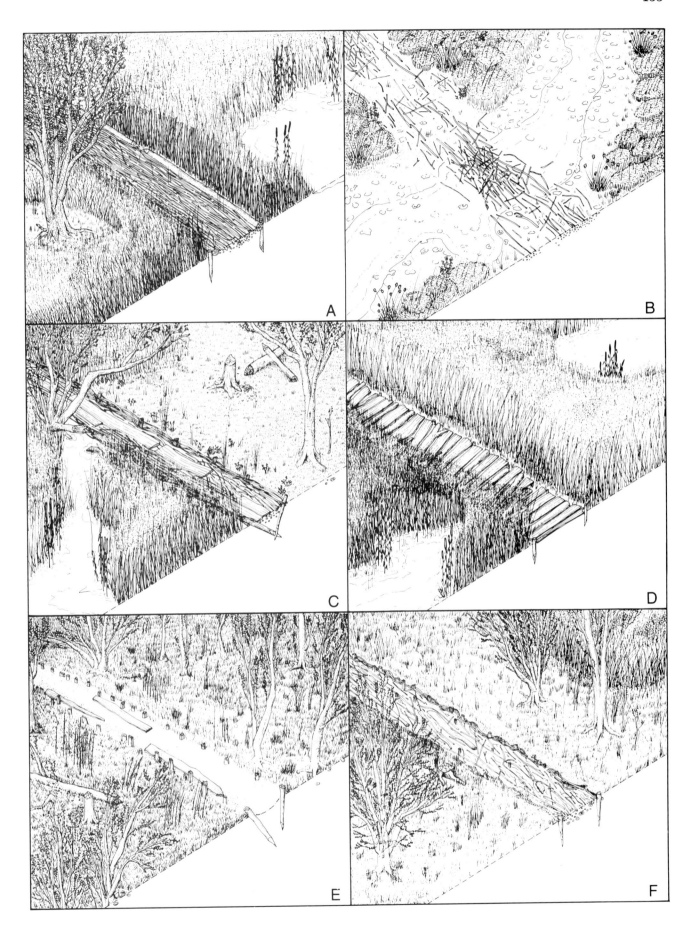

Figure 10.20   Goldcliff: Reconstruction of the types of trackways and other linear structures in their environmental setting. (A) Trackway 1, (B) Trackway 1311 at Goldcliff West, (C) Trackway 1108, (D) Trackway 1130, (E) Double Post Row 970, (F) possible Trackway 1103. Drawing by S J Allen

156

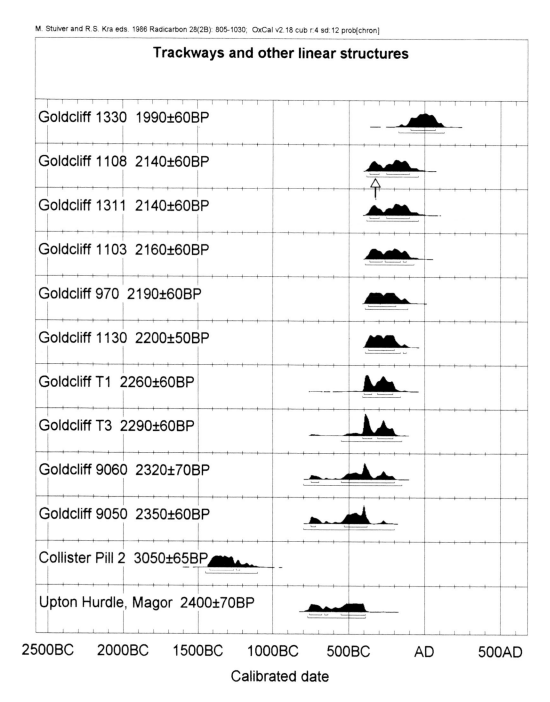

M. Stuiver and R.S. Kra eds. 1986 Radicarbon 28(2B): 805-1030; OxCal v2.18 cub r:4 sd:12 prob[chron]

Trackways and other linear structures

Goldcliff 1330	1990±60BP
Goldcliff 1108	2140±60BP
Goldcliff 1311	2140±60BP
Goldcliff 1103	2160±60BP
Goldcliff 970	2190±60BP
Goldcliff 1130	2200±50BP
Goldcliff T1	2260±60BP
Goldcliff T3	2290±60BP
Goldcliff 9060	2320±70BP
Goldcliff 9050	2350±60BP
Collister Pill 2	3050±65BP
Upton Hurdle, Magor	2400±70BP

2500BC   2000BC   1500BC   1000BC   500BC   AD   500AD

Calibrated date

Figure 10.21 Goldcliff: The calibrated date ranges of trackways and other linear structures, prepared using the calibration curves in Stuiver et al 1986 using OxCal v2.18. An arrow marks the dendrochronological date range of Structure 1108 between 336 and 318 BC

uncertain; the impression was that they lay close to the interface but they have not been investigated in sufficient detail to be confident;
(iv) in clayey peat above the main peat, two examples (1108 and 1130).

It should be noted those in (ii) have been so categorised if it appears that wood was stratified within peat. However, in the case of 1311 and 1330 there is beetle evidence (Chapter 14) which indicates that at the time of the trackways the area was already subject to marine influence. We do, therefore,

need to make a distinction between the relationship to the crude stratigraphic sequence and the more detailed picture available for certain contexts where we have environmental evidence. Similarly, Haslett *et al* (1998b) have emphasised that Foraminifera may signal marine influence in advance of transitions from peat to clay.

The data presented does show that trackways occur within a range of types of environmental setting from organic peat to clays and the gradations between. Peats will have formed beyond the range of tidal influence, or very high within the intertidal zone since accumulation depends on the balance between organic and minerogenic supply (Allen 1995). Palaeoenvironmental evidence for some marine influence at the time of many trackways, particularly 1311, 1330, 1108, and 1130, suggests that they lay very high within the intertidal range. There is not a clear relationship between stratigraphic context and the type of track. Surprisingly, Type A brushwood tracks occur in Stratigraphic Contexts 2–4. Some of the more complex track types (C and E–F) occur within the fen wood peat in Stratigraphic Context 2 and also, where it was beginning to be inundated by the sea, Stratigraphic Context 4.

We have no clear relationship between trackway type and stratigraphic context, but evidence of a relationship between track type and peat type, which may relate to the mechanical properties of the substrate. There are cases where different types of tracks were constructed in apparently the same environmental and stratigraphic context. We could infer from this that people were using the trackways for different purposes, or constructing them at different times of year when contrasting conditions obtained, although most of the trackways were of wood cut in winter (see Chapter 12). Alternatively, perhaps different methods of construction conveyed a different message to those who used, or observed, the structures.

Trackway dating

Ten tracks, or possible tracks, of the nineteen have been radiocarbon dated and another is dated by peat above and below. The calibrated ranges of the trackway dates are shown in Figure 10.21. Most have ranges in the period between 400 Cal BC and 100 Cal BC, in common with the building dates shown in Figure 9.1. Trackway 1108 has a much more precise dendrochronological date between 336 BC and 318 BC (Chapter 11), which is indicated by an arrow. That track leads towards Building 4, which has an identical radiocarbon date. We can, thus, suggest that the dendrochronological date of 1108 probably also applies to Building 4, but that is not certain. Trackway 1330 appears later with a calibrated range between 170 Cal BC and 130 Cal AD. It, thus, seems to postdate the adjacent Building 7 which is the earliest radiocarbon dated rectangular structure. The Trackway 1330 date supports the evidence of the Goldcliff West buildings in suggesting that activity here was more long-lived than in the Building 1–4 area. On Figure 10.21 the Goldcliff trackway dates are compared with the two other dated trackways in the estuary (Chapter 16), the Upton Hurdle Track, which is two or three centuries earlier than most Goldcliff examples, and a short length of track at Collister Pill-2, which is around 900 years earlier than most of the Goldcliff examples.

We have seen that the trackways of the 1st millennium BC (ie excepting the boat plank struc-ture) occur in three distinct stratigraphic contexts. The very similar dates for the tracks in these different contexts indicates that, in this case, the stratigraphy is picking up chronological subtlety beyond the precision of the radiocarbon dating. There is also no obvious chronological pattern in the types of trackways, nor would we necessarily expect one in view of what has already been said about the tendency for trackway Type A to occur in very different stratigraphic contexts.

Trackway geography

Most of the linear wooden structures seem likely to be trackways. They are one of our main clues as to the ways in which the late-1st millennium BC landscape was used and its various components articulated. The problem at Goldcliff is that the evidence is exposed in a narrow strip, a transect of ancient landscape which stretches for kilometres, but is often only a few metres wide. We have demonstrated that it is possible to trace linear structures inland below the overlying clays, and some of them can also be traced to seaward by pegs which penetrate underlying deposits. Until further erosion occurs we will be ignorant of what lies buried by clay to the north. However, the geography of the linear trackways does provide a fruitful basis for deduction. We do know that some of the trackways lead to rectangular structures: 1108 leads to Building 4 and, at Goldcliff West, Trackway 1311 leads from near Building 6 in the direction of Building 8. It is not, therefore, unreasonable to suggest that other trackways may lead in the direction of structures or activity areas. The radiocarbon evidence implies that most trackways are broadly coeval. It may be, therefore, that where trackways converge they point to the site of a structure or activity area. At Goldcliff West two trackways converge on Building 6, although the dating evidence suggests 1330 may be later. In a similar way, the sites of Bronze Age settlements have been hypothesised round the Somerset Levels on the evidence of convergent trackways (Coles and Coles 1986, fig 35). Brunning's (Chapter 12) evidence that the more complex structures, 1108, 970, and 1103, were partly made from debris of other building projects enhances the likelihood that these trackways, in particular, led to buildings, which we know was the case with 1108.

Figure 10.22 explores the notion of convergence. The trackways are in bold black and each is projected by a broken line. Trackway 1108 is straightforward: it leads from Building 4 for 75m south. Trackway 970 leads in a similar direction. Presumably both trackways led in the direction of some activity, the site, or sites, of which have now been eroded away, perhaps fish traps or the landing place of boats. The clearest grouping of tracks is 1–9, a concentration which invites comparison with that found on the Somerset Levels at Tinney's Ground (Coles and Orme 1978, fig 31) and parts of the Derryoghil trackway complex in

158

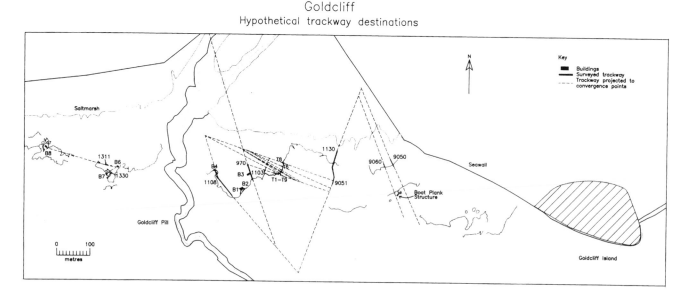

Figure 10.22 Goldcliff: The geography of trackways. Drawing by B Taylor

Ireland (Raftery 1996, fig 220). Trackways 1–9 have been shown to be at slightly different levels within the peat. This implies that the concentration of trackways represents multiple remakings. The orientations suggest that this is not remaking of a single route, but several. If we project their lines to seaward: T1 converges with T2–5 at various points between about 10–30m east of the present peat edge, and with others at 65–110m. T1 would converge with T6 at *c* 65m and T8 would converge at 150m. It is not suggested that all of the trackways necessarily converged on one point. However, the fact that there is convergence may suggest the existence of some focus of activity, probably between 10m and 60m east; here there is a palaeochannel with large tree trunks (9054, CD 10.3), but we do not know if it is contemporary with the trackways.

Inland, it may be speculated that the closely spaced group T2–5 seems likely to lead to some focus of activity. Perhaps also significant may be the convergence points of T6 and T8 which, projection suggests, occurs *c* 42m west of the present peat edge. T1 could lead to the area of Building 3, but the general direction of the others hints at the existence of buried structures or activity areas, inland from the known buildings.

It is not clear whether 1130 and 9051 are a single trackway or successive tracks along a similar line but, either way, a significant route has been identified stretching seaward for 100m. If projected, T1 and T8 would converge at roughly the seaward extent to which 9050 has been traced. Further east along the

peat shelf there is the series of enigmatic peg structures of which two are linear and have radiocarbon dates which indicate they are broadly contemporary with the other structures, while 9050 is clearly a trackway which heads out into the estuary. The neighbouring 9060 might be the remains of an eroded or dismantled track which would converge with 9050 some 30m to landward.

Looking at the broader scale pattern created by the trackways as a whole may also provide some guide to the way the wider landscape was being used. Surprisingly, and unlike the Somerset Levels trackways (Coles and Coles 1986), the main trend is not towards the dryland of the former Goldcliff Island. The island extended further seaward in the Iron Age (Chapter 2), but only the Trackway Group 1–9 led in that direction and, if projected, would have reached the island about 120m south of the present seawall. However, if convergence means anything, they were probably heading for something much nearer than the island. The main trend of the other routes is out into the Estuary, and for this the most likely purpose is fishing, fowling, and landing places for boats. There may even have been a ferry across the estuary, participating in the networks of riverine and estuarine boat communication of which Sherratt (1996) has written. Where were they travelling from? The clues we have suggest other buildings inland and some likely situations are suggested by the previously noted convergence points. These areas need to be monitored with particular care as erosion proceeds in the years ahead.

11 Dendrochronological dating *by J Hillam*

11.1 Introduction

Dendrochronology was undertaken for three reasons: (i) to provide precise dates for the timber structures, (ii) to produce a site chronology, or chronologies with which to date prehistoric timbers from other sites, and (iii) to extract non-chronological information about the woodlands around Goldcliff and the use of timber at the site with which to supplement evidence produced by other specialists. Oak timbers with sufficient rings for analysis were selected from the structures and contexts outlined in Table 11.1; full details of the samples are given in Table CD 11.1.

11.2 Methods

The samples were first frozen for at least 48 hours to consolidate the wood; they were then cleaned with a Surform plane which highlights the boundaries of the annual growth rings. If the cross-sections are still not clear, an edge may be pared with a Stanley knife. The only exceptions to this procedure were the samples of boat planks. These were not frozen prior to the surfacing of their cross-sections since freezing is thought to prohibit the successful conservation of the timber by breaking down the wood structure. Instead the cross-sections were pared using a razor blade. From a dendrochronological point of view this is not ideal since it is preferable to surface the whole cross-section. However, it proved adequate with the Goldcliff boat planks.

Samples unsuitable for dating purposes were rejected at this stage. These included non-oak samples, samples with unmeasurable ring patterns due to knots or narrow rings, and those with <40 rings. Normally samples with <50 rings are rejected because their ring patterns may not be unique (Hillam *et al* 1987). However, analysis of Iron Age timbers from Fiskerton in Lincolnshire (Hillam 1985a and 1992) had showed that samples with 40–50 rings can sometimes be dated reliably, provided that there are several timbers per structure. In view of the scarcity of prehistoric tree-ring data, it was also felt that the maximum amount of data should be collected from the site and, therefore, analysis was extended to those samples with 40–50 rings.

The ring widths were measured to an accuracy of 0.01mm on a travelling stage connected to a microcomputer which uses a suite of dendrochronology programs written by Tyers (1997). The ring width data were plotted as graphs. Crossmatching was carried out, first visually by comparing the graphs on a light box, and then using a computer program to measure the amount of correlation between two ring sequences. The program uses crossmatching routines which are based on the Belfast CROS program (Baillie and Pilcher 1973, Munro 1984). Generally *t*-values of 3.5 or above indicate a match, provided that the visual match between the tree-ring graphs is acceptable (Baillie 1982, 82–5). *t*-values *c* >10 usually indicate an origin in the same tree, although *t*-values <10 may be produced when different radii are measured on the same trunk. Visual matching can sometimes aid the decision as to whether timbers come from the same tree, but inevitably some same tree samples will go undetected by dendrochronology.

Dating is achieved by averaging the data from the matching sequences to produce a structure or site master curve, and then testing that master for similarity against dated reference chronologies. A site master is used for dating whenever possible because it enhances the general climatic signal, at the expense of the background noise, from the growth characteristics of the individual samples. Any unmatched sequences are tested individually against the reference chronologies. As the analysis progressed and a working master chronology was produced for Goldcliff, new sequences were first tested against this in the search for crossmatching. Matching was accepted if the sequence to be dated matched visually and statistically with the working master, and with the individual components of that master. Figure 11.1 shows the relationship between

Table 11.1 Summary of Goldcliff wood used for dendrochronological analysis

Group	Number of samples selected for analysis
Main peat shelf	
Building 1 and associated timbers	15
Building 2	1
Double Post Row 970	1
Trackway 1108	6
Trackway 1149	1
Boat planks (2) in Structure 1124	3
Goldcliff West	
Building 6	47
Building 8	1
Goldcliff East	
Bog oaks	4
Mesolithic site	
Bog oaks	3

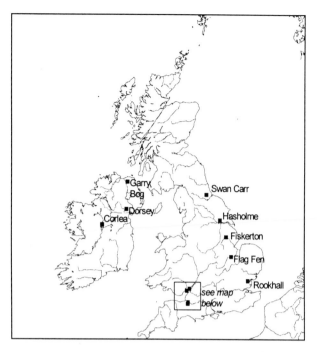

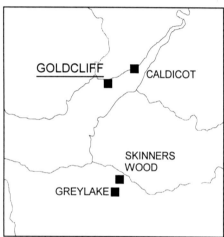

Figure 11.1 Maps showing Goldcliff in relation to the other sites discussed in the dendrochronology report

Goldcliff and the other sites discussed in terms of crossmatching.

Once tree-ring dates have been obtained, calendar dates can be assigned to each of the annual rings within the sample, but the date of the outer ring is not necessarily equivalent to the year of felling. If a sample has bark or bark edge, the date of the last measured ring is the date in which the tree was felled. A complete outer ring indicates that the tree was felled during its period of dormancy between autumn and early spring (referred to as 'winter felled'). A partially formed ring indicates that the tree died in late spring or summer (known as 'summer felled') or, if the springwood is just beginning to form, in spring (Baillie 1982, fig 2.1). Partially formed rings are not measured so, for spring- and summer-felled trees, there will be a one-year discrepancy between the date of the measured ring sequence

and the felling date. It is not always possible to distinguish between an incomplete ring and a complete narrow ring and, therefore, the season of felling is often indistinguishable. Sometimes the outer edge of a sample may be damaged because of the delicate nature of sapwood and, whilst it is known that bark edge was originally present, a few outer rings may have been lost. In cases such as these, the felling dates are precise to within a few years. Where bark edge is absent, felling dates are calculated using the sapwood estimate of 10–55 rings (Hillam *et al* 1987). This is the range of the 95% confidence limits for the number of sapwood rings in British oak trees over 30 years old. Where sapwood is absent, felling dates are given as *termini post quem* (tpq) by adding 10 years, the minimum number of missing sapwood rings, to the date of the last measured heartwood ring. This is the earliest possible felling date but the actual felling date could be much later, depending on how many heartwood rings have been removed during conversion of the trunk into its component timbers.

The estimation of felling date ranges gives some indication of when a tree was felled. This information must then be related to the date that the timber was used. At this stage, factors such as seasoning, reuse, and/or stockpiling have to be considered. Seasoning is unlikely to have had an impact at Goldcliff since timber was usually felled and used green until relatively recently (eg Hollstein 1980). However, the reuse of timber has been a common practice since prehistoric times and stockpiling may also occur. Therefore, although the production of tree-ring dates is an independent process, the interpretation of these dates can sometimes be improved by drawing on other archaeological evidence such as that provided by the wood technologist.

The above gives a brief introduction to dendrochronology. Further information about the history, principles, and methodology of dendrochronology can be found in Baillie (1982) and Hillam (forthcoming a).

11.3 Results

The results are summarised below. Further details can be found on the accompanying CD 11.1–11.7 and/or in the archive report (Hillam forthcoming b).

Buildings 1 and 2, and associated timbers

When the ring sequences were checked for similarity, eight were found to match (Fig 11.2, Table 11.2), six from Building 1, 543 from Building 2, and 526 which was located near Building 1 (Fig 7.3). Their ring widths were averaged to produce a master curve of 202 years. The unmatched sequences were tested against the master, but no further matches were found.

The master curve and any unmatched sequence were compared against dated chronologies over the period 2000 BC–AD 300. These are numerous in the

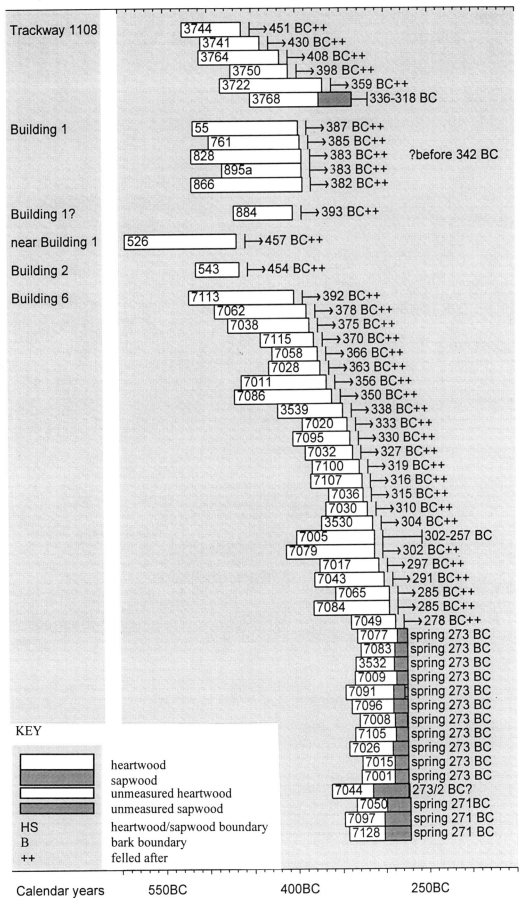

Group   Span of ring sequences and felling dates

Figure 11.2 Bar diagram showing the relative positions of the dated Iron Age ring sequences; bars are arranged in order of felling date

Table 11.2 *t*-value matrix showing the level of agreement between the matching ring sequences from the 1991 excavation

	0055	0526	0543	0761	0828	0866	0884	0895
Dates BC	516–397	593–467	513–464	498–395	518–393	518–392	470–403	483–393
0055		4.69	4.92	4.87	10.03	4.48	6.18	8.91
0526			3.70	4.82	3.52	4.47	\	–
0543				6.23	–	6.20	\	–
0761					4.10	9.07	–	3.27
0828						3.89	7.73	7.71
0866							3.39	–
0884								7.16
0895								

Values <3.0 are not shown; \ is overlap <15 years

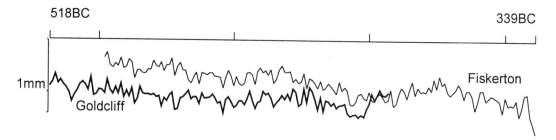

Figure 11.3 Tree-ring match between the master from Buildings 1 and 2 and the chronology from Fiskerton, Lincolnshire. The vertical scale is logarithmic

period 250 BC–AD 300 because the data are derived from Roman timbers. They are less numerous in the prehistoric period. Fortunately, the Goldcliff master gave a very good match with the chronology from the Fiskerton causeway in Lincolnshire (Hillam 1985a, 1992). Its ring sequence gave a *t*-value of 7.8 with Fiskerton over the period 518–392 BC (Table 11.3), and the match was confirmed by an excellent visual agreement (Fig 11.3). Other reference chronologies provided extra confirmation that the match was correct. The Hasholme chronology, derived from the Hasholme logboat in East Yorkshire (Hillam 1987), and three chronologies from Ireland, all showed similarity with some of the Goldcliff ring sequences, particularly those from Building 1 (Table CD 11.2). The Irish chronologies are from two archaeological sites, Corlea and Dorsey (Baillie 1995, 64–67), and from Garry Bog 2, which is made up from bog oaks (Brown *et al* 1986). Interestingly, the 8-timber master from Goldcliff gave lower *t*-values with Ireland and Hasholme than did the original 4-timber master which was made up from samples 55, 761, 828, and 884. This gave *t*-values of 4.0 and 4.8 with the Irish long chronology (Brown *et al* 1986) and Hasholme, respectively.

Building 6

The southeast corner of Building 6 was excavated in 1992 and three posts were sampled for dendrochro-

nology. No dating was forthcoming. The whole structure was excavated in 1993 (Fig 8.6), and the decision made to conserve the timbers for display. It was, therefore, decided to select a further six to eight of the most suitable timbers in the hope that these would provide a date for the structure. In accordance with accepted dendrochronological practice (Hillam forthcoming a), samples with full sapwood and long ring sequences were selected. Some crossmatching was obtained but no dating. Additional timbers were sampled in groups until all those suitable for dendrochronology had been examined. The result before the last few timbers had been sampled was that two master curves were produced, one from timbers from the outer part of one or more trees and the other from the inner part of the tree or trees (Fig 11.4). There was a firm link between the inner tree group and other Goldcliff masters, plus a tentative link between the inner and outer tree masters. If matters had rested at that point, some of the Building 6 timbers would have been dated but the date would have been very imprecise. However, analysis of the final group of timbers confirmed the internal link between the two groups (Table 11.3).

For the purpose of this report, the results will be presented as though the samples were examined as part of a single group. A total of 39 samples were dated (Fig 11.4 and Table CD 11.3) and combined to produce a 250-year chronology. This gave *t*-values of 5.3 and 5.1 with the masters from Buildings 1 and 2 and Trackway 1108, respectively, over the period

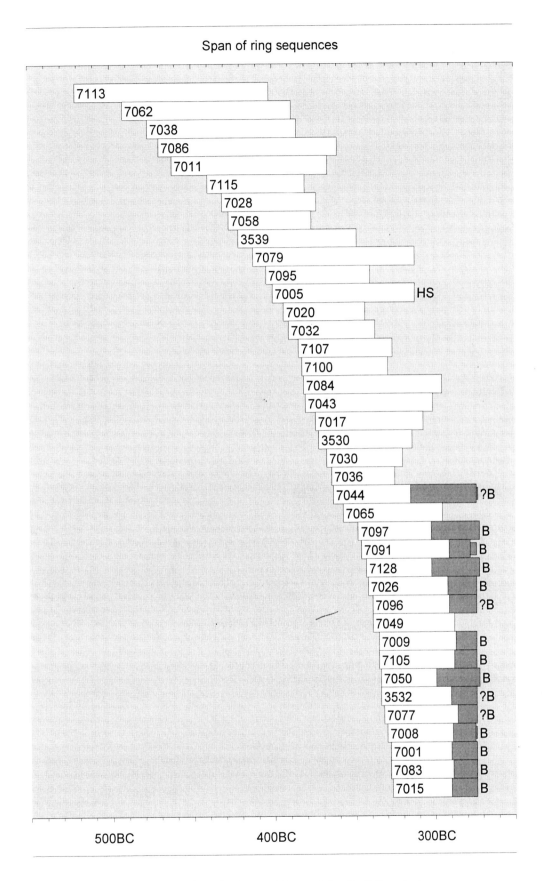

Span of ring sequences

Figure 11.4 Bar diagram showing the relative positions of the Building 6 ring sequences arranged by start date. Key as for Figure 11.2

Table 11.3 Dating the Iron Age master curves: *t*-values with dated reference chronologies

Chronology	Date span	Building 6			Buildings 1 and 2	Trackway 1108	Site master
		Early	**Middle**	**Late**			
England							
Fiskerton (Hillam 1992)	498–339 BC	7.58	4.25	–	7.76	4.88	8.14
Hasholme boat (Hillam 1987)	588–323 BC	–	–	–	–	4.43	–
Swan Carr (Brown and Baillie 1992)	115–381 BC	–	–	–	–	3.42	–
Ireland							
Corlea trackway (Baillie 1995)	446–148 BC	4.80	4.22	–	3.58	3.89	5.79
Dorsey (Baillie unpubl)	570–319 BC	–	–	–	–	3.38	3.03
Garry Bog-2 (Brown *et al* 1986)	890–231 BC	–	–	–	3.61	4.08	–
Goldcliff							
Building 6 early (inner tree group)	521–360 BC		12.31	\	5.21	5.24	
Building 6 middle (intermediate group)	421–295 BC			5.95	–	–	
Building 6 late (outer tree group)	363–272 BC			\		–	
Buildings 1 and 2	593–392 BC					9.28	
Trackway 1108	528–336 BC						

Values <3.0 are not shown; \ is overlap <15 years

Table 11.4 *t*-value matrix showing the level of agreement between the ring sequences from trackway 1108

Date BC	3722 485–369	3741 507–440	3744 528–461	3750 473–408	3764 509–418	3768 451–336
3722		3.58	4.69	6.04	5.15	5.39
3741			5.02	4.54	7.68	\
3744				\	5.66	\
3750					6.26	4.17
3764						3.35
3768						

\ is overlap <15 years

521–272 BC. It also matched Fiskerton with a *t*-value of 6.5 and Corlea trackway in Ireland with a *t*-value of 5.5.

Trackway 1108

Six timbers were analysed from Trackway 1108. These had ring sequences between 66 and 116 years, all of which crossmatched to give a 193-year master curve (Table 11.4). This master crossmatched that from Buildings 1 and 2 with a *t*-value of 9.3 when the trackway master spanned the period 528–336 BC. The correlation values between the trackway master and reference chronologies are given in Table 11.3.

Other structural timbers

Samples from five other structural timbers proved suitable for dendrochronology (Table CD 11.1). Sam-

ple 3837 from Trackway 1149 had 86 rings; 7165 from Building 8 had 48 rings, and 7334 from the Double Post Row 970 had 76 rings. None of these could be dated.

The boat fragments from Structure 1124

Boat Plank 3436 produced two samples, G2 and H2, each of which was measured along two different radii. Only one radius was measured along sample M2 from Plank 3438. H2, with 104 rings, had the longest ring sequence; G2 and M2 had 65 and 82 rings, respectively. Their ring patterns crossmatched to give a master chronology of 113 years. The level of correlation between G2 and H2 from Fragment 3436 was similar to that between G2/H2 and M2 from 3438 (Table 11.5). The two planks are, therefore, probably from the same tree.

When the master was tested against dated chronologies, there was no match with any of the other

Table 11.5 *t*-value matrix showing the level of agreement between the ring sequences from Goldcliff boat fragments

Dates BC	3436G2 1130–1066	3436H2 1130–1027	3438M2 1139–1058
3436G2		8.39	7.26
3436H2			7.65
3438M2			

Goldcliff structural timbers. However, high *t*-values were found with several chronologies over the period 1139–1027 BC (Table 11.6). These were confirmed by the visual matches. The Goldcliff sequence showed particularly good agreement, not only with the oak and ash chronologies from the nearby Caldicot Castle Lake excavations, but also with the oak chronology from the Flag Fen/Fengate excavations in Cambridgeshire (Fig 11.1).

The bog oaks

Seven bog oaks were suitable for measurement, two from the Mesolithic site (Fig 4.2) and five from Goldcliff East. Two samples from Trench 31 were rejected because they were not oak; others from the Mesolithic shelf and Goldcliff East were rejected, either because their rings were unmeasurable, or they had insufficient rings. Some of those that were measured also had rings which were difficult to measure accurately. This may be part of the reason why none of the bog oak sequences have been dated.

The only crossmatching was between 2076 and 2077 from Goldcliff East. These gave a *t*-value of 5.3 and were combined to produce a 223-year master. Neither of the samples was difficult to measure so there can be no doubt about the accuracy of the tree-ring data, but, despite being tested against all available reference chronologies from Britain and Ireland, this master remains undated.

The analysis of 82 oak timbers from Goldcliff, therefore, resulted in the production of three new tree-ring chronologies: a 322-year Iron Age chronology spanning the period 593–272 BC (Table CD 11.4), a Bronze Age chronology for the period 1139–1027 BC (Table CD 11.5), and an undated bog-oak master

of 223 years from Goldcliff East (Table CD 11.6). The latter is made up from only two timbers, but it may date in the future and provide useful reference data.

11.4 Interpretation of the tree-ring dates

The Iron Age timbers

When the tree-ring dates associated with Buildings 1 and 2 are examined, they can be seen to fall into two groups (Fig 11.2). The end dates for 543 from Building 2 and 526, woodworking debris just north of Building, are 464 BC and 467 BC respectively. Allowing for a minimum of ten missing sapwood rings (see Hillam *et al* 1987), these timbers were felled after 454 BC and 457 BC, respectively, and could potentially be the earliest Iron Age timbers to be dated. This is interesting in view of other evidence for various phases of activity in the Building 1 and 2 area (p 99). However, neither piece had sapwood so they could have been cut significantly later.

The last rings on the dated samples from Building 1 itself range from 397 BC to 392 BC. Such similar end dates suggest the timbers are contemporary and could indicate that only the sapwood rings are missing (Baillie 1982, 57). If that were the case, and the sapwood estimate of 10–55 rings is applied, this would give a felling date after 382 BC (by adding 10 to 392 BC) and before 342 BC (by adding 55 to 397 BC), and thus a construction date for Building 1 towards the middle of the 4th century BC (Table 11.7). In Chapter 7 it was suggested that Buildings 1 and 2, although parallel, may not have been absolutely contemporary. There are differences in construction technique and overlapping eaves also seem unlikely. The dendrochronological evidence gives some support to this by suggesting Building 2 may have been constructed earlier but because there is no sapwood it does not represent proof.

Trackway 1108

Of the dated timbers from this trackway, 3768 is the only one which has sapwood. It has a felling date range of 336–318 BC which suggests that the

Table 11.6 Dating the Goldcliff boat chronology. *t*-values with dated reference chronologies

Chronology	Date span	*t*-value
Belfast long chronology (Brown *et al* 1986)	5289 BC–AD 1983	3.7
Caldicot ash chronology (Hillam 1997)	1169–990 BC	5.7
Caldicot oak chronology (Hillam 1997)	1131–998 BC	4.8
Croston 2, Lancs (Brown and Baillie 1992)	1584–970 BC	4.1
Flag Fen/Fengate, Cambs (Neve 1992)	1406–937 BC	4.3
Greylake, Somerset (data Howard pers comm)	1108–952 BC	3.1
Rookhall, Essex (Hillam unpubl)	1264–1106 BC	3.1
Skinners Wood, Somerset (Hillam 1993)	1162–983 BC	3.9

Table 11.7 The dating of the timber structures as indicated by dendrochronology

Bronze Age	
Boat planks from Structure 1124	After 1017 BC
Iron Age	
Building 2	After 454 BC
Building 1	After 382 BC and possibly before 342 BC
Trackway 1108	336-318 BC
Building 6	Spring 273 BC
Building 6 (?)repairs	Spring 271 BC

trackway leading to Building 4 is slightly younger than Building 1. Dendrochronology cannot help with the dating of Building 4 itself since there were no timbers suitable for dendrochronology.

Building 6

Fifteen samples from this Goldcliff West structure had complete sapwood. The outer rings of all these timbers, with the possible exception of one (7044), were just beginning to form indicating that the timbers were felled in spring. Although the exact timing of the onset of growth each year will vary from tree to tree depending on the genetic makeup of the tree, and from year to year depending on climate, this event is likely to occur about April just prior to the opening of the leaves (Baillie 1982, fig 2.1; Varley and Gradwell 1962).

Most of the timbers with complete sapwood were felled in spring 273 BC. These seem to be scattered randomly around the structure as well as including a timber from one of the inner scatters which may represent a support for the roof ridge (Fig 12.4). Three other timbers were felled in spring 271 BC, and perhaps represent repairs to the structure. These are 7050 from the northwest corner, 7097 from the northeast corner, and 7128 from western inner scatter (Fig 12.4). The outer edge of 7044 was slightly damaged and it was not possible to be exact about the time of felling. The last measured ring was 274 BC, but there was another ring which was not measured.

This timber, therefore, may have been felled in winter 273–272 BC or in spring 272 BC. There was no archaeological evidence to indicate that 7044, 7050, 7097, or 7128 were different from the timbers felled spring 273 BC.

The Bronze Age boat fragments from Structure 1124

None of the boat fragments had sapwood, making the estimation of a precise felling date impossible. Allowing for a minimum of ten missing sapwood rings, the timber for the boat was felled some time after 1017 BC (Fig 11.5).

11.5 The timbers

With the exception of Building 6, the relatively small number of samples per structure makes it impossible to derive any valid information about the size and age of tree used at Goldcliff. The tree-rings may, however, indicate the conditions in which the trees were growing.

The average ring widths from the boat fragments in Structure 1124 varied between 0.67mm and 0.86mm, indicating that the timbers came from slow-grown trees and suggesting that where these trees grew conditions were limiting to growth in the Bronze Age. As in the Iron Age, this may be due to wetness (see below).

On the main peat shelf, the Iron Age samples from, or near, Building 1 and Trackway 1108 had relatively narrow rings, as did the single samples from Structure 970 and Trackway 1149 (Table CD 11.1). None of these had average ring widths >1mm, and many were considerably less, which suggests the trees were subject to some form of stress. This could be because they grew in a dense woodland environment and/or because they were subject to adverse conditions. Since alder, a tree of damp conditions, was the dominant timber in Buildings 1, 2, and 4, it is possible that conditions were rather too wet for oak. The similarity between the ring sequences from 1108 and those from Buildings 1 and 2 (Table 11.7) suggests that a single source of timber was being exploited for the complex on the main peat shelf.

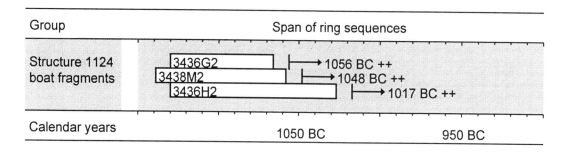

Figure 11.5 Bar diagram showing the relative positions of the ring sequences from the Goldcliff boat fragments; bars are arranged in order of felling date

The sample from Building 2 had wider rings (1.77mm/year) but with only one sample it is impossible to know how representative this is of the Building 2 timbers. Sample 406 had an average growth rate of 1.54mm/year; it was plank which probably eroded from Building 1, 3m to the east.

The timbers used at Goldcliff West grew under conditions more favourable for the oak trees, with average ring widths from Building 6 generally varying between 0.98mm and 2.34mm. The timbers in this structure were identified as 65% oak and 18% hazel, the remainder being made up from ash, elm, field maple, Pomoideae, and willow/poplar. Alder was not represented at all. This may suggest that around 273 BC, conditions around the site were unsuitable even for alder and, therefore, oak may have been brought in from some more favourable site. The only timber from Building 6 with average ring widths well under 1mm is 7044. This is also the only timber which was identified as having been possibly felled in winter, perhaps indicating a different source to the other oak timbers.

It is obvious from the Building 6 tree-ring samples that relatively large and mature oak trees were used to produce the timbers. Figure 11.4 shows the relative positions of the dated ring sequences arranged in order of their start dates. There is no overlap between the rings of the top eight timbers, for example, and the bottom sixteen, indicating that the top group were from the inside of a tree, or trees, whilst the bottom group were from the outside. The timbers in the middle of the bar diagram are intermediate to these two groups. This indicates that the tree, or trees, were split radially and then each segment sub-divided into two and, in some cases, perhaps three pieces.

The first ring of 7113 was within 10 years of the centre of the tree, and the complete chronology is 250 years long. This indicates a tree aged about 260 years old when felled. (It could be slightly older if 7113 came from near the crown of the tree, since it would have less rings than would a sample from near the bottom of the trunk.) Size of tree could be anywhere between 0.5m and 1.2m in diameter. Such a tree could easily produce the timbers necessary to build the structure. However, the ring patterns are not particularly similar (Table CD 11.3). Examination of the t-value matrix for Building 6, the visual matches, and the samples themselves, indicates that some of the timbers are from the same tree. Possible same tree groups are:

3530\7030
7008\7009\7049\7077
7032\7036
3539\7086\7113\7115

Since dendrochronology cannot always detect timbers from the same tree (see above), more of the timbers may be from the same tree. Even so, it is likely that several trees were used in the construction of Building 6; the surplus could easily have been used

for other purposes, including firewood. Crossmatching between the Building 6 ring sequences (Table CD 11.3) is sufficiently good to indicate that a single woodland was being exploited. The only exception is 7044, the timber which could have been felled in winter and which came from a much slower-grown tree than the others.

Sample 7165 from nearby Building 8, unfortunately not intact when excavated, had relatively wide rings averaging 2.24mm/year.

11.6 Discussion

The only other two Iron Age sites in the United Kingdom with wooden remains which have been dated by dendrochronology are the Fiskerton causeway and the Hasholme logboat mentioned above (Hillam 1992). The Hasholme boat, the tree for which was felled or died during 322–277 BC, is younger in date than the Goldcliff timbers from the main peat shelf and slightly older than Building 6 from Goldcliff West. The Fiskerton causeway has felling dates ranging from 456 BC to at least 375 BC. Its period of use may, therefore, correspond with Buildings 1 and 2. The tree-ring match between Goldcliff and Fiskerton is very striking (Fig 11.3) and is almost as good as the internal match between the Building 1 master and that from Trackway 1108, for example. There is also very good matching between the individual ring sequences from Goldcliff and the Fiskerton master.

Although timbers from several Bronze Age sites have been dated, this is the first time that boat timbers of that date have been dated by dendrochronology. Samples have been examined in Sheffield from the remains of similar boats from Caldicot in Gwent (Parry and McGrail 1991), North Ferriby in East Yorkshire (Wright 1990), and Dover in Kent (Bennett 1992), but without success. In the case of the Ferriby boats, this may be because of the condition of the timber when it was finally analysed (Hillam 1985b), whilst access to good cross-sections must have contributed to the lack of dating of the Dover boat (Groves personal communication). The success attained at Goldcliff encourages the hope that more Bronze Age boats will be dated in the future.

11.7 Conclusion

There are relatively few prehistoric archaeological sites in England and Wales which have produced tree-ring dates. For the Bronze Age, there is a group of sites with ring sequences ending around 1000 BC. The Goldcliff boat fragments belong to this group, which also includes nearby Caldicot and Flag Fen/Fengate in Cambridgeshire. In the Iron Age, the Goldcliff structural timbers from Buildings 1 and 2 are broadly contemporary with the Fiskerton causeway from Lincolnshire, and slightly older than the Hasholme logboat discovered in East Yorkshire, whilst Building 6, constructed in 273 BC or just after, is the youngest Iron Age structure so far dated in Britain. The two Goldcliff chronologies, spanning the periods 1139–1027 BC and 593–272 BC, may prove useful in dating timbers from other sites in the future.

Acknowledgements

The tree-ring analysis of the Goldcliff timbers received funding from Cadw; it also forms part of the English Heritage-funded research project aimed at producing a prehistoric tree-ring chronology for southern Britain. I am also grateful to Martin Bell and Richard Brunning for information about the site, and to Mike Baillie and Dave Brown for providing unpublished tree-ring chronologies. Further data were made available through the EU Environmental Research Programme, contracts EV5V-CT94-0500 and ENV5-CT95-0127. Thanks also to Cathy Groves for analysing some of the bog oak samples and for helpful discussions about the site.

12 Wood and woodworking at Goldcliff *c* 400–1 BC

by R Brunning, S Johnson and R Morgan

12.1 Introduction to wood studies

In this project the overwhelming predominance of artefacts and material cultural remains was wood, forming prehistoric structures. Given the vulnerability of the remains in the intertidal area, the emphasis throughout was on making a record of the wooden structures as exposed in plan, and carrying out strategic small-scale excavations to investigate their character and obtain samples of wood and environmental samples. Buildings 1, 2, 5, and 6 were totally excavated. Samples were taken of Buildings 3, 4, 7, and 8 and small-scale excavations took place on most of the nineteen trackways. The scale of excavation of each structure varied greatly from those producing single posts for radiocarbon dating to those producing >100. Over the seasons of work (1990–94) *c* 1159 pieces of wood were lifted; these have been identified by Johnson (Section 12.2), who has also looked at samples from some structural wood which was not lifted (eg Buildings 3, 4, 7 parts of Trackway 970) and the submerged forest. The lifted wood was examined for evidence of woodworking by Brunning (Section 12.3). Morgan (Section 12.4) has looked at 745 pieces for tree-ring studies, mostly pieces of unsplit wood with bark preserved and pieces where sampling would not compromise the wood conservation strategy. Thus, each specialist examined somewhat different proportions of the material from a given context, so the sample sizes described in each of the individual studies also vary. The large amount of data generated by study of this wood is represented in graphs and plans in the text, supported by many tables of data and plans of some of the less important structures on CD 12. This chapter includes drawings of 89 pieces of wood, representative, as far as possible, of the main structures excavated and the types of wood and woodworking within them. An additional collection of 52 wood drawings is contained on the supporting CD.

Of the total lifted assemblage of around 1159 pieces, a sample of 503 pieces (43%) has been selected for conservation. All the wood from Building 6 (144 pieces) is being conserved by the National Museum of Wales. Philip Parkes has been responsible for conservation of the rest of the assemblage at the Department of Archaeology, University of Wales, Cardiff; this too will be housed in the National Museum. This includes a large sample of 270 pieces from Buildings 1, 2, and 5, 20 pieces from Trackway 1108, 17 pieces from Building 8, and smaller numbers from other buildings and trackways. Most of the 57% of the assemblage which had not been identified for conservation had regrettably to be disposed of in 1998 once the studies reported in this chapter were completed. The exceptions are small numbers retained from structures which have not been radiocarbon dated and small groups of material retained for teaching purposes.

A study of the degradation processes of the wood has been published elsewhere by Blanchette and Hoffman (1993). That Scanning Electron Microscope based study showed a relatively intact overall cell structure, but with severely degraded cell walls, with evidence for the activities of erosion and tunnelling bacteria rather than fungal activity.

12.2 Wood identifications
Su Johnson

12.2.1 The submerged forest

Surveys were made of the submerged forest in four areas where samples were taken of each stump or tree trunk. In this way it has been possible to produce maps of the composition of the fen woodland. (For earlier work on the composition of the submerged forest see Allen 1992.) Such evidence provides, in the early periods, a valuable insight to the composition of coastal wildwood and ecology (Wilkinson *et al* 1997, Bell 1997). In the later periods the composition of these submerged forests provides special opportunities for comparison with the other environmental evidence reviewed in Chapters 13–15 and with the evidence for the use of wood in the prehistoric structures outlined in this chapter.

The earliest woodland sampled, long predating the structures discussed in this chapter, is the peat shelf above the Mesolithic site where the trees predate the transition to raised bog *c* 4900 BP. This essentially Mesolithic forest was planned and sampled, the distribution of the species being shown in Figure 4.2. One hundred and twenty-two pieces were identified, 86 stumps and 36 trunks. Alder predominates in the trunks (58% compared with birch 28%), but among the stumps there are more birch (47%) compared with alder (37%). Willow (8%), oak (14% trunks, 6% stumps), and hawthorn family (1%) are also present. Thus, species of wet conditions predominate, although the oaks imply this location on the edge of the island was drier than much of the later submerged forest to the west considered below. There is some spatial difference in the composition of this woodland (Fig 4.2): alder and birch occur over the whole area, with willow on the southern part and oak and hawthorn family on the northern part. The contrast

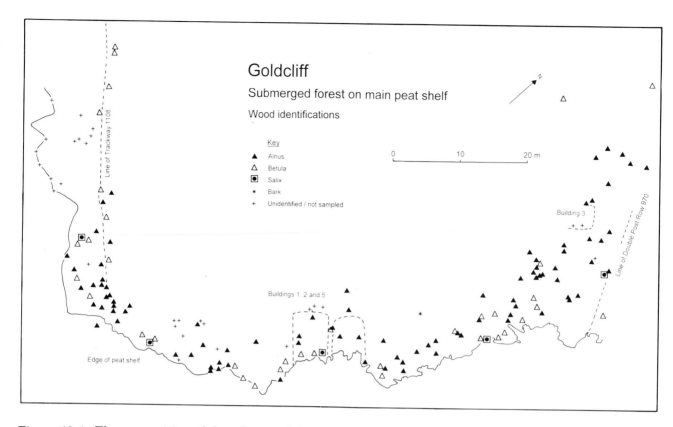

Figure 12.1 The composition of the submerged forest in the area of Buildings 1–4, between Structures 1108 and 970. Drawing by S Johnson. Alnus *(alder);* Betula *(birch),* Salix *(willow)*

is likely to be temporal; the oak and hawthorn family are at a slightly higher level where the peat is less eroded. This reminds us that where we see a submerged forest exposed, we can not assume that all those trees were coeval because erosion and oxidation are greater closer to the peat edge, and here earlier peats tend to be exposed.

The area most intensively sampled was the Iron Age peat shelf between Structures 1108 and 970, the area around Buildings 1–4 (Fig 12.1). In all, 121 samples were examined: 64% were alder, 31% birch, and 5% willow. Prior to the making of the structures, conditions were obviously sufficiently dry for a few decades so that trees tolerant of wet conditions could grow. The submerged forest between Structure 1103 and Trackway 1 was similarly mapped (CD 12.1) and 24 stumps identified. Of these, 54% were alder and

46% were willow, reflecting a wetter phase of the submerged forest near the point where wood peat gave way to reed and sedge communities.

Seventeen stumps were examined at Goldcliff West. These were from the Building 8 area (Fig 8.17), a distinct wood layer below the level of the building and exposed by the erosion of part of the building. All of these were birch and indicate a phase when the raised bog dried out sufficiently for temporary colonisation by trees.

12.2.2 The buildings

Preservation and completeness of buildings varied considerably, so there are big differences in the number of samples available for identification.

Table 12.1 Submerged forests, wood identification

Species	Peat shelf A	Peat shelf B	Goldcliff West	Mesolithic site	
	Stumps	Stumps	Stumps	Trunks	Stumps
Alder	78	13		21	32
Birch	38		17	10	41
Willow	5	11			7
Oak				5	5
Hawthorn type					1
Total	121	24	17	36	86

Note: Peat shelf A between 1108 and 970, Peat shelf B between 1103 and Trackway 1

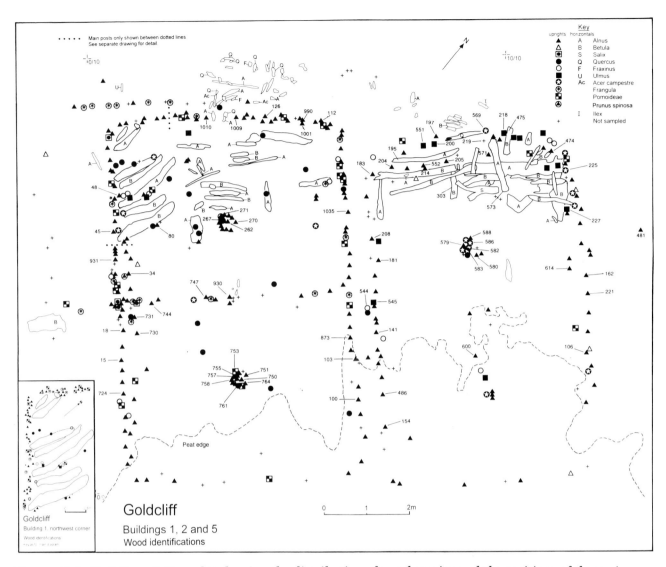

Figure 12.2 Buildings 1, 2, and 5 showing the distribution of wood species and the positions of those pieces which are illustrated, or are discussed in the dendrochronological report, or Chapter 12. Inset: northwest corner of Building 1. Drawing by S Johnson. Alnus *(alder),* Betula *(birch),* Salix *(willow),* Quercus *(oak),* Fraxinus *(ash),* Ulmus *(elm),* Acer campestre *(field maple),* Frangula *(alder buckthorn),* Pomoideae *(hawthorn family),* Prunus spinosa *(blackthorn),* Ilex *(holly)*

Buildings 1 and 5 (Fig 12.2, CD 12.2)

A total of 409 pieces of wood from in and around Building 1 were identified, including posts and stakes from the walls and interior, wattle, flooring, and woodworking debris. Ten species were present with alder by far the most common (56%). Alder accounted for c 75% of the walls and post settings, and c 60% of the wattle and flooring. Oak was the next most common (11%) and occurred more often as internal posts than in the walls. About half of the woodworking debris was oak. Other species present accounted for <10% each. Birch, which made up 6% of the assemblage as a whole, accounted for 13% of the wattle and 30% of the flooring. In the south end, alder is the main species used, with only a few oak, ash, and hawthorn family. In the north end, which is better preserved, there is a greater variety of wood used. Just over 9% of the assemblage consisted of alder buckthorn, a species which occurs only rarely elsewhere at Gold-cliff. This species occurs in the north wall, the northern ends of the east and west walls, and in the two lines forming the possible Structure 5.

The wood identifications do not show clear evidence of repair, the double line of posts along the west wall could be an internal feature. Building 5 is apparently defined by the distribution of alder buckthorn (Chapter 7), but if this building consists of the central partition, the north part of the east wall and the lines of posts outside the west and north walls, it becomes difficult to explain the alder buckthorn in the west wall.

Building 2 (Fig 12.2, CD 12.3)

There are 140 samples from this structure and, as in Building 1, the most common species was alder (56%). Birch accounted for 13% of the assemblage, about half on the floor. Both elm and field maple were more common than in Building 1 at c 9% each, and oak accounted for only c 3% of the assemblage.

It is likely that Building 2 was repaired, as suggested by the apparent replacement of the axial posts and north wall. However, the differences in wood identifications are not sufficient on their own to suggest which parts are original and which repairs. Possibly the outer north wall is the repair.

Much of the wood for Buildings 1 and 2 could have originated in the surrounding alder carr woodland discussed above.

Building 3 (CD 12.4 and 12.5)

This building was constructed of vertical elements of varying sizes, divided into those which, in the field, were defined (not always consistently) as posts and stakes/pegs. It should also be noted that some of the pieces described as 'pegs' could be wattle. Seventy-two samples from in and around this structure were identified, 58 from the building itself and a further 14 pieces, which may, or may not, have originally been part of the structure, came from the area around the building (CD 12.6). Of the samples from the structure itself, 20 were from the floor, 35 from upright elements, and 2 from woodworking debris.

The building was constructed mainly from alder (58%) and birch (34%), with alder the more common in the upright elements and birch in the floor timbers. There was also one ash peg, two alder buckthorn pegs/stakes, and a piece of alder buckthorn of unknown function. The species composition of wood from outside the building is similar to that from the building itself, alder and birch, with one piece of field maple.

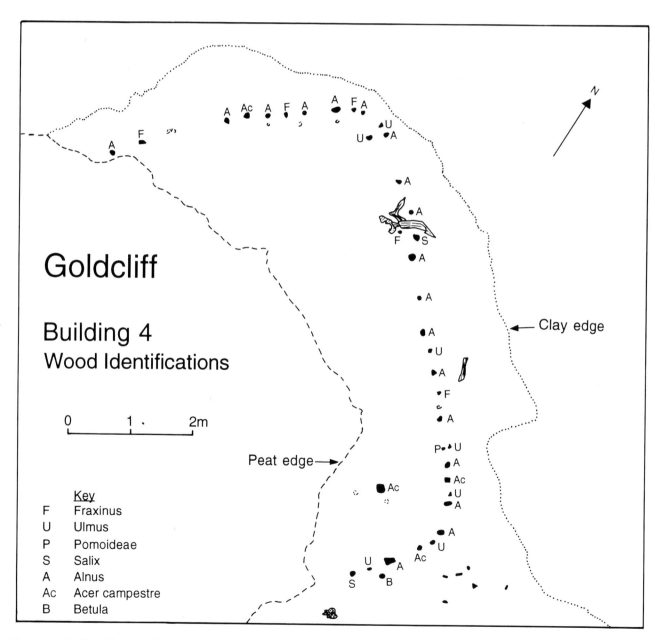

Figure 12.3 Building 4 showing the distribution of wood species. Drawing by S Johnson. Fraxinus (ash), Ulmus (elm), Pomoideae (hawthorn family), Salix (willow), Alnus (alder), Acer campestre (field maple), Betula (birch)

This building was of similar composition to the surrounding fen woodland (Fig 12.1). The tree stumps on this part of the peat shelf are mostly alder and birch, with some willow (which does not occur in Building 3). Alder buckthorn and field maple have not been identified in this woodland, but it has not been possible to sample every stump.

Building 4 (Fig 12.3, Table CD 12.4)

Thirty-eight samples were taken from the surviving north end of this building. These show a pattern of more or less evenly spaced alder roundwood (occasionally split timber), in most cases separated by one or two posts or stakes of other species. This pattern

is not as evident along the short remaining section of the east wall where the sequence is willow round-wood, split elm, split alder, maple roundwood, split elm, alder roundwood. Inside the northwest corner of the building there are several extra non-alder posts which are on a slightly different alignment to the main wall line and may represent a repair.

Building 6 (Fig 12.4, CD 12.4)

All the structural timbers from Building 6 have been identified except for eleven pieces from the southwest corner which were eroded out by the sea between the 1993 and 1994 excavations. The wall line was constructed largely from split oak and hazel round-

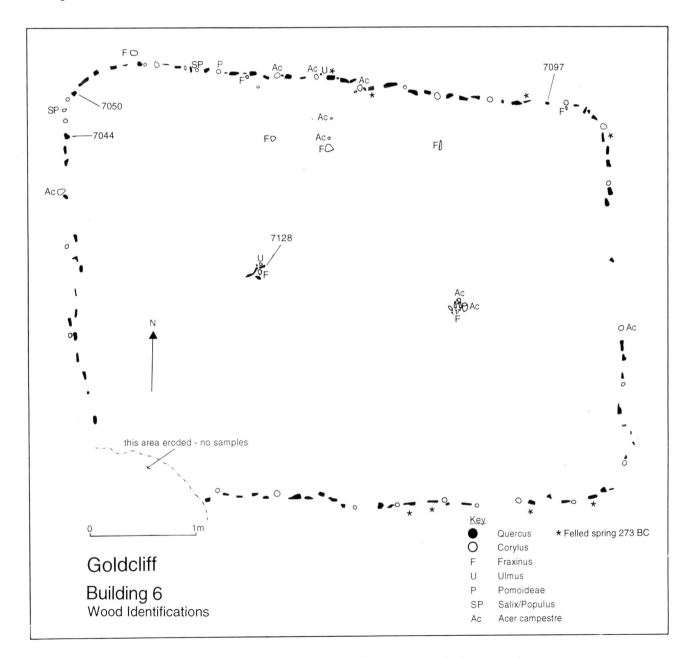

Figure 12.4 Building 6 showing the distributions of wood species and the location of pieces dendrochronologically dated. Drawing by S Johnson. Quercus *(oak),* Corylus *(hazel),* Fraxinus *(ash),* Ulmus *(elm),* Pomoideae *(hawthorn family),* Salix/Populus *(Willow/poplar),* Acer campestre *(field maple)*

wood posts, with a few other species used for the roundwood posts along part of the northwest wall. The assemblages from the two central roof supports are quite different. The western setting was composed of four pieces of oak, one of ash and one of elm, whereas the eastern setting was of three pieces of ash and two of field maple. Other than the post settings, the only internal timbers were some split ash and field maple roundwood pieces at the northern end. The use of oak and hazel as split timber and roundwood posts, respectively, is remarkably consistent around most of the wall line, which may mean that these two species were selected for those particular uses. The northwest wall line, where roundwood posts of woods other than hazel were used, is apparently original rather than a repair. Perhaps the supply of hazel was inadequate to finish the building, so other species were used. The wood was probably obtained from a fairly dry woodland, of contrasting composition to the submerged forest east of the Pill, and the careful arrangement of the different species may indicate that the building was in some way special.

Building 7 (Fig 8.14, CD 12.4)

All 21 of the surviving timbers were sampled. Almost half were alder, with three samples each of oak, ash, and field maple, and one each of elm and hawthorn family. It is thought that much of this building has been eroded and there is no clear pattern to the distribution of wood types.

Building 8 (Plan CD 12.7, Table CD 12.4)

By the time this building was sampled, a large part of it had been eroded, leaving only 21 verticals. Almost half were ash, and 28% were field maple, with three elm and two oak. The wood is likely to have come from a drier woodland than the alder carr suggested for the buildings east of the Pill.

12.2.3 Trackways and linear structures

Trackways 1108 and 1149 (Plan CD 12.8, Table CD 12.9)

There were 124 samples from these two trackways, 108 from 1108 and 16 from 1149. The range of species present in both is similar. Alder is slightly more common than field maple, although it is only more common as brushwood. Oak and field maple are more common as both horizontals and upright elements, and ash and elm also occur as upright elements more often than alder. The distribution of the species, and the fact that most of the more common species were used for different structural elements, suggests that there was little selection of species for different purposes. Species composition suggests no obvious difference between the two structures.

Double Post Row 970 (Fig 12.5, Table CD 12.10)

Along a length of around 10m, approximately 72% of the posts from this structure were sampled, giving a total of 110 pieces. Most were from posts, stakes, and pegs, with only thirteen from possible horizontals. Eight species were present, three of which accounted

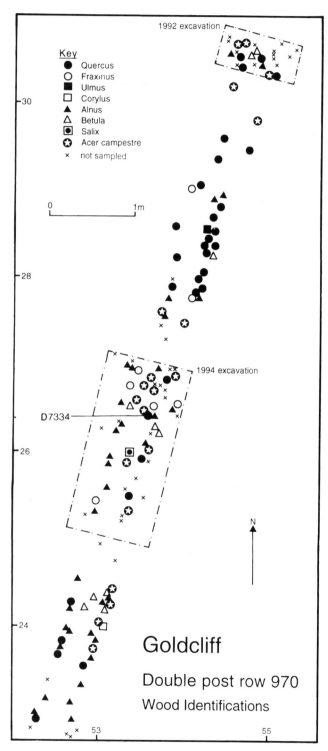

Figure 12.5 Double Post Row 970 showing the distributions of wood species. Drawing by S Johnson. Quercus (oak), Fraxinus (ash), Ulmus (elm), Corylus (hazel), Alnus (alder), Betula (birch), Salix (willow), Acer campestre (field maple)

for >80% of the assemblage. Alder was again the most common (35%), and oak accounted for 27%. Field maple was less common (19%), but included all but one of the definite horizontal elements. Birch made up around 9% of the assemblage and ash c 6.5%. Elm, hazel, and willow each occurred only once.

There are some apparent patterns in the distribution of the different species in this structure. Alder is more common than oak in, and to the south of, the 1994 excavation trench; north of this trench oak is the more common. Birch appears to occur in small groupings: one in the 1994 trench and one just to its south. A further two birch samples occur in the 1992 trench with a single post, or stake, between the two trenches. Field maple has less well defined groups, although there is a distinct group of horizontals and stakes/posts at the north end of the 1994 trench. The apparent grouping of some species suggests the possibility of construction in stages, which is interesting as the overall plan shows short straight lengths which are not precisely aligned. One possibility is that the trees were selected in a fairly random fashion, but all the usable wood from one tree was used before going on to the next, possibly by different people working on each side or on different lengths of the row. This could explain the apparently different character of the different lengths and of the two lines, especially south of the 1994 trench.

Structure 1103 (Plan CD 12.11, Table CD 12.12)

This structure was probably a trackway or fence comprising vertical stakes, brushwood and some larger horizontal pieces. In places the 'brushwood' appears to have been woven around the uprights. A total of 112 samples were identified and nine species were present. All the species were represented in the 'stake' category, but there was less variety among the other structural elements. Alder made up 70% of the assemblage and was used for all structural elements. Willow (11%) occurred mostly as brushwood, with one stake and one horizontal. The only other species occurring as elements other than stakes were ash (one brushwood sample) and field maple (one post and one brushwood sample). The pattern of species distributions does not clarify the nature or phasing of this enigmatic structure. The abundance of alder is probably because it was the most common local timber source; tree stumps in the surrounding contemporary submerged forest are all alder and willow, and woodchips were present around the structure, so some wood was worked on the spot.

Trackways 1–9 (Plan CD 12.1, Table CD 12.13)

This group of trackways, exposed over 45m of the eastern part of the main peat shelf, were all of similar construction, brushwood with some larger, lateral horizontals and some vertical pegs and stakes. The

number of identification samples from these trackways varied between 86 from Trackway 4 to one from Trackway 3, with none from Trackways 2 and 7. One hundred and ninety-one samples were identified but only four species were present. Alder was the species used most often in all but Trackways 5 and 9, and was the only species found in the samples from Trackways 1, 3 (one sample only), and 8. The brushwood sample from Trackway 5 consisted entirely of willow, which was slightly more common than alder in Trackway 9 and accounted for c 10% and 20% of the samples from Trackways 6 and 4. In this trackway group there are too few samples from the larger structural elements to suggest preferential use of different species for specific elements, although alder is generally the most frequent, and sometimes the only species used. Overall, alder accounted for 75% of the wood in the samples from these trackways, and willow another 22%.

Alder buckthorn occurred in two trackways: as a single post/stake in Trackway 4 and as brushwood in Trackway 9. Birch occurred only as single pieces of brushwood in Trackways 4 and 6. Apart from the single alder buckthorn post/stake all the larger elements in the trackways' construction were of alder or willow (mostly alder) and the buckthorn and birch occurred in very small numbers as brushwood. The tree stumps between Trackway 1 and Structure 1103 are all alder and willow, which strongly suggests the use of trees growing in the immediate area of the trackways.

Palaeochannel 9053 and area (Plan CD 12.14, Table CD 12.15)

A total of 21 samples from this area of wood debris and probable pegs were identified. Twelve of these were described as structural and one as natural, but it has not been possible to assign the remaining eight to either category. The most numerous species were alder, birch, and willow, but the most interesting occurrences were the single examples of lime and holly, both of which are very uncommon at Goldcliff. The lime is particularly interesting since it apparently came from a tree trunk, presumably derived from woodland of a different composition to that examined in detail to the west around Trackways 1108 and 1, but with similarities to material from Trackway 9051 (below). It may be that some at least of this wood has been eroded from a much earlier submerged forest.

Trackways 1130 and 9051 (Table CD 12.16)

These two trackways have been traced and sampled over a distance of around 100m. Ninety-four pieces of wood from the trackways have been identified and show significant differences in the species composition between 1130 and 9051. Sixty-three samples were taken from the northern end of the trackway

(Trench 22 and northwards), in which only four species were present. Over 60% of this assemblage was birch, 22% alder, and 14% willow, there was also a single hazel peg. Thirty-two samples were taken from the area south of Trench 22, in which twelve species were present. Ash, alder, hazel, and birch were most common (four to six occurrences each), oak, field maple, elm, and lime all occurred twice and there was one example each of willow, willow/poplar, ivy, and hawthorn family. The difference in species composition, and slight difference of alignment of 1130 and 9051, suggests they are two different structures and different sources of wood are suggested, either in time, or space. Some of the species are also generally uncommon in the Goldcliff samples: the hawthorn family is uncommon away from Buildings 1 and 2, hazel occurs only occasionally in the trackways, lime is also rare (seven examples in the Goldcliff assemblage), and the ivy sample is the only one from the site. The eroded appearance of some 9051 horizontal wood in the field suggests that driftwood or wood from an earlier submerged forest may have been used. If so, the woodland from which it was derived was very different, drier, and more mixed, than the predominantly alder and birch with willow characteristic of the surviving Iron Age submerged forest.

Structures between 9066 and 9050 (Table CD 12.17)

Structure 9066 (Table CD 12.17, Plan CD 12.18)
Twenty-four pegs from this small, semi-circular grouping were identified. Most were alder (around 70%) with one or two each of ash, hazel, birch, and blackthorn. The distribution of alder defines a semi-circular area suggesting perhaps a light hide or shelter.
  Structure 9062 (Table CD 12.17, Plan CD 12.19)
Sixteen samples from this amorphous structure were identified, twelve were described as pegs or stakes and the rest as debris. Six species were present, although only alder, elm, and hazel occurred more than once. There was one occurrence of mistletoe, apparently used as a peg.
  Structure 9061 and Context 9055 (Table CD 12.17, Plan CD 12.20)
Seven samples from 9061 were identified, three were alder and there were single samples of ash, hazel, alder buckthorn, and bark. An ash peg and oak and alder horizontals were identified from Context 9055, approximately 4.5m north of 9061.
  Structure 9060 (Table CD 12.17, Plan CD 12.21)
This double peg row (?eroded trackway) produced sixteen pegs and two horizontals which were identified. All but two of the pegs were willow, the remaining two and one of the horizontals were alder, the other elm.
  Trackway 9050 (Table CD 12.17, Plan CD 12.22)
Samples from fourteen stakes and 28 horizontals and brushwood were identified from this clearly defined trackway. Around 82% of the stakes were alder and

the rest willow. All the samples from pieces described as horizontals were alder and all those described as brushwood were willow.

Comment on structures between 9066 and 9050

Overall, almost half of the wood from this group of structures was alder and almost 30% willow. Hazel (six pieces) is uncommon at Goldcliff (except in and around Building 6), blackthorn (one sample) is even more uncommon on the site in general, and the mistletoe sample from Trackway 9050 is the only one recorded from the site. Only two of the structures (9050 and 9060) have been dated and appear to be broadly contemporary. There is nothing in the wood identifications which might suggest a different date for the other structures, which were of more enigmatic form.

12.3 Wood and woodworking at Goldcliff *c* 400–1 BC
Richard Brunning

12.3.1 Methodology and characterisation of the assemblage

Each piece of wood lifted or sampled was given an individual wood number, with the exception of some group numbered woodchips and brushwood. After cleaning, the dimensions, morphology, and woodworking information were recorded on wood recording sheets. Cross sections were drawn of all the converted timbers and woodworking debris. The converted material was described according to the method of splitting, such as radial, tangential, half or quarter split. Some of the radials from very large trees had been sub-divided tangentially. These were termed 'reduced radials'. The knottiness of the wood was assessed on a scale of 1–5 with 5 being very straight grained and 1 very knotty.

The sampling and recording was undertaken according to the latest professional guidelines (Coles 1990, English Heritage 1996). For the sake of brevity the common English names are used for the wood species.

The recording methodology followed that used in the Somerset Levels and other prehistoric sites in Britain and Ireland (Coles *et al* 1985, Orme and Coles 1983, Brunning and O'Sullivan 1997, O'Sullivan 1997). The worked points of timbers were classified according to the number of sides they had been worked on to produce 'pencil', 'wedge' or 'chisel' shaped ends. The number, length, width, and cross-sectional shape of the tool facets were noted. Where the tool blade had come to a stop in the wood leaving a small step, this curvature or 'jam curve' was traced as a record of the blade shape. Small ridges and grooves left by irregularities in the cutting blade were only present on a very small number of timbers. Their presence on the bottoms of the axial posts and absence from the stakes set at lower depth, suggests that these 'tool signatures' may be one of the first features to be lost to decay (Sands 1997).

The wood assemblage from the Iron Age layers at Goldcliff was derived from the remains of the rectangular buildings and linear features which are interpreted as trackways. In addition, there is a small amount of artefactual material, mainly from the palaeochannel around Building 6. Much of the horizontal material exposed on the surface was in a very poor state of preservation. The worked tips of the pegs and stakes were in a better condition, although many of the more slender points were buckled and bent as a result of a combination of driving into place while still green, together with subsequent compression from overlying sediments.

12.3.2 The buildings

Woodworking information was recorded from 631 items from the rectangular buildings. This was comprised of 566 structural elements, 9 pieces of flooring, and 56 pieces of woodworking debris. These figures do not include the material recovered from the palaeochannel around Building 6, where 24 pieces of woodworking debris and artefacts were recorded.

The proportions of the different buildings analysed

varied considerably. Buildings 1, 2, 5, 6, and 8 had virtually all their surviving timbers studied. A much smaller proportion of Building 3 was analysed, and Buildings 4 and 7 were just sampled for species identification, with only one axial post from Building 7 being extracted for woodworking analysis. In addition, the buildings all suffered from varying degrees of erosion. Buildings 1 and 2 were the most complete, with some flooring material surviving and the smaller wall stakes still present in the northern end of Building 1. Building 6 also retained most of its wall line, but the other structures had probably lost many of their wall posts.

Building 1 (Figs 12.6–12.8, Table CD 12.24, additional wood drawings CD 12.25)

A total of 300 pieces of wood were analysed, consisting of 249 structural elements, 45 pieces of woodworking debris, and 6 pieces of flooring. The structural elements can be divided into four main categories, the large wall posts, the smaller wall stakes, the central posts and their packing, and the stall divisions and possible internal aisles. The separation of the posts and stakes is somewhat subjective as the smallest posts and largest stakes are very similar.

The large wall posts were almost all roundwood

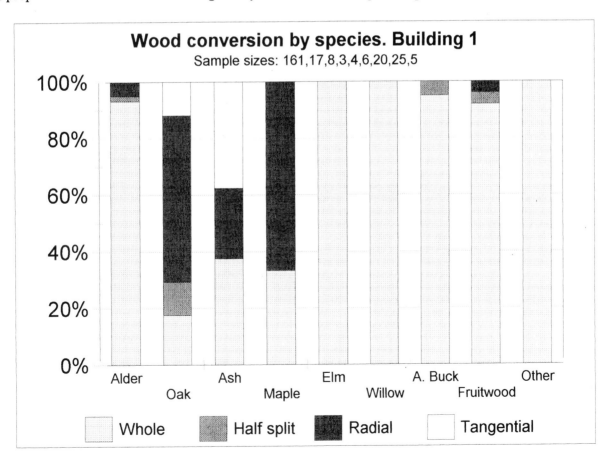

Figure 12.6 Wood conversion by species in Building 1. Fruitwood = Pomoideae. Drawing by R Brunning. For a table of the data see CD 12.24

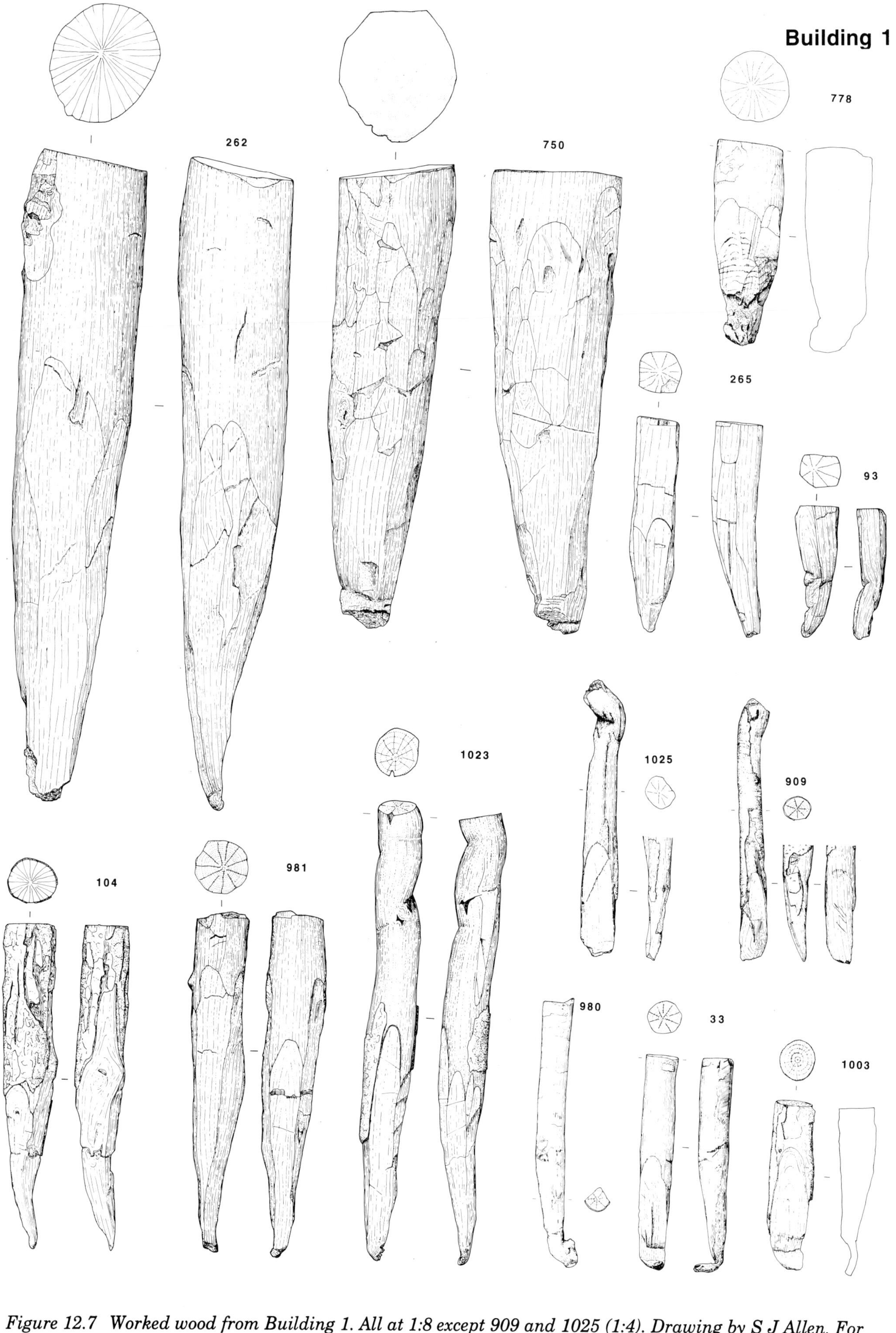

Figure 12.7 Worked wood from Building 1. All at 1:8 except 909 and 1025 (1:4). Drawing by S J Allen. For additional wood drawings see Figure 12.8 and CD 12.25

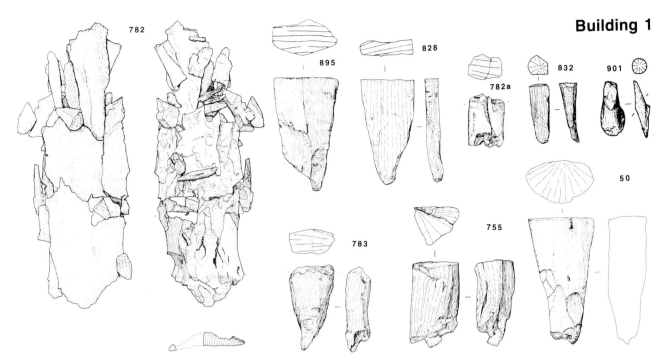

Figure 12.8 Worked wood from Building 1. All at 1:8 except 901 (1:2), trimmed branch. Drawn by S J Allen. For additional wood drawings see Figure 12.7 and CD 12.25

(96%), with the vast majority being alder (82%). Hazel (7%) and fruitwood (4%) were the only other species present in significant numbers, with the remainder of the roundwood composed of single examples of many different species. The converted posts consisted of one radially split ash and two alder and one oak which had been tangentially split.

The 92 smaller stakes in the wall line were also mainly roundwood (94%). The converted material comprised two tangential and one radial pieces of ash, two radial alder, and single half-split examples of alder buckthorn and fruitwood. The roundwood was again mainly alder (57%), but also contained a much larger proportion of alder buckthorn (14%) and fruitwood (20%) and a significant willow element (6%).

The central posts and most of their supporting timbers were roundwood, all being alder except two pieces of fruitwood (Pomoideae) and one blackthorn. The other supports comprised five alder and one oak radials, and single examples of half-split alder and oak.

The stalls and potential aisles had quite a different composition. The timbers which might be the remnant of two rows of aisle posts are all radially split oak, with a single exception which is a tangential oak timber. The most northerly stall division is formed by four radially split timbers, three of oak and one field maple (Fig 12.8: 828, 895). The second stall division is more varied with four roundwood stakes (two of ash, one alder, and one elm) and single split pieces of ash, alder, elm, and fruitwood.

The large wall posts, central post groups, and the stall and aisle posts all had cut ends with surviving facets at shallow angles mainly of 1–16°, the shallow

blows forming the top of the point while the shorter, more steeply angled facets, cut across the heartwood at the tips. In the majority of cases (62%), this produced a pencil type point, with many fewer examples of wedge or chisel shaped points (Fig 12.7: 262). Roughly half the timbers were cut to a point over all their surviving length, but where this was not the case the length of the cut points varied between 58mm and 870mm. In some cases long shallow cuts were observed high up on one or two sides of the posts, though not contributing significantly to the pointing process, or removing side branches.

The smaller wall stakes had points that were mainly chisel shaped (77%) (Fig 12.7: 33, 1003), with a smaller number of wedge points (19%) and hardly any pencil points (4%). The points were cut over short lengths of 29–222mm with the majority <100mm. The surviving facets showed a small number of steeply angled (5–30°) blows were used to sever the stems and point the tips.

A large proportion of the flooring consisted of birch logs that were too decayed and compressed to be useful for woodworking analysis. Of the remaining six pieces, one was a birch log, another a half-split piece of alder buckthorn, and the rest were alder. Of the latter, one was quarter-split, one radially, one tangentially split, and one left in the round. One of these split alder planks (Fig 12.8: 782) appeared to have been pegged down through two holes, but this plank was in such a poor state of preservation that the dimensions of these apparent perforations could not be determined. The 'pegs' consisted of a small radial oak fragment (Fig 12.8: 782a) and a small alder fragment. The piece of alder that was not split was also badly decayed but may have been cut flat on at least one side.

The woodworking debris was recorded in three separate areas associated with Building 1, and consisted of woodchips and small offcuts. Eight pieces came from within the north door, seven others from elsewhere inside the building, and the largest concentration, of 30 pieces, outside the north wall. The assemblage within the building consisted of one radial and four tangential pieces of alder, a half-split alder buckthorn fragment, and a tangential ash piece. The group from within the door was also mainly of alder, of which three were tangential fragments and one quartered. In addition, were a radial oak fragment and a half-split piece of ash, the other two elements being small woodchips of unidentified species. The 30 pieces from the area north of Building 1 were very different to the other two groups, as over half their number were oak woodchips and small offcuts, with a mixture of radial, tangential, and intermediate cross sections. Most of the rest of this group consisted of other radial and tangential woodchips and off-cuts of field maple, ash, alder, and elm. The other debris in this assemblage consisted of a quarter-split piece of ash and two cut branches, one alder and the other alder buckthorn. The debris from all these groups were mainly

100–220mm in length and 20–55mm in width. Only a few examples lay outside these dimensions.

Building 5 (Figs 12.11 and 12.12, CD 12.29)

A total of 33 pieces of wood were studied from the two lines of stakes thought to represent the walls of this building. The line to the north of Building 1 supplied ten examples, and the remainder were derived from the line which crossed the centre of that building. Some of the latter group may, however, actually be part of the west wall of Building 1.

All of these stakes were left in the round, with bark still present in most cases. The species composition was dominated by alder (52%) and alder buckthorn (33%), with the latter being more prevalent in the northern row. Willow was the only other identified species.

The material varied in quality from very straight-grained to quite knotty. The points were formed by cuts over relatively short lengths of 40–196mm, delivered by shallowly angled blows between 1° and 20° (Fig 12.12). These formed a mixture of chisel shaped points and simple pencil shaped points, together with a small number of wedge shaped ends. This pattern is probably a reflection of the small size of most of this assemblage.

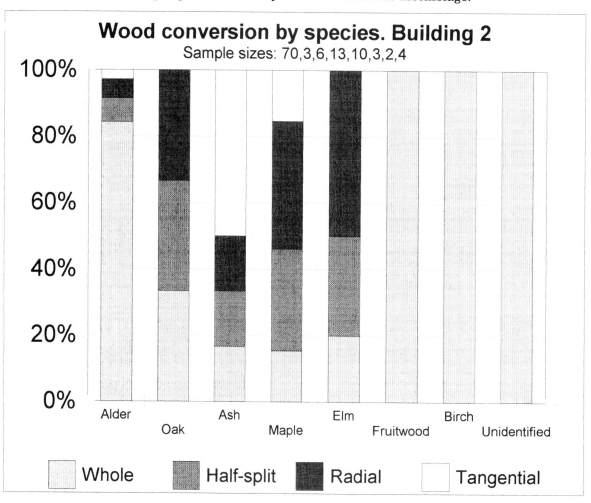

Figure 12.9   Wood conversion by species from Building 2. Drawing by R Brunning. For a table of the data see CD 12.26

Building 2

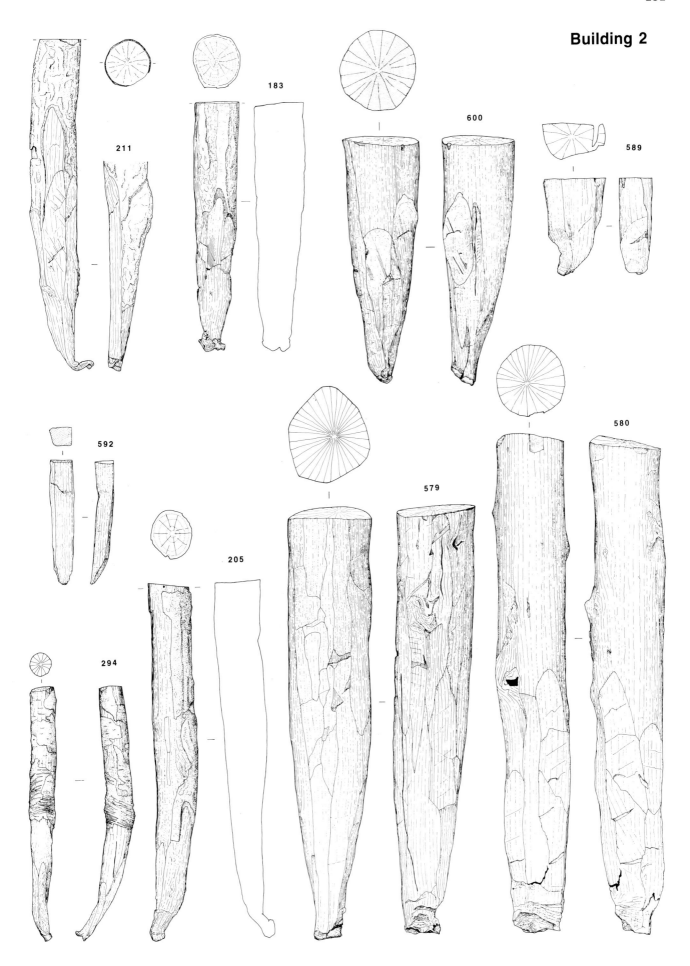

211
183
600
589
592
205
579
580
294

Figure 12.10 Worked wood from Building 2. All at 1:8. Drawing by S J Allen. For additional wood see CD 12.27

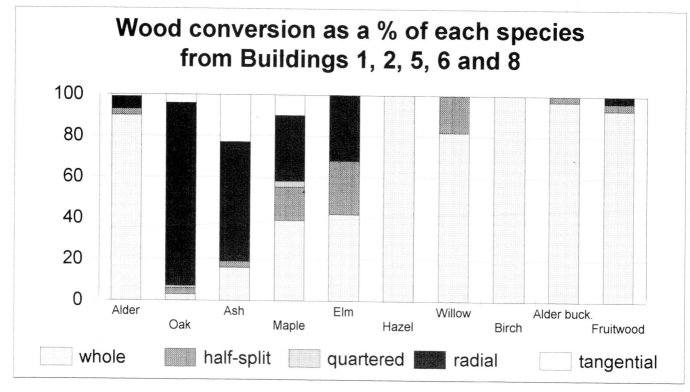

Figure 12.11 Wood conversion as a percentage of each species from Buildings 1; 2; 5; 6, and 8. Drawing by R Brunning). For a table of the data see CD 12.28

Building 2 (Figs 12. 9–12.11, CD 12.26 and 12.27)

A total of 119 pieces were studied from this building, of which 111 were wall or central posts, 3 were pieces of flooring, and another 5 were woodworking debris. All the flooring material was birch, two of the pieces being roundwood logs still retaining their bark and the other (475) squared off on two faces. The woodworking debris consisted of four tangentially split alder off-cuts from within the building and one small radial birch fragment from the area to the north of the building.

The posts varied in quality from quite knotty to fairly straight grained, with the oak, ash, and field maple elements being more straight grained than the average. Most (67%) of the posts were roundwood, still retaining some bark. Of these, 80% were alder, with the remainder composed of small numbers of elm, birch, fruitwood, ash, field maple, and oak. The converted timbers consisted of roughly equal numbers of half-split and radially split examples, comprising 13% and 14% of the total, respectively. Other tangential or intermediate conversions accounted for the other 6% of the total assemblage. These three categories of converted timbers were mainly formed of roughly equal numbers of alder, elm and field maple, together with smaller numbers of ash and oak. A concentration of the non-alder timbers is apparent in the northeast corner of the building and in the northern central post group.

The vast majority (77%) of the points on the posts were pencil shaped, still retaining numerous axe facets almost all formed by blows angled between 1° and 20°(Fig 12.10:579, 580, 600). The care taken in

fashioning the points is further demonstrated in the length over which the timbers were cut to a point, which varied between 180mm and 830mm, with many examples being cut over their entire surviving length. The other points were evenly split between wedge and chisel shapes. These also displayed numerous surviving facets, testifying to a considerable effort taken to form tapering points.

Building 3 (Fig 12.12)

The excavation of this building was very limited so few timbers were lifted for analysis. They consisted of seven stakes and one piece of wattling, all in the round, and eight pieces of roundwood and offcuts thought to represent flooring. The stakes and wattling were all alder, as was the woodworking debris, which consisted of two half-split and two tangential pieces.

The ends of both the vertical and horizontal components had been simply severed to produce chisel shaped points, with the exceptions of one pencil and two wedge shaped points (Fig 12.12:3412, 3415, 3416). The cutting angles on the remaining facets were moderately steep, between 5° and 30°, resulting in short points cut over 65–125mm.

Building 6 (Figs 12.4, 12.13, and 12.14, CD 12.30)

The timbers studied from this building consisted of 143 posts from the walls, partitions, and central posts. The walls were formed from split oak planks,

Building 3 & area

Building 4

Building 5

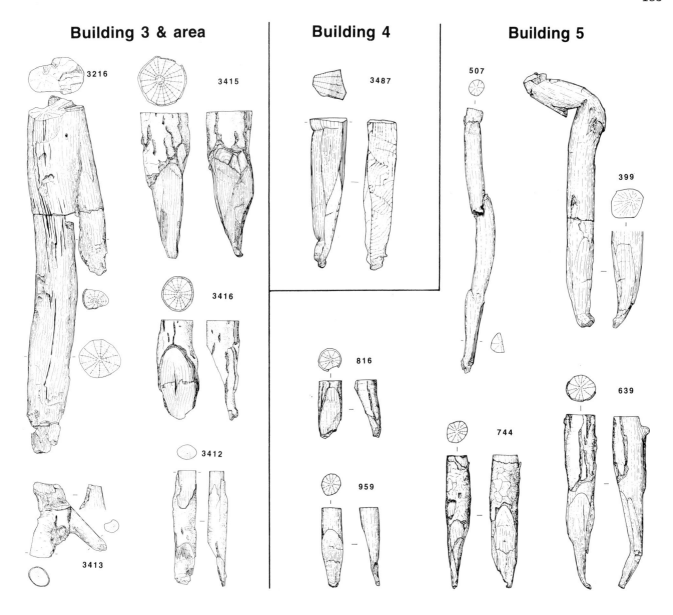

Figure 12.12 Worked wood from peat shelf south of Building 3, Building 3, Building 4, and Building 5. All at 1:8 except 3415 and 3416 (1:4). Drawing by S J Allen. For additional wood drawings from Building 5 see CD 12.29

apparently divided into short stretches by round-wood posts. The latter were predominantly hazel, with a smaller number of field maple and a single example of fruitwood. The oak planks were derived from very large trees and were the product of tangential sub-division of larger radially split timbers (eg Fig 12.13: 3532, 3537, 7077, 7091, see discussion below).

The southern central post group consisted of a large, radially split ash timber supported by four split oak planks and a small piece of elm. The northern group was formed around a large half-split piece of field maple supported by three split ash timbers and one field maple roundwood. The evidence for partitions consisted of one intermediate split and four radially split pieces of ash and two field maple posts, one roundwood and the other quarter-split.

The quality of the timbers varied considerably

between the species. The maple and elm were generally very knotty timbers, while the hazel varied from quite knotty to fairly straight grained. In contrast, the ash was consistently straight grained, and the oak was very straight grained with virtually no knots.

The points on the posts were mainly pencil (eg Fig 12.13: 7081) (56%), or wedge shaped (eg Fig 12.13: 3538, 3539) (31%), with the smaller number of chisel shaped points mainly present on the round-wood (Fig 12.13: 3528, 3531). The split wood was usually cut down over a short length on the narrowest sides, leaving a comparatively small number of surviving facets on the wood. The only posts displaying large numbers of facets were a split oak (7110) with *c* 33 facets and a roundwood field maple (7112) with 21 facets; both posts were from the northern end of the building.

184

Building 6

Building 7

Building 8

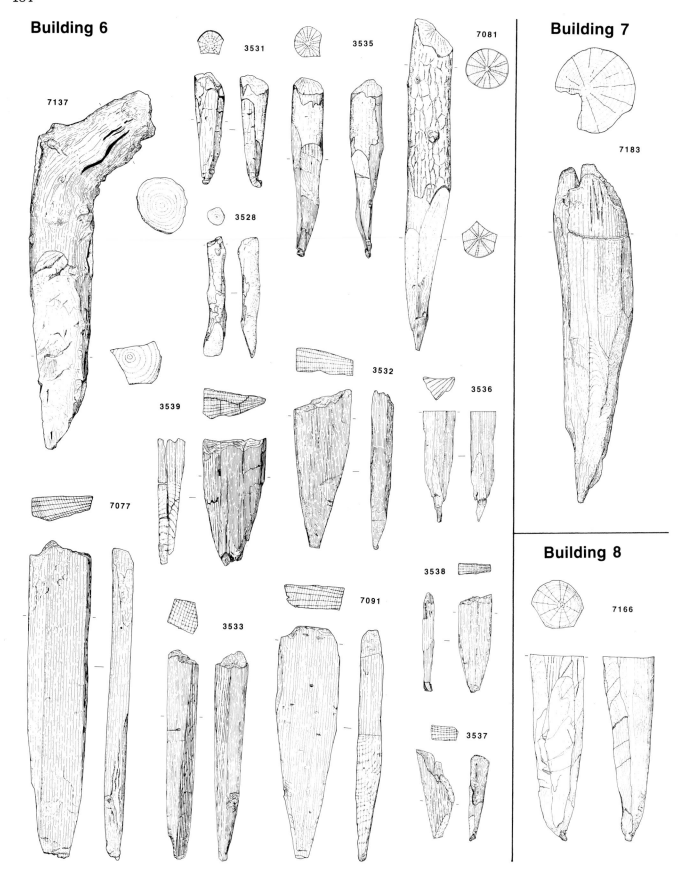

Figure 12.13 Worked wood from area around Building 6 and Buildings 6, 7, and 8. All at 1:8 except 3528 (1:4). Drawing by S J Allen

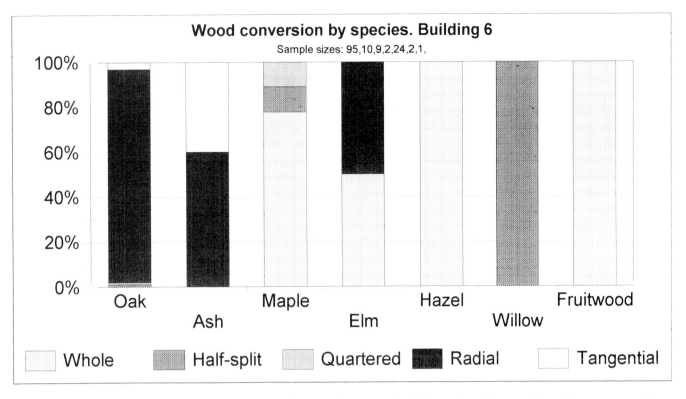

Wood conversion by species. Building 6

Sample sizes: 95,10,9,2,24,2,1,

Legend: Whole — Half-split — Quartered — Radial — Tangential

Species: Oak, Ash, Maple, Elm, Hazel, Willow, Fruitwood

Figure 12.14 Wood conversion by species Building 6. Drawing by R Brunning. For a table of the data see CD 12.30

Building 7

The only piece analysed was the axial post (Fig 12.13: 7183). This was a straight grained ash roundwood post that had been cut to a pencil point with numerous shallow angled blows between 1° and 10°. This had produced a pencil shaped point which still retained traces of 34 axe facets.

Building 8 (Fig 12.13 and 12.15, CD 12.31)

A total of 21 pieces were studied from this building, all of which were vertical stakes. This assemblage was dominated by radially split ash, oak, and field maple timbers, with the ash predominating. Some of these timbers appear to have been formed from radially split planks which were subsequently further reduced tangentially. This process resulted in some very small stakes being produced, especially among the ash. The only other converted wood consisted of one tangentially split piece of field maple and two half-split elm timbers. The remaining four pieces were ash, maple, and elm roundwood, all of which still retained traces of bark.

The points of the stakes were formed by cuts at fairly shallow angles of 1–20° over lengths of 39–98mm. These formed pencil or wedge shaped points on all the timbers except for the small split ash pieces which were simply cut across to form chisel shaped points.

12.3.3 Buildings discussion

Species selection

The main factors which governed the use of different tree species on the Goldcliff site were:

- geographical availability of each species
- social/economic access to each species
- usefulness of a particular species in performing a required function.

The species composition of the buildings provides an interesting contrast to the trackway evidence below. The presence of alder buckthorn and fruitwood in significant amounts in Building 1 and the possible Building 5 is surprising, given their low rate of use in the trackways. They were used whole as small stakes in between the larger wall posts and may have been similarly utilised in other buildings where such structural elements have not survived. Presumably local availability and the small size of these species were the main factors in such a pattern of use. Their low usage in the trackways does, however, suggest the possibility that they were deliberately chosen for this role.

Willow was only used sparsely in the buildings, and its main role as small wall stakes was probably primarily dictated by its easy local availability rather than a deliberate selection. The wide variety of species used for the small stakes in Building 1 suggests that any species of a suitable size nearby was used. More care was taken for selection of the

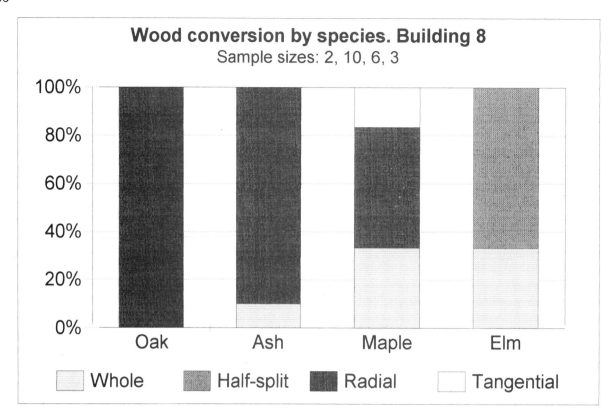

Figure 12.15 Wood conversion by species Building 8. Drawing by R Brunning. For a table of the data see CD 12.31

main wall posts. Birch trees appear to have been available in a suitable size locally but were only used as flooring material. This is probably a reflection of their lack of strength and very rapid speed of decay in wet conditions.

The species composition of the main structural elements of the buildings suggests a division between Buildings 6 and 8, and the rest of the structures. Buildings 6 and 8 contain no alder posts or stakes in contrast to all the other buildings where alder is dominant. This predominant use of alder is not surprising as the environmental evidence suggests that it was present in the immediate vicinity in some abundance. Alder rots easily except in damp conditions or underwater (Edlin 1970, 187, Rackham 1980, 105), a factor which may have commended its use in the very wet contemporary environment. It can grow to a substantial size, which allowed its use as major wall posts and for the main roof supports. A combination of ease of felling (Coles and Orme 1985, 7), broad size range, good preservation in the wet, and local availability made the use of alder a logical choice for both large and small structural elements. The surprising point is that it did not fulfill this role in two of the buildings.

The consistent use of four other tree species, oak, ash, field maple and elm, for large structural members can be seen in all the buildings except Building 3 and the putative Building 5. This, together with the trackway evidence, suggests that these species were available in reasonably local woodlands. Their proportion of the total structural elements appears to change in relation to the position of the buildings in

the landscape, which may in fact be related to chronological differences. On the wood peat, Buildings 1, 2 and 3 displayed small percentages of these species, 12.5%, 29.5%, and 2%, respectively, with none from Building 5. In contrast, Building 4 at the edge of the wood peat had 41% and Buildings 6, 7, and 8 had 80.5%, 62%, and 100% respectively. This suggests that, either alder was less readily available on the raised bog areas, or that a better source of oak, field maple, ash, and elm was closer to Buildings 6, 7, and 8, or that other socio-economic factors had dictated a change in wood usage. The difference in growth rates between the oak from buildings in the raised bog and wood peat areas suggests that different woodlands were being exploited to produce these oak timbers (Chapter 11).

The precise use of these four species is also interesting. In Building 1 the oak, field maple and elm are mainly used as internal timbers in the structure, as aisle posts or for the walls of stalls. In Building 2 the large numbers of elm and field maple appear to have occurred as part of the rebuilding of the structure (see below). In contrast, in Building 8 all four species may have been utilised as timbers in the original wall line.

It is Building 6 that displays the most segregated use of different species. Here the walls are formed almost entirely of split oak divided into short sections by single hazel or, more rarely, field maple posts. The axial posts are a mixture of ash, maple, and oak piles and the evidence for partitions is formed by ash and maple posts. This pattern is unusual as it does not appear to be a sound use of resources. The regularly spaced hazel posts would appear to have an important structural function, but hazel is not a good load bearing timber and rots very quickly. Oak has many good qualities as a timber, including large size, ease of conversion into planks, great strength, and resistance to rot. Large oak timbers are, therefore, usually retained for functions which represent the best use of these qualities. The use of large split oak planks for the walls of a prehistoric building is unheard of in Britain. Wattle and daub buildings are the norm, being easy to erect, and it appears that the other buildings at Goldcliff made use of this technique.

The incorporation of a large amount of very useful and, therefore, socially 'valuable' oak planks in Building 6 suggests that either the building had a special purpose, or that its builders had easy access to such material, or that time constraints forced the builders to use materials which they would otherwise have reserved for other functions. The first possibility is unlikely as there is nothing to suggest that Building 6 had a different function from the other structures. There is also little to suggest that this one structure was built by a different group who had easier access to a supply of oak timbers. Even if a ready supply of oak planks had become available for some reason when the building was planned, it would not explain the strange use of hazel.

The most likely explanation seems to be that a new building was required in a hurry. Building the normal wattle structure would take too long, so a ready supply of hazel poles and oak planks was used to allow rapid construction. This would explain the use of the hazel and oak, and may provide a reason for the distinctly skewed alignment of the building. The building was needed quickly so the quickest method was chosen, even if it was not the most efficient or practical. A traditional design inappropriate to the materials was followed, and the structure was hastily set out. The dendrochronological evidence may support this theory (see Chapter 11).

Conversion and timber preparation (Fig 12.11)

The minimum of preparation appears to have taken place in forming the structural elements of the buildings. This can be seen as a consistent theme in prehistoric woodworking, varied only when it is over ridden by social factors. The alder, willow, hazel, birch, alder buckthorn, and fruitwood used in the buildings were mainly left in the round with their bark still in place. There were some occasional half-split pieces but only alder had significant numbers of radial or tangentially converted timbers. This was probably a reflection of the ease of splitting this species and the larger size of the alder trees being used.

The elm timbers used were also often left in the round and, when converted, were usually half-split or simply radially split with both the bark and the thin feather edge on the inside retained. Elm does not split well if knotty but the dominant factor in this pattern was probably its relatively limited size. Field

maple was also mainly used in the round or as simple half-split timbers, but additionally occurred as radially or tangentially split examples, often with both bark and feather edge removed. This may reflect a slightly larger size range than was represented in the elm.

The other two significant species used, oak and ash, can both grow to large sizes and are relatively easy to split along the radial plane. These two factors, combined with the intrinsic strength of these woods, account for the small number of roundwood, half-split, or quartered examples. The majority of timbers of these species were radially converted, with a significant proportion of tangentially split pieces also present in the ash assemblage. Generally, the ash timbers seem to have been derived from smaller trees than the oak examples, and more often retained bark or feather edge on the split pieces. The ash posts from Building 8 were more unusual in that they included many examples of radially split timbers that had subsequently been further sub-divided tangentially. This resulted in some quite small stakes being used in this structure.

In all the buildings the oak timbers were predominantly derived from radially split planks that had been sub-divided tangentially to produce smaller but still substantial planks. This was best seen in the large assemblage from Building 6 where analysis of the pattern of the rays in the cross sections of these timbers suggests that radial splits from very large trees were being sub-divided two or more times to create the planks forming the walls of the building.

The cross section evidence, combined with the dendrochronological results, suggests a complex pattern of oak tree use. A small young oak of c 900mm diameter, felled in 273 BC was used to produce Timbers 7049 and 7009. In that same year of felling a very large tree, at least 1.7m in diameter, was cut down to produce 7015, 7083, and 7026. Similar large trees were cut down in 271 BC and during the winter of 273–272 BC, as shown by Timbers 7050 and 7044. The cross sections of Timbers 7011 and 7028 suggest they were from a tree c 1.6m in diameter in 360 BC. If this tree was felled in 273 or 271 BC, as seems likely, then it still had about another 90 years worth of growth to add.

A minimum of four, and probably more, oak trees were, therefore, used to produce the timbers for Building 6. Even one of the large trees could have supplied the material for the whole building with some to spare. The presence of two felling years in this material may suggest a period of repair as suggested by Hillam, Chapter 11. This seems unlikely, however, as the oak would not have decayed in this short a time and single posts are unlikely to have worked free. This is supported by the lack of any evidence for later periods of possible repair in the tree-ring information. A different explanation could be that the material for the building construction was drawn from a stockpile of oak timbers. This is probable because the number of trees involved in the construction were far more than were needed. If the timbers from trees felled in spring 273 BC, winter

273–272 BC and 271 BC were all used as part of the original building phase, this suggests a rare example of seasoning, or at least semi-seasoning of wood in the prehistoric period. The presence of a timber stockpile would also fit with the theory that the unusual choice of materials for Building 6 was partly determined by a need to build quickly using readily available material. Perhaps a grander building project or woodland clearance had produced the glut of oak timbers that made this possible.

Aside from the splitting of some timbers, the main form of preparation evidenced on the Goldcliff building material was the formation of pointed ends to ease the insertion of posts and stakes. As is evident from the rest of the woodworking evidence, the minimum expenditure of effort seems to have gone into this process. The smaller diameter material is often cut to a chisel shaped point with a small number of blows, while the larger pieces are cut on two or more sides to form wedge or pencil shaped ends. Split pieces are normally cut down on their narrowest faces to form a point, with just one or two blows on the other sides to finish the point.

There are very few changes in the styles of point formation. Building 6 appears to have had less effort expended on forming points to its structural elements than Buildings 1 or 2. To an extent this may be a product of the dominance of narrow split planks which require fewer blows to form a point. However, the pattern can also be seen on the roundwood and the central posts, which suggests that it may represent a different style of working. There is little difference between the point formation of timbers in Buildings 1 and 2, and the higher numbers of chisel points in the former structure are a product of the presence of smaller wall stakes in the building. The only significant difference appears to be between the Axial Post 579 in Building 2 and all the other axial posts in Buildings 1 and 2. Post 579 still retains the traces of 107 axe facets at its tip, whereas the other axial posts all have less than 30. The care taken in the preparation of 579 may be because it was a repair (see below).

Building design

The design of the Goldcliff buildings (see also Chapter 9) is centred around earthfast load bearing wall posts, forming a wall line with no right angled corners, and supporting a roof held up by a small number of axial posts. As such, it shares some important characteristics with Iron Age roundhouses in Britain. The relatively small size of the buildings and short roof span did not require structurally important aisle posts.

These characteristics separate the Goldcliff buildings from most contemporary continental examples. There, the only similar examples are the smaller buildings associated with larger houses or isolated in the countryside, which also have large load-bearing posts in the walls (Audouze and Büchsenschütz 1991, 66). These buildings all have right-angled corners,

however. One much larger building at Verberie in Oise has even more similarities to the Goldcliff structures as it has two axial posts and walls containing load bearing posts which also form rounded corners (Audouze and Büchsenschütz 1991, 66–7). These have been taken to represent a western European group between the central European rectangular buildings and the British roundhouse.

The internal layout of the Goldcliff buildings is only shown in a fragmentary state in Building 1, where there is evidence for stalls and what may be two rows of aisle posts, which are likely to have functioned more as terminals to the stalls than as roof supports. The row of stakes running across the centre of the building is suggested as a remnant wall line from Building 5 but, if it is in fact part of Building 1, it may represent a central division with two gaps along the aisles. The existence of stall partitions, mats for the collection of dung, and doorways through the short sides of buildings have been suggested as the essential characteristics of stables (Therkorn 1987, 209). These are all evident in Building 1 at Goldcliff and may have existed at the other less well preserved structures. Building 6, for example, has some traces of stalling and all the buildings appear to be entered along their short sides.

The construction of the walls varied, notably between Buildings 1 and 2 and Building 6. The former two buildings had walls composed of closely spaced large posts. The evidence from the best preserved parts of Building 1 suggests that the gap between these posts was filled with stakes of 20–60mm diameter which formed the vertical components of possible wattlework which bound the whole wall line together. The wattlework may have dictated the presence of rounded corners, although continental examples and evidence from Glastonbury suggest that wattle walls with right angled corners were perfectly possible (Brunning 1995). A more important reason may have been the prevailing cultural architectural tradition which emphasised curving walls. Certainly, it seems hard to think of a purely functional reason for the curved corners of the plank built walls of Building 6.

No horizontal wattle elements were discovered but this is easily explained by the high level of erosion. The vertical stakes of Building 1 were often set at very shallow angles, 81% exhibiting an angle <60°. They were generally inclined slanting upwards anti-clockwise around the wall line, but this may be a product of later erosion patterns rather than their original orientation. No evidence of daub was found associated with the walls, as was also the case in the Assendelver Polders (Therkorn 1987, 191).

The walls of Building 6 are unusual in their composition dominated by split oak planks (see species selection above). The sections show that many of the shallowest set vertical wall timbers in this building may have been lost to erosion. This, taken together with the evidence from the best preserved parts of the walls, suggests that they were originally formed entirely by vertical posts with no horizontal wattling. The split timbers varied greatly in size with widths between 30mm and 185mm and thicknesses between 9mm and 65mm. This, together with the orientation of the planks, suggests that the planks could not have overlapped or been held together with tongue and groove joints. Aside from the stability engendered from being driven into the ground, a wall plate would be required at the top of the wall to hold the planks in place, bind the walls together and spread the weight of the roof. The form of this top wall plate is uncertain (see Chapter 9).

Repair

There are several pieces of evidence to suggest that the Goldcliff buildings required periodic repairs. This can be compared with the buildings studied in the Assendelver Polders project, most of which showed evidence of repair, either in the form of extra roof supports, buttressing of walls, or replacement of wattles (Therkorn 1987, 194). Possible dendrochronological evidence for repair to Building 6 has been noted.

In Building 1, just over half the large wall posts were inclined between 80° and dead vertical. The other posts were slightly more inclined, but the lack of a pattern suggested any slump occurred after the building has ceased to be a structural entity.

In Building 2, however, only 29% of the main wall posts were between 80° and dead vertical. A consistent downward inclination to the west, southwest, or northwest is evident especially in the north wall. This north wall shows evidence of having been replaced at least once, with a later and more complete wall line possibly being formed outside the original line. This is supported by the species composition of this possible wall rebuild which is dominated by field maple, elm, and ash, in contrast to the rest of the walls which are dominated by alder. If Building 2 had wattle walls similar to those suggested for Building 1, it would have been very hard to remove individual wall posts. If significant repairs were needed, it seems more likely that a whole wall section would have to be dismantled and replaced.

The doubling up of the axial posts in this building also supports this possibility, as it appears that the group centred around 579 may have been connected with the slight shift further north of the northern wall. This is supported by the presence of field maple around the post, and the common orientation of Axial Posts 579, 600, and the wall posts in the north end, which suggests that they may have slumped while still a coherent unit. Some other posts such as 543 and 544 on the west side may represent later attempts to stabilise the walls.

Woodworking debris

Woodworking debris was only recovered in significant numbers from within and around Building 1.

Woodchips were noted amongst the flooring of the building by Parkhouse during the initial cleaning. Little such material remained at the time of the main excavation. The material that was recovered from within the building consisted mainly of alder fragments with only three pieces of oak or ash. Roughly half the material was recovered from the doorway of the building, suggesting that it may have been placed there in response the greater amount of wear to the floor in that area. This material may represent debris from the initial construction of the structure, or from early repairs.

The 30 pieces of debris from the area immediately to the north of the building (Fig 7.3) were of a different character. Over half their number were oak woodchips and small offcuts, with a mixture of radial, tangential and intermediate cross sections. Most of the rest of this group consisted of other radial and tangential woodchips and offcuts of field maple, ash, alder, and elm. The debris from all these groups was mainly 100–220mm in length and 20–55mm in width. This evidence seems to suggest an origin in the finishing of timbers either within, or just outside, the building. The high level of oak, ash and field maple, and the low representation of alder suggest that this material was not generated by repairs to the main wall line. During excavation it was noted that several thin lenses of clay separated the debris. This suggests that the debris was produced by an activity that occurred over several seasons.

Nine pieces of woodworking debris were recovered from the palaeochannel deposits around Building 6. The woodworking debris consisted of four ash, two elm, and single examples of field maple, alder, and fruitwood. The ash, alder, and maple debris could have been produced by dressing split planks or forming points on such planks. The two elm examples may have derived from pointing a roundwood post. The alder buckthorn was an undiagnostic half-split fragment. With the exception of the single alder piece, all of this debris could have been produced by the process of forming points on the non-oak posts of Building 6. If this was their source the evidence suggests that the oak posts were pointed at a different time, and/or a different location. This would fit with the possibility that the material was drawn from a stockpile, and that the points were made when the wood was still green and, therefore, easier to cut.

12.3.4 Trackways

Little or no woodworking information was recorded from Trackways 1, 2, 3, 5, 7, 9, 1208, 1311, 1330, 9050, and 9061. The other linear structures had varying numbers of pieces studied. The double Post Rows 970 and 1103, the linear Structures 1108 and the corduroy Trackway 1130 all had large numbers of timbers recorded, while the quantity of material from the other features was quite small. From all the trackways the number of items sampled and identified to species was greater than the quantity lifted and subject to woodworking analysis. Full species identification results should, therefore, be sought in the preceding section (12.2). In many cases the horizontal and smaller vertical trackway components had been very close to the surface, and consequent decay and erosion had removed a lot of surface detail making the precise recording of tool-marks difficult.

Linear structure 1108 (Fig 12.16, CD 12.32)

Wood records were made for 52 stakes or pegs and 35 horizontal components. Both the horizontal and vertical components possessed an overwhelming proportion of converted to unconverted wood (2.1:1). The species composition of the stakes was unusual as it was dominated by oak and field maple, with lesser numbers of ash, elm, alder, and a single blackthorn. The maple, alder, ash, and oak all occurred as roundwood but, except for the alder, they were all more common as split wood. Radial splits

were common on the oak, maple and ash (eg Fig 12.16: 3458, 3754, 3772), with more simple half- or quarter-splits favoured by the maple, and elm. The only tangential fragment was a piece of elm. Despite the relatively small size of the material (10–50mm diameter/width) the points had been finished with shallow blows of 5–20° over lengths of 80–180mm and one cut >502mm. Pencil, wedge, and chisel points existed in almost equal proportions.

Very little whole roundwood was used for the horizontal wood. What occurred was dominated by alder, with only single examples of oak, elm, willow, and birch. The converted material was mainly radially split. Oak was the most common species split in this way, the only other examples being two of alder and one of field maple. Only a couple of oak and maple pieces were split tangentially. Simpler half or quarter reductions were seen in a small number of alder, maple, elm and ash. The points were a mixture of wedge and chisel shapes, with the latter most commonly seen on the roundwood where only a few steeply angled blows had severed the stems. Cutting angles varied between 10° and 50° forming points

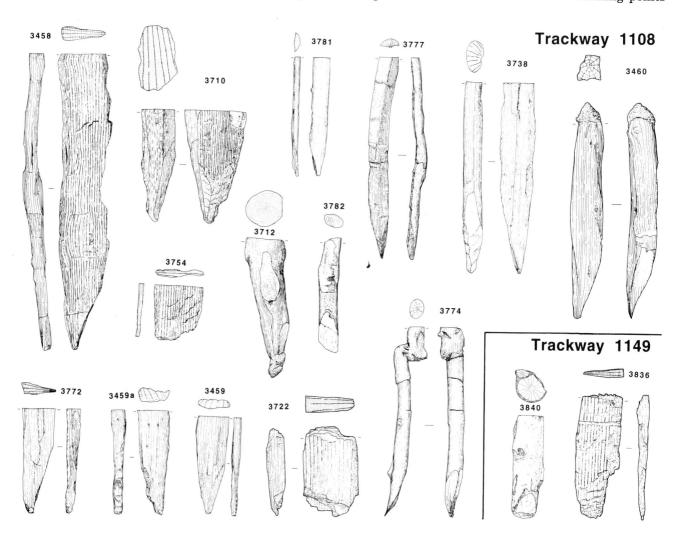

Figure 12.16 Worked wood from Trackways 1108 and 1149. All at 1:8 except 3710, 3712, 3782, and 3840 (1:4). Drawing by S J Allen. For additional wood drawings see CD 12.32

25–30mm long. This is in marked contrast to the vertical components and, therefore, it does not appear that any of the horizontal material includes reused stakes. The points are just where the stems have been cut to length.

While most of the material from this trackway was in the 10–50mm size range, there was some evidence for the use of larger trees. Two of the radially split oak pieces must have come from trunks well over 70mm in diameter. Most of the split material was very thin and quite short (160–340mm) and may represent the offcuts from working larger timbers which were used for other purposes elsewhere. One tangentially split timber (3780) appeared to have broken at one end where a hole, 25mm in diameter, penetrated the wood. This suggests the possibility that this piece may be reused or was originally intended for a different function. Another piece (3857) had many cut marks over its surface, suggesting that it may have been used as a chopping board, perhaps during the cutting of the points for the stakes.

Linear Structure 1149 (Fig 12.16)

Twelve pieces of wood were analysed from this structure. They consisted of six pegs and six horizontal elements, all of which were converted pieces, except for one very knotty piece of alder roundwood. Field maple, elm, and alder were the main species, together with a single piece of oak. All the converted material was radially split (eg Fig 12.16: 3836) or axed apart from quarter-split pieces of elm and maple, a tangential elm fragment, and a piece of alder with an irregular cross section. Many of the horizontal pieces were pieces of woodworking debris, and the pegs were also quite small and could have been derived from a similar source.

Double Post Row 970 (Fig 12.18)

From this structure 32 stakes and ten horizontals were studied for woodworking. Half the horizontal wood was roundwood of ash, alder, willow, and birch. The remainder were five pieces of field maple, four radially split and one tangentially. By contrast, the vertical elements had only a small proportion of unconverted wood. Ash, alder and birch comprised what little roundwood there was, while oak, field maple and alder formed all the split timbers with the single addition of one split ash piece. The vast majority of the converted wood had been split radially, with tangential and half- or quarter-split examples forming only one third of the group. The cut ends of the horizontals were simple wedge or chisel shapes cut across at angles of 1–40°. Pencil shaped points formed over half the ends of the stakes with the remainder being roughly equal amounts of wedge and chisel points. The points were formed mainly by cutting at shallow angles of 1–25° and

comparative care seems to have been taken in fashioning tapering points. The pencil points generally retained over ten facets and up to 22, reflecting the effort involved in their production.

Some of the roundwood was very knotty, but otherwise the material was quite straight grained and knot free, including the alder. The converted wood was derived from trees of 85–140mm diameter for the horizontals and 110–180mm for the verticals. The alder and maple radial splits generally retained their outer rings but the oak radials were often reduced. Some of the field maple, oak, and alder may have been offcuts from the working of larger timbers.

Linear Structure 1103 (Fig 12.18, CD 12.33)

A large assemblage of wood from this structure was analysed, comprising 54 horizontal components and 49 stakes or pegs. The horizontal wood was mainly alder, with a small amount of willow and a single piece of ash. The only converted pieces were seven alder timbers, four split radially and three tangentially. The stakes and pegs exhibited a much wider range of species and more converted than unconverted wood. The roundwood was mainly alder again, with small numbers of oak, ash, willow, birch, hawthorn, and buckthorn. The majority of the converted wood was also alder, but the additional species were oak, field maple, elm, ash, and birch. Radial splits were by far the most numerous, with less than half the wood being split tangentially, halved or quartered.

The cut ends on the roundwood from the vertical and horizontal material were almost all chisel shaped cut at shallow angles of 10–25° over lengths of 38–121mm (Fig 12.17: 3333). This material was generally quite small, between 10mm and 29mm, and was very knotty. In contrast, the converted material was moderately to very straight grained with few side branches, and points of pencil or wedge shape. With the exception of the oak and one of the alder pieces which had been reduced, all the converted wood retained the outer rings and often bark. The size of the parent trees for this material varied from 80mm to 170mm in diameter. The knotty roundwood could have come from the branches of trees, the trunks of which may have supplied the split material. Many of the split alder horizontal pieces appeared as though they were offcuts from the formation of larger timbers. Two of the tangential pieces of alder had crude joints, which may suggest that they were reused timbers. A small, slightly oval indentation existed in 3359, which was a small piece broken at both ends. The indentation was 18mm in diameter and 11mm deep and was slightly angled. It may have functioned as a hole to accommodate a peg or treenail as part of a joint but its fragmentary nature defies conclusive attribution. The other piece, 3355 (Fig 12.17) is larger, 286mm × 35mm × 13mm, but is also broken at both ends. One end may be

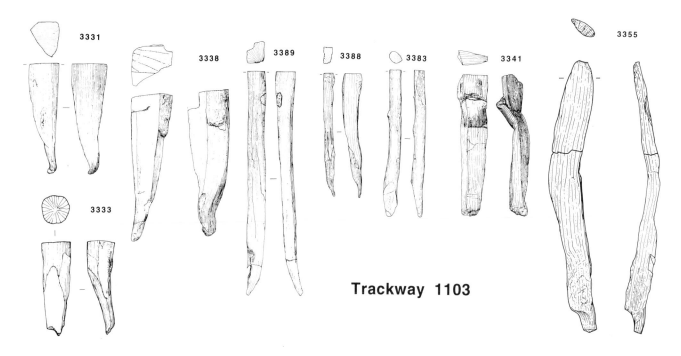

Trackway 1103

Figure 12.17 Worked wood from Linear Structure 1103. All at 1:8 except 3331, 3333, 3338, and 3341 (1:4) and 3355 (1:2). Drawing by S J Allen. For additional wood drawings see CD 12.33

broken across a lap joint, which appears to have been gouged rather than axed out. Although the timber curves significantly, it has been axed flat on its inner face and along at least one of its sides. This suggests that it once performed a function as part of a more complex structure.

Trackway 4

Only five horizontals were studied from this structure, four alder and one willow. They were all quite knotty roundwood that had simple chisel points leaving single facets which had severed the relatively small stems at angles of 2–20° over lengths of 50–93mm.

Trackway 6 (Fig 12.18)

Woodworking information was only recorded from six elements of this structure. All of these were moderately knotty pieces of roundwood alder, or willow, which were used as horizontal elements. The cut ends present were simple chisel types severed with blows delivered at angles of 10–20° (Fig 12.18: 3901, 3912).

Trackway 8

Only three stakes/pegs and eight pieces of brushwood were analysed from this structure. All this material was alder roundwood of quite a knotty character. Most of the roundwood was relatively small

(15–35mm diameter) with the exception of three larger pieces of 80mm, 110mm and 130mm. The only cut ends were two simple chisel points from the brushwood with short steep cuts of 30°.

Palaeochannel 9053

Fifteen pieces were analysed from this structure, of which eleven were horizontal and the other four were interpreted as vertical stakes or pegs. All the material was roundwood, mainly of alder with lesser numbers of willow and birch. With only one exception, all the pieces analysed were very, or moderately, knotty and several appeared to be small cut branches. The diameters varied from 25mm to 60mm, with the larger material coming from the horizontal components. No worked ends were recorded on the vertical 'stakes' but six survived on the horizontals, with four chisel points and two wedge-shaped ends.

Trackway 1130 (Fig 12.18)

This corduroy track produced 57 pieces for woodworking analysis, of which five were stakes or pegs and the rest horizontal members. Unusually, the assemblage was dominated by birch, with alder and willow providing lesser contributions, and hazel only one item. Whole roundwood dominated both the horizontal and vertical components. Apart from a single radially split piece of birch and a small tangential willow fragment, the converted material was all simple half- or quarter-split birch and alder

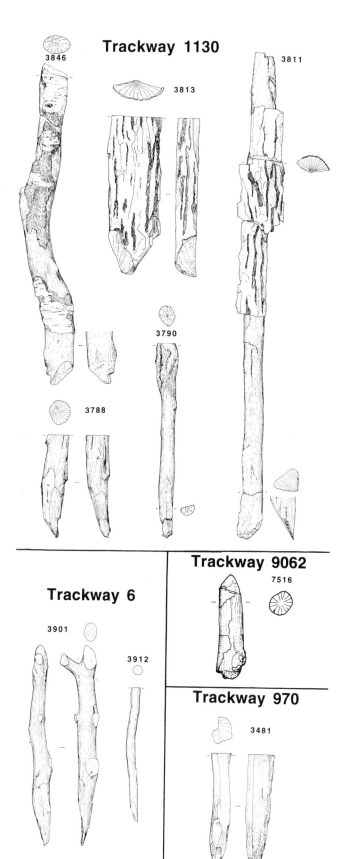

Trackway 1130

3846

3813

3811

3790

3788

Trackway 6

3901

3912

Trackway 9062

7516

Trackway 970

3481

Figure 12.18 Worked wood from Trackways 1130 and 6 and Structures 9062 and 970. All at 1:8 except 7516 (1:2). Drawn by S J Allen

(eg Fig 12.18: 3811, 3813). Chisel shaped points predominated and were mainly used on the smaller diameter material, where they left single facets. The larger trunks, up to 90mm in diameter, exhibited more wedge and pencil points, and one was cut over a length of >380mm. Cutting angles varied between 1° and 30° and, with one exception, the cut lengths ranged from 38mm to 180mm. The cut ends on the horizontal material appeared just to be a product of severing the trunks rather than deliberately forming a point. The wood varied widely in its quality, with some being very knotty while others were relatively straight grained.

Trackway 9051

Only three pieces were analysed from this structure. They were a half-split piece of willow used as a stake and two roundwood pieces of hazel and hawthorn brushwood. The willow had a pencil shaped point, and the brushwood had wedge and chisel points. All the material was quite knotty.

Structure 9066

The assemblage analysed from this structure included five 'pegs', five horizontals, eight pieces of bark, and nine very small twigs of alder and birch. The larger material was mainly alder, with two ash pegs and single pieces of hazel and blackthorn among the horizontal material. The only clear tool facets were on two of the pegs, where they made simple chisel points. In general the material was very small and extremely knotty, with even the larger components having diameters of only 10–40mm. The vast majority of this material shows no signs of human working, and the smaller material does not appear to be of suitable quality for basketry. It, therefore, appears that the 'structure' may merely consist of a very small number of insubstantial pegs amongst naturally deposited unworked wood. Their function cannot be determined, but the few pegs may be the vestigial traces of a trackway.

Structure 9060

Fifteen pegs were studied from this structure, twelve of willow, two alder, and one elm. All the material was roundwood between 18mm and 30mm in diameter and very variable in quality from extremely knotty to quite straight grained and branch free wood. Apart from two wedge-shaped points, all the cut ends were simple chisel shapes made by blows delivered at shallow angles of 3–15° over lengths of 50–170mm from the tips. The shallow cutting angles and simple points were a product of the small size of the wood.

Table 12.2 Wood conversion by species used in trackways

Conversion type	Alder	Oak	Field maple	Elm	Ash	Willow	Birch	Hazel	Other	Total
Whole	107 (70)	5 (19)	8 (22)	2 (15.5)	14 (64)	41 (93)	30 (70)	7 (100)	5 (83)	219 (65)
Half	14 (3)	1 (4)	6 (17)	3 (23)	1 (4)	2 (5)	7 (16)			14 (4)
Quarter	7 (5)	2 (8)	5 (14)	3 (23)	2 (9)		3 (7)		1 (17)	23 (7)
Radial	26 (17)	17 (65)	14 (39)	2 (15.5)	5 (23)		3 (7)			67 (20)
Tangential	7 (5)	1 (4)	3 (8)	3 (23)		1 (2)				15 (4)
Totals	151	26	36	13	22	44	43	7	6	338

Percentage in brackets

Structure 9062 (Fig 12.18)

Eleven pegs and two horizontals were studied from this structure, although not all the pegs were identified. The pegs were all roundwood, mainly of alder with some ash, willow, and hazel. The horizontals were a radially split piece of alder and a tangentially split elm fragment. The points had been formed by a small number of steeply angled blows (35–50°) producing chisel points. The wood was quite variable in knottiness and fairly small, between 10mm and 45mm in diameter. One peg (7516) had been whittled to a point with a knife which had left long narrow (3mm) facets around the whole circumference.

12.3.5 Trackways discussion

The species selection, conversion, and preparation techniques used on the trackway material (Table 12.2) shed light on the local woodland, its utilisation, and general woodworking activity in the area. Brief characterisation of the material from the different trackways is shown below (the proportion of converted to unconverted wood is shown in brackets):

1149 (11:1) Virtually all split fragments of maple, elm, alder, and oak. Much of the material may be woodworking debris.

1108 (2.1:1) Large amounts of oak, maple, and alder, and some elm, and ash. Much of the split material may be offcuts.

970 (2.2:1) Mainly maple alder, and oak, including a lot of offcuts and split material. Some ash and birch present.

9051 (0.5:1) Only three pieces.

1103 (0.47:1) Alder, willow, and ash, with some elm, maple, and oak. Alder woodchips and offcuts present.

1130 (0.43:1) Some alder and willow, but mainly split and whole birch.

9062 (0.2:1) Alder, elm, and hazel. Horizontals split, verticals roundwood.

T 4 (0:1) Alder and willow roundwood.

T 6 (0:1) Alder and willow roundwood.

T 8 (0:1) All alder roundwood.

9053 (0:1) Mainly alder, birch, and willow.

9066 (0:1) Only a small proportion is probably from a structure.

9060 (0:1) Mainly willow.

Three main factors probably governed the use of different tree species on the Goldcliff site:

- geographical availability of each species
- social/economic access to each species
- usefulness of a particular species in performing a required function.

The predominant use of alder and willow in all the structures suggests that the first of these factors was the most important on the site. The small use of hazel suggests that this species was not available locally in any quantity, as it would be eminently suitable for many of the structures present (Coles and Orme 1985). Its absence may also be one reason for the lack of any hurdle trackways at Goldcliff.

The presence of larger, timber producing trees is shown in the use of oak, field maple, ash, and elm These species are only used in significant numbers in four of the structures analysed (1149, 1108, 970, and 1103). These structures are built in a different way to the other trackways and the use of these species may have been governed by the requirements for fairly large, strong and durable vertical components, in contrast to the smaller stakes and pegs used in the other tracks. However, alder was also used in large numbers for the same functions in these structures and, given its abundant local availability, it could probably have supplied all the required material. The presence of woodchips and offcuts from the production of larger timbers in these four structures suggests that much of this material may, in fact, represent the utilisation of the by-products of woodworking associated with more substantial structures such as buildings. The positions of these trackways in relation to the known buildings, several of which are of the same date (compare Figures 9.1 and 10.21), supports this possibility, and suggests that the other trackways of contrasting materials may not lead to buildings. The fact that the structure closest to a building (Trackway 1149) was almost entirely composed of converted material, including woodworking debris, enhances this possibility.

Dendrochronological analysis has shown that the oak timbers in 1108 and Buildings 1 and 2 were probably derived from the same woodland source (Chapter 11). The presence of a small number of reused timbers in 1108 and 1103 suggests the possibility of repair or dismantling of such structures. As these reused timbers are horizontal elements, they be may later additions to the linear structures.

The corduroy trackway (1130) is an example where the particular qualities of tree species may have dominated the wood selection. The birch logs used would have rotted quickly in the damp conditions, but this may not have been a problem in a structure which would have probably had a short life expectancy anyway. The birch may have been used because it grew to a moderately large size but was not particularly useful for other structures such as buildings. The other large timber producing species, such as alder, oak, field maple, elm and ash, were used in large sizes in the buildings rather than the trackways. Where birch trunks were included in buildings, it was mainly as flooring in Buildings 1 and 2. In building a substantial corduroy trackway (1130) and flooring their buildings, the Iron Age inhabitants of Goldcliff displayed a wise use of the available woodland resources, where the poor qualities of birch dictated its use as a source of expendable material of large size.

The use of willow, birch, hazel, blackthorn, and hawthorn in the round (Table 12.2) was probably largely due to their small size. Interestingly, ash was also used, mainly in the round, which may suggest that large trees of that species were not available locally. Alder probably grew locally in a fairly small state, but many trunks were large enough to be split down radially for use in the trackways.

The oak, field maple, and elm pieces were mainly present in the form of split wood. The elm was split in many different ways, with radials being the least frequent type. This may reflect the small size of the parent trees, or the fact that when knotty this species is very hard to split evenly. In contrast, the oak and field maple were mainly radially split. This was the easiest way to produce timbers from large trees of these species without sawing. As mentioned earlier, many of the alder, oak, and maple appeared to be offcuts from the production of larger timbers. These account for much of the tangential material of these species.

12.3.6 The evidence for woodworking tools (Fig 12.19, CD 12.34)

The evidence for woodworking is very limited because it is mainly derived from the pointed ends of

stakes. Only the artefactual material and the converted timber provide evidence for more diverse woodworking tools and techniques.

Seven different profiles of the cutting edges of tools have been identified from the 'jam curves' seen on the Iron Age material from Goldcliff (Fig 12.19). The jam curves represent the cutting edges of the tools used to form a point on the timbers, and/or cut the wood to the desired length. These profiles do not necessarily represent the full blade width of the tool being used. In most cases the width of the toolmarks is limited by subsequent adjacent blows, and by the curvature of the timbers. The latter is especially important as it is only in one case (Timber 580) that the full width of the blade appears to have cut into the wood.

The two different possible types of tool represented by the profiles are axes and billhooks. The flattest blade profiles (A and B) may well have been made by billhooks like the straight-bladed examples from

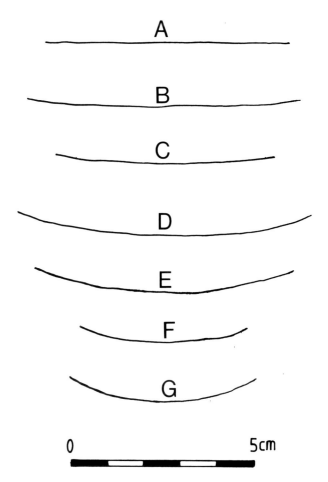

Figure 12.19 Profiles (actual size) of tool blades as revealed by 'jam curves'. The associations of profiles with structures were as follows: (A) Trackway 9051, Buildings 1 and 2, (B) Building 8 and Trackway 9060, (C) Building 2, (D) Buildings 1 and 2, (E) Buildings 1, 2, and 7 and Structure 9053, (F) Building 2, Trackway 1103, and 9053, (G) Building 1. For details and dimensions of the individual pieces of wood see CD 12.34. Drawing by R Brunning

Meare and Glastonbury (Gray and Bulleid 1953, 236, Bulleid and Gray 1917, 366). If axes created these profiles they must have been abnormally straight bladed or large. A comparable jam curve to Profile B was recorded from the Iron Age Derraghan More trackway in Ireland with a similar width of 80mm (O'Sullivan 1997, 310).

The very small number of pre-Roman iron axes recorded from Britain means that it is hard to ascribe the different profiles to recognised types. The most common profile (E) and the widest profile (D) would fit within the curvature and blade width of both iron socketed axes and shaft hole axes from southern Britain (Darbyshire 1995, 290–354). If the profile of 580 does represent the full blade width of the tool, it would suggest that the axe in question was more likely to have been one of the smaller socketed axes than the larger shaft hole types. The absence of wider axe blade profiles reinforces the evidence of the British metalwork concerning the absence of the wide triangular bladed socketed axes which are the most common type in Continental Europe (Darbyshire 1995). Socketed iron axes as narrow as 40mm are known from southern Britain, so the blade widths of the highly curved profiles, F and G, may be close to the full blade width. The commonest profile (E) is very similar to several of the jam curves recovered form the Iron Age trackways of the Mountdillon bogs in Ireland (O'Sullivan 1997, 310). The late Bronze Age or early Iron Age evidence from Oakbank crannog provides profiles similar to types E and F but not to any of the straighter types (Sands 1997, 66).

The converted timber would have been split with mallets and wedges. Two wooden mallets of this period, which were recovered from Glastonbury, could have performed this function (Bulleid and Gray 1917, 322). Although some examples of possible iron wedges are known from Britain (Darbyshire 1995, 547), it is far more likely that seasoned oak wedges were used. Axe handles could have been used as wedges to start the splits, and the butts of some axes show signs of burring by hammering (Darbyshire 1995, 351). No evidence of sawing was seen on any of the timbers.

The use of other tool types is mainly derived from the artefactual material, except for the apparent use of a knife to fashion a peg (Fig 12.18: 7516) from Structure 9062. An adze may well have been used to fashion the inside face of the stave (Fig 8.12: 3541), and a chisel may also have been used in the formation of the basal groove in the same vessel. A chisel may also have been used to form the 7mm wide grooves on the top of the wall Post 3443b. However, the exposed position of this piece raises the possibility that the grooves are a result of more recent damage. A width of only 7mm would also be much smaller than the known Iron Age chisels (Darbyshire 1995, 484–501).

One edge of a curving indentation occurs at the end of a split oak timber (3452) from Context 1105. This feature is 22mm wide and 23mm deep and may represent the remains of an augered hole, although its broken state means this cannot be proved. Of the very small number of augers known from Britain, one spoon bit type has a blade 23.5mm wide (Darbyshire 1995, 508–523). A draw knife or shave may have been used to fashion the possible oak and elm handles (Fig 8.12: 5072 and 5103). Both such tools have been recovered from Iron Age contexts in Britain (Darbyshire 1995, 399–405).

12.4 Tree-ring studies and the character of the wood used in some of the buildings and trackways
Ruth Morgan

Introduction

The two adjacent structures, Buildings 1 and 2, have been the subject of intensive wood analysis; partial sampling of other rectangular post settings has also provided limited information about wood exploitation and use. Buildings 3 and 8 are described here; the results from very restricted study of Buildings 4 and 6 are mentioned, but further detail should be sought in the wood identification and woodworking reports above.

This report also includes descriptions of the wood, particularly roundwood, from sixteen trackways and linear structures of Iron Age date on the western peat shelf at Goldcliff. They were constructed long after the tracks so far known in the Somerset Levels (Morgan 1988), but were broadly contemporary with the transverse oak plank tracks at Corlea-1 and Derraghan in Co. Longford (Raftery 1990, 1996).

The aims of the analysis of both the building and trackway wood have been to :

- determine the character and location of the original woodland
- analyse the nature and extent of the selection of wood
- identify any evidence for woodland management
- attempt to establish a relative chronological framework from the tree-ring evidence.

A total of 408 wood samples have been examined from the six buildings and 360 from the trackways and linear structures, by deep-freezing and surfacing the transverse section of each post or stem with a Surform plane, which reveals the growth rings of the tree very clearly if well-preserved. The precise diameter, number of rings, and the character of the growth pattern (fast or slow, uniform or variable, stage of growth of the outermost ring to determine the season of cutting) were recorded. The wood discussed here represents around 60–70% of that lifted and identified. It must be stressed that most of the discussion here is focused on the roundwood, as the type of evidence collected cannot be determined on, for example, split radial planks which were the main component of Building 6. This report, therefore, gives only partial evidence. Reference should be made to CD 12.35 (Column 3) to identify the proportion of the sample on which the results are based.

These results should be read in conjunction with the conclusions of the species identification (Johnson, Chapter 12.2), the study of woodworking (Brunning, Chapter 12.3) and the dendrochronological dating of oak (Hillam, Chapter 11).

12.4.1 Buildings

Building 1 (Table CD 12.35 and 12.36)

A total of 232 wood samples (approximately 63% of the total identified) came from this rectangular structure, primarily from wall posts and stakes (CD 12.2). See Figure 12.2 for the locations of pieces of Buildings 1 and 2 noted in the text. In addition to the dominant alder, alder buckthorn (*Frangula alnus*) was common in the possible Structure 5, and the group of Pomoideae (which includes the microscopically indistinguishable *Pyrus, Sorbus,* and *Crataegus*) also provided a quantity of stakes. The other woods examined from among the stakes included very small quantities of willow, blackthorn, field maple, ash, and elm; birch was used mainly for horizontal floor planks and oak for posts of unknown function inside and outside the building. Around 83% of the wood considered here was roundwood.

Elements of Building 1

West wall

The west wall included at least two lines of posts, and is here divided into the main wall (23 alder and 2 ash posts) and inner wall (13 alder and 4 other woods), as well as 33 stakes of varied species (CD 12.36).

Figure 12.20 reveals that the main wall posts were consistently 60–100mm in diameter, the inner posts were slighter at 40–60mm and the stakes were 20–40mm. The range of age and size (Figs 12.20 and 12.21) clearly shows the separation of the three components by size and species. Ages ranged from c 5 to 80 years, following what appears to be a natural age progression. Most of the stakes were aged 5–25 years and posts 20–40 years. It is clear that the trees were carefully selected for size; for example the alder buckthorn stakes were the same diameter as the alder and Pomoideae, but were much more mature (slower-grown).

North wall

The north wall was represented by 12 alder wall posts (6 posts from each side of the probable entrance) and 41 stakes of various species. The posts were generally 60–120mm in diameter and aged 20–50 years, the stakes 20–50mm across and aged 10–30 years (Figs 12.20 and 12.21). While all the stakes were similar size, variations in age between species

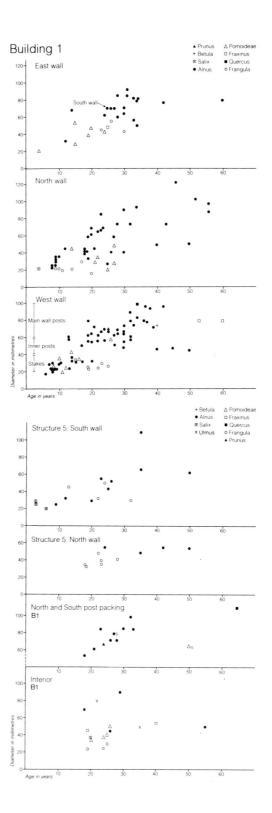

Figure 12.20 Scatter diagrams indicating the relationship and distribution by size (vertical axis) and age (horizontal axis) of the wood used for posts and stakes in the different elements of Buildings 1 and 5. Drawing by B Garfi. Prunus spinosa *(blackthorn),* Betula *(birch),* Salix *(willow),* Alnus *(alder),* Pomoideae *(fruitwood),* Fraxinus *(ash),* Quercus *(oak),* Frangula *(alder buckthorn)* Ulmus *(elm)*

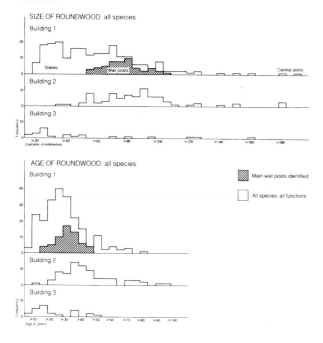

GOLDCLIFF

SIZE OF ROUNDWOOD: all species

Figure 12.21 Histogram showing the range in size (above) and age (below) of wood of all species from Buildings 1, 2, and 3. Drawing by B Garfi

showed different growth rates: the alder buckthorn were <20 years old and the Pomoideae >20 years. In the west wall this was reversed. The possible door posts (1009 and 1010) varied in size: 1009 was more substantial at 105mm across, compared with 1010 at 75mm.

South wall
Only one post was sampled from the eroded wall, an alder trunk 70mm across and 25 years old.

East wall
This single line of posts provided 30 samples, including 16 alder posts, which were 50–90mm across and aged 25–35 years. Eleven stakes of varied woods were 30–50mm in diameter and 15–30 years old (Fig 12.20).

North and south axial posts and packing
The northern group included main alder Post 262, 170mm in diameter and 80 years old, and Post 270, which was a split radial from a tree around 190mm across and about 63 years old. Both represent large alders, a tree which does not usually reach a great age, but can grow rapidly to a substantial size. Post 262 showed signs of fungal attack. Its growth rate was variable, while 270 had grown rapidly, suggesting different sources for the trees. Packed around the posts were 10 mainly roundwood stems included 8 of alder, 1 oak, and 1 blackthorn. The trees were 55–100mm across and of varied age (18–60+ years), clustering as in the wall posts at 60–90mm and 20–30 years (Fig 12.20). Alder 271 was a split half trunk,

and Oak 267 was a split quarter. The southern axial post (750) was a substantial alder trunk 190mm across and *c* 55 years old, flanked by larger pieces (751 and 758) and packed with eleven smaller pieces of radially split and roundwood alder, Pomoideae, and split oak (dendrochronologically dated Piece 761). Original tree age and size was estimated at 10–110 + years and 20–120mm.

Internal structures in the northwest corner
Seven horizontal floor planks made of birch and alder were examined; they were crushed and poorly preserved, making age and size difficult to determine. Four were thought to be split quarters, and three roundwood, from trees up to 200mm across. Stakes of seven different wood species, probably whatever was available, formed a parallel east–west line to the south of a series of split oak planks which were dendrochronologically dated; the stakes were unusually quite concentrated in age at 20–30 years, and of varied size (Fig 12.20).

Outside Building 1

A range of wood samples came from the north and west of the building, including split oak and varied roundwood, mainly 25–50 years old and 45–140mm across.

Possible Building 5

Two parallel stake lines, one across the building and one north of the building are interpreted as a possible separate structure, Building 5. Among the 28 samples examined (CD 12.35) were a majority of alder and alder buckthorn, with some willow, a wood hardly found elsewhere and not of great durability. All were roundwood, except for two alder posts which were originally from large trees >100mm across: Post 930 was almost a split quarter, and Post 744 a boxed heart, both from trees *c* 40 years old. The stakes were wide-ranging in age, up to 50 years (Fig 12.20); the willow was very young (possibly the remains of wattle infill), the alder buckthorn 15–30 years, and the alder 10–50 years. The stakes were, however, quite consistent in size, between 20mm and 60mm across, and were probably carefully selected, though very slight for any type of roof support. Among these stems was a high proportion of probably summer cut wood (14%), and only 11% suggested winter cutting.

Tree-ring studies: Buildings 1 and 5

During wood analysis, it became clear that some of the alder posts contained sufficient growth rings of satisfactory quality to merit ring-width measurement. To succeed in cross-matching some variation from ring to ring, suggesting that recurrent patterns might be discernible, must be present. The aim of this

Table 12.3 Tree age and character of the rings in alder samples from Building 1

Group	Typical age range	Character of rings	Ring-widths	Sample numbers (locations Fig 12.2)
1	30–40	Very sensitive	0.1–2mm	Wall posts: 15/18/45/103/112/724/1035/873/990/1010
2	c 25	Very sensitive	0.1–2mm	730/731/747/931
3	50–70	Sensitive	<1mm	Wall posts: 34/48/100/1001/1009 Internal: 80/755/757/764/750/744
4	50–70	Sensitive	1–3mm	North post/wall: 126/270/262

study was not absolute dating, as in oak, but an attempt to establish an internal dating framework, to determine relative relationships between the posts: whether they were from trees growing at the same time, in the same woodland, and cut down together, or whether they revealed a variety of sources and cutting dates which might suggest repairs and additions. The relative tree-ring dating of roundwood has the potential, as has been shown in a number of projects, eg at Fiskerton (Hillam 1992) or Alvastra in Sweden (Bartholin 1987), to provide very precise internal dating frameworks for wooden structures.

Alder has been used for tree-ring study in several locations, eg from the Somerset Levels trackways (Morgan 1980 and 1988) and Scottish crannogs, where Crone (1988, 144) concluded that 'only alder with strong dominant growth patterns are susceptible to cross-matching'. Alder's intermittent growth can cause poor year-to-year correlation, while giving hints of contemporaneity through longer cycles of growth which are difficult to prove. The standard measure of similarity used for oak, the *t*-value (Baillie 1982, 1995) is not so appropriate to a wood with such wide variations from ring to ring as alder; here a simple measure of the percentage of corresponding rises and falls is used (eg CD 12.38), but it may be more effective to use some form of smoothing.

The rings are termed 'growth rings' here, in recognition of the less clearly seasonal and less reliably annual growth of diffuse-porous woods such as alder, by comparison with the ring-porous oak. Many alder samples also revealed 'locally present' rings, often very narrow rings which cannot be identified around the entire circumference of the trunk; where these are common, even the measurement of multiple radii cannot resolve the final record for the tree, and some were abandoned for this reason.

Frequently too, the latest rings immediately below the bark were very suppressed, leading to the suspicion that they were not annual. The writer and others (Crone 1988) have observed this in other contexts, and noted that they lead to a lack of confidence in their reliability as annual indicators. This suppression may be related to competition with other trees, or possibly to the infestation of alder by sapfly larvae (Elling 1966, Crone 1988), which burrow round the cambium where new wood is produced and affect the tree's ability to create new

wood cells. Thus, relative felling dates of the Goldcliff alder are treated cautiously, and are given a standard deviation of ± 2 years to allow for the possible loss or misinterpretation of rings.

Measurements were finally made on 27 alder samples (CD 12.37), including eighteen wall posts, the north and south axial posts and some packing pieces, and some internal stakes. The posts had 25–80 growth rings. The tree age and character of the rings enabled grouping of the alder samples, as shown in Table 12.3.

These groups could either represent different sources and different woodland types, growing under

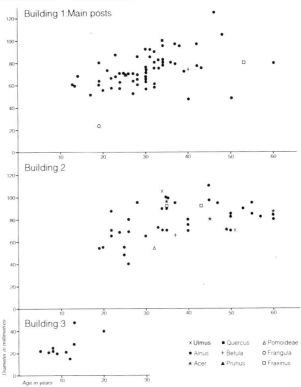

Figure 12.22 Distribution by age and size of the main wall posts in Buildings 1, 2, and 3. Drawing by B Garfi. Ulmus (elm), Alnus (alder), Acer campestre (field maple), Quercus (oak), Betula (birch), Prunus spinosa (blackthorn), Pomoideae (fruitwood), Frangula (alder buckthorn), Fraxinus (ash)

200

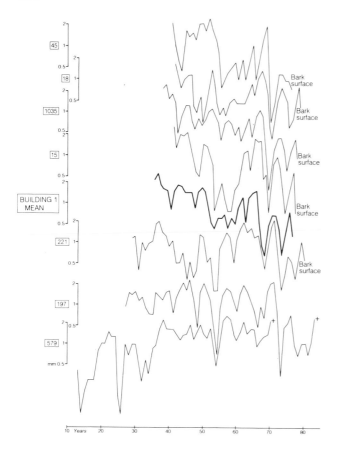

Figure 12.23 *Ring-width patterns of four alder main wall posts from Building 1, with their mean curve (in bold) and three cross-matching patterns from Building 2 posts (221, 197, 579). Drawing by B Garfi*

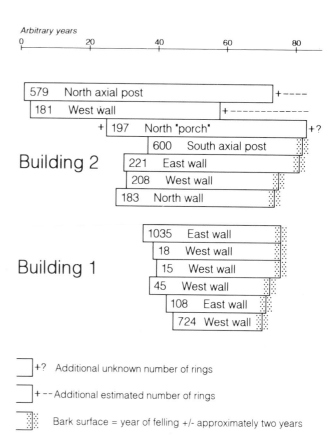

Figure 12.24 *Bar chart indicating the relative time scales of the cross-matched alder groups in Buildings 1 and 2. Drawing by B Garfi*

variable conditions which led to differing rates of growth, or the variations could be chronological.

Visual comparison of the measured patterns revealed the correlation of six records from wall posts in Group 1 above (15/18/45/103/724/1035) from the east and west walls (Figs 12.23–12.24). The most mature post (1035) became the key pattern to linking the others, and their similarity to each other is shown by the correlation values which averaged 72% (CD 12.38).

Other corresponding ring records (though not with the group above) were from Posts 112 and 1009 in the northeast wall (61%). The patterns of other posts, such as 873 and 990, suggest that they may be contemporary, but their ring patterns were not similar enough or could not be finally resolved to be absolutely certain.

All posts were measured out to their bark surface and, where correlated, showed apparently varied cutting dates. However, the standard deviation of ±2 years is applied to allow for the suppressed growth (one sample revealed four more rings on one radius than another), rather than try to interpret these as precise relative years in which the trees were felled, which would suggest the difficult practice of adding, or replacing, key wall posts in the building. It must be concluded that alder is not sufficiently reliable for very precise relative dating, and the varied end years shown in Figure 12.24 could be contemporary; the

cross-matching does at least show that some of the trees used for wall posts grew at the same time, and probably in the same woodland.

The north (262) and south (750) posts were both from mature slow-grown trees, and their ring-patterns showed no correspondence with each other, nor with the group based on the wall posts. This does not exclude the possibility that they were growing at the same time, but they probably represent carefully selected trees which could have been stockpiled, or even inserted later; the evidence is inconclusive. The split alder post packing piece (270) came from a, possibly, much older tree with fast growth (rings of 1–2.5mm, on average), and its final 40 or so rings showed some correspondence with the above post group, but could not be firmly fitted into the series.

Three split pieces of alder from south post packing (755/757/764), the rings of which spanned some 60 years, revealed sufficient similarity to suggest that they originated in the same tree. It was initially surmised that, if they matched the Post 750, they could be part of the same tree; there were some similarities but as the split pieces had more rings than 750, they must either have come from lower down the trunk, or from a different tree.

No cross-matching was evident in the patterns from the alder wood in the northwest corner (Post 80) or the possible Building 5 (744/747).

Tentative identification of the season of cutting from the stage of growth of the outermost ring indicated quite a significant amount of apparently summer cut wood, particularly in the west wall posts and stakes. A total of 24% of posts examined from the whole building were cut in winter and 11% in summer. If this interpretation of the stage of growth is correct, it would suggest construction using wood from a variety of sources and collected over several seasons.

Building 2 (Table CD 12.35, 12.39–12.41)

A total of 88 wood samples were examined, approximately 62% of those identified, and included 61 wall posts, some floor planks and internal posts and stakes. Figure 12.2 shows the locations of the pieces mentioned. Alder was again the dominant wood species; small amounts of field maple, elm, birch, and ash, and single samples of willow, Pomoideae, and oak were also examined. Around 71% of the samples examined here were roundwood, the remainder having been modified in some way. Winter was identified as the cutting season of 14% of the examined wood, and only 2% may have been cut in summer.

Elements of Building 2

West wall
The west wall posts were of varied species: roundwood of alder and a little elm, and radially split oak and ash. They revealed a wide variation in tree maturity (20–80 years), but were quite consistent in size at around 70–90mm (posts from all walls shown in Figure 12.22, from individual walls in CD 12.40). The largest post (181) reached 120mm across. The oak piece was a radial split from a tree of unknown original age, dendro-dated to after 454 BC (Chapter 11). It stood in a group of four posts of different species; the ash and oak posts lie just west of the wall line and effectively outside the building.

North wall
Most of the alder inner wall posts (six to the west and three east of the entrance) were roundwood and fell into a concentrated size range of 80–100mm, varying in age from 25–60 years. The one exception was the eastern door post (571), a split half alder trunk 130mm across, though only 36 years old. The outer row of posts was characterised by the use of field maple and elm, and a higher proportion of split wood from larger trees than the alder; eg the split half post (219), the 'boxed heart' elm post (218) originally 150mm across, the radial alder plank (197), and the quartered elm (551). There appears to have been no attempt to pair size or species of posts across the entrance; the eastern group were more substantial in size, with Post 571 at 130mm, Post 218 at 150mm, and Post 569 at 105mm, compared with Post 200 at 105mm, and Post 205 at 90mm in the west. Tree age was also greater in the field maple and elm than in most of the alder.

East wall
The posts of regularly spaced alder, with some field maple and ash, were consistent in size between around 70mm and 100mm in diameter, and aged 20–60 years, concentrated between 30 and 40 years. A partial line of inner posts suggested a double or repaired wall; of the four examined, three were alder roundwood 55–70mm across (so less substantial than the main wall posts), and one a small elm radial plank.

South wall
One post of alder from the centre of the eroded south wall was 100mm across and 35 years old. A possible remnant of an inner line, Post 948, was 47 years old and 90mm across, so consistent with the wall posts.

Flooring
A series of floor planks provided 15 samples, 9 of birch, 4 of alder and 1 each of willow and elm. Due to poor preservation, no count, or only an approximation, of tree age was possible. The planks were roundwood, or halved or quartered roundwood, or tangentially split. For example, transverse birch Plank 214 was compressed roundwood from a tree about 90mm across and of indeterminate age. Birch Plank 303 at right angles was probably a split quarter from a tree 90mm across and c 25 years old. Alder Plank 573 may have been roundwood 90mm across. Small birch Plank 475 was a trimmed split quarter from a tree over 150mm across and >35 years old. Alder Plank 195 was roundwood 77mm across and 31 years old, consistent in size with the wall posts.

North and south axial posts
The northern group provided five alder and three field maple samples. The main post (579) was 170mm across and aged c 60 years. Nearby alder Post 580 was also large at 155mm across and >50 years old. The packing material around ranged from an alder roundwood stake 34mm across, to radially split field maple Slat 586 from a tree >170mm across and >100 years old, to a squared trunk from a tree >120mm across. The south axial post (600) stood alone, and was 176mm across (similar in size to north Post 579), but only c 40 years old. A scatter of posts just to the south included a squared quarter trunk of ash, an elm roundwood post, and a piece of split alder from a substantial tree.

Outside Building 2

One alder post (481) lay beyond the east wall; it was 86mm across and 41 years old.

Tree-ring studies: Building 2

A total of 19 alder, 4 elm, 3 field maple, and 1 ash ring-width records were collected from wall posts, both axial posts and packing materials (CD 12.41); records spanned between 25 and >80 years.

Alder
Three ring records from wall posts (221 east wall, 208 west wall, and 183 north wall) have been tentatively matched with the pattern of the southern axial post (600), and with longer series from the north axial post (579), west wall post (181), and north wall post (197) (Fig 12.23). None of the last three extended out to the bark surface. The relative end years of the series shown in Figure 12.23 varied over a span of *c* 10 years, and for the reasons already explained, may be consistent with common cutting years, or may indicate slight variation. Post 197, however, was almost certainly cut later, as it was a small radial piece from a larger tree. The correlations between the ring patterns (CD 12.38) are not as high as for those within Building 1, averaging 65%, but they do suggest at least a common source for some of the wood. The ring patterns were compared with those from Building 1, and revealed some clear similarities, as shown in Figure 12.23. The relationship between their relative time spans and end years is as illustrated in Figure 12.24, and implies the general contemporaneity and common source of some of the wood used in both buildings, though they do not imply precisely identical cutting years or dates of construction; the wood may have been cut down over a period of years and stored for use.

Elm and ash
Of the elm posts (CD 12.41) measured, Post 200 was a mature and slow-grown tree of 70 years and 105mm across, and Post 218 was 150mm across and aged *c* 90 years. Their ring patterns showed similar trends with periods of very slow uniform growth, and sudden bursts of sensitive growth, as did Post 227 from the east wall (a radial split from a tree *c* 180mm across and >95 years old). However, there was no evidence from the patterns to confirm that they were growing at the same time. Post 545 was a much less mature (at 34 years) and more vigorously growing tree which had reached 105mm. The wide variation in tree maturity no doubt made cross-matching less likely to succeed, but elm wood from other contexts has not proved very successful for tree-ring analysis, and it may be a tree which is insufficiently sensitive to local conditions.

Field maple
Three field maple records came from Post 225 in the northeast corner, and north post packing Pieces 582 and 583; the last two showed sufficiently similar patterns to suggest they could have originated in the same tree, but the designation of bark surface on 583 in Arbitrary Year 60 and the last (but not final) ring of 582 in Arbitrary Year 63 indicates that this is

unlikely to be the case. The tree which provided 582 was probably cut down some years later, within the same woodland as 583.

Building 3 (Table CD 12.39)

A total of 24 samples were examined (33% of the total identified); ten were alder and alder buckthorn stakes from the north wall and the rest were birch and field maple stakes and horizontals found in the vicinity of the building. The alder samples were roundwood of relatively consistent size, *c* 20–30mm diameter and <15 years old (Figs 12.21 and 12.22). Rings were wide, signifying rapid growth. There was also a group of large posts or trunks 100–160mm across outside the building. The season of cutting was tentatively identified in nineteen samples (79%) as winter; none suggested summer cutting.

Building 4

Only one ash radial piece 87mm wide with >45 rings was examined.

Building 6

Sampling of Building 6 for this study was only partial and reference should be made to other reports (Chapters 11 and 12.2–12.3). A total of sixteen samples included only six roundwood of fast-grown alder and hazel (*Corylus avellana* L.), 9–67mm across; the three hazel posts from the wall were cut in winter, 68mm across and 20–28 years old. The use of hazel for this purpose can be remarked on, as this wood species is rare at Goldcliff, despite being so dominant elsewhere eg at nearby Caldicot (Nayling and Caseldine 1997).

Building 8 (Table CD 12.39)

A total of nineteen, mainly ash and field maple samples, included only five of whole or halved roundwood, so original tree size and age could not be determined; numbers of rings suggested mature trees of 50–100 years or more. The wood was fast-grown. The largest stake was an ash radial split from a tree of >230mm in diameter and >65 years old. The species and maturity of the wood allowed some ring-width measurement: three elm stakes (7152 from the northwest corner, and 7162 and 7166 from the southwest corner) were measured over 74–99 years, all extending out to near the bark surface, but a decline in growth rate over their last 40 years or so led to an almost flat growth profile and no possibility of correlation. Two ash stakes (7150 from the northwest corner and 7167 from the middle of the south wall) revealed uniform rates of growth of 1–1.5mm annually and showed no correspondence

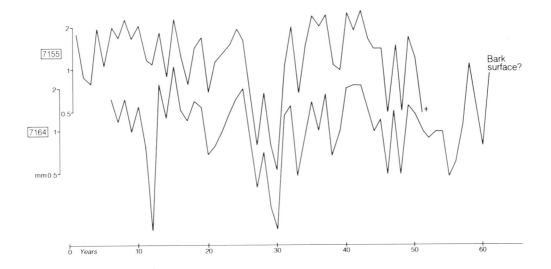

Figure 12.25 Ring-width patterns of two field maple radial planks from Building 8, so similar that they probably came from the same tree. Drawing by B Garfi

over their 65–93 year time span. Two field maple samples (7155/7164) with 50–60 rings revealed more promising sensitive growth patterns and proved likely to have originated in the same tree (correlation value of 86%), as illustrated in Figure 12.25. The two posts lay some distance apart, 7155 at the northwest corner and 7164 at the southwest corner of the building.

Discussion of evidence from the buildings

Evidence indicates that alder was favoured for the walls of the buildings, an excellent choice as it is dense, strong, and durable under wet conditions, and was clearly easily available. The main alder wall posts of Building 1 were produced from carefully selected trees 60–80mm across and aged 20–40 years; the inner (rebuilding or strengthening) lines of alder posts were also 20–40 years old but slighter at 40–60mm, which suggests they were the smaller stems from the same or similar woodland. The stakes of varied species between the wall posts were 10–20 years old and 20–40mm across. The alder main wall posts of Building 2 were less consistent in species and size, and were larger and older than those of Building 1:

	Building 1	Building 2
Average age (years)	32.7	41.7
Average diameter (mm)	77.4	84.0

The wood was also generally slower-grown (with narrower rings) in Building 2. This variation in tree development suggests different woodland sources and/or different periods of time for the wood in both buildings. It is clear from the preserved tree stumps

(Fig 12.1) and palynological records that alder and birch woodland was growing on the peat shelf just prior to construction of the buildings.

Tree maturity was very varied; the most mature alders used in the structures reached a size of over 200mm and an age of 80 years, and all ages were represented, suggesting collection from the whole range of natural woodland. Oaks probably exceeded 250 years in age, and there was evidence of field maples >100 years old.

The Building 3 stakes resemble the alder and Pomoideae stakes of Building 1 in size and age; the stakes of the proposed Building 5 were also 20–40mm across, but much more widespread in age up to c 50 years.

Growth rates were generally fast and regular, though becoming more variable in the later years of the more mature alder, suggesting a well-maintained water supply and relatively unstressed and favourable conditions for growth. The alder buckthorn revealed more uniform growth rates than the alder; both trees enjoy wet and acid soils, but may have been responding to different conditions or growing at a different time. They contrast with the narrow-ringed oaks from Buildings 1 and 2, a species which would have disliked wet conditions if growing locally. The split wood from larger timber trees (oak, ash, field maple, elm), such as that used in Building 8, may have been imported from higher, drier ground on Goldcliff Island, or to the north.

The roundwood in the buildings gives the overall impression of having been selected for size from very local woodland, which shows no evidence of prior exploitation or management.

The tree-ring records from alder, field maple, ash, and elm, aimed at providing an internal relative dating framework, have demonstrated the suitability of alder and field maple, in particular, to provide clearly measurable rings and cross-matching ring patterns under certain conditions. Elm and ash had a tendency to be insensitive.

Groups of cross-matching alder main wall posts from each of Buildings 1 and 2 show that some of the trees used were growing at the same time, probably in the same woodland. Uncertainty over identifying final rings has removed some of the evidence for precise cutting years. Various strands of information from other sources suggest that the buildings were probably not constructed at the same time, and that Building 2 was probably the earlier. The tree-ring links could support this theory by suggesting that Building 1 was built (or repaired) at the same time as repairs were carried out to Building 2, which led to a doubling of the wall lines and axial posts (when 579 was installed, see the woodworking report). A group of stock-piled poles felled in the same wood could have been cut to length and used as needed, making it difficult to link their felling date with their use date.

The theory that the wood of both buildings came from various sources at different times is further supported by the variation in cutting season noted in the roundwood (CD 12.35), with Building 1 revealing 11% summer cutting and Building 5 as high as 14%, whereas Building 2 had only 2%, and all the roundwood in Buildings 3 and 8 was cut in winter.

12.4.2 Trackways and linear structures

Structure 1108

This structure of small diagonally driven posts has been dendrochronologically dated to 336–318 BC (Chapter 11); vertical elements suggested multi-phased construction, but this could not be determined from the wood examined, which totalled 74 samples (68% of those lifted, Table CD 12.35). The wood was very varied in species and cross-section. Among the roundwood, field maple and ash were more mature (17–38 years) than alder and oak (<5 years) (Fig 12.26). Selection for size for certain functions is probable, the older stems being 30–50mm across and the younger 10–20mm, but the spread is wide (Fig 12.27). The remains of the horizontal track surface consisted largely of field maple roundwood of 30–40mm diameter. Season of cutting was determined in 33% of all samples (mainly alder and field maple); 30% were probably cut in winter and 3% in summer.

Structure 1149

This structure may be an extension of 1108, but sample numbers were insufficient to confirm this. The thirteen samples (81%) were of six different wood species; many were radially split fragments. Original trees must have been aged c 15–85 years, and three stems were probably winter cut.

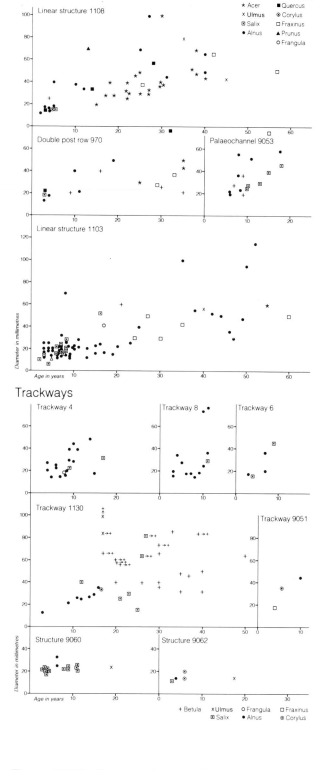

Figure 12.26 Scatters showing the range in age (horizontal axis) and size (vertical axis) in all wood species from the tracks and linear structures (roundwood only). Drawing by B Garfi. Betula (birch), Acer campestre (field maple), Ulmus (elm), Salix (willow), Alnus (alder), Pomoideae (fruitwood), Quercus (oak), Corylus (hazel), Fraxinus (ash), Prunus spinosa (blackthorn), Frangula (alder buckthorn)

Trackways and other linear structures

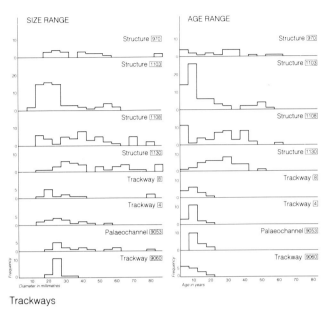

Trackways

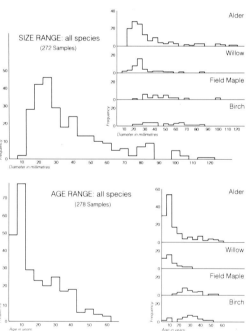

Figure 12.27 Histograms showing the overall range in age and size of all the trackway roundwood, and also in alder, willow, field maple, and birch individually. Drawing by B Garfi

Double Post Row 970

A total of 39 samples (35%) consisted largely of field maple and alder with some oak and birch. The wood varied greatly in cross-section; original tree size varied from roundwood stems of 10mm up to trunks of 230mm or more. Age/size comparisons among the roundwood (Figs 12.26 and 12.27) suggests that any available wood of around 20–50mm across was collected; at this size, age varied from 3 to 35 years (up to over 60 years). Of the mostly alder roundwood

samples, twelve (36%) were winter cut and only one possibly summer. The wood gives the impression of a very varied assemblage, perhaps gathered as available from a variety of woodland sources (with very varying rates of growth). There was little evidence of exploiting the properties of the different wood species, other than splitting those which cleave easily (oak or field maple). Ring-widths of two adjacent radially split field maple horizontals (7318/7319) and one alder post (7351) were measured, each with around 50 rings; the sensitive field maple ring patterns clearly corresponded and suggested an origin in the same tree, possibly supporting the theory of construction teams laying track sections (Johnson, Chapter 12.2).

Linear Structure 1103

This linear alignment was represented by 93 samples (83%), including 63 alder used for structural elements, 12 of willow brushwood, and the remaining 18 of 7 other species. The dominance of alder and willow suggests the cutting of very local woodland, and is confirmed by nearby tree stumps of the same species. The distribution by age and size of the stems, based on the 61% roundwood, indicated three categories of wood each of which seemed to serve a specific function (Figs 12.26 and 12.27):

(i) a cluster of small alder and willow stems <20 years old and 10–25mm in diameter, used as brushwood to weave around the posts and as packing material;
(ii) larger pole-sized horizontals forming the walking surface and vertical pieces of many species selected for size of 30–70mm across, with a wide spread in age up to 60 years;
(iii) some large alder trunks 100–120mm across and 40–50 years old holding the structure in place.

The wood gives the clear impression that size governed its selection. Felling season was determined in 61% of the wood; 55% was winter cut and 6% could have been cut in summer. A third of the wood was classed as wide-ringed or fast-grown (not clear from Figure 12.26 as much was split wood), and 20% revealed uniform growth, suggesting favourable conditions. Recorded ring-width patterns of two alder posts *c* 50 years old (3345/3353) did not reveal any clear similarity.

Brushwood tracks

Trackway 1 Nine alder roundwood samples were examined (75%), four aged 7 years and the others 20–40 years; they were 16–85mm across and of varied growth rate. Five were probably winter cut.

Track 4 This brushwood track of alder with a little willow and alder buckthorn may have been two-phase, but this could not be determined from the wood, of which eighteen samples (20%) were examined. The more substantial longitudinal pieces (3883/3884/3885) were 40–50mm across and aged 10–15 years, and they were supported by lighter material of 4–9 years and 15–30mm across (Figs 12.26 and 12.27). About half the stems were wide-ringed and growth rates varied; thirteen (72%) samples were winter cut and two possibly summer. The alder brushwood shows a very similar range in age and size to that from brushwood track Tinney's A in the Somerset Levels (Morgan 1988, fig V.17).

Track 6 This track of longitudinal brush covered by a walking surface of larger timber was represented by only six roundwood alder and willow samples (12%). They were 3–27 years old, 16–100mm across (Fig 12.26), wide-ringed, and all cut in winter.

Track 8 All fourteen alder roundwood stems (100%) from this brushwood track were cut in winter and most were fast-grown. In size the wood fell into two groups, substantial longitudinals of 80–100mm across though only around 10 years old, and a concentrated group of stems 15–35mm across and 3–11 years old (Figs 12.26 and 12.27). The wood gives the impression of careful selection for the purpose, unlike some of the other tracks.

Palaeochannel 9053

This unstructured spread of wood provided sixteen samples (76%) of fast-grown alder, willow, and birch roundwood aged 6–18 years and 19–76mm across (Figs 12.26 and 12.27). Horizontal pieces were generally of alder or willow 40–50mm in diameter and uprights were of willow 25mm across. The majority of stems were <10 years old, but there is no concentration to suggest any form of selection. Most of the stems (81%) were cut in winter, with 12% possibly cut in summer.

Trackway 1130

The 47 samples (76%) examined from this corduroy track were of birch, alder, and willow, used apparently randomly along the track. One piece of hazel was used as a post. Birch was dominant but is not a durable wood, especially when split, so its widespread use suggests a quick and temporary structure. The birch stems were large, 30–90mm across, slow-grown and mature at 20–50 years (Fig 12.26); the alder tended to be young, <20 years, and fast-grown, 20–40mm in diameter. The willow was 20–30 years old but varied in size from 16mm to 82mm. There was no clear indication of selection for size in any of the wood (Fig 12.27). Of the wood with preserved bark surface, 53% suggested winter cutting, with one possible example of summer cutting. Other tracks of similar construction type include the earlier Corlea-6 track in Co Longford (Raftery 1990) of oak and ash roundwood on a birch substructure, or the Abbot's Way in the Somerset Levels (Coles and

Orme 1976, Coles 1980) made mainly of ash, hazel, and alder; in the latter the trees were 60–100mm across and 65% of the wood was split roundwood.

Trackway 9051

Only three roundwood samples (9%) were of willow, ash, and hazel, 4–10 years old and 18–43mm across. The wood was fast-grown; two stems were winter cut and one possibly summer. This track was a possible extension to 1130, but there were insufficient samples to draw conclusions on the basis of age, size, growth rate, or woodworking style; differing alignments and use of species suggests they were not the same.

Structures between Track 1130 and Boat Plank site 1124

Wood from 9066 Five samples (21%) of alder, ash and hazel were aged 3–13 years and 12–30mm across.

Structure 9062 From this area of roundwood pegs came eight samples of hazel, alder, elm, and ash (50%); all were roundwood except one small tangential piece of ash. Ages varied from 3 to 50 years and size from 12mm to 42mm (Fig 12.26), thus growth rates also varied greatly.

Structure 9061 Only one roundwood alder peg 9 years old and 29mm across, and cut in winter, was examined.

Structure 9060 This double row of roundwood pegs provided fifteen samples (83%), largely of willow with a little alder and elm. The stems fell into groups aged c 4 years, c 8–11 years, and one at 19 years, although diameters were very consistent at 20–25mm (Figs 12.26 and 12.27) and the wood was clearly collected for its appropriate size. The wood was fast-grown and was probably collected at varied times of year, as eight stems (53%) suggested winter cutting and six summer. Comparison of the details of opposing pegs showed that 7483 and 7484 were both willow of 4 years and 23mm across, and 7490 and 7491 were both willow of 9 years and 23mm across (but one cut winter and one (?) summer), but Pegs 7486 and 7487 were the same size and aged 4 and 8 years, respectively (both cut summer), and 7488 and 7489 were different species, willow of 4 years and 20mm across and alder of 7 years and 25mm across (both cut winter). The evidence does not suggest that one pole was cut into pieces for paired pegs, but rather that they were pre-prepared and, thus, mixed in species and age. The single horizontal Piece 7475 was of elm 19 years old and 24mm across, the same size but more narrow-ringed than the other wood.

Discussion of the trackway evidence

The tracks fell into two groups on the basis of materials:

(i) brushwood structures dominated by the use of young alder and willow stems on average 25mm across and 5–10 years old;

(ii) more complex and substantial structures using round and split wood of a variety of species from often large and mature trees.

Generally the wood displays such varied characteristics as to suggest a wide variety of sources and cutting times, to provide a ready supply of suitable sized material for the required purpose. Brushwood may have been collected as required and judging by the species from close to the construction site, but the split timber was probably stock-piled, reused, and left over from other activities; the extensive use of birch in Trackway 1130 hints at the often temporary and short-term nature of such structures. Also it was noted that the choice of wood species did not always reflect the most effective use of its properties.

Most of the track wood appears to have been cut in winter, but in one or two structures such as 9060 there is a proportion of summer cut wood, suggesting supplementation of existing supplies with fresh material. This could hint at summer construction while water levels were lower, but could equally suggest all-year-round collection for all-year-round construction.

Selection for size was apparent only in Structure 1103 and Trackway 9060 (Fig 12.27), and age concentrations were noted in Structure 1103 and Trackway 4. The overall ranges indicate the use of wood of approximately 15–40mm in diameter, and the majority of stems aged <10 years though with large amounts up to 40 years old. Examined by wood species, the alder and willow demonstrated very similar ranges (<20 years old, and peaking in size at 15–30mm), whereas the field maple and birch were wide-ranging in size and more mature (25–40 years). There were no suggestions of any previous woodland management, and the wood gives the overall impression of rapid collection from any available source, whether freshly cut or recycled, almost regardless of features or properties.

13 The vegetation history of the Goldcliff area *by*
A Caseldine with contributions by K Barrow and J James

13.1 Introduction

A number of factors have influenced the vegetation development in the Goldcliff area. These include autogenic (self-producing), climatic, hydrological, anthropogenic, and sea level change. These influences are superimposed upon each other, with one or more playing a major role in determining the contemporary vegetation. The vegetation provides parameters within which human communities could operate, providing opportunities and limitations, and hence influencing activities. Changes occur, requiring a response; some of these were over a longer period, others were short, no more than a brief interruption in a period of otherwise comparative stability. These changes vary spatially as well as temporally.

The following account is based on the results of 21 pollen diagrams and accompanying stratigraphic evidence, with additional detailed plant macrofossil analysis. A brief description of the sampling strategy is included in the text but, because of the large number of sequences analysed and the consequent space constraints, full details of the stratigraphy, pollen zonation, and plant macrofossil results for each site, are provided on CD 13.1. After a brief consideration of interpretative issues, there follows a synthetic discussion in which the results are discussed chronologically, and in the broader context of other work carried out in the region (Fig 13.1). Particular reference is made to the investigations of Smith and Morgan (1989) carried out to the east of Goldcliff Point. Other studies which help to place the Goldcliff work in the wider regional context are those further 'inland' at Barland's Farm and Vurlong Reen (Walker *et al* 1998) and Caldicot (Caseldine and Barrow 1997), and further along the coast at Uskmouth (Aldhouse-Green *et al* 1992) and Caldicot Pill/Sudbrook (Scaife 1993 and 1995).

13.2 Sampling strategy

Samples were taken with the aim of recovering a full environmental record, both of local and regional changes, from the Mesolithic to the Iron Age. Particular emphasis was placed on the recovery of samples from the main concentration of structures of Iron Age date to obtain evidence of the spatial variation in the vegetation communities at that time. The Iron Age evidence is described from p 226 after an account of the vegetation history associated with the archaeological sites of Mesolithic to Bronze Age date.

All the samples were from archaeological sites, and

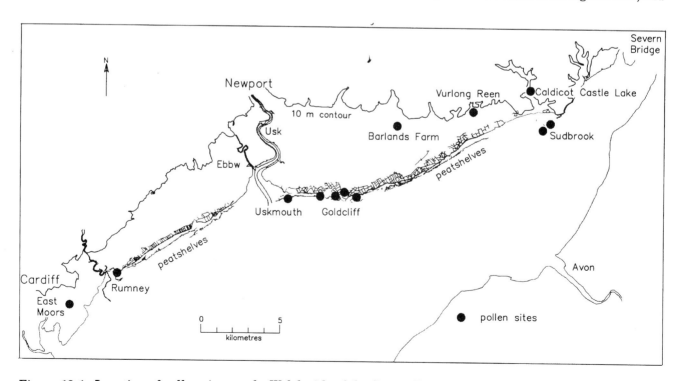

Figure 13.1 Location of pollen sites on the Welsh side of the Severn Estuary

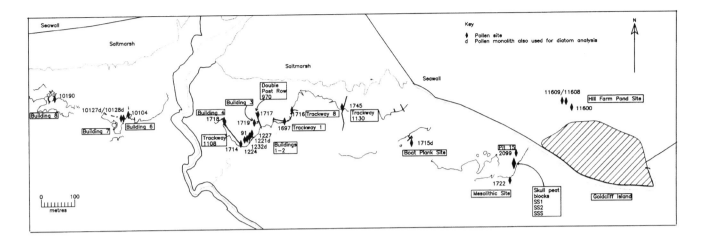

Figure 13.2 Location of Goldcliff pollen sites

their distribution is shown in Figure 13.2. Pit 15 was dug essentially to recover a long environmental sequence which would enable the sequence from the Mesolithic site to be linked with the later sequences from the Iron Age sites, and would provide a comparison with the environmental record, already prepared by Smith and Morgan (1989), to the east of Goldcliff Island. A human skull was found in that sampling pit. Shorter sequences were taken from the later prehistoric sites, with the aim of showing the environmental conditions shortly before, during and after the period of activity, depending on the deposits available at the particular site. The longest and most detailed sequence from this part of the site is from Building 2, which provides a continuation of the earlier environmental record from Pit 15.

The general stratigraphic sequence has already been discussed in Chapter 3 and simplified stratigraphies are given in the pollen diagrams. Detailed stratigraphic descriptions are provided on CD 13.1. The earliest records are from sites on the edge of Goldcliff Island. A pollen monolith (1722) from the Mesolithic site included head deposit, buried soil, estuarine clay, and wood peat, with the upper deposits corresponding to the basal deposits in a pollen monolith (2099) from Pit 15. Bulk samples were also taken from the occupation levels at the Mesolithic site for plant macrofossil analysis. The pollen monolith (2099) from Pit 15 provided a long dated sequence, comprising estuarine clay, wood peat, and raised bog deposits, covering the later Mesolithic, Neolithic, and Bronze Age. In addition, two pollen sequences (Series 1 and 2) from the block of raised bog peat containing the skull were analysed and plant macrofossil samples were also examined in order to clarify the context of this find. A pollen monolith (11600) of Neolithic and Bronze Age date at Hill Farm Pond on the edge of Goldcliff Island comprised a woody peat between clay deposits, with charcoal present both at the base and on the surface of the peat. The rest of the sites examined all lie to the west of Goldcliff Island and the pollen records are Bronze and Iron Age in date. A monolith (1715) was

taken from the palaeochannel deposits from beneath the late-Bronze Age Boat Plank Structure 1124 and analysed for pollen and plant macrofossils. The remaining sites that were sampled lie further to the west and are all Iron Age in date. Stratigraphically, Buildings 1 (Monoliths 1232 and 1224), 2 (Monoliths 1221 and 1227), and 3 (Monolith 1719), and Trackways 1108 (Monolith 1714), 1 (Monolith 1697), 8 (Monolith 1716), and 1130 (Monolith 1745), and Double Post Row 970 (Monolith 1717), all occurred on the upper peat shelf. The monoliths were taken through the peat band and into the underlying clay, and at Building 2 one of the monoliths (1221) extended down into the underlying raised bog peat, enabling comparison with the top of the pollen sequence (2099) from Pit 15.

Monoliths were taken from both inside and outside of Buildings 1 and 2 to determine the vegetational development at the site. In particular, emphasis was placed on the analysis of pollen from the 'occupation' levels. Similarly, detailed investigations were undertaken to ascertain the nature of the 'reed matting' samples from the floors of Buildings 1 and 2 in an attempt to elucidate their use. Samples from Building 3, the trackways, and double post row were taken to investigate the vegetational development along the peat shelf and the environmental conditions when the structures were in use. Monolith 1718 was taken from Building 4 because the auger survey indicated that peats below the building lay at the limits of a late-Bronze Age marine transgression, so the sequence in this area needed to be clarified in relation to the sequences on the peat shelf to its east and on the west side of Goldcliff Pill. Two monoliths (10127 and 10128) were examined from Building 6 at Goldcliff West, primarily to determine the environmental conditions contemporary with, and immediately following, occupation at the site. A longer, earlier sequence (10104) from Building 6 was investigated by students (unpublished), as was a sequence (10190) from Building 8 (unpublished). A sample, contemporary with track level, from each of Trackways 1311 and 1330, which had originally been taken for beetle analysis, was also examined for plant macrofossils to ascertain the local conditions.

13.3 Methods

Pollen analysis

Subsamples of 1ml were used for pollen analysis. Laboratory preparation followed standard procedures (Moore et al 1991), including disaggregation in 10% NaOH, micro-sieving and treatment with HF and HCl to remove minerogenic material, and Erdtman's acetolysis. *Lycopodium* tablets were added to enable pollen concentrations to be calculated. The samples were mounted in either silicone oil or glycerine jelly. The pollen was identified using either a Leitz Laborlux or Vickers M15 microscope. Routine counting was at a magnification of × 400, with crucial identifications at × 630 or × 1000. Generally, at least 400 Total Land Pollen (TLP) grains were counted but, where pollen was sparse, counting ceased either after 500 or, in a few cases, 1000 *Lycopodium* spores had been counted. Charcoal fragments were also counted in some diagrams. Pollen identification was by comparison with a reference collection and identification atlases, notably Moore et al (1991). Nomenclature is based on Bennett (1994) and Bennett et al (1994). Diagrams were prepared using TILIA and TILIAGRAPH (Grimm 1991). Trees, shrubs, heaths, and herbs are expressed as a percentage of TLP. The other groups are expressed as a percentage of that group plus TLP. Local Pollen Assemblages Zones (LPAZs) have been identified and are indicated in summary in each pollen diagram, with the full supporting descriptions on CD 13.1. The relationships between diagrams and zones are summarised in Tables 13.1 and 13.2. A chronological framework for the analysis is provided by a series of radiocarbon dates which are marked on the pollen diagrams and on the archaeological sections in other chapters showing the contexts of the botanical samples. Full details of the radiocarbon dates are given in Appendix II. Because of the number of diagrams and space constraints, only selected taxa pollen diagrams are presented in the text, Figures 13.3–13.21, with full diagrams on the CD 13.2–13.22.

Plant macrofossil analysis

Most of the samples examined were subsamples removed from either the pollen monoliths, 'reed matting' samples, or samples from the Mesolithic charcoal layer. Details of the location of the samples are given on CD 13.1. The quantities examined are given in the relevant tables. Depending on whether they were peats or clays, the samples were allowed to soak in either sodium hydroxide or hydrogen peroxide, respectively, prior to sieving. The samples were washed through a stack of sieves with 2mm, 1mm, 500μ, and 250μ meshes. A few samples were examined from beetle samples that had already been processed (see Chapter 14 for details of initial processing). In the case of 1731, 1751, 10133, and 10134, a subsample of the residues and the whole of the flots were examined. The whole of 10100 was scanned.

The remains were sorted and identified using a Wild M5 microscope and, where a higher magnification was necessary, a Leitz binocular microscope. Identification was by comparison with modern reference material and standard identification texts, including Berggren (1969 and 1981), Beijerinck (1947), Bertsch (1941), and Schoch et al (1988). Nomenclature follows Stace (1991). A brief description of the results is given on CD 13.1, with the full data presented in Tables CD 13.23–13.33, including a table (CD 13.23) summarising the ecological habitats.

The macroscopic plant remains from the pollen sievings, and from occasional additional small samples taken to verify the composition of the peat, were also examined and this information is incorporated in the stratigraphic descriptions on CD 13.1.

13.4 Interpretative considerations: taphonomy and human activity

It is beyond the scope of this report to discuss in detail the factors that have influenced the formation of the pollen and plant macrofossil records at Goldcliff, but it is essential to be aware of their significance. In terms of the pollen record, apart from factors such as differential pollen production and dispersal, the changing nature of the depositional environment is of particular importance, especially so in coastal deposits, such as Goldcliff, where intercalated peat and clay deposits occur with 'occupation' deposits.

Various models of pollen production, dispersal, and deposition have been put forward in relation to peat and lake deposits (Andersen 1970 and 1973, Tauber 1965 and 1967, Moore et al 1991, Price and Moore 1984, Jacobson and Bradshaw 1981). The registration of anthropogenic activity has been discussed by Edwards (1979, 1982, and 1993). In addition, Scaife and Burrin (1992) have considered the sources of pollen in alluvial sediments in a rural, anthropogenically-affected catchment, and this model has been modified further at Caldicot (Caseldine and Barrow 1997), where there is a possible tidal influence. At Goldcliff the estuarine/marine deposits are likely to contain a greater proportion of allochthonous and reworked pollen compared with the peat deposits, whilst the pollen records from the deposits from the buildings, in particular, are likely to contain pollen brought in by people or animals. Factors influencing the registration of human activity taking place on the dryland in the diagrams at Goldcliff are the distance from the activity, ie the 'mainland' and Goldcliff 'island', and the nature of the local vegetation, ie alder woodland or the much more open raised bog or

Table 13.1 Correlation of earlier local pollen assemblage zones at Goldcliff

Date 14 C years BP	West Building 4 1718	Building 2 1221	Boat Plank Site 1124 1715	Pit 15 2099	Skull Peat Block Series 1	Skull Peat Block Series 2	Mesolithic Site 1722	East Hill Farm Pond 11600
2600	GC1718.3c Corylus–Quercus	GC1221.2 Corylus–Calluna–Alnus						
2720			GC1715.2c Poaceae–Quercus–Chenopod. GC1715.2b Poaceae–Quercus–Cyperaceae GC1715.2a Poaceae–Corylus–Cyperaceae GC1715.1 Quercus–Alnus–Chenopod.					GC11600.3 Alnus–Poaceae–Chenopod.
3200	GC1718.3b Calluna–Corylus GC1718.3a Corylus–Alnus–Quercus							GC11600.2b Alnus
3360	GC1718.2 Corylus–Calluna							
3500	GC1718.1 Corylus–Calluna–Quercus							
3640				GC2099.8				
3680		GC1221.1 Corylus–Calluna–Tilia		Corylus–Calluna–Poaceae				
3800				GC2099.7 Corylus–Calluna–Ulmus	GCSS1.3 Corylus–Poaceae	GCSS2.3 Corylus–Poaceae		GC11600.2a Alnus–Quercus–Ulmus
4300					GCSS1.2 Corylus–Calluna	GCSS2.2 Corylus–Calluna		GC11600.1 Corylus–Alnus–Tilia
4520				GC2099.6 Corylus–Calluna–Alnus	GCSS1.1 Betula–Corylus–Calluna	GCSS2.1 Betula–Alnus–Corylus		
4900				GC2099.5 Betula				
5190				GC2099.4 Alnus–Betula				
5660				GC2099.3 Alnus			GC1722.3 Alnus	
5720				GC2099.2b Salix GC2099.2a Cyperaceae–			GC1722.2b Salix GC1722.2a Salix–	
5820				Poaceae– Quercus–			Cyperaceae	
5920				Salix GC2099.1 Alnus– Quercus– Poaceae– Chenopod.			GC1722.1b Chenopod.– Pinus– Quercus GC1722.1 Chenopod.– Corylus– Pteridium	

Table 13.2 Correlation of later local pollen assemblage zones at Goldcliff

Date (14 C years BP)	West Building 6 10128	Building 6 10127	Building 4 1718	Trackway 1108 1714	Building 1 1224	Building 1 1232	Building 2 1221	Building 2 1227	Building 3 1719	Double Post Row 970 1717	Trackway 1 1697	Trackway 8 1716	East Trackway 1130 1745
	GC10128.3b *Calluna–Corylus–Chenopod.*	GC10127.2 *Alnus–Quercus–Chenopod.* GC10127.1b *Chenopod.–Poaceae–Plantago* GC10127.1a *Chenopod.*		GC1714.3 *Poaceae–Chenopod.*	GC1224.3b *Poaceae–Corylus–Plantago* GC1224.3a *Poaceae–Cyperaceae–Plantago*	GC1232/4b *Corylus–Poaceae* GC1232.4a *Corylus–Poaceae–Cyperaceae*	GC1221.7 *Poaceae–Plantago–Corylus*	GC1227.3 *Poaceae–Chenopod.*	GC1719.6 *Corylus–Poaceae*	GC1717.4b *Chenopod.–Poaceae* GC1717.4a *Corylus–Poaceae–Chenopod.*	GC1697.3b *Chenopod.–Cyperaceae–Poaceae* GC1697.3a *Cyperaceae–Poaceae–Chenopod.*	GC1716.3 *Poaceae–Cyperaceae–Chenopod.*	GC1745.3 *Chenopod.–Poaceae–Cyperaceae*
2150	GC10128.3a *Calluna–Corylus–Chenopod.*		GC1718.4 *Poaceae–Corylus*	GC1714.2c *Poaceae–Alnus–Betula* GC1714.2b *Alnus–Betula* GC1714.2a *Alnus–Salix–Poaceae*									
2200	GC10128.2 *Poaceae* GC10128.1 *Calluna–Corylus*				GC1224.2b *Betula–Poaceae* GC1224.2a *Alnus–Betula*	GC1232.3b *Alnus–Betula* GC1232.3a *Betula–Alnus*	GC1221.6b *Alnus* GC1221.6a *Betula–Alnus*	GC1227.2 *Betula–Alnus*	GC1719.5 *Alnus*	GC1717.3 *Alnus–Poaceae*	GC1697.2 *Poaceae–Alnus Poaceae*	GC1716.2 *Poaceae–Cyperaceae*	GC1745.2 *Poaceae–Cyperaceae*
2360				GC1714.1 *Poaceae–Chenopod.*	GC1224.1 *Poaceae–Chenopod.–Quercus*	GC1232.2 *Poaceae–Chenopod.–Quercus* GC1232.1 *Corylus*	GC1221.5 *Poaceae–Chenopod.–Quercus*	GC1227.1 *Poaceae*	GC1719.4 *Poaceae–Chenopod.–Quercus* GC1719.3 *Corylus–Poaceae* GC1719.2 *Poaceae–Corylus*	GC1717.2 *Poaceae–Chenopod.–Quercus* GC1717.1 *Corylus–Poaceae*	GC1697.1 *Quercus–Poaceae–Chenopod.*	GC1716.1 *Poaceae–Chenopod.*	GC1745.1 *Poaceae–Chenopod.*
2460							GC1221.4 *Corylus–Poaceae* GC1221.3 *Poaceae–Corylus* GC1221.2 *Corylus–Calluna–Alnus*		GC1719.1 *Corylus–Calluna*				
2600			GC1718.3c *Corylus–Quercus*										
3000			GC1718.3b *Calluna–Corylus* GC1718.3a *Corylus–Alnus–Quercus*										
3360			GC1718.2 *Corylus–Calluna*										
3500			GC1718.1 *Corylus–Calluna–Quercus*										
3680							GC1221.1 *Corylus–Tilia–Calluna*						

saltmarsh environments. The identification of human activity is also more complicated in coastal areas where species, which in other contexts are often labelled as anthropogenic indicators (cf Behre 1981), eg Chenopodiaceae and *Artemisia*, are likely to occur naturally. Finally, the extent of human activity revealed by the archaeological work is likely to have had an impact on the local wetland vegetation communities; however, given the extent of natural coastally related environmental changes such anthropogenic effects are, in this context, difficult to identify.

Similar considerations to those of pollen also apply to seeds. The plant macrofossil record is dependent on the production, dispersal, and germination characteristics of the species involved. In the case of peat deposits, most of the seeds can be considered to be relatively local in origin, although clearly there will be some variation within this with seeds adapted for dispersal by the wind likely to be from a slightly wider area. In fluvial deposits, the ability of the seeds to float is important in determining how far they may be transported, and seeds may be transported over very great distances (Cappers 1993). However, investigations of recent point bar samples from along a river led to the conclusion that the majority were probably local in origin (Field 1992). In estuarine deposits, seeds may also have been transported over a greater distance. A number of present day studies of seed dispersal within tidal saltmarshes have been made. It is suggested that, within the saltmarsh, the net movement of seeds is landwards, ie from lower to upper saltmarsh, whereas in the mudflats the net transport is seawards (Huiskes *et al* 1995). However, it is also suggested that considerable numbers of seeds are not transported at all, particularly where shelter is provided by vegetation. In addition to the dispersal of lower saltmarsh species in the upper saltmarsh by tides, it has been proposed that cattle and geese could

be important in the dispersal of some lower saltmarsh taxa (Bakker *et al* 1985). At Goldcliff, in addition to the natural factors operating, the plant macrofossil record, notably from the buildings, is likely to have been influenced by the transport of plant material by humans and animals, as evidenced by the large numbers of animal footprints at Goldcliff West.

13.5 Discussion

The environmental record from Goldcliff spans some 6500 years from the Mesolithic through to the Roman period. The last period is beyond the scope of this report and will be discussed elsewhere. Multiple diagrams for some periods enable detailed consideration of local changes spatially (Fig 13.2), as well as temporal comparisons to be made (Tables 13.1 and 13.2), and the whole study is considered in relation to other pollen investigations in the region (Fig 13.1). The evidence is considered chronologically and demonstrates the increasing impact of human communities in the area through time, with the earlier vegetation changes, up to the 'elm decline', showing only limited evidence of interference, although the archaeological evidence clearly demonstrates the presence of Mesolithic communities.

13.5.1 Mesolithic environmental changes c 6500–5900 radiocarbon years BP

The Mesolithic site and contemporary environment c 6500 radiocarbon years BP

The earliest evidence is from the Mesolithic site dated to the early- to mid-7th millennium radiocarbon years BP on the western edge of the former Goldcliff

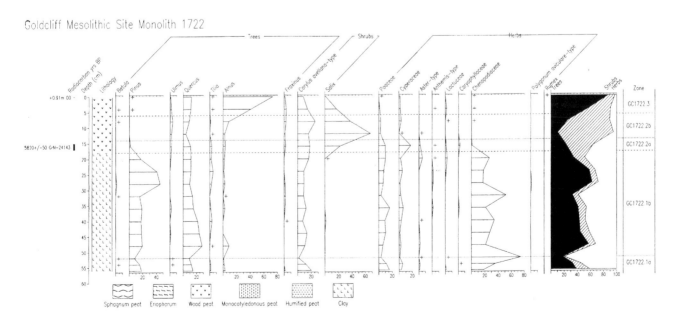

Figure 13.3 Percentage pollen diagram (selected taxa) from Monolith 1722 from the Mesolithic site. Stratigraphic key for all sites

Island. Pollen failed to survive in the land surface on the head deposit on which the occupation occurred, but a possible indication of the contemporary vegetation, or just after, is provided by pollen, although in very low concentrations, preserved in a relatively thin band of charcoal-rich clay at the estuarine/Mesolithic soil boundary. High representation of Chenopodiaceae (goosefoots) pollen in the basal zone, GC1722.1a (Fig 13.3, CD 13.2, monolith location on Fig 4.4) indicates local saltmarsh development and confirms the estuarine nature of the deposit, as do the relatively high values for *Pinus* (pine), discussed further below. Initially Poaceae (grasses) values are quite high (*c* 15% TLP), suggesting reedswamp may have developed in the area as water levels rose, but the values decline as a stronger marine influence is exerted. Since the site is on the edge of the 'island' it is likely that the 'dryland' taxa will, to a large degree, reflect the local vegetation, but it is on the western flank and if the prevailing wind direction was westerly then this might reduce the local influence and a predominantly regional picture be represented. The evidence suggests that on the drier ground a woodland comprising *Quercus* (oak) with some *Ulmus* (elm), *Tilia* (lime) and *Fraxinus* (ash) and an understorey of *Corylus avellana* (hazel) occurred. Herbaceous pollen that can be positively attributed to human activity occurring on the dryland is lacking, but *Pteridium* (bracken) values are relatively high and could reflect a response to burning. Similarly, the growth of *Corylus* could also have been stimulated by human activity. That burning did happen locally is apparent from the very abundant macroscopic charcoal recorded at the site and its association with Mesolithic artefacts, although the scale of activity is less easy to decipher (Chapter 4 and further discussion below). A map (Fig 17.4b) illustrates the possible vegetation communities in the area at this time.

The charcoal identified from the site is dominated by *Corylus*, with substantial amounts of Pomoideae (hawthorn type), *Quercus*, and *Ulmus*. The relatively high representation of *Ulmus* is of interest because it is absent from the basal pollen level and only just registers in the following level. This would tend to suggest that elm was, or had been, a more important constituent of the island woodland than indicated by the pollen record and that, either local woodland containing this species, or wood collected from such woodland, had been burnt. Although the pollen record largely post-dates the charcoal record there is agreement in that both indicate oak woodland and hazel scrub. The discrepancy in terms of Rosaceae species is not surprising, given that these species are insect pollinated and poor pollen producers. *Alnus* (alder) is absent from the charcoal record but is present from the base of the pollen diagram, demonstrating the presence of alder carr in the region. Its presence is in keeping with evidence from elsewhere in the British Isles for the migration and establishment of alder (Bennett and Birks 1990, Chambers and Elliott 1989).

The virtual absence of pollen, beetles (Chapter 14), and limited plant macrofossils (Table CD 13.24, sample locations Fig 4.5) indicates that conditions were basically unsuitable for preservation, and that dry conditions prevailed at the time of occupation, but some plant remains do hint at a marine influence. The waterlogged remains that do survive are generally relatively resistant to decay. Seeds of *Sambucus nigra* (elder) are the most frequent. *Urtica dioica* (common nettle) seeds are also present. Both these taxa in later periods are associated with human activity and disturbed and nitrogen-rich soils. Their occurrence here may, therefore, be the result of human activity. Whether or not the *Sambucus nigra* seeds could represent deliberate collection of elderberries by humans must remain open to speculation, as they could equally well have been brought onto site by birds or by natural processes, particularly if growing locally.

Other evidence for woodland is provided by *Moehringia trinervia* (three-nerved sandwort), a woodland herb of well-drained nitrogen-rich soils. *Stachys sylvatica* (hedge woundwort) is also common in woods on richer soils. Of the remaining taxa, *Atriplex* spp. (oraches) and *Polygonum aviculare* (knotgrass) could be associated with disturbed ground and/or represent saltmarsh communities. The presence of swamp/fen is indicated by *Lycopus europaeus* (gypsywort) and *Carex* spp. (sedges). Apart from the charred hazelnuts, a few charred seeds were also recovered from the site and probably reflect local vegetation that had become burnt accidentally, or could represent grassy material used as tinder. *Juncus* sp. (rushes), Poaceae, and *Bolboschoenus maritimus* (sea club-rush) are present, suggesting reedswamp and saltmarsh.

Radiocarbon dates for the site, apart from for the hazelnut dated to 5415 ± 75 BP (OxA-6682), vary from 6760 ± 80 BP (OxA-6683) to 6420 ± 60 BP (SWAN-28) and correlate well with dates from charcoal and an oak tree associated with a thin peat layer at Goldcliff East, but no pollen work has been carried out on this. Further east at Caldicot Pill/Sudbrook (Scaife 1993 and 1995) pollen has been analysed from organic muds overlain by marine silts and from a thin surface peat and demonstrate a change from estuarine conditions to a range of freshwater environments comprising freshwater aquatic, marginal aquatic and damp oak/hazel fen carr woodland. Dates from the organic muds and clay peat contact are 6360 ± 70 BP (BETA-79887) and 6660 ± 80 BP (BETA-79886), respectively.

Marine inundation *c* 6400–5900 radiocarbon years BP

The pollen and lithostratigraphy in Pollen Column 1722 clearly record a period of relative sea level rise and marine inundation post dating occupation of the site. The end of this period and the formation of a peat is dated to 5820 ± 50 BP (GrN-24143). At the

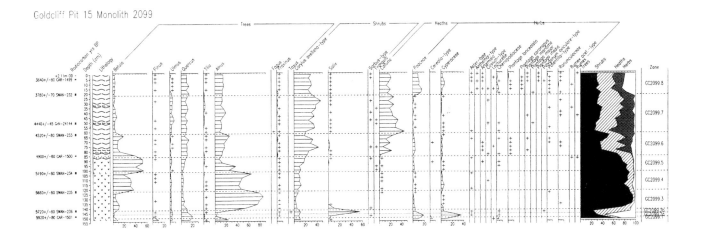

Figure 13.4 Percentage pollen diagram (selected taxa) from Monoliths 2099, 2100, and 2101 from Pit 15

base of Pollen Diagram 2099 (Fig 13.4, CD 13.3) from Pit 15 (monolith location Fig 5.3) peat initiation is dated slightly earlier to 5920 ± 80 BP (CAR-1501).

Estuarine/marine sediments are more complex taphonomically than peats. The pollen present may be largely allochthonous and derived from several environments away from the site of deposition, although there may also be substantial amounts of saltmarsh taxa represented. In addition, there may be reworking and hiatuses in the depositional sequence as a result of erosion of the sediments themselves (Scaife 1995). In terms of pollen source in estuarine sediments, it has been suggested that most pollen enters the estuary from the atmosphere (Brush and Brush 1994), although other studies have suggested a greater input entering through rivers and streams (see Brush 1989 for discussion). It has also been suggested (Brush and Brush 1994) that, even allowing for resuspension, the pollen settles within several kilometres of entry into the estuary. Patterns of vegetation and land use may, therefore, be preserved within the pollen record.

In Zone GC1722.1b Chenopodiaceae values are exceptionally high in some levels, reflecting saltmarsh. Poaceae may also reflect saltmarsh or reedswamp communities. Aquatics (see CD 13.2), such as *Menyanthes* (bogbean) and *Potamogeton* (pondweed), also suggest the presence of fresher water plant communities, although certain *Potamogeton* species can tolerate brackish water.

Pinus, which was well represented in the earlier Zone GC1722.1a, is even more strongly represented in GC1722.1b. Over-representation in estuarine/marine sediments is well recognised because of its buoyancy in comparison with other types of pollen (Hopkins 1950). Representation is similarly recorded at other sites, both on the Welsh (Scaife 1993 and 1995, Caseldine 1993) and the English side (Godwin 1943, Scaife 1987) of the estuary. Because of its long distance transport capability, in the air as well as water, the position of *Pinus* in the vegetation of the region is uncertain (see below). *Pinus* representation

in Wales during the early–mid Flandrian is very variable (Moore 1978, Walker 1982, Caseldine 1990).

Low pollen concentrations are recorded throughout GC1722.1b. Apart from *Pinus,* the arboreal pollen is again dominated by *Quercus* and *Corylus avellana*-type with small amounts of *Ulmus, Tilia,* and *Fraxinus,* suggesting a wooded landscape of mixed deciduous forest, with elm and lime perhaps forming a significant component. A similar picture is recorded in the basal Zone GC2099.1 (Fig 13.4, CD 13.3, Table 1) from Pit 15, which was similarly located close to the island edge. One difference that emerges is that, whereas *Alnus* values are low, generally less than *c* 5% TLP in GC1722.1b, in GC2099.1 *Alnus* reaches over 20% TLP, perhaps indicating some alder carr development and fresher water conditions to the north. A high level of *Alnus* is also recorded in the basal level from Goldcliff 1 (Smith and Morgan 1989). A reduced brackish/marine influence in the immediate vicinity of Pit 15 is indicated by much lower Chenopodiaceae values, although saltmarsh is clearly indicated, as is the presence of swamp communities. The end of the marine phase, indicated by a reduction in Chenopodiaceae pollen, is evident in several diagrams from the area, including Goldcliff East (Smith and Morgan 1989), Uskmouth (Caseldine 1993), and Barland's Farm (Walker *et al* 1998).

Although microscopic charcoal is recorded throughout this period, other indicators of human activity are less certain. *Quercus* shows a general decline and *Fraxinus* increases briefly, whilst at the same time *Ulmus* and *Tilia* decline before recovering again later, but pollen values are low and, given the depositional environment, it is perhaps wise not to read too much into these changes. *Corylus avellana*-type values remain relatively constant throughout Zone GC1722.1b after an initial decline and recovery. Herbaceous taxa, which could be attributed to the effects of human activity, are largely absent, apart from a peak in Cerealia-type pollen in the basal level in GC2099.1 which, particularly given the context, is probably attributable to wild saltmarsh/coastal grasses which produce Cerealia-type pollen rather than cereals (see Dickson 1988 for discussion).

Whilst evidence for exploitation of dryland vegetation communities in the area is difficult to identify, the pollen records indicate the opportunities offered by the wetland vegetation, notably the saltmarsh communities for grazing and hence hunting. Direct evidence for Mesolithic utilisation of the saltmarsh environment is provided by artefacts and human and animal footprints throughout the intertidal area (Allen 1997a). At Uskmouth, pollen (Caseldine 1992) and foraminifera (Culver and Lundquist 1992) from the fill of footprints in clays predating 6250 ± 80 BP (OxA-2627) confirm the mudflat and saltmarsh nature of the environment (Aldhouse-Green et al 1992).

13.5.2 Peat development and later Mesolithic and earlier Neolithic vegetation changes c 5900–4900 radiocarbon years BP

Peat initiation c 5900–5650 radiocarbon years BP

Following a period of rapid sea level rise in the early Holocene, resulting in the estuarine/marine deposits discussed above, sea level rise slowed leading to an expansion in coastal wetlands and an advancement of the shoreline seawards c 6000 radiocarbon years BP. This change is recorded at both the Mesolithic site and Pit 15 where ultimately a wood peat developed as fresher water conditions prevailed. Radiocarbon dates of 5920 ± 80 BP (CAR-1501) from Pit 15, 5820 ± 50 BP (GrN-24143) from the Mesolithic site, and 5950 ± BP (CAR-659) from Site 1 at Goldcliff East demonstrate that peat initiation was more or less synchronous on both sides of Goldcliff Island, although at Site 2 Goldcliff East (Smith and Morgan 1989) and Hill Farm Pond, lying at higher levels, peat development was later. Dates for peat initiation at other sites are similar, with dates of 6250 ± 80 BP (OxA-2627) and 6260 ± 90 BP (CAR-1178) for an organic mud and 5810 ± 80 BP (OxA-2628) for the base of the peat at Uskmouth (Aldhouse-Green et al 1992), and 5920 ± 50 BP at Barland's Farm (Walker et al 1998). At Caldicot Pill/Sudbrook dates on wood are 6040 ± 70 BP (BETA-54829) and 5760 ± 70 BP (BETA-54827) (Scaife 1995). The change from estuarine environments to semi-terrestrial/terrestrial peats appears, therefore, to have been broadly contemporaneous along much of the northern shore of the estuary c 6000 radiocarbon years BP. A rather later date of 5190 ± 80 BP (SWAN-32) at Goldcliff West relates to the resumption of peat growth after a marine transgression rather than initial peat inception (Chapter 3). Further west still, at Rumney, an auroch skeleton dated to 4060 ± 70 BP (CAR-851) is from clay deposits below middle Wentlooge peat, and an intertidal environment is suggested on the basis of pollen and foraminiferal analyses (Green 1989).

In GC1722.2a from the Mesolithic site, but more strongly represented in GC2099.2a from Pit 15, an increase in Poaceae pollen is accompanied by marked peaks in Cyperaceae (sedges) and Sparganium type (bur-reed) pollen, indicating an expansion in reed and sedge communities, and the beginning of peat development, prior to the establishment of a Salix (willow) dominated community in zones GC1722.2b and GC2099.2b. Salix cinerea is frequently an early invader in the colonisation of swamp and fen (Rodwell 1991a, 80). A comparable succession was also recorded from the other side of Goldcliff Point at Site 1, Goldcliff East. In both areas at this time Alnus values are low, perhaps masked by the local on-site vegetation. This episode of willow domination is then replaced by the growth of alder with willow possibly continuing to colonise seawards. At Pit 15 radiocarbon dates of 5920 ± 80 BP (CAR-1501) and 5720 ± 80 BP (SWAN-236) bracketing Zone GC2099.2 suggest that the period of colonisation and dominance of willow lasted around 200 radiocarbon years. A similar succession was also recorded at Uskmouth, but with Salix playing a less significant role (Caseldine 1992). The occurrence of Chenopodiaceae pollen at low levels attests to a continued marine presence and saltmarsh communities in the area, although at both the Mesolithic site and Pit 15 the conditions were essentially fresh water, perhaps with an occasional brackish influence.

A number of hazelnuts (Table CD 13.25) were recovered during excavation within the peat overlying the Mesolithic site. Since Corylus was not recorded in the wood identified from the wood peat (Chapter 12), it is likely that they represent the growth of hazel on the dryland at this time. It is possible they may have been transported by wind or water, but rodents also contributed. Examination of the nuts revealed gnaw marks attributable to bank vole (Clethrionomys glareolus), wood mouse (Apodemus sylvaticus), and dormouse (Muscardinus avellanarius). Hazelnuts that had been gnawed by dormouse and bank vole were found around track level at the Neolithic Sweet Track in Somerset (Caseldine 1984).

The dry ground of the island and the mainland to the north appears to have continued to support mixed deciduous woodland throughout Zones GC1722.2a, GC1722.2b, GC2099.2a, and GC2099.2b, with continuous pollen curves for Ulmus and Quercus and Corylus avellana-type suggesting elm as well as oak formed a significant part of the woodland community, with an understorey of hazel. In contrast, the representation of Tilia is poor. A similar picture is recorded from most of the other sites in the area, apart from Vurlong Reen (Walker et al 1998, Walker and James 1993) where very high Tilia values point to deciduous woodland dominated by lime on the nearby dryland. Apart from a low incidence of charcoal, evidence for human activity is lacking at these and other sites. Cerealia-type pollen recorded at Site 1 Goldcliff East (Smith and Morgan 1989) is more likely to be from wild coastal grasses rather than cereal cultivation, given the context.

For human communities in the area, the wetland landscape was changing considerably from one of open saltmarsh to carr woodland, with concomitant opportunities for exploitation altering significantly. Although a zone of saltmarsh would have persisted, during this period an expansion of freshwater habitats seawards was occurring, creating a much wider band of swamp, fen, and carr woodland between the estuary and dryland.

The local vegetation changes during the following carr woodland phases reflect factors such as vegetation succession and competition rather than local human activity. Although direct marine inundation in the area of Pit 15 is limited during this period, the influence of related changes in water-level on the vegetation succession is evident.

At Pit 15 a radiocarbon date of 5720 ± 80 BP (SWAN-236) dates the end of Zone GC2099.2b and the beginning of GC2099.3, a zone dominated by very high *Alnus* values, reflecting the establishment of alder carr. The absence of *Salix* later in the zone suggests it was ultimately shaded out by the alder canopy (Rodwell 1991a, 80). The presence of wetter pools is indicated by small peaks in *Potamogeton*. Low amounts of Poaceae and Cyperaceae indicate local grasses, including reed, and sedges, and other taxa such as *Hedera* (ivy), *Filipendula* (meadowsweet), *Potentilla* (cinquefoil), and *Lysimachia* (loosestrife) also reflect a carr environment, as do frequent Pteropsida (fern) spores. The same change in the dominant woodland is recorded in GC1722.3 at the Mesolithic site where alder also replaces willow, but even between these two sites 34m apart (Fig 4.2) there is some difference in the local woodland record. *Betula* (birch) is present in noticeable amounts in GC2099.3, particularly at the beginning, suggesting it invaded before the development of a thicker alder canopy restricted its establishment (Rodwell 1991a, 80), but hardly present in GC1722.3, although *Betula* seeds, albeit designed for dispersal over a greater distance than many seeds, in the peat at GC1722.3 attest to the relatively close proximity of birch woodland. *Betula* although part of the carr woodland at Goldcliff East (Smith and Morgan 1989), is clearly less significant, and in the Barland's Farm area (Walker *et al* 1998) appears to be even less important. At virtually the same date (5740 ± 70 BP (BETA-63595)) as the expansion of *Alnus* at 2099, peat development and alder carr occurred at Vurlong Reen-1 (Walker *et al* 1998). Here again, *Betula* registers only sporadically. In contrast, *Betula* reaches significant amounts in the basal wood peats at Uskmouth (Caseldine 1992), dated to 5810 ± 80 BP (OxA-2628). From the evidence, therefore, there was clearly some variation in the nature of the wet woodland in the region, with *Betula* a more important component in the western part of the area.

Away from the immediate environs of the wetland, the dryland woodland community seems to have remained little changed, with oak and elm predominating. Representation of all the dryland trees and shrubs is lower in GC2099.3 than the previous zone, but this reflects the expansion and filtering effect of *Alnus* locally. However, *Ulmus* shows only a minor reduction, perhaps indicating it played a more significant role in the woodland. Representation of *Tilia* is sporadic, apart from at Vurlong Reen (Walker *et al* 1998, Walker and James 1993) where values remain high (see discussion above). Although there is a decline in dryland trees and *Corylus*, there is no definite pollen evidence for human interference with the vegetation. Poaceae pollen is present in low amounts but this is probably largely from local reed communities. Herbaceous pollen is otherwise poorly represented. There is a small amount of macroscopic and microscopic charcoal present at the top of GC1722.3 and low amounts of microscopic charcoal in GC2099.3.

The continued presence of Chenopodiaceae in GC1722.3 from the Mesolithic site is perhaps a reflection of the closer proximity of that site to the contemporary estuary than Pit 15 where Chenopodiaceae pollen is absent during GC2099.3.

Vegetation changes during the carr woodland phase c 5650–5200 radiocarbon years BP

A fall in *Alnus* pollen and increase in *Betula* to almost an equivalent amount at the beginning of GC2099.4, dated to 5660 ± 80 BP (SWAN-235), marks the end of a phase, lasting c 60 radiocarbon years, of almost total alder dominance and the beginning of an expansion in birch fen woodland. A sedge dominated understorey is indicated by an increase in Cyperaceae pollen and *Carex* seeds. Possibly the alder was beginning to become moribund and dying as a result of a combination of depression of the underlying peat and a rising water table related to an increase in sea level. Clay was noted in the stratigraphy at the end of Zone GC2099.4, dated to 5190 ± 80 BP (SWAN-234), demonstrating the site was subject to marine inundation. The date is identical to that at Goldcliff West (5190 ± 80 BP (SWAN-32)) for the resumption of peat growth after a much longer marine transgression. At Goldcliff West pollen and stratigraphic evidence (unpublished student project) and beetle evidence (Chapter 14) indicate local fen woodland was much less significant.

At Site 1 on the eastern side of Goldcliff Island (Smith and Morgan 1989), a marine episode is recorded as starting shortly before 5530 ± 90 BP (CAR-657) and lasting to c 5400 radiocarbon years BP. At Site 2, peat accumulation started at 5660 ± 80 BP (CAR-778), coinciding with the increase in *Betula* in GC2099.4. Again *Alnus* dominates, with *Betula* of much less significance at both Sites 1 and 2, although a slight peak is recorded towards the end of the zones. An increase in *Betula* also occurs shortly after 5380 ± 50 BP (BETA-72510) at Barland's Farm and *Betula* is marginally more frequent after 5340 ± 70 BP (BETA-63594) at Vurlong Reen, but levels are very low (Walker *et al* 1998). As in the previous period, throughout the region alder dominates but birch is more important, if almost imperceptibly so, in some areas.

During GC2099.4 occasional *Calluna* (heather) grains and increasing *Sphagnum* moss spores hint at the beginnings of ombrogenous bog development.

On the dryland the woodland is little changed until the end of Zone GC2099.4 when a brief decline in *Ulmus* to *c* 1% TLP is recorded. Some minor peaks in charcoal occur around this time, but there are no open ground indicator species recorded and the apparent fall in *Ulmus* may be due to a peak in *Alnus* at the end of this zone and increase in *Betula* at the beginning of the next (GC2099.5) rather than the result of human activity or disease. Concentration values (unpublished) are lower for *Ulmus* and *Quercus* but higher for *Alnus* and *Betula* suggesting, either a real reduction in the former two taxa, or the filtering effect of the last local two taxa. Equally, the latter may have had a significant effect in preventing the registration of any open ground taxa associated with any small-scale activity. This event is dated *c* 5190 ± 80 BP (SWAN-234) and *Ulmus* quickly recovers in the following Zone GC2099.5, while *Alnus* declines. *Ulmus* then declines again, but this time accompanied by clearance indicator taxa (see 'elm decline' discussion below). Slightly earlier than this (*c* 5250–5500 radiocarbon years BP) the presence of charcoal and open-habitat taxa, notably *Rumex* (docks) at Vurlong Reen (Walker *et al* 1998), is interpreted as possible evidence for human interference with the vegetation. This carr woodland phase, lasting *c* 470 radiocarbon years, was somewhat longer-lived than the previous one.

The end of the carr woodland phase *c* 5190–4900 radiocarbon years BP

Within Zone GC2099.5, *Betula* takes over as the most prominent taxon, taking advantage, along with the other fast-growing species, *Salix* and *Frangula* (alder buckthorn), of opening of the tree canopy (Rodwell 1991a, 81), as *Alnus* suffers a steady decline. Ferns, notably *Osmunda regalis* (royal fern), would have been conspicuous in the field layer, whilst an increase in *Sphagnum* spores, most marked at the end of the zone, and continuous representation of *Calluna* in low amounts indicate the establishment of ombrogenous nuclei. Traces of clay in the stratigraphy indicate a brief marine episode, perhaps little more than an exceptionally high tide or storm surge, at the beginning of the zone. An increase in Poaceae pollen may reflect an expansion in local reedswamp. The occurrence of occasional Chenopodiaceae pollen during the zone suggests a continued marine influence nearby, but a peak in *Typha* (bulrush) at the end of the zone suggests fresher water conditions locally. Whilst at Pit 15 carr woodland gives way to bog, at Goldcliff East (Smith and Morgan 1989), the vegetation succession pro-

ceeds from fen to bog without an intervening carr stage.

Ulmus values commence GC2099.5 at <1% TLP but increase later, as do *Quercus* and *Tilia*, coincident with a decline in *Alnus* pollen, suggesting a recovery in elm, and that lime became more prominent in the dryland woodland. Evidence for human activity at most is very slight, with no apparent impact on the woodland in the pollen diagram. Poaceae values are higher, which indicates an increase in grassland, but this could as well represent local wetland changes (see above) as an increase in dryland grassland. Cerealia-type pollen towards the end of the zone and just before the 'elm decline' could equally be attributable to one of the wild species of the *Hordeum*-type (barley) pollen found in coastal habitats, but the date is not unacceptable in terms of early cereal found at other sites in Britain (Edwards 1993 and 1989, Edwards and Hirons 1984), and the presence of *Rumex* in the level above could indicate some human disturbance. *Quercus* pollen concentrations (unpublished) are lower in these two levels (88cm and 92cm) than the previous level but, whilst pollen concentrations are falling generally, *Ulmus* and *Tilia* concentrations peak at 92cm before falling at 88cm, the beginning of the 'elm decline'. These changes are discussed further below in relation to the 'elm decline'.

The increase in *Ulmus* in GC2099.5 is also mirrored in GC1.3 from Goldcliff East (Smith and Morgan 1989), as is the increase in *Quercus* and *Tilia*. An increase in *Quercus* and *Tilia* is also evident at Barland's Farm (Walker *et al* 1998), whilst *Ulmus*, from being absent towards the end of LPAZ BF3, does reappear at low levels. At Vurlong Reen, *Ulmus* values are also very low around this time but *Tilia* values are high, in fact much higher than in the other diagrams from the area.

The carr woodland phase: comparison of the pollen record with the wood identification and beetle results

In addition to the pollen evidence from Goldcliff, tree stumps and trunks have been identified (Chapter 12.2) from the wood peat. *Alnus* and *Betula* together dominate the assemblage, with smaller amounts of *Quercus*, *Salix*, *Fraxinus*, and Pomoideae (*Sorbus* type pollen). The results are in keeping with the pollen record and confirm the basic vegetation succession, although the resolution is not as fine. *Salix* appears to occur at the lowest level in the peat, with *Alnus* dominating. *Betula* is also relatively frequent at this level but is then dominant at a higher level recorded in the field as 'Sphagnum bog'. The presence of oak wood demonstrates that some of the *Quercus* pollen is derived from oak growing within local alder carr woodland rather than dryland habitats, but there is also no evidence, at least in this area, that oak ever dominated the 'wet' woodland.

The pollen evidence for the whole of the carr

woodland phase is broadly in agreement with the beetle evidence for woodland (Chapter 14), both dry and wet, apart from the underestimation of alder in the beetle record compared with the pollen and wood records. In contrast, the beetle evidence may provide firmer evidence for the relatively local presence of pine in the area. The variability in occurrence of *Pinus* during the Mesolithic in Wales has already been referred to, as has the apparent over-representation of *Pinus* in the estuarine sediments (p215). In the pollen records covering the carr woodland phase *Pinus* is present only sporadically, but this may be partly a result of the filtering effect of the local woodland, and it is possible from the beetle evidence that, rather than the *Pinus* pollen being from some distance away, there was some comparatively local pine.

13.5.3 The development of raised bog and Neolithic and Bronze Age vegetation changes c 4900–2600 radiocarbon years BP

The development of raised bog

A marked decline in *Betula* and increase in *Calluna* at the beginning of GC2099.6 indicates that, after 1000 years of carr woodland, a marked change in the wetland landscape occurred, although this probably took place over 100–150 years as birch woodland was replaced by the growth of raised bog, and an open landscape dominated by *Calluna*, *Eriophorum* (cottongrass), and *Sphagnum* moss took over, as confirmed by the beetles (Chapter 14). For the human communities in the area this would have presented very different opportunities in terms of hunting and grazing (see below).

These changes are dated to 4900 ± 60 BP (CAR-1500) at Pit 15 and are consistent with changes occurring to the east of Goldcliff Point at Site 1 (Smith and Morgan 1989) dated to 5020 ± 80 BP (CAR-652), but somewhat later at Site 2 c 4300 radiocarbon years BP, although 'transition bog' occurs from c 5100 BP. Raised bog growth was widespread throughout the wetland area and, although a much more open landscape would have existed, it is clear from the pollen record that areas of wet fen woodland persisted where run-off resulted in a higher nutrient level, giving a more diverse landscape. Indeed, *Alnus* increases steadily and *Betula* peaks at the end of Zone GC2099.6, probably reflecting carr woodland growing along the edge of the island. The possible distribution of the vegetation communities during the raised bog phase in the Goldcliff area is illustrated in Fig 17.4c.

The 'elm decline' and Neolithic clearance c 4900–4500 radiocarbon years BP

Coinciding with these substantial changes in the wetland were changes on the dryland. A decline in

Ulmus, beginning shortly before 4900 radiocarbon years BP, equates with the 'elm decline', an event widely recognised in pollen diagrams from Northwest Europe, reflecting either the effects of disease equivalent to the recent elm tree disease, anthropogenic activity, or a combination of both (see Edwards 1993 and Peglar 1993 for review of evidence). It is generally thought that disease played a major role but it is possible that human activity and animal browsing may have weakened or damaged the trees, thereby aiding the spread of the disease, whilst the use of regenerating elm suckers or coppice shoots from diseased trees could have prevented their recovery to maturity. The possible earlier decline, discussed above, could suggest human disturbance in the area c 200 radiocarbon years before the main 'elm decline'. The decline is accompanied by the appearance of *Plantago lanceolata* (ribwort plantain) in zone GC2099.6, and suggests some opening up of the forest cover. A small peak in *Fraxinus* may reflect increased flowering as a result of this. *Tilia* also declines around this time but *Quercus* values remain high, although concentration values (unpublished), along with those of most other taxa, including Poaceae, decrease. *Corylus avellana*-type pollen increases, then declines, indicating an expansion in hazel woodland or increased flowering, which could perhaps be related to management practices such as coppicing and/or burning as charcoal also increases. Alternatively, the increase could be associated with an expansion in *Myrica gale* (bog myrtle).

A slight increase in Poaceae compared with the previous zone occurs, and it is probable that this increase is due to an opening of the forest cover on the dryland rather than a further expansion in reed or saltmarsh communities. *Plantago lanceolata* is present throughout the zone and, with *Potentilla* and Ranunculaceae (buttercup), could indicate grassland and grazing. Indeed after the initial increase, Poaceae values gradually decline during the zone which is consistent with grass production falling as grazing continued and intensified (Groenman-van Waateringe 1993). Around mid-zone Cerealia-type pollen is recorded but *Artemisia* (mugwort) and Chenopodiaceae pollen, possibly from weeds of cultivation, occur earlier than this and could suggest cultivation took place over a longer period. Alternatively, these taxa could reflect saltmarsh habitats. However, given the changes in woodland cover an anthropogenic interpretation is in this case preferred. Towards the end of the zone minor peaks in *Ulmus*, *Quercus*, and *Fraxinus* indicate some regeneration. The record broadly matches that recorded by Smith and Morgan (1989) on the other side of the island, the major difference being that there is not a distinct decline in *Quercus* in the relative pollen diagram, although *Quercus* concentrations do decrease, and agricultural indicator species are generally less well represented. The difference between the two records could simply reflect differential land use on the two sides of the island, or the filtering effects of local vegetation. However, the absence of a clear decline in *Quercus* here does not support Smith and Morgan's argument that because tree types other than elm are affected, the 'elm decline' itself may relate to anthropogenic activity.

The appearance of *Rumex* at the beginning of the 'elm decline' and a temporary peak in *Pteridium* in the level above in GC2099.6, and possibly the occurrence of Cerealia-type pollen at the end of GC2099.5, may approximate to Smith and Morgan's clearance and opening up of the forest Phase A. Similar representation for *Artemisia* and Chenopodiaceae and *Plantago lanceolata*, but poorer representation for Cerealia-type and other weeds, notably *Rumex,* in the remainder of GC2099.6, equates with their agricultural Phase B. The *Ulmus* curves from Pit 15 and their Site 1 correlate well. The minor woodland regeneration recorded towards the end of GC2099.6 is in agreement with a temporary rise recorded in mid GC1.4b, dated to shortly after 4660 ± 80 BP (CAR-650), and before a more sustained recovery in woodland taxa, particularly *Ulmus*, and equates with Smith and Morgan's Phase C regeneration episode.

This clearance episode at Pit 15 appears to have lasted *c* 400 radiocarbon years, ending *c* 4520 ± 80 BP (SWAN-233). Elsewhere in the Estuary, at Vurlong Reen (Walker *et al* 1998), a period of woodland decline, particularly involving the clearance of *Tilia*, and farming activity appears to have lasted from *c* 4800/4900 to 4250 radiocarbon years BP. The representation of *Ulmus* at both this site and Barland's Farm, where a comparable clearance episode lasts from *c* 4800/4900 BP–*c* 4400/4500 radiocarbon years BP is poor. The end of this episode is possibly represented at the beginning of Phase I at Caldicot (Caseldine and Barrow 1997) where low *Tilia* and *Ulmus* and the presence of Cerealia-type and *Plantago lanceolata* are dated to pre-4670 ± 80 BP (CAR-1323) in Column 6, suggesting a relatively short period of activity in that area.

Woodland regeneration and the later Neolithic and early Bronze Age *c* 4500–3700 radiocarbon years BP

By the beginning of this period (*c* 4500 radiocarbon years BP) raised bog was well established in the area. Zone GC2099.7 from Pit 15 is distinguished by a further decline in *Alnus* and *Betula* pollen, after an increase at the end of GC2099.6, suggesting a reduction in wet woodland as the bog encroached even further, but some carr woodland probably persisted along the edge of the island. At the same time, an increase in *Ulmus* followed by an increase in *Tilia* suggest abandonment and regeneration on the dryland, possibly on Goldcliff Island, as well as elsewhere in the region. *Ulmus* is well represented and attains even higher values than previously, which would suggest that this reflects local, rather than regional, changes. *Corylus avellana*-type pollen fluctuates slightly but overall shows a steady in-

crease. Evidence for agricultural activity is very limited with *Plantago lanceolata* absent throughout the zone. However, some form of 'forest farming' (cf Edwards 1993) may have occurred at this time. By this time, also, raised bog was well established in the area, and would have provided a grazing resource, even if the stocking rate was relatively low. Frequent charcoal in the pollen record from this zone and the other zones from the raised bog peat indicates burning in the area, and the presence of charred macrofosssil remains suggests at least some of the charcoal can be attributed to the burning of the wet heath. Whether this represents natural events, accidental, or deliberate management practices is uncertain, but similar results have been recorded at other lowland bogs (Wells *et al* 1997). The possibility of deliberate burning in prehistoric times to maintain heath and increase grazing potential has generally received more attention in relation to upland areas in Britain (Caseldine and Barrow 1998, Moore 1973, 1975, and 1993), although the continental literature puts far more emphasis on the maintenance of lowland heaths by burning (Kaland 1986). The end of the Zone GC2099.7 is dated to 3780 ± 70 BP (SWAN-232).

Further possible evidence for environmental conditions during this period comes from a site on the edge of Goldcliff Island, Hill Farm Pond, and Pollen Diagram 11600 (Figs 13.5, CD 13.7, monolith location on Fig 3.7). A radiocarbon date of 4320 ± 80 BP (SWAN-133) dates peat initiation just after the beginning of Zone GC11600.2a. Pollen Zones GC11600.1, GC11600.2a, and possibly GC11600.2b, may, therefore, correlate with GC2099.7 from Pit 15. GC11600.1 corresponds to a sandy clay deposit. Pollen failed to survive in the basal level examined (48cm), and concentrations were very low in the lowest levels of GC11600.1. High counts of *Corylus avellana*-type pollen indicate hazel scrub locally, whilst quite high values for *Alnus* suggest alder fringing the 'island' edge. Mixed deciduous woodland on the dryland is indicated, with *Ulmus* and *Tilia*, as well as *Quercus*, relatively well represented. This suggests this zone belongs to the regeneration phase, but Poaceae values occur in noticeable amounts and *Plantago lanceolata*, *Plantago coronopus* (buck's-horn plantain), and Chenopodiaceae are present. There are two possible interpretations for their presence. Either they could represent limited agricultural activity or they could reflect a slight marine influence, with aquatics towards the end of GC11600.1 (see CD 13.7) demonstrating a trend towards fresher water conditions prior to peat development. However, the evidence for hazel scrub and quite frequent *Pteridium* spores, indicating bracken, suggests colonisation following clearance and abandonment. Charcoal also indicates the presence of human activity and Neolithic flints were found at the base of the wood peat, providing further support for the first hypothesis.

Whilst raised bog continued to dominate at Pit 15, the beginning of GC11600.2a, dated to just before *c* 4300 radiocarbon years BP, is marked by a sharp rise

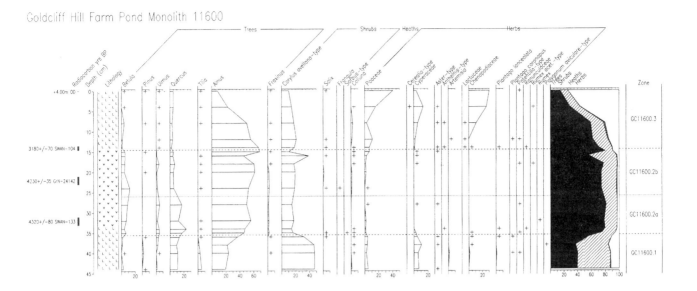

Figure 13.5 Percentage pollen diagram (selected taxa) from Monolith 11600 from Hill Farm Pond

in *Alnus* as alder carr and peat developed at the site. *Alnus* pollen dominates, but an increase in *Betula*, followed by a decline whilst *Salix* increases in GC11600.2b, indicates changes within the carr woodland. The latter changes dated to 4230 ± 35 BP (GrN-24142) coincide with the appearance of fine clayey bands within the peat, suggesting the site was subject either to occasional marine inundation, or later reworking, although the pollen record does not reflect this. Alternatively, activity on the island may have led to some hillwash. *Fraxinus* pollen forms a continuous curve throughout GC11600.2a and much of GC11600.2b. This may simply reflect ash growing within carr woodland, although representation of ash increases where there is opening of the forest cover and there is a very slight increase at the GC11600.2a/2b zone boundary, coinciding with a decline in *Quercus* and *Ulmus* shortly before 4230 ± 35 BP (GrN-24142). The low incidence of clearance indicator species supports the carr woodland proposition rather than the latter, but the domination of *Alnus* may mask what was going on the dryland. However, during GC11600.2a and GC11600.2b *Quercus*, *Ulmus*, and *Corylus* clearly made up the dryland woodland, which is also suggested by the pollen record from GC2099.7, as is the possible reduced level of clearance activity. *Tilia* is poorly represented in comparison with GC2099.7, and in comparison with the previous zone (GC11600.1) and it seems less likely that *Tilia* was growing on the island at this time, at least in significant amounts (see discussion below). A decline in *Ulmus* towards the end of GC11600.2b could equate with a decline at the GC2099.7/8 pollen zone boundary dated to c 3780 radiocarbon years BP (see below).

Elsewhere in the region a similar recovery is found in *Ulmus* to that recorded at the beginning of GC2099.7. This occurs in the latter half of GC1.4b at Goldcliff East (Smith and Morgan 1989) beginning

c 4660 ± 80 BP (CAR-650), with an *Ulmus* maximum dated to 4440 ± 80 BP (CAR-649), equivalent to 4440 ± 45 BP (GrN-24144) in GC2099.7. *Tilia* also increases at Pit 15 and Goldcliff East, but not to the same extent as *Ulmus*. Similar representation occurs at Goldcliff West (unpublished student project). In contrast, at Vurlong Reen I and II the regeneration phase is marked by a recovery in *Tilia* rather than *Ulmus* and is dated to 4230 ± 70 BP (BETA-63593) and 4260 ± 70 (BETA-63597), respectively, and at Barland's Farm to 4480 ± 60 BP (BETA-7258), where *Ulmus* representation is stronger but still less than that for *Tilia* (Walker *et al* 1998). At Caldicot (Caseldine and Barrow 1997), an increase in *Tilia* is dated to 4670 ± 80 BP (CAR-1323). Much further west, *Tilia* is well-represented in an undated diagram from East Moors, Cardiff (Hyde 1936).

The pollen evidence from sites in the region (Figs 13.1 and 13.2) suggests slight variations in the type of woodland and the time when different areas were cleared. The end of GC2099.7 is dated to 3780 ± 70 BP (SWAN-232), when a decline in *Tilia* and *Fraxinus* accompanies the *Ulmus* decline as well as a brief fluctuation in the curve for *Quercus* and a decline in *Corylus avellana*-type, suggesting clearance of woodland containing elm, lime, ash, and oak, but recovery of oak before further clearance. At Goldcliff East Site 1 (Smith and Morgan 1989) the *Ulmus* curve fluctuates with a decline in *Ulmus* dated to 3780 ± 70 BP (CAR-647) and a decline in *Tilia*, with *Corylus*, marginally later at 3670 ± 70 BP (CAR-646). At Building 2, to the west of Pit 15 and Monolith 2099, *Ulmus* values are already very low at the beginning of GC1221.1 (Fig 13.13, CD 13.12, monolith location Figs 7.11 and 7.12) and a decline in *Tilia* at the beginning of GC1221.2 is dated to 3680 ± 70 BP (SWAN-134). At Barland's Farm (Walker *et al* 1998), a decline in *Tilia*, *Corylus avellana*-type, and *Ulmus* occurs shortly before 3740 ± 60 BP (BETA-72507) but

Quercus increases, suggesting oak may have temporarily spread into cleared areas. A decline in *Quercus* is then accompanied by a brief increase in *Corylus*, suggesting a short-lived expansion in hazel or increased flowering, perhaps related to management practices. A marked impact on lime woodland occurs *c* 3910 ± 70 BP (BETA-63592) at Vurlong Reen (Walker *et al* 1998), although a slight recovery in *Tilia* and more marked recovery in *Corylus avellana*-type is recorded a little later, followed by clearance *c* 3500 radiocarbon years BP, presumably particularly of hazel scrubland. At Caldicot (Caseldine and Barrow 1997) by the beginning of Phase II, some time during the earlier Bronze Age, *Tilia* values were also much reduced, suggesting clearance of *Tilia* woodland. The decline in *Tilia* was, therefore, widespread in the region during the early Bronze Age and is in keeping with a decline in *Tilia* widely identified in British diagrams and attributed to anthropogenic activity (Turner 1962). Alternatively, a reduction in summer temperatures may have played a role, at least in part (Walker *et al* 1998, 74). A further possible factor is paludification (marsh development). Waller (1994) has discussed the effects of paludification on *Tilia* representation, particularly in coastal areas where sea level rise has led to paludification and increased the size of the wetland zone. Given that the decline is equally pronounced at sites on the wetland edge and elsewhere, this explanation is not supported by evidence from the Severn. However, representation of *Tilia* prior to the decline is very variable, relating both to the location of lime woodland in the area and the location of the pollen sites. High counts for *Tilia* at Caldicot and Vurlong Reen, sites close to dryland, point to local limewood. At Barland's Farm representation is not as high and may indicate a reduction in lime in the woodland to the west of the previous area, but may also relate to the greater distance between the site and dryland. It is even more poorly represented in 2099 from Pit 15 and Goldcliff Site 1, suggesting a greater distance between the pollen source and these sites and that, therefore, any lime woodland on Goldcliff Island was very limited in extent. A view supported by the pollen record from Hill Farm Pond, although high *Alnus* values may have affected *Tilia* registration.

Bronze Age environmental changes *c* 3700–3000 radiocarbon years BP

The remaining zone at Pit 15 GC2099.8, dated from *c* 3780 ± 70 BP (SWAN-232) to 3640 ± 60 BP (CAR-1499), shows a marked increase in frequency of herb pollen, particularly Poaceae, Cyperaceae, and Chenopodiaceae, along with the decline in arboreal taxa, although raised bog persisted at the site. In addition, a number of weed taxa are represented, including *Plantago lanceolata* and other *Plantago* spp, Ranunculaceae, *Potentilla*, *Artemisia*, and *Rumex* spp, and an increase in *Pteridium* occurs. These taxa, as well as being indicative of agricultural

activity, are also found in saltmarsh and swamp or fen communities. There are several possible interpretations, including the possibility of some slight mixing of sediments, as there was evidence of erosion of the peat at the top of the column, and some traces of clay within the peat. Equally, the pollen may reflect an increasing marine influence. Confirmation that peat went on growing in the area after *c* 3600 radiocarbon years BP is provided by a radiocarbon date of 3180 ± 70 BP (SWAN-104) from charcoal on the peat surface at Hill Farm Pond, assuming there is no hiatus between the charcoal and peat. A fall in *Ulmus* and a brief increase in *Corylus avellana*-type towards the end of GC11600.2b may date to *c* 3700 radiocarbon years BP and reflect local activity, and charcoal below marine clay at Hill Farm is dated to 3670 ± 60 BP (CAR-1505). This supports the possibility that the increased representation of herbaceous taxa in GC2099.8 may also derive, at least partially, from agricultural activity.

Zone GC2099.8 also corresponds quite closely with the beginning of GC1.4d at Goldcliff East (Smith and Morgan 1989), which lasts until *c* 3130 ± 70 BP (CAR-644) and also shows an increase in weed taxa and *Pteridium*. The full equivalent zone is, therefore, not recorded at 2099 nor is the Goldcliff East reed peat, reflecting a retrogressive succession, which occurs at the end of GC1.4d; this confirms that some erosion has occurred at 2099 (Chapter 5). At GC1.4d the *Phragmites* (common reed) peat is followed by a marine clay marked by an increase in Poaceae, Cyperaceae, and Chenopodiaceae and other herbaceous taxa in GC1.5, indicating brackish swamp and saltmarsh communities. Although the increase in herb taxa during GC2099.8, GC1.4d, and GC1.5 may be partially attributable to an increasing marine influence, it is likely that the herbaceous taxa also reflect an increase in interference with the woodland and agricultural activity in the region from *c* 3700 radiocarbon years BP, and more particularly on Goldcliff Island, given the pollen and charcoal evidence from Hill Farm Pond and Trench 2. The stronger representation of herbaceous taxa in GC2099.8 than GC1.4d may, therefore, partially relate to the location of the two sites and possible activity on the island, Pit 15 (2099) being closer to the island but outside any carr woodland influence which could have filtered out any dryland pollen.

This period is also represented in pollen records 1221 (Fig 13.13, CD 13.12) and 1718 (Fig 13.9, CD 13.15, monolith location on Fig 7.16), from Buildings 2 and 4, respectively, where raised bog continued to develop and where fluctuations in the arboreal record provide further evidence for interference with the woodland cover. Shortly after the beginning of GC1221.2 a fall in *Quercus, Fraxinus,* and *Corylus avellana*-type followed by a fall in *Ulmus* accompanied by an increase in Poaceae and peaks in *Plantago lanceolata, Artemisia,* and *Pteridium,* and the presence of Chenopodiaceae and *Rumex,* point to further clearance and agricultural activity estimated at some time *c* 3300–3500 radiocarbon years BP. Coinciding with these changes is a peak in microscopic charcoal, providing additional evidence for human activity. However, Chenopodiaceae pollen and other taxa, such as *Plantago maritima* (sea plantain), could equally represent saltmarsh environments, and a thin band of clay, suggesting a very brief marine inundation, does occur just before their appearance in the pollen record. Increasing *Alnus* values during this period in GC1221.2 could be registering an increase in alder carr as a result of a rising water table. The same minor clearance episode, represented by a decline in *Quercus* and appearance of *Plantago lanceolata*, appears to be recorded during GC1718.2 and is dated to *c* 3360 ± 40 BP (GrN-24147) to 3500 ± 30 BP (GrN-24148). *Alnus* also increases during this period, but there is no evidence for the brief marine inundation recorded in GC1221.2.

A similar sequence indicating possible clearance activity is also evident at Building 6 at Goldcliff West (unpublished student project), and at Goldcliff East (Smith and Morgan 1989) is discernible towards the end of GC1.4d and dated *c* 3440 ± 70 BP (CAR-645). Following an increase in *Quercus, Fraxinus,* and *Alnus*, suggesting a brief recovery in oak and ash woodland and expansion in alder later in GC1221.2 from Building 2, a decline in all three taxa occurs *c* 3000–3100 radiocarbon years BP. The presence of *Plantago lanceolata*, Ranunculaceae, and Chenopodiaceae again suggests human activity but the end of GC1221.2 coincides with the end of raised bog *c* 2580 ± 70 BP (CAR-1438) and the deposition of estuarine clay. Chenopodiaceae pollen and other taxa could equally well represent saltmarsh and swamp habitats and an increasing marine influence. The brief regeneration episode mid-zone in GC1221.2 is also represented in GC1718.3a from Building 4 and is followed by a clearance and agricultural phase during GC1718.3b. This is followed by a slight

regeneration episode *c* 3000 ± 40 BP (GrN-24146) before a further decline in *Quercus*. Stratigraphic changes from a *Sphagnum* to a reed peat begin around this time. Chenopodiaceae pollen, which is present in GC1718.3a and GC1718.3b, peaks at the end of GC1718.3c and *Potamogeton* pollen is consistently present. It seems likely that these changes are related to sea level rise which elsewhere is represented by the deposition of clay. At Goldcliff West at Buildings 6 and 8 (unpublished student project), where raised bog continued to persist, a possible minor clearance episode is estimated at around 3100–2900 radiocarbon years BP.

At Goldcliff East (Smith and Morgan 1989) and Hill Farm pond estuarine clays were deposited *c* 3100 radiocarbon years BP and, as discussed above, changes in the pollen records prior to this may indicate agricultural activity. Elsewhere in the region, at Barland's Farm and Vurlong Reen (Walker *et al* 1998), there is further evidence for clearance activity. At Barland's Farm, where clay deposition is recorded *c* 2900 ± 60 BP (BETA-72056), from *c* 3700 radiocarbon years BP there is a steady decline in dryland arboreal taxa, accompanied by an increase in *Plantago lanceolata* and *Rumex*. At Vurlong Reen open-habitat taxa are more frequent from *c* 3900 radiocarbon years BP, although dryland arboreal taxa fluctuate. Slightly inland, at Caldicot, the pollen evidence (Caseldine and Barrow 1997) suggests pastoralism with some cultivation.

The environment of the skull

During the excavation of Pit 15, part of a human skull was discovered within peat below a palaeochannel cut into the peat (Chapter 5). The date of 3095 ± 40 BP (OxA-7744) for the skull is close to the date of

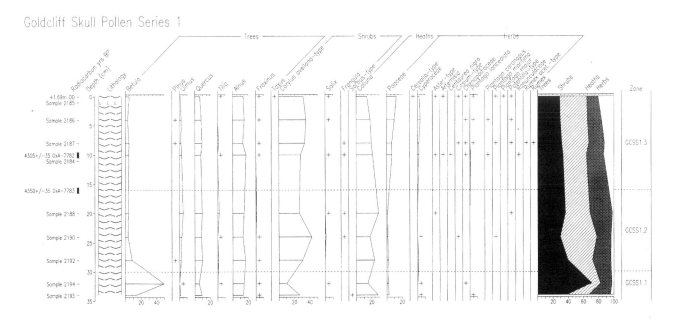

Figure 13.6 Percentage pollen diagram (selected taxa) from Sample Series 1 taken directly above and below the skull in the peat block

Goldcliff Skull Pollen Series 2

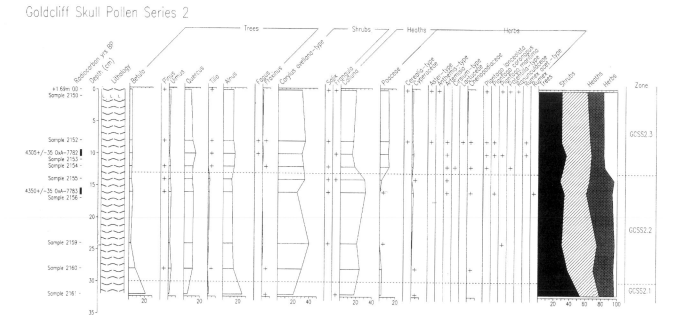

Figure 13.7 Percentage pollen diagram (selected taxa) from Sample Series 2 taken from c 9cm to the side of the skull in the peat block

3130 ± 70 BP (CAR-644) for the transgressive contact at Goldcliff East, suggesting the palaeochannel is contemporary with that event. However, the radiocarbon date of 4350 ± 35 BP (OxA-7783) from the peat below the skull and the date of 4305 ± 35 BP (OxA-7782) from above are somewhat earlier than the skull but in keeping with the pollen record from the peat. This problem of a discrepancy between the date of human remains and associated peat has been encountered at other sites, including Lindow Moss (Turner and Scaife 1995).

Two series of samples (Fig 5.3b), Series 1 from directly above and below the skull and Series 2 from approximately 9cm to the side, were examined as well as a sample from within the skull. The pollen records demonstrate the skull lay within raised bog peat. A peak in *Betula* at the end of GCSS1.1 (Figs 13.6, CD 13.4) and relatively high *Betula* and *Alnus* values in the only level of GCSS2.1 (Figs 13.7, CD 13.5) correspond with the increase in *Betula* and *Alnus* recorded just before the GC2099.6/7 zone boundary (Table 13.1) dated to 4520 ± 80 BP (SWAN-233). An increase in *Ulmus* in both GCSS1.2 and GCSS2.2 equates with the regeneration of elm evident in GC2099.7 (p 220). *Ulmus* is also well represented in GCSSS (Fig CD 13.6), the sample from within the skull. An increase in *Tilia*, dated to 4440 ± 45 BP (GrN-24144) in GC2099.7, occurs slightly later in all three zones, and relatively high *Tilia* values are also recorded from the pollen sample from within the skull. Both the pollen and the radiocarbon dates, therefore, indicate the skull is in peat of Neolithic date. The remaining zones, GCSS1.3 and GCSS2.3, are from peat lying directly above and from peat above a level equivalent to halfway up the skull, respectively (compare Figs 13.6, 13.7 and Fig 5.3b). The zones are characterised

by an increase in Poaceae, increased frequency of other herb taxa, and a reduction in *Tilia*, although *Ulmus* remains at >1% TLP. Although these zones are similar to GC2099.8, dated from 3780 ± 70 BP (SWAN-232) to just after 3640 ± 60 BP (CAR-1499), *Ulmus* values are higher, which suggests the zones might be earlier and this is confirmed by the date of 4305 ± 35 BP (OxA-7782) near the beginning of them. The greater representation of herbaceous pollen, including the presence of Chenopodiaceae pollen which is typical of saltmarsh, and lower *Tilia* and *Ulmus* values in these zones compared with the latter half of GC2099.7, which from the radiocarbon dates should be contemporary, may be accounted for by traces of clay in the peat. The clay may possibly have been intruded from above, bringing with it later pollen, or mixing of older and later peat, either by natural processes or human activity, although the appearance of the peat did not suggest major disturbance. The evidence from the plant macrofossils is similar, with some hints of disturbance, but not markedly so.

The peat surrounding the Series 2 pollen samples was also examined for plant macrofossils (Table CD 13.26). The plant remains are in close agreement with the pollen evidence. The assemblage is dominated by raised bog taxa including *Calluna vulgaris*, *Erica tetralix* (cross-leaved heath), *E. cinerea* (bell heather), *Eriophorum vaginatum*, and *Sphagnum*, with wetter conditions suggested in the upper samples by the presence of *Rhynchospora alba* (white beak-sedge) and *Menyanthes trifoliata*. In the lowest samples a few *Betula* seeds are recorded, broadly coinciding with the higher *Betula* pollen values. Occasional clay lenses were noted down to 9cm, with a trace of clay down to 25cm, and possible hints of saltmarsh occur in the upper samples with the occasional seed of *Atriplex*, *Plantago major* (greater plantain), and *Potentilla anserina* (silverweed). These taxa are also associated with waste ground, and the presence of *Urtica dioica, Polygonum aviculare,* and Chenopodiaceae at skull level may also relate to disturbance at the site and human or animal activity, since cattle hoof prints were noted in the edge of the channel (Chapter 5).

The slight disturbance of the peat above the skull can probably be accounted for by the later palaeochannel. One possible explanation for the fact that the peat towards the base of the skull shows less evidence of disturbance is that the skull was either deliberately pushed into the bottom of the channel by humans, or accidentally pushed down by the trampling of animals, ie cattle.

Bronze Age marine inundation *c* 3000–2600 radiocarbon years BP

The pollen records from the clays dating to after *c* 3000 radiocarbon years BP, Goldcliff East GC1.5 (Smith and Morgan 1989), Hill Farm Pond GC11600.3, and Barland's Farm BF7 (Walker *et al* 1998), all strongly indicate saltmarsh and swamp vegetation communities. At the same time *Alnus* values decline reflecting a decrease in the extent of alder carr in the area. This is clearly demonstrated during GC11600.3 where *Alnus* values fall from >60% TLP to <10% TLP. It is also evident at Vurlong Reen (Walker *et al* 1998). The decline in *Alnus*, as mentioned above, also registers in the pollen records from Buildings 2, 6 and 8 as water levels rose and by *c* 2600 radiocarbon years BP at Building 2 marine inundation had occurred. In the palaeochannel deposits at Caldicot (Caseldine and Barrow 1997) a decline in *Alnus* is recorded during Phase V, commencing *c* 3000 BP and, although there is a brief recovery during Phase VI, a marked decline occurs at the beginning of Phase VII,

a zone with dates lying in the range 2750–2400 radiocarbon years BP.

From around 3000 radiocarbon years BP, as noted earlier, there is increasing evidence for clearance and agriculture at the end of zone GC1221.2 from Building 2 and, during GC1718.3c, from Building 4. At Goldcliff East (Smith and Morgan 1989) the increase in herbaceous taxa during GC1.5 is probably attributable to agricultural activity as well as the development of saltmarsh. The same may apply at Barland's Farm (Walker *et al* 1998) where open-habitat taxa increase during a period of clay deposition after about 2900 radiocarbon years BP. Dryland arboreal taxa also decline at Vurlong Reen (Walker *et al* 1998). At Caldicot, in addition to the pollen evidence (Caseldine and Barrow 1997) for pastoralism and cultivation, faunal remains associated with the archaeology confirm the former and seeds of possible weeds of cultivation support the latter.

To summarise, the evidence shows that between *c* 3500 and 2600 radiocarbon years BP the Goldcliff area was subject to increasing marine inundation, leading to an increase in saltmarsh and reedswamp communities. Against this background of events, clearance was taking place throughout the area with evidence for both pastoralism and cultivation. It is suggested the marine transgressive phase in the area to the east of Goldcliff Pill is related to a palaeochannel, probably of Bronze Age date (Chapter 3), in the area of Auger Hole 44 (Fig 3.4). Two thin bands of *Phragmites* peat occur in the area to the east of the auger hole and lying within the intervening clay was a palaeochannel containing the boat plank site.

Boat Plank Structure 1124

The pollen record (Figs 13.8, CD 13.8) from the boat plank platform site (1124) (Chapter 6), dated to 2720

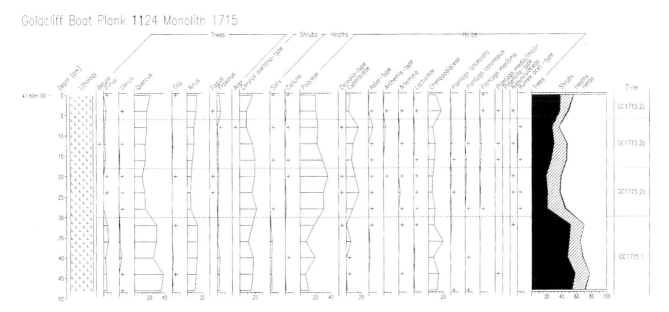

Figure 13.8 Percentage pollen diagram (selected taxa) from Monolith 1715 from Boat Plank Structure 1124

± 70 BP (CAR-1434), is from a small palaeochannel cutting the lower peat and predates the platform (monolith location Fig 6.7). It shows similarities with the assemblages from the estuarine clay discussed above; Chenopodiaceae pollen reflecting saltmarsh is well represented throughout the diagram. Additional information about the local environment is provided by macrofossil remains from the pollen residues and separate, larger, plant macrofossil samples (Table CD 13.27). The interpretation of the pollen record from estuarine sediments has already been discussed (p 215) and is discussed further below (p 228). Again, *Pinus* is probably over-represented but, compared with the record from the Mesolithic, is much less frequent, suggesting a reduction in *Pinus* in the region by this time. During the earliest zone GC1715.1 arboreal pollen values, notably *Quercus*, are high. A slight fall in *Quercus* around the middle of the zone is followed by a further fall at the end. Both these falls in *Quercus* could relate to clearance of oak woodland, and it is tempting to see these changes as broadly contemporary with the changes recorded at other sites, discussed above, during the period *c* 3500–2600 radiocarbon years BP, particularly the GC1715.1/GC1715.2a boundary fall in *Quercus* as perhaps equivalent to *c* 3000 radiocarbon years BP or slightly later. Around this time a more or less continuous record begins for *Plantago lanceolata* and other herbaceous taxa increase in frequency, reflecting a possible increase in agriculture on the dryland in the area and/or an increase in saltmarsh and swamp communities locally. During GC1715.1 plant macrofossil remains are very sparse and include only a few Poaceae seeds and *Phragmites* rhizomes. Plant macrofossils (20–25cm) from a clayey peat, coinciding with GC1715.2a, are much more frequent. The increase in Poaceae pollen is probably attributable to *Phragmites* reed and grassy saltmarsh. An increase in Cyperaceae pollen coincides with seeds of sedges, particularly seeds of *Bolboschoenus maritimus,* which suggest stands of sea-club rush either separately or with *Phragmites*. Although both can tolerate brackish conditions, sea club-rush can tolerate higher salinities. Other taxa represented, such as *Salicornia* spp (glassworts), *Ruppia maritima* (beaked tasselweed), *R. cirrhosa* (spiral tasselweed), *Aster tripolium* (sea aster), *Mentha* spp (mint), *Hydrocotyle vulgaris* (marsh pennywort), and *Ranunculus sceleratus (*celery-leaved buttercup*),* are typical of a *Bolboschoenus maritimus* community (cf Rodwell 1995) but are also found in either saltmarsh or reedswamp communities. The *Bolboschoenus maritimus* community is found alongside creeks in the upper saltmarsh (Rodwell 1995), a similar situation to this. It can tolerate occasional to frequent inundation with brackish water and grow in standing water more than 50cm deep (Rodwell 1995, 210).

A plant macrofossil sample from immediately below the level of the boat plank, and coinciding with GC1715.2c, was from a less organic blue–grey clay. A fall in Cyperaceae pollen and increase in Chenopodiaceae pollen suggests a stronger marine influence than in GC1715.2b. An apparent increase in *Potamogeton* type pollen (see CD13.8) is probably attributable to *Triglochin maritima* (sea arrowgrass) which was present in the plant macrofossil record along with *Juncus* sp and *Bolboschoenus maritimus*. The whole sequence of marine to brackish–freshwater to increasingly marine, which is indicated by the botanical evidence, is confirmed by the diatom record (Chapter 15).

Essentially, the boat plank site seems to have been constructed across a palaeochannel containing increasingly marine sediments. The immediate environment would have been one of mudflat, saltmarsh and reedswamp, lying some distance from raised bog (see Fig 3.4), with such taxa poorly represented in the pollen record. In the preceding period on the dryland there is evidence for mixed farming with indicators of grassland and Cerealia-type pollen, although there is a very slight and gradual recovery of arboreal pollen during GC1715.2b and GC1715.2c. However, this could reflect reworked pollen and the increasing marine influence rather than an increase in woodland. Radiocarbon and dendrochronological dates for the structure suggest it is contemporary with activity at Caldicot *c* Phases VI and VII. Zone GC1715.2 is not dissimilar to CM.5a and CM.5b from Column 1 at Caldicot (Caseldine and Barrow 1997), with relatively low arboreal taxa and similar representation of herbaceous taxa.

At the same time as the boat plank platform was constructed in a palaeochannel surrounded by saltmarsh and mudflat in the immediate area, raised bog continued to grow in the area of Buildings 1, 2, 3, and 4 and further west at Buildings 6 and 8. The possible environmental conditions around this time are illustrated in map Fig 17.4d.

13.5.4 The later prehistoric vegetational and environmental changes c 2600–2350 radiocarbon years BP

Marine inundation and peat development c 2600–2450 radiocarbon years BP

The later sequence of events at Goldcliff is represented in several diagrams (Table 13.2), enabling a more precise picture of the spatial variation in the local vegetation communities and environmental changes to be determined. In the area of Buildings 1 and 2 (Fig 7.11, Section 216) the stratigraphic and pollen evidence demonstrates that raised bog continued to grow until *c* 2580 ± 70 BP (CAR-1438), when the deposition of clay indicates that here too a change to marine/estuarine conditions occurred. Here this was a relatively short-lived episode and coincides with a marked increase in Poaceae pollen in GC1221.3 from Building 2, which suggests an increase in reedswamp, confirmed by *Phragmites* remains within the top of the peat and within the clay, and possibly grass dominated saltmarsh/sea meadow in the area. Chenopodiaceae pollen, though present, is not strongly represented, whereas at Building 3 a comparable zone, GC1719.2 (Fig 13.15, CD 13.14, monolith location on Fig 7.16), is identifiable in which Chenopodiaceae values exceed 1% TLP. This suggests a stronger marine influence, although the deposit itself is a yellow *Phragmites* mud with blue–grey clay, indicating the site was towards the limits of inundation, which is confirmed by borehole evidence (Fig 3.4). Again, the dominant local community appears to be reedswamp. The occurrence of ericaceous pollen and *Sphagnum* spores in these zones is attributable to the continued presence of contemporary raised bog communities to the west and/or erosion of the raised bog surface.

The decline in *Alnus* witnessed towards the end of GC1221.2 starting *c* 3100 radiocarbon years BP results in low *Alnus* values in GC1221.3 and, as has already been discussed (p 223), reflects either a natural decrease in alder as a result of an increasing relative sea level and inundation, or clearance of alder woodland fringing the dryland to the north, or within the wetland itself. The possible evidence for clearance activity dating from *c* 3000–3100 radiocarbon years BP has also been discussed (p 223). *Quercus* continues the decline started in GC1221.2 into GC1221.3 and *Corylus avellana*-type also declines sharply, perhaps reflecting clearance of oak woodland with hazel understorey and hazel scrubland, although some of the *Corylus avellana*-type pollen is probably attributable to *Myrica gale*, ie bog myrtle communities. A slight increase in *Quercus* pollen in GC1221.3 could indicate a brief recovery in oak woodland, although this is not recorded in the comparable zone GC1719.2 at Building 3, but the latter is represented by only one level. Cerealia-type pollen and other herb taxa possibly indicate mixed agriculture on the dryland in the region.

A brief return to fresher water conditions and a relative fall in sea level is demonstrated by the formation of a slightly woody, *Cladium* (great fensedge) and *Phragmites* peat recorded in lithostratigraphies at Buildings 1, 2, and 3 and Double Post Row 970. This corresponds with Zones GC1232.1 (Fig 13.11, CD 13.9, monolith location on Figs 7.6 and 7.12), GC1221.4, GC1719.3, and GC1717.1 (Fig 13.16, CD 13.19, monolith location on Fig 10.6), respectively (Table 13.2). Locally, *Cladium* and *Phragmites* communities dominated, with occasional fen woodland reflected in the varying frequency of *Betula* pollen, most strongly represented in GC1221.3 and almost absent in GC1717.1. *Corylus avellana*-type pollen is abundant in all these zones, with much of it appearing to be *Myrica*, suggesting that, rather than a period when hazel scrub increased markedly, bog myrtle communities were expanding. *Myrica gale* is found in both *Cladium* sedge swamp and in *Phragmites australis–Peucedanum palustre* and *Phragmites australis–Eupatorium cannabinum*, tall-herb fen communities where *Phragmites* or *Cladium* usually dominate (Rodwell 1995). It is also found in fen woodland (Rodwell 1991a) and mire communities

(Rodwell 1991b). Minor changes in other arboreal taxa vary from site to site but interpretation is limited because the zones are short. In GC1221.4 from Building 2 there is more evidence of an increase in *Quercus* pollen at the end of the zone than in the comparable zones in the other diagrams where an increase does not really occur until the following zones. *Fraxinus* is relatively well represented in GC1719.3 and GC1717.1 from Building 3 and Double Post Row 970, respectively, compared with in GC1232.1 and GC1221.4 from Buildings 1 and 2. The former may indicate increased flowering or the spread of ash into formerly cleared areas. The difference in representation may reflect the geographical relationship of the pollen sites to the cleared areas, although the distance apart of the sites is only around 60–80m and the distance from dryland, apart from Goldcliff Island, is around 5.5km. Agricultural indicator species such as *Plantago lanceolata* and Cerealia-type are present but reduced in comparison to the previous zone which would accord with the possible evidence for an increase in scrub. This episode, like the previous one, was also short-lived before a return to marine/estuarine conditions. The end of the zone is dated to 2460 ± 70 BP (SWAN-135) at GC1221.4, a date comparable with that of 2470 ± 60 BP (BETA-63590) at the top of the peat at Vurlong Reen (Walker *et al* 1998) and also marking clay deposition.

Marine inundation *c* 2450–2350 radiocarbon years BP

The return of estuarine/marine conditions, after the brief fresher water phase, is represented at a number of sites (Table 13.2). At Building 2, where peat development resumed *c* 2360 ± 70 BP (SWAN-136), estuarine/marine conditions lasted *c* 100 radiocarbon years. A sharp increase in Poaceae pollen (Zone GC1221.5) coincides with clay deposition and is largely attributable to local reedswamp, although some pollen may derive from saltmarsh and dryland communities. *Phragmites* remains confirm the continued presence of reedswamp communities, although subject to marine inundation. Low Chenopodiaceae values initially suggest a weaker brackish/marine influence before relatively strong representation demonstrates an increase in saltmarsh habitats locally. An increase in Cyperaceae pollen suggests sedge as well as reedswamp communities. *Juncus* seeds, indicating rushes, are also present. Low amounts of ericaceous taxa and *Sphagnum* spores suggest the continued presence of raised bog, either actively growing or eroding in the area and this is confirmed by the evidence from Building 4 (see below) and the diatom evidence (Chapter 15). An increase in *Phragmites* remains towards the end of the clay phase reflects a succession leading to fresher water conditions and the formation of a peat. A decrease in marine conditions is also indicated by diatoms (Chapter 15). The same sequence, although in less detail, occurs in GC1232.2 and the later part in GC1224.1 (Fig 13.12, CD 13.10, monolith location on Figs 7.9 and 7.12), both from Building 1. An almost identical sequence of local events also occurs at Building 3, GC1719.3, to the east and Double Post Row 970, GC1717.2. This period of clay deposition is also recorded in more or less detail at Trackway 1108, Zone GC1714.1 (Fig 13.10, CD 13.18, monolith location on Fig 10.1), to the west of Buildings 1 and 2, and to the east at Trackway 1, Zone GC1697.1 (Fig 13.17, CD 13.20, monolith location on Fig 10.11), Trackway 8, Zones GC1716.1 and GC1716.2 (Fig 13.18, CD 13.21, monolith location on Fig 10.12), and Trackway 1130, Zone GC1745.1 (Fig 13.19, CD 13.22, monolith location on Fig 10.14).

A trend towards more marine conditions is discernible from sites towards the eastern end of the current peat shelf, possibly related to a palaeo-channel in the area of Auger Hole 44 (Fig 3.4). Saltmarsh communities are most strongly represented in GC1716.1 and GC1716.2 from Trackway 8, and GC1745.1 from Trackway 1130, where Chenopodiaceae values are consistently *c* 5% TLP or more. At Trackway 1, Cyperaceae pollen is more significant, suggesting more sedge swamp in that area. At some of these sites limited plant macrofossil evidence complements the pollen records for local environmental conditions.

At Trackway 1108 (Table CD 13.31) a sample (230–280mm) from clay contains relatively few remains but reflects *Phragmites* swamp and fen communities (cf Rodwell 1995) in the area, with *Phragmites* remains and seeds of *Juncus* sp, *Mentha*, and *Apium* spp (marshwort) well represented and small amounts of *Lythrum salicaria* (purple loosestrife), *Cladium mariscus,* and *Eupatorium cannabinum* (hemp agrimony). At Trackway 8 (Table CD 13.33) a similar reed assemblage is recorded from clay (190–240mm) just below the peat and includes *Apium* spp, Poaceae, *Typha* spp, *Lycopus europaeus*, (gypsywort) *Juncus* spp, and *Atriplex* spp seeds. The last indicates a brackish influence. There is only a hint of birch woodland in the area, provided by a single *Betula* seed.

The interpretation of pollen from estuarine/marine deposits, and the greater taphonomic problems involved compared with a peat, has been discussed earlier (p 215). Clearly, from the stratigraphic, pollen, and diatom evidence (see above), there is some eroded and reworked material but some indication of the reliability of the pollen record from these upper clays, as a reflection of the contemporary environment, can be gained by comparison with the earlier clay pollen record. Although concentrations are considerably lower than in the peats, pollen preservation was relatively good in the clays. *Pinus* values are higher than in the peats and, as noted earlier, this over-representation is probably attributable to the effects of water transport. However, the values are considerably lower than during the Mesolithic, suggesting a real decrease in the amount of pine in the pollen catchment area, which is consistent with the evidence from South Wales for a reduction in pine since the Mesolithic (eg Barton *et al* 1995).

Low amounts of *Alnus* and *Betula* pollen in the clays probably relate to fen carr woodland to the north. In Zones GC1221.5 from Building 2, GC1719.4 from Building 3, and GC1717.2 from Double Post Row 970, all zones covering the full estuarine/marine episode, an increase in *Quercus* pollen is recorded followed by a decrease. Higher *Ulmus* values coincide with the increase in *Quercus*. *Corylus avellana*-type values are markedly lower in the zones from the clays. A slight increase during GC1221.5 from Building 2 corresponds with the first increase in *Quercus* and could indicate an increase in hazel woodland but hardly registers at other sites. Overall, the evidence suggests some regeneration of oak woodland followed by clearance on the dryland, but the possibility of pollen from the reworking of older peat means the results must be treated with caution. Herbaceous taxa, including *Plantago lanceolata* and Cerealia-type, indicate agricultural activity on the dryland. Pollen evidence for this period from other sites in the region is lacking, apart from Caldicot where at the end of Phase VII (approximately *c* 2400 radiocarbon years BP) a very slight regeneration episode is recorded. Here pastoralism is considered of major importance but with some evidence for cultivation (Caseldine and Barrow 1997).

The local vegetational sequence of events recorded in the peats at Building 4 can be related to the period of clay deposition at the other sites. As mentioned previously, during Pollen Zone GC1718.3c *Potamogeton* is consistently present and a peak in Chenopodiaceae at the end of the zone suggests a rising water table and increasing marine influence. Stratigraphically, the pollen column from Building 4 can be linked with the period of clay deposition through Trench 25 (Fig 10.3) which contains Linear Post Alignment 1149 where 50mm of peaty clay below 200mm of peat probably correlates with the end of GC1718.3c.

13.5.5 The upper peat and the building and trackway environment c 2350–2000 radiocarbon years BP

A relative fall in sea level or still stand resulted in a short period of peat development in the area between Trackways 1108 and 1130 (Fig 13.2) which had formerly been subject to inundation (Fig 3.4). This is of particular significance because, associated with the end of this episode, is a period of intensive human activity represented by numerous trackways, buildings, and other structures. During this time the ensuing vegetation communities varied considerably from site to site, reflecting varying extents of marine influence. The evidence will basically be considered from west to east in the main Goldcliff area, with the evidence from the buildings largely discussed first, followed by the trackways, and then the evidence from Goldcliff West.

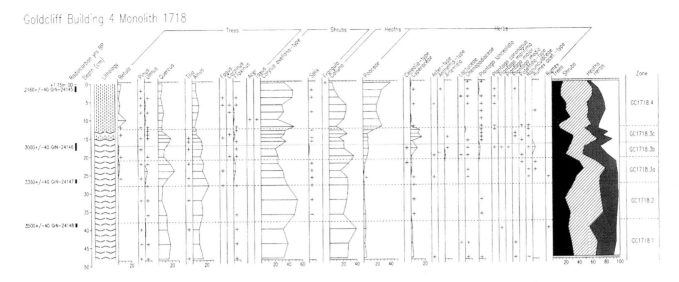

Figure 13.9 Percentage pollen diagram (selected taxa) from Monolith 1718 from Building 4

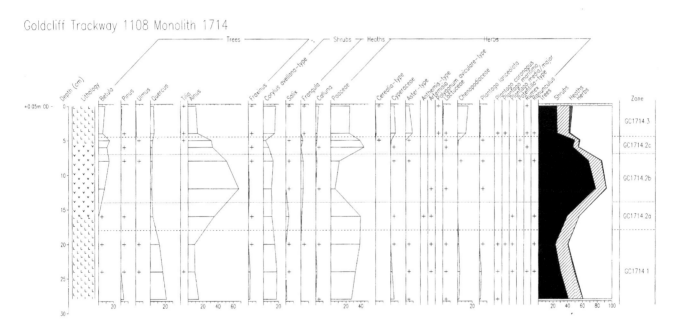

Figure 13.10 Percentage pollen diagram (selected taxa) from Monolith 1714 from Trackway 1108

The local environment

Building 4

Whereas, at most of the sites in the main area, the beginning of this phase is marked by a transition from clays to peats, at Building 4 a continuous peat sequence (Fig 7.16) is recorded and a *Phragmites* peat ultimately replaces a *Sphagnum–Calluna* peat. As noted above, a small peak in Chenopodiaceae pollen, coinciding with increasing Poaceae values at the end of GC1718.3c (Fig 13.9, CD 13.15) may correspond with the marine transgressive phase. A small peak in *Betula* near the beginning of GC1718.4 registers an increase in birch woodland in the area, probably correspond-ing to the development of carr woodland recorded at

the other sites along the upper peat shelf, but then values drop to low levels. Other arboreal pollen is also poorly represented, apart from *Corylus avellana*-type, much of which could be *Myrica*. Relatively high *Calluna* values, at least initially, indicate the relatively close proximity of raised bog for much of the period. The presence of Chenopodiaceae pollen at the same time as a decline in *Calluna* occurs in GC1718.4 suggests a steadily increasing marine influence towards 2160 ± 40 BP (GrN-24145), a trend also indicated at the other sites in the area. *Urtica dioica* seeds, noted in the stratigraphy, and *Lythrum* pollen are typical of reed-swamp but also occur in fen communities which may also have been present locally. *Phragmites–Urtica* fen is described as forming part of the reed dominated vegetation found above saltmarsh strandlines, particularly in the southwest (Proctor 1980, Rodwell 1995, 246).

No 'floor' deposits were recovered from the building (Chapter 7) but the very close similarity between the radiocarbon date for the top of the peat and the building shows there has been little erosion of the peat here. Although wood identified from the building (Fig 12.2) indicates it was largely made from local wetland trees, notably *Alnus*, other taxa, namely *Ulmus* and *Acer campestre* (field maple), and possibly *Fraxinus*, suggest that some wood was brought in from dryland habitats, as well as confirming the limited pollen record for the presence of these species in the region at the time.

Trackway 1108

At the site sampled for pollen at Trackway 1108 (Fig 10.1), a trackway leading northwards towards Building 4 and lying to the west of Buildings 1 and 2, the stratigraphic sequence is interrupted by the marine episode discussed above. The transition from estuarine conditions to peat is marked by a muddy clay with high Poaceae values, an absence of Chenopodiaceae pollen, increasing *Alnus* values, and a peak in *Salix* at the boundary between GC1714.1 and GC1714.2 (Fig 13.10, CD 13.18), suggesting a change to fresher water conditions with reedswamp and colonisation by willow and alder. *Alnus* values rising to >60% TLP coincide with the development of a wood peat. As *Alnus* values decline later in the zone, *Betula* values increase indicating a change in the local woodland. These changes are mirrored in the plant macrofossil record (Table CD 13.31) with first *Alnus* remains and later *Betula* seeds abundant, although *Betula* seeds are well-designed for wind transport and may be over-represented at the site. The rest of the plant macrofossil assemblage from 150mm to 200mm supports the pollen evidence, reflecting the transition from reedswamp to fen carr with taxa such as *Phragmites*, *Mentha* sp, *Hydrocotyle vulgaris*, *Lychnis flos-cuculi* (ragged robin), *Lythrum salicaria*, and *Cladium mariscus*. *Rubus fruticosus* (bramble) and *Solanum dulcamara* (bittersweet) recorded from 70–120mm are typical of carr woodland.

The period of trackway construction coincides approximately with pollen levels 40–60mm. In the column from which the samples were taken (Fig 10.1) the trackway lay at the base of the overlying clay within a muddy deposit which was sampled separately from the clay. The column was from the southern end of the track whereas, to the north, an apparent continuation of the structure (1149) lay within peat (Chapter 10). At 50mm and 60mm Poaceae pollen dominates, suggesting a reed dominated environment and this is borne out by the record in the field of *Phragmites* remains lying along the structure. A steady decline in *Alnus* may be related to a rising sea level or be partially attributable to utilisation of local woodland to make the trackway. *Alnus* is the most frequent wood type identified from the trackway (Chapter 12.2). Similarly small oscillations in the curves for *Betula*, *Frangula*, and *Salix* may also be related to the use of local birch, alder

buckthorn, and willow wood in the trackway, although elm, field maple, and possibly oak must have been brought from dryland. The macrofossil sample (50–70mm) examined from the muddy deposit contained thousands of *Juncus bufonius* (toad rush) and *Juncus gerardii* (saltmarsh rush) seeds. The former is a pioneer species typically found in muddy deposits, including saltmarsh, and where trampling occurs, perhaps reflecting the use of the trackway. Other taxa, including *Atriplex* spp, *Aster tripolium*, and *Bolboschoenus maritimus*, also indicate brackish conditions. These conditions are more strongly indicated in the sample above (0–50mm) and the assemblage from Sample 1731 which contains large quantities of *Bolboschoenus maritimus*, *Atriplex* spp and other brackish/saltmarsh taxa such as *Ranunculus sceleratus*, *Polygonum aviculare*, *Suaeda maritima* (annual sea-blite), and *Spergularia* spp (sea-spurrey). The sample was also examined for beetles (Chapter 14), which give similar results. Small amounts of *Calluna* and *Erica* sp suggest the local presence of, or erosion of, raised bog. Whether or not the presence of the trackway and associated activity encouraged the presence of taxa such as *Atriplex* spp, *Plantago major* and *Polygonum aviculare* is difficult to say; these would occur anyway in saltmarsh communities but on dryland could occur as weeds in disturbed ground. The pollen record is in close agreement with the plant macrofossil evidence. Poaceae values are relatively high whilst Cyperaceae, Chenopodiaceae, and *Aster* type values increase in GC1714.3, reflecting the change to brackish conditions and the development of saltmarsh. To summarise, in the area sampled, the trackway dated to 2140 ± 60 BP (CAR-1438) appears to have been constructed at the transition from carr woodland to saltmarsh. A possible reconstruction of the environmental conditions at the trackway is illustrated in Figure 10.20C.

Buildings 1 and 2

Four diagrams, two from inside and two from outside the buildings, demonstrate the environmental sequence at Buildings 1 and 2, to the east of Trackway 1108 (Figs 7.12, 13.11–13.14, CD 13.9 and 13.10, CD 13.12 and 13.13). Again, the establishment of carr woodland is evidenced by the formation of a wood peat. The end of the estuarine phase and the reappearance of freshwater conditions, is demonstrated by high Poaceae values, abundant *Phragmites* remains, and low Chenopodiaceae values at the end of Zones GC1221.5, GC1224.1, GC1227.1, and GC1232.1, a trend also indicated by diatoms (Chapter 15). In all four diagrams the development of woodland is marked by an increase in both *Betula* and *Alnus* pollen, with initially the former slightly more abundant than the latter, suggesting that in this area birch was an important component of the local vegetation compared with at Trackway 1108 or Building 4. Later in the sequences, excluding 1227, *Alnus* predominates and *Betula* declines, to a greater or lesser extent depending on the diagram, before increasing again, although not returning to former levels. The whole sequence is discussed in more detail below but

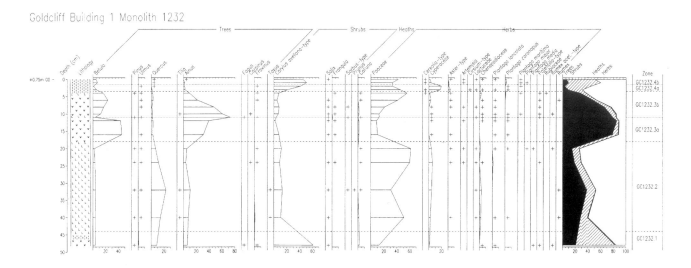

Figure 13.11 Percentage pollen diagram (selected taxa) from Monolith 1232 from Building 1

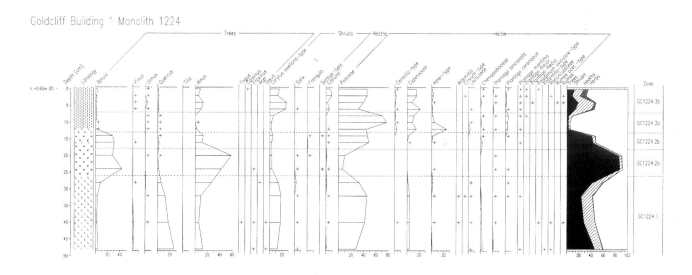

Figure 13.12 Percentage pollen diagram (selected taxa) from Monolith 1224 from Building 1

the variations between the diagrams clearly reflect differences in the local vegetation. In 1227 the pollen sequence from the peat is truncated in comparison with the other diagrams, which confirms that the later peat has been eroded.

At Building 2 (Fig 7.11) the establishment of alder and birch carr woodland, Zone GC1221.6, is dated to *c* 2360 ± 70 BP (SWAN-136). A date of 2270 ± 70 BP (CAR-1351) from a peat sample (1249) nearby, described as 80–100mm below occupation material, provides an approximate date for the top of the peat. Initially *Betula* dominates (GC1221.6a) but then *Alnus* takes over as the dominant tree (GC1221.6b). Other taxa typical of this fen woodland (cf Rodwell 1991a *Salix cinerea–Betula pubescens–Phragmites australis* woodland) present in the pollen record include *Viburnum opulus* (guelder-rose), *Rhamnus cathartica* (buckthorn), *Sorbus*-type, *Solanum dulcamara*, *Lysimachia vulgaris*-type, and *Sphagnum*. A very thin clay band was noted around 100mm

indicating a brief period of marine inundation, confirmed by diatoms (Chapter 15), perhaps a storm surge or very high tide. This appears to have had little effect on the vegetation, which is consistent with alder's ability to tolerate a certain degree of salinity (Ranwell 1974). *Alnus* is commonly preferentially frequent in semi-swamp/pseudo-swamp carrs and its dominance is likely to be due to other factors (p217 and cf Rodwell 1991a). This zone is also represented in GC1232.3 from Building 1 and GC1224.2 from 500mm west of Building 1. In 1232 a thin band of clay containing marine and brackish diatoms (Chapter 15) was noted *c* 110mm and, again, this coincides with a peak in *Alnus,* accompanied by a small peak in *Frangula* and a marked decline in *Betula* at the GC1232.3a/3b boundary, again, perhaps suggesting a competitive advantage for *Alnus* at the expense of *Betula*. However, the dominance of *Alnus* appears to have been short-lived because *Alnus* then shows a steady decline while *Betula* shows some recovery. *Salix*

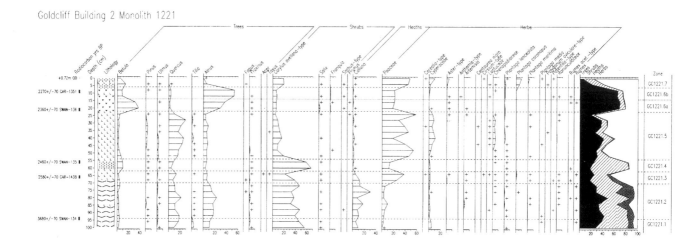

Figure 13.13 *Percentage pollen diagram (selected taxa) from Monolith 1221 from Building 2*

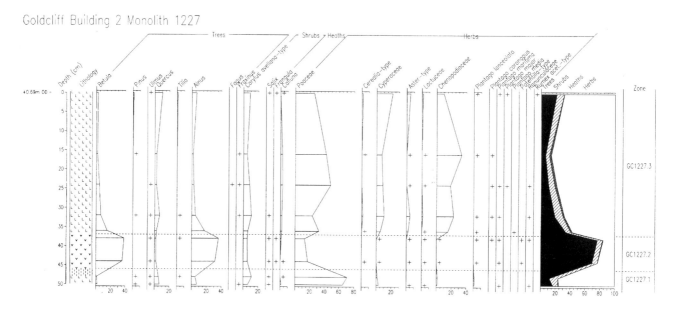

Figure 13.14 *Percentage pollen diagram (selected taxa) from Monolith 1227 from Building 2*

is more or less consistently present during this period GC1232.3b. Although the decline in *Alnus* could relate entirely to natural environmental changes, it is possible that human activity could have played a role. A steady increase in Poaceae suggests an increase in reed and a more open environment. Chenopodiaceae pollen is constantly recorded, suggesting a marine influence. The increase in Poaceae pollen culminates in a peak *c* 60% TLP at 4cm. This level coincides with a thin band of muddy clay and a peak in Chenopodiaceae pollen confirms its marine origin, as does the diatom evidence (Chapter 15). A similar sequence is represented in GC1224.2 where *Alnus* declines at the beginning of GC1224.2b but *Betula* values are maintained, Poaceae values increase and Chenopodiaceae pollen is present and a clay band is recorded at *c* 140mm. Again the decline in *Alnus* may be related to sea level change, other natural factors, or human activity. Changes in the

frequency of *Frangula* and *Salix,* evident in all the diagrams during this period, may relate to competition and the overtopping of these shrubs by the developing canopy (Rodwell 1991a), or possibly reflect anthropogenic activity.

The same basic sequence, with a decline in *Alnus* and slight increase in *Betula,* occurs at the beginning of GC1221.7. from Building 2. Comparison with Diagrams 1224 and 1232 suggests that either alder may have remained dominant slightly later at 1221, or that possibly part of the upper record is less complete, perhaps related to earlier occupation at Building 2. It has also been proposed that there may have been an earlier structure (Building 5) at the site (Chapter 7) and there is a possibility that the fall in *Alnus* could relate to its construction. Accompanying the decline in *Alnus* is a decrease in *Frangula,* a wood type also used in Building 5, in 1221 and 1232 but slightly later than the *Alnus* decline in 1224. Alternatively, the decline in *Alnus* could relate to the construction of Buildings 1 or 2, although this seems less likely, given the plant macrofossil evidence (discussed below), or other structures in the area. *Alnus* was the most frequent wood used in making the posts of the buildings whereas the floor timbers were largely *Betula* (Chapter 12). At the end of GC1232.3b and GC1224.2b a distinct fall in *Betula* pollen is recorded which probably relates to occupation at the site. From the pollen records most of the other wood types used in making the buildings, ie *Salix, Frangula,* and possibly Pomoideae (*Sorbus*-type pollen), *Fraxinus,* and *Quercus,* could also be from local woodland, but *Ulmus* and *Acer campestre* are likely to be from dryland, as might be the *Quercus, Fraxinus,* and Pomoideae.

The pollen records from the top of the peat are supplemented by plant macrofossil samples taken from beneath timbers regarded as flooring, as well as a sample (130) taken at the base of a sequence taken through the 'reed matting'. The results from the macrofossil samples (Tables CD 13.28 and 13.29) largely bear out the pollen evidence, with *Betula* seeds frequent and *Alnus* remains relatively rare, although the different dispersal characteristics of these species need to be kept in mind. Other species typical of a fen woodland community which are present include *Hydrocotyle vulgaris, Eupatorium cannabinum, Lycopus europaeus,* and *Typha* sp, as well as moss, including *Sphagnum*. However, in addition, species such as *Bolboschoenus maritimus, Aster tripolium, Atriplex* spp, and Poaceae species reflecting a brackish environment are represented. As these samples were taken from as far as possible 'sealed contexts', it seems reasonable to assume that these remains represent saltmarsh plants beginning to grow at, or near, the site or brought in with a high tide which had flooded the site. The latter is supported by the stratigraphic evidence for clay deposition. Small amounts of *Calluna* could reflect incipient raised bog.

The 'occupation period'

Most of the remaining evidence from Buildings 1 and 2 relates to occupation at the site. Interpretation of the evidence is complicated because of the difficulty of deciphering what is present 'naturally' and what is present because of human, or animal, intervention. The possibility of the buildings being used by animals was proposed at an early stage during the excavation and other lines of evidence, notably the beetles (Chapter 14) and mites (Chapter 15) have confirmed this. The evidence from the plant remains is more subtle, but adds further support. In a recent paper Kenward and Hall (1997) have discussed the interpretation of stable manure from archaeological sites, but the evidence is largely from urban and/or dryland sites where it is much more obvious that material has been brought onto site and is out of context. At Goldcliff the plant evidence for human/animal activity is less likely to be so obvious. Natural vegetation

growing at the site, or close to it, is the material most likely to have been exploited and utilised. Pollen taxa could be present either because of (i) vegetation growing around the site, (ii) vegetation brought onto it by natural processes such as wind or water transport, (iii) vegetation growing close to the site being brought onto the site deliberately by humans, (iv) pollen brought in on the feet of humans or animals, or (v) dung from animals. A possible interpretation of the environmental conditions at Building 1 is given in Fig 17.6.

The pollen evidence

The final zones from Pollen Monoliths 1232 and 1224 from Building 1 are from deposits regarded as largely representing occupation material. The distribution of these samples is shown in Figure 7.12. This material is primarily an organic deposit of reeds and probable 'dung' with some clay. The record is rather longer from 1224. The pollen records show broad similarities and slight differences, as might be expected, given the nature of the material and the likely differences in taphonomic processes, particularly if the building was roofed, since GC1232 is from within and 1224 is from outside Building 1. In addition, samples described as 'dung' from 'reed matting' Sample 91 (Fig CD 13.11) was also examined. In both GC1232.4a, from 'reed matting' comprising well preserved stem material (see below), and GC1224.3a, a mixture of reed and 'dung', high counts of Poaceae and Cyperaceae are recorded, although the prominence of these differs between the two diagrams, ie Poaceae values fall slightly in 1232.4a and Cyperaceae reach *c* 20% TLP, whilst in GC1224.3a Poaceae values peak and Cyperaceae are *c* 10–15% TLP. In the following Zones GC1232.4b (reed and 'dung') Poaceae begin to increase again and Cyperaceae fall to low levels whereas, in GC1224.3b (reed and 'dung'), Poaceae are lower than in the previous zone but Cyperaceae more or less maintain similar values. These differences are probably attributable to the reed material present, the amount of 'dung' within the sample, and whether or not the sample contained any clay brought in with reed or introduced by flooding. Support for this view is provided by 'dung' Sample 91 which has Poaceae and Cyperaceae values comparable with GC1232.4b. High Cyperaceae counts reflect the presence of *Bolboschoenus maritimus,* whilst the high Poaceae values can be accounted for by *Phragmites* reed-swamp and saltmarsh grasses represented in the plant macrofossil record (see below). Other pollen taxa also indicate saltmarsh. A peak in *Aster*-type pollen is recorded at the beginning of both GC1232.4a and GC1224.3a and is reasonably well represented in all the zones, as well as in 'dung' Sample 91. High *Plantago coronopus* values are recorded during GC1224.3a and GC1224.3b, although slightly lower in the latter, GC1232.3b, and 'dung' Sample 91. Along with records from GC1221.7 (Building 2) and

10127 (Building 6), this is the strongest representation from Goldcliff of *Plantago coronopus,* compared with the other diagrams covering this period. *Plantago coronopus* occurs in middle and upper saltmarshes as well as coastal grasslands and it seems likely that the high values may be accounted for by dung from cattle grazing in mid to upper saltmarsh. Cattle grazing can, in fact, lead to an increase in *Plantago coronopus.* Cerealia-type pollen is recorded in all the zones and is discussed further in relation to the plant macrofossil evidence. High *Corylus avellana*-type pollen values are recorded in GC1232.4b and 'dung' Sample 91. This suggests that hazel and/or *Myrica gale* communities were being browsed. Sheep/goat droppings examined for pollen and seeds from the Roman site Nieuwenhoorn 09–89 in the Netherlands consisted almost entirely of pure *Myrica gale* (Brinkkemper 1991). Apparently sheep are considered to dislike the taste of bog myrtle whereas goats do not. Sheep are present at Goldcliff but the presence of goat is uncertain (Chapter 15).

Representation of tree pollen is extremely poor in Zones GC1232.4a, GC1232.4b, GC1224.3a, and GC91 from 'dung' Sample 91, reflecting the nature of the material. However, in GC1224.3b *Alnus* is present in small but significant amounts and *Quercus* is consistently present at >1% TLP. A small peak in *Ulmus* occurs and it is also constantly present throughout the zone. This sub-zone may simply postdate the record from 1232, although an increase in *Corylus avellana*-type pollen at the beginning of GC1224.3b may correspond with the high *Corylus avellana*-type values in GC1232.4b and GC91 and the difference in representation relate to the fact that 1224 is outside the building rather than inside. *Calluna* pollen may similarly reflect this difference, with *Calluna* present in significant amounts in GC1224.3b but absent in GC1232.4b and only present in GC91. *Calluna* remains were present in Sample 200 described as 'reed matting' from outside the building (see below). The final zone GC1224.3b may represent an organic deposit of reed and 'dung' more heavily trampled and exposed to marine inundation than in the building.

The final zone, GC1221.7, from Building 2 also comprises occupation deposits, although examined in less detail than at Building 1. The penultimate sample occurs at the boundary between the underlying peat and 'reed matting' and resembles the end of GC1232.3b and beginning of GC1232.4a, otherwise the pollen assemblages are similar. Arboreal pollen values are very low, apart from *Corylus avellana*-type pollen, and *Plantago coronopus* relatively frequent.

The fourth Diagram 1227, from Building 2, clearly lacks these deposits and suggests erosion (also suggested by the section in Figure 7.11) of the earlier wood deposits as well (see above). Arboreal pollen is low and Poaceae and Chenopodiaceae, and to a lesser extent Cyperaceae, pollen is high, reflecting saltmarsh and swamp communities. *Plantago* spp are present as is *Aster* type, but not at the frequency recorded in the final zones of the other diagrams. The high Chenopodiaceae values reflect a strong estuarine/marine influence and the different circumstances to those represented in the other three diagrams.

The 'reed matting'

In addition to the analysis of pollen, plant macrofossils were examined from 'reed matting' samples (Table CD 13.29) and their distribution is shown in Figure 7.12. The first set of samples included sequences down through the 'matting' in Building 1, a sample from outside of the building, and a sample from Building 2. The second set were samples from just above the 'timber flooring' and were much smaller. They were examined to complement beetle work and to test the previous results.

The samples, apart from 130 discussed earlier, all show a similar assemblage, although the frequency of particular taxa varies from sample to sample. The samples from within the buildings contained well preserved vegetative remains which appeared to consist essentially of stem material predominantly of *Phragmites australis*, with *Bolboschoenus maritimus* present. The samples could be peeled apart and traces of blue–grey clay and, what appeared to be, 'dung' were visible. Sample 200, from outside the building, differed in appearance, with much more fragmented reed remains, resembling the deposit at the top of Pollen Monolith 1224, and was probably an organic deposit containing dung and trampled reed. The samples, therefore, contain material probably brought in by human and animal agencies and natural agencies, notably tidal, although fresh water flooding from inland of the site is also a possibility.

The vegetative remains within the samples comprised both longer stems, including seed heads, and much more fragmented material, the last as might be expected from trampling, or in dung. Of the seeds, large quantities of *Bolboschoenus maritimus, Juncus* spp and Poaceae occurred, with *Phragmites australis* and *Agrostis* sp (bents) particularly abundant in the Poaceae. Other species which were particularly frequent were *Aster tripolium* and *Plantago major.* *Atriplex* spp, *Lycopus europaeus, Triglochin maritima,* and *Schoenoplectus tabernaemontani* (grey club-rush) were also reasonably well represented. Basically, the seed assemblage suggests a *Bolboschoenus maritimus* community, but many of the species recorded could also be found in *Phragmites* reedswamp or fen communities or a water-margin community (cf Rodwell 1995), whilst others could represent other saltmarsh communities. *Lycopus europaeus* is essentially a freshwater species whereas *Atriplex, Aster, Spergularia, Salicornia,* and a number of other taxa could derive from other saltmarsh communities. It is perhaps worth noting that *Lycopus europaeus* seeds float very well and it is possible that they may have been washed in from a little way away, as may other taxa. The transport of seeds between different saltmarsh levels is well established (Bakker *et al* 1985), both from tidal dispersal and transport by cattle. Flotation experiments have also demonstrated differential dispersal of saltmarsh taxa, with some taxa remaining afloat for only a few hours, whilst others remained afloat for days or weeks (Koutstaal *et al* 1987). Although both *Plantago major* and *Juncus bufonius* occur in saltmarsh and other wet environments anyway, both these taxa occur in trampled contexts in dryland contexts and may have benefited from such activity in the area. The grasses recorded are of particular interest because they include species, although scarce, which produce Cerealia-type pollen. They include *Arrhenatherum elatius* (false oat-grass), *Elytrigia* spp (couches), and *Hordeum secalinum/H. marinum* (meadow/sea barley). However, part of a possible *Avena* (oat) caryopsis may indicate some cultivated cereal was brought onto the site (cultivated, as opposed to wild, oat can only be determined by the presence of chaff).

The plant remains suggest that a range of communities varying from brackish to fresh water, ie local saltmarsh, swamp, and fen communities, were being exploited and their presence is confirmed by the evidence from other sites in the area (see below). The evidence suggests that much of the reed had been collected from swamp communities, perhaps in the area of Trackways 1 to 1130, supplementing reed at the site itself. Present-day studies demonstrate that *Phragmites australis* can be found in fresh to brackish or tidal waters, being moderately tolerant of saline conditions (Rodwell 1995). It can grade into the *Bolboschoenus maritimus* community which appears to be more tolerant of wetter and more saline conditions. The *Bolboschoenus maritimus* community can occur at a variety of levels within saltmarshes and it is found at a number of sites around the British Isles (Chapman 1960, Gimingham 1964). Both communities can occur in or around the upper saltmarsh and sometimes in inverted zonations in estuaries (Rodwell 1995). *Bolboschoenus maritimus,* as well as *Phragmites*, is frequently recorded where there is some freshwater input (eg Birks 1973, Gimingham 1953 and 1964) and it grades into other swamp types on estuarine foreshores, and in sheltered sea-lochs in Western Scotland gives way sharply to *Alnus* woodland (Rodwell 1995, 210). In the Fal estuary, Cornwall (Ranwell 1974), *Bolboschoenus maritimus* is recorded throughout the saltmarsh to tidal woodland transition, occurring from 0.18m OD to 2.44m and above, OD (Newlyn). Other taxa represented at Goldcliff and the levels at which they occur in the Fal estuary include *Agrostis stolonifera* 1.08–2.69m OD, *Aster tripolium* 1.60–2.26m OD, *Juncus gerardi* 2.06–2.63m OD, *Lycopus europaeus* 2.76m OD and above, and *Hydrocotyle vulgaris* 2.77m OD and above. Both *Phragmites* and *Bolboschoenus* communities occur where there is grazing.

There is no doubt that the buildings were used by cattle, from the presence of cattle dung within the stem material, confirmed by the mite (Chapter 15) and beetle (Chapter 14) evidence. Cattle and sheep bone (Chapter 15) are also present. The good state of preservation of much of the stem material might at first appear surprising given the use of the building, but from observations of animal behaviour in the Moel-y-Gaer house at Butser Iron Age Farm, it can be accounted for by the fact that cattle and sheep spend a lot of their time just standing (Reynolds personal communication 1992 in Macphail and Goldberg 1995). Also, if the building was primarily used for cattle, as indicated by the beetle and mite evidence, then the stems are more likely to survive, whereas the sharper hooves of sheep would have resulted in more reworking and fragmentation (Bottema and Reynolds personal communication 1992 in Macphail and Goldberg 1995).

Given the evidence from the structures, it seems likely that their location relates to the exploitation of saltmarsh for grazing, a well-established use (Chapman 1960, Adam 1990). Grazing would have had some impact on the vegetation communities in three ways. It results in defoliation, trampling, and the deposition of dung and urine (Looijen and Bakker 1987). There have been a number of present day studies of the utilisation of saltmarsh environments, demonstrating that the timing of the maximum herbage accumulation, herbage utilisation, and terrain use varies considerably from community to community, eg cattle were found to spend a lot of time resting in an *Artemisia maritima* community but did not eat it (Looijen and Bakker 1987). It is possible that certain species/communities may have expanded at the expense of others in the Goldcliff area as a result of grazing, but such changes are difficult to identify with certainty in the palaeoenvironmental record. However, cattle grazing enhances species diversity, and trampling leads to bare soil, providing access for new species, especially lower saltmarsh species (Bakker 1985). Generally, there is an increase in species diversity in the pollen record from the estuarine deposits at Goldcliff. The relatively high counts of *Plantago coronopus* pollen have already been referred to and *Plantago coronopus* may increase as a result of grazing. Similarly, the *Juncus gerardi* community is known to expand where grazing occurs in saltmarshes (Bakker 1989, Adam 1990).

Some evidence for the season of use is provided by the plant remains from the reed matting. Seed heads of *Bolboschoenus maritimus* and *Juncus gerardii* were found amongst the material, and the large seeds of *Bolboschoenus* were clearly held tightly in place, sandwiched between stems and, therefore, contemporary with deposition of the material. Clapham *et al* (1987) give the time of flowering for *Bolboschoenus* as July and August and fruiting time August and September. Fitter (1987) gives the flowering period as June–August and the author has found *Bolboschoenus* already flowering at Borth Bog in late May 1998. *Juncus gerardii* also flowers around June–July. This would suggest the reeds were deposited and the buildings in use between July and August (assuming flowering and fruiting times are comparable with today). *Phragmites australis*, generally less well represented in the seed record from the samples, flowers in August–September, although other factors such as seed preservation are possibly involved.

Sample 200 from outside Building 1 differs from the samples within, primarily in containing noticeable amounts of *Calluna* remains, and the final pollen zone (GC1224.4b) also contains small quantities of *Calluna* pollen. It is possible some heather was brought onto the site deliberately, or transported naturally. As mentioned above, the sample contained much more fragmented material, as did the deposit at the top of Pollen Monolith 1224. Archaeological evidence suggests trampling around the building which would help to account for this. The sample is interpreted as representing a heavily trampled organic deposit containing reed and dung and subject to tidal inundation.

Similar assemblages have been recorded from Iron Age and Roman sites in The Netherlands, although the exact location and nature of the sites differ from Goldcliff. The late-Iron Age site of Rockanje 08-52 was located on raised bog similar to buildings and trackways at Goldcliff West (see below), but dung from the byre area of the house was strongly dominated by saltmarsh taxa (Brinkkemper 1991, 80). Reed stems were also abundant, although reedswamp species were rare. The native Roman settlement of Nieuwenhoorn 09-89 was also constructed on raised bog, but dung samples were dominated by *Bolboschoenus maritimus* (Brinkkemper 1991, 80–84). The samples are described as showing 'splendid horizontal layering', a feature shared with the reed matting samples from Goldcliff, and are considered to represent the deliberate spreading out of bundles, largely comprised of *Bolboschoenus maritimus*. It is suggested that the delicate layering would not have survived trampling and the lack of homogenisation and fragmentation may be explained by the rapid spreading out of the material but, as discussed above, it is feasible for stem material to be well preserved in byres, particularly if used by cattle. Above these samples are further dung samples which contain large quantities of *Juncus gerardii*, *Aster tripolium*, *Plantago major*, *Atriplex patula / prostrata*, *Lycopus europaeus,* and *Juncus bufonius*, similar to the assemblage at Goldcliff.

Building 3

At Building 3, 38m north of Building 2, a woody peat also developed following a period of clay deposition. However, the pollen column (Fig 7.16) from within the building suggests some variations in the composition of the local woodland. Low *Betula* values at the beginning of GC1719.5 (Fig 13.15, CD 13.14) indicate birch was either absent, or only a minor component of the vegetation, compared with the area of Buildings 1 and 2, whereas an increase in *Salix* pollen

suggests that willow was significant and was playing a colonising role. Continued high values for *Salix* also suggest that conditions were perhaps wetter at this site. However, *Alnus* reaching over 60% TLP demonstrates that alder was important locally. An increase in *Betula* pollen in the upper pollen levels is also represented in the pollen sievings by the appearance of birch seeds and bark in the stratigraphy and corresponds with the higher *Betula* values recorded at Buildings 1 and 2 (GC1232.4b, GC1224.3b). The decline in *Alnus* is also similar.

The pollen evidence from the final zone shows other similarities with the three diagrams from Buildings 1 and 2. As mentioned above, *Betula* values are slightly higher at the beginning of GC1719.6, and *Corylus avellana*-type and Poaceae values increase, as in GC1221.7, although Poaceae not to the same extent. However, there are differences, Cyperaceae values increase only slightly, *Plantago coronopus* is absent and pollen of Chenopodiaceae and *Aster* type only appears in the final level GC1719.6. Unlike the diagrams from Buildings 1 and 2, 1719 does not include any deposits which were identified in the field as possible 'occupation deposits'. The final level was quite clayey, indicating the site was subject to tidal influences, confirmed by the saltmarsh taxa, as in the final zones from Buildings 1 and 2. The survival of timber flooring in the building, and comparison with the records from Buildings 1 and 2, does, however, confirm the pollen record extends up to the use of the building. There is a decline in *Alnus*, *Betula*. and *Frangula*, between 40mm and 0mm. They are the species identified from the building itself (Chapter 12), so it could represent clearance to make the building, indeed cut wood was recorded on the peatshelf to the south (Chapter 7). *Calluna* values of >1% TLP suggest the presence of raised bog in the area, and the higher frequency of *Corylus avellana*-type may be attributable to an increase, or closer proximity, of bog myrtle rather than increase in hazel.

Double Post Row 970

At a distance of 5m east of Building 3 similar conditions are also recorded at Double Post Row 970 (Fig 10.6) where *Betula* is largely absent in pollen zone GC1717.3 (Figs 13.16, CD 13.19), which corresponds with the upper peat layer. *Alnus* percentages, although showing a distinct peak, are lower than at the previous site and Poaceae percentages are higher and, together with the stratigraphic evidence, it seems likely that locally the vegetation was reed with occasional trees of alder and willow, as is shown in the possible environmental reconstruction in drawing Figure 10.20E. As at Building 3, *Salix* is again well represented. The structure dated to 2190 ± 60 BP (CAR-1440) is considered to relate to this carr woodland phase (Chapter 10) from the presence of some horizontal wood stratified within the peat, although a thin layer of clay is recorded from beneath

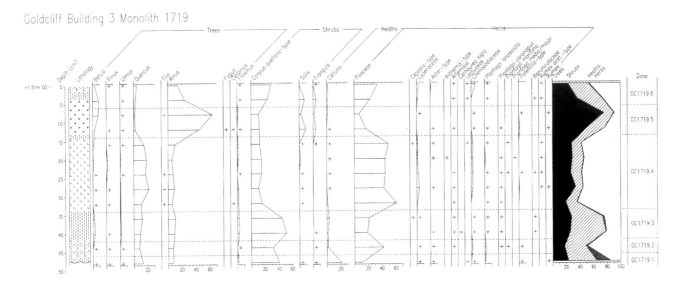

Figure 13.15 Percentage pollen diagram (selected taxa) from Monolith 1719 from Building 3

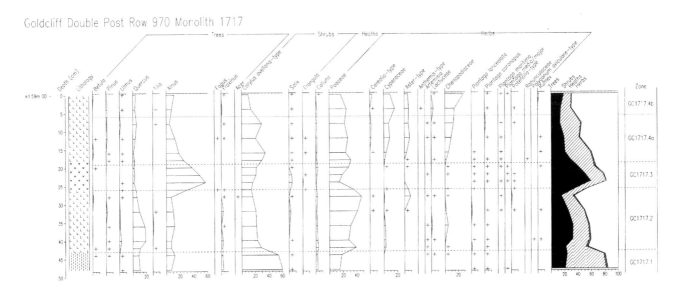

Figure 13.16 Percentage pollen diagram (selected taxa) from Monolith 1717 from Double Post Row 970

one piece. It is also suggested that the depressed peat between the verticals may have been compressed by planking, now lost, which would support the view it was a trackway, but other possible interpretations are noted in Chapter 10. The contorted appearance of the surface in Section 335, from which the pollen monolith was taken, is possibly attributed to compression by the structure itself. The wood assemblage from the structure is dominated by *Alnus* and *Quercus* and, to a lesser extent, *Acer campestre*, with small amounts of *Betula*, *Fraxinus,* and *Ulmus*, and *Corylus* and *Salix* represented by a single piece each. Again, this suggests both the utilisation of local woodland and wood brought from dryland communities. It is difficult to identify any abrupt changes in the pollen record which might definitely signify human interference with the local vegetation. *Alnus* shows a steady decline during GC1717.3 rather than

a sharp fall, but *Salix* and *Frangula* values do fall to <1% TLP. It is possible that the continued steady decline of *Alnus* at the beginning of GC1717.4a, coinciding with clay deposition, reflects some erosion and reworking, attributable to the disturbance noted above, and led to the smoothing of the pollen curve for *Alnus*, although other curves do not seem to be affected.

The decline in *Alnus*, moderately high Poaceae, increasing Cyperaceae and Chenopodiaceae, and stratigraphic change to clay indicate a return to estuarine conditions and brackish swamp and salt-marsh. The site is very close to Building 3 and the evidence from the final zone there (GC1719.6) is in agreement with the evidence from the end of GC1717.3 and beginning of GC1717.4, with an increase in Poaceae at the end of GC1717.3 and increase in *Corylus avellana*-type at the beginning of

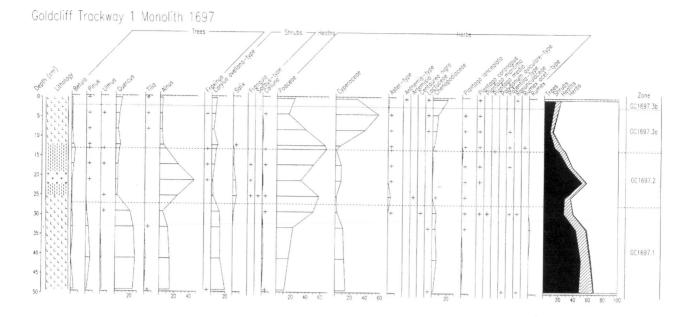

Figure 13.17 Percentage pollen diagram (selected taxa) from Monolith 1697 from Trackway 1

GC1717.4 and values of >1% TLP for Chenopodiaceae and *Aster* type. This is in accordance with a similar sequence of events at Buildings 1 and 2.

Between Double Post Row 970 and Trackway 1 lies Structure 1103, and the wood evidence from there, largely *Alnus* with a small amount of *Fraxinus* and *Salix, Acer, Quercus, Ulmus*, Pomoideae, *Betula,* and *Frangula*, when compared with the pollen records from the sites to the west, supports the view that wood was being used both from wetland and dryland environments.

Trackway 1

The trend towards a reduction in woodland and wetter conditions eastwards is also borne out by evidence from Trackway 1 (Fig 10.11), where the upper peat is largely *Phragmites* with some wood. In the field, the trackway was considered to be constructed at the junction between fen woodland and reedswamp (Chapter 10). *Alnus* values show a further reduction compared with those at Double Post Row 970, with a maximum *c* 45% TLP in GC1697.2 (Fig 13.17, CD 13.20). *Salix* representation is still relatively high. The dominance of reedswamp is reflected both in the high Poaceae values and stratigraphic record. Three macrofossil samples (Table CD 13.32) provide more detailed information about the environmental conditions prior to, contemporary with, and postdating the trackway. The trackway was recorded as consisting of brushwood, with the surface of the track directly overlain by blue clay in Trench 3, from which the samples were taken, although to the east there had been a little peat growth overlying track wood (Chapter 10).

The pollen record corresponding with the peat shows a clear succession, with a peak in *Salix* followed by a peak in *Alnus*. Poaceae values, which have been high, fall as *Alnus* peaks but then rise again. Peaks in *Sparganium* and *Typha* occur during mid-zone (see CD 13.20). The reduction in *Alnus* is accompanied by a slight increase in *Betula* in the latter half of the zone. The lowest macrofossil sample (180–230mm), from the peat below the trackway, corresponds with the earlier part of GC1697.2 and contains seeds of *Alnus, Betula, Solanum dulcamara, Carex, Sparganium,* and *Typha* and agrees with the pollen record for carr of alder, willow, and birch with reed, sedges, bulrushes, and bur-reed. The following sample (130–180mm), coincident with the brushwood of the trackway, contains a similar assemblage including seeds of *Alnus, Betula, Typha,* and *Sparganium* but in addition small amounts of *Atriplex, Plantago major,* and *Bolboschoenus maritimus*, suggesting a change towards brackish conditions. Given the wet environment it is possible the brushwood may have sunk slightly into the peat. The track surface seems to lie at the peat/clay interface in a *Phragmites* muddy peat, reflected in an abundance of Poaceae pollen. The upper macrofossil sample, including the surface of the trackway and the overlying clay, sees an increase in *Bolboschoenus maritimus* and *Atriplex* and the appearance of *Aster tripolium* and *Salicornia*, and coincides with the beginning of a massive increase in Cyperaceae pollen (reaching >50% TLP) and marked increase in Chenopodiaceae pollen, demonstrating the establishment of a *Bolboschoenus* swamp community, more tolerant of brackish conditions than *Phragmites*, and saltmarsh. Evidence for any activity associated with the track is difficult to identify given that that 'weedy' species could occur there naturally. However, the presence of *Urtica dioica* and *Plantago major* could perhaps be associated with such activity.

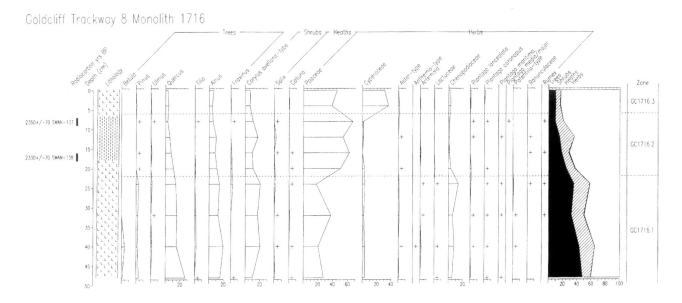

Figure 13.18   Percentage pollen diagram (selected taxa) from Monolith 1716 from Trackway 8

A small peak in *Plantago lanceolata* pollen at track level could also represent activity. The possible environmental conditions contemporary with the trackway suggested by the botanical evidence are represented in Figure 10.20A. The location and date of the track (2260 ± 60 BP (CAR-1349)), is consistent with the date for the top of the peat at Building 2. As previously, the wood of the structure indicates the use of local resources, ie *Alnus*, as does the evidence from Trackways 4, 5, and 6, with varying amounts of *Alnus, Betula, Salix,* and *Frangula* (Chapter 12).

Whilst the pollen assemblage from GC1697.3 indicates sedge swamp was more significant at Trackway 1 than at Double Post Row 970, Zone GC1717.4, the representation of *Corylus avellana*-type pollen and *Calluna* is much poorer, probably reflecting the slightly greater distance from raised bog and possibly bog myrtle communities which survived to the west. The trend towards wetter and more saline conditions accompanied by changing vegetation communities is confirmed by the evidence from two sites still further to the east and closer to the possible palaeochannel.

Trackway 8

At Trackway 8 (Fig 10.12) estuarine/marine conditions give way to a *Phragmites* peat but with no development to a wood peat. *Alnus* values during GC1716.2 (Fig 13.18, CD 13.21) are reduced to <10% TLP whilst Poaceae values are >50% TLP, demonstrating the presence of reedswamp. Although Chenopodiaceae values are less than in GC1716.1, they are consistently >1% TLP, suggesting the site is nearer to marine/estuarine conditions. The trackway itself clearly lies within the peat (Chapter 10) and was, therefore, constructed through a reedswamp community. Radiocarbon dates for the top and bottom of the peat are 2350 ± 70 BP (SWAN-137) and 2330 ± 70 BP (SWAN-138), respectively, and suggest the peat formed in a relatively short period of time before marine inundation occurred again. They also suggest that peat initiation occurred synchronously with that at Buildings 1 and 2 but that there peat development may have lasted longer and led to the formation of a wood peat. Alternatively, peat development could have lasted for the same period of time but not have developed to the same successional stage because of wetter conditions. Macrofossil evidence (Table CD 13.33 100–150mm) from around track level is in agreement with the pollen record and confirms the nature of the local environment of the trackway with seeds of *Phragmites, Typha* sp, *Hydrocotyle vulgaris, Lycopus europaeus,* and *Juncus* sp, all taxa typical of a *Phragmites australis* community. Wood for the structure must have been brought from nearby and it is all *Alnus* (Chapter 12). At this site *Betula* is absent from the pollen record during this period. The presence of *Betula* seeds is, as previously mentioned, probably largely attributable to the ability of birch seeds to be transported by the wind and suggests birch growing a little distance away, perhaps towards Buildings 1 and 2. Low amounts of *Salix* suggest the presence of willow locally and at Trackway 9, 22m to the south, almost equal amounts of *Salix* and *Alnus* wood were identified (Chapter 12). *Frangula* was also present but not recorded in the pollen record. The evidence from this site is in agreement with the beetle evidence from Trackways 4 and 6 (Chapter 14), which suggests they too were built in reedswamp.

A macrofossil sample (20–70mm) from the clay above the peat contained frequent seeds of *Bolboschoenus maritimus,* as well as several *Schoenoplectus tabernaemontani* seeds, which coincided with high Cyperaceae pollen counts, suggesting brackish swamp, as at Trackway 1. Other taxa, such as *Typha* and *Hydrocotyle vulgaris*, also indicate swamp and occasional seeds of *Atriplex* spp, *Spergularia,* and *Aster tripolium* suggest a saline influence.

Trackway 1130

At the final site, Trackway 1130 (Fig 10.14), examined for pollen in the main area, clay dominates the stratigraphy, interrupted by only a narrow band of *Phragmites* peat in which Poaceae pollen dominates (GC1745.2) (Fig 13.19, CD 13.22). The peat lies below the level of the trackway, dated to 2200 ± 50 BP (CAR-1504), which coincides with a band of laminated clay containing thin bands of peat with *Phragmites* rhizomes, reflected in Poaceae values of >50% TLP in GC1745.2. Chenopodiaceae values fall slightly from the previous zone, GC1745.1, but still attain values of *c* 5% TLP in the peat and peat/clay of GC1745.2, demonstrating saltmarsh nearby and a brackish influence. Cyperaceae values rise and suggest an increase in sedge communities. Plant macrofossils from beetle Sample 1751 (Table CD 13.33, sample location on Fig 10.14) taken from around track level are in agreement with the pollen evidence for brackish reed and sedge swamp and saltmarsh communities, with taxa such as *Phragmites australis, Bolboschoenus maritimus, Schoenoplectus taber-*

naemontani, Salicornia sp, and *Atriplex* spp represented. The beetle evidence also indicates reed-swamp subject to inundation by saline water (Chapter 14). The dating evidence suggests that this deposit correlates with the upper part of the peat band at Buildings 1 and 2 and dated at Building 2 to 2270 ± 70 BP (CAR-1351). At this site the track was constructed through reed/sedge swamp which was already subject to marine inundation. The local conditions suggested by the botanical and beetle evidence are illustrated in Figure 10.20D

Values for *Alnus* drop to <10% TLP during GC1745.2, whilst *Salix* declines from >2% TLP during GC1745.1. A small peak in *Betula* occurs in mid-zone. Whether these small fluctuations in arboreal taxa relate to trackway construction is difficult to say but wood identified from the trackway is mainly *Betula* with some *Alnus* and *Salix* (Chapter 12).

Above track level an increase in Chenopodiaceae and decline in Poaceae suggests an increase in saltmarsh locally and a stronger marine influence. *Plantago lanceolata* and *P. coronopus* increase at, or just above, the wood level and could be related to activity. The comparatively high counts of *P. coronopus* in dung samples from the buildings has already been noted (p 233), and the fact that *P. coronopus* may increase in saltmarsh communities as a result of grazing.

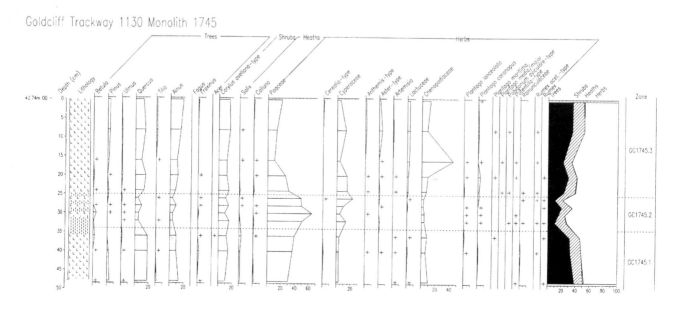

Figure 13.19 Percentage pollen diagram (selected taxa) from Monolith 1745 from Trackway 1130

Summary of vegetation changes along the upper peat shelf

The evidence suggests that peat initiation occurred more or less synchronously along the peat shelf, but that the ensuing vegetation succession varied from site to site, with the relationship between the location of the site and contemporary sea level playing a significant role. The basic succession from the underlying clay is marine conditions with saltmarsh, followed by reedswamp and, later, carr woodland with occasional marine inundation during a brief period of relative sea level fall. As sea levels started to rise again, reedswamp increased and fresh water conditions became increasingly brackish until ultimately saltmarsh developed. It was during the final stage of the carr woodland, the succeeding reedswamp, and early stages of saltmarsh development that there was such a concentration of human activity on the upper peat shelf east of Goldcliff Pill. Much of this activity was apparently related to the exploitation of saltmarsh for grazing. A possible reconstruction of the environmental conditions existing at this time and their spatial extent is shown in Figures 17.4e and 17.5.

The regional environment

The evidence suggests a largely open environment during the period c 2350–2100/2000 radiocarbon years BP. High tree pollen counts occur in zones associated with wood peats but are attributable to local carr woodland. Dryland tree taxa are poorly represented. *Quercus* values are considerably lower than in the previous estuarine phase and lower than in the peat phase preceding this, suggesting further woodland clearance. Values for tree pollens are marginally higher in the reed peats, reflecting the different depositional environment. *Ulmus*, *Tilia*, *Fagus* (beech), *Fraxinus*, *Carpinus* (hornbeam), and *Acer* occur sporadically, demonstrating their presence in the remaining woodland and most of these wood types are represented in the structures. The relatively frequent occurrence of *Plantago lanceolata* grains in the upper peat band indicates pastoralism on the dryland, but there is only limited evidence for cultivation.

In the overlying clay deposits an apparent increase in the frequency of dryland tree taxa occurs, but this may represent reworked material rather than a real increase in woodland. Herbaceous taxa, including *Plantago* spp, *Rumex*, Asteraceae, and Cerealia-type are much more frequent, and may reflect either the local saltmarsh communities or agricultural activity on the dryland.

13.5.6 Goldcliff West environmental changes

The local environment

Building 6
Whilst in the area of Buildings 1 and 2, marine inundation of raised bog had occurred by around 2500–2600 radiocarbon years BP, and reedswamp had replaced raised bog at Building 4, at Goldcliff West raised bog continued to persist. At Building 6, the top of a long pollen column (10104) was dated to c 2700 radiocarbon BP, demonstrating erosion of the peat, but evidence broadly contemporary with activity at the building is available from two monoliths (10127 and 10128). Monolith 10128 is from the peat deposits at the edge of the channel, whilst 10127 is from the channel itself (monolith locations on Fig 8.10). The ecological setting of Building 6 suggested by the pollen, as well as other lines of evidence, is illustrated in Figure 17.6.

Pollen Zone GC10128.1 (Fig 13.20, CD 13.17) essentially reflects a raised bog environment with only a hint of marine influence. The beginning of the zone is radiocarbon dated to 2260 ± 50 BP (GrN-24141). Overlying the peat of this zone, a band of clay demonstrates a marine incursion, and this is borne out by an increase in pollen of Poaceae and Chenopodiaceae in GC10128.2. *Phragmites* rhizomes indicate a brief development of reedswamp. A return to high *Calluna* and *Sphagnum* values, and the absence of Chenopodiaceae pollen, in GC10128.3a indicates raised bog, but a radiocarbon date of 2460 ± 35 BP (GrN-24140) suggests this is eroded material. Above this the deposit comprises a mixture of peat and clay and appears to represent *Sphagnum* peat which has become mixed with estuarine clay as a result of later inundation, confirmed by diatoms (Chapter 15), and trampling, indicated by cattle footprints in this area (Fig 8.13). The pollen assemblage comprises relatively high amounts of *Calluna* and *Sphagnum* as well as Chenopodiaceae reflecting this mix. It was within this mixed deposit that artefacts and animal bones were found (Chapter 8). A partially articulated cow skeleton lay at a level approximately equivalent to the top of the monolith. Marine inundation would ultimately have resulted in the cessation of raised bog growth.

The pollen record 10127 (Fig 13.21, CD 13.16) from the channel is strongly dominated by a saltmarsh assemblage which is consistent with the diatom record (Chapter 15). Detailed plant macrofossil evidence is also in close agreement, as is the beetle evidence (Chapter 14). Chenopodiaceae pollen is well represented throughout the diagram but with the strongest representation in GC10127.1a (Context 1319). *Atriplex* and *Salicornia* seeds are abundant (Table CD 13.30). These, and *Spergularia*, *Suaeda maritima*, *Aster tripolium*, *Triglochin maritima*, and others reflect a saltmarsh environment. In contrast, *Calluna*, *Erica*, *Eriophorum*, and *Sphagnum* indicate erosion of the adjacent raised bog surface and the occasional charred remain suggests earlier burning. Both erosion and burning are also indicated by the soil micromorphological evidence (Chapter 15). In the following sub-zone GC10127.1b, which is a clay with peaty bands (Context 1320), *Plantago* spp, notably *Plantago coronopus*, and in the latter half of the zone *Plantago maritima*, are more strongly represented, perhaps reflecting the creation of favourable habitats as a result of activity. Seeds of

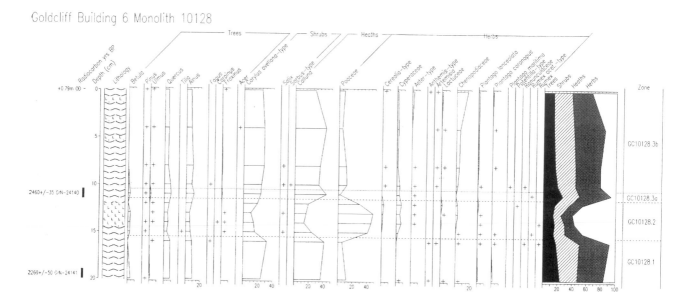

Figure 13.20 Percentage pollen diagram (selected taxa) from Monolith 10128 from the palaeochannel around Building 6, Goldcliff West

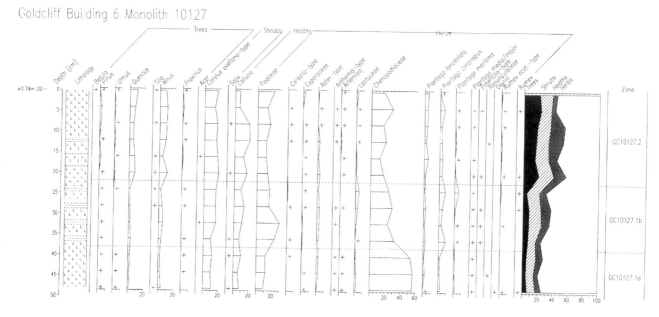

Figure 13.21 Percentage pollen diagram (selected taxa) from Monolith 10127 from the palaeochannel around Building 6, Goldcliff West

Plantago coronopus are present. Artefacts were concentrated in this context (Chapter 8) and it is considered to represent either contemporary activity or erosion of material shortly after occupation. The plant macrofossil assemblage is similar to that from the previous sample, but with an increase in ericaceous remains, reflecting the higher peat content of the sample. An increase in grass seeds corresponds with a peak in Poaceae pollen, and pollen and plant macrofossils of Chenopodiaceae are still frequent. Positive botanical evidence for human activity is slight, much stronger evidence provided by the beetles (Chapter 14), but one or two taxa may be imports. The presence of *Aphanes inexpecta* (slender parsley-

piert), which occurs in cultivated and bare ground may be attributable to human or animal activity.

In the second zone (GC10127.2), which is from the later fill (Context 1303), all the tree pollens, including *Pinus*, increase, and *Plantagos* are slightly less frequent. Pollen concentrations are lower and, with the increased presence of *Pinus* and higher arboreal counts, suggest a stronger marine influence, possible reworking and/or a larger regional pollen source and some possible woodland regeneration. Diatoms indicate a greater marine influence (Chapter 15). The plant macrofossil assemblages from this zone are similar to the previous assemblages, although in lower concentrations. Confirmation of the local presence of *Plantago maritima* is provided by one seed. The residues from beetle Sample 10100, which contained cattle lice and human fleas (Chapter 14) from this context, were also examined and provided a larger plant macrofossil assemblage, with most species better represented and some additional taxa. Again, the botanical evidence for activity at the site is less obvious than that from the beetle record, but some taxa might reflect enhancement of already existing habitats, eg bare ground/mud favouring certain taxa, or be imports such as eg *Potentilla anserina* and *Plantago major,* which are saltmarsh taxa, *Rubus fruticosus,* which could reflect either natural habitats or disturbance at the site, *Prunella vulgaris* (selfheal), which occurs in grassland or disturbed ground, *Linum catharticum* (fairy flax), which commonly occurs in calcareous grassland but can occur on moorland, and a *Triticum dicoccum/T. spelta* (emmer/spelt wheat) spikelet fork, indicating cultivation of wheat on the dryland and the transport of either crops or crop processing waste to the site. *Rumex acetosella/acetosa* pollen in GC10127.1b and GC10127.2 could also relate to sorrell/docks growing on site as a result of trampling and disturbance of the peat surface rather than activity on dryland.

The arboreal pollen records from 10128 and 10127 are low and reflect a largely regional picture. *Quercus* was the most frequently used species in making Building 6 and is relatively well represented in the pollen record, ie *c* 5% TLP during GC10128.2. Hazel is the second commonest wood used at the site and *Corylus avellana*-type pollen is *c* 25% TLP, but this includes *Myrica,* whereas the remaining taxa *Fraxinus, Acer, Ulmus, Salix/Populus,* and Pomoideae are generally present at <1% TLP. *Alnus* is not present at Building 6 but is present in the pollen record during GC10128.2 at *c* 5–10% TLP and is the most frequent wood recorded at Building 7. At Building 8, *Fraxinus* is the most frequent wood identified. The difference in wood types used in structures at Goldcliff West compared with the main Goldcliff area seems to reflect the lack of 'local' wood available in the Goldcliff West area and the greater reliance on dryland resources, although *Alnus* was used in the possibly earlier Building 7 (Fig 9.1).

Trackways 1330 and 1311

The remaining botanical evidence from Goldcliff West is from two beetle samples taken at track level (Table CD 13.30). Sample 10133 (location on Fig 8.14) was from Trackway 1330 which crossed the floor of the palaeochannel surrounding Building 7 and ran in the direction of Building 6. The sample contained *Sphagnum* moss, *Eriophorum,* and ericaceous stems and *Myrica,* reflecting a raised bog environment and, in addition, a range of saltmarsh taxa, including *Bolboschoenus maritimus, Aster tripolium, Salicornia* sp, *Spergularia* sp, *Glaux maritima* (sea milkwort), *Triglochin maritima, Atriplex* sp, *Ranunculus sceleratus, Juncus bufonius, Juncus gerardii, Sonchus asper* (prickly sow-thistle), and *Plantago major,* suggesting marine inundation. Small amounts of clay were noted adhering to the woody remains and it seems the trackway was subject

to marine inundation during, or immediately after, its life. Sample 10134 (location on Fig 10.19) from Trackway 1311, a brushwood track to the west of Building 6 running in the direction of Building 8, produced a similar plant assemblage to Sample 10133. It comprised largely *Sphagnum* moss leaves with a little *Calluna, Eriophorum,* and *Myrica,* reflecting raised bog, but saltmarsh taxa were also represented. Again, the evidence suggests the track was constructed when occasional inundation was occurring, or just before. The beetle evidence (Chapter 14) is in agreement with strong evidence for saltmarsh and brackish environments. A possible representation of the local landscape at this time is given in Figure 10.20B.

Summary of the local environmental conditions at Goldcliff West

The evidence suggests raised bog persisted at Goldcliff West at a time when the area of Buildings 1–3 was subject to a number of inundation episodes. The evidence from the trackway sites is particularly useful in determining the conditions around the main period of activity, as it is possible that the final natural peat deposits may have been eroded along with any 'flooring' at the buildings, although the presence of artefacts within the peat at the edge of the surrounding palaeochannels and the peat radiocarbon dates suggest this was limited. No distinct episode of reed development was evident in the top of the peat at Goldcliff West. However, the evidence suggests that by the time of occupation marine inundation was beginning to take place in this area as well, ultimately preventing any further growth of the raised bog, as such vegetation cannot tolerate saline conditions. The occurrence of *Myrica gale* remains confirms that part of the *Corylus avellana*-type pollen is *Myrica* and may indicate an expansion of bog myrtle as a result of drainage changes and drying out of the bog as gullies/palaeochannels developed during the transgression. A broad parallel to the evidence from Goldcliff West is that from the late-Iron Age site near Rockanje (08-52) in the Netherlands, where the subsoil comprised raised bog plants but, rather than the initial stages of occupation coinciding with this phase, as at Goldcliff West, the habitation is considered to coincide with saltmarsh (Brinkkemper 1991, 101).

The regional environment

As in the main Goldcliff area dryland tree taxa are poorly represented in the pollen record leading up to and broadly contemporary with occupation at Goldcliff West, suggesting a largely open environment. The increase in arboreal taxa in the second half of the pollen record from 10127 may represent an increase in woodland, but is more likely a reflection of the increased marine input. *Plantago lanceolata* does, in fact, increase at this time. This, and other, herbaceous taxa may reflect grazing either on dryland or in the saltmarsh. Cultivation on the dryland, perhaps on the island, is indicated by Cerealia-type pollen and confirmed by a *Triticum* spikelet fork.

13.6 Conclusions

The palaeobotanical records provide evidence both for environmental change in the 'local' wetlands and on the dryland, both the mainland to the north and Goldcliff Island. Sea level change and human impact, combined with autogenic, hydrological, and climatic factors, were major influences in the vegetational history and landscape development of the area. The changes to the landscape are considered again in the final chapter which includes summaries of landscape change through time in the form of maps and reconstruction drawings of the possible environmental conditions during the Iron Age. Within the wetlands, a relative fall in sea level between the later Mesolithic and Bronze Age gave rise to a vegetation succession from saltmarsh through reedswamp, carr woodland to raised bog (Fig 17.4a, b, c). During the Bronze Age, a relative increase in sea level resulted in inundation in the area of Goldcliff Island and the deposition of clays, whilst at Goldcliff West raised bog communities were maintained (Fig 17.4d). Another, but much briefer, episode of relative sea level fall during the late Bronze Age/early Iron Age, again gave rise to a succession from saltmarsh to reedswamp, which in some areas, eg Buildings 1 and 2, progressed to carr woodland, whereas in others eg Trackway 8 never developed beyond reedswamp (Figs 17.4e, 17.5). In contrast to the earlier period the succession did not proceed to raised bog. A renewed relative rise in sea level led to a retrogressive succession and a return to saltmarsh (Fig 17.3f). Superimposed on these changes in the wetland vegetation is the impact of human activity. The presence of charred plant macrofossil remains, notably in the raised bog peats, points possibly to deliberate manipulation and management of the environment. The main archaeological evidence is associated with the retrogressive succession from fen woodland, reedswamp to saltmarsh of the upper peat band. Confirmation that the decline in 'local' arboreal pollen recorded in the peats at this time is at least partially attributable to human interference is provided by the archaeological wooden structures. Evidence from Buildings 1 and 2 suggests the use of local reed as flooring/bedding for cattle. Although less easy to distinguish with any certainty in the palaeobotanical record, it is possible that grazing may have had some impact on the local vegetation, notably the saltmarsh.

The pollen record also provides evidence for the impact of human activity on the dryland in the region, with some evidence for activity on the 'local' Goldcliff Island, as opposed to the more distant mainland. Pollen evidence for environmental impact is slight during the Mesolithic period, although archaeological evidence clearly indicates activity and exploitation of the environment on and around Goldcliff Island. The nature of the environment, lowland woodland, makes any changes less easy to identify. A Neolithic clearance episode, lasting several hundred years, registers throughout the area, both on Goldcliff Island and the mainland, with some variation in the duration and nature of the agricultural activity recognisable. A period of regeneration occurs during the later Neolithic but this may relate to a change in agricultural practice rather than a diminution in human activity. Clear differences occur in the composition of the woodland in the region at this time with *Tilia* particularly important in the area of Vurlong Reen and Caldicot. Increasing activity occurs during the Bronze Age with at least two periods of renewed clearance activity and regeneration discernible. By the Iron Age, more extensive clearance had occurred. Although the strongest evidence is for pastoral farming, evidence for cereal cultivation in the area occurs from the Neolithic onwards.

14 Beetles as indicators of past environments and human activity at Goldcliff

by D N Smith, P Osborne, and J Barrett

14.1 Sampling, processing, and analysis

Introduction

Most of the contexts examined at Goldcliff contained the remains of a range of insects of which the majority were beetles (Coleoptera). These insect faunas have been studied in the hope that they can be informative on two aspects of the archaeology:

(i) to aid reconstruction of the past vegetation and environmental history of the peat shelf, and to put the various structures present into their specific environmental context;
(ii) to attempt to try to detect the nature of human activity in both the wider environment and around the archaeological buildings and structures themselves.

The work presented here is the result of the combined efforts over 6 years of three palaeoentomologists (Peter Osborne, David Smith, and Jayne Barrett). In terms of palaeoentomology, Goldcliff is one of the most extensively analysed sites in Wales, and probably in Britain outside of an urban settlement. It is certainly one of the most studied in terms of its insects for this period of prehistory.

Sampling

The size of the ancient landscape at Goldcliff, approximately 1200m along its broadest front, with all its buildings, structures and natural peats, presents the palaeoentomologist with a substantial problem in terms of sampling. When sites are sealed in deep peats, the most practical sampling strategy for insect remains is to sample regularly throughout the whole depth of the deposit and examine these samples as if they represented a geological sequence. This was clearly inappropriate to the situation at Goldcliff; with so many individual archaeological sites this strategy would produce more material than could possibly be examined.

Consequently, Goldcliff deposits were sampled as if they were an archaeological problem, rather than a geological one. The majority of samples collected were directly associated with archaeological contexts. In total five trackways and three buildings were sampled in this way. The exceptions to this are the two deep 'pollen pits' which were cut though the whole of the depth of the peat shelf. These are Pit 15 through the peat shelf above the Mesolithic site, and Trench 79 through the depth of the peat shelf under Building 6 at Goldcliff West. In both cases a continuous column of 100mm consecutive samples was collected (Figs 5.3 and 8.4).

On average, the samples were approximately 10kg in weight. The samples from Building 1, however, were very small. Collected during the 1991 excavation, they ranged between 1kg and 0.5kg.

Processing and identification

The work which forms the basis of this paper was carried out in three stages. The floor deposits recovered in the 1991 excavations were initially processed and identified by Peter Osborne at the Department of Earth Sciences, University of Birmingham. On his retirement the 1993 samples were passed to David Smith at the Department of Ancient History and Archaeology, University of Birmingham, and these were examined in 1994 with funding from Cadw. The three samples from Trackway 1108 were examined in late 1994 by Jayne Barrett as part of her undergraduate dissertation. Finally, in 1997 David Smith examined more of the floor material from Building 1.

In all cases, the samples were soaked in water overnight and then paraffin floated using the procedures first outlined by Coope and Osborne (1968) and expanded on in Kenward et al (1980). The insect remains were sorted from the flot using a low power microscope and the insect fragments, mainly beetles, were identified by using a number of entomological keys and by direct comparison with the Gorham Collection of British Coleoptera housed at the Department of Ancient History and Archaeology, University of Birmingham.

Analysis

In total, 413 different species of beetle have been identified from the deposits at Goldcliff. CD 14.1 presents the general species list for the site. The taxonomy follows that of Lucht (1987). Also included in this table is a 'sketch' ecology for each species and the specific hosts of the wood and plant feeding species. The full lists of the insects and weights and volumes of material processed from each of the samples examined are presented in five additional tables (CD 14.2–14.6).

In order to allow the data to be summarised visually, each species has been assigned an ecological code. These codes are given in the tables and CD 14.1. The scheme used is an amalgam of two such presently in use (Kenward 1978, Robinson 1981 and 1983). Although inelegant, it was, however, necessary since the insects from some of the contexts encountered are derived from both the natural environment and from materials associated with human occupation. The codings for those species from the natural environment are a variation of the codings proposed by Robinson (1981 and 1983). Those species from an aquatic environment are expressed as a percentage of the entire fauna, and the terrestrial elements of the fauna have been calculated as a percentage of the non-aquatic species present, following the procedure outlined by Robinson (1981 and 1983). The aquatic species have been further divided into two new categories: those associated with predominately acid waters (aw) and saline waters (sw). The scheme of coding provisionally proposed by Kenward (1978) for insects from human occupation deposits has also been used here, but follows the updated coding presented by Kenward and Hall (1995). In addition, the recent sets of codes proposed by Kenward (1997) indicating the degree of synanthropy (association with humans) of any particular species is also included here. CD 14.1 Column 2 also contains information on the relative rarity of the insects recovered from Goldcliff. This information, and the codes used, are derived from Hyman and Parsons (1992 and 1994). A key to all of the ecological codes used, in the analysis at Goldcliff, and an explanation of their meaning, is presented in CD 14.1. The proportions of these ecological groups are presented as tables and figures when each sampling location is discussed in the text below.

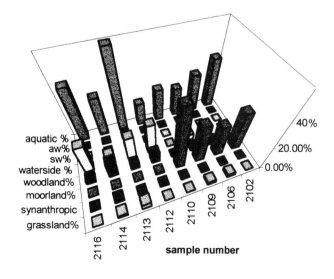

Figure 14.1 The main ecological groups of beetles in the sequence from Pit 15

14.2 The insect faunas from the peat shelves

Pit 15. The section through the peat shelf north of the Mesolithic site (Fig 5.3)

In total, sixteen samples were taken as a continuous column throughout the depth of the peat shelf at this location. Due to the obvious repetition of the faunas in the upper part of the sequence, only nine of the samples from this column were analysed. The species from these samples are listed in CD 14.2. The proportions of the ecological groups which are present in the samples (excluding Sample 2121, which included only one species) from this section are presented in Table 14.1 and illustrated in Figure 14.1.

1.60–1.40 m below the datum (Samples 2121 and 2116)

These two samples represent the lowest layers of this sequence, and they both contained the stems of water reeds. Sample 2121 lies just above the blue estuarine clay which underlies the peat. The sample only produced one insect fragment of no interpretative value. Sample 2116 produced a small fauna of insects, amongst them water beetles, which suggest the presence of a fresh water marsh. There are slight indications of the vegetation which may have grown in this locality. The chyrsomelid *Plateumaris braccata* feeds on *Phragmites* (Koch 1992). Similarly, *Phalacrus caricis* is a 'smut beetle' which feeds on mould growth, normally on species of sedge (Thompson 1958). Lastly, the small weevil *Tanysphyrus lemnae* feeds on duck weeds (*Lemna* spp) which float on the open surface of still waters. There is minimal evidence for the presence of surrounding woodland based on a single individual of *Scolytus rugulosus*. The scolytids are 'bark beetles' which feed under the bark of a range of trees. *S. rugulosus* is one of the least 'fussy' of the genus and feeds on a wide range of small trees and shrubs (Koch 1992).

1.30–1.00 m below the datum (Samples 2114, 2113, 2112)

This group of samples came from a section of the sequence where there were the abundant remains of tree limbs, much of it birch. The majority of the insects clearly indicate the presence of still, or even stagnant waters. In essence a continuation of the local environment seen above. Amongst the relatively large numbers of water beetles present in these faunas are *Hydroporus dorsalis, H. scalesianus* and *Hydraena testacea* which are commonly found in slow flowing and fresh waters (Friday 1988). Many other species, such the Hydrophilidae and the Helodidae, indicate decaying vegetation and leaf matter gathering at the water's edge in swamps.

Table 14.1 The main ecological groups present in the samples from Pit 15

Group (%)	2116	2114	2113	2112	2110	2109	2106	2102
Aquatic (a)	42.31	30.77	59.62	17.58	25.00	22.22	29.41	38.10
Acid water (aw)	0.00	0.00	1.92	0.00	0.00	0.00	0.00	0.00
Saline water (sw)	0.00	0.00	0.00	0.00	0.00	0.00	0.00	0.00
Waterside (ws)	23.33	8.89	19.05	24.26	0.00	4.76	5.56	0.00
Woodland (w)	3.33	13.33	4.76	8.82	0.00	2.38	2.78	0.00
Moorland (m)	0.00	0.00	0.00	0.74	50.00	30.95	25.00	30.77
Synanthropic (s)	0.00	2.20	0.00	0.73	0.00	0.00	0.00	0.00
Grassland (g)	0.00	2.22	4.76	0.00	0.00	2.38	2.78	0.00

The patterns seen in this table and figure are described in detail below.

Finds of *T. lemnae* suggest the presence of duckweed on the water's surface. However, in Sample 2113 there are two species of water beetle, which may indicate different water conditions. Both *Hydroporus melanarius* and *H. neglectus* are associated with peaty and leaf-filled pools, often in woodland (Friday 1988, Nilsson and Holmen 1995). *Hydroporus dorsalis* is apparently found in similar circumstances but is particularly associated with shaded waters (Balfour-Browne 1940, Friday 1988).

A similar pattern is shown by the terrestrial insects from these deposits. Amongst the ground beetles (Carabidae), the *Agonum* species, *Pterostichus vernalis*, and *P. minor* are all found at the edges of fresh water amongst stands of rich, emergent vegetation (Lindroth 1974). Several species of Pselaphidae, Scydmaenidae, and Orthoperidae probably share this habitat. The plant feeders from these deposits again suggest the presence of *Phragmites* vegetation. Sedges, however, may be the dominant species within the waterside vegetation, to judge from the relatively large numbers of individuals of sedge feeding species present, such as *Plateumaris sericerea*, *P. caricis*, and *Thryogenes*. One exception to this harmonious picture may be *Pterostichus diligens*. Although it is found in this type of environment, it is more common on boggy ground by acid pools (Lindroth 1974 and 1986). On the continent and in Scandinavia it is also found under alder and willow in wet woodland (Lindroth 1986).

The most distinctive aspect of the faunas recovered from this level is the clear rise in the number and range of species associated with woodland (see Table 14.1 and Fig 14.1). Many of the species present, such as *Melasis buprestiodes*, the various Anobidae, *Colydium elongatum*, and *Cercylon*, are associated with hard woods such as beech and oak, though they are occasionally taken from other tree species, especially birch (Koch 1992). Other species found appear to show a clear preference for birch, in particular *Bolitophagus reticulatus* and *Scolytus ratzburgi* (Hyman and Parsons 1992). *Hypophloeus unicolor* is also associated with beech and oak on dry land, but is also found in birch on raised bogs and heathland (Hymen and Parsons 1992). Lastly, the relatively large numbers of *Hylurgops paliatus* and *Rhyncolus clo-*

ropus (*Eremotes ater*) suggest the presence of pine in the area (Duffy 1953, Bullock 1992). Surprisingly, given the clear evidence for their presence in the pollen record from these layers (Chapter 13), there is no indication of either alder or willow from the insect faunas. Why this may be, and the difficulties in using this fauna to suggest the nature of the tree cover locally, are discussed below. Equally the implications of this fauna in terms of palaeoentomology and ecology are also discussed below.

1.00–0m below the datum (Samples 2110, 2109, 2106, 2102)

These samples cover the top metre of the section. They all contain a similar fauna. There is a sharp rise in the number of species with moorland habitats and a decline in those associated with woodland (Fig 14.1). Species which suggest the presence of moorland include *Plateumaris discolor*, which feeds on cotton grasses, and *Micrelus ericae*, which feeds on heathers (Koch 1992). The Carabidae *Bradycellus ruficollis* and *Agonum ericeti* are also normally found on sandy ground below heathers on moor and heathlands (Lindroth 1974). The presence of peaty pools is again suggested by the occurrence of *Hydroporus melanarius*.

The implications of these faunas

It would seem that during the period represented there is a succession from marine to reed swamp to carr woodland and through to raised bog. This appears to be one of the more common directions of the hydrosere succession in coastal and estuarine environments suggested by Walker (1970).

In essence, this is a similar succession to that seen in the pollen cores examined from Goldcliff East by Smith and Morgan (1989). However, there is no archaeoentomological evidence for the marine regression at 5000 BP seen in Smith and Morgan's palynological results here at Goldcliff West. Even if the 100mm sample which covered this period contained a mixture of marine deposits and fresh water

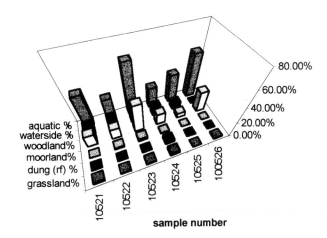

Figure 14.2 The ecological groupings of beetles from the submerged woodland above the Mesolithic site

peats, there should still be estuarine species present in the fauna. There also seems to be no conclusive evidence for a return of sedge beds and a redevelopment of carr after this transgression, as suggested by Smith and Morgan's results at Goldcliff East. However, it is possible, given the 100mm thickness of the samples taken, that the sedge peat may become mixed with the overlying wood peat. This is a result of a common problem with insect remains. The large samples required often mean that 'short lived' events such as this can be potentially lost below the 'resolution horizon'.

The drowned woodland on the peat shelf above the Mesolithic site

In order to increase our knowledge of the woodland taxa present at Goldcliff, a series of six bulk samples (10521, 10522, 10523, 10524, 10525, 10526) were taken from around a number of tree stools preserved in the exposed surface of the peat shelf (Fig 4.2) in the autumn of 1995. Unfortunately, due to marine erosion, no bark stripping or bore hole probing could be undertaken. The beetle taxa present are listed in CD 14.2. The proportions of the ecological groups in these faunas are presented in Table 14.2 and Figure 14.2.

When considering these faunas it is important to grasp that this work on the drowned forest above the Mesolithic site is merely the sampling of the wood horizons within the longer sequence of Pit 15. This explains why the woodland faunas examined below occur in larger proportions than they do in all but one of the samples from Pit 15.

In terms of the general environment, many of the aspects seen in the faunas from between 1.30m and 1.00m below datum in Pit 15 (see above) are repeated here. Again, there are several species which suggest the presence of fresh water pools and this pattern is also confirmed by a number of new species. Amongst these are *Hygrotus decoratus, Hydroporus palustris, Porhydrus lineatus* and *Acilius sulcatus*. Noticeably, the three *Hydrochus* species present are all associated with stagnant water. In terms of the vegetation within the bodies of water, *Tanysphyrus lemnae* suggests duckweed was present in some areas, *Donacia versicolorea* suggests broad leafed pond weed (*Potamogeton natans*) also occurred. The presence of stands of waterside vegetation is confirmed by many of the ground beetle species found in these deposits, particularly the two species of *Oodes*. Similarly, the species of *Donacia* and *Plateumaris* suggest the presence of a sedge bed.

However, it is the nature of the woodland fauna which is of interest to us here. These species are listed below in Table 14.3, along with the types of trees on which they are normally found (the individuals from between 1.30m and 1.00m below the datum in Pit 15 are also included in this table).

The Goldcliff forest fauna: its nature and comparison with other forest faunas

Eight of the woodland species from the forest fauna at Goldcliff are considered as rare or endangered at the present time (Hyman and Parsons 1992). However, their presence here is not surprising. The prominence of timber feeding taxa in the Red Data Books (Shirt 1987, Hyman and Parsons 1992) indicates that mature woodland has now become a declining feature in our modern landscape. Additionally, most of the woodland species at Goldcliff are associated with dead and decaying stumps and timbers. The 'tidy maintenance' of woodlands by modern foresters means that this important biotype of dead and decayed wood has certainly declined in

Table 14.2 The ecological groupings from the submerged woodland above the Mesolithic site

Group (%)	10521	10522	10523	10524	10525	100526
Aquatic (a)	41.82	28.17	63.23	26.32	35.71	54.20
Waterside (ws)	12.50	13.73	14.04	11.90	8.33	0.00
Woodland (w)	15.63	13.73	36.84	14.29	5.56	26.67
Moorland (m)	0.00	1.96	3.51	1.19	0.00	0.00
Dung (rf)	0.00	0.00	0.00	3.57	0.00	0.00
Grassland (g)	3.13	1.96	1.75	3.57	0.00	1.67

Table 14.3 The woodland associated beetles from the foreshore at Goldcliff
listed under the species of trees on which they are normally found

Tree species	Coleoptera	MNI	%
General woodland	Haplocnemus nigricornis Ampedus nigrinus Dalopius marginatus Cercylon spp. Spindus dubius Aspidiphorus orbiculatus Gyronobius planus Anobium punctatum Grammoptera ruficornis Phleoephagus lignarius	27	–
Quercus / Fagus (oak/beech)	Melasis buprestoides Colydium elongatum Xyletinus longitarsis Phloiotrya vaudoueri Prionyhus melanarius Hypophloeus unicolor Leptura scutellata Dryocoetes villosus Curculio vernosus Rhynchaenus avellanae	21	40.3
Pinus spp (pine)	Hylurgops plaiatus Rhyncolus lignarius	12	23.07
Salix (willow)	Dorytomus spp	4	7.6
Betula (birch)	Bolitophagus reticulatus Hypophloeus unicolor Scolytus ratzeburgi	8	15.3
Ulmus (elm)	Ptelebius vittatus	2	3.8
Fraxinus (ash)	Hylesinus oleoperda	2	3.8
Corylus (hazel)	Curclio nuncum	1	1.0
Tilia (lime)	–	0	0
Alnus (alder)	Agelastica alni Dryocoetes villosus	2	3.8

MNI is Minimum Number of Individuals.

presence, even within modern forests (Buckland and Dinnin 1993).

The Goldcliff woodland fauna differs from other woodland sites of similar or earlier dates in Britain. The most dramatic of these, the submerged pine and birch forest at Bronze Age Thorne Moors, South Yorkshire, has produced an insect fauna which contains eighteen species that are now extinct in Britain (Buckland 1979, Whitehouse personal communication). These are species, such as *Rhysodes sulcatus, Isorhiporus melasoides, Prostomis mandibularis,* and the three extinct species of *Eremotes.* Today they are found only in the isolated pockets of undisturbed primary woodland in Central Europe and are described as being *'urwaldrelikt'.* It is widely assumed that this type of woodland and its associated insects are relics of the time when undisturbed and continuous forest was present across Europe (Buckland 1979, Buckland and Dinnin 1993).

Evidence for dramatic flooding and burning at Thorne Moor wastes during the Bronze Age may mean that the site is something of an exception when compared with the contemporary forests in the lowland river valleys of Britain (Whitehouse 1997, Howard *et al* in press). However, a number of other sub-fossil faunas suggest that although the insect faunas of Bronze Age Thorne Moors may be exceptional, they do follow a general rule. The forest faunas from both the Neolithic and Bronze Age Stileway site in the Somerset Levels (Girling 1985), and Neolithic deposits at both Runnymede Bridge and Mingies Ditch, Oxfordshire (Robinson 1991 and 1993), all contained a range of woodland species, which today are either rare or extinct. Some of these are good candidates for *'urwaldrelikt'* species status. Amongst these species are the lime feeder *Ernoporus caucasicus,* and the alder feeder *Agelastica alni,* as well as *Ryncolus lignarius* and a range of scolytids. A similar pattern has been seen in a number of Neolithic faunas from around Leicester and Nottingham (Howard *et al* in press).

The poor comparison, however, between these lowland woodland faunas and the Goldcliff woodland fauna should not surprise us. The situation at Goldcliff is an exception. Here the landscape appears to have been scattered fen woodland set in a dynamic mosaic of shifting estuarine environments rather than continuous lowland forest. The 'broken' nature of the environments present at Goldcliff may be limiting the occurrence of many woodland species at this site. The fauna of the old forest, in particular the decaying wood element, is not able to disperse itself across unwooded and open environments (Buckland and Dinnin 1993). Equally, in prehistory this site would have been at least 6km from the nearest continuous woodland, apart from the small area on the island.

The comparison of the nature of the woodland suggested by the beetles and pollen at Goldcliff

If the host preferences for the woodland insect species at Goldcliff (Table 14.3) are taken at face value, it suggests that the local woodland was dominated by oak or beech, and included to a lesser degree some pine and birch. This reconstruction is in contrast to that suggested by the pollen from this sequence (Chapter 13) which suggests that locally the area was initially dominated by a thick willow and alder carr, in which later birch came to predominate. The pollen record from this section also records small amounts of the pollen of oak and ash throughout, probably derived from dry woodland on Goldcliff Island. The reconstruction of the woodland suggested by the pollen is also confirmed by the timber identification from the area of the foreshore above the Mesolithic site (Section 12.2 and Fig 4.2), although these results indicate that a limited number of oaks may have grown on the local bog surface itself.

Why is there an apparent contrast in the suggested reconstruction of the nature of this woodland between the insect results and those from the pollen and wood identification? There are two possible reasons:

(i) Both Girling (1985) and Robinson (1993), who investigated deposits in the Somerset Levels and in the Thames Valley, found that alder is often underrepresented in fossil insect faunas. Both suggested that this is because a comparatively low number of species feed on alder. For example, Bullock (1992) suggests that the 93 species which feed on oak outnumber the potential twelve which feed on alder. It is probably the contrasting numbers of feeders which is responsible for different pollen and insect results at Goldcliff. It is likely that the insect fauna developing in a few bog oaks is overshadowing that from the alder, even though alder carr is the predominant tree cover in the area initially;

(ii) It would seem possible that the majority of those insect species which suggest the presence of pine, elm, ash, and hazel, are actually derived not from the locally adjacent fen woodland but rather from the dryland slopes on Goldcliff Island, or perhaps from further afield. The presence of these species, the majority with flight potential, is actually not very surprising given that at this sampling location the bed rock of the prehistoric island of Goldcliff is within 10–30m.

The subsequent disappearance of this aspect of the insect fauna at Goldcliff is explained by the pollen analysis at this sampling site (Chapter 13). It is evident that, during the development of the raised bog that followed this carr phase, woodland clearance occurred on Goldcliff Island.

Trench 79: The section through the peat shelf below Building 6 at Goldcliff West

In total fourteen samples were taken as a continuous column through this depth of peat (location on Fig 8.4). It was clear in assessment that there would be a replication of results, so only a limited number of samples were fully examined. The upper two samples from this column were given particular attention since they lay directly under Building 6. A table of species recovered is presented in CD 14.3. The proportions of the main ecological groups for these samples are presented in Table 14.4 and Figure 14.3.

0.55–0.14m below OD (Samples 10124 and 10121)

Although these deposits produced relatively small faunas, they contain many of the same species found in the bottom of Pit 15 which indicate the presence of reeds and sedges growing in a fresh water swamp. There is some indication, however, of more acidic conditions in Sample 10121, with the presence of five individuals of *Hydroporus melanarius*, a species which favours more acidic water.

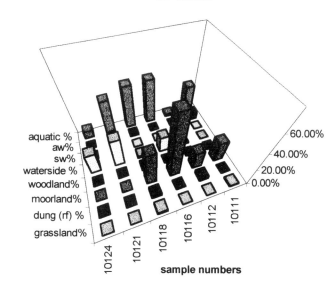

Figure 14.3 The ecological groupings of beetles from Trench 79

Table 14.4 The ecological groupings from Trench 79

Group (%)	10124	10121	10118	10116	10112	10111
Aquatic (a)	8.33	36.59	45.95	46.51	2.33	29.25
Acid water (aw)	0.00	4.88	1.35	0.00	0.00	7.55
Saline water (sw)	0.00	1.22	0.00	0.00	1.16	0.00
Waterside (ws)	22.73	30.77	2.50	17.39	1.19	0.00
Woodland (w)	0.00	0.00	2.50	0.00	0.00	0.00
Moorland (m)	0.00	0.00	37.50	69.57	19.05	22.67
Dung (rf)	0.00	0.00	2.50	0.00	3.57	0.00
Grassland (g)	0.00	0.00	2.50	0.00	0.00	1.33

It is clear from this table and figure that there are a number of patterns discernible.

0.06m below the datum to 0.85m above (Samples 10118, 10116, 10112, 10111)

The remaining samples from this section clearly suggest that the fresh water swamp had become a raised bog by this stage. Many of the indicators for the presence of acidic moorland conditions and vegetation which were seen in the upper samples from Pit 15 are also here. Two notable additions to this raised bog fauna are *Chilocorus bipustulatus* and *Haltica* cf *ericeti* which are both found on heather, though the former is sometimes also taken from pine.

A few species suggest the presence of salt marshes in the vicinity. However, these individuals are present only in small numbers and are known to be very active fliers. This may suggest that these salt marshes were some distance away. Amongst these are *Octhebius marinus*, which, as its name suggests, is normally found in shallow saline pools (Hansen 1987). *Hydrovatus clypealis* and *Bembidion varium* are also a common inhabitant of salt marshes (Lindroth 1974). *Tachys parvulus*, although not limited to salt marshes, appears also to have a coastal distribution (Lindroth 1974).

There are no indications of the presence of tree cover in the area, (except possibly for *C. bipustulatus*). There is also little sign of human impact on this environment, aside from the presence of a small number of *Aphodius* 'dung' beetles. It is possible that these may indicate the use of this raised bog for grazing, but the ability of these dung beetles to fly across large areas may mean that the grazing land could be much further afield.

Implications of these faunas

As was seen in Pit 15, it would seem that a fresh water marsh quickly gave way to a raised bog in this area of the Gwent Levels. However, unlike the pattern seen in Pit 15, there is no obvious intervening period where a wet carr woodland developed.

There is a stark contrast between the faunas in the top two samples (10112, 10111) from this section and those from the fills of the palaeochannels which surround Building 6 (Trench 17, 73, 75 described below). There are none of the saltmarsh or synanthropic species which dominate in the palaeochannels. This suggests that there is a clear break in both time and environment between the top two samples and the deposits of estuarine clay which overlay them. This supports the idea of erosion of the bog surface between the time of the use of the buildings and their subsequent burial below estuarine clay.

14.3 The insects from the trackways at Goldcliff

Nineteen trackways lie on the surface of the peat shelf at Goldcliff. The results presented here are from trackways which were dated, and where sampled material seemed to be contemporary with the trackways and would help reconstruct the environment that they crossed.

Trackway 4 and Trackway 6

In total, five samples associated with two brushwood timber trackways were examined (Samples 1746, 1748, and 1754 from, respectively, above, at, and below the level of Trackway 4, and Samples 1756, 1757 from, respectively, at and below the level of Trackway 6). These trackways were part of a group of eight which crossed the same 50m area of the eroding western peat shelf (Fig 10.8). They were constructed from roundwood and brushwood bundles laid along the axis of the trackway and held in place with wood pegs. The list of species recovered from these deposits is presented in CD 14.4. The proportions of the ecological groups recovered is presented in Table 14.5 and Figure 14.4.

The two trackways studied here are considered together since they produced similar faunas. The majority of the species present clearly suggest that these trackways were laid across an area of dense *Phragmites* swamp in a body of reasonably fresh water. The large numbers of carabid species found in

252

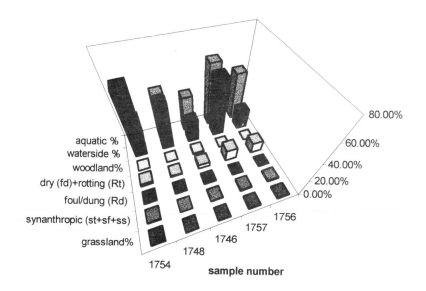

Figure 14.4 The proportions of the ecological groups of beetles from Trackways 4 and 6

Table 14.5 The proportions of the ecological groups from Trackway 4 and 6

Trackway number Group (%)	4 1754	4 1748	4 1746	6 1757	6 1756
Aquatic (a)	24.56	44.29	35.45	60.67	46.72
Waterside (ws)	66.28	46.15	22.32	57.63	19.18
Woodland (w)	0.00	0.00	1.34	0.00	0.00
Dry rotting (fd + rt)	2.91	1.28	4.46	11.86	10.96
Foul/dung (rd)	0.58	0.00	0.45	0.00	0.00
Synanthropic (st + sf + ss)	1.74	0.00	0.45	1.69	1.37
Grassland (g)	1.74	0.00	0.00	1.69	1.37

these samples are common in dense stands of tall reeds and sedges. Particular to this environment are *Elaphrus uliginosus, Bembidion semipunctatum,* and *Oodes gracilis* (Lindroth 1985). Many of the carabids present, such as *Agonum thoreyi, Odacantha melanura* and *Dromius longiceps,* are often found in thick rafts of dead water reeds, as are occasionally *Leistus rufescens* and *Agonum fuliginosum.*

The water beetles are all from non-acid waters, often with dense stands of emergent waterside vegetation. Many of the species present favour stagnant 'brown' waters full of dead and decaying vegetable matter. Examples of these are *Hygrotus inaequalis, Hydroporus memnonius* and *H. scalesianus, Porhydrus lineatus, Coelestoma orbiculare,* and *Ochthebius bicolon* (Balfour-Browne 1940, Hansen 1987, Harde 1984, Friday 1988). *Agabus bipustulatus* prefers less stagnant, slow flowing, fresh waters (Hansen 1987, Harde 1984). Other species suggest some areas of open and deeper water, eg *Colymbetes fuscus* and the *Gyrinus* (Whirligig) species (Girling 1982).

However, it is the large numbers of *Plateumaris braccata* which very precisely suggests the nature of the surrounding environment (this species accounts

for the obvious dominance of the 'waterside' ecological grouping in Table 14.5 and Fig 14.4). *P. braccata* only feeds on *Phragmites communis,* the common reed (Koch 1992). *Silis ruficollis* is also commonly found on *P. communis. Carex* and *Scirpus* sedges are also indicated by the presence of the *Notaris* and *Limnobaris* weevils. There are suggestions of woodland in the area, probably at some distance. Both the *Polydrusus* and *Curculio* species are associated with trees, oak in the case of the latter (Koch 1992). Similarly, there may have been rough grassland or disturbed ground in the area, again perhaps at some distance. The larvae of *Strophosoma melanogrammum* feed mainly on docks, *Hypera plataginis* on vetches, and *Sitona flavescens* on *Trifolium* clovers (Koch 1992).

The implications of these faunas

It is clear that these trackways were crossing an area of dense fresh water reed marsh. The absence of wood-boring species in these trackways at Goldcliff may be of significance. Robinson (1992) has suggested that timber structures that are quickly waterlogged after their construction fail to develop

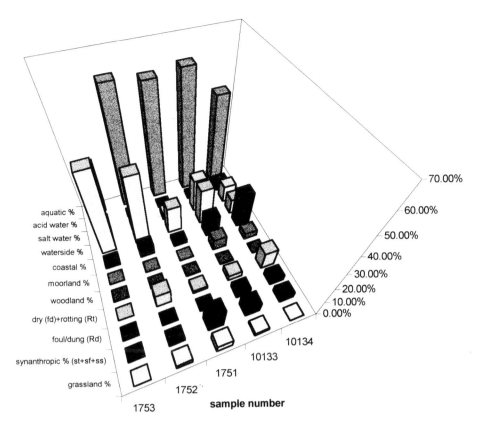

Figure 14.5   The proportions of the main ecological groups of beetles from Trackways 1130, 1330, and 1311

Table 14.6   The proportions of the main ecological groups from Trackways 1130, 1330, 1311

Sample number Trackway number Group (%)	1753 1130	1752 1130	1751 1130	10133 1330	10134 1311
Aquatic (a)	26.87	60.82	58.60	60.49	46.30
Acid water (aw)	0.00	0.00	0.00	1.23	4.63
Salt water (sw)	7.46	3.01	3.82	18.52	9.26
Waterside (ws)	46.94	39.16	15.38	20.31	8.62
Coastal (c)	2.04	5.59	1.54	10.94	18.97
Moorland (m)	0.00	0.00	0.00	6.25	3.45
Woodland (w)	0.00	0.00	0.00	0.00	0.00
Dry (fd) + rotting (rt)	0.00	8.39	1.54	3.13	10.34
Foul/dung (rd)	0.00	0.00	0.00	3.13	3.45
Synanthropic (st + sf + ss)	0.00	1.40	12.31	6.25	3.45
Grassland (g)	0.00	2.80	4.62	1.56	0.00

the expected populations of wood borers such as the 'woodworm beetle' *Anobium punctatum*. It would seem that these trackways, therefore, worked their way beneath the water surface, either with use, or as the result of a sudden change in water level. This appears to have been the case with many of the Somerset Levels trackways, where wood borers were typically absent, except in cases where infestation had clearly occurred before the timber was laid (Girling 1980). This may be why there is such a concentration of trackways at this point on the peat shelf, as one sank beneath the surface another was

built to replace it, as indeed some differences in the stratification of the trackways suggest (Chapter 10).

Trackway 1130

Trackway 1130 (Samples 1753,1752,1751) ran in a north–south direction, and was 145m to the east of the Trackways 4 and 6 mentioned above (Fig 10.14). The trackway was 1m wide and of a corduroy construction. The samples examined formed a continuous column. Sample 1753 came from a marine clay which was the basal deposit in the section through the trackway; Sample 1752 was from a peat just underlying the trackway and Sample 1751 comes from the level of the trackway (Fig 10.14). The species lists for this trackway is presented in CD 14.4. The proportions of the ecological groups found are presented in Table 14.6 and Figure 14.5.

The faunas recovered are somewhat different in their nature to those from Trackways 4 and 6 discussed above. Some aspects are, however, familiar. Some of the water beetles present are associated with still water in reed marshes. Amongst these are *Hygrotus inaequalis, Noterus calvicornis, Acilis sulcatus, Octhebius minimus,* and *O. bicolon.* There is also evidence for the presence of *Phragmites* water reeds throughout with *Plateumaris braccata* and phalacrids present. It is, however, noticeable that *P. braccata* occurs in considerably larger numbers in Sample 1752 which was from the underlying *Phragmites* peat just below the trackway. This appears to tie in with reed bed growth suggested by the plant macrofossil and pollen analysis from this section (Chapter 13).

A number of the insects present suggest that there was marine influence before, during, and after the construction of this trackway. This is shown by the relatively high proportions of species which are associated with salt water and coastal conditions in all of these samples (Table 14.6 and Fig 14.5). Amongst the former are *Ochthebius dilatatus* and *O. viridis,* both species which are commonly found in salt water pools of varying levels of salinity (Hansen 1987). Amongst the latter are the ground beetle *Bembidion varium* which is often found on exposed clay in amongst patchy areas of sedges and grasses, mostly in salt marshes (Lindroth 1985), as is *Brachygluta* cf *helferi* (Pearce 1957). This estuarine aspect of the fauna remains constant throughout the depth of the section, suggesting that some degree of salinity was maintained even during the period of maximum reed peat development.

Trackway 1330

This trackway lay to the north of Building 7 (Fig 8.14) and appears to have been a brushwood construction crossing the palaeochannel. Only Sample 10133 was examined for insects. The species lists are presented in CD 14.4. The proportions of the ecological groups found are presented in Table 14.6 and Figure 14.5.

The estuarine environment is even more pronounced in this sample than in the faunas from Trackway 1130. There is an increasing dominance of species associated with salt marsh and brackish water. These include *Ochthebius marinus,* the two *Ochthebius* species already mentioned, the dytsicid *Hydroporus tessellatus* and also the mud burrowing *Heterocerus fossor* and *H. maritimus* (Friday 1988, Hansen 1987, Clarke 1973). Also present is a range of species that are found on clay in salt marshes. These are species such as the carabids *Bembidion*

assimile and *Bembidion minutum,* and *Pogonus chalceus,* and the staphylinids *Bledius capito* and *Bledius occidentalis.*

There are several insects from another ecological group present. *Bradycellus ruficollis* and *Micrelus ericae* are both species associated with heather and moorland. Their presence here suggests that the establishment of this trackway occurred during the time of transition between raised bog and fully estuarine conditions. This would suggest that the saline tolerant species of insect discussed above were deposited during periodic salt water inundation at times of high tide.

Also present are a few individuals which are either 'culture favoured' or synanthropic in origin, eg *Typhaea stercorea,* the Lathridiidae, and the Cryptophagidae. The presence of these species most likely reflects the close proximity of Building 7.

Trackway 1311

This is a discontinuous brushwood track (Fig 10.19) which runs to the west of Building 6 in the direction of Building 8 (Sample 10134). The species list for this trackway is presented in CD 14.4. The proportions of the ecological groups found are presented in Table 14.6 and Figure 14.5. The insect faunas bear a strong resemblance to those from Trackway 1330. This suggests that this trackway ran though the same, or a very similar environment to 1330.

Trackway 1108

This structure was first seen as a linear post alignment which was traced for 100m south of Building 4 (Fig 7.2). A series of posts was driven diagonally from either side of the structure and then brushwood had been laid in the V between the opposed diagonal posts. This feature has been interpreted as a trackway. Unlike many of the trackways of prehistoric Europe, it has the distinction of leading to a specific structure, Building 4.

In total, three samples from layers associated with this structure were examined (Fig 10.3). Sample 1732 was from a wood peat which underlay the trackway. Sample 1730 was from a layer of peat intermixed with estuarine clays from just below the brushwood which formed the track surface. Sample 1731 was from the reeds which covered the brushwood itself. The faunas recovered are presented in CD 14.4. The proportions of the ecological groups present are presented in Table 14.7 and Figure 14.6.

The majority of the species present are very similar to those seen above from Trackways 1130, 1330 and 1311. They indicate that this area of Goldcliff was near a salt marsh at the time of the deposition of this material and, again, that construction may have occurred during the transition between peat growth and the establishment of fully estuarine conditions as inundation occurred.

**Table 14.7 The ecological groupings
from Trackway 1108**

Group (%)	732	1730	1731
Aquatic (a)	26.67	44.72	29.52
Salt water (sw)	1.67	14.07	9.52
Waterside (ws)	9.09	14.55	5.41
Coastal (c)	6.82	5.45	9.46
Woodland (w)	0.00	1.82	2.70
Rotting general (rt)	15.91	20.00	9.46
Rooting dry (rd)	0.00	6.36	16.22
Foul/dung (rd)	0.00	2.73	2.70
Synanthropic (st)	0.00	4.55	5.41
Synanthropic (sf)	0.00	1.82	5.41
Synanthropic (ss)	2.27	3.64	10.81
Grassland (g)	0.00	0.91	1.35

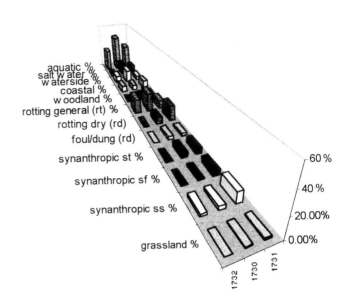

*Figure 14.6 The ecological groupings of beetles
from the Trackway 1108*

One aspect of these faunas is surprising. A number of species are present which are strongly associated with human habitation. In particular *Typhaea stercorea*, *Aglenus brunneus,* and *Anobium punctatum* are all present. It would seem unlikely that these species would be able to live and breed in material lying in the open, let alone on an exposed salt marsh. Perhaps their presence is related to the buildings to the north and east of that trackway. Material containing this fauna may have been washed from these buildings, either whilst they were in use, or when they subsequently collapsed. In essence, the deposit around the base of this structure may represent tidal material. This could also be the explanation for the presence of a number of species which are not common inhabitants of salt marsh. These include the dytsicids *Hydroprus scalesianus* and *H. palustris,* which normally occur in fresh or fen waters. This may also include the various species of phytophage such as the *Apion* and *Kateretes*, which are typical inhabitants of grassland rather than foreshore. Many of these, and others like them, are often encountered as accidental in shore or river drift.

There also are, however, a number of other possible explanations for the presence of this synanthropic fauna at this location. It may be that there is an as yet undetected structure in the near vicinity. Another, more speculative, explanation for the presence of these species may be that they represent material which was dropped whilst being carried to or from Building 4 along the trackway. If so, this may not only indicate the type and condition of material present in Building 4, but the actual route that it took to get there.

Comments on the trackway faunas

It is clear that Trackways 1108, 1130, 1330, and 1311 came under some degree of marine influence just before, during, or just after, construction. It is possible that these salt marsh and saline tolerant species of insect are deposited during times of periodic high tide. They certainly indicate that these trackways were built during the transition between raised bog and fen development and the re-establishment of fully estuarine conditions at Goldcliff. It is also clear, from the persistent occurrence of the synanthropic species, that these structures are probably associated with the activities occurring within the buildings themselves.

14.4 The insects from the Iron Age buildings

The interior of Building 1

During 1990 and 1991 the material covering the round wood flooring of Building 1 was sampled. In total, thirteen samples from this floor have been analysed for their insect faunas (Samples 1003, 1004a, 1004b, 143, 99, 153, 130, 17, 1176, 1195, 1173, 1183, and 1186, location on Figure 7.12). Several of these appear to have lain directly above the timbers (1003, 130, 17, 1176, 1186, 1195). The remaining samples (143, 99, 153, and 130) formed a continuous sequence through the material overlying the floor, and Samples 1173 and 1183 formed a short sequence from between two of the floor timbers.

These samples were studied on two occasions. Peter Osborne examined Samples 1003, 1004a, and 1004b in 1991 just before his retirement (these three samples formed the basis of the study described in Smith *et al* 1997). Additional samples were analysed by Smith in 1997. Although these samples were comparatively small (often only 1–2 kg), they produced relatively large insect faunas. This itself suggests that large insect populations developed and

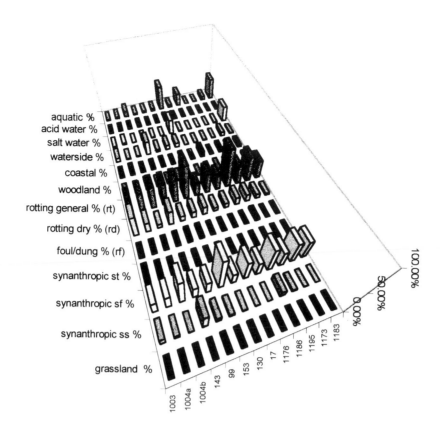

Figure 14.7 The ecological groupings of beetles from the interior of Building 1

Table 14.8 The ecological groupings from the interior of Building 1

Group (%)	1003	1004a	1004b	143	99	153	130	17	1176	1186	1195	1173	1183
Aquatic (a)	1.33	2.56	9.09	1.71	2.86	3.41	36.73	3.49	18.75	0.00	0.00	5.41	31.37
Acid water (aw)	0.00	0.00	0.00	0.57	0.00	0.00	1.02	0.00	0.00	0.00	0.00	0.00	0.00
Salt water (sw)	1.00	2.56	0.00	1.14	1.43	0.00	6.12	1.16	0.00	0.00	0.00	1.35	5.88
Waterside (ws)	5.98	1.02	1.52	21.32	4.06	7.11	6.60	0.51	0.51	1.02	1.02	5.58	1.52
Coastal (c)	1.01	2.63	0.00	0.58	1.47	0.00	1.61	0.00	7.69	0.00	2.94	1.43	2.86
Woodland (w)	0.34	0.00	3.33	0.58	0.00	2.35	0.00	0.00	0.00	1.72	0.00	0.00	2.86
Rotting general (rt)	25.93	31.58	36.67	36.63	36.76	55.29	19.35	31.33	23.08	62.07	29.41	40.00	28.57
Rotting dry (rd)	33.67	15.79	6.67	24.42	8.82	10.59	12.90	6.02	7.69	12.07	11.76	7.14	2.86
Foul/dung (rf)	0.67	0.00	0.00	1.16	2.94	2.35	0.00	0.00	0.00	0.00	2.94	0.00	0.00
Synanthropic (st)	7.74	5.26	3.33	1.74	2.94	0.00	0.00	0.00	0.00	0.00	0.00	0.00	0.00
Synanthropic (sf)	21.21	23.68	46.67	20.35	22.06	58.82	19.35	34.94	23.08	41.38	26.47	35.71	31.43
Synanthropic (ss)	12.79	5.26	0.00	27.33	8.82	3.53	1.61	0.00	0.00	10.34	2.94	0.00	0.00
Grassland (g)	0.34	0.00	0.00	0.00	1.47	1.18	1.61	0.00	0.00	0.00	0.00	0.00	0.00

that this material must have been biologically very active. The insect fauna is displayed in CD 14.5. The proportions of the ecological groups present are presented in Table 14.8 and Figure 14.7.

The additional samples from Building 1 studied in 1997 confirm many of the conclusions drawn in Smith *et al* (1997). Again, the majority of the insects recovered from this material are clearly associated with decaying organic matter, clearly demonstrated by the relatively high proportions of ecological groups rt, rd, rf in Table 14.8 and Figure 14.7. The majority are inhabitants of either dry 'hay-like' material or

mildly mouldering plant matter. Amongst these species are *Xylodromus concinnus*, *Typhaea stercorea*, the Cryptophagids, the Lathridiids, and *Ptinus fur*. Other species such as the Histeridae are present, some hydrophilids (eg *Cercyon haemorrhoidalis and C. annalis)*, and several species of the staphylinids (eg *Oxyetylus scultptus*, the *Lithocarius, Leptracinus*, and *Neobisnus*) all of which are thought to be associated with decayed and wet organic material. The contribution of these latter species to the nature of the overall insect fauna is reflected in the relatively high proportions of the general rotting ecological group (rt) (Table 14.8 and Figure 14.7). This picture of a squalid interior is even stronger if the *Trogophloeus* species are considered as part of this community (Kenward in Hall *et al* 1983, Kenward and Hall 1982, Kenward and Hall 1995, Smith *et al* 1997), rather than species from the external environment.

Also clear from Table 14.8 and Figure 14.7 are the relatively large numbers of synanthropic species which are present in this material. The most noticeable are *Aglenus brunneus*, *Typhaea stercorea,* and *Ptinus fur,* which Kenward (1997) holds to be strongly synanthropic. The presence of this community of human dependent, or at least 'culture favoured', species clearly suggests that this material had a human origin, rather than, a natural origin, for example as part of any subsequent reed bed that developed after the abandonment of the site.

In addition to confirming the results of Peter Osborne's initial examination, and the interpretations of this presented in Smith *et al* (1997), these new samples do appear to throw some additional light on a number of questions concerning the use of Building 1.

It is noticeable that the samples from the lower levels of the flooring material and from between the timbers of the floor contain larger proportions of aquatic insects than the other samples (Table 14.8, Fig 14.7). This is particularly the case with species such as *Octhebius dilatus* and *Paracymus aeneus,* which are both found on mud and detritus at the edge of saline pools in salt marshes (Hansen 1987). This could indicate that the lowest part of these flooring deposits remained wet throughout. The deposition of plant material onto this surface may have been a deliberate attempt to try to ameliorate the wet conditions. The brackish nature of this seepage is also indicated by some of the species of mite identified by Schelvis (Chapter 15).

There is also confirmation for the suggestion made in Smith *et al* (1997) that this mat of decaying vegetation was made up of mainly water reed collected from the local reed beds. There is a persistent presence of species such as *Odacantha melanura*, *Dromus longiceps,* and *Silis ruficollis,* which are often associated with *Phragmites* (Lindroth 1985, Harde 1984). Other species of insect present are also found in dense stands of emergent waterside vegetation. Amongst these are *Notaris scirpi*, which is associated with club rushes (*Scirpus* spp), and *Phalacrus caricis*, the *Thryogenes* species and *Limnobaris pilstriata,* which are all often associated with *Carex* rushes.

The 1997 analysis of additional samples from the floor of Building 1 produced results that, to a very limited degree, may indicate one aspect of how this building was used. All, or part, of the buildings may have been used as a byre. Several of the species present are members of a community that Kenward (Hall and Kenward 1990, Kenward and Hall 1995, Kenward and Hall 1997) has tentatively suggested are associated with well rotted, compacted stabling materials in the archaeological record. Amongst these are some of the *Cercyon* species present, *Acritus nigircornis, Oxytelus sculptus,* the *Leptacinus, Neobisnus,* and *Monotoma* species. It is worth remembering, however, that these species, although consistently present, occur only in low numbers at Goldcliff. Equally, some aspects of Kenward's stabling material fauna are missing here (in particular the *Anthicus* species). Also Kenward and Hall (1997) clearly indicate that this fauna should not be relied upon without additional evidence for stabling from the archaeological record itself. In particular, they lay stress on the presence of hay meadow species amongst the plant remains as a confirming source of information. Unfortunately, at Goldcliff the majority of the plant remains present are from the local marshes, which are also likely to have provided bedding and fodder for animals, making it difficult to distinguish introduced material from that which grew naturally on the site. Further confirmation of this weak signature for the presence of animal dung comes from the mites (Chapter 15).

There is another possible indicator of the presence of stabling material. This is the occurrence of *Damalinia* biting lice in these deposits. These parasite species have been used to suggest the presence of stabling material at a number of archaeological sites (Buckland *et al* 1993, Kenward and Allison 1994, Kenward and Hall 1997). Only two hind bodies of lice, both of which were unidentifiable to species, were discovered in the samples prepared for beetle analysis. During his study of the mite fauna from the same deposits, however, Schelvis (Chapter 15) recovered a considerable number of identifiable fragments of the cattle louse *Damalina bovis*. This clearly suggests the presence of cattle at the site, and probably within Building 1 itself. The presence of these parasites would also appear to rule out the suggestion that this deposit consists of collapsed roof thatch, since it seems unlikely that cattle lice would be present in roofing material.

The external environment of Buildings 6 and 8

Both Buildings 6 and 8 are surrounded by palaeochannels. That around Building 6 was cut into brown peats and filled with a grey stiff clay. That around Building 8 was a shallow channel in the peat with a thin clay at the surface. The edges of the Building 6 channel and the floor of the Building 8 channel were covered with animal footprints (Figs 8.13 and 8.17). The contents of the palaeochannels, including the insect remains, are thought to be broadly contemporary with, or slightly later than, the buildings they surround (Chapter 8). In total, three trenches across the palaeochannel around Building 6 were sampled. In 1993, three samples were obtained from Trench 17 (Samples 5505, 5504, and 5503, Fig 8.11). These three samples formed the study described in Smith *et al* (1997). In 1994 three samples from Trench 73 also were recovered, a sample from the pure grey clay in

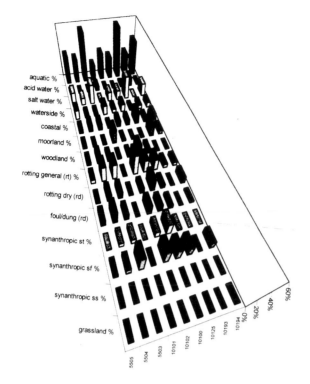

Figure 14.8 The ecological groups of beetles from the palaeochannels around Buildings 6 and 8

the top of the palaeochannel (Sample 10100), another from the mixed 'puddled' layer at the outer edge of the channel (Sample 10102), and the last from the peat underlying the channel (10101). Only one sample of material (10125) was obtained from the clay in the top of the channel in Trench 78 (Fig 8.10). In terms of the channel around Building 8, only two samples were obtained (Fig 8.19). Once again these consisted of a sample from the clean clay in the channel (10193), and again from the peat underlying the channel (10194).

The insect species recovered from this channel are listed in CD 14.6. The proportions of the ecological groups present in these palaeochannels are presented in Table 14.9 and Figure 14.8.

The additional samples from Trenches 73 and 77 from around Building 6 appear to confirm the reconstruction made in Smith *et al* (1997). This suggested that the insect faunas recovered consisted of three aspects. The first of these was the presence of coastal and saline tolerant insect species. The samples from within all of the channels examined here contain halobiotic water beetles such as *Ochthebius marinus* and *O. dilatus* and *O. viridis*. Species such as *Heterocerus maritimus*, the staphylinid *Bledius occidentalis* and the scarabaeid *Aphodius plagiatus* all suggest the presence of areas of open mud and sandy ground (Clarke 1973, Tottenham 1954, Jessop 1986). Equally, the carabids *Pogonus chalceus*, *Bembidion minimum* and *Dyschirus salinus* are all found on clay areas between sparse growths of salt marsh plants such as *Salicornia* (Glassworts) and *Atriplex* (Oraches) (Lindroth 1985).

Other species such as *Bembidion varium* and *Agonum nigrum* are often found in areas of sedges and rushes, sometimes in salt marshes. Also associated with these plants are the Chrysomelidae *Plateumaris sericea* and the curculiondid *Limnobaris pilistriata* (Koch 1992). The latter species is also salt tolerant (Koch 1992). The hydophilids *Cercyon littoralis* and *C. depressus* are found beneath seaweed on the foreshore (Hansen 1987). The presence of other salt marsh plants is suggested by some of the species present. *Mecinus collaris* feeds only on *Plantago maritima* and *Blitophaga opaca* probably feeds on sea beet in coastal situations.

In Smith *et al* (1997) it was suggested that the surrounding environment was therefore salt marsh. Now that the stratigraphy, pollen, and plant macrofossil history of the site is more clearly understood, it seems that these buildings were not sited initially

Table 14.9 The ecological groups (%) from the palaeochannel around Building 6

Sample Building Trench	5505 6 17	5504 6 17	5503 6 17	10101 6 73	10102 6 73	10100 6 73	10125 6 77	10193 8	10194 8
Aquatic (a)	31.76	27.03	56.36	17.36	30.33	24.58	57.98	26.67	40.16
Acid water (aw)	0.00	0.00	0.00	4.86	0.82	0.00	1.68	10.00	2.10
Salt water (sw)	16.89	8.49	23.03	1.39	10.66	11.02	26.89	0.00	14.70
Waterside (ws)	10.89	2.65	2.78	10.92	5.10	8.99	2.00	4.55	6.14
Coastal (c)	3.96	7.41	6.94	1.68	6.67	5.62	14.00	4.55	7.02
Moorland (m)	1.98	0.00	0.00	16.81	1.18	0.00	0.00	22.73	5.26
Woodland (w)	2.97	8.47	4.17	0.84	1.96	12.36	4.00	0.00	0.44
Rotting general (rt)	4.95	19.05	19.44	0.00	25.49	15.73	14.00	4.55	4.39
Rotting dry (rd)	0.99	7.94	8.33	0.84	5.49	15.73	4.00	0.00	7.89
Foul/dung (rf)	7.92	15.34	6.94	0.00	11.37	7.87	4.00	0.00	2.19
Synanthropic (st)	0.99	5.29	6.94	0.00	7.84	14.61	2.00	0.00	0.00
Synanthropic (sf)	3.96	7.41	20.83	0.84	18.43	14.61	12.00	0.00	9.21
Synanthropic (ss)	0.00	1.59	0.00	0.00	0.78	0.00	0.00	0.00	0.44
Grassland (g)	0.99	1.59	0.00	1.68	0.78	2.25	2.00	0.00	2.19

in a salt marsh as such. Rather, it seems they were initially in an area of undulating raised bog in which the channels and its fringes were subject to marine inundation at extreme tides. It also seems that this marine environment became more dominant in the latter periods of the site's use. It is during this later period that many of the upper samples of clean clay from these palaeochannels, insect faunas from which are described here, were deposited.

The second aspect suggested in Smith *et al* (1997), that of the presence of considerable numbers of beetles associated with animal dung, is also repeated in all of the channel fills examined. This is mainly due to the large numbers of *Aphodius* dung beetles present which account for the relatively high proportions of the rotting/foul ecological group (rf) seen in Table 14.9 and Figure 14.8. This clearly suggests that grazing animals were present in the area, a point made very forcibly by the finds of cattle hoof prints in the channel edges (Fig 8.13).

Several of the species present, particularly those from the various synanthropic ecological groups (see Table 14.9 and Fig 14.8), would appear to have their origins within the building. This may be particularly the case with the species, such as some *Cercyon*, the *Monotoma*, the Cryptophagids, the Lathridiids, *Typhaea stercorea*, *Aglenus brunneus*, and *Anobium punctatum*, which have a close association with human settlement. Equally, members of the group of insects which Kenward (Hall and Kenward 1990, Kenward and Hall 1995, Kenward and Hall 1997) has suggested may be associated with stable manure are present. Overall, this is the same group of species which were found in Building 1 and suggests that the internal environment of Building 6 may have been similar. What is not clear is if these insects fell into the channel, were washed there, or represent the dumping of material by humans into the palaeochannel.

The latter explanation may seem to be case with Sample 10100 from the grey clay in Trench 73. This sample contained a relatively high proportion of synanthropic species but, more importantly, the remains of fifteen individuals of *Damalina bovis*. This species of lice lives only on cattle. If it is accepted that this sample represents material from inside the structure, the presence of so many parasites of stock may suggest that Building 6 had a stabling role. Interestingly, this material also contains two individuals of the human flea, *Pulex irritans*. Kenward (Kenward and Hall 1997) has noted that human fleas are often found in material which has been interpreted as stabling material, presumably dropped from passing humans, or perhaps developed on from their larval form.

14.5 The implications of the synanthropic faunas at Goldcliff

In Smith *et al* (1997) a number of general propositions about both the site at Goldcliff and the

implications of the insect faunas found were put forward. The more extensive study of the insect remains presented here has perhaps strengthened some of the statements made in that paper.

The possible use of the buildings at Goldcliff

The expanded insect analysis described here has produced a number of additional pieces of evidence that may suggest, in part, a byre role for these buildings. Although this evidence is somewhat circumstantial, its repetition in both the internal deposits in Building 1 and the external palaeochannel of Building 6 may be of significance. However, it also should be borne in mind that occasionally insect faunas such as this can continue to exist after a building has been abandoned (Smith 1996a, 1996b). This may be the case, particularly where grazing stock are concerned. However, the presence of human fleas on site would suggest that the contents of the buildings are contemporary with the human activity within them. Lastly, these buildings may also have had a range of other functional and social uses that do not leave such a distinct signature in the entomological record.

The origin of the synanthropic fauna at Goldcliff

In Smith *et al* (1997) comment was made upon the possible origin of the synanthropic fauna at Goldcliff. This centred upon the proposition put forward by Kenward and Allison (1995) and Kenward (1997) that these species could arrive on site in two ways, by gradual accretion from the surrounding environment or by direct importation in carried goods and materials. Many of the arguments made which suggested that this fauna's origin was the result of the latter process still hold true. In particular, the apparently short life, certainly of Building 6, and the improbability of these species naturally occurring in a saline environment still support this proposition. However, at the time of writing Smith *et al* (1997) it was not possible to say if a large or small amount of material was brought onto site. It was suggested that if these individuals arrived as a dead, or dying, population then a large volume of material would be needed. The alternative to this would be that a 'founding' population arrived in a small amount of material brought in and subsequently bred itself up, under favourable humanly created conditions in the buildings, to relatively high numbers. It now appears that the second scenario may have been the case. Subsequent examination of the plant remains from the buildings has suggested that the majority of the vegetation present came from the wetlands around the sites rather than from dryland hay meadows (Chapter 13). This would appear to suggest a predominantly local origin for the majority of this material. Equally, there is now evidence that some of the insects present were part of a breeding population. Some of the *Cercyon*, the Staphylinids and several of the *Typhaea stercorea*, Cryptophagids, Lathridiids, and *Aglenus brunneus* found were soft bodied and wrinkled which suggests that they were teneral (newly hatched). Kenward (1978) feels that this is a sign of a breeding population.

In Smith *et al* (1997) it also was suggested that the absence of Ptinidae may be due to the fact that they were, by chance, not part of this original founding population. However, subsequent finds of *Ptinus fur* in the materials from the buildings at Goldcliff clearly suggest that, although in very low numbers, it was present.

The synanthropic fauna and the length of occupation of the site

In Smith *et al* (1997) the presence of such strong synanthropic faunas at Goldcliff appeared to go against the grain of Kenward's (Kenward and Allison 1994, Kenward 1997) suggestion that the diversity of the synanthropic population present could be used to indicate how long a settlement had been continuously occupied. The logic underlying this proposition was that insect species would accrete from the natural environment at a relatively slow speed. The more diverse the fauna the longer the settlement had been continuously occupied. These insect faunas at Goldcliff, isolated from their natural habitat and clearly developing within a short-lived structure, would appear not to have had the time or the potential to accrete from the surrounding environment. In addition, the other aspect of Kenward's proposition suggests that a very diverse fauna on a short-lived site indicates that a large volume of material must have been moved onto the settlement. However, in the case of Goldcliff, there is the possibility that a small breeding population arrived on site in a limited amount of material. As a result, it would seem that Kenward's (1997) highly creditable and constructive suggestions need to be carefully considered on a site-by-site basis.

Species of biological importance

A number of the species recovered from this site have a biological interest and are rare in Britain today.

Tachys bisulcatus This species's status within this country is at present uncertain. Hyman and Parsons (1992) suggests that it is a non-established immigrant species, or that it is of doubtful occurrence in this country. At present the only record for this species, according to Lindroth (1974), is from Durham and he considers it to be an importation. The present record would tend to contra-indicate this, but a single record is insufficient evidence on which to base a claim for native British status.

Oodes gracilis This is a species which is now thought to be extinct from the British fauna. Today it is found in the warmer areas of Central and Southern Europe and it is thought to be particularly temperature sensitive (Lindroth 1986). Its occurrence in deposits associated with the Bronze Age Somerset Levels trackways has been used to suggest higher temperatures during this period (Girling 1976 and 1984), though its decline may also be due to habitat loss (Buckland and Dinnin 1993).

Agelastica alni This bright purple species feeds only on alder leaf. Its status in Britain is somewhat unclear. Harde (1984) suggests that it is extinct as a species in Britain, but Hyman and Parsons (1992) think that it may still be present in one or two isolated areas. It has not been taken since 1946. However, it seems to have been more common in the past with a number of Neolithic and Bronze age finds (Girling 1977 and 1980, Robinson 1993) and some Neolithic sites in the Trent catchment (Smith unpublished).

Hydroporus scalesianus Shirt (1987) lists this small water beetle as vulnerable (Red Data Book status RDB2). Today it is limited to a few relict habitats in fen and fen carr, mainly in Norfolk. It appears to be in decline as a result of habitat loss mainly due to drainage. However, its presence at Bronze Age Church Stretton (Osborne 1972), Thorne Moor (Buckland 1979), and at many of the Somerset Levels sites (Girling, 1976, 1977, 1980, and 1984) suggests that it may have been more widespread in the past.

Also present is a range of species associated with dead wood which today are considered to be rare (Hyman and Parsons 1992). These include *Hypophloeus unicolor* (*Corticeus unicolor* in the British catalogue–RDB 3), *Colydium elongatum* (RDB 3), *Prionyhus melanarius* (RDB 2), *Bolitophagus reticulatus* (RDB3), and *Drycoetes alni* (RDB3). Their decline today probably owes much to the removal of dead wood and to the loss of woodland in general. In terms of the geological record, many of these species have only been recovered from sites on the Somerset Levels (Girling 1985) or at Thorne Moors (Buckland 1979).

Bledius occidentalis This robust staphylinid species occurs at a few sandy areas on the south coast of England. Shirt (1987) considers it to be rare (Red Data Book status: RDB 3) but Hyman and Parsons (1994) suggests that since *Bledius* colonies tend to move around within a site, they may be easily overlooked during a periodic survey. Its status is best described as insufficiently known (Red Data Book Status: RDBK).

Rhopalomesites tardyi (*Mesites tardii* in Kloet and Hincks 1977) This large weevil is considered to be scarce at present in this country (Red Data Book Status: Notable A in Hyman and Parsons 1992). It is uncommon but widely spread throughout the country where its distribution is coastal. It occurs in firm driftwood on the shoreline (Warren and Key 1991) and in a range of dead timber in coastal woodlands (Hyman and Parsons 1992). There has been some speculation that this distribution might suggest that it has been recently introduced to this country in drift wood, though this has been questioned (Buckland and Dinnin 1993). However, its occurrence here suggests that it has a far longer history in this country. This is also supported by a 11th century AD record of this species from Dublin (Coope 1981).

A number of other species encountered, often in some numbers, at this site are considered to be scarce today (Red Data Book Notable A and B in Hyman and Parsons 1992, 1994). This is again probably due to recent contraction of their various habitats. These species are *Elaphrus uliginosus, Bembidion semipunctatum, Odacantha melanura, Dromus longiceps, Aphodius plagiatus, Plateumaris braccata*, and *Mecinus collaris*.

15 Other environmental evidence from Goldcliff, mainly concerning the setting and activities in and around buildings of the later 1st millennium Cal BC *by M Bell, N G Cameron, M G Canti, A Caseldine, J Crowther, G M Cruise , S J Dobinson, Y Hamilakis, C Ingrem, R I Macphail, and J Schelvis*

15.1 Introduction
Martin Bell and Astrid Caseldine

Waterlogged intertidal contexts such as the peats and clays at Goldcliff contain a potentially very wide range of sources of palaeoenvironmental evidence which complement one another in the study of coastal change and human activity (Bell 1997). Where many sites exist within a long and complex sequence, finite resources dictate a selection of the techniques employed and those parts of the sequence to be examined. The approach at Goldcliff was based on three central palaeoenvironmental studies: pollen and macrofossils in Chapter 13, and insects in Chapter 14. Those studies were intended, so far as possible, to provide an outline of the sequence as a whole. This chapter presents the results of smaller scale palaeoenvironmental studies generally focused on more specific research questions. The first paper on diatoms complements the botanical and beetle chapters by providing a more precise indication of water conditions and salinity than was possible from the other sources. That section includes one column from the Bronze Age boat plank site, but the other columns are from in and around the Iron Age Buildings, with one column from Trackway 1108.

All the other studies in this chapter are focused mainly on the Iron Age buildings and the problems of their ecological setting and the activities associated with them. Some of the studies were planned from the outset, others (mites, micromorphology, and mineralogy) were undertaken following a post-excavation meeting in September 1997, when it became clear that the originally planned palaeoenvironmental programme was unlikely to resolve what was going on in the buildings. That issue was addressed in two main ways. Firstly, the sediments were examined using micromorphology, mineralogy, phosphates and magnetic susceptibility. Secondly, faunal analysis was carried out on mites, which provide complementary evidence to the originally planned work on beetles, and animal bones. The bone studies indicate the range of activities associated with the keeping and hunting of animals.

15.2 Diatom analysis of sediments
Nigel Cameron and Simon Dobinson

Introduction

Diatom analysis is a technique established in intertidal archaeology, particularly in the reconstruction of former water quality. It has, for example, been used in recent years to reconstruct salinity and other aspects of water quality from sediments associated with coastal archaeological sites in the Severn Estuary Levels (Cameron 1997, Cameron and Dobinson 1998).

In this study, diatom analysis has been applied to sediments associated with Buildings 1 and 2, the palaeochannel around Building 6, and the Boat Plank Structure 1124 (locations on Fig 13.2). The sediments investigated were sub-sampled from five monoliths. The primary aim of using diatom analysis was to determine the salinity conditions under which the sediments accumulated. In addition, it was hoped that other aspects of diatom species ecology, such as the relationship with other water quality parameters, or habitat, would assist in the interpretation of the environments in which the sediments formed, and in the interpretation of the taphonomy of the deposits.

15.2.1 Methods

Diatom preparation and analysis followed standard techniques (Battarbee 1986). For assessment and counting, slides were examined using a Leitz research microscope at a magnification of ×1250 or ×1000 under phase contrast illumination. An assessment of 38 sub-samples from the monoliths indicated that diatom percentage counts would be possible for 37 of these samples. Previous investigations have led us to expect that peat samples are usually non-diatomaceous. However, here this was not generally the case and we, therefore, had many more samples to count than expected. In order to make counts, analyse, and report on all 37 samples, a reduced diatom sum was used so that efforts could be spread across all monoliths. Where possible, a total of approximately 120 diatom valves was counted for each slide. However, in the few cases where diatom concentrations were very low, a smaller sum was counted (c 75 valves), and in these cases was considered to be adequate, given the low species diversity.

Where necessary, diatom identifications were confirmed using diatom floras and taxonomic publications held in the collection of the Environmental Change Research Centre (ECRC), UCL. The floras most commonly consulted were Cleve-Euler (1951–55), Hendey (1964), Hustedt (1930–66), and van der Werff and Huls (1957–74). The principle source of data on species ecology used was Denys (1992).

Data were entered into the AMPHORA diatom database at the ECRC, where these data, slides, and cleaned valve suspensions are available for examination. The program TRAN (Juggins 1993) was used for data manipulation and diagrams were plotted using TILIA and TILIAGRAPH (Grimm 1991).

Diatom species-salinity preferences were classified using the halobian groups of Hustedt (1953 and 1957, 199). This species-salinity classification is based upon Hustedt's observations of diatom distributions across salinity gradients on North Sea coasts, but has been expanded to include more taxa than in the original publications. The salinity ranges of the main halobian groups are summarised below:

(i) Polyhalobian: >30g l⁻¹ ie high salinity
(ii) Mesohalobian: 0.2–30g⁻¹ ie estuarine brackish
(iii) Oligohalobian to halophilous: optimum in slightly brackish water
(iv) Oligohalobian to indifferent: optimum in freshwater but tolerant of slightly brackish water
(v) Halophobous: exclusively freshwater
(vi) Unknown: taxa of unknown salinity preference.

Diatom halobian groups are indicated above the percentage diatom diagrams and the halobian group composition is summarised at the right-hand side of each diatom diagram.

15.2.2 Results and discussion

The samples prepared and sediment descriptions are listed at the beginning of each monolith sub-section. (All depths are in centimetres below the top of the monolith.) Full stratigraphic descriptions are given in CD 13.1.

Boat plank site Monolith 1715

Eight samples were analysed (Fig 15.1) from this 50cm monolith, which was also analysed for pollen and taken immediately below the structure (location on Fig 6.7).

Ocm, 4cm, and 8cm are clay, Context 1125
16cm and 24cm are peaty clay, Context 1127
32cm, 40cm, and 48cm are clay, Context 1129

The sequence appears to be divided into three phases of salinity: a marine-dominated assemblage at the base, a brackish–fresh and marine phase above and, at the top, a marine-dominated assemblage, with a recovery of halophilous taxa (*Navicula cincta*) at the surface.

The basal section, comprising the samples from 48cm to 32cm, Context 1129, are dominated by polyhalobous taxa which represent over 80% of the total diatom assemblage in the lower two samples. Oligohalobous indifferent and oligohalobous halophilous to indifferent taxa are absent in these two basal samples. The percentage of polyhalobous taxa declines at 32cm, but remains relatively high at over 60%, whilst the percentages of mesohalobous to oligohalobous indifferent groups increase.

The samples from Context 1127 at 16cm and 24cm have increased percentages of mesohalobous to oligohalobous indifferent taxa (c 30%), with reduced percentages of polyhalobous diatoms (c 30%). Poorer preservation is apparent, with an increased percentage of taxa of unknown salinity group. The majority of the latter appear to be freshwater taxa. Despite the continued presence of planktonic and semi-planktonic marine taxa, the shift in species composition in the middle part of the sequence suggests that there was a decrease in the salinity at the site of deposition during the period of accumulation, and is in agreement with the botanical evidence (Chapter 13).

In the top part of the sequence, samples from 0cm, 4cm, and 8cm depth, respectively, the percentages of polyhalobous taxa return to relatively high values (55–75%). Oligohalobous indifferent taxa decline to values of <5%, and there are slightly reduced abundances of mesohalobous taxa. In the two uppermost samples halophilous taxa increase, reaching a maximum abundance of >15% in the top sample (*Navicula cincta* is the main halophilous taxon at this level). However, the dominance of marine (polyhalobous) planktonic diatoms in the uppermost samples shows a strong marine influence. These samples are in the same layer as the boat plank structure and indicate that tidal, estuarine conditions predominated.

Goldcliff Building 1 Monolith 1232

Eight samples were analysed from Monolith 1232 (Fig 15.2), which was also analysed for pollen. These come from within the building (location on Figs 7.6 and 7.12). Diatom concentrations were found to be high enough to allow diatom counts to be made for all of these samples.

Ocm is peat
2cm is reed matting
4cm is peaty clay/mud
6cm is wood peat
11cm is very thin clay band (sample quite peaty)

18cm is transition from peat to clay
24cm is organic clay/mud
28cm is clay

The four basal samples, below 10cm depth, are dominated by polyhalobous taxa (>50%). The dominant marine diatoms are the tychoplanktonic species *Paralia sulcata* and *Cymatosira belgica*. A number of other polyhalobous and mesohalobous taxa, both planktonic and non-planktonic, are represented. Freshwater taxa are present in all four of the basal samples, but generally have low abundances. The transition from peat to clay at 18cm, although dominated by marine diatoms, has higher numbers of freshwater diatoms (oligohalobous indifferent diatoms >20%) including taxa such as *Navicula variostriata* and *Pinnularia viridis*.

In the upper part of the sequence the percentages of polyhalobous and polyhalobous to mesohalobous taxa decrease and they comprise only c 10% of the diatom assemblage at 0cm depth. Between 11cm depth and 4cm depth a range of mesohalobous diatoms, including *Navicula digitoradiata* (small form) and *Nitzschia valdestriata*, increase to almost 20% of the total diatoms. Halophilous taxa such as *Navicula eidrigeana*, followed by *Navicula cincta*, become dominant in the upper part of the sequence and comprise almost 60% of the diatom assemblage at the top of the monolith. Oligohalobous indifferent species decrease from almost 25% at 6cm depth to just >10% at 0cm depth. A high percentage of taxa at 4cm depth were poorly preserved and identifiable only to generic level.

Overall there is a clear transition from a predominantly marine tidal environment to one of brackish waters and this follows to some extent the clay–peat transition observed in the lithostratigraphy. A terrestrial/aerophilous diatom input is apparent from the increase in *Hantzschia amphioxys* towards the surface.

An important issue related to this sequence is concerned with the nature of the flooding at the level of the reed matting (2cm) and perhaps the peaty-clay mud (4cm) immediately below this floor. Sedimentary, beetle, and pollen evidence also indicates flooding episodes during the life of the building and may, in addition, be represented by the clay band at 4cm. The presence of aquatic diatom assemblages corroborates this, whilst the presence of aerophilous (semi-terrestrial) taxa and the poor preservation of the assemblage at 6cm can be related to the dry conditions that would have predominated. The diatom evidence at these levels shows an increase in halophilous (high conductivity, but essentially, freshwater taxa) as opposed to estuarine–brackish (mesohalobous) species. The dominance of the former rather than the latter salinity group, along with the decreasing importance of marine planktonic diatoms, suggests that the flooding did not come directly from the estuary, but was perhaps related to local increases in water-level in a shallow freshwater–brackish environment.

Goldcliff Building 2 Monolith 1221

Six samples were analysed (Fig 15.3) from Monolith 1221, which was also analysed for pollen from Building 2 (location on Figs 7.11 and 7.12):

0cm and 4cm are peat
10–14cm is very thin clay band at a depth of 10cm on one side of the sample column and 14cm on the other
22cm and 24cm are organic clay/mud (transition from peat to clay)
28cm is clay

The level of diatom preservation is better in the three basal samples which are associated with clay, or the transition from peat to clay. Diatom preservation in the upper three samples, which are from a peat, is poorer and this is reflected in the high numbers of valves identifiable only to generic level.

As in Monolith 1232, Monolith 1221 reflects a shift from high percentages of polyhalobous taxa (>55% at the base of the monolith) to mesohalobous taxa, reaching almost 30% at 10–14cm, and then halophilous taxa (*Navicula cincta* comprises almost 80% of the diatom assemblage) at 0cm. The marine assemblages at the base of the sequence are dominated by *Paralia sulcata* and *Cymatosira belgica* and comprise from >55% down to 35% of the diatom assemblage. However, as well as significant abundances of mesohalobous (maximum c 15%) and halophilous (maximum >20%) taxa in the basal samples, a number of oligohalobous indifferent taxa (maximum >25%) are abundant at 22cm and 24cm. Halophobous taxa are also present in these samples.

A number of the oligohalobous indifferent and halophilous taxa, common at 22cm and 24cm depth, are aerophilous and are usually associated with terrestrial habitats. These species include *Navicula mutica, N. perpusilla, N. contenta, Hantzschia amphioxys, Nitzschia terrestris, Nitzschia recta, Pinnularia borealis* var *rectangularis*. Further, the halophobous *Eunotia* spp and *Frustulia rhomboides* var *saxonica* are typical of acid, oligotrophic waters or bog surfaces. Based on diatom evidence alone these mixed assemblages are difficult to interpret, but the diatoms from terrestrial and acid, oligotrophic habitats suggest that, as well as being tidal, the depositional environment was subject to inwash from the landward side, reworking of older or younger deposits, or lay at an acid site which was inundated by the sea. There is evidence that, contemporary with these samples, a raised bog, which at this site was inundated at c 2580 BP, survived a few hundred metres to the west.

As mentioned above, preservation in the upper part of this sequence is poorer than in the lower samples. This is to some extent reflected in the numbers of valves identifiable only to generic level and consequently in the higher numbers of diatoms of unknown salinity preference. There is, however, a decline in the numbers of polyhalobous and mesohalobous taxa. *Fragilaria* and *Nitzschia* spp (both genera in this instance probably representing freshwater taxa) are abundant at 4cm depth, and the halophilous species, *Navicula cincta*, comprises >75% of the diatom assemblage at the top of the monolith. In the two uppermost samples marine and brackish taxa are present, but at low percentages compared with the basal section of the sequence. It is likely, therefore, that the two samples from the upper part of the monolith represent a predominantly freshwater habitat with less tidal influence. *Navicula cincta*, the dominant species in the top sample, is typical of high conductivity fresh–brackish water. The species' non-planktonic lifeform, along with its abundance, suggests that it is unlikely to have been transported beyond its lifetime range and may, therefore, represent the local aquatic environment. Whatever the case, the uppermost diatom assemblages provide evidence for reduced salinity in the upper part compared with the lower section of the sequence. The diatom assemblage at 0cm in Monolith 1221, like that associated with the floor in Monolith 1232, suggests freshwater of high conductivity rather than flooding directly from the estuary (although the low percentage of *Paralia sulcata* indicates that this may have occurred). On the other hand, the poorly preserved freshwater/aerophilous dominated assemblage at 4cm in Monolith 1221 is consistent with often dry conditions.

Palaeochannel around Building 6 Monolith 10128

Nine samples were prepared from this sequence (Fig 15.4) which was also analysed for pollen (the location is shown on Figure 8.10). This monolith was from peat with clay layers, immediately to the south of the palaeochannel edge:

    0cm, 4cm, and 8cm are peat with clay
    10cm is peat
    12cm and 14cm are clay
    16cm is peat, 16cm is clay lens (?footprint)
    20cm is peat

All except the basal sample (20cm) contained countable diatoms. Intensive scanning of coverslips prepared for the latter sample revealed a single valve fragment of *Paralia sulcata* and another of *Rhopalodia gibberula*. These are polyhalobous and mesohalobous to halophilous species, respectively.

The peat and clay in the remainder of the sequence contains a mixture of diatom assemblages. However, all are dominated by polyhalobous, mesohalobous, or halophilous taxa. Oligohalobous indifferent diatoms are relatively uncommon and reach a maximum of only c 10%. A number of these freshwater taxa, for example the *Pinnularia* spp, are likely to originate from a terrestrial source. *Nitzschia* sp 1, one taxon common at the base of the sequence, could not be assigned to any salinity group.

Overall then, it appears that the sequence represents brackish to marine conditions with a number of non-planktonic *Navicula* species, notably *Navicula cincta*, common or abundant throughout. The constant input and abundance of planktonic, polyhalobous taxa such as *Cymatosira belgica*, *Paralia sulcata*, and *Rhaphoneis minutissima* indicates the tidal nature of the site. However, there is the possibility of reworking of material, and for example at 12cm and 14cm depth the polyhalobous component is significantly reduced to c 10%.

The diatom salinity groups of the parallel samples taken from peat and from the clay lens at 16cm are similar despite the difference in sediment type. Both are dominated by marine, brackish and halophilous taxa; however, the sample represented on the diatom diagram as the uppermost of the two is from the clay and contains a richer species assemblage than the sample from the peat, represented as the lower sample at 16cm. For example, in the mesohalobous group the clay sample contains several more *Navicula* and *Nitzschia* taxa than the peat sample. This is as one would expect from previous experience of relatively poor diatom preservation in peats.

The upper 10cm of Monolith 10128 corresponds to an occupation horizon and contained bones and woodchips. Both diatom and stratigraphic evidence suggest there were tidal conditions at this time. During the period of occupation, freshwater (oligohalobous indifferent) diatoms are absent, or present only in low numbers, whilst halophilous diatoms, associated with freshwater of high conductivity, are abundant (Maximum abundance of c 35%). At the same time the mesohalobous to polyhalobous groups associated with the estuary comprise over 40% of the diatom assemblages.

Palaeochannel around Building 6 Monolith 10127

A total of seven samples was analysed for diatoms from Monolith 10127 (Fig 15.5), which was also analysed for pollen (location shown on Fig 8.10). This monolith was taken mainly through the clays in the palaeochannel which overlie and largely postdate the material of Monolith 10128:

    0–16cm is clay, Context 1303
    24–32cm is peaty clay, Context 1320
    40–48cm is clay, Context 1319

All the samples were found to contain a significant percentage of polyhalobous diatoms, rising from 25% to 30% at the base of the sequence, to a maximum of 60–65% at the top of the sequence. A similar pattern is seen in the increase in abundance of polyhalobous to mesohalobous diatoms, whilst mesohalobous taxa show an overall decrease from c 15% to 25% at the base of the sequence to c 10% at the top. Halophilous taxa are relatively uncommon with percentages of <5% and a maximum at 24cm. The diatom halobian group profile is, to some degree, influenced by the

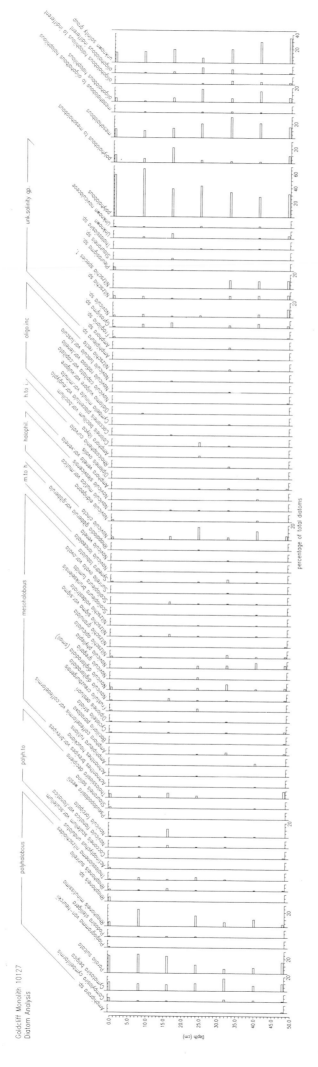

Figure15.5 Goldcliff: Diatom analysis Monolith 10127

large number of taxa of unknown salinity group which reach a maximum of almost 35% in the basal sample. The abundance of this unknown category reflects both the poor preservation of some taxa (identified only to generic level) and, in the case of *Nitzschia* sp 1 in the lower part of the core, a taxon which is of unknown salinity preference.

Therefore, the diatom diagram shows an apparent increase in salinity from the base of the core to the top, with brackish and halophilous diatoms more common in the lower half of the sequence. Marine planktonic taxa, which are common at the same time, then become dominant in the upper half of the core. Taken together with the relative rarity of freshwater taxa, it appears that the sequence represents a brackish to marine habitat influenced by tides throughout, but with an increasing level of marine influences towards the top. This is consistent with the results of other analyses (Chapters 13 and 14), which indicate that this sequence represents a marine transgression.

15.2.3 Conclusions

Following a diatom assessment, diatoms were found to be present and, to some degree, countable in 37 out of 38 sub-samples. Preservation was generally good in the clays and surprisingly good in a number of peaty samples. Analysis has been carried out on five monoliths. All sites and almost all samples show some degree of marine diatom input throughout. Generally, oligohalobous indifferent taxa are present at relatively low abundances and the non-planktonic diatom component is dominated by mesohalobous and halophilous taxa. Monolith 1715 has maxima of marine taxa at the bottom and top of the profile, with brackish to freshwater taxa increasing in the middle part of the sequence. Halophilous taxa then increase towards the surface. The levels associated with the Bronze Age boat plank structure show a strong marine–estuarine influence and indicate that there were, at least periodically, tidal conditions.

Salinity trends are also apparent in the later samples eg Monoliths 1232 and 1221, respectively, show declines in polyhalobous taxa from the base to the top of the profile whilst less saline taxa, particularly oligohalobous–halophilous taxa, increase in abundance towards the top. The uppermost levels of both of these sequences are associated with floors. The predominantly high conductivity freshwater nature of flooding is, therefore, of significance. Monolith 10128 has a mixed diatom assemblage of polyhalobous, mesohalobous, and halophilous components. The dominant non-planktonic component is of non-marine taxa, but there are few true freshwater (oligophalous indifferent) diatoms. The upper 10cm of Monolith 10128 corresponds to the period of bone and worked wood deposition, and the abundance of polyhalobous and mesohalobous diatoms in these samples suggests that there were tidal conditions at the time. Monolith 10127, like Monolith 10128,

contains very few freshwater species and shows a trend of decreasing mesohalobous and halophilous diatoms and increasing polyhalobous diatom percentages from the bottom to the top of the profile, respectively. This sequence ties in with the marine transgression interpreted from other evidence such as the high values for Chenopodiaceae pollen associated with salt-marsh.

The trends interpreted here are based predominantly on the evidence of diatom assemblages. As commented upon in the discussion, a number of taphonomic factors have influenced these assemblages. Sediment mixing processes may have introduced non-contemporaneous diatoms to assemblages of different ecological character. Transport by tidal or freshwater flow will have introduced allochthonous valves into the local diatom assemblage. This is particularly likely in the case of the marine planktonic component. Differential preservation of diatom valves is evident, with heavily silicified valves being preferentially preserved. However, a number of taxa across the salinity spectrum are robust, so the almost complete absence of taxa of one salinity group can probably be taken to represent ecological rather than taphonomic factors. This is especially so where some relatively fragile taxa of the group are also preserved. The possible input of diatoms from acidic (bog) habitats is discussed for Monolith 1221 and is supported by data from other sources.

15.3 Soil micromorphology
Richard Macphail and Gill Cruise

15.3.1 Introduction

Two contexts were examined through soil micromorphology:

(i) organic sediments within Building 1 (Fig 7.12), three undisturbed samples taken from macrofossil samples from Context 901 (Sample 11 is 0–20mm, 91 is 20–40mm, 65 is 40–50mm);

(ii) palaeochannel fills that exhibited animal footprints (Trench 17) to the north of Building 6 (Fig 8.11), a series of four lateral Kubiena samples from the various fills over a 2m length of the trench, from the south to north sides (Sample 5508, 5507, 5509, and 5510).

Methods were as specified in Section 4.9.

15.3.2 Results

Soil micromorphological analysis of all contexts on the site, Mesolithic (Chapter 4) and Iron Age, identified six main microfabric types as specified on CD 4.8 (M1a–M6b: see key to soil micromorphology), four anthropogenic inclusions (AI1–4), clay (estuarine silt and clay), five organic materials (O1–5), and eight pedofeatures (P1–8). Their frequency and abundance are reported upon for Iron Age palaeochannels in CD 15.1.

Organic layers within Building 1

Three micromorphological samples were taken of Context 901 (locations on Fig 7.12) at the following depths: Sample 11 at 0–20mm, Sample 91 at 20–40mm, and Sample 65 at 40–50mm. All are composed of layered plant remains (brackish swamp types, Chapter 13, CD Plates 15.12 and 15.13). The only mineral component present is a little fine silt. Examination under UVL found no autofluorescent materials.

Palaeochannel fills

Samples are described upwards and laterally, towards the centre of the fill.

Sample 5508 is composed of three layers (CD 15.1). The lowermost layer is composed of partially humified (reddened and isotic) and locally fragmented peat (M6a), mixed with many clay and coarse silt infills (P2). Some peat has been very finely fragmented into amorphous components, and possible burrows are present (S4). The reddish humified peat has also been affected by post-deposition impregnation by crystalline iron carbonate – siderite (see below, CD Plate 15.5). Above, estuarine silts and clays are dominant, but contain frequent plant (organs, tissues, and amorphous) fragments, some being sub-rounded with embedded silty mineral material (M1b). Beds are not horizontal, some being strongly curved (concave–convex–concave over some 25mm) with very pale grey lower fills of the concave parts. At the top of the sample, fragmented humified peat is intercalated with estuarine silts and clays (M6b). Pseudomorphs of probable vivianite (hydrated iron phosphate) occur in the upper two layers (P6). Very few to few woody roots are present throughout (O4).

Laterally, in Sample 5507, layered peat composed of *Sphagnum imbricatum* is dominant, and this has been rooted by *Calluna* (Chapter 13, CD Plate 15.6). Some peat layers and woody roots appeared to be charred (O1, O2). Cracks in the peat are infilled with poorly sorted clay, silt, and a little fine sand, with much dark, detrital organic matter (P2).

Towards the channel centre, Sample 5509 is dominated by laminated estuarine clay and silt, with frequent laminae of detrital, fragmented, and humified peat (CD Plates 15.8 and 15.9). Sample 5510 is also composed of laminated estuarine clay and silts with fine laminae of fine detrital peat and 10mm thick layers of amorphous peat, with fine detrital and charred peat inclusions (CD Plates 15.10 and 15.11).

15.3.3 Discussion

Organic layers within Building 1

Although parasite evidence of cattle stabling in Building 1 is convincing, there is no soil micromorphological evidence from the samples taken (0–50mm) of a byre floor *sensu stricto*. For example, at the Moel-y-Gaer stable at Butser Ancient Farm, the stable crust is formed of layered plant fragments, dung, intercalated fine sand, and silt (from trampling), cemented by calcium phosphate (Macphail and Goldberg 1995, plate 3, Macphail and Cruise in press). At Goldcliff, layered plant remains alone are present, along with only a scattering of fine silt. No humified organic matter (or possible dung), as found within the trampled palaeochannel, was present in the samples examined. The few fine silts themselves are best interpreted as naturally occurring estuarine silts deposited within an organic sediment. Crowther (below) found little chemical evidence of this context being a byre floor, and Caseldine (Chapter 13) found macro-fossils, suggesting brackish swamp plants. Insect studies (Chapter 14 and Schelvis this chapter) do, however, suggest the presence of dung. Although there is no evidence for dung from the micromorphological samples examined, it is possible that the plant material was used as foundation/bedding to provide a drier surface.

Palaeochannel fills

Samples were taken across and through the palaeochannel round Building 6. The base of Sample 5508 shows good evidence of drying out and desiccation of peat, alongside its humification. Cracks in the peat also became infilled with coarse silty material. It is possible that the peat also became biologically worked, but no clear excrements are apparent. Ensuing sediments are mixed estuarine silts and clays, with intercalated detrital organic matter, and fragmented humified peat and other humified organic matter. It is not inconceivable that: (i) disturbance of the humified peat, and (ii) shredding of organic matter as found in the overlying curved mineralogenic beds that have a pale initial 'fill', are all related to animal trampling, the pale fill resulting from initial infilling of a hoof impression. It is also a strong possibility that some of the humified organic material has a dung origin (cf reference dung types from Butser Ancient Farm). The presence of animals in the palaeochannel (footprints) is recorded in this trench. The former likely presence of rare pseudomorphs of vivianite may be purely coincidental, vivianite being found in many estuarine deposits, but the poorly sorted and disorganised manner in which the organic fragments occur in the curved (hoof impression) bedded estuarine silts is akin to animal trampled floor material from Butser (cf Macphail and Goldberg 1995, plate 6). The presence of unsorted, sub-rounded, organic fragments and mixed organic and mineral material, is also more likely to relate to animal trampling than purely natural sedimentation. Samples 5509 and 5510 show mainly clay and silt sedimentation, with some included humified peaty soil fragments, possibly as evidence of animal disturbance and dunging locally. As noted by Caseldine (Chapter 13), the organic constituents of bedding and dung are clearly likely to be the same as the natural plants growing locally.

In Sample 5507, *Sphagnum* peat formation alongside heather growth is an indication of natural organic sedimentation. Nevertheless, here too, the charring of peat layers and woody roots of *Calluna* and the inclusion of charcoal within the moss peat, may relate to anthropogenic activity, although this was not necessarily coeval with the structure and might represent earlier management of the bog vegetation by fire. There is evidence that the peat bog was affected by drying out, desiccation, and humification. Animal trampling is recorded in the sediments of the palaeochannels, with animals having an erosive effect on the peat bog.

Acknowledgements

The authors acknowledge funding support by St David's College, University of Wales, Lampeter and wish to thank Nick Barton, Martin Bell, Astrid Caseldine, and John Crowther for their collaboration and discussion. Marie-Agnès Courty and Paul Goldberg are thanked for their discussion of the thin sections.

15.4 Mineralogical analysis of samples from Buildings 1, 6, and surroundings
M G Canti

One of the problems posed by the site is the function of the buildings and whether they housed animals. Faecal spherulites have provided indications elsewhere of the presence of animal dung (eg Matthews *et al* 1996, Boschian 1997). They are very small (5–15µm), radially crystallised spheres of calcium carbonate deposited in the animal gut by digestive processes (Canti 1997, Brochier 1983). The Goldcliff deposits were examined to see if the dung question could be resolved and, at the same time, the opportunity was taken to look at aspects of the mineralogy and post-depositional processes occurring in the sediments.

15.4.1 Scanning method

The samples were dried and sieved through a 250µm mesh. A small quantity of the powder was then dispersed in methyl salicylate (RI-1.537) and examined at low and medium power under plane polarised and cross polarised light. This is the equivalent of a thin section scan, except the materials are not held in their field positions. It has the advantage that unknowns can be examined by other means as well.

15.4.2 Results

The samples from Building 1 were all very similar. These are as follows and their locations are shown on Figure 7.12: Samples 100, 133, 1180, 1178, 87, 85, 109, 6, 1232 (2 levels), 1224. The hand samples consist of more or less leafy organics with recognisable reed-like materials in some cases. These are generally not decomposed enough to be dung. Under the microscope, the samples are c 90% dark unidentified organics (plant material) with few sand grains (up to c 100µm) and c 10% silt grains (mostly c 10–30µm). A few diatom fragments (10–15µm thick rods with a central airspace) can be seen, along with occasional phytoliths and euhedral gypsum ($CaSO_4$, see test below) crystals. There are no spherulites. The variation between these samples is insignificant, consisting mostly of slight differences in the colour of the organic matter or relative quantities of the components.

Sample IV (1223, west of Building 1, Fig 7.12)

The hand sample has similar organics to the above, but also contains a number of 1–3mm, light brown, rounded, soft, and friable aggregates. Under the microscope, the general appearance of the sample is also the same, but with very large numbers of 3–7µm, yellowish, equidimensional crystals. These are the crushed remains of the light brown aggregates, and consist mostly of jarosite ($KFe_3(SO_4)_2(OH)_6$) with a little quartz and gypsum (see test below).

Sample I (10102, Palaeochannel round Building 6, Fig 8.10)

This contains significantly more mineral grains than all the other samples, a fact clearly visible in the hand sample. Under the microscope, the components are more varied and included larger numbers of phytoliths and diatoms. Although there are no spherulites, composite dung-like organic fragments are present containing minute high-birefringence prismatic crystals (probably calcium carbonate). These crystals have been noted in numerous modern dung samples, and are currently being investigated as another possible digestive deposit similar to spherulites. A few prismatic calcium oxalate crystals from plants are also present. Most modern dung samples contain some calcium oxalate, as a small proportion comes through the herbivore digestive tract unscathed by digestive acids (see Canti 1997). The sample also contains a few gypsum crystals.

Gypsum test

Optical testing is not a guarantee of gypsum identification, so one crystal was photographed on the SEM and checked with EDXRA. The results (CD 15.14–15.16) show euhedral crystals composed of calcium, sulphur, and oxygen as expected. Perfect crystal faces are apparent beneath extraneous fragments adhering to the surface (CD 15.14). This clearly implies that the crystal has grown in situ and has not been transported at all. Most of the gypsum crystals noted in the slides were similarly perfect. Gypsum grows under a number of conditions, but the most likely at Goldcliff is the oxidation of pyrites producing sulphuric acid, which forms gypsum on contact with the calcium carbonate from shells:

$$Fe_2S + H_2O + CaCO_3 = FeOH + CaSO_4 + CO_2$$

The pyrites would have originally formed under the reducing conditions likely to have developed when so much organic matter was buried under sediment. Bacterial activity and biological substrates generally are closely linked to this type of pyrite formation (Altschuler *et al* 1983, Canfield and Raiswell 1991, Wuttke 1992). The gypsum growth could occur at any time between the original pyrite deposition and the present day, whenever the removal of overlying sediments allowed more oxygen to reach the stratigraphy again.

Jarosite test

EDXRA was carried out on the minute crystals from Sample IV (1223) (see CD 15.17–15.19) and showed Fe, K, S, Si, Al, and O. Assuming the aluminium was coming from traces of clay in the sample, these elements could be explained by crystals being a mixture of jarosite and quartz. XRD showed these two phases to be present, as well as a trace of gypsum. Jarosite represents a different manifestation of the neutralisation of sulphuric acid arising from the oxidation of pyrites (see Bouma *et al* 1990, Dent and Pons 1995). Its presence (rather than gypsum) probably depends on variations in Ca and K available in the sediment and the pH of the surrounding solution. Broadly:

$$Fe_2S + H_2O + K = KFe_3(SO_4)_2(OH)_6$$

pH test

The current pH of each sample was determined using a meter calibrated with standards at pH 7 and pH 4. About 20g of the sample was dispersed in distilled water and measured after 1 hr and 3 hrs to check stability. The results (CD 15.19a) show the high level of variation (range 7.5–2.4, mean 4.5) typical in situations where pyrite is oxidising. It must be stressed that these do not necessarily represent the

pH values of the stratigraphy in situ, as further oxidation may have occurred since excavation. However, with the exception of Sample 1 (10102, pH 7.5), it is likely that the field pH values would have become generally too low for spherulite preservation once pyrite oxidation had started in the ground.

15.4.3 Conclusion

Samples from Building 1 appear to be variably rotted leaf material that has undergone taphonomic processes associated with acidity from pyrites oxidation. Faecal spherulites, had they ever been present, could not have survived these low pH values in the field (see Canti 1997 and in press). Sample 1 is notably different in having a higher pH, as well as containing more mineral material and fine biogenic (?)calcium carbonate in organic aggregates. This material may well be another form of faecal mineralisation and the aggregates closely resemble dung remains.

15.5 Phosphate and magnetic susceptibility studies
John Crowther

15.5.1 Introduction

Spatial and depth variations in the total phosphate (phosphate-P) concentration and magnetic susceptibility of soils and sediments can often provide valuable insight into former patterns and temporal sequences of human activity. Phosphates, which are present in all organic matter (including plant material, faeces, and, especially, bones), are relatively insoluble and tend to become 'fixed' within the mineral fraction of soils/sediments as organic decomposition (mineralisation) occurs. Where such inputs have been concentrated and mineralisation has occurred, signs of phosphate enrichment may remain detectable for periods of 10^3 years; cf Proudfoot (1976), Hamond (1983), and Bethell and Máté (1989). Magnetic susceptibility (χ), on the other hand, largely reflects the concentration of magnetic forms of iron oxide (eg maghaemite) in sediments, which is dependent upon the presence of iron and of alternating reduction–oxidation conditions which favour the formation of magnetic minerals. Enhancement is particularly associated with burning (Tite and Mullins 1971).

Unfortunately, estuarine sediments and peats present difficulties for both types of analysis. In the case of phosphate, mineralisation is slow under seasonally or permanently waterlogged conditions, and phosphate concentrations within poorly decomposed organic material such as dung are, therefore, unlikely to be markedly different from the natural peats. Areas of phosphate enrichment associated with the peats are, therefore, likely only to reflect the presence of bone. With magnetic susceptibility, the problem is that peats and heavily gleyed minerogenic sediments contain low concentrations of iron. χ values are, therefore, generally very low and, even if substantial prehistoric enhancement did take place, the effects of this will have diminished as a result of subsequent gleying. Where elevated levels are recorded, it is important to establish that this is due to enhancement rather than variations in overall iron content (Crowther and Barker 1995). This involves the determination of the maximum potential magnetic susceptibility of samples (χ_{max}) and calculation of the percentage fractional conversion (χ_{conv}), viz (χ/χ_{max}) × 100.0 (Tite 1972, Scollar *et al* 1990).

Despite these unpromising circumstances, analysis was undertaken on samples from two locations: (i) Buildings 1 and 2 and (ii) Trackway 1108. Phosphate-P was determined following alkaline oxidation with NaOBr (Dick and Tabatabai 1977). χ_{max} was achieved by heating samples at 650°C in reducing, followed by oxidising, conditions (Crowther and Barker 1995). Loss-on-ignition (LOI) at 375°C for 16 hours was used to estimate organic matter content (Ball 1964), and pH (1:2.5, water) and particle size were determined by standard methods (Avery and Bascomb 1974).

15.5.2 Results and discussion

The detailed analytical results are presented in CD 15.20–15.27.

Buildings 1 and 2

Various natural sediments (peats and estuarine clays) and possible flooring materials were examined in the hope that they might provide some insight into the function of the two buildings. Attention, in particular, focused on the layer of reeds that extended across the floor of the buildings, and the possibility that certain organic deposits associated with this layer might be animal dung. Samples ($n = 61$) taken across the supposed occupation layer within Buildings 1 and 2 and the immediately adjacent area are all organic rich, with LOI values ranging from 30.9–78.2% (CD 15.21). The χ values are consistently low (maximum, $0.050\mu m^3\ kg^{-1}$) and provide no evidence of burning, which is consistent with the lack of charcoal recorded during the excavation and subsequent laboratory sieving.

The majority of the phosphate-P concentrations are <$0.400mg\ g^{-1}$. The principal areas of phosphate enrichment (maximum $3.45mg\ g^{-1}$) occur outside the buildings, to the north and west of Building 1 (Fig 15.6), a pattern that is in keeping with the distribution of bone finds (Fig 7.12), and might be associated with the dumping of midden material. The only signs of phosphate enrichment within the buildings are in the north-west corner of Building 1. Although this certainly lends support to there having been animal stalls in this part of the building, the results need to be treated with caution, for two reasons. First, the higher concentrations could, to some extent, reflect the generally better preservation of the floor in this part of the building; ie surface layers, which tend to be more phosphate-rich (Crowther 1997), may have

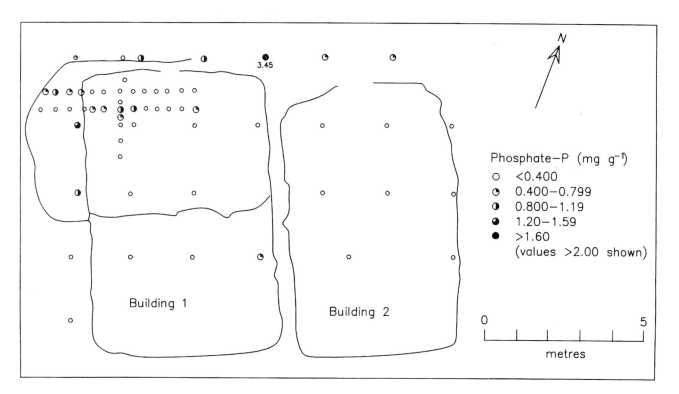

Figure 15.6 Goldcliff: Phosphate-P survey of Buildings 1 and 2

been eroded elsewhere. In this respect, however, it should be noted that the upper part of Monolith 1232 from the eastern corner of Building 1 (CD 15.22) revealed an increase in phosphate-P concentrations up though the reed layer (range 0.398–0.555mg g^{-1}) and into the thin layer of overlying peat (maximum 0.744mg g^{-1}). The lack of phosphate enrichment within the reed layer in this particular section raises questions about its interpretation as a flooring layer, though concentrations as high as 1.36mg g^{-1} were recorded in samples of the reed layer from elsewhere within Building 1 (CD 15.23). Certainly, if it was a flooring layer, then the activities that took place on it do not appear to have led to a significant increase in phosphate concentrations across the entire ground surface of the building.

Secondly, as noted above, dung deposits will not necessarily exhibit much higher phosphate-P concentrations than the natural peats. Indeed, the mean phosphate-P concentration of nine samples, including some from beneath floor timbers (CD 15.24), that were recorded during the excavation as being possible dung (Context 942), is only 0.447mg g^{-1} (s dev, 0.194mg g^{-1}), which is not significantly different from the other organic contexts sampled in the spatial surveys. This finding at first sight appears to be at odds with the results from Monolith 1224 (CD 15.25), located just outside the west wall of Building 1 (Fig 7.9), and extending through a section of Context 942. Phosphate-P concentrations within this context are in the range 1.14–1.41mg g^{-1}, which are much higher than those recorded in the spatial survey or in Monolith 1232. While such enrichment might be associated with dung, the fact that even higher values (1.33–1.84mg g^{-1}) were recorded in the overlying peat suggests that other phosphate-rich material may be affecting the results. Bone, possibly derived from midden deposits (see above), is the most likely source, and it is quite conceivable that this has significantly augmented the phosphate concentrations of the peats and dung-like deposits in the upper part of this monolith. The phosphate evidence relating to the reed layer and possible dung deposits is, thus, somewhat equivocal.

Phosphate-P concentrations in the underlying clay (CD 15.26) are mostly <0.500mg g^{-1} (maximum, 0.810mg g^{-1}) and display no discernible pattern. Traces of phosphate enrichment, thus, appear to have been confined within the layer of peat and organic deposits.

Trackway 1108

Samples taken along a 2.70m transect line across Trackway 1108, 1992 Trench (Fig 10.1) revealed no evidence of phosphate enrichment (CD 15.27).

Acknowledgements

Laboratory analysis was undertaken by Ian Clewes and John James.

15.6 Remains of mites (*Acari*) from the Iron Age site
Jaap Schelvis

15.6.1 Introduction

Research on remains of invertebrate animals in general and arthropods in particular from archaeological, or palaeontological, contexts can take place at different levels of completeness and thoroughness. At the one extreme it is an attempt to extract all invertebrate remains from a given sample, identify as many of these remains as possible to species level and subsequently integrate all ecological implications of the finds in a full scientific publication. It goes without saying that this very useful and time-consuming exercise can only be carried out during training sessions. Strict deadlines and budgetary limitations do not allow this type of analysis to be carried out during contract research. At the next level of research, a selection is made of the groups of invertebrates to be studied in a particular archaeological or palaeontological setting. From these groups, a representative part of the fauna is extracted from the samples to answer given questions. The third, and lowest, level of research is the assessment aimed at the validation of samples. In this case, a representative part of the invertebrates are extracted from (a part of) the samples. On the basis of these analyses, a basic report is produced in which the following questions are being answered:

- Are there any remains of invertebrates preserved in the deposits?
- How is the density and quality of preservation of these remains?
- Are there any taxonomic groups among the remains which could shed light on the archaeological questions of the site?

Usually assessments are carried out in order to select samples for further analysis. Ideally, this already takes place during the fieldwork allowing the sampling strategy to be modified according to the results of these studies.

The arthropod study presented in this report is a combination of the lower two levels of research. The presence of arthropod remains had already been demonstrated by work on Coleoptera (Chapter 14). A number of samples were selected for further analysis focusing on the mite remains on the basis of preliminary scans of the arthropod faunas of ten samples taken from archaeologically relevant features.

15.6.2 Material and methods

A total of ten samples was initially studied to assess the potential of the acarine remains. The samples varied in size from <1kg to almost 5kg (Sample 10102, from which a 2.0kg subsample was studied)

Table 15.1 Mite samples from Building 1 and Building 6 palaeochannel

Sample	Building	Coordinates/context	Depth (mm)	Weight (kg)
87	Building 1	1.8/7.7	0–20	1.2
85	Building 1	1.8/7.75	20–40	1.0
109	Building 1	1.8/7.75	40–60	1.1
6	Building 1	1.8/7.75	80–100	0.6
100	Building 1	1.4/8.3	0–40	2.8
133	Building 1	1.4/8.3	40–60	1.8
1178	Building 1	1.4/7.25		0.845
1180	Building 1	1.6/7.5		0.446
1223	West of B 1	Context 942		2.5
10102	B6 palaeochannel	Context 1320		2.0 (5.0)

Table 15.2 Preservation density and species diversity of mite samples

Sample	Preservation	Density	Diversity	Parasites	Gamasids	Value
87	+ +	+ +	+ +	+ +	+ +	4
85	+ +	+	+	–	+ +	3
109	+ +	+ +	±	–	+	2
6	+ +	+	±	–	+ +	2
100	+ +	+ +	+	+	+	3
133	+ +	+ +	+	–	+	3
1178	+	±	–	–	+	2
1180	+ +	+ +	+	–	+	2
1223	+ +	+ +	+	+	+	3
10102	+	+	+	+	+ +	3

and were taken both from reed layers in and outside Building 1 (Fig 7.12) and the palaeochannel around Building 6 (Sample 10102, Fig 8.10). Table 15.1 summarises the details of the samples.

From these ten samples the chitinous remains were extracted by wet-sieving on 1.0mm and 106µm. The fraction between these two sieves was then subjected to a paraffin flotation (adapted version by Schelvis 1992a of the method originally published by Kenward *et al* 1980). The float consisting of chitinous remains mixed with some inevitable botanical debris was subsequently sorted under a low power (×8–×16) stereo microscope in industrial methylated spirit. The result of these scans was recorded on scansheets. From each sample about 100 mite remains, as well as all remains of ectoparasitic insects, were transferred to a microscope slide containing 80% lactic acid. The lactic acid makes the remains more or less transparent, thereby facilitating the identification process. The remains were then identified by means of Grandjeans Half Open Slide Technique, as described by Balogh and Mahunka (1983), using a transmitted light microscope at a magnification of ×100–×400. Identifications were based both on relevant keys (Siepel in preparation for the Oribatida and Karg (1971 and 1989) for the Gamasida) and on direct comparison with the Scarab reference collec-

tion comprising >400 species of mites and ectoparasitic insects.

15.6.3 Results

As the research question in this case focused on the presence of animal excrement in the deposits, the target groups were the predatory mites characteristic of dung, the General Dung Indicating (GDI) and Possible Dung Indicating (PDI) species (as defined by Schelvis 1992b) and the ectoparasitic insects. The presence and species diversity of these groups was, therefore, the main criterion in the selection of the samples. Other parameters used in the validation of the samples were the density and quality of preservation of the remains. The combination of these characteristics of each sample results in the allocation to one of the following five values used to select the most promising samples for further analysis:

(i)   useless sample, eg zoological sterile or contaminated by recent arthropods;

(ii)   usable sample, just enough remains of sufficient quality to possibly answer certain questions;

(iii) useful sample, enough remains of sufficient or good quality to probably answer certain questions;

(iv) good sample, more than enough remains of good quality to answer certain questions;

(v) excellent sample, a high density and diversity of very well preserved remains. It would be a scientific waste not to study this sample in more detail.

Table 15.2 summarises the various characteristics of the ten samples which were scanned. Preservation, density and species diversity were estimated on a scale ranging from very poor (– –), poor (–), mean (±), good (+) to excellent (+ +). The presence of parasitic insects and gamasid mites is indicated by the number of pluses (0, 1, 2 or 3 for none, few, mean, or many remains, respectively).

On the basis of the assessent criteria presented in Table 15.2, six samples (85, 87, 100, 133, 1223, 10102) were selected for further analysis, allowing both a comparison of the indoor acarine fauna with the outdoor fauna and a detailed study of samples from various places and depths within Building 1 (see Figure 7.12 for location). A table listing species and attribution to ecological groups is given on CD 15.28. In the following sections the results of the selected samples will be discussed.

Sample 85

This 1.0kg sample was overlying the Samples 109 and 6 and underlying Sample 87, a sequence through the reed matting. This sample was found to contain several dung indicating gamasids such as a representative of the genus *Macrocheles*, *Trichouropoda orbicularis*, *Uroobovella pyriformis*, *Uroobovella difoveolata*, and *Nenteria stammeri*. Although the latter two species were once described as Producer Indicating species for horse excrement (Schelvis 1992b), they have been found since in dung deposits produced by various domestic animals. The oribatid remains in this sample indicate a rather foul environment: *Oppia nitens* and *Ramusella clavipectinata* together forming Ecological Group XIX optimally represented in anthropogenic habitats rich in decaying organic matter. Other oribatids found include characteristic inhabitants of peat bogs such as *Limnozetes foveolatus* and *Hydrozetes* sp as well as species typically found in brackish grassland such as *Punctoribates hexagonus* and *Scutovertex pilosetosus*.

Sample 87

This sample consisted of a layer of 20mm of deposit overlying the 20mm of reed deposit of Sample 85. The quality of preservation of the chitinous remains in the two samples was equally high; however, in Sample 87 the density of arthropod remains and the species diversity were considerably higher than in Sample 85. Apart from the gamasid species already mentioned above (Sample 85), this sample was also found to contain the remains of the dung indicating species *Androlaelaps casalis* and a second species of *Macrocheles* with a length of c 900µm, possibly another dung indicator *M. glaber*. Two other gamasid species found in Sample 87 are not typical inhabitants of excrement. One is commonly found in decaying organic matter (*Uropoda orbicularis*) and the other one is a rare species recorded in Central Europe from 'garden soils' (*Dinychus woelkei*). More than fifteen species of oribatids were recorded including the ones found in Sample 85. The extra species were again indicative of peat bogs (*Limnozetes ciliatus*) and brackish habitats (*Latilamellobates incisellus*).

Sample 87 also yielded the remains of at least 23 individuals of the cattle biting louse *Damalinia bovis*. Because of the high host specificity of the *Damalinia* lice, it can be concluded from this find that cattle were present at the site and, in view of the restricted dispersal capacity of lice, even within Building 1.

Sample 100

Like Sample 87, this sample was taken from the top of a reed layer sequence, although the original deposit was probably thicker. Although the species diversity in this sample was somewhat lower than in Sample 87, the characteristics of the arthropod fauna were rather similar. One gamasid which was not recorded in the other two samples is *Uroobovella marginata*, a General Dung Indicating species according to Schelvis (1992b). Also similar to Sample 87 was the presence of *Damalinia bovis* although the density of the remains was much lower; only six individuals in a sample more than twice as big as Sample 87.

Sample 133

Another sample from the reed matting similar to Sample 85, but two samples below this. Again the gamasid fauna is dominated by dung indicating species. Compared with Sample 85, the only difference is that *N. stammeri* is replaced by *A. casalis* and that another female individual of the rare *D. woelkei* was recorded. The similarity found in the gamasid fauna is not present among the Oribatida. The oribatid fauna of Sample 133 is far more diverse than the one in Sample 85. Well over twenty species were recorded, most of which were again indicative of open wet environments with a considerable marine influence such as *Oribatella arctica litoralis*.

A notable feature of Sample 133 was the relatively high frequency of remains of Pseudoscorpionida. The mouthparts of these small predators are not uncommon in archaeological deposits but in this case there were also 'complete' abdomens and even some almost complete individuals. Pseudoscorpionida are relatively common in deposits rich in decaying organic matter such as compost heaps.

Sample 1223

Sample 1223 was taken from Context 942 west of Building 1. It resembled the previous samples from within Building 1 as far as the oribatids are concerned. This is of course not surprising since the oribatid remains reflect the ecological conditions of the local environment rather than the characteristics of the deposit itself. Since the samples are dated to about the same period the oribatid fauna should be similar. Most of the species found in Sample 1223 were indeed the same as in the previous samples. There were, however, some extra species such as *Poroliodes farinosus, Adoristes ovatus, Liacarus coracinus*, and *Ceratoppia bipilis*. The first three species are characteristic for wooded environments. *A. ovatus* and *L. coracinus* are representatives of Ecological Group III, optimally represented in 'dry and moist, rarely wet, litter as well as moss in woodland' (Schelvis 1990), and *P. farinosus* is considered to be a typical arboricolous species living at the lower regions of tree trunks (Strenzke 1952). The fourth oribatid species which was not found in the other samples was *C. bipilis*. This highly xerophilous species inhabits mosses growing on trees and shrubbery. Furthermore, *C. bipilis* is one of the few species which is regularly found on and in old thatched roofs (Strenzke 1952 and personal observations).

The gamasid fauna of Sample 1223 was different from the ones found in the indoor samples. Only a handful of individuals of the two dung indicators *Trichouropoda orbicularis* and *U. pyriformis* were recorded. The rest of the hundreds of gamasids were immature stages of *Uropoda orbicularis*. This common gamasid is regularly found in all sorts of foul places such as middens and compost heaps which it can easily reach because of its phoretic behaviour. Phoretic mites cling to other animals (usually flying insects) in order to exploit new habitats. *U. orbicularis* uses a number of flies (Diptera), including the house fly *Musca domestica*, to move about.

Again, this sample was found to contain the remains of cattle lice. The density of the remains (MNI = 4) was even lower than in Sample 100. The other samples containing *D. bovis* all yielded both heads and abdomens. In Sample 1223, only the more vulnerable abdomens were found and not the relatively sturdy heads. The reason for this difference in distribution of body parts remains a mystery.

Sample 10102

This sample was from the palaeochannel round Building 6, for location see Figure 8.10. Both the density and the quality of preservation of the arthropod remains in this sample was somewhat lower than in the other samples. The species found

were, however, essentially the same as those found in the samples taken from Building 1. Two oribatid species not recorded in the other samples were *Nanhermannia coronata* and *Hermannia subglabra*. The latter species is a highly characteristic species of the marine littoral and *N. coronata* is found in peat bogs.

The gamasid fauna of Sample 10102 was dominated by dung indicating species such as *U. pyriformis, U. difoveolata* and *A. casalis*. However, some 'compost' species were also present, such as *U. orbicularis* and single representatives of the genera *Pergamasus* and *Parasitus*. The latter two taxa also contain species living in excrement so without an identification to species level (which was unfortunately not possible in this case) the amount of ecological information provided by these finds is very limited.

The analysis of the sample confirmed the presence of cattle lice in this sample already demonstrated by David Smith (Chapter 14). A total of fifteen remains of *D. bovis* representing at least ten individuals produces a density which is higher than in the Samples 100 and 1223 but still considerably lower than in Sample 87.

15.6.4 Discussion and conclusions

The ten samples taken for analysis of the mites at Goldcliff were indeed all found to contain considerable numbers of acarine remains. A first scan led to the selection of six samples (85, 87, 100, 133, 1223, 10102) to be studied in more detail. The other four samples were two from below the Samples 85 and 87 as well as two taken at different places from the reed matting in Building 1. The other samples showed a lower density of mite remains (6 and 1178) and a lower quality of preservation (1178). Furthermore, they all had a lower species diversity in the target group Gamasida and none of them yielded remains of ectoparasitic insects.

The samples from the floor levels in Building 1 (85, 87, 100, and 133) all produced an acarine fauna which undoubtedly originated from a deposit containing excrement. The high relative abundance of Gamasida (as compared with Oribatida) together with the presence of various dung indicating species are indications for such a deposit. The mite remains did not allow the identification of the animal which produced the excrement. However, the presence of cattle lice in the two topmost samples from the floor deposits (87 and 100) leave little doubt that the buildings were used by domestic cattle. There were no other specific indications found for the presence of domestic animals or humans. The only other 'parasite' in three out of the four samples was the predatory mite *Eulaelaps novus*, which is found on small rodents and in their nests.

The sample taken from the palaeochannel round Building 6 was very similar to the samples taken within Building 1. Again, high numbers of dung indicating Gamasida, in combination with cattle lice, lead to the same conclusion that domestic cattle will have been present near Building 6. From the evidence it is not possible to determine whether the cattle were actually housed in Building 6 on the basis of a sample taken from the palaeochannel. However, on the basis of the similarity of the arthropod fauna to the samples taken from the floor deposits of Building 1 this seems to be a plausible assumption.

The deposit just outside Building 1 to the west represented by Sample 1223 seems to be different from the other deposits studied. Although there were again some cattle lice present, the mite fauna was not found to be characteristic of a true dung deposit as indicated by the very low relative abundance of only two dung indicating species. On the basis of the acarine remains Sample 1223 seems to be taken from a deposit rich in decaying organic matter (such as a compost heap or midden), possibly mixed with some excrement.

Even though the research question focused on the origin of the floor deposits and those groups of arthropods likely to shed light on this question, there were other finds which are at least worth mentioning. The oribatid mites found in the samples allow a local environmental reconstruction dominated by ecological groups optimally represented in wet, open and marine influenced habitats. Only in Sample 1223 were there any substantial indications for more wooded surroundings of the site. In this sample there was also a remarkably high density of the oribatid *Ceratoppia bipilis*, a species associated with thatched roofs.

The general conclusion of this study is that on the basis of the mite remains the floor deposits of Building 1 (and probably also of Building 6) represent stabling material mixed with the excrement of domestic cattle.

15.7 Humans and animals *c* 450–270 Cal BC
Yannis Hamilakis

15.7.1 Introduction

This section reports and discusses the available mammalian zooarchaeological evidence from the Iron Age contexts of the site, aiming to contribute to the investigation and elucidation of certain research questions which are central to the overall project: the nature and character of occupation, the possibility of a seasonality pattern, the human involvement with animals in 'economic' or other practices, the function of building structures. As it can be shown below, despite its small size, this sample presents an interesting picture which significally complements and strengthens many of the results and arguments emerging from the other categories of archaeological material. The small size of the sample, however, is a serious limiting factor for further elaborate discus-

sion; this limitation should be taken into account in any consideration of this material.

15.7.2 Recovery and methodology

The material discussed here comes from careful trowel excavation, mostly outside the buildings. Given the location, large-scale sieving was not considered feasible. It should be expected, therefore, that our material is subject to recovery bias which would have affected small elements of medium-size mammals, small mammals, birds, and fish (Payne 1972, Levitan 1982). Having said that, however, given the nature of the deposit (peat), bone, as any other hard material, was easily detectable during excavation. Indeed, this is verified by the fact that some bird bones were collected (see report by Ingrem below), as were some small mammals. Furthermore, when sieving was carried out in the laboratory using large numbers of mainly reed samples from the floors of Buildings 1 and 2 (through 0.5mm mesh), only one or two additional fragments were recovered. It is also worth noting that the examination of the residues from the extensive sampling for botanical remains which was carried out in the laboratory yielded very few, largely unidentified fragments of mammalian bones and no bird or fish. This can be contrasted with the samples from the Mesolithic levels of the site, which produced a considerable amount of fish bones (see report in Chapter 4). So, while recovery bias must be considered, careful excavation and specific sedimentary conditions, guarantee that this is not such a serious limiting factor in this case. As for the absence of certain categories of material (such as fish), parameters other than recovery should be considered (see below).

The material was analysed at the Environmental Archaeology Laboratory of the Department of Archaeology, University of Wales, Lampeter. The comparative collection of the Department as well as atlases and specialist studies (Schmid 1972, Hillson 1986) were consulted during the identification. Only the stratified material was analysed.

Quantification follows a modified version of the Number of Identified Specimens (NISP), which could be termed Minimum Number of Anatomical Units (MNAU) and which is similar to the concept of 'diagnostic zones', as defined by Watson (1979). According to this procedure, the following anatomical units were counted: skull (only when a significant portion of it and/or features such as horn cores/antler or maxillary teeth are present), horn core/antler, maxilla, mandible, teeth (only premolars and molars), atlas, axis, scapula (mainly glenoid articulation and the area around it), pelvis (acetabular area) proximal humerus, distal humerus proximal femur, distal femur, proximal radius, distal radius, ulna, proximal tibia, distal tibia, proximal metacarpal, distal metacarpal, proximal metatarsal, distal metatarsal, astragalus, calcaneum, phalanx-1, phalanx-2, phalanx-3. For long bones, proximal and distal include their respective halves of the shaft. Long bones with both halves present were recorded as two fragments. Vertebrae were counted as such only when the centrum was present, and ribs when the articulation and the area around it was present. Vertebrae (with the exception of atlas and axis) and ribs were not identified to species. This procedure, despite some problems, is easy to apply, takes into consideration butchery practices and fragmentation patterns, and reduces the possibility of interdependence. For comparative purposes, MNI (Minimum Number of Individuals) figures are also given, following the simplest form of the procedure (the most abundant left or right-hand element).

Ageing is based on epiphyseal fusion (following Silver 1969) since there are no ageable mandibles or mandibular teeth in the assemblage. The serious problems with this procedure have been well rehearsed in the zooarchaeological literature (eg Watson 1978, Maltby 1982, Moran and O'Connor 1994) and they should be kept in mind in the consideration of the results. In addition to the categories 'fused' and 'unfused', the category 'fusing' has been included for the cases where the epiphysis has just fused and the fusion line is very prominent and clear. This feature could be quite interesting since it provides evidence for absolute ageing, rather than relative one ('younger than' or 'older than') as with the 'fused' and 'unfused' categories. I also divided the material into two broad groups, 'neonatal/early juvenile' and 'older'. The first category refers to bones coming from very young animal, some of which may be older than the animals usually attributed to the category of 'neonatals' (0–6 weeks old). In our case (and based on comparisons with material in the reference collection), the category may include bones coming from animals up to 4–5 months old.

Butchery was recorded following Binford (1981) and Fischer (1995). In addition to the conventional chop and cutmarks, the category 'sawmark' was used to describe 'persistent cutting (sawing) at a particular location' which can produce a distinctive mark characterised by 'multiple, closely spaced, parallel or nearly parallel cutmarks that cumulatively create a deep incision' (Fischer 1995, 17). Measurements were taking according to the conventions suggested by von den Driesch (1976).

15.7.3 Results

Provenance and preservation

The material (289 fragments in total, CD 15.29) comes mainly from the excavated areas outside the Buildings, especially Buildings 1, 2, and 6. A small number of bones comes from other isolated contexts, including a red deer skull and antler from a palaeochannel at Goldcliff East (Appendix I, Map 16, 1093). These two are broadly dated to late Bronze Age and

Iron Age. It must be noted that only two fragments come from inside the buildings: a 'neonatal/early juvenile' pelvis of a cow (northeast corner of Building 1), and a 'neonatal/early juvenile' left tibia of a cow (floor of Building 1). There is also a partly articulated cattle skeleton (Fig 8.9, 5053), north of Building 6 (see below).

The general preservation of the material (CD 15.36) is good. There is, however, a high percentage (c 18%) of gnawed bones, nearly all of them by carnivores with one exception where rodent action seems more likely. This high rate of carnivore damage (which is found in many large and robust bones) may have affected the material in many ways. It may have resulted in the total destruction of many small size elements, especially from the medium and small mammals. Moreover, it may indicate that the material remained exposed for sometime before burial and it may have been spatially displaced, reducing the possibility of finding material in primary contexts. Other preservational traces such as cracking, soil erosion, and root etching are fairly minimal.

Species' and anatomic elements' representation

The species' and anatomic elements' representation for the site as a whole are presented in Tables CD 15.30–15.31. Cattle is by far the most abundant species forming c 58% of the sample. Its predominance becomes clearer if the microfauna is excluded. MNI figures also show clearly this predominance. Other domesticated species are represented in very low numbers and include sheep/goat (8%) and horse (3%). The fragments of sheep/goat were found around Building 6 and Buildings 1–2. This underrepresentation of sheep/goat may be due, to some extent, to the high rate of carnivore damage, or to the recovery bias; but even allowing for these processes, the predominance of cattle is still quite noticeable. The two horse bones (three anatomical units) were found north of Buildings 1 and 2, and east of Building 6, but in some distance from it. Dog is surprisingly not represented directly by bones, but its presence is implied in the plentiful gnawing traces.

The wild fauna is represented by red deer which occurs as concentrations of antler fragments (counted as one anatomical unit); in one case the antler fragments were accompanied by a fragmented skull (208, Goldcliff East); the other two concentrations occurred north of Building 1 near its entrance, and 14.5m north of Building 2. In this second case (Fig 7.2), substantial pieces of antler up to c 25m were recovered. These pieces seemed to have formed part of the same fully developed antler which was fragmented recently. The occurrence of a skull suggests that red deer was hunted rather than simply collecting shed antler. Moreover, the full development of the antler is considered to indicate that killing occurred during summer or autumn (eg Albarella 1997, 5).

Other wild fauna is represented by rather ambiguous cases, one possible wolf fragment (in two anatomical units) and one possible fox tooth. To this, the concentrations of clearly intrusive, water vole bones (mainly skull and teeth) should be added.

As far as the representation of body parts is concerned, cattle as the main species is represented by nearly all parts of the body. This representation indicates that the animals were killed at the site, rather than being brought as body parts from elsewhere. The very low occurrence of certain body parts, such as phalanges, and teeth is of interest. The possibility that this pattern is the result of the recovery and preservational bias should be seriously considered. This may explain the lack of the phalanges but it does not satisfactorily account for the very low occurrence of mandibles and mandibular teeth, robust elements which are found in relatively large quantities in most sites. This pattern raises the possibility that these elements (along with phalanges) were discarded during the primary butchery stage, which may have occurred in another context of the site. Moreover, it is noticeable that primary 'meaty' cuts such as upper limbs are very well represented. The extremely small size of the sample means, however, this suggestion cannot be explored further.

Ageing

Given the methodological problems with ageing based on epiphyseal fusion, reliable discussion on ageing should be based only on attribution in broad ageing categories (Moran and O'Connor 1994). In that sense, the data in CD 15.32 are on a relatively sound basis. It is clear that more than half of the ageable cattle bones come from very young animals, either neonatal or early juvenile (up to 4–5 months). This may reflect to some extent infant mortality but, since a significant number of bones were older than the typical 'neonatal' ones, it may indicate a deliberate strategy of killing young animals. This possibility has two interesting implications: (i) that cattle were raised at the site, confirming further the picture drawn from the body part representation; (ii) that this kill-off pattern reflects a specific animal husbandry practice with emphasis on the production of milk as well as meat, a strategy which, it is assumed, requires the killing of calves (but see McCormick 1992 for a different view). Furthermore, given the presence of a significant proportion of neonatal and early juvenile animals, we can assume that the site was occupied during the spring and the summer (accepting spring as the calving season), and that a significant amount of animals may have been killed during late summer/early autumn. This, however, does not necessarily mean that the site was exclusively occupied in the spring and the summer. As it can be seen from CD 15.33, there are several bones coming from older animals, some even past 3–4 years of age. Were we to test the seasonality hypothesis, we would

need a much larger sample with dental ageing data which could show peaks in the mortality pattern at certain ages, corresponding to certain times of the year.

Butchery and fragmentation

Butchery and fragmentation information is presented in Tables CD 15.34 and 15.35, respectively. The limited evidence for butchery provides clear indications for a range of activities: use of deer antler for tool making; disarticulation of cattle and sheep/goat body parts to make them more manageable for cooking, and possible skinning of cattle.

The fragmentation information presented in CD 15.35 (for postcranial elements only) is a simplified picture which summarises a diversity of forms. The category 'cylinders' here include only the true cylinders, that is the long bones which have had both their epiphyses gnawed off by carnivores. The category 'other' include a range of fragments such a splinters of long bones, fragments of shaft and epiphyses etc. The category 'complete' includes also bones which are nearly complete (minus some carnivore damage etc) The figures on complete bones and the mid-shaft breaks require some comment. The relatively high number of complete bones is explained by the fact that the majority of cattle bones come from neonatal/early juvenile animals. It may, therefore, represent natural deaths which have not been further modified by humans, and/or juvenile animals killed for food, and because of their small size they required no further human modification and management for cooking, or they were not considered worth breaking up for marrow extraction. The mid-shaft breaks by contrast (which come from mature animals), indicate possibly deliberate breakage for marrow extraction: in most of these cases, the fragmentation pattern is very similar to what in the literature has been termed 'true spiral or helical fracture' (spiral fracture with rough structure surfaces) (Lyman 1994, 319 where more references can be found). This is usually associated with breakage when the bone was fresh. Given that the specific fragments bore no carnivore gnawing marks at the fracture surfaces, carnivore action, the major non-human modifying agent in the assemblage, can be excluded. Taking into account the fact the depositional matrix is peat, is seems unlikely that trampling or other sedimentary factor was the fracturing agent. It seems more likely, therefore, that these fractures represent human action: the breaking up of mature cattle bones for marrow extraction.

Size

The few metrical data from measurable mature bones are given in CD 15.37. It is clear that these data cannot be used to discuss reliably the size of animal populations, breeds etc. Comparison with other assemblages showed that cattle are smaller in size compared with assemblages such as late-Iron Age Owslebury (Maltby 1987) and Danebury (Grant *et al* 1991); horse is smaller than that from mid–late Iron Age Market Deeping (Albarella 1997) and Iron Age Ashville (Wilson *et al* 1978), but slightly bigger than that from middle-Iron Age Mingies Ditch (Wilson 1993). The small size of cattle and horse in relation to other Iron Age settlements may be related to differences in chronology (most of the sites compared with Goldcliff are late Iron Age), or in the nature and character of occupation.

The articulated cattle skeleton

As was mentioned earlier, north of Building 6, at the south end of Trench 74, a partial semi-articulated cattle skeleton was found (Fig 8.9, 5053). It consists mainly of parts of the axial skeleton (vertebrae and ribs), and some parts from the fore upper limbs (humerus, radius–ulna). It seems to belong to an animal of 12–18 months of age (on the basis of epiphyseal fusion, especially the distal humerus which was just coming into fusion). No cut marks or other anthropogenic traces were found on the skeleton; it had been attacked, however, by carnivores which left clear traces on the bones and they may have removed and redistributed the missing parts of the skeleton. No other features or artefacts directly associated with this skeleton were found.

15.7.4 Conclusions and discussion

Despite its extremely small size, the assemblage provides some very interesting clues for the relationships between animals and humans at Iron Age Goldcliff. The inhabitants occupied a landscape which, in addition to its wetland, estuarine character included some woodland around it, as indicated by the presence of red deer. They raised mainly cattle, although they did keep other animals such as horse and dog (indirect evidence from the gnawing marks), and had access to sheep/goat meat. The predominance of cattle in the bone assemblage confirms the picture gained from other evidence, such as animal footprints and entomological remains (Figs 8.13 and 8.17). The inhabitants occupied the site in the spring and the summer, as indicated by the larger number of very young animals, but although it seems possible, we cannot state with certainty based on zooarchaeological evidence that the site was occupied exclusively during spring and summer.

It seems possible that cattle were exploited for milk as well as meat. The animals were raised, killed, and processed on the site. The carcasses were butchered to make them more manageable for cooking and some bones were broken up for marrow extraction. There is also some indication of skinning. Other animal parts were also used, eg sawn antler for tool making. The fact that almost no bones were found inside the buildings makes it unlikely that these buildings were used for human inhabitation including food processing, preparation and consumption; if this was the case we would expect to find the discarded food refuse. Food consumption (and other activities such as tool making) did, however, take place around the buildings.

Some of the characteristics of the assemblage seem quite distinctive, if they are to be compared with other assemblages from Iron Age Britain. In most other assemblages sheep/goat seem to predominate (Davis 1987, 181, Grant 1984a). Cattle seem to appear in high percentages (but still lower than sheep) in lowland areas with heavy soil (Davis 1987, 181). The specific environmental conditions are likely to be at least partly responsible for the predominance of cattle at Goldcliff, given the wetland nature of the landscape which makes it suitable for cattle but not so for sheep/goat. The environmental conditions, however, may not necessarily explain the very low occurrence of sheep/goat and the total absence of other common Iron Age domesticates such as pig (suitable for wetland environments). For example, a late-Iron Age site with similar environmental setting such as Meare East in Somerset Levels, produced an assemblage in which sheep/goat predominates and pig is present in relatively high numbers (Levine 1986). It is, therefore, possible that the predominance of cattle in the Goldcliff assemblage may reflect either only part of the animal husbandry practices of the community (implying the raising of other species and subsequent deposition of their bones in other settlements used by the same community), or a conscious decision of the community to concentrate on cattle and utilise very little of the other species available to them.

One of the main debates involving animals and humans in Iron Age Britain in recent years focuses on the 'symbolic' manipulation of animal skeletons and part skeletons, in 'special' structured depositions, sacrifices etc (eg Hill 1995, Grant 1984b, 1991, Wilson 1992). In this assemblage, the case of the partial articulated skeleton of a cow discussed above could be taken to signify such a special deposit. In our case, however, there are no contextual indicators of a ritualised deposition: associated artefacts or structures, other associated animal or human remains, anthropogenic traces on the bones etc. It would be a mistake, however, to write off this find, as well as other categories of faunal data, as simply 'normal', 'subsistence' related etc. As some of the above writings recognise (eg Hill 1995), it is theoretically unsound to create a dichotomy between subsistence and ritual, 'normal' and 'special' deposits. As masses of anthropological and ethnographic literature should have taught us, this dichotomous thinking is a product of the recent western intellectual tradition and it is not necessary helpful in elucidating British (or any other for that matter) prehistory. The animal remains analysed here would have undoubtedly been used for sustenance, but at the same time they would have participated in the rituals of everyday life, in the meaningful social interactions of the Iron Age inhabitants of Goldcliff. There is strong evidence for ritual deposition of human and probably animals on the edge of Goldcliff Island around half a millennium earlier than these buildings (Chapter 5).

It has also been suggested (based on 'ritual' finds from a number of sites) that wild animals such as deer, and domesticates such as horse and dog, occupied a special position in the cosmology of Iron Age people (eg Hill 1995, 57). The finds of these animals in our assemblage are not adequate for exploring further this idea. We do have, however, direct evidence for the hunting of red deer, which for the inhabitants of Goldcliff would have meant more than the provision of raw material for tool making. Hunting in a number of agricultural societies acquires a prominent social and cosmological significance, mainly because it signified the encounter with 'remote' realms and is seen as having close affinities with warfare. Consequently, hunters enjoyed the authority deriving from their special skills in manipulating these 'remote' realms (eg Cartmill 1993, cf Hamilakis in preparation). It is quite likely that the occupants at Goldcliff vested hunting with similar meaning, although, as before, we cannot take this idea further with the evidence at hand.

Finally, the absence of fish remains requires comment. Recovery cannot be held responsible for the total absence of fish remains for reasons already given. It seems, however, that this phenomenon is not unique to Goldcliff. Serjeantson et al (1994) have noted recently in a thorough study that this is a more general trend in British later prehistoric sites, and they have suggested some possible explanations for this, including the destruction of bones as a result of fish processing, and the possibility of trading fish with sites inland. These suggestions should be examined further and tested but we would maintain that it is theoretically naive to believe that the availability of resources should necessarily mean that humans exploited them as food (or for other subsistence activities). It is commonplace in anthropological literature (cf Hamilakis 1998) that for an edible item to become 'food' it should occupy a certain position in that society's ideological and cosmological realm and framework. Goldcliff may be an ideal site for exploiting marine resources but its Iron Age inhabitants may not have considered fish as food. This does not necessarily mean that fish was 'tabooed', simply that fish was not socially defined as an food item which could enter one's body.

Acknowledgements

Thanks are due to Astrid Caseldine for information and help, and to Dale Serjeantson and Claire Ingrem who agreed to study the bird bones at short notice.

15.8 The bird remains
Claire Ingrem

The bird bones were identified to species and anatomical element using the comparative material at the Faunal Remains Unit, Southampton University (FRU), anatomical elements were recorded to side and standard measurements taken where possible according to Cohen and Sarjeantson (1996).

The material recovered from Iron Age contexts consisted of ten bird fragments (CD 15.38). Eight bones were derived from a partial duck skeleton which are a good match with mallard (*Anas platyrhynchos*). Other duck species were ruled out by comparisons with measurements of the humerus, ulna, coracoid, and carpometacarpus of those of known species (Woelfle 1967); mallard was again the best match. In addition, the humerus of a wader smaller than a dunlin (*Calidris alpina*) was recovered which was not identifiable to species. The remaining bird bone, a carpometacarpus, was only identifiable as a passerine.

The partial duck skeleton consisted of eight bones from the right forelimb and upper body of the bird, the furcula, a central body element, and a left scapula (CD 15.39).

Both duck and wader are commonly found in estuaries and sea shores (Peterson et al 1993). It is, therefore, not surprising to find them at an Iron Age coastal site. None of the bones show evidence of butchery or burning, but this does not preclude the possibility that they constitute food remains. Cut and/or chop marks are only occasionally found on bird bones, a consequence of their generally small size. All of the duck bones came from one context (1004 in the northwest corner of Building 1) and, with the exception of the furcula and left scapula, represent the right wing. The presence of a central and left sided bone suggests that the whole skeleton was initially present, but due to depositional and preservational factors only the right forelimb has survived.

15.9 Conclusions
Martin Bell and Astrid Caseldine

Wooden structures of the later 1st millennium Cal BC are generally on, or close to, the latest middle Wentlooge peat surface below upper Wentlooge minerogenic sediment. The environmental evidence shows that the change from peat to clay is not a sudden marine transgression. Some flooding and marine influence occurred before the peat clay transition and the archaeological structures are in the upper part of the sequence in which the flooding is attested. Diatoms indicate that the flooding which affected Building 1 was only slightly brackish. Schelvis (personal communication) notes that mites indicating marine influence might have been introduced with plant material rather than washed in. The same species are, he notes, found in The Netherlands on the top of dwelling mounds which were probably never flooded. Diatoms indicate that the area outside Building 6 was subject to greater brackish and marine influence. In the areas of Buildings 1, 2, and 6 the combination of clay lenses within the peat and a range of biological evidence in and around the buildings indicate that periodic inundation occurred and that implies occupation may have been seasonal.

A main objective of work presented in this chapter was to clarify the activities associated with the rectangular buildings. The mites indicate that the whole of the sampled reed layer in Building 1 related to floor and use layers and are not likely to have derived from collapsed roofing or later natural reed growth (Schelvis personal communication). Micromorphological evidence did not support the field interpretation of dung and byre layers in Building 1. However, sampling for this study was of the clearly defined reed layer rather than fine detrital plant material which was, in places, present within the reeds. Dung sphericles were not preserved, phosphate studies showed only small-scale enhancement of floor levels. The ability of both these techniques to detect byre deposits is limited in this context by a combination of generally low pH and waterlogged conditions. Despite the inconclusive results of those studies, there can be little doubt that Building 1 housed animals, given the presence of mites indicative of excrement, and particularly cattle lice. Interestingly, this evidence was most abundant in the upper floor samples, suggesting the possibility that use as a byre was a secondary function of this building.

The bone evidence supports the footprints in indicating that the predominant animals kept were cattle and the presence of neonatals and young animals suggests activity may have been mainly in spring and summer. The absence of evidence for fish in any Iron Age context is striking given the location, and the good preservation of other bone, despite generally low pH.

16 The intertidal peat survey *by H Neumann with contributions by M Bell and A Woodward*

16.1 Aims

Work at Goldcliff between 1990 and 1994 had produced a remarkable concentration of intertidal prehistoric archaeology of many periods, mostly in a 1.5km strip of foreshore. A central question posed by these discoveries was how they compared with the Welsh Severn Estuary as a whole; was Goldcliff exceptional in some way, or did it highlight the archaeological richness of a much wider area? The answer to that question was important for two main reasons: from the perspective of the Goldcliff Project to put that work in a wider context, and because background survey was badly needed in a landscape threatened by a diverse range of development proposals. As noted in Chapter 1, there had by this stage been many discoveries by Upton and others, but most had not been investigated in detail, so there was a clear need for a review of the area as a whole. The intertidal survey was a lot more geographically wide ranging but much less detailed than the earlier Goldcliff survey.

The intertidal survey was possible through the support of the Board of Celtic Studies (BCS) of the University of Wales, which funded the survey over 15 months from October 1995 to December 1996. The main tasks were to: (i) synthesise previous research, drawing from published sources as well as museum and Sites and Monuments Records (SMR), (ii) create a detailed mapbase of the extent and morphology of the peatshelves using air photography, and (iii) conduct a systematic field survey over the entire length of the peat exposures, enabling the recording of the sites previously discovered by Upton and others, and revealing new sites. Field survey assistance and more detailed survey of specific sites was funded by Cadw, (iv) create databases of archaeology, dating evidence, and palaeoenvironmental information, linked with the maps.

16.2 Field survey, mapping programme, and databases

In view of the known archaeological richness and complexity of the peat exposures, it was decided to restrict the survey to the prominent coastal exposures which stretch along the 25km intertidal zone of the Gwent Levels (Fig 16.1). The western edge of the survey area was, thus, defined by the Rhymney River east of Cardiff, the eastern edge by the bedrock outcrop at the edge of the Gwent Levels at Sudbrook Point. This has meant that some peat exposures have

not been included, notably those up the Rivers Rhymney, Usk, or Severn.

Archaeological discovery in the intertidal zone is governed by marine erosion which picks out more resistant peat layers on which many of the sites have been found. The peatshelf is a narrow exposure, mostly 15–25m wide, and extends over most of the foreshore, interrupted where rivers, pills, and palaeochannels dissect the shelf. The seaward edge of the peat shelves may be only a few centimetres high where the peat shelves are thin, but erosive cliffs up to 2m high occur elsewhere. Mud cover varies from tide to tide, both in extent and thickness, visibility of the peat surface depending on weather conditions. There was a need to develop methodologies appropriate to an area inundated twice daily by the sea in which the extent of site exposure is constantly changing.

Field survey was preceded by a mapping programme based on a set of 1:10,000 colour stereopair air photographs, paying particular attention to the morphology of the peatshelf and location of palaeochannels. These were digitised on AutoCAD, producing a vector based multi-layered map of the area. It is based on the OS National Grid and allows the generation of 10 figure grid references. The preliminary 1:5000 base maps, thus, created were taken into the field and further details on morphology of the peatshelves, palaeochannels, and stratigraphy added to complete the mapping programme. The preliminary maps contained sufficient detail to enable navigation and accurate location of previously discovered sites. The maps were then updated and geometrically rectified to produce a base map accurate to within 5–10m. In areas with a particular density of finds, Electronic Distance Measurement (EDM), Global Positioning System (GPS) survey, and conventional planning, provided further accuracy and detail.

Archaeological discoveries and information on the peat types and thickness of the shelf were added during the field survey, which took place over 2 months in February and March 1996, when increased storminess and higher tidal extremes had cleared much of the superficial mudcover. However, much of the newly mapped information was based on the observations of Upton, who has made many discoveries during his regular visits to the area over 20 years, especially after storm episodes. This highlights the need to visit at times determined by the whims of nature and the importance of locally knowledgeable fieldworkers. Some areas were revisited over a period of 2 years following the initial

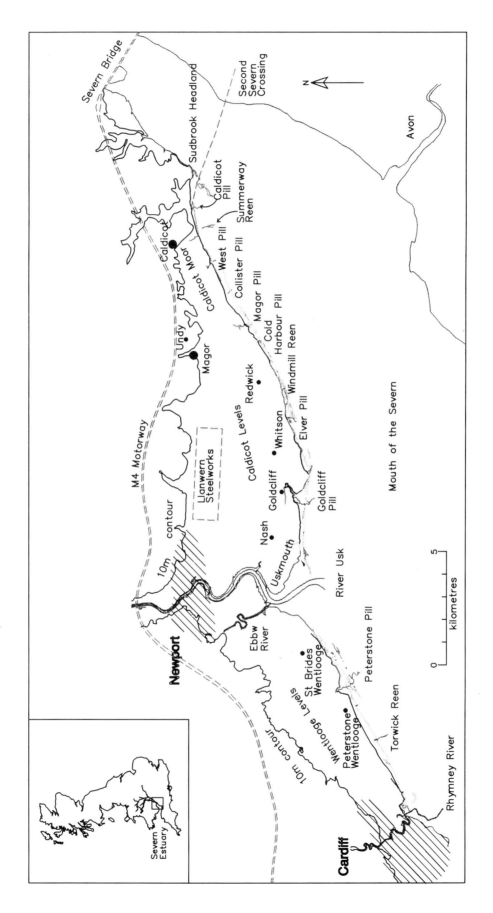

Figure 16.1 The Gwent Levels and Severn Estuary, showing modern settlements, pills, and, seaward of the seawall in grey, the intertidal peat shelves. Drawing by B Taylor

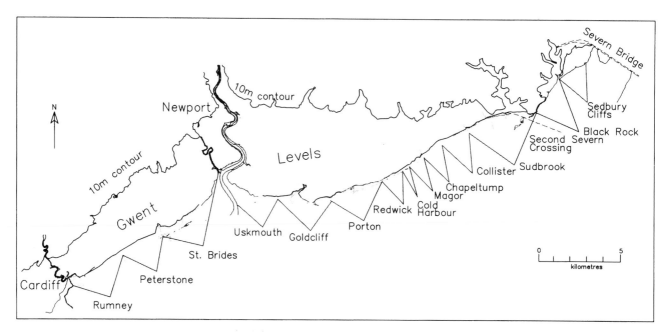

Figure 16.2 Intertidal survey: Survey units for the map base in Appendix I. Drawing by H Neumann and B Taylor

Table 16.1 Intertidal Survey: structure of database

Archaeological finds	Radiocarbon dates	Dendrochronology	Bibliography
SERN	SERN	SERN	Author
Location	Location	Location	Title
Broad class	Lab-code	Date	Journal/book
Type	C14 date BP	Felled	Topic
Site name	Calibrated date BC	Season of felling	Location
Context	Material	Species	
NGR	NGR	Number of rings	
Period	Description	Species	
Date	Site name	NGR	
Method	Source	Site name	
Description	Type	Description	
Source		Source	
Archive number			
NOTES	NOTES	NOTES	ABSTRACT

survey in March 1997, October 1997, and February 1998, when further excavation and survey work was carried out on sites identified during the first survey.

The result was the first detailed map of the intertidal area, on which the location of palaeochannels, extent of peat exposure, mud cover and stratigraphy, as well as archaeological finds were marked. The intertidal area was divided into fourteen geographical units which are largely defined by existing archaeological site names and parish names (Fig 16.2). Each of these geographical areas is represented by one or more maps in Appendix I, Maps 1–26. This mapping programme is the foundation of our attempt to regard discoveries, not in isolation, but within a contemporary environmental context.

It will also facilitate future monitoring of the peat-shelves and saltmarshes in terms of erosion, changes in mud cover and location of new discoveries.

Many discoveries in the intertidal zone had not been systematically recorded. Only partial information was held in various archives, while several sites were only known about locally as anecdotal evidence. In order to facilitate academic research and the recognition of the sites for management purposes, there was a need to collate all the information on a comprehensive database. This was achieved on dBaseV, which is compatible with existing formats of the SMR and National Monument Records (NMR), and allows this information to be linked to the existing vector map through the implementation of a Geographical Information System (GIS). The database is divided into five units or tables, comprising (i) archaeology, (ii) radiocarbon dates, (iii) dendrochronological dates, and (iv) a bibliography (Table 16.1). The record of archaeological finds forms the core of the database, providing information about the type of find as well as its context, source, location by National Grid Reference (NGR), and text modules linked to each entry offer more detailed description.

The latest development, carried out by Barbara Taylor, has been to produce the Compact Disc (CD) which accompanies this volume. On the CD is an interactive map integrating the information from the database with the maps, photographic records, and film to create a multimedia research tool. The map base and the linked database together present more detailed information supporting the synthesis in this chapter. This system is designed to evolve as new data becomes available, which is inevitable given the dynamic nature of the estuary.

16.3 Dating

Table 16.2 outlines the archaeological periods in terms of radiocarbon and calibrated years. The main dating tool is radiocarbon analysis which, including Goldcliff, provides a total of 174 dates, of which 70 are from archaeological finds and 104 from environmental sequences. They derive from the peat near archaeological sites, pollen diagrams, wooden structures and posts on the peat, and within palaeochannels, charcoal scatters, bones, and antler. Dates in this chapter are quoted as uncalibrated radiocarbon dates followed by the laboratory code, and calibrated ranges within two standard deviations using OxCal (v2.18) (Bronk Ramsey 1994 and 1995). A full list of dates is given on CD 16.1. The dates obtained from peat and archaeological samples range from the late Mesolithic through to the recent period. Figure 16.3a shows that environmental dates obtained from peat and some animal bones cover almost the full range of the period between 6660 and 2180 radiocarbon years BP with a few later dates, some derived from driftwood or palaeochannel fills.

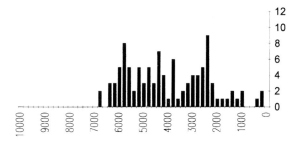

a) Environmental C14 Dates

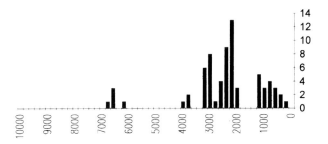

b) Archaeological C14 Dates

Figure 16.3 The range of radiocarbon dates from the intertidal peat shelves (a) environmental dates, (b) archaeological dates, x-axis is radiocarbon years BP in units of 200, y-axis is number of dates. Drawing by H Neumann

There are very few archaeological radiocarbon dates for the Mesolithic; they are from Goldcliff and one Mesolithic antler tool (Fig 16.3b). Only one very late-Neolithic date (from Peterstone Palaeochannel 3) highlights the general scarcity of Neolithic finds in the estuary. There is a cluster of dates for the later Bronze and Iron Age wooden structures and charcoal between 3180 and 1930 radiocarbon years BP, and another for medieval and some post-medieval fishing structures, and two boat finds between 830 and 1730 radiocarbon years AD. Apart from Goldcliff (Chapter 11), all dendrochronological dates are from medieval and later sites.

Table 16.2 Archaeological periods in terms of radiocarbon years Cal BC/AD and Cal BP

Period	Radiocarbon year BP	Cal BC/AD	Cal BP
Recent	post c 200	post c 1750 Cal AD	200–0
Post medieval	300–200	1550–c 1750 Cal AD	400–200
Medieval	900–300	1070–1550 Cal AD	880–400
Early medieval	1650–900	410–1070 Cal AD	1540–880
Romano-British	2000–1650	50–410 Cal AD	1900–1540
Iron Age	2550–2000	800 Cal BC–50 Cal AD	2750–1950
Bronze Age	3850–2550	2300–800 Cal BC	4250–2750
Neolithic	5000–3850	3900–2300 Cal BC	5800–4250
Mesolithic	10,800–5000	10,000–3900 Cal BC	12,000–5800
Palaeolithic	<10,800	<10,000 Cal BC	<12,000

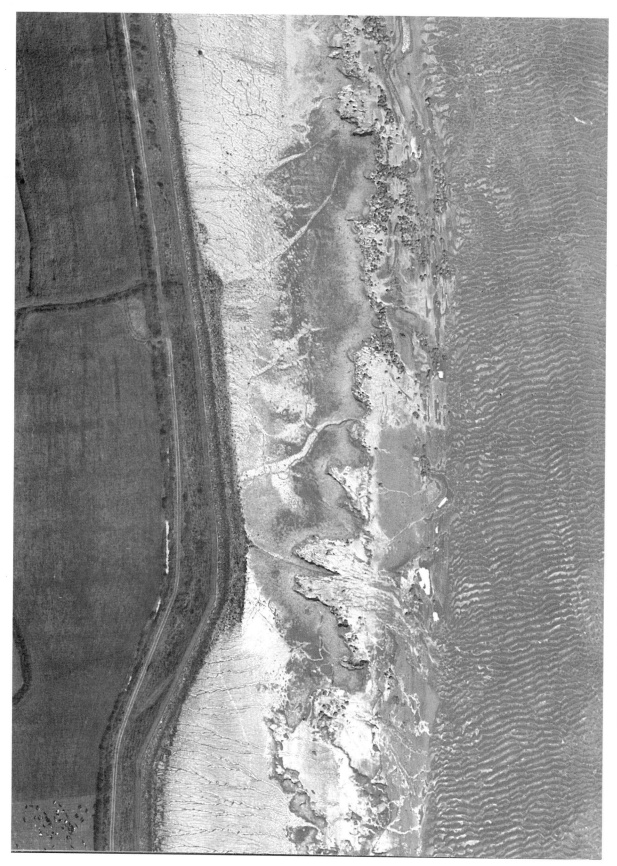

Figure 16.4 Redwick: The intertidal peat shelf. For a plan of the same area see Figure 16.8. Photograph by Aerofilms Ltd 1993, extract of 8/3824

Figure 16.5 Redwick: Section of the cleaned peat edge 45m south of Building 1. Photograph by M Bell

16.4 The peat sequence

The intertidal peatshelves are the most distinctive part of the Holocene sequence (Fig 16.4). Around 6000 BP terrestrial peats started to develop and extend seawards. Temporary retreats led to a fluctuating coastline and deposition of marine clays of variable thickness within the peat. This peat complex, provisionally termed the middle Wentlooge Formation (Allen and Rae 1987, 191) consists of a single peatbed further inland (eg Vurlong Reen, Walker *et al* 1998) and near bedrock outcrops on the foreshore (eg Goldcliff Pit 15, Chapter 5). In many areas the lower part of the peatbed is frequently intercalated with layers of estuarine clay representing relatively short-lived phases of marine incursion. This resulted in a series of peatshelves forming a stepped sequence where the intermittent clay has been eroded (eg Uskmouth, Magor and Peterstone Pill), or several peat layers being exposed in section in a cliff of the main peatshelf (eg at Redwick, Fig 16.5). These lower peatshelves are usually thinner than the upper shelf, up to 0.05–0.2m thick, are often discontinuous and characteristically consist of reed peat which only occasionally developed into alder carr. The main phase of peat formation resulted in a more continuous succession with peat reaching a thickness of almost 2m. This variation is due to a number of factors including spatial variation in the type of coastal wetland at the time of formation, differential compaction, and truncation of the upper layers, for which there is evidence at Rumney, Peterstone, and Goldcliff.

The early stages of peat formation were interrupted by phases of marine inundation. The timing and length of such phases is not well understood because radiocarbon dates are mostly from the upper layers of the peat, where the archaeological finds are concentrated. Dates from a distinct lower peatshelf have been obtained at Goldcliff, Magor, and Uskmouth, and they range from 5680 ± 70 BP (Beta-73059, 4720–4350 Cal BC; lowermost peat at Magor Pill, Allen and Rippon 1997) to 6770 ± 70 BP (Beta-60761, 5740–5490 Cal BC; oak in basal peat at Goldcliff East, Chapter 2). Sequences of dates spanning almost 3000 years are available from pollen diagrams at Vurlong Reen (Walker *et al* 1998), Goldcliff East (Smith and Morgan 1989), and Goldcliff Pit 15 (Fig 5.3). From the Mesolithic onwards the accreting estuarine mudflats were colonised by reed swamps, which developed into alder carrs and as the fens expanded seawards during the Neolithic and Bronze Age, raised bog became established. This formed a relatively stable ecosystem for a millennium and a half. Superimposed on this overall succession towards an ombrotrophic bog were minor interruptions during marine transgressions which caused wetter conditions and a temporary reversal of the succession with the establishment of fen woodland over the raised bog, or the deposition of estuarine sediments. Dates from the onset of the raised bog peat come from Goldcliff, ranging from 4900 ± 60 BP to 4740 ± 80 BP (Car-1500 and Car-651, 3820–3450 Cal BC, Smith and Morgan 1989). At Vurlong Reen, further inland, the raised bog develops at a later date of 3950 ± 70 BP (Beta-63592, 2700–2200 Cal BC, Walker *et al* 1998). The surface of the peat, which was followed by inundation, dates at Goldcliff between 2580 ± 70 BP (Car-1438, 910–410 Cal BC), 3440 ± 70 BP (Car-645, 1950–1530 Cal BC, Smith and Morgan 1989) and at Vurlong Reen 3640 ± 60 BP (Car-1499, 2200–1880 Cal BC) and 2510 ± 60 BP (Beta-63590, 810–410 Cal BC, Walker *et al* 1998), suggesting that a raised bog was in existence for c 2–2.5 millennia. The temporal differences in the timing of the transgression may reflect the undulating surface of the bog or, in some cases, dates taken from truncated levels. Locally, there is a relatively short-lived phase of renewed peat formation at the closing stages of the life of the bog, resulting in a thin upper peat (eg at Cold Harbour-1) and a more developed fen wood peat (eg at Goldcliff) before final burial by marine clays.

The entire middle Wentlooge peat complex is 3–5m thick (Fig 3.4). Its base ranges as low as −1.85m: the upper contact between peatshelf and marine sediments varies between 0.75m OD (Goldcliff, Building 1) and 4.13m OD (Chapeltump). Differential compaction and distortion of the sediments and peat, however,

Table 16.3 Types of intertidal peats by area (ha)

Site	Reed peat	Woody peat	Raised bog	Oak forest	Total
Rumney	8.05	5.17			13.22
Peterstone	2.98	1.54	0.57		5.09
St Brides	3.08	0.22			3.30
Uskmouth	2.51	2.21	0.79		5.51
Goldcliff	0.81	1.04	7.84	0.30	9.99
Porton	0.61	7.34	3.99		11.94
Redwick/Cold Harbour	0.25	0.17	2.06		2.48
Magor	0.09	1.41	1.20		2.70
Chapeltump/Collister	2.68	1.13		1.72	5.53
Sudbrook	0.02				0.02
Total	21.08	20.23	16.45	2.02	59.78
%	35.3	33.8	27.5	3.4	100

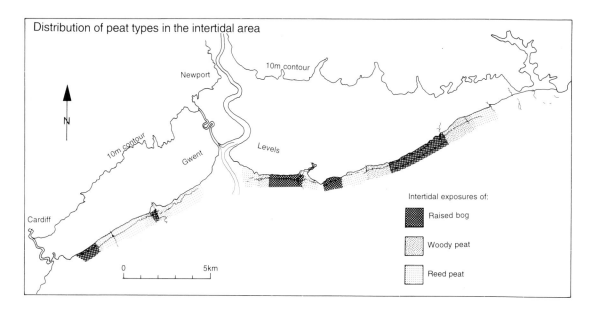

Figure 16.6 Distribution of peat types in the intertidal area. Drawing by H Neumann

means that these heights do not reflect the elevations at the time of deposition (Allen forthcoming c).

Types of peat

The exposed area of the peat in the intertidal area from the edge of the modern mud to the seaward ledge of the peatshelves is approximately 60ha. This figure was estimated from the maps based on air photo transcripts and field survey on a scale of 1:5000 using a 10m × 10m raster. This figure can only be a rough estimate due to the variable conditions in the estuary; it includes only the visible part of the peatshelf and not areas covered with a thick modern mudcover and recent saltmarsh. During the systematic field survey, the type of peat was noted, and this showed the peat surface is locally very variable; raised bog peat often includes areas of alder peat that have either developed on top of the bog peat, or are contemporary with it. In some places the raised bog peat has been eroded, leaving underlying woody peat exposed. Areas of predominantly reed peat sometimes have patches of woody fen peat, reflecting spatial variation within the former wetland.

The values for the different peat types in Table 16.3 are based on the dominant type of peat over a large area, excluding patchy and localised variations. Raised bog comprises 27.5% of the total area and occupies a relatively substantial, thick, peatshelf. Woody peat occupies 33.8% of the area and generally comprises alder, birch, and willow. Locally drier areas supported oaks, including a 600m long exposure between Chapeltump and Collister Pill (Maps 23–24), and at Goldcliff East. Reed peat also occupies large areas (35.3%) and is characterised by relatively flat and thin exposures with occasional clay content within the peat. A description of the changing

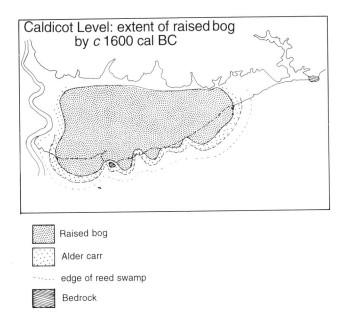

Caldicot Level: extent of raised bog
by c 1600 cal BC

░ Raised bog

∴ Alder carr

----- edge of reed swamp

▨ Bedrock

*Figure 16.7 Hypothetical extent of raised bog,
alder carr, and reed swamp in the Caldicot Level
c 1600 Cal BC. Drawing by H Neumann*

character of the peat exposures along the intertidal transect from Rumney in the west to Sudbrook in the east is given in CD 16.2.

The main types of peat exposed in the intertidal area are summarised in Figure 16.6. The intertidal exposures represent a transect across the former bog. The relatively straight line of this transect cuts across various inlets, palaeochannels and low-lying areas of the former bog. Towards its seaward margin and the rivers, the raised bog was bounded by fen carr and reed swamp, representing the different spatial zones of vegetation succession. Based on the information of peat types occurring in the intertidal area and geomorphological characteristics, the former maximum extent and shape of the great bog can be estimated and this is illustrated, for the Caldicot Level, in Figure 16.7. The greatest uncertainty is associated with the distance which the bog extended seawards. Coastal reed swamps fringing the bog may have extended many hundreds of metres, even kilometres, towards the River Severn. At Magor Pill there is evidence that the Romano-British shore was not less than 0.8km seaward of today's shore (Allen and Rippon 1997, 356)

Therefore, the present exposures of different peat types (Fig 16.6) are time-transgressive, representing marginal carrs and swamps that were contemporary with the bog and, to a lesser extent, earlier stages of the succession to raised bog.

The main exposures of raised bog are in three main areas: Rumney Great Wharf (ST 236778–ST 242781), Uskmouth/Goldcliff (ST 350822–ST 382822), and the largest exposure between Windmill Reen to Cold Harbour Pill (ST 408830–ST 435844), which includes Redwick–Cold Harbour–Magor–Chapeltump. A small exposure of raised bog peat is also evident immedi-

ately west of Peterstone Pill (ST 276797–ST 280801). Where raised bog developed, the peatshelf averages 0.5–1.0m in thickness, generally displaying a succession from reed swamp to raised bog. At Uskmouth, Goldcliff, Magor, and Chapeltump exposures of two or more discrete shelves indicate an interruption in peat formation by a marine transgression which led to the deposition of a layer of marine clay within the lower part of the peat.

In the late Bronze Age and early Iron Age, over a period of several hundred years, the raised bog became gradually inundated and buried by estuarine sediments (upper Wentlooge Formation), marking the demise of the ombrotrophic bog in favour of saltmarsh. There is a thin layer of peaty clay at the transition between raised bog peat and the blue–grey estuarine clay. In some locations this thin layer has been noted during excavations (at Rumney-3, Redwick-2, Cold Harbour-1, Chapeltump-1, and Collister Pill-1) and, where it is still preserved, it often contains pottery sherds and charcoal. In some areas another thin peat developed following initial inundation and before final burial by the upper Wentlooge clays. This peat is sometimes associated with archaeological remains. There is evidence of a thin upper peat between Redwick-1 and Cold Harbour Pill, an organic clay above the main peat is represented at Rumney-1, where it contains archaeology, while at Goldcliff a peat postdating the raised bog is present between Goldcliff Pill and the former island, and is associated with the main concentration of Iron Age archaeology.

In the areas between the raised bog exposures the peat is much thinner or absent. These include Peterstone Great Wharf (ST 242781–ST 276797), St Brides (ST 284802–ST 303815), Porton (ST 382822–ST 408830) and a 800m long exposure of reed peat west of Collister Pill (ST 457856–ST 462858). At Peterstone peat is now absent, but this is the result of erosion in historic times, as collapsed blocks of peat found in the fills of rectangular pits indicate the former presence of two layers of fen peat up to 0.2 m thick. In the other areas reed peats are exposed, which occasionally develop into fen wood peat but generally do not exceed 0.2m.

The peatshelf is breached by the Rivers Usk and Ebbw at Newport, and bounded by the Rhymney River at Cardiff to the west. Five pills drain the levels in a north–south direction and dissect the peatshelf at Peterstone, Goldcliff, Cold Harbour, Magor, and Collister. Peat exposures are also visible in some of the lower, tidal sections of the rivers Taff/Ely, Rhymney, Wye, and the lower Severn (Hewlett and Birnie 1996). In addition there are a number of palaeochannels of former rivers, the largest at Rumney (ST 246783), Porton (ST 420835), and Chapeltump (ST 445851). Former courses of the present pills are also still visible as palaeochannels such as at Elver Pill, Magor Pill (Allen and Rippon 1997), and to some extent Goldcliff Pill, although here uncertainties remain as to its former course (Chapter 3). The former bog was drained by a dense network of smaller, sinuous channels that are clearly visible on air photographs and on the ground. These palaeo-channels are filled with grey marine silts and clays.

16.5 Archaeology of the peats and associated sediments

A great many archaeological finds are located on Maps 1–24 in Appendix I and listed in the gazetteer of sites on the CD. The main sites will be discussed briefly in this section. Some sites are dated by the typology of pottery or metalwork, rather more by radiocarbon dates. An indication of the approximate date of many other sites is provided by their relationship to the stratigraphic sequence outlined above. However, some significant differences from area to area have been noted in the dates of peat inception and cessation, so dates based only on stratigraphic relationships are within quite broad bands. Because many sites are only dated stratigraphically, this section is structured under the main stratigraphic units: Pleistocene deposits, lower Wentlooge minero-genic sediments, archaeology *within* middle Wentlooge peats, archaeology *on* middle Wentlooge peat surfaces, finds from palaeochannels cutting middle Wentlooge peat. Within these headings, finds are subdivided according to site.

16.6 Archaeology in the Severn Gravels before 10,000 BP, Palaeolithic

Six Palaeolithic finds were recorded from Sudbrook within a gravel deposit (Aldhouse-Green 1993). No additional Palaeolithic artefacts were identified during this survey. Recently, the potential of the Severn Gravels for Palaeolithic archaeology has been assessed as part of a wider survey of English and Welsh rivers (Wymer and Harding 1997).

16.7 The lower Wentlooge Formation 10,000 BP–*c* 4600 Cal BC, Mesolithic

This was a period of predominant marine influence characterised by expanses of coastal mudflats and saltmarshes. During the early part of the Holocene the laminated clays of the lower Wentlooge Forma-tion were being laid down and their Foraminifera and pollen content suggest intertidal sandy mudflats with open contact to fully marine conditions (Ald-house-Green *et al* 1992). The only occupation is on the fringes of Goldcliff Island (Chapter 4). A wider Mesolithic presence is indicated by human footprints preserved in the well-laminated silts of the former mudflats. Three trails have been described in detail at Uskmouth-1 (Aldhouse-Green *et al* 1992), where the lowermost peat overlying the footprints was dated to 6140 ± 100 BP (OxA-3307, 5240–4940 Cal BC). Further trails of human footprints were re-

corded from Magor-2; peat slightly below the foot-prints was dated to 5720 ± 80 BP (OxA-2626, 4780–4360 Cal BC, Aldhouse-Green *et al* 1992). When the site was revisited during the field survey several new footprints had become visible as well as bird prints, possibly of crane. Allen (1997a) also recorded human footprints from laminated silts at Goldcliff-1343, Redwick-5, and Magor-8. Possible dog prints were also found near the footprints crossing a palaeochannel at Magor-8.

Animal footprints have been noted on the lower foreshore in many locations. Red deer hoofprints apparently following the course of a palaeochannel are particularly well preserved at Redwick (Map 21). Allen (1997a, fig 18) has identified several sites where animal tracks are well preserved, including deer and aurochs at the mouth of the Usk (Map 11), aurochs at the edge of a palaeochannel at Porton (Map 20) and along a stretch of foreshore west of Magor Pill (Map 22). During the intertidal peat survey an in situ deer antler was also found in the same location and another at St Brides at the western side of Uskmouth (SB-2).

The footprints show the Mesolithic mudflats would have provided a rich and open hunting ground for game, birds and fish. An antler mattock dated to 6180 ± 80 BP (OxA-4574, 5260–5000 Cal BC, Ald-house-Green and Housley 1993) was found in the vicinity of the footprints at Uskmouth. Two other stray finds of axes/adzes from the foreshore at Goldcliff East and Porton (1094 and PO-1) were noted in Chapter 4.

Marine sediments at the base of the middle Wentlooge peats extend as far inland as Barland's Farm and Vurlong Reen (Walker *et al* 1998), testify-ing the extent of these mudflats over much of the Gwent Levels behind the seawall. Our survey area, where this stratigraphic level is now exposed in the intertidal zone, would have been a considerable distance from dryland sites. Mesolithic settlement was likely to have been situated at the edge of the mudflats, either on the adjacent dryland fringe now concealed under middle and upper Wentlooge depos-its, or near elevated bedrock outcrops such as Goldcliff Island. Sudbrook is another suitable spot, although no Mesolithic finds are as yet recorded here.

16.8 Archaeology within middle Wentlooge peat complex *c* 4600–1700 Cal BC

The lower part of the middle Wentlooge complex is later Mesolithic and at Goldcliff one flint and charcoal are present within the base of the peat (Chapter 4). Some of the unstratified Mesolithic finds noted in the previous section could also derive from the base of the middle Wentlooge peat.

Neolithic artefacts are confined to occasional un-stratified artefacts from the lower foreshore eg a polished rhyolite axe (M-11, Map 22) found 'opposite the Magor sewage works on the mud beyond the peat'

(Green 1989, 195, fig 4), and a Neolithic flake (SU-2, Map 26) found on the muddy foreshore at Sudbrook (Godbold and Turner 1993, fig 2). A fragment of a leaf-shaped or barbed and tanged arrowhead (Rumney-C1.1), recovered and assigned to the Neolithic from a beach on the peatshelf at Rumney (Fulford *et al* 1994, 196 and fig 9), is also likely to have been eroded from deposits close by. The human skull from Alexandra Docks, Newport (NP-11, Map 10) is also of later Neolithic date (Chapter 5).

The only in situ Neolithic finds are a few struck flints at the same horizon as a charcoal layer dated to 4320 ± 80 BP (Swan-133, 3350–2650 Cal BC) at the base of wood peat on the Goldcliff headland (Chapter 3). Evidence for a Neolithic presence on the nearby dryland comes from pollen analysis at Goldcliff which shows evidence for grazing and later mixed farming following the elm decline (Smith and Morgan 1989), and at Vurlong Reen which shows a *Tilia* decline and subsequent expansion of grass and herbaceous taxa which may be indicative of human interference around 3900–4300 BP (Walker *et al* 1998). Other environmental evidence includes the remains of aurochs (RU-12, Map 1) from Rumney (4060 ± 70 BP, Car-851, 2880–2460 Cal BC; Green 1989) and a complete articulated skeleton (U–7, Map 12) at Uskmouth (4660 ± 70 BP, Car-1096, 3640–3130 Cal BC; Whittle and Green 1988). Both animals probably died naturally rather than as a result of human agency. Both were recovered from the marine clays that intercalate the base of the middle Wentlooge peats. Foraminifera evidence at Rumney suggests that the clays in which the aurochs were found derived from intertidal marshes and sand or mudflats, and the pollen assemblage contains a high proportion of taxa typically found in saltmarshes, which indicate a prevailing marine environment near the mouths of major rivers.

Although later Bronze Age archaeology is well represented on the surface of the peatshelves, in situ earlier Bronze Age finds are almost as elusive as those of the Neolithic. There is, however, a collection of unstratified surface finds that are of interest. Two middle-Bronze Age side-looped spearheads were found on the surface of the lower blue clay where the peat was locally absent: one at Rumney (RU-9, Map 1), and another at the lower foreshore at Portland Grounds (PO-2, Map 17). An early–middle Bronze Age unlooped 'shield pattern' palstave (PO-12, Map 20) of Acton Park type was found on Portland Grounds near Redwick, lying loose on the surface of a peat bed 'from which it had evidently been eroded' (Green 1989). Savory (1954) recorded a middle Bronze Age barbed and tanged arrow-head (CO-11, Map 25) which was picked up on the beach of West Pill by Mr K R Hodges. The stray finds on the lower foreshore are likely to have been derived from another context, most probably the peatshelves of the middle Wentlooge Formation or associated palaeochannels. In the absence of evidence for their original context they could be interpreted as lost objects, a continuation of the diffuse dryland Bronze Age

artefact scatters in Gwent summarised in Lillie (1991). Given their wetland context it also needs to be considered whether ritual deposition was involved, as it may have been with some of the Bronze Age metalwork deposited in a palaeochannel at Caldicot (Nayling and Caseldine 1997). Alternatively, some of the metalwork may have been eroded from settlements on the wetland.

The environment of deposition in the early part of the Bronze Age would have been one of continued presence of alder carr and raised bog. On dryland the most sustained phase of woodland clearance occurred during the early part of the 4th millennium BP, ie in the early–middle Bronze Age (Walker *et al* 1998). The absence of any in situ archaeological sites within the peat of Neolithic or earlier Bronze Age date is striking. Many surfaces within the peatshelf are exposed and, although not specifically dated, their stratigraphic position shows that many must be broadly Neolithic or earlier Bronze Age. This demonstrates either the illusive nature or low density of activity on the coastal wetlands at this time. Even so we must not forget that the archaeological visibility of this phase is bound to be less than that of later periods, because most peats of Neolithic or earlier Bronze Age date are covered by continued later peat growth.

16.9 Archaeology on the surface of the middle Wentlooge peat complex *c* 1500–300 Cal BC

Sites described in the following paragraphs have been discovered on top of the middle Wentlooge peat. Under this heading are included sites from a peaty clay horizon on the surface of the main peat. In many areas this represents the land surface immediately prior to burial by the upper Wentlooge marine sediments. There is, however, evidence that hiatuses exist where the top of the sequence has been eroded. It is also clear that the contact between the peat and clay is time asynchronous, as some areas were flooded earlier than others. The exposed peat surface which was surveyed during the BCS and other surveys, therefore, represents later stages in the coastal wetland, but in some areas the very latest peat to form may have been eroded.

Sites are described for each location; previous research is summarised first, followed by more detailed description of new sites revealed during the BCS survey under their appropriate site heading.

16.9.1 Rumney (Map 2)

Summary of previous work

A late-Bronze Age small roundhouse (Rumney-3.1) constructed of split oak posts *c* 5m in diameter was recorded next to a tidal creek at Rumney by Allen (1996a, 10 and 1996b, 8). The youngest part of one post was dated to 3080 ± 50 BP (Beta-46951, 1460–1210 Cal BC). Within the upper peat and the lowermost few centimetres of silts directly overlying the peat a scatter of fire-cracked stones, charcoal, pottery, and bone (Rumney-3.2) was collected. When the site was revisited during the survey no further pottery was found. The site was close to the seaward edge of the peatshelf, partly truncated and the upper layer of the peat and the silt appeared to have already been eroded.

Approximately 350m to the west of the roundhouse Allen (1996b, 2–6) recorded a scatter of charcoal, fire-cracked flints, cattle bones, and fragmentary pottery (Rumney-1). This was in dark grey silts overlying the main peat and at the edge of an active palaeochannel. It was interpreted as a temporary encampment on active saltmarsh adjacent to a tidal channel (Allen 1996b, 9). A radiocarbon analysis on the charcoal fragments from this site yielded an Iron Age date of 2250 ± 60 BP (Beta-39437, 410–160 Cal BC), although some of the pottery appears to be of late-Bronze Age type.

170m west of the roundhouse Allen recorded (1996a, 10, 1996b, 6–8) another site from within the topmost few centimetres of the peatshelf. This occurred in an area of a water-filled hollow with a mass of hard, baked silt, fire-fractured pebbles, fragments of pottery and a ball of hard-baked clay (Rumney-2), and was interpreted as a hearth from a temporary encampment.

Rumney-4

A small peat island 0.6m in diameter, isolated by erosion of the peat shelf, had around it five stakes in an area 1.6m × 1.4m (CD 16.3). The one stake lifted had a pointed end. These posts are presumably the surviving fragment of some sort of eroded structure.

Rumney-6

An island of peat c 1m across seaward of the main shelf had been protected from erosion by a surrounding rectangular arrangement of sixteen split timbers defining an area 1.6m × 1m, within which was some horizontal wood. It was planned in March 1996 by the writer (Neumann and Bell 1997, 8, CD 16.4) and replanned and excavated in 1997 by Nigel Nayling, to whom we are grateful for information. He found that the timbers generally sloped inwards and the peat surface was at c 3.1m OD. A radiocarbon date is awaited.

Rumney-16 and -17

Two other features of similar dimensions were located during the survey in 1996: an outline of peat within the underlying estuarine clay defined a square c 1m × 1m. At Rumney-17 two small round-

wood posts were located along one side and the peat extended at least 0.07m vertically into the clay. At Rumney-16 no posts were visible.

Rumney-7

The intertidal peat survey has recorded three features within the peat c 100m northwest of the roundhouse. They consist of shallow, c 0.4m × 0.6m wide and a few centimetres deep, depressions within the peat exposing underlying clay, with an orange discoloration and fire-cracked flints and some charcoal. At one of the features (Rumney-7.1) a large piece of charcoal was embedded within the peat immediately adjacent to the feature. They may be hearths similar to Rumney-2.

Conclusions

The peatshelf around Rumney is suffering from severe erosion. It is clear from the range of discoveries which have been made that the area was a significant focus of Bronze Age settlement and activity. The Rumney-1 site suggests that this may have continued into the Iron Age. By the time of its discovery, the site was already partly eroded and it has since suffered further. Circular areas of peat are eroding away and those areas gradually coalescing to create small islands of surviving peat, some of which, like sites Rumney-4 and Rumney-6, survive longer because they are partly protected by structural wood. What remains of the archaeology in this area is in imminent danger of being lost, in particular, the vulnerable silts that directly overly the peat surface and contain much of the occupation debris associated with the wooden structures. The landward edge of the peatshelf, where the overlying upper Wentlooge and Rumney Formations are retreating, provides significant potential for future discoveries.

16.9.2 Redwick-1: Rectangular buildings
Martin Bell and Heike Neumann

No archaeology had previously been published from this area. Recording of wooden structures on the peat shelf discovered by Upton was a priority for the BCS survey, particularly because the structures were similar to those at Goldcliff (Chapters 7–9). During February 1996, at a time of reduced mud cover, four structures were located and marked by pegs, making them easy to relocate for planning during 25–29 March 1996 when there was 50–100mm of mud. The objectives of this exercise were to make as complete a plan as possible of what was exposed and take samples for radiocarbon dating, but otherwise to adopt a minimally invasive strategy. Upton developed the technique of removing the worst of the mud using farmers' slurry scrapers. The peat surface was

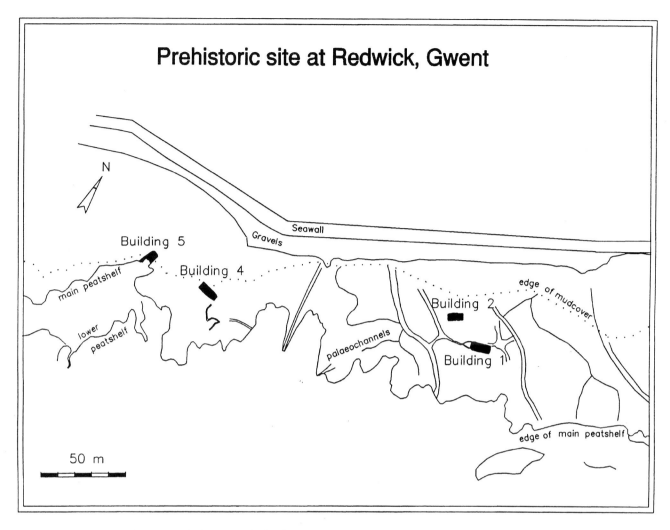

Figure 16.8 Redwick: Plan of the peat shelf showing the locations of Buildings 1, 2, 4, and 5. For an air photograph of the same area see Figure 16.4. Drawing by H Neumann

then cleaned, using trowels and plastic spatulae. Each post located was marked by a waterproof label.

Using these methods a team of about six were able to clean and plan an area averaging 12m × 5m in one or two 6 hour tidal shifts. This site was easy to clean because there was almost no natural wood in the peat. The structures were planned using a local grid of steel pins for each structure and conventional drawing frames. The relationship between the structures, the palaeochannels, and the peat edges etc were mapped from air photographs and detail added by EDM survey (Fig 16.8).

Comments on the shape, size, and character of wood should be regarded as provisional in the case of unexcavated wood because they are based on the eroded stumps. Excavation generally shows that timbers are larger than they had appeared on the surface. Seven pieces of wood were excavated and four of these radiocarbon dated.

Figure 16.5 shows the stratigraphic sequence exposed by the eroding peat shelf. The buildings lie on its surface. For a drawn section and stratigraphic description see Neumann and Bell (1997, 12–13). Many tree stumps are exposed at the front of the peat

shelf on its surface. Further back, *c* 10m from the edge, overlying peat contains no wood and in the area of Building 1 small twisted heather stems and *Eriophorum* show the buildings were on raised bog. They are at *c* 2.4m OD.

Building 1

This building contrasted with the others in that its wall line was marked by a shallow gully (Bell and Neumann 1997, Fig 8), defining a roughly rectangular area, 11.5m × 4.5m, with rounded corners and apparently slightly bowed side walls (Fig 16.9). The building is defined by three large axial posts, of diameters 0.12m, 0.13m, and 0.17m. Seventeen other vertical pieces of wood occur along the line of the gully defining its perimeter. Of these, eleven appear to be roundwood and seven split timber; ranging in size from 20mm to 70mm, with an average of 50mm. The verticals were unevenly disposed, most being at the west end and north side. It is possible that not every vertical was spotted because the building was planned in torrential rain, the gully was waterfilled,

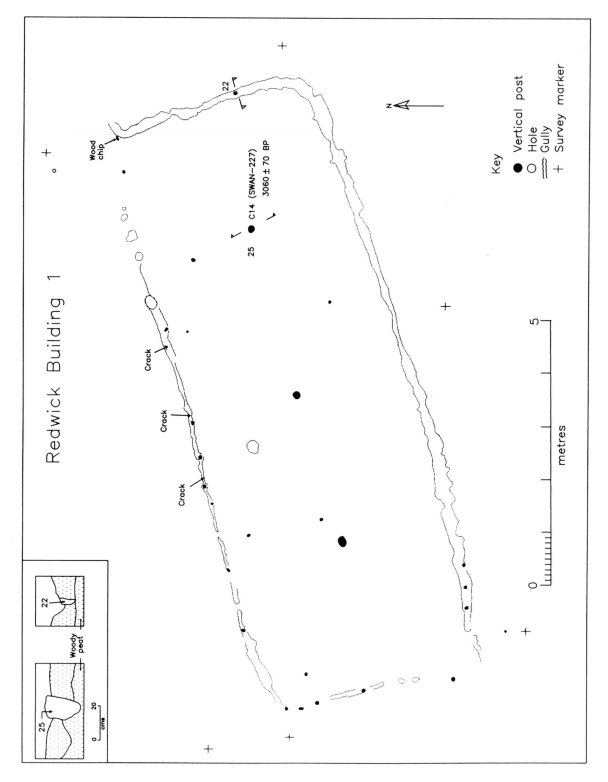

Figure 16.9   Redwick: Building 1 plan with inset sections of Axial Post 25 and Post 22. Drawing by M Bell, H Neumann, and B Taylor

and some timbers had to be located by touch! The impression is that the building had been significantly more eroded at the south side and east end. Upton reports (personal communication) that when originally found there was much more wood along the wall lines. Within the area are six other posts, possibly representing internal divisions.

The gully feature averages *c* 0.2m wide and 50–100mm deep; its base is very irregular and deeper areas probably represent lost posts. The gully is not restricted to the building but forms part of a network of slight channels on the peat surface (Fig 16.8). This is probably a secondary feature relating to a crack in the peat which was very clear in places along the former wall line, a post-depositional feature observed in some Goldcliff West structures (Fig 8.18).

No finds apart from a woodchip were made in cleaning this building. Two timbers were excavated,

a small split timber (22) on the east side, and the eastern axial post (25), from which branches had been trimmed with an axe. The end was not pointed but trimmed flat and was battered. A radiocarbon date was obtained on a sample from this *Betula* post: 3060 ± 70BP (SWAN-227, 1510–1100 Cal BC).

Sections of the two excavated posts show that woody peat appears at a depth of *c* 0.15m below the peat surface, confirming an earlier transition from alder wood to raised bog.

Building 2

Also rectangular *c* 8.9m × 3.8m, with three large axial posts of diameter 0.12m, 0.11m, and 0.11m (Fig 16.10). The western axial post had a square post of sides 50mm beside it, perhaps a support post or

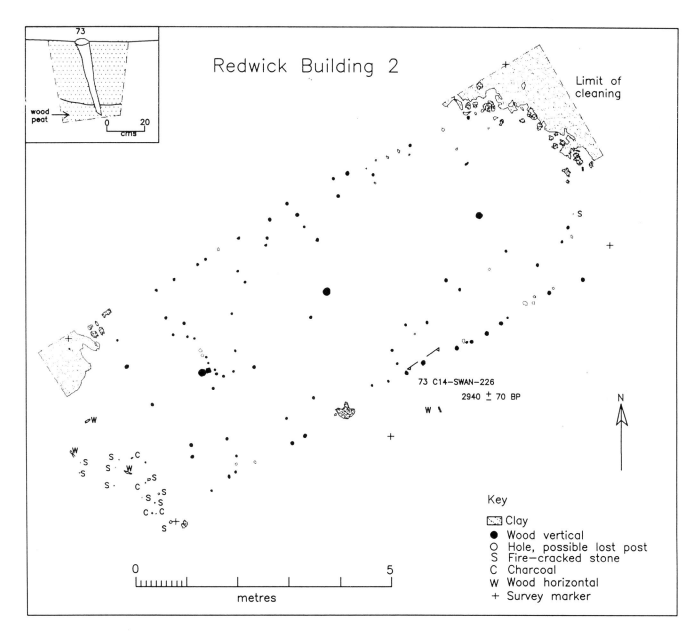

Figure 16.10 Redwick: Building 2 plan with inset section of Post 73. Drawing by M Bell, H Neumann, and B Taylor

packing. The walls were of 46 posts, roundwood with 15% split timber, the average diameter 40mm (Bell and Neumann 1997, fig 10). Holes of similar size along the wall line may represent the positions of lost posts; one contained wood fragments. The eastern end of the south wall was particularly well-preserved. Of the east wall there was little trace and the west wall was represented by just five posts.

Within the area of the building are another 33 posts, all but one roundwood, averaging 30mm in diameter. Several of these form lines at right angles to the walls and may represent subdivisions. The clearest sub-division is a rather irregular line running north from the western axial post which separates an area 1.2m wide by 1.8m in the northwest corner. Two other lines on the north wall suggest the possibility of subdivisions 1.4m and 1.5m wide.

Post 73 was excavated near the middle of the south wall. This was roundwood 55mm in diameter, pointed by a single axe blow; it was identified as *Corylus avellana* and radiocarbon dated 2940 ± 70BP (SWAN-226, 1390–940 Cal BC). In the section excavated for this post wood peat occurred at a depth of 0.3m, suggesting a thicker layer of raised bog peat than in the area of Building 1 to the south.

The building appeared to be on a slight peat rise around which, in places, was grey clay, which at the northeast and northwest corners is shown on the plan. The junction between the peat and the clay is highly irregular and characterised by small patches of clay within the peat. Some of these are of sufficiently regular shape to be identified as cattle footprints.

A scatter of artefacts occurred around the building as shown on Figure 16.10. Most were in peaty clay outside its west end: ten fire-cracked stones; charcoal; small roundwood fragments, possibly wattling; and a woodchip. The presence of many more posts, footprints and artefact scatters at Building 2 suggest that it has been less truncated by erosion than Building 1.

Building 3

Three posts in a line 0.5m long were noted in February 1996 but as they have not subsequently been relocated, it is unclear whether they represent part of another structure.

Building 4

A rectangular structure which appears to measure 12.4m × 3.4m (Fig 16.11). The wall lines are represented by 38 pieces of wood of average diameter 35mm. Of these, 19% were split timber and the remainder roundwood. There are a number of circular holes, some of which may represent the positions of lost wood. Along the inferred wall line are areas where posts are lacking, and the position of the walls is, in places, uncertain.

Two large axial posts of diameters 0.13m and 0.14m are present, 6m apart. Since this distance is much greater than those in other rectangular structures in the estuary it seems probable an intermediate axial may have been lost. The western axial post (206) had a packing of two pieces of split timber and a fire-cracked stone. At the west end is Feature 1 which was excavated. It had a peaty clay fill which contained two bones, a piece of charcoal and a fire-cracked stone. Two pieces of oak planking had been driven into this feature well below the depth of the feature fill. Plank 209 was 0.61m long by 0.11m wide and 30mm thick; Plank 210 was 0.47m long by 0.1m wide and 20mm thick. A probable interpretation for these timbers is that they represent packing for a substantial post which was subsequently removed; it is on a line with the two axial posts and probably served that purpose.

The eastern axial post (205) was excavated and had a flattish base created by many shallow curving axe scars. A radiocarbon date was obtained for this *Quercus* post: 2930 ± 70BP (SWAN-225, 1390–930 Cal BC). In excavating this post a small hollow on the surface to the east was removed. Beneath this hollow, sealed by peat, was a water-rounded boulder 0.22 by 0.18m with a slightly dished surface. This was 0.3m from the axial post and might, at an earlier stage, have served as a pad, or packing stone, for the post. Below the stone was distinctive reedy plant material, very well preserved. The presence of a large stone in this peat seems very likely to relate to human activity. The fact that it was sealed within the peat suggests continued peat growth during the period of activity; this suggests that further traces of this building, and the activities associated with it, may still lie buried in the peat.

Feature 3 lay within the suggested floor area, it was a roughly rectangular area 0.6m × 0.5m and 50mm deep. Its edges were straight in places and may have been cut with a spade. The fill was clay with peat and some charcoal; there were possible cattle footprints, both within the feature and just outside it. Adjoining this feature and outside the Building to the south– west were distinct cracks of the peat surface, which in places contained clay. Unlike Building 1 the cracks had no relationship to wall lines.

There were some pieces of roundwood of average diameter 30mm in the interior, which make no clear pattern, but together with some holes which could represent lost wood, they hint at internal sub-division in the northwest corner. Within the east end of the building was an area where the peat had been charred, indicating perhaps the position of a hearth.

At the west end of the building peaty clay overlay the peat and there were some possible animal footprints at this interface. Clay patches were also present at the east end. Outside the building to the north and west were fire-cracked stones, charcoal, and roundwood fragments, suggesting that occupation horizons may survive in places.

297

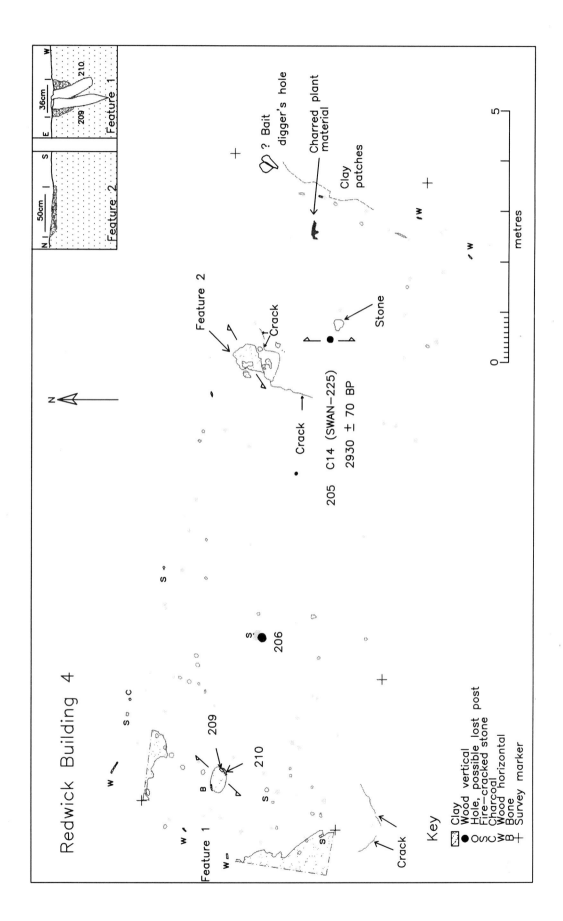

Figure 16.11 Redwick: Building 4 plan with inset sections of Features 1 and 2. Drawing by M Bell, H Neumann, and B Taylor

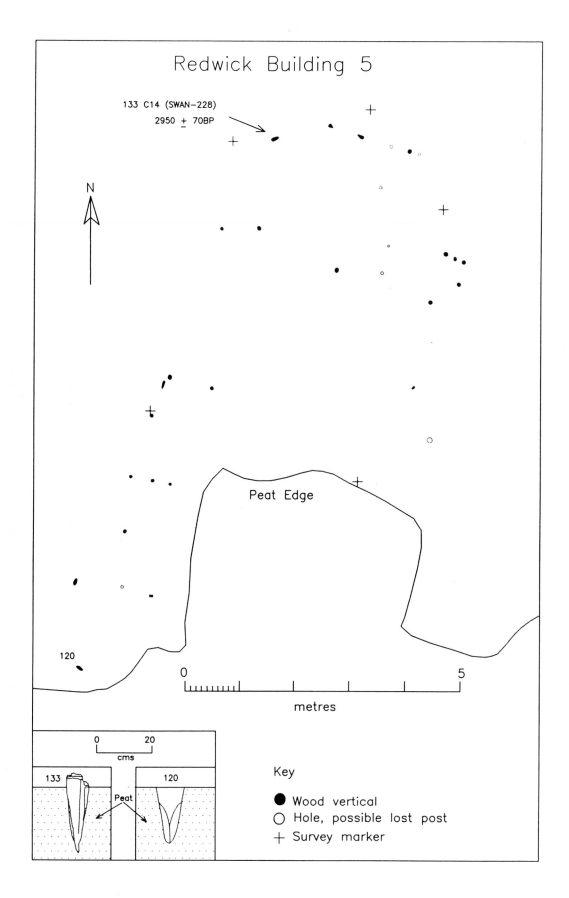

Figure 16.12 Redwick: Building 5 plan with inset sections of Posts 133 and 120. Drawing by N Evans, H Neumann, and B Taylor

Building 5

Defined by 23 pieces of roundwood and split timber marking a rectangular area 10.6m × 4m (Fig 16.12). There were seventeen pieces of roundwood, of average diameter 40mm, and seven pieces of split timber, averaging 80mm × 20mm. The long dimension of the structure was truncated to seaward by the eroding peat edge. The surviving end gave the impression of being curved. There were no substantial axial posts but it seems likely that the structure represents the truncated remains of a building of the same general type as those previously described. Two posts have been excavated; 133 was a split oak timber 80mm × 30mm, radiocarbon dated: 2950 ± 70BP (SWAN-228, 1400–990 Cal BC). The building is of particular interest because it contains a greater proportion of split timber, at least some of which is oak, and it may have future dendrochronological potential.

Other features

About 20m west of Buildings 1 and 2 the peat shelf was crossed by a sinuous palaeochannel some 3m wide which had a fill of grey clay (Fig 16.8). Its floor was very muddy at the time of our fieldwork but Upton has found bone and pot boilers here.

Fieldwalking and other finds

In October 1996 the peat shelf at Redwick was largely clear of mud and the opportunity was taken to fieldwalk an area c 0.5km long with six people spaced at intervals of 5m. The teams walked across the peat shelf from north to south moving 30m to the side with each crossing. The exercise did not bring to light any new structures, although at the time of searching some areas still had significant mud cover, especially north of Buildings 4 and 5, which we have never seen without thick mud. Additional structures have been reported by Upton in the past and were presumably mud covered at this time.

The fieldwalking did produce a few bones and fire-cracked stones, some stratified in the peat surface, some unstratified in the general area of the buildings. A thumbnail scraper was found unstratified on the peat surface 12m north of Building 2 (Bell and Neumann 1997, fig 12). Although small scrapers are often associated with the early Bronze Age, similar forms occur in middle Bronze Age contexts at Brean Down (Saville 1990, figure 109, no 21). An earlier find from nearby may also be relevant: a Bronze Age palstave of Acton Park type was found 'loose on the surface of a peat from which it had evidently been eroded' (Green 1989), some 550m west of the Redwick site. Using Burgess's (1974, fig 26) dating of Acton Park, the palstave could be a century or two earlier than the Redwick structures. Whether or not directly related to the site, the find is further evidence of middle Bronze Age activity. The rectan-

gular buildings at Redwick are the only close parallels for those investigated in greater detail at Goldcliff and the wider issues raised by the two sites are discussed in Chapter 17.

16.9.3 Other sites at Redwick (Map 21)

Redwick-2

Some 210m east of Redwick-1 a scatter of charcoal was identified within the thin clay/peat layer which here forms the transition between the main peat and the overlying clay. A small area of this was cleaned and planned in October 1996 in heavy rain. Embedded within this layer were wood chips and a pointed split timber stake which had been driven into the peat at an angle; its broken top end was sealed by the overlying clay. The site has not been dated but the stratigraphic context is the same as the nearby dated site of Redwick-1, and stakes obliquely driven into the peat are also a feature of Cold Harbour-1, suggesting possible contemporaneity and a wider spatial extent of this type of activity than originally realised. Similar charcoal scatters with their associated finds have been interpreted as temporary encampments representing isolated and intermittent activity. In the light of the other evidence for occupation at Redwick, they may represent the fringes of larger multi-activity occupation sites nearby.

Other observations at Redwick

Several charcoal scatters, as well as other finds of bones and pottery found over the years by Upton within the clay fill of the nearby palaeochannels, indicate intensive activity in this area. In some of the palaeochannels vertical posts and pieces of horizontal wood were observed and may represent the crossing places of palaeochannels. None of these observed to date could, however, be described as a clearly defined trackway. Mudcover has prevented relocation and further investigation of these. In the area north of the dense network of palaeochannels (Map 21), the upper Wentlooge marine clays still cover the underlying raised bog peat. Along the contact between the upper Wentlooge clays and the peat the potential for further discoveries of small artefact scatters still preserved in the easily eroded peat/clay transition is high. Continued monitoring of this area is recommended.

16.9.4 Cold Harbour: previous research (Maps 21–22)

Two sites have previously been recorded from the Cold Harbour Pill area. Cold Harbour-1a comprises two small charcoal concentrations a few centimetres thick from a shallow circular depression within raised bog peat and dated to 2900 ± 60 BP (Car-991, 1300–920 Cal BC, Whittle 1989). They were associated with several fragments of fire-cracked flints, pottery, and pointed stakes, within a clayey peaty layer at the interface between the peatshelf and overlying marine clays of the upper Wentlooge Formation; one small stake was found penetrating below a charcoal scatter, six other small stakes driven into the peat at an oblique angle in the immediate area. A possible cattle hoof print is also noteworthy as the first of many such finds to be documented and associated with one of the estuary's prehistoric sites (Whittle 1989). This site has been interpreted as a temporary encampment. It became buried by a 0.1m thick layer of marine clay, overlying which was a thin peat layer before the whole sequence was buried by the upper Wentlooge clays. The BCS survey with Upton located another charcoal scatter with evidence of stakes 360m west of Cold Harbour Pill (Cold Harbour-1b).

The second previously investigated site was a trackway excavated by Stephen Parry in 1987–98, and there are brief summaries of the results by Marvell (1987, 1988a and b) and Parry (1987). A report on this site has been prepared by Martin Locock and we are grateful to him for information (Locock 1998a). This structure, Cold Harbour-3 (GGAT Excavation 21 Site A, PRN 4328g), was also located within a peaty clay layer above the main peatshelf, and that peat is described as partly sealed by a second much thinner peat. This is a phenomenon which we have observed in a number of places between here and the Redwick settlement. The site is described as two interconnecting trackways; the first was on a *Phragmites* surface and comprised a number of layers of brushwood pegged along one side; the second comprised pairs of stakes driven into the peat to form a V-shape on which planks could have been supported (Marvell 1987), similar to Goldcliff Trackway 1108 (Chapter 10). During the current survey we made no further discoveries in the area where Parry located Cold Harbour-3, so that this site has probably been eroded away.

16.9.5 Chapeltump (Map 23)

Summary of previous work

Excavations in the late 1980s revealed evidence of Bronze Age activity to the east of Chapeltump palaeochannel. In 1986 a substantial roundhouse c 10m in diameter, was excavated near a palaeochannel at Chapeltump-1 (Whittle 1989). It consisted of an inner and outer ring and a central post. A small pottery assemblage, fire-cracked flints, three struck flints, and charcoal fragments were recovered from within a clayey peat directly overlying the woody peat in the area just north of the structure. The central post was dated to 3170 ± 70 BP (Car-992, 1620–1260 Cal BC) and one of the stakes to 2910 ± 70 BP (Car-402, 1370–920 Cal BC) assigning it to a

similar age range to the roundhouse at Rumney-3. Only 80m to the east of this site Upton discovered some occupation debris in 1985 and limited excavations were carried out by Newport Museum and Cardiff University at Chapeltump-2. More detailed excavation in 1986 revealed a pottery assemblage totalling 184 sherds from the interface between the peat and overlying estuarine clay (Trett 1988a). Woodward (forthcoming) shows that the formal characteristics of this assemblage are best matched among the Unit 5b and, particularly, the late Bronze Age Unit 4 assemblage at Brean Down (Woodward 1990). Other finds include bone points, worked roundwood pegs, a small lithic assemblage, a human bone (left femur of adult male), dated to 3080 ± 70 BP (Car-956, 1520–1130 Cal BC), and an oak post dated to 2830 ± 70 BP (Car-961, 1220–830 Cal BC; Trett and Parry 1986). As suggested by Whittle (1989, 211) the range of dates suggests continued interest in an area favoured by occupation. This notion is further strengthened by the Iron Age date for the Upton Hurdle trackway which lies 40m south-southwest of Chapeltump-1.

Chapeltump-3

Another wooden post structure 30m west of the Chapeltump-1 roundhouse was noted during the BCS survey in February 1996. It consisted of a semicircular arrangement of seven posts in the woody peat at the edge of a palaeochannel. This structure could have formed part of another roundhouse of similar dimension but truncated by erosion at the palaeochannel edge. When the site was revisited in March 1996 to survey the area, newly deposited mud concealed all the posts. A large oak stump noted alongside the structure previously was marked and its position surveyed.

16.9.6 Collister Pill–1 Roundhouse
Martin Bell

A roundhouse beside Collister Pill (Map 24) had been observed by Upton, but each time the area was visited it was covered by thick mud and nothing was seen. On 26 January 1998, following storms, Upton and the writer visited the site and found two roundwood verticals on the peat surface. The surrounding peat was cleaned with a slurry scraper, revealing that the two originally observed posts were not part of the roundhouse, which was found just 1m away! On that visit about two thirds of the circle were cleaned and a sketch plan made.

We returned to the site on 14 February 1998 with a team totalling six for 2 days. A 10m square grid of steel pins was established and the mud cover, then between 20mm and 100mm, was removed with slurry scrapers, trowels and plastic spatulae. The clean peat surface revealed an inner and outer circle of posts. A piece of white plastic was cut to the size

301

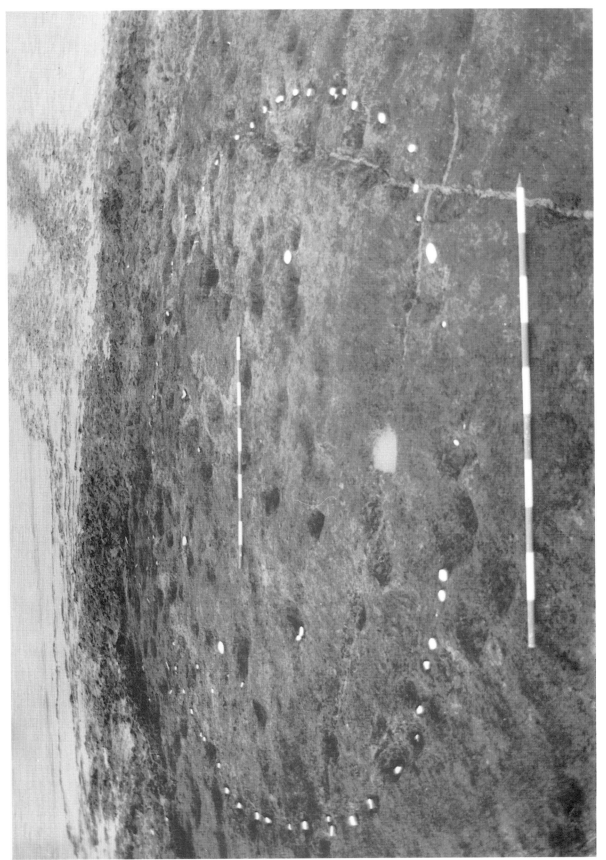

Figure 16.13   Collister Pill roundhouse: February 1998. The position of each post is marked by a plastic outline of the correct size. Scale 2m. Photograph by E Sacre

Figure 16.14   Collister Pill roundhouse: Plan made February 1998. Drawing by S J Allen

and shape of each post and pinned to its top to produce the photograph in Figure 16.13; without the plastic the posts would not have been visible in the dark peat. The building was planned (Fig 16.14) and each piece of wood sampled for identification, although this has not yet been done. One post only was excavated, the southern of the inner post ring which has been sampled for dating but not yet dated.

The inner ring of posts was 3.6m in diameter formed by five roundwood posts of average size 0.1m. The spacing suggests that they were originally about 1.5m apart, if so two may have been lost. The outer circle was 6m in diameter and formed of 57 much smaller roundwood posts ranging in diameter from

30mm to 70mm, with most measuring 40mm. In parts of the wall these were regularly spaced at c 0.3m. In places where they were closer, some may be wattles. A gap at the south-southeast probably represents an entrance, because it is flanked by a post 0.12m in diameter, larger than others in the outer wall. The adjacent gap is 1.6m wide but within this gap there were two tiny pegs, the gap between them just 0.6m. Beside a gap in the northeast segment were three posts just outside the wall line which might suggest an original gap or other feature. Outside the building 1m south are two pairs of posts just 40mm apart separated by 1.7m; they clearly go together and we may imagine something like a forked rack, perhaps for drying just outside the entrance. To the west are two isolated posts.

Within the building were six small roundwood posts of diameter *c* 30mm; these might be the remains of furnishings or subdivisions. One group creates an area *c* 0.6m × 1.4m × 1m beside the west wall; this might have served as a very light pen for animals or have retained the bedding for one person. There was no trace of any flooring within the building. The interior was devoid of finds. There was, however, a scatter of fifteen pottery sherds (report by Woodward, Chapter 16.11), charcoal and four fire-cracked stones just outside the northwest segment of the wall line, where an area 3m × 1m was excavated to a depth of 50–100mm. A total of six fire-cracked stones were found outside the roundhouse to the northeast.

The roundhouse was at 3.15m OD, 50m west of Collister Pill where the peat shelf was 40m wide. On the seaward edge of the peat there was submerged forest but the trees reduced inland. Two small stumps were located 3.2m south of the roundhouse but the roundhouse itself is on wood-free raised bog peat. Within the roundhouse the section of a hole, probably dug by bait diggers, revealed the following sequence from the top down: peaty clay (70mm); *Phragmites* peat (20mm); blue clay (40mm); main peat. The outcrops of peat and clay on Figure 16.14 relate to different levels within this sequence. The peat surface was marked by a prominent rectilinear pattern of cracks filled with grey clay and at the surface sometimes sand, gravel, and shells. On the southern side it seems that these cracks have caused some dislocation to the curve of the roundhouse wall. Such cracks are widespread in the Collister Pill area but it is uncertain whether they relate to the effect of desiccation and cracking in prehistory or off-loading effects relating to the erosion of overlying clay and peat exposure in more recent times. Either way, the cracks must increase the overall vulnerability of this peat to future erosion.

On 21 April 1998 a pit was excavated 2m north of the roundhouse to a depth of 1.15m. The purpose was to obtain pollen monoliths for a M Res dissertation being prepared at Reading University by Rachel Burbridge (1998). This showed that the peat was 0.82m thick. At its top was 50mm of organic peaty clay, containing pottery and charcoal. Cleaning of this layer in plan exposed a probable cattle hoofprint. The upper 0.25m of the peat were wood free, below wood increased, and it is this lower woody peat which is exposed as submerged forest to the south. A marked charcoal band occurred 0.2m from the pit base. Rachel Burbridge's analysis showed that there were three charcoal peaks within the peat, the most prominent in the upper 20cm. The evidence suggests that burning, probably of the wetland vegetation, occurred in two places prior to the roundhouse, and this may hint at an earlier history of human activity in the area. The already noted clay laminations in the bait diggers' hole, and the presence of Chenopodiaceae in the top part of Rachel Burbridge's

sequence, confirms that the use of the roundhouse occurred in the initial stages of the marine transgression which ended the long life of this bog.

The plan of this building is of a very familiar type: the double ring roundhouse, the most ubiquitous building type on dryland sites in the Bronze Age and Iron Age (Guilbert 1981). The inner ring of more substantial posts carries much of the weight of the roof; the slighter, numerous outer posts would have been woven together to create a strong wattle wall. One or two thin pieces of horizontal roundwood are likely to be the remains of wattles but there was no greater concentration of clay along the lines of the walls; presumably, if the structure was daubed then any surfaces relating to daub collapse must have been eroded away. Buildings of this type have been constructed experimentally at the Welsh Folk Museum St Fagans, Castell Henllys (Mytum 1986), Butser (Reynolds 1979), and elsewhere, demonstrating the strength and success of this building form. Being waterlogged, this example must be one of the most complete examples recorded, although it is at the small end of the size range and lacks a porch, sometimes taken as characteristic of residential structures. Larger but incomplete examples of the same structural type are represented by other waterlogged Severn Estuary examples at Chapeltump, where parts of the inner and outer rings remained (Whittle 1989) and Rumney Great Wharf, where only one ring of substantial posts was found (Allen 1996a and b). All three roundhouses were associated with a scatter of charcoal, fire-cracked stone, and Bronze Age pottery. The Rumney and Chapeltump structures have radiocarbon dates in the later Bronze Age and the pottery from Collister Pill is similarly thought by Woodward (Chapter 16.11) to be later Bronze Age.

Collister Pill-4 (Map 24)

A skeleton of a young sheep was found in situ in peat. Stratigraphically it is likely to be Bronze Age. It may have died there naturally and become embedded in growing peat.

16.10 Archaeology in palaeochannels on the middle Wentlooge peat complex

It is clear from the numerous palaeochannels on the peatshelves that the raised bog and carr wetland were drained by sinuous channels commonly a few metres in width. In some cases levées can be recognised, such as at the western palaeochannel at Magor and some of the palaeochannels immediately east of the Redwick structures. These levées are characterised by slight rises of the peat surface which run along the edges of channels and drop away from the channel line. These channels provided the inroads for the marine transgression and as the transgression progressed, they were gradually filled with silts. The presence of later Bronze Age pottery suggests that the infilling of the channels by tidal waters depositing estuarine silts commenced during the later Bronze Age and was completed in the Iron Age, when we see a trackway being laid across the fill of one of these channels.

16.10.1 Rumney: previous research (Map 2)

The only previously recorded Bronze Age finds have been at Rumney (Rumney-14, Map 2). In a clay-filled palaeochannnel on the peat, *Bos* bone and fragments of a Bronze Age pot and jar were recovered (Newport Museum, acc no 91.28.1–4).

16.10.2 Rumney-5 (Map 2)

During the intertidal survey a wooden structure was found. This consisted of two *c* 1m lines of split timbers across a sinuous palaeochannel; they were 0.8 m apart (Bell and Neumann 1997, fig 4, CD 16.6). One line was slightly bowed, pointing in a downstream direction. A plan was made of the structure but in 1997 it was further investigated by Nayling, to whom we are grateful for information. He describes the southern (downstream) row as consisting of four split uprights against which vertical planks of wood had apparently been retained by three partially collapsed uprights. A radiocarbon date is awaited. Nayling also investigated other palaeochannels at Rumney in 1997.

16.10.3 Peterstone palaeochannels (Map 4)

A series of four palaeochannels was identified within the estuarine mud to the south of Peterstone Great Wharf during the field survey in March 1996 when the area was relatively clear of mud. The intertidal area to the south of the saltmarsh is at 2.2 m OD. The peatshelf is largely absent in this area. Occasional exposures along the eroding edge of the saltmarsh and within palaeochannels are patchy and only a few centimetres thick. It is clear, however, that these channels once drained a fen or marsh where peat was forming. Channels 1 to 3 were the subject of survey and recording during 1997 and an interim report was published in Bell and Neumann (1997). The wooden structures in these palaeochannels have since been radiocarbon dated.

Peterstone-1

Some 33 pieces of wood were recorded along a 32 m stretch of the palaeochannel (Fig 16.15): two were posts 10cm or more in diameter, two split timbers, and the remainder small roundwoods, mostly more or less vertical within the channel fill. Peterstone-1

Feature 1 consisted of six small pegs in a rectangle, 0.5m × 0.8m when originally recorded within the clay fill of the palaeochannel (Neumann and Bell 1997, fig 5). It was relocated in March 1997, with only four pegs and the possible impression of a fifth; a gully may have eroded away a sixth peg (Fig 16.15). Given the size of the geometric form, pegs to hold in place fishing baskets or nets seems a plausible hypothesis. Peg 458 was dated to 3000 ± 70 BP (GrN-24150, 1420–1040 Cal BC) assigning it to the Bronze Age. Peterstone-1 Feature 2 had a concentration of round-wood verticals, small pieces of thin horizontal round-wood, in an area 0.8m × 0.7m; some horizontals appeared to have been woven round the verticals in the fashion of wattles (Fig 16.15). It may have been part of a light woven fence running, at least partly, across the channel; it might also represent the crushed and eroded remains of a basket-like structure.

A wooden object (Peterstone-1.3) was recovered from within the clay fill of the palaeochannel (Fig 16.16). The object is in three pieces and appears to have been fashioned from a piece of radially split wood which would have been more than 0.89m long. The shape of the object is similar to a paddle but the rounded end is less wide and fatter than would be expected for this purpose. Comparisons with paddles from other sites suggest that it may be a dual purpose implement to serve both as a paddle and a punting pole, which could account for its worn and rounded end (Bell and Neumann 1997, 15). Although the identification of this artefact as a paddle is tempting, in view of its context within a palaeochannel and with the nearby possible fishing structures, its unconventional shape makes this identification uncertain. It might have served many other functions as a digging stick, or a tool for making holes in the mud for the emplacement of posts.

Peterstone-2

Palaeochannel 2 (Fig 16.17) is marked by a ridge of peat, its upper surface concave and the ridge curving seaward where this peat also became eroded. Its continuation as a clay-filled channel could be followed for 25m beyond the extant peat ridge. Close to the saltmarsh it was cut by a linear ditch 1.65m wide. Three other short sections of ditch (Peterstone-6) in the area are of similar alignment; Allen (1987a, fig 3) interprets ditches in this area as Romano-British. In the area where peat remained eleven vertical posts and pegs were recorded within the channel but did not form a recognisable pattern. Within the channel there were also nine bones, including an antler, a fire-cracked stone (Peterstone-2.3) and some twisted wood fibres which are probably the remains of a withy tie (Peterstone-2.2). Three sherds of pottery were recovered from the clay-fill of this channel by Upton during a small excavation in March 1997 (Peterstone-2.1); for these Woodward suggests a late-Bronze Age date (Chapter 16.11).

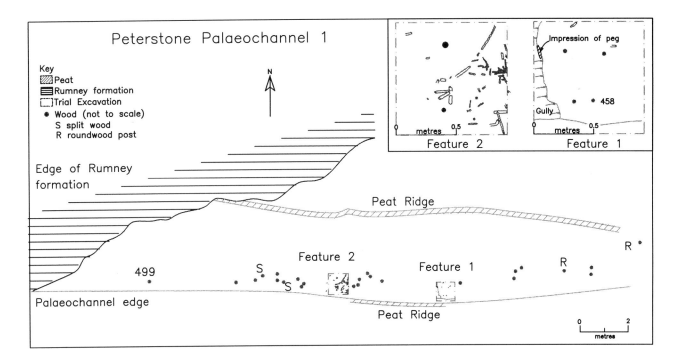

Figure 16.15 Peterstone Palaeochannel 1: showing the location of wood in the palaeochannel, including Features 1 and 2 (shown enlarged) and the location of Object 499. Wood 458 has a radiocarbon date of 3000 ± 70 BP (GrN-24150). Drawing by H Riley, H Neumann, and B Taylor

Peterstone-3

The west end of this channel is overlain by the Rumney Formation and saltmarsh. The palaeochannel extends from this as a raised peat ridge, which can be followed east as a low clay ridge and beyond this by intermittent wood posts and bones (Fig 16.18). A total of twenty posts, six bones, and four stones were recorded in this length. The posts were irregularly placed but a linear row of eight split uprights was aligned along the north side of the channel. One of these, Vertical 523, has been dated to 3910 ± 60BP (GrN-24149, 2580–2200 Cal BC) which would place it within the late Neolithic/early Bronze Age. It was a timber of square section and an end pointed by many axe blows, the dished profile of which suggested to Brunning that they may have been made with a bronze axe. This post alignment represents an important find as it is the earliest dated in situ archaeological find for the Neolithic/early Bronze Age, a period for which we have very little evidence in our study area as a whole.

An undated ditch appears from below the Rumney Formation and approaches the palaeochannel diagonally. Unfortunately, erosion appears to have bottomed the ditch out just north of the point at which they would converge. This ditch is another of the series of probably Romano-British ditches (Peterstone-6) in the Peterstone area (Allen 1987a, fig 3).

Palaeochannel 3 can be traced, in places where the overlying Rumney Formation has been eroded away, curving west where it appears to join Palaeo-

channel 4 (Map 4). This again takes the form of a peat ridge, and beyond this a low ridge of clay. The only finds from that channel are a *Bos* jaw and one other bone.

Conclusions

The Peterstone palaeochannels are in a stretch of the foreshore which had been unproductive of finds, yet these discoveries, made over just 2 days of fieldwork under only moderately favourable conditions of mud cover, have been surprising. They confirm the impression from elsewhere in the estuary that prehistoric communities made wooden structures within palaeochannels probably for fishing purposes. The radiocarbon dates from these structures suggest a long tradition of use and a diversity of structures and activities. The time scale of activity has been pushed further back with the discovery of an in situ late-Neolithic/early-Bronze Age structure. This demonstrates the importance of palaeochannels as sources of evidence for earlier activity that may be more obscured on the peat shelf where visibility may be restricted by continuing peat growth. The artefacts from Peterstone suggest the probability of a settlement nearby. One of the wooden structures has a similar date to the roundhouse at Rumney, 2.5km to the west. If we are correct in inferring that a peat once existed in this area and was largely eroded away some time before deposition of the overlying Rumney Formation, then it is possible that settlement traces have gone with it, leaving only remnants in the

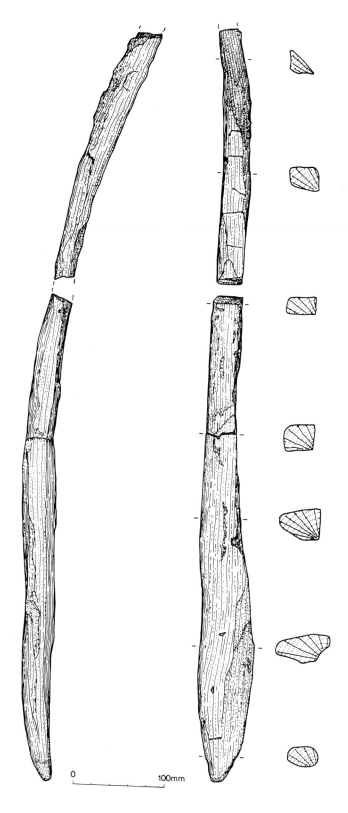

Figure 16.16 Peterstone Palaeochannel 1: Wooden Object 499. Drawing S J Allen

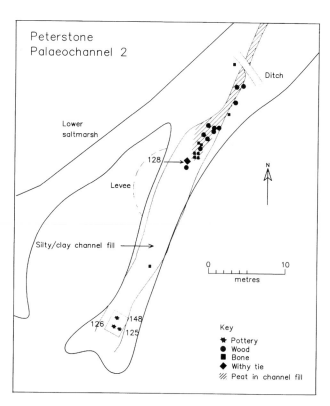

Figure 16.17 Peterstone Palaeochannel 2: solid black outline transcribed from air photographic cover. Grey lines and artefacts picked up by GPS in 1997. Drawing by H Riley and B Taylor

adjacent palaeochannels. However, artefacts occur both in the peat and in the underlying clay channel fill suggesting that occupation may not be purely confined to the period of peat formation. The presence of a late-Neolithic/early-Bronze Age structure suggests that the area between Rumney and Peterstone, where the peat has been largely eroded, may still hold potential for further discoveries of earlier periods for which visibility is restricted in most other areas.

16.10.4 Cold Harbour-2 (Map 21)

A clearly defined group of post settings within a palaeochannel. Here the surface of the peat shelf is marked by a channel with a fill of consolidated grey clay (Map 21). When the area was visited after a storm in February 1996 a distinct pattern of wooden elements was observed. This consists of a linear, but somewhat irregular, fence-like line of roundwood verticals (Neumann and Bell 1997, figs 13, 14) running along the south side of the channel with a group of thin roundwood verticals at the east end (Fig 16.19). A little beyond the west end of the line is an area of roundwood verticals which define a roughly circular area 0.7m in diameter (Figs 16.20 and 16.21). In October 1996 a small trench 0.3m × 0.6m was excavated across part of this structure. This showed that it consisted of pointed pieces of roundwood 0.5m or more long around which, at the top, were woven thin pieces of roundwood to form a basket-like structure (Fig 16.21). One of the vertical pieces of roundwood (no 230) provided a radiocarbon date of 2520 ± 60 BP (SWAN-241, 790–530 Cal BC). Adjoin-

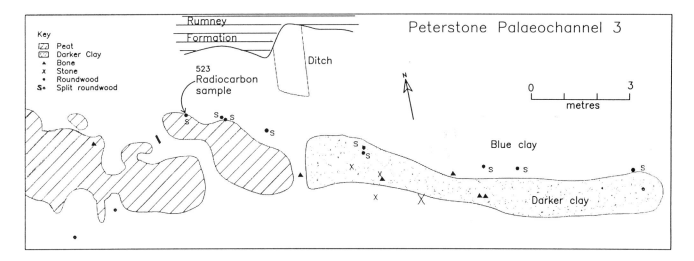

Figure 16.18 Peterstone Palaeochannel 3: Line of the palaeochannel, shaded, and along its line, posts, bones, and stones. Wood Sample 523 has been radiocarbon dated 3910 ± 60 BP (GrN-24149). Drawing by S J Allen and B Taylor

ing the previously described area is a more irregular area, *c* 1m in diameter, of thin roundwood verticals. On the edge of the channel, which is within 1m of these structures, the peat clay edge is marked by small circular areas of clay on peat. These appear to be cattle footprints. Other roundwood verticals and bones are found scattered elsewhere in the channel and in an area of mixed peat and clay on the south side of the channel.

The woven structure at Cold Harbour Pill is of considerable interest in demonstrating, for the first time, that a wooden structure within a palaeochannel on the peat surface is of early Iron Age date. This structure seems most likely to be some sort of fish trap, possibly involving a fence-like arrangement and woven baskets.

16.10.5 Magor: previous research (Map 22)

Following the discovery by Upton and Trett of Iron Age pottery from the general area around the eastern palaeochannel at Magor Pill in 1985, one narrow channel was sectioned and described at Magor-1 (Whittle 1989, 217–20). The channel was cut approximately 0.8m into the main peatshelf and filled with marine clay. Stratified in the upper part of the fill was a small assemblage of Iron Age pottery, most notable a well preserved bucket-shaped pot assigned to the 3rd–1st centuries BC. Other finds included animal bone, including horse, and a wooden peg. The unabraded pottery was thought to belong to a period of transgression and to derive from an occupation close by on the wetland (Whittle 1989, 221). Allen (forthcoming b) has examined a further pottery assemblage from the Magor Pill area which includes late-Iron Age calcite tempered ware. He hypothesises that this assemblage may derive from a seasonal animal herding camp on the silt marshes.

16.10.6 Magor-9 and -10 (Map 22)

Approximately 150m to the east of the Magor Pill eastern palaeochannel Upton reported a possible hearth on the surface of the raised bog peat and a brushwood trackway in its vicinity. The hearth (Magor-9) was concealed under mud when visited in February 1996, but some of the wood from the trackway (Magor-10) protruded from the edge of the mudcover. These conditions only allowed the location of these features to be recorded and it has not been possible to revisit the site under more favourable conditions. Stratigraphically the hearth is likely to be Bronze Age, being on the surface of the bog itself, and it is possible that the trackway can also be allocated to that period, or the Iron Age.

16.10.7 Chapeltump: previous research (Map 23)

Some unusually large horse skulls have been reported washed out in the Chapeltump palaeo-channel (Chapeltump-4); one specimen is held at Newport Museum, another was collected during the survey. The stratigraphic context of these skulls from within the palaeochannel seems to suggest an Iron Age date. The area deserves monitoring in view of the evidence from elsewhere (noted in Chapter 5) for 'special deposits' including horse bones of Iron Age date. Given the fact that these horse skulls have been described as large, and the prevailing view is that most horses in this period were the size of small ponies (Maltby 1996, 23), the context and character of these horse skulls also requires further investigation. It has been suggested that the rearing of horses for military use was an important aspect of the economy of the reclaimed levels in the Roman period (Allen and Fulford 1986), but perhaps this tradition extends

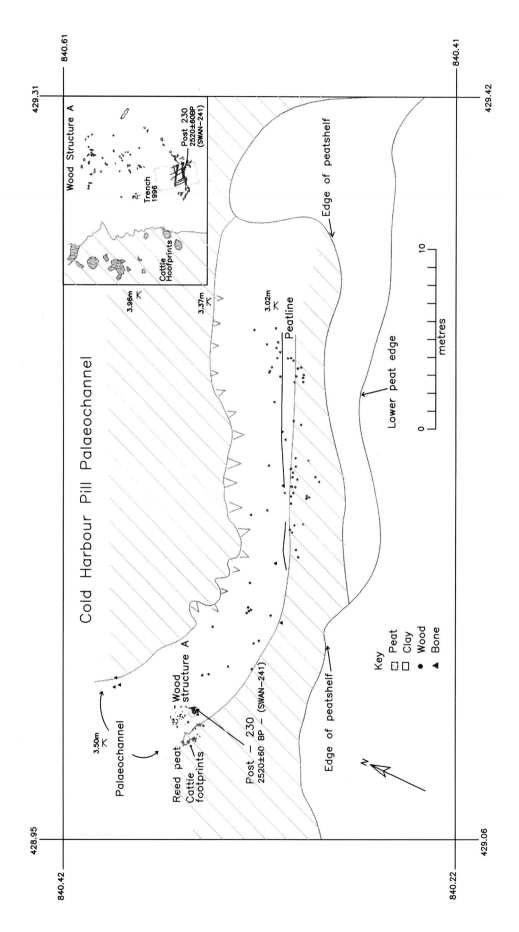

Figure 16.19 Cold Harbour Pill-2: Palaeochannel showing along the south side of the channel many wood stakes. Inset Wood Structure A. Drawing by H Neumann, M Bell, and B Taylor

Figure 16.20 Cold Harbour Pill 2 Palaeochannel: Wood Structure A, a roughly circular area of thin roundwood pieces. Scale 0.3m. Photograph by M Bell

further back than previously thought. From the same channel other animal bones and Iron Age pottery have been found by Upton.

A trackway, the 'Upton Hurdles' (Chapeltump-5), named after its finder, was excavated in 1985 from within the Chapeltump palaeochannel and was dated to 2400 ± 70 BP (Car-960, 770–390 Cal BC; Trett and Parry 1986). It was located at 2.45m OD within estuarine silt. It consists of at least two woven wooden hurdles and could be traced over a distance of 3m. The hurdles were *c* 1m wide and secured by five pegs driven vertically through the hurdle (Trett 1988b).

Figure 16.21 Cold Harbour Pill 2 Palaeochannel: Wood Structure A in section

16.10.8 Collister Pill-2 (Map 24)

This was investigated as a representative of a class of site for which there were hints in many places: a palaeochannel crossed at right angles by a few pieces of brushwood and with one or two pegs. This brushwood trackway was exposed in a palaeochannel 4.5m wide (Figs 16.22 and 16.23). The channel ran across the main woody peat and had a fill of mixed peat and clay. The trackway led from the peat edge across the clay and peat fill of the channel and comprised 44 pieces of brushwood, mostly oriented at right angles to the palaeochannel. Most of the wood was horizontal, but a few pieces may represent pegs which held the brushwood in position. Some pieces were overlain by peat and may have been driven into the peat by trampling; one of the horizontals appears to have been broken in two underneath a hoof print. The trackway was dated to 3050 ± 65 BP (GrN-24152, 1450–1100 Cal BC) and appears to have been constructed at the final stages of the bog immediately prior to it being submerged by the upper Wentlooge clay.

16.10.9 Collister Pill-3 (Map 24)

A substantial palaeochannel was marked by a 19.2m wide gap in the peat shelf and filled by clay. From this channel Upton had reported discoveries over several years including wood, stone, and pottery from the east edge of the channel (Fig 16.24). Bank-parallel cracks, similar to those recorded in a

Figure 16.22 Collister Pill 2: A palaeochannel which is crossed by a light brushwood trackway. Scales 0.45m and 1m. Photograph E Sacre

palaeochannel at Magor Pill (Allen and Rippon 1995, fig 23), and changes in the colour, particle size, and organic matter content of the clay channel fill, marked successive palaeochannel edges. Activity appears to have taken place at one such edge where three 0.1m wide pieces of roundwood projected from the eroding clay fill of the channel at a steep angle dipping towards the eastern channel edge. One of these (Wood 551) was dated to 2390 ± 60 BP (GrN-24151, 770–380 Cal BC). Between these posts and the channel edge a concentration of thirteen, mostly angular and clearly fire-cracked stones, lay stratified within the channel fill. Further south of this area other fire cracked stones lay scattered in the same channel. There were also four pieces of roundwood pegs 20mm in diameter and one piece of bone. In 1994 and 1997 Upton recorded the position of three sherds of Bronze Age pottery (Chapter 16.11) in relation to the wood (Fig 16.24). Another sherd has been found unstratified on the surface of the same channel to the south.

The parallel roundwood elements and pegs might suggest either a trackway or jetty at the edge of a channel. The association with burnt stone, pottery and bone is not something which has been recorded in relation to trackways elsewhere in the estuary,

and the size of the roundwoods suggest that they were supporting a more substantial structure than the known trackways. Burnt stones occur elsewhere in the estuary, notably in association with the Redwick Bronze Age settlement and in the fill of the palaeochannel at Caldicot (Nayling and Caseldine 1997, 246). Burnt mounds representing much larger concentrations of similar burnt stones are of frequent occurrence in western Britain and Ireland during the Bronze Age and are generally associated with watercourses. This structure seems likely to have been associated with some specific activity in the Iron Age and it is probable that there was an area of settlement, whether temporary or permanent, nearby. Similar finds of pottery, fire-cracked stones, and wood in the Magor-1 palaeochannel (Whittle 1989) were also assigned to the Iron Age. The Collister Pill structure is of the same date as the Upton Hurdle trackway (2400 ± 70 BP) in the Chapeltump palaeochannel, less than 2km to the west. The evidence from Collister Pill-3 is a further indication of Iron Age settlement activity in this area.

On the opposite side of this palaeochannel and 87m seaward Upton discovered a wood structure which he and Bell roughly cleaned and recorded on 26 January 1998 (CD 16.5). It was linear, 1.05m across, the exposure just 0.1m thick. It comprised 27 pieces of roughly vertical roundwoods of diameter 10–15mm (one 40mm) around which nine horizontals of diameter 10–20mm appeared to have been woven. This seems likely to have been a hurdle which could have formed a track sloping down into the palaeochannel, or some sort of wattlework fishing structure as envisaged at Cold Harbour Pill-2.

16.10.10 Saddle quern from West Pill (Map 25)
Martin Bell

Late in 1997 Upton found a large saddle quern (Collister-8) 120m west of West Pill. The findspot was visited on 26 January 1998 and the impression left by removal of the quern was clear. The surrounding area was cleaned with a slurry scraper which showed that it had been stratified in sandy grey clay in which there were some small peat pebbles and pieces of wood, and 5m away a 1m × 1m raft of peat. Accordingly, it is thought likely that the find comes from a palaeochannel. Cattle footprints were present 5m from the quern, and 31m to its east was the partially articulated skeleton of a Bovid.

The quern (Fig 16.25) is made on a slab, 0.63m × 0.30m × 0.08m high, of fine grained silicified sandstone in which there appear to be some small pebble sized inclusions. A dished upper surface 0.46m long has been produced by working; the lower part of the dished area is 22mm lower than each end. At the narrower end there is rough chipping in places round the sides to remove irregularities. Also at the narrower end, and down each side, there is evidence

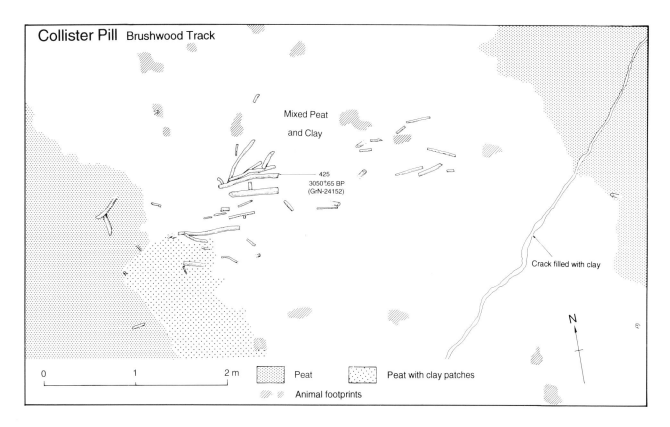

Figure 16.23 Collister Pill 2: A palaeochannel crossed by a light brushwood trackway. Drawing by S J Allen

of a pronounced polish on the dished surface. Most of the dished area within this margin has been extensively pecked with a sharp object to create an irregular grinding surface. The polish down the margins indicates that this pecking is a reworking of an earlier smoothed surface. Pecking seems to have taken place in lines down the long axis. Within the pecked area the higher points, which often represent the larger inclusions, have been flattened and polished. The concentration of working, wear, and polish at the narrower end indicates that the user was positioned there, the opposite end being irregular and unworked. Although this object could have been used for a range of grinding and polishing purposes, its character and the pattern of wear suggests a saddle quern for grinding grain. Such querns were in use from the Neolithic until the middle Iron Age; there are examples from Glastonbury Lake Village (Roe 1995). The find is not directly datable, but a barbed and tanged arrowhead was earlier found at West Pill (Savory 1954) so it seems probable that there was an eroded Bronze Age site in this area. The quern findspot, more than 1km from the edge of the wetland, is of particular interest since it implies that activities such as crop processing may have taken place within the wetland.

16.10.11 Post-prehistoric finds

Investigation of these was not a particular objective of the survey but even so Romano-British ditches,

fish traps, stone strews, and rectangular pits were recorded; some wrecks of probable post-medieval date were also noted. These finds are summarised, in the context of work on later periods, by others in CD 16.7–9.

16.11 Bronze Age pottery from Collister Pill 3, Peterstone Palaeochannel 2, and Collister Pill Roundhouse
Ann Woodward

A total of 21 sherds of middle-Bronze Age to early-Iron Age date were recovered from three separate sites. The three small assemblages are described and discussed separately.

Collister Pill Roundhouse

A total of fourteen sherds, of average weight 15g, were found as a scattered group northwest of the roundhouse (see Fig 16.14). These sherds may all have derived from a single vessel. Their matrix is slightly laminated and micaceous and contains a medium density of grog and very rare large inclusions, some apparently limestone, and some smooth pebbles. The hard inclusions may have been incorporated accidentally. The material was mainly fresh, but three sherds were slightly abraded and one had been refired.

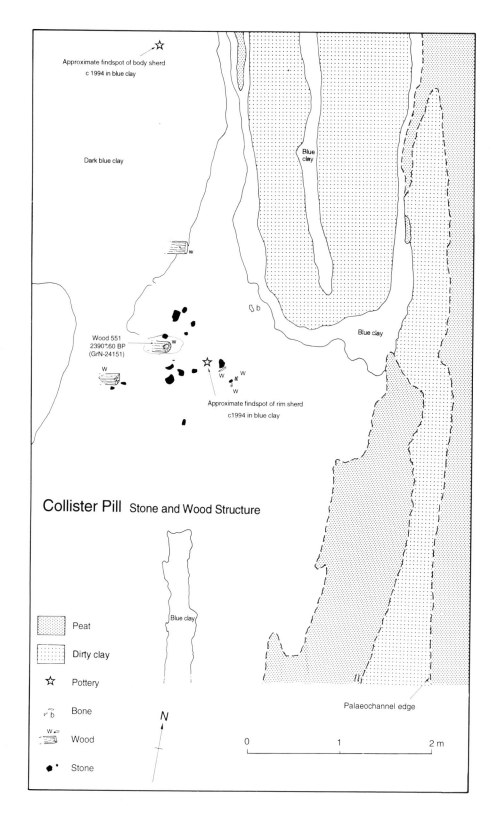

Figure 16.24   Collister Pill 3: Large palaeochannel with pieces of roundwood, burnt stone, and pottery near its edge. Drawing S J Allen

Fig 16.26a: Flattened rim sherd (11% of circumference surviving) from a small plain vessel. Find 123A.

Fig 16.26b: Simple base angle, interior surface absent. Find 128: this simple thick-walled small vessel, or vessels, can be matched at the nearby site of Chapeltump-2 where flattened rims and simple

bases occur in similar grog-tempered fabrics (above p300 and Woodward forthcoming, 7, 10–13, 19–20). The Chapeltump-2 assemblage was dated by radiocarbon analysis to the middle-Bronze Age period, and is similar in date to the timber roundhouse found at Chapeltump-1 (Whittle 1989). Such pottery is also found at Lesser Garth Cave, Glamorgan (Savory

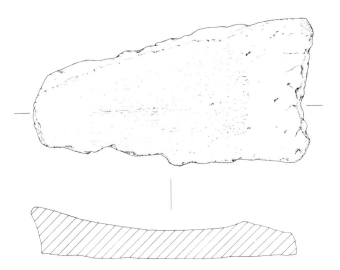

Figure 16.25 West Pill: Saddle quern, Scale 1:8. Drawing by J Foster

1980b, fig 72) and, across the Severn, on sites such as Brean Down, Units 4 and 5b (Woodward 1990, figs 91 and 95). Much of the Trevisker-related assemblage from Brean Down Unit 5b was decorated, but plain vessels were also present.

Collister Pill Palaeochannel 3

Four large sherds of average weight 141g were recovered. The fabrics were coarse and dark in colour. The main inclusions were a sparse scatter of medium to large angular fragments of white and translucent calcite. The sherds were fresh, except Sherd 2 (not illustrated) which was refired. The average rim circumference represented is 11%.

Fig 16.26c: Rim to belly fragment from plain, ovoid jar with a plain, tapered, and everted rim.

Fig 16.26d: Rim, shoulder, and upper wall from a tall, plain, straight-necked jar with a high, rounded shoulder. The simple rim has a slight internal bevel.

Fig 16.26e: Rim and shoulder from an extremely large, plain jar with a flat-rimmed, vertical, thin-walled neck standing above a rounded shoulder. There is a distinct moulding on the interior surface at shoulder level.

The three vessels represented belong to a very specific group of straight-necked, thin-walled jars of large size. In Wessex such jars occur predominantly in assemblages of early-Iron Age date. For instance, they are common in the Cadbury 6 and Cadbury 7 levels of the Site D ditch cutting at Cadbury Castle, Somerset (Barrett, Freeman, and Woodward, forthcoming), at Ham Hill, Somerset (Morris 1987, fig 3, form J1) and in Danebury ceramic phases 3 and 4 (Cunliffe 1984, form JB2). Danebury provides the best dated sequence and, according to the latest interpretation of the radiocarbon dates there, Cunliffe offers a 5th–4th century BC date for these two

ceramic phases (Cunliffe 1995, 18). Although such vessel profiles do not occur in the late-Bronze Age assemblages of the Thames Valley, they are found in late-Bronze Age groups further west. Thus, we may draw attention to the vessels from Brean Down Unit 4 (Woodward 1990, fig 96, 108 and fig 97, 116) and the rather smaller straight necked jars found within the earliest assemblage at Thornwell Farm, Gwent (Woodward 1996, fig 26, 21–22). All these western assemblages are characterised by calcareous inclusions, and the calcite-tempered pieces from Collister Pill-3 are remarkably similar to some of the material from Brean Down Unit 4. Stylistically, therefore, these sherds could be of late-Bronze Age or early-Iron Age date: the radiocarbon date suggests, however, that they belong in the later sector of this period range.

Peterstone Palaeochannel 2

Three sherds, two of which join, were of average weight 21g. Two separate vessels are probably represented although the fabrics are similar, containing rare small- to middle-sized inclusions of white calcite in a sandy matrix. The vessels were thin-walled, and the interior and exterior surfaces were carefully smoothed. All three sherds were very fresh.

Fig 16.26f: Simple rim from a fine vessel, decorated with wide, slightly uneven, incised horizontal grooves; 9% of circumference represented. Find 125.

Fig 16.26g: Two joining decorated wall sherds from the belly of another similar fine vessel. The decoration includes one complete zone, roughly executed incised cross-hatch bounded by two triple sets of horizontal grooves and the beginning of another set of horizontal grooves below. Finds 126 and 148.

These vessels are similar to some of the highly decorated pots from Brean Down Unit 5b, where deep horizontal grooving and cross-hatch motifs both occur (Woodward 1990, figs 89 and 90). This would indicate a middle-Bronze Age date for the Peterstone-2 vessels, and this is confirmed by the result of the radiocarbon determination from Palaeochannel 1.

16.12 The sequence of prehistoric activity

The survey of both the character of peat exposures and the types of archaeological finds has shown that the density of archaeological finds is closely linked with the palaeoenvironmental context. The highest density occurs on raised bog peat and includes round and rectangular buildings, assemblages of charcoal, fire-cracked flint, bone and worked wood.

The network of palaeochannels on the surface of the bog also contains a distinct set of finds. Most commonly these comprise post alignments, woven structures, bone, fire-cracked flint and some pottery. Many palaeochannels, in particular those in the vicinity of rectangular buildings, have cattle hoofprints around the edges. Trackways crossing

314

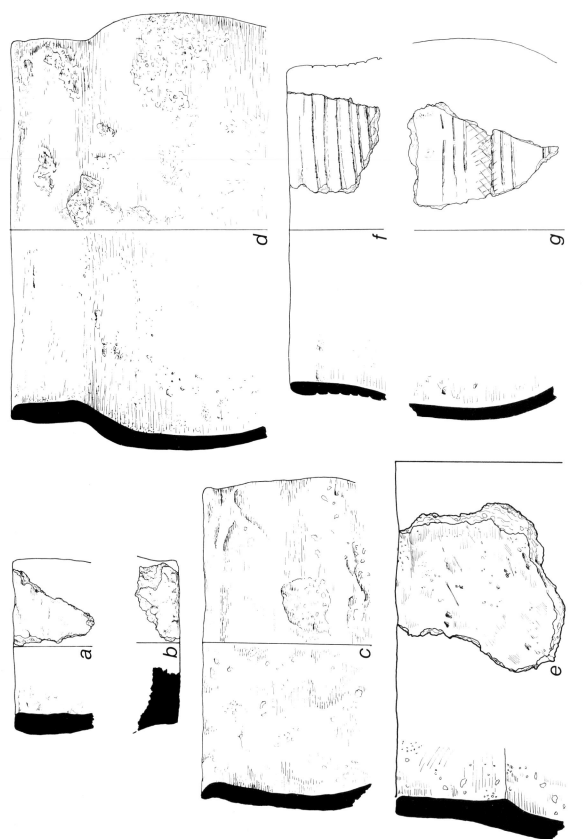

Figure 16.26 Pottery: (a–b) Collister Pill Roundhouse, (c–e) Collister Pill Palaeochannel 3, (f–g) Peterstone Palaeochannel 2. Scale 1:2. Drawing by J Foster

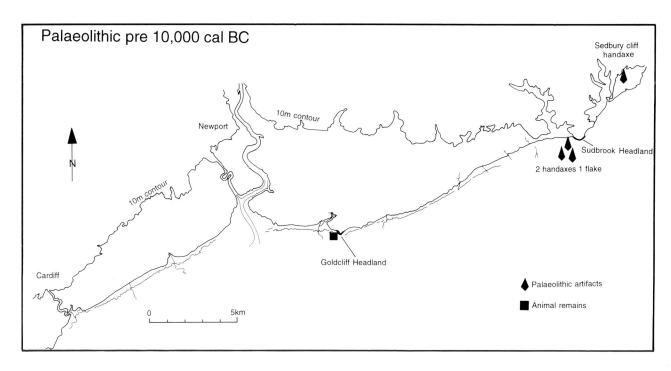

Figure 16.27 *Distribution of Palaeolithic finds. Drawing by H Neumann*

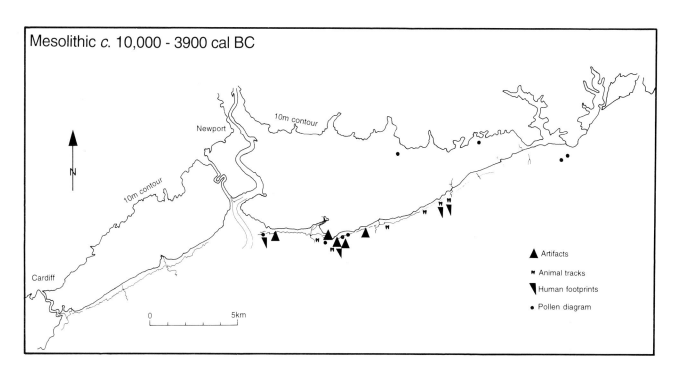

Figure 16.28 *Distribution of Mesolithic finds c 10,000–3900 Cal BC. Drawing by H Neumann*

these channels have been identified at Chapeltump and Collister, but the highest density occurs at Goldcliff where they are not generally associated with palaeochannels but were built on reed peat, wood peat, and raised bog peat (Chapter 10).

The survey of other areas of reed and fen wood peat between the main areas of raised bog peat (St Brides, Porton, Collister Pill to Sudbrook) and around major river outlets has shown that these areas are lacking in situ prehistoric archaeology.

Palaeolithic (Fig 16.27)

Palaeolithic finds all originate from Pleistocene gravels exposed on the eastern margins of the Gwent Levels at Sudbrook and Sedbury cliffs (Green 1989, Aldhouse-Green 1993). This is a reflection of site visibility. When the levels became increasingly flooded as a result of sea level rise from the early Holocene onwards, the Palaeolithic landscape was buried. Pleistocene deposits are exposed on the

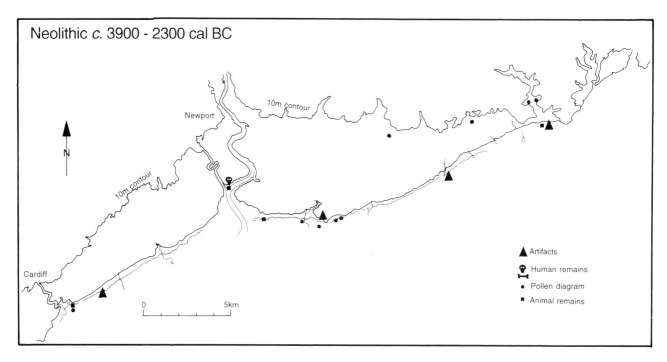

Figure 16.29   Distribution of Neolithic finds c 3900–2300 Cal BC. Drawing by H Neumann

margins of bedrock outcrops, as at Sudbrook, with finds of Palaeolithic tools, and Goldcliff with Pleistocene raised beach, head, and animal bones but no archaeology.

Mesolithic (Fig 16.28)

The only occupation site from this period is at Goldcliff (Chapter 4). During the early and middle Mesolithic sea level rose rapidly and laminated clays and silts accumulated in estuarine mudflats over large expanses of the Gwent Levels: the lower Wentlooge Formation. Animal hoofprints in this deposit attest to the presence of red deer, aurochsen, and dog/wolf (Allen 1997a and b, 503), as well as human footprints (Aldhouse-Green et al 1992). Although the foreshore beyond the peatshelves was not investigated systematically within the scope of this survey, human and animal tracks were recorded at many locations near the edge of the peatshelves, with particular concentrations east of Uskmouth, Redwick, Cold Harbour, and Magor. Unstratified finds of axes/adzes at Goldcliff East and Porton, together with the footprint sites and an antler mattock at Uskmouth, may well represent forays from a dryland site, eg on Goldcliff Island, towards the surrounding open estuarine mudflats. The earliest radiocarbon dates from the base of the peat at Uskmouth (6140 ± 100 BP, OxA-3307), Goldcliff (5950 ± 80 BP, Car-659), Magor (5720 ± 80 BP, OxA-2626), and Sudbrook (6660 ± 80 BP, Beta-79886) show that these mudflats were beginning to be colonised by reed swamps and alder carrs before the end of the Mesolithic.

Neolithic (Fig 16.29)

This is a period for which at present we have remarkably little evidence of human activity; just previously noted isolated artefacts and evidence of clearance and charcoal horizons at Goldcliff Island. Aurochsen skeletons found at Rumney, Uskmouth, and Sudbrook also date to the Neolithic but these are probably wild animals which became naturally enmired. The only in situ archaeology thus far discovered is from the end of the Neolithic when there is evidence at Peterstone of a wooden structure in a palaeochannel.

Bronze Age (Fig 16.30)

Finds from this period are the most common on the peatshelves. Three major areas of Bronze Age settlement have been identified: Rumney Great Wharf, Redwick/Cold Harbour, Chapeltump, and Collister Pill. All are located on raised bog and are associated with buildings and occupation debris. In most cases artefacts including charcoal, bone and wood, and sometimes pottery were preserved in a peaty clay layer immediately overlying the surface of the raised bog. Where this layer was eroded, more resistant wooden posts relating to building structures were still clearly visible. Two types of building have been identified. Roundhouses are found at Rumney Great Wharf (Allen 1996a and b), Chapeltump (Whittle 1989), and Collister Pill; such structures are typical of this period. The other type are rectangular wooden buildings at Redwick. Other artefact scatters at Rumney (Allen 1996a and b) and wooden posts with bone and charcoal scatters at Cold Harbour (Whittle

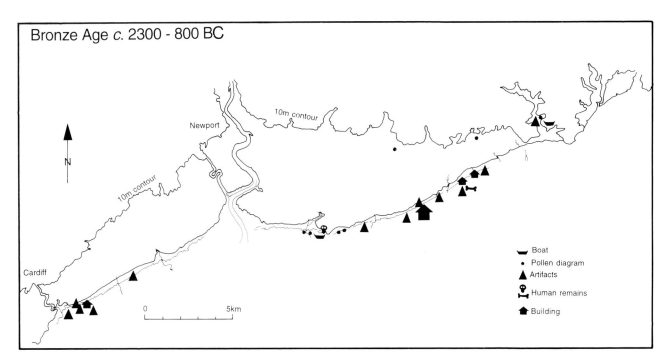

Figure 16.30 Distribution of Bronze Age finds c 2300–800 Cal BC. Drawing by H Neumann

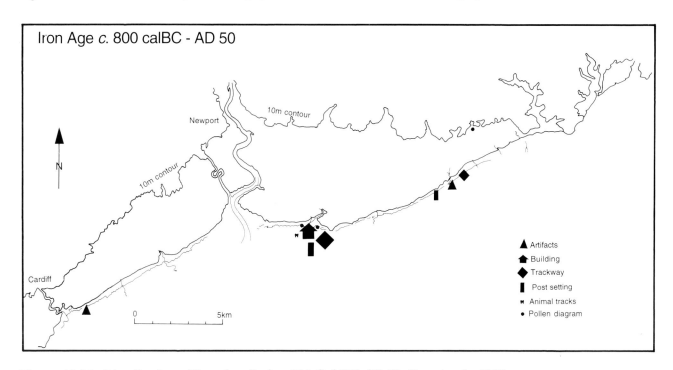

Figure 16.31 Distribution of Iron Age finds c 800 Cal BC–AD 50. Drawing by H Neumann

1989) have been interpreted as temporary encampments on the raised bog, although it is also possible that these sites represent the edges of settlements which have been eroded to seaward, or are buried to landward. Palaeochannels on the bog surface at Rumney, Peterstone, and Collister have yielded bone, fire-cracked flints, and Bronze Age pottery, and probable fishing structures. It is clear that from the middle Bronze Age the coastal bog was not only utilised but, for the first time, there is evidence for occupation by prehistoric communities. The evidence

leaves little doubt that settlement took place on the bog surface and the variety of wooden structures and artefact scatters attests the diversity and widespread distribution of activity during this period.

Iron Age (Fig 16.31)

Iron Age evidence is concentrated at Goldcliff. A further category of Iron Age site was identified during the survey at Cold Harbour Pill-2 where a palaeochannel contained a line of roundwood verticals and a woven structure which are thought to relate to fishing. Iron Age pottery and a single wooden post had previously been recorded in a palaeochannel at Magor (Whittle 1989). Other Iron Age finds associated with palaeochannels are pottery at Chapeltump-4, and a trackway at Chapeltump-5. Charcoal collected from eroding silts at the horizon of the topmost organic band at Rumney-1 produced an Iron Age radiocarbon date, although the pottery is of late Bronze Age type, and was interpreted as a short-lived camp or occupation on saltmarshes adjoining the banks of an active tidal creek (Allen 1996a and b).

Thus, by comparison with the preceding Bronze Age, Iron Age activity is limited and, with the exception of Goldcliff, appears to be associated with the utilisation of palaeochannels and occurrence of wooden trackways. Palaeochannels were in the process of silting up, and there is some evidence that the accretion of saltmarshes was underway. What this may represent is a retreat of settlement activity in the face of marine incursion. The coastal resource remained to be utilised but a shift of emphasis towards other types of activity occurred, such as the utilisation of tidal creeks for fishing and the increased need for trackways to facilitate access. Interestingly, all the trackways for which we have radiocarbon dates so far (Fig 10.21) are Iron Age. They may represent attempts to maintain networks of communication and access to areas that became increasingly wet in the face of the relentless marine transgression which, by the middle–late Iron Age, had inundated the whole of the former bog.

The saltmarshes that dominated the Gwent Levels during the deposition of the upper Wentlooge estuarine clays have been drained and claimed for cultivation since Roman times, which suggests that inundation of the Levels, which started in the Bronze Age, was accelerated and completed over a period of several hundred years during the Iron Age. Evidence at Goldcliff suggests that, where areas of raised bog remained, activities related to rectangular buildings continued in line with Bronze Age tradition, although the lack of archaeology pointing towards domestic activity could indicate a trend towards more seasonal utilisation of the bog. Continued inundation saw the ultimate abandonment of activity even in these areas.

16.13 Assessment of erosion and vulnerability

Erosion is the dominant coastal process in the survey area and, although areas of saltmarsh accretion exist, they do not appear to expand onto the area of the peatshelves. The erosive activity of the sea is the single most important cause for the gradual depletion of the peatshelves in the estuary. Erosion is not a recent phenomenon; historic and archaeological evidence for the erosion of saltmarshes and set backs

of sea walls are documented from early medieval times (Rippon 1996a, 97–99), highlighting the dynamic nature of estuarine coastlines. The present diminution of the peatshelf is the combined result of exposure to the tides twice daily, currents during high tides and wave impact during rising tides. These effects can be exacerbated during stormy weather when the strength of the wave impact is that much stronger. The peat itself, compacted by overlying upper Wentlooge silts and clays, is more resistant to erosion than the marine sediments in which it is embedded and, therefore, forms a plateau with a distinct edge, shielding the underlying sediments to some extent and, more importantly, forming a buffer between the erosive force of the sea and the sea wall which protects the low-lying Gwent Levels. Despite its relative resistance to erosion, however, the shelf is retreating and at constant risk from the sea, being located in an area of strong currents and extreme tidal range.

Types of erosion

The two dominant types of erosion recognised in the estuary are undercutting, followed by fracture and surface flaking. Flaking occurs on the peat surface as a result of wave action, exacerbated probably by the drying of the peat surface during low tides, especially during high tidal ranges, on higher peatshelves, and warm weather. Drying causes shrinkage, cracking, and, during the following high tide, fragments of peat lift off. This results in the removal of top layers and truncation. This type of erosion is particularly prevalent at Rumney, Redwick, and has also been observed at Goldcliff (Bell 1995). In areas where the peat is very thin, truncation of peat can create 'holes' in the peatshelf, exposing the underlying clays. Where this occurs, for instance east of Collister Pill, shallow pools are created on the peatshelf. As the exposed soft underlying clay erodes more quickly than the peat, these patches expand rapidly. In some areas a former relatively thin peatshelf has been completely eroded such as at Peterstone Great Wharf. Occasionally a ledge of clay is still visible indicating where the peat used to be and, where this has happened, the exposed underlying clay is rapidly eroding through gullying and wave abrasion. Wave splash is particularly strong at the edge of the peatshelf. Here the waves from the incoming tide tend to break along the edge and the force of the water impacts laterally on the vertical face as well as the surface. Lines of weakness along horizontal cracks are created, speeding up the process of lifting loosened flakes off the peat and the result is a sloping peat surface.

The peaty-clay layer overlying much of the raised bog peat is particularly vulnerable to truncation. The clays and silts that bind the peat together are very easily washed out causing rapid disintegration of this horizon. This is of particular significance as the upper peaty clay has been shown to include much of the occupation assemblages associated with buildings. At Cold Harbour a large area of this peaty-clay still exists, protected by a modern mudcover and is occasionally exposed after a storm when the mudcover is temporarily removed.

Erosion of the clays and silts underlying the peatshelf causes more readily visible and dramatic erosion resulting in the collapse of large sections. As the peat becomes undercut at the seaward cliff face, entire sections of peat can break off. During storms these effects are exacerbated and accelerated, sometimes leading to the rapid loss of larger areas, which had been thought relatively stable. Areas where a steep clay cliff below the main peat is exposed are particularly vulnerable. At Magor Pill a large area below the present peatshelf is littered with peat floats of substantial size, suggesting that undercutting of the peatshelf and rapid erosion is a severe problem in this area. Similar erosion is also evident in the Redwick/Cold Harbour area.

At Goldcliff rapid erosion also led to the removal of whole peat blocks. Following a storm this had taken place in a series of curved plates and the peat had lifted off on a horizontal plain. The peat appeared to have cracked along pre-existing, in situ cracks in the peatshelf. These cracks were filled with marine clay and, as the clay eroded, gullying within these cracks formed areas of weakness. Similarly, changes in the peat types, eg from reed peat to woody peat, or thin layers of clay deposited during a marine transgression, may cause lines of weakness within the peat which would explain the horizontal lifting off of whole peat blocks (Bell 1995).

Erosion on a smaller scale is also caused by rigid objects driven into the peat which create eddies and wave splash that have a stronger impact on the peat than waves just flowing over a smooth horizontal surface. Wooden posts driven into the peat or larger stones lying on the peat are surrounded by small depressions or gullies which deepen over time. Unfortunately, the wooden posts of prehistoric buildings or post settings are often affected by this process and consequently lost. This process also has implication for more recent coastal management structures on the peatshelves such as breakwaters or revetments which can cause accelerated erosion in vulnerable areas where the peat is very thin.

The extent of erosion

The observations made during the rapid survey have shown that the peatshelf is gradually being eroded into a progressively narrower strip which is also becoming thinner. Most of these observations have been made within the space of 2 years during which some of the survey areas have been visited repeatedly. However, to assess the extent of erosion more quantitatively, monitoring of certain locations over a longer period of time is necessary in order to take into account the episodic character of erosion. Analysis of air photographs taken over several decades or historical cartographic sources could be used to give a large scale assessment of the loss of areas. More detailed and qualitative as well as quantitative assessments of erosion can only be achieved with the help of an accurate map base which does not exist for many intertidal areas. It is hoped that the maps created during this survey will serve to facilitate future erosion assessments.

Previous work on historic maps and air photographs can give us some insight into the extent of retreat since the late-18th century. At Rumney Great Wharf rapid retreat of the marsh edge is documented

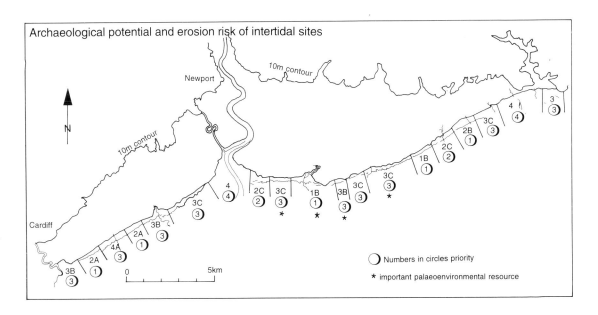

Figure 16.32 Map of the archaeological potential and erosion risk of intertidal sites in the Welsh Severn Estuary. Drawing by H Neumann

from a series of air photographs and maps from the Commissioners of Sewers, suggesting that the coastline retreated 300m between 1831 and 1989, an average rate of 1.9m per annum (cf Parkhouse and Parry 1990, fig 7). Cartographic sources document the retreat of the coastline in the order of 340m between 1844 and 1951 at Peterstone, 630m between 1851 and 1951 at Caldicot, and 550m between 1777 and 1951 at Sudbrook (WALSC 1954, cf Rippon 1996a, 107), a retreat of between 3.2m and 6.3m per annum.

During excavations at Goldcliff erosion was monitored over a 4 year period and here the average rate of erosion was 1.24m (Bell 1993, 88). Observations made at Goldcliff between 1993 and 1994 exemplify that storms can result in episodic acceleration within a short space of time, causing the loss of areas 12m × 18m and 15m × 9.5m, and damaging some of the rectangular buildings.

Assessment of threat

The threats to the archaeology and palaeoenvironmental resource of the intertidal peatshelves can be divided into the natural threats resulting from erosion and deposition and those posed by developments for industrial and commercial development and maintenance of sea defences. The threat from development affecting the intertidal area directly (eg strengthening of sea defences, proposed Severnside Airport) and indirectly (eg impact of shifting currents caused by gravel and sand extraction and Severn Barrage) is acute and the risk from erosion is ongoing. The following assessment concentrates on the degree of erosion in relation to the archaeological value of stretches of the foreshore. The aim is to assign a degree of priority in terms of monitoring sections of the peatshelves from which any additional development threats can be assessed.

To achieve this, sections of the coastline have been assigned a value for their archaeological importance and the degree of erosion that is taking place at a specific section. In combining both values, priorities can be assigned, with the highest priority given to areas of archaeological importance and where there is a threat from erosion. The distribution of erosion risk, archaeological potential, and with the priority of areas in terms of monitoring are illustrated in Figure 16.32. This is based on values assigned as follows:–

Archaeological potential
1: high density of unique finds of international importance
2: high density of finds of national and regional importance
3: moderate density of finds
4: few or no known finds

Erosion risk
A: rapid retreat of more than several metres over a decade
B: moderate retreat and erosion of surface

C: some erosion
D: area appearing stable

1st priority
Archaeologically important and under threat from erosion, rescue survey or excavation recommended or, in the case of Goldcliff, monitoring of planned sites

2A: Rumney (Map 2), Peterstone (Map 4)
1B: Goldcliff (Maps 13–15), Redwick (Map 21)
2B: Chapeltump/Collister Pill (Maps 23–24)

2nd priority
Archaeologically important, moderate or little threat from erosion, regular monitoring recommended.

2C: Uskmouth (Maps 11–12), Magor Pill (Map 22)

3rd priority
Moderate archaeological value, with some erosion threat, occasional monitoring recommended.

3: Sudbrook (Map 26)
3B: Rumney (Map 1), Peterstone (Maps 6–7), Goldcliff East (Map 16)
3C: Peterstone/St Brides (Maps 7–9), Uskmouth (Map 12), Porton (Map 17–20), Collister/Sudbrook (Map 25)
4A: Rumney (Map 3)

4th priority
Little peat or archaeology known and limited erosion risk

4: Newport (Map 10)

16.14 Recommendations

In order to fully appreciate and utilise the unique archaeological and palaeoenvironmental resource of the Severn foreshore, there is a need to respond to the immediate threat to potential and existing sites. This can only be achieved by regular monitoring of high priority areas. This has proved to be most effective after high spring tides and after periods of storms and tidal extremes. Conditions can be favourable at any time during the year but the months of January–April often experience storms and the highest tidal extremes. There is a need to engage and work together with locally knowledgeable enthusiasts as well as professionals. Much of the information gained so far has been on the basis of voluntary work, particularly by Derek Upton. Such work should be actively encouraged and some provision made for allocating funds for recording and monitoring.

The mechanisms and extent of erosion have not yet been quantified and revisiting of specific sites over the whole length of the foreshore is recommended, in particular those of high priority. Setting up marker posts, survey, and the use of photographic or video recording are some methods that can facilitate the quantification of retreat rates, and to qualify the type of erosion.

Many questions about the types of activity that occurred in the prehistoric coastal wetland are still unanswered, in particular the importance and use of fishing, seasonality, and the mechanisms and speed of the environmental changes that occurred during the transformation from raised bog to estuarine sedimentation. The value of detailed archaeological work, coupled with palaeoenvironmental investigation has been demonstrated at Goldcliff, but palaeoenvironmental work is needed elsewhere. One such area of priority is the Redwick/Cold Harbour site where so much new and unprecedented archaeological evidence has been investigated recently. With the emergence of prehistoric fishing structures, post settings and pottery in palaeochannels, work should be intensified with systematic collection of artefacts and ecofacts, by means of sieving for example. This is particularly valuable in the vicinity of existing buildings and settlement sites. There is a need to facilitate rescue excavation of sites under threat and emphasis should be placed on both the archaeological and environmental record, the context and microgeography of the adjacent area within which the archaeology is found is as important as the archaeology itself.

The categories of research priority defined above and in Figure 16.32, are intended to direct attention to those areas where recording and monitoring are particularly needed. It is not justifiable to use these categories to identify areas as archaeologically unimportant in the context of planning and development proposals. As Maps 1–26 show, every part of the coastal zone has produced some finds and, therefore, has archaeological potential. Our knowledge of this landscape is constantly developing. Areas such as Peterstone, Collister, and West Pill, which appeared relatively poor in finds until about Easter 1997 have, since then, produced important material. The fundamental conclusion of this survey is that any and every part of the Welsh Severn Estuary, including the reclaimed areas behind the seawall, is of such archaeological potential that any development proposals should be accompanied by assessment of their archaeological implications.

17 Discussion and conclusions *by M Bell*

17.1 Introduction

Conclusions from individual parts of the site, periods, and studies have been included where appropriate at the end of the chapters concerned. It is not intended here to summarise the results of the project as a whole, rather to select key themes, particularly those which link the detailed Goldcliff case study to the wider picture now available from the intertidal survey.

17.2 Formation processes in intertidal archaeology

This section outlines what we have learnt of the distinctive formation processes of the intertidal archaeological record: how the sea, and other factors, create the context for archaeology and bury and exhume sites. Examples of some of the main archaeological contexts and processes are illustrated schematically in Figure 17.1. Here we concentrate on the processes affecting peat shelves. Processes involved in artefact erosion and reworking in a broader intertidal zone have been modelled by Allen (1997c).

Peat topography

The raised bog surface at Goldcliff West showed a pronounced pattern of hummocks of very varied size, surrounded by a net-like pattern of encircling depressions. We have found no evidence that these channels were created by human agency and have concluded that this microtopography is of natural origin. Trudgill (1974) reports a similar pattern of hummocks and anastomosing channels on desiccated peat on Godney Moor on the Somerset Levels. That study concluded the topography was not related to that of underlying clay but represented a natural drainage pattern of the bog. Trudgill observed that the Godney channels carried water from November to May and were prone to poaching by cattle, an analogy perhaps for the many footprints surrounding Buildings 6 and 8.

Site burial

Most of the sites discussed here are on peat and have been buried by the upper Wentlooge marine transgression. Detailed palaeoenvironmental investigation at Goldcliff Buildings 1, 2, and 6 shows that there was marine influence within the upper part of the peat and within the horizons associated with activi-ties. In places, encroaching marine influence involved erosion of occupation horizons. Around Gold-cliff Building 6 (Fig 8.10) a palaeochannel cut into artefact horizons and artefacts were reworked. The surface of some trackways may also have been washed away (eg Goldcliff 1108). When sites have been truncated, it is sometimes not clear whether this took place at the time of the original transgression, or during the more recent exhumation of the peat. Elsewhere the transgression was of a gentle nature preserving flooring and trackway surfaces, eg Goldcliff Buildings 1 and 2.

Trackways tend to be associated with slightly raised areas of the peat (eg Fig 10.9). It is thought that this is mainly because vertical structural wood makes the peat less compactable. An alternative explanation, which needs to be kept in mind, is that structures, both trackways and buildings, may have protected peat surfaces from erosion at the time of the original transgression, and this may have contributed to the slightly raised areas on which these structures sit. Such is the case with prehistoric sites on peat in the Federsee in Germany (Schlichterle personal communication).

The only evidence we have for deliberate disman-tling of buildings is that Redwick Building 4 had at least one axial post removed. Parts of other struc-tures, such as Goldcliff Building 5, could have been reused but this is speculative. It is odd that wall posts were not reused, given that during the transgressive phases wood is likely to have been in short supply out in the wetlands, and the wider survey indicates some continuing use of these locations during the salt-marsh phase. Perhaps there was some social prohi-bition against demolition and reuse. Evidence for the collapse of the buildings is very limited; a few posts in the northeast corner of Goldcliff Building 2 had collapsed inwards and been squashed into the floor. A little other timber within Goldcliff Buildings 1 and 2 might be roofing, but most is demonstrably floor-ing. There is no great pile of timber which would have been associated with the collapse of these structures, either at Goldcliff, Redwick or the roundhouse structures. What we find on the peatshelf at Goldcliff are just a few scattered cut pieces which might have been washed from the buildings, but are perhaps more likely to derive from woodworking on the spot. We must, therefore, envisage a situation in which the ruins of buildings were standing, visible perhaps for decades, within steadily accumulating saltmarsh, just as the fish traps of earlier generations are visible today. When pieces collapsed and broke off they were washed away on the tide, or oxidized in accumulating minerogenic sediments less favourable for their preservation.

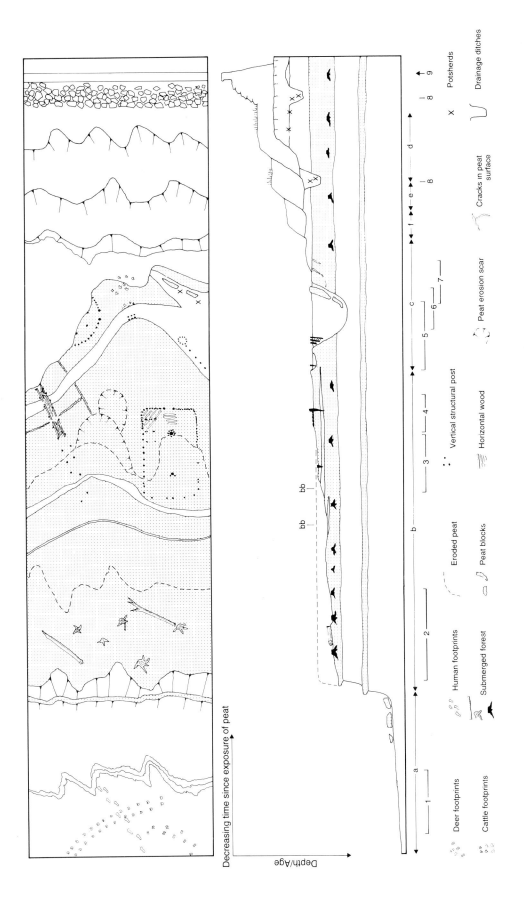

Decreasing time since exposure of peat

Depth/Age

Deer footprints	Human footprints	Eroded peat	Vertical structural post	Potsherds
Cattle footprints	Submerged forest	Peat blocks	Horizontal wood	Drainage ditches
			Peat erosion scar	Cracks in peat surface

Figure 17.1 Schematic plan (top) and section (bottom) to illustrate some of the main contexts in which intertidal archaeology is found and the exhumation processes of the intertidal archaeological record. Sedimentary formations: (a) lower Wentlooge laminated silts, (b) middle Wentlooge peats and clays, note clay lenses within the peat at bb, (c) upper Wentlooge silts and clays, (d) Rumney Formation, (e) Awre Formation, (f) Northwick Formation. Archaeology etc: (1) footprints of humans and animals, (2) submerged forest exposed, (3) truncated rectangular building, (4) building floor and trackway surface exposed, (5) palaeochannel with wooden structures (?fishing) and trackway, channel contains reworked potsherds, (6) roundhouse part buried by upper Wentlooge Formation, (7) cattle footprints at middle Wentlooge surface and palaeochannel edges, (8) ditches within the upper Wentlooge Formation (some Romano-British), (9) seawall. To the right prehistoric archaeology is buried by formations (d)–(f). Drawing by S J Allen

Site exhumation and erosion

Following the original transgression, peat surfaces may have been exhumed and undergone erosion during subsequent transgressions. This happened at Peterstone (Chapter 16) where the palaeochannel complex with its archaeology was planed off some-time in the medieval or post-medieval period, prior to the deposition of the Rumney Formation. Indeed, it is implicit in the Allen model of sedimentary formations (eg Fig 3.1) that some sites will have undergone successive episodes of truncation.

The effects of erosion we can document most clearly in relation to the recent exposure of the sites as summarised in Figure 17.1. Peats are more resistant to erosion than clay layers and this produces the peat shelves. We have observed a number of processes involved in erosion of the peat. By cutting into underlying clays the more resistant peats are under-mined and then collapse as blocks (Bell 1995, fig 58). More insidious is the effect of drying and oxidation: peat dries out on hot days, pieces flake off, and are washed away. Particularly obvious is the effect of freezing episodes when the surface of peat and clay becomes frozen, lifts and, on thawing, is washed away. We have observed but not quantified these processes but it seems probable that over the period of decades for which peat shelves are exposed they will have made a significant contribution to the lowering of the peat surface. Further back from the peat edge we have observed evidence for the develop-ment of vertical and associated horizontal cracks through which the retreating tide drains. In other areas (eg around Collister Pill sites, Fig 16.14) we are uncertain whether cracking relates to dessication of the peat in prehistory, or recent times. Either way it establishes planes of weakness which are being exploited by erosion. Particularly evident among erosion processes is the lifting off of great curved plates of peat up to 10m across which may be up to 0.5m thick at the peat edge and decrease in thickness back from the edge. Removal of plates such as these destroyed part of Building 8 in 1994 (Fig 8.17). Smaller plates become detached from the surface of the peat shelf, as in one corner of Building 6 and the erosion edges then expand (Fig 8.4). The most destructive erosion of peat plates observed during this project around Building 8 appears to have occurred in May–July 1994, an exceptionally hot period, suggesting perhaps that the effects of desiccation, as well as the force of waves, may contribute to this form of erosion. The processes responsible for erosion of these peat rafts are under further investigation by John Allen (personal com-munication).

The range of erosive processes outlined has been acting on the peats at the shelf edge for a much longer period and they are consequently eroded to a lower level than the peats back from the edge (Fig 17.1). Thus, the surviving peat surface on the edge is generally, significantly earlier than that to landward where the peat surface becomes successively

younger. This is often evident because to seaward one finds successively earlier successional stages with wood, or reed, peat exposed. The peat shelf overlying the Goldcliff Mesolithic site is a particu-larly extreme form of the phenomenon; the peat shelf at the edge dates to c 4790–4540 Cal BC (GrN-24143; Fig 4.4) and the peat surface at Pit 15 is 2240–1880 Cal BC (Car-1499; Fig 5.3). These observations about erosion highlight the importance of wider strati-graphic evidence in situations in which the radiocarbon dating of intertidal peats is used in studies of sea level change. It is not, however, always the case that exposed peat surfaces are time trans-gressive. Sometimes marine erosion exploits textural changes within peats and can, thus, etch out and expose peat surfaces of a specific date. These are most easily recognised where there are brief wood-land phases within raised bog or reed peat, for example a short-lived birch wood exposed by erosion below Goldcliff Building 8 (Fig 8.17).

On the peat surface structures to seaward are eroded to a lower level, and may be represented only by a few post bases (Fig 17.1) or in other cases, such as Redwick 1, many posts appear to have been oxidized, or washed away. In places where they have been buried by later clays or peat growth, floor levels and trackway surfaces survive. Where trackways have been excavated below upper Wentlooge clay, preservation is found to be very much better than on the exposed peat shelf (compare Figures 10.15 and 10.16). Thus, surface exposures do not do justice to the quality of the intertidal archaeological resource. Some structures appear to have been significantly truncated by erosion. The floor levels of Goldcliff Buildings 6–8 have gone and some peg alignments are probably the eroded remains of trackways (eg Goldcliff 9060).

Site visibility

The survival and visibility of archaeology differs greatly spatially and temporally according to sedi-mentary context (Fig 17.1). Footprints are very apparent in the laminated lower Wentlooge Forma-tion, also where they are picked out by clay in peat at the middle Wentlooge surface; they also occur in some of the later minerogenic formations (Allen 1997a), particularly in our experience at the very base of the upper Wentlooge Formation. It is likely that animals were around at other times and we have noted occasional evidence in other contexts, for instance possibly in section at the Goldcliff Meso-lithic site (Fig 4.4). Wood structures exist within the minerogenic horizons, as we have seen with the Goldcliff boat plank site and the Upton Trackway but they are much rarer in these contexts than in peats. Structures are likely to have survived where they lay below the normal watertable, or well within the normal tidal range. Structures in palaeochannels, such as Cold Harbour Pill-2 and the Peterstone channels, are more likely to be preserved than

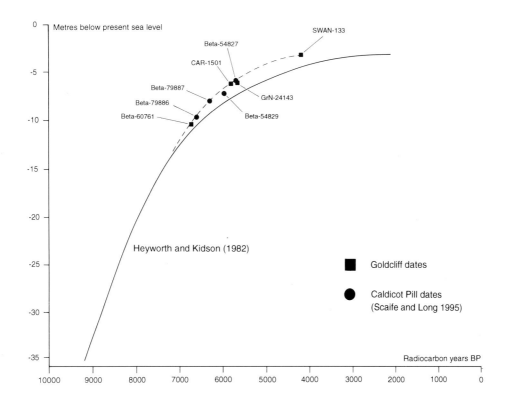

Figure 17.2 Dated indicators of past sea level from the edges of Goldcliff Island (Table 17.1) compared with the sea level curve of Heyworth and Kidson (1982) and dated peats at Caldicot Pill (after Scaife and Long 1995)

adjacent sites on the high saltmarsh, where any timber is likely to have oxidised and activity may be represented just by charcoal or pottery scatters or, more often perhaps, by artefacts swept into adjacent palaeochannels. It is evident that prehistoric activity occurred at the time of the upper Wentlooge minerogenic phase, but it is much less visible archaeologically and it is consequently unclear how widespread this activity was. In the context of Netherlands wetland sites, Louwe Kooijmans (1985) has likewise observed there is a tendency for archaeology associated with transgressive phases to be less visible because of the erosive effects of the transgression itself. Those erosive effects are very apparent in the Severn Estuary in the form of the many palaeochannels which cut the surface of the peat, the most intensively investigated example being round Goldcliff Building 6.

17.3 Positive and negative sea level tendencies at Goldcliff

The implications of compaction

There are many dates from archaeological contexts at Goldcliff relating to periods of lower sea level. Most are from on top of, and within, peats. The decreasing height of peat surfaces away from Goldcliff island (Fig 3.6) show that where the Holocene sedimentary surface is thickest OD relationships

have been very significantly affected by compaction. Similar compaction effects have been recorded by Haslett *et al* (1998a) on a bedrock margin at Nyland in the Somerset Levels and compaction phenomena are discussed more generally by Allen (forthcoming c).

The effects of differential compaction are emphasized by the decreasing height of the upper peat shelf between Trackways 9050 and 1108. Radiocarbon dates show that all the structures on this peat shelf are broadly coeval (Fig 3.4), yet there is a consistent altitudinal decrease to the west resulting in an overall height difference of 2.9m. In that case the auger survey indicates that the height difference probably relates, not so much to total Holocene sedimentary thickness, but to the decreasing thickness westwards of a lens of minerogenic sediment which inundated the raised bog during the Bronze Age and is thickest on either side of Auger Hole 44. If the same thickness of peat and clay were laid down over a given unit of time, then, following the effects of the greater compressibility of peat, the clay surface will be higher. Thus Trackway 9050 is underlain by 3m of Bronze Age minerogenic sediment, whereas Structure 1108 is underlain by 0.25m, which may largely account for the overall difference of *c* 2.9m in the OD heights of the two contemporary structures. In this way the extent of various minerogenic influxes within the peat is seen as a key factor creating differences in the OD heights of the peat surface.

Table 17.1 Peat dates from Goldcliff

	Site	Fig ref.	14C date	Lab code	Calibrated date	OD height	Mean sea level (m)*
a	Goldcliff East	2.1	6770 ± 70 BP	Beta- 60761	5740–5490 Cal BC	–3.7m	–10
b	Pit 15 peat base	5.3	5920 ± 80 BP	Car-1501	5060–4660 Cal BC	0.68m	–5.62
c	Mesolithic site peat base	4.4	5820 ± 50 BP	GrN-24143	4790–4540 Cal BC	0.71m	–5.59
d	Hill Farm Pond peat base	3.7	4320 ± 80 BP	SWAN-133	3350–2650 Cal BC	3.7m	–2.6

a and, possibly, d are either directly on head; b, c, and, possibly, d are on mineragenic sediments overlying head. *Mean sea level has been calculated by subtracting the MHWST at Newport + 6.3m OD from the OD height of the sample.

Sea level change

Sea level curves for the Bristol Channel and Severn Estuary have been prepared by Hawkins (eg 1973) and Heyworth and Kidson (eg 1982) and these studies have recently been refined and critically examined in the course of site specific studies by Jennings *et al* (1998) at Porlock, and Haslett *et al* (1998a) in the Axe Valley. The very obvious effects of compaction, which became apparent as a result of detailed stratigraphic investigation and dating at Goldcliff and the work by Haslett et al (1998a), calls into question the reliability of some of the date and height records which are the basis of sea level curves. Of all the dates from Goldcliff it could be argued that the only ones which are really reliable as indicators of the altitude of sea level in the past are four dates given in Table 17.1 for the onset of peat inception at different heights around the edges of the former island. Figure 17.2 plots the points and compares them with Heyworth and Kidson's (1982) sea level curve for the Bristol Channel. The Goldcliff points plot on average about 1m above the curve, as do the four peat dates from Caldicot Pill plotted on the same diagram after Scaife and Long (1995, fig 36). Such differences are likely to arise because the Heyworth and Kidson (1982) graph included sites subject to compaction.

Although the effects of compaction mean that only a few of the Goldcliff dates provide good evidence of the specific altitude of past sea level the well-dated sequence does provide evidence of positive and negative sea level tendencies. Peat/clay contacts represent transgressive episodes, ie positive tendencies, and clay/peat contacts represent regressive episodes, ie negative tendencies. Figure 17.3 presents separate sequences for six main areas of the site from east (left) to west (right), and on the left is an attempt to generalise the results of the sea level tendencies for the Goldcliff sequence as a whole. Every episode does not register at each site, one reason for this being that, following the development of the raised bog, transgressions occur earlier, and are more numerous to the east. This is considered to be because the bog grew to a higher level in the west. There is also the question of whether, in the early stages of a transgression, peat was eroded. The summary diagram assumes erosion at Pit 15, where there was a palaeochannel. The date of the main peat

clay transgression is derived from the two very closely similar dates from Hill Farm and Goldcliff East (Smith and Morgan 1989); in the latter there is pollen evidence for rising water tables which strengthens confidence that the sequence has not been truncated. The summary of sea level tendencies in Figure 17.3 should be seen as a working model to be tested and refined by continued fieldwork and dating. Some of the changes may relate to local factors (eg the effects of palaeochannels), others, as we shall see below, are broadly contemporary with changes elsewhere and are likely to reflect more widespread patterns.

17.4 Environmental change at Goldcliff

The temporal sequence of marine transgressive and regressive phases and their relationship to the archaeological finds are summarised in Figure 17.3. The changes are related to a spatial dimension in Figure 17.4a–f which maps the landscape in six selected time frames covering the period between *c* 5800 Cal BC and 1 BC/AD. In referring to this diagram it should be appreciated that it is based on extrapolation from spatially restricted data. The area from which we have both stratigraphic information and dates is a comparatively narrow coastal band, supplemented by the larger triangular area of the Wetland Reserve for which we have some stratigraphic information but no dates (Fig 17.4). The result of this is that resolution on an east–west dimension is high, whereas scaling of the north–south dimension is uncertain, and it is possible that zones should be compressed, or in most cases probably appreciably stretched north–south. Allen and Fulford (1987) estimate, from current erosion rates, that the prehistoric shore may have been more than 2km seaward, although, as the reconstructions make very clear, that interface was, in prehistory, a constantly fluctuating boundary. The maps only extend to the east side of Goldcliff Island, not as far as the Smith and Morgan (1989) pollen sites some 600m further east.

Map a, c 5800 Cal BC: This illustrates the scene prior to any known archaeology. The area would have been mudflat or saltmarsh with the bedrock island of Goldcliff rising from it covered in wildwood.

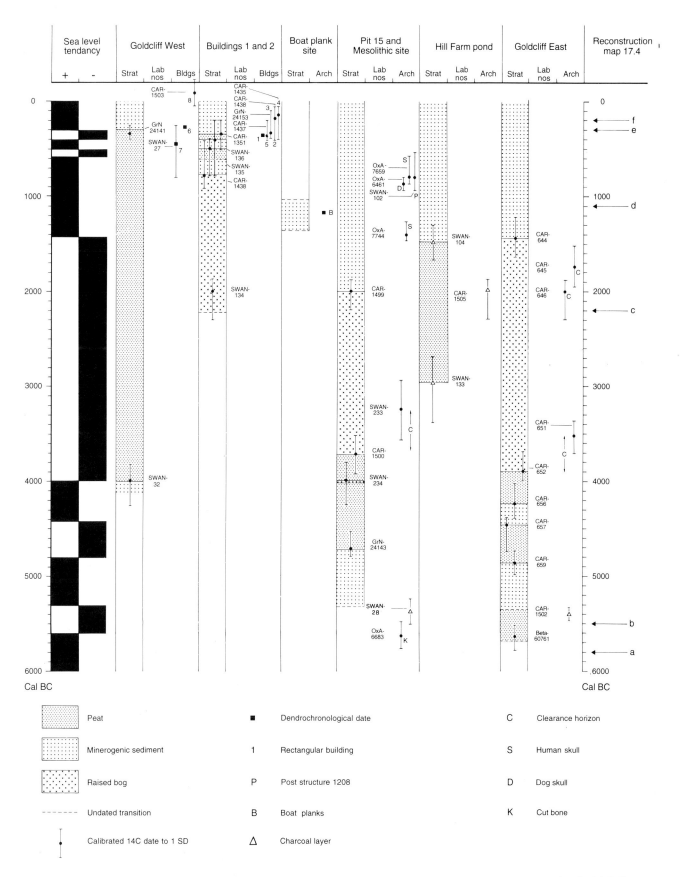

Figure 17.3 Summary of the sequence of peats and minerogenic sediments in six areas of the Goldcliff site and their relationship to the dated archaeological sites. On the left is a summary of this sequence in terms of positive and negative sea level tendencies. Letters on the right correlate this temporal diagram with the reconstruction maps in Figure 17.4

328

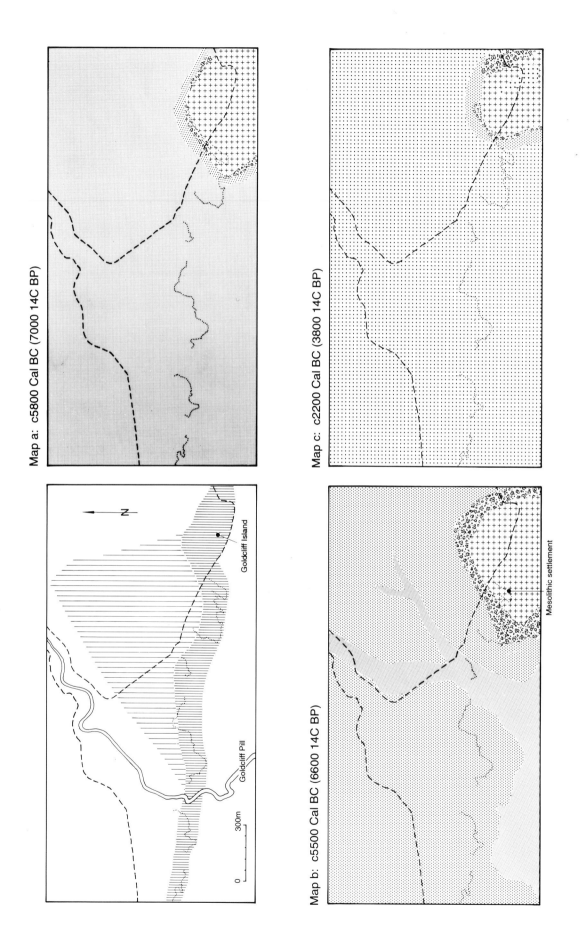

Map a: c5800 Cal BC (7000 14C BP)

Map c: c2200 Cal BC (3800 14C BP)

Map b: c5500 Cal BC (6600 14C BP)

Goldcliff Island

Goldcliff Pill

N

300m

0

Mesolithic settlement

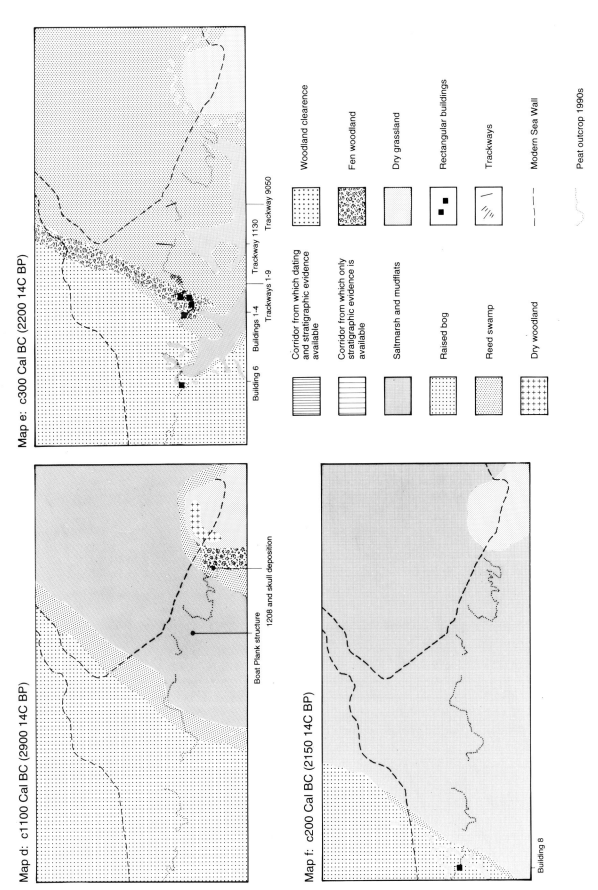

Map d: c1100 Cal BC (2900 14C BP)

Map e: c300 Cal BC (2200 14C BP)

Map f: c200 Cal BC (2150 14C BP)

Boat Plank structure

1208 and skull deposition

Building 6   Buildings 1-4   Trackway 1130

Trackways 1-9   Trackway 9050

Building 8

Corridor from which dating and stratigraphic evidence available

Corridor from which only stratigraphic evidence is available

Saltmarsh and mudflats

Raised bog

Reed swamp

Dry woodland

Woodland clearence

Fen woodland

Dry grassland

Rectangular buildings

Trackways

Modern Sea Wall

Peat outcrop 1990s

Figure 17.4   Reconstruction of the Goldcliff environment. Top left the area from which evidence is extrapolated. Maps show the changing environment (a) before 5800 Cal BC, (b) c 5500 Cal BC, (c) c 2200 Cal BC, (d) 1100 Cal BC, (e) c 300 Cal BC, and (f) after c 200 Cal BC. Drawn by S J Allen

Map b, c 5500 Cal BC: This is the time of the earliest known Mesolithic activity. Dry woodland on the island was already being modified by the effects of anthropogenic burning. The earliest known activity began during a regressive phase marked by peat growth over former saltmarsh and eventually oak colonisation of peat round the island fringes. Beyond this a great expanse of reedswamp is represented by the widely distributed reed peat found now at *c* –3m OD. The auger survey shows that this peat is not continuous, so we may envisage channels which probably introduced some marine influence into parts of the mainly freshwater *Phragmites* swamp. However, the positions of channels on this map are schematic. Four out of the five Mesolithic dates correspond to the period of the regressive phase, but the hazelnut date (OxA-6682) implies that activity may have continued later in the series of transgressive and regressive cycles which continued until 4000 Cal BC. During the two regressive phases (*c* 5700–5300 Cal BC and 4850–4400 Cal BC), the landscape was as shown in Figure 17.4b. During the two transgressive phases (*c* 5300–4850 Cal BC and 4400–4000 Cal BC) the landscape was as shown in Figure 17.4a. The rate of sea level rise decreased *c* 4000 Cal BC and for about 2500 years the rate of peat growth exceeded that of sea level rise, producing a vast bog.

Map c, c 2200 Cal BC: The map shows raised bog development at its most extensive as it was between *c* 3800 and 1500 Cal BC. During the life of the bog, an unknown distance to seaward of the area mapped there would have been channels introducing marine influence, fringed with reedswamp and perhaps a few trees. Similar communities fringe the island. Further to seaward there would have been saltmarsh and mudflats. Throughout the life of the raised bog there were specific episodes of clearance on the island (see below) but that impact increased after *c* 2000 Cal BC, and by *c* 1500 Cal BC tree cover on the island had been much reduced.

Map d, 1100 Cal BC: This is the time of the boat plank structure. At *c* 1500 Cal BC the bog on either side of the former island, at Goldcliff East and Hill Farm, had been inundated. This was the minerogenic horizon which, west of the island, centred on Auger Hole 44, in which area a palaeochannel seems to have existed. The boat plank structure probably crossed a minor tributary of that channel. At this time marine influence extended some 400m west of the boat plank site, where we may suppose there was scattered fringing reedswamp and trees and to the west the raised bog continued to grow. By the time of Map d the island was largely grassland with some trees and fringing fen woodland.

Skull deposition and Structure 1208 were at the island edge. We know that Skull 1214 was inserted into earlier peat. Skull 497 was in peat which has not been directly dated. It is consequently uncertain whether skull deposition occurred in an area of bog which survived up to this time, or whether these activities were associated with saltmarsh conditions, as the relationship between the skull dates and the

stratigraphy summarised in Figure 17.3 might suggest. Either way these activities occurred at the island/wetland interface.

Map e, c 300 Cal BC: This is the time of the main concentration of prehistoric activity. It was a regressive phase during which the area between the raised bog and the island was colonised mainly by reed peat. Most of the trackways provided communication across this swamp. To its east was a 200m wide band of fen wood peat on which Buildings 1–3 and the more complex of the trackway forms (1108, 970, 1103) were located. Marine influence was introduced episodically by channels to the south. The areas of Buildings 1–3 was subject to multiple small-scale inundation episodes before and during the main period of activity. That activity was brought to an end by the transgression which at Building 2 is dated *c* 360 Cal BC, which corresponds to the dendrochronological date of Building 1. Radiocarbon dates for Buildings 2–5 indicate that parts of this area may have been inundated rather later, possibly *c* 200 Cal BC. To the west the raised bog continued to grow and it was here that Buildings 6–8 were located. Even here there are the first signs of marine encroachment onto the flanks of the bog in the area of Building 6 at 273 BC. We have no pollen sites close to the island which cover this period, but by this time it is thought to have carried mainly grassland with some scattered trees.

Map f, after c 200 Cal BC: By this time the marine transgression had significantly advanced, extinguishing the reedswamp and the fen woodland and leaving Building 8 on the edge of the remnant bog, its surrounding palaeochannels receiving marine influence from time to time. The radiocarbon dates suggest that the main locus of activity gradually migrated to the west with the encroachment of marine influence. Use of a wider range of dryland wood sources for Buildings 6 and 8 might be because, by this time, all the fringing fen woodland had been inundated, or cleared necessitating the bringing of timber from more distant sources.

When the bog at Goldcliff was finally inundated remains uncertain. The latest peat date is *c* 300 Cal BC from the Building 6 area. The Building 8 date is 200–500 years later. If that building was constructed on the peat, as the field evidence seemed to suggest, it could imply bog growth into the late Iron Age or early Romano-British period. However, that is perhaps rather a sweeping conclusion to draw on the basis of one radiocarbon date.

But what of Goldcliff Pill, today a prominent landscape feature cutting across the area under consideration (Fig 17.4)? The auger transect shows clearly that the Pill cannot have been in its present position between 5000 and *c* 500 Cal BC. We have found no evidence of a prehistoric palaeochannel of a comparable size elsewhere, but there are several smaller channels within about 600m west of the island. It seems that in prehistory the drainage may have been carried, not by a single channel, but by a series of smaller channels. The headward erosion of one channel around Hole 44 may have cut through the earlier raised bog peat and contributed to the marine incursion represented by Figure 17.4d. It is possible that a channel opened up on the line of the present pill at about the time of Building 6; gullying and movement of the peat evident around this building could have been related to the headward migration of a major channel at this time. Alternatively, the pill could have been artificially created, or enhanced, by the Romans to facilitate drainage of the inland area; in that context the finding of the Goldcliff Stone beside the Pill is noteworthy because it is generally agreed that it marked some linear construction by legions from Caerleon (Knight 1961). A major new drainage channel, or a seawall, might appropriately be marked in such a way, especially where it signified the Roman taming of a landscape which had previously been ancestral grazing land (Bell 1996). A third possibility is that the present line of the pill is post Roman. Stephen Rippon (CD 16.9; 1996a, fig 12) has identified an early boundary line, which crosses the Pill, and which he thinks may be of Roman, or post-Roman, origin. Rippon's identification of this possible earlier, pre-Pill, element in the landscape palimpsest reinforces the evidence presented here for the Pill's post-prehistoric origin. The apparent mobility and complex history of Goldcliff Pill contrasts with Magor Pill which can be documented in a similar position from Iron Age to recent times (Allen and Rippon 1997).

17.5 Reconstruction of the 1st millennium BC environment
(Figs 17.5–17.7)

Figure 17.5 is a panoramic reconstruction of the landscape at around the time of the most concentrated activity c 300 Cal BC. The scene is deliberately foreshortened north–south to illustrate the range of ecosystems, each of which is likely to have been wider to seaward. Dry ground in the distance is actually some 6–9 km away. In one scene it illustrates the setting of a range of structures, some of which were not contemporary: dendrochronological evidence indicates that Building 6 was probably 70–100 years later than Building 1 and Building 8 may have been 200–400 years later than the other buildings. The boat plank structure (1208) and evidence for skull deposition are some 700 years earlier. They are shown on the same drawing, not to imply contemporaneity, but to give an impression of the ecological context in which those activities took place. More detailed reconstructions of the most intensively investigated Buildings 1 and 6 are shown on Figures 17.7 and 17.6, respectively.

The three reconstructions view the scene at high tide with marine influence extending up the channels at times as far as the buildings and trackways. In the western area Buildings 6–8 were situated on raised bog, a landscape of hummocks, three of the largest with buildings, and encircling depressions. By the time of Building 6 (Fig 17.6) marine influence was already being introduced from the encircling palaeochannel, the surroundings of which were much trampled by cattle. Building 4 is situated east of the raised bog in an area of *Phragmites* peat (Fig 17.5) with Trackway 1108 running south near the boundary between the *Phragmites* peat and a band of fen woodland to the east. Within the fen wood are Buildings 1–3 and linear Structures 970 and 1103. At the time of the buildings part of the woodland was cleared for timber, and other trees may by this time have been dying because of the effects of episodic inundation.

Figure 17.7 shows Building 1 in its surroundings. Underlying the building is the remains of the putative earlier Building 5. This reconstruction is based on the assumption that Building 2 was earlier than 1 and by this stage was ruined, although the chronological relationship between the two buildings is far from clear, as discussed in Chapters 7 and 9. The buildings sit on slight hummocks with encircling depressions through which marine influence is introduced, depositing a strandline of detrital plant material at the hummock edge. Cattle graze the fen sward and the saltmarsh to seaward. Calves may have been housed in the building and the scene shows milking at the entrance to the building. In the background small boats are seen out on the estuary, some perhaps communicating with communities on the English side in the far distance 10km away.

East of the fen woodland (Fig 17.5) is a great tract of reedswamp through which run Trackways 1–9, 1130, and 9050. These maintain access between the drier fen woodland and channels to seaward. In the channels it is likely that boats were landed and maintained, as we know they were some 700 years earlier at the time of the boat plank structure. The setting of that earlier structure is shown within saltmarsh; it crosses a minor palaeochannel. To the east another earlier structure (1208) is reconstructed hypothetically as a platform for the exposure of human bodies. Skull deposition took place at the wetland island interface 300–1000 years before the trackways and buildings shown to the west.

By 300 Cal BC the island was largely cleared, although the field boundaries shown are imaginary. The dry ground in the distance was, by this time, largely cleared pasture, probably with smaller areas of arable fields, and significant surviving woodland, probably in the steeper valleys which were exploited for some of the wetlanders' timber requirements. At the left in the distance we have added a hillfort, a site such as Tredegar Camp, Newport (Whittle, E 1992) actually 9km away but enjoying dramatic views across the levels landscape, which it is likely to have exploited.

17.6 Environmental change: wider comparisons and possible causes

Environmental changes in the Goldcliff sequence in

West

East

a   b   c   d   e   f   g   h

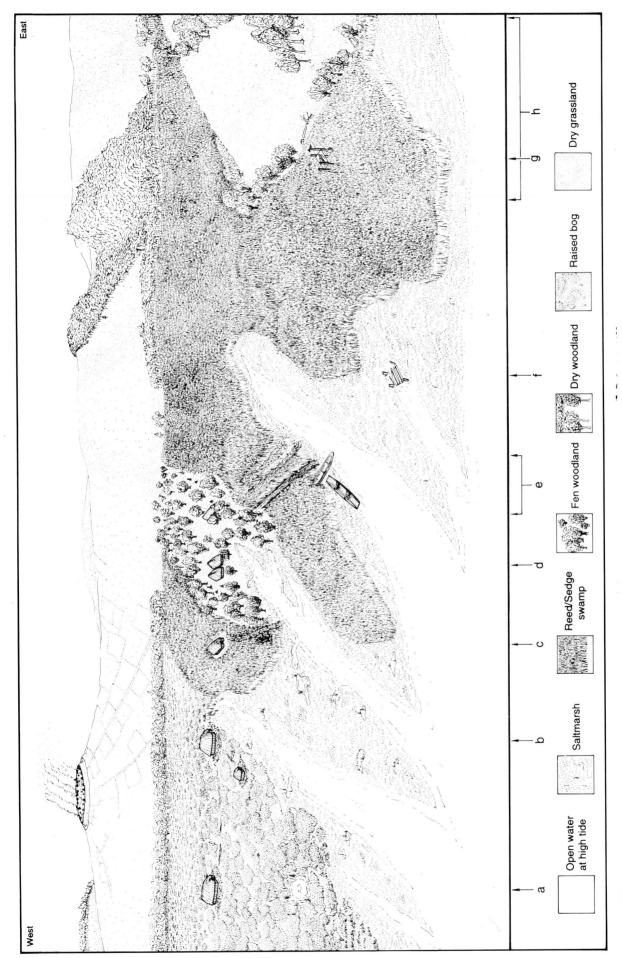

| | Open water at high tide | | | Reed/Sedge swamp | | | Fen woodland | | | Dry woodland | | | Raised bog |
| | Saltmarsh | | | | | | | | | | | | Dry grassland |

Figure 17.5   Reconstruction of the landscape c 300 Cal BC also showing the environmental setting of some structures (f and g) of earlier date and one structure (a) which may be later. (a) Building 8, (b) Building 6, (c) Building 4, (d) Buildings 1 and 2, (e) Trackways 1–9, (f) Boat plank structure (post 1170 BC), (g) Structure 1208 (c 920–510 Cal BC), (h) former Goldcliff Island. Drawn by S J Allen

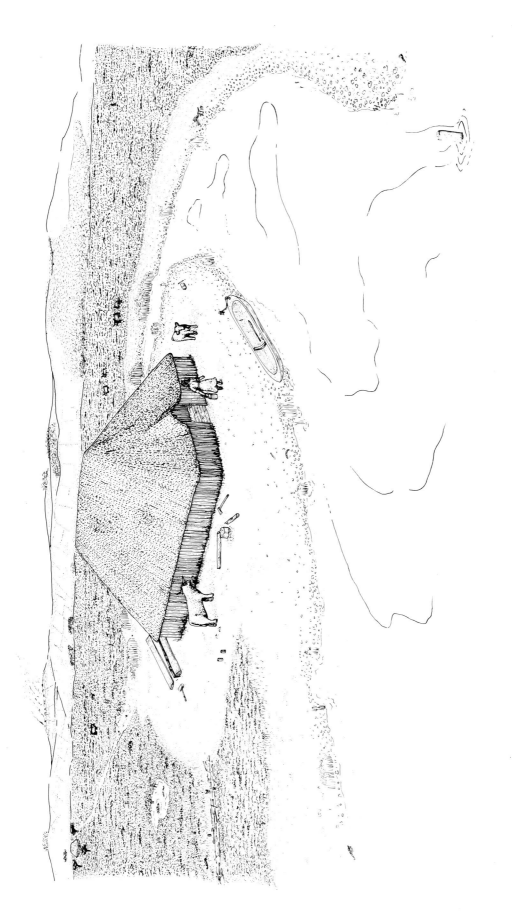

Figure 17.6 Building 6 c 273 BC in its ecological setting. Drawing by S J Allen

Figure 17.7 Building 1 c 382–342 BC in its ecological setting. Drawing by S J Allen

certain cases relate to local factors such as the position of palaeochannels, which are none the less important in understanding the context of archaeological sites. There are also organic–minerogenic–erosive–depositional changes which appear to be broadly coeval in the Severn Estuary and beyond. Increasingly precise dating enables us to test to what extent changes are contemporary and may therefore relate to wider Holocene sea level and climate changes.

The lower Wentlooge Formation resulted from rapid early Holocene sea level rise which, by c 5600 Cal BC had reduced to the extent that peat formation occurred. Alternating peat and clay deposition occurred at Goldcliff until 4000 Cal BC. For the next 2500 years at Goldcliff peat deposition exceeded sea level rise. The onset of this phase at 4000 Cal BC represents the point at which sea level curves for the Bristol Channel (most recently Jennings et al 1998, fig 9; Haslett et al 1998a, fig 1) show a marked reduction in the rate of rise.

In the Severn Estuary we have yet to establish to what extent transgressions and regressions occurred during the main period of peat formation from 4000 to 1500 Cal BC. At Goldcliff all we have within the peat are clay bands millimetres in thickness which could represent either the landward margins of transgressions or deposition during rare storm surge events, which can give rise to tides more than 2m above predicted levels and could, therefore, have led to brief inundations of the bog. Elsewhere on the Welsh side of the Estuary, variations in the extent and thickness of peats may well relate to transgressive and regressive phases, the chronology of which has yet to be established. On the south side of the estuary at Brean Down (Bell 1990), an alternating sequence of blown sands and stabilisation phases between 2000 and 700 Cal BC may represent different manifestations of transgressive and regressive episodes. However, the evidence so far available does not indicate a simple relationship between the estuarine and dune sequence. Sand deposition spans the later phase of peat formation and extends into what appears to have been a transgressive phase at Goldcliff.

After 1500 Cal BC there is an increased number of trackways in the Somerset Levels. At about the same time inundation of the bog began to take place at several sites in the Welsh Severn Estuary. The Bronze Age settlements at Redwick, Chapeltump and Rumney-3 are likely to have been inundated between c 1300 and 900 Cal BC and the survey (Chapter 16) revealed widespread evidence of activity on the peat surface during the later Bronze Age. That transgression lasted for about 800 years but at Goldcliff was interrupted by two short lived regressions c 600 and 400 Cal BC. The main period of Iron Age activity was associated with the latter. Following this episode even the raised bog at Goldcliff West, which had not been inundated during any of the three transgressions between 1500 and 500 Cal BC, was inundated in the area of Building 6, c 271 BC, and Building 8 apparently later.

The question is, are the short-lived 1st millennium BC regressions at Goldcliff local phenomena, or more widespread? The regression c 300 Cal BC may occur elsewhere: an artefact scatter in an organic band at Rumney-1 has a similar date, and there is a thin peat overlying the raised bog in the Redwick/Cold Harbour area which has not yet been dated. As originally defined the upper Wentlooge Formation is the minerogenic horizon overlying the mid-Holocene peat and clays. At Goldcliff the date of that transition varies by between 1000 and 1500 years, pointing to a more complex sequence of environmental changes in the 1st millennium BC than previously envisaged.

Notwithstanding the fact that the upper Wentlooge may represent more than one separate inundation, the deposition of this sediment body was of large spatial scale and reflects very rapid sedimentation in the 1st millennium BC. It seems to have affected virtually the whole Gwent Levels, including the inland sites of Barland's Farm and Vurlong Reen (Walker et al 1998), in all perhaps 800km². It is also broadly coeval with a major episode of flooding in the Somerset Levels where, between c 850 and 550 BC, a marine incursion occurred up the Axe valley (Housley 1988). Marine incursions are apparent in many other coastal wetlands around this time, for instance in the East Anglian Fenland (Hall and Coles 1994, 92) and the Humber wetlands (van de Noort and Ellis 1998).

Inundation of the middle Wentlooge peat is the most significant change, not just because of its scale but because so much of the archaeological evidence is concentrated during this period. The middle–upper Wentlooge transition is also associated with the development of palaeochannels which are now filled with upper Wentlooge clay. The effects of these channels on the hydrological stability of the bog need to be considered. They would have provided drainage for the bog but also created inroads for marine incursions during high tides. Any drainage channels within the Gwent Levels would eventually merge into a tidal creek system, and the location of the boundary between freshwater drainage and tidal creeks depends on sea level. During a marine transgression the tidal creek system would encroach further inland, perhaps as far as the raised bog and result in the deepening of channels. Allen (1992b, 128) notes that the burial of the bog was preceded by the erosional widening of palaeochannels and has outlined the ways in which this occurred (Allen 1997a). The effects of these processes would have been exacerbated if, as a result of more stormy conditions and associated higher sea level, coastal erosion was cutting into the margins of the bog, disrupting its hydrology. Channels draining the bog margin would have become increasingly incised, leading to desiccation and the development of cracks and gullies on the bog surface. Gullying and cracking would have led to desiccation and improved drainage thus creating, for a time, a drier peat surface more suitable for settlement. We have strong evidence for gullying around Building 6 and widespread evidence of cracks from the intertidal survey. However, it should be acknowledged that further work is needed to establish to what extent the cracks are prehistoric, or postdate exhumation of the peat.

The changes described are self limiting. The short-term effects of improved drainage in creating a drier surface would have been counteracted by the effects of peat shrinkage and compaction, which would have led to a progressive lowering of the peat surface. This phenomenon is well documented following the drainage of bogs, for instance in the Fenland 'a drop of 3.25m between 1848 and 1932, as the peat wastes and shrinks after drainage' was recorded by Godwin (1978, 38). The effects of compaction are equally significant at Goldcliff where we have suggested compaction from 5.5m to 1.8m, a drop of 3.7 m (Chapter 3), although that is the product not just of peat shrinkage but metres of clay overburden.

The effect of the processes described would be a relative lowering of the bog surface and, with time, more frequent inundation by the sea. It follows that either a rise in relative sea level, or increased storminess triggering erosion and desiccation, could have produced the observed sedimentary change, although it is highly probable that both processes were in this case combined.

Lowering of the peat by desiccation and compaction would mean that the peat surface was lower in the tidal range and, thus, subject to increasing rates of sedimentation. This process reversed the initial improved drainage by blocking the channels, a process which seems to have been well advanced by the Iron Age when one of the channels was crossed by the Upton Track.

There is a similarity between the periods of major sedimentation in the Severn Estuary and the extensive River Severn catchment which has been the subject of particularly detailed palaeohydrological study (Gregory 1983, Gregory *et al* 1987). The Severn and its tributaries show a marked increase in alluviation from *c* 1000–1 Cal BC, up to five times modern sedimentation levels (Shotton 1978, 31, Brown 1987, 304). These changes occur at a time when the Severn catchment, in common with much of the Midlands and northern Britain, was subject to increasing clearance with the result that an anthropogenic explanation for increased alluviation has been favoured. However, there is recent evidence that, on some sites in the Lower Severn, the increase in sedimentation was sea level related (Hewlett and Birnie 1996, 59). It occurs during the same period that the rapid deposition of upper Wentlooge clay occurred in the estuary. That change was on such a scale that it seems inconceivable that it could be related solely, or even mainly, to increased sediment supply from the River Severn. If greatly increased sedimentation in the Severn River and Estuary do turn out to be coeval, that would strengthen the case for regarding climate-related factors as a greater influence than clearance history. At the moment the relative contribution of the two factors is far from

clear. The case does, however, emphasise the potential value of extending catchment scale studies of river systems to estuarine contexts, which offer particular opportunities for the identification of extra regional factors such as sea level or climate, particularly because estuaries have contexts which can be precisely dated by dendrochronology, especially if they contain archaeological sites.

17.7 People and wetland environmental change

Dynamism is one of this estuarine environment's most important characteristics. This created the context and limits of possible human action and the diversity and ecological productivity which made this an attractive place for people. The diversity of resources reflects differing frequencies of inundation: from the resources of the open water, to those areas of mudflat which were inundated at each tide, those saltmarshes inundated only every 2 weeks by spring tides, those more rarely inundated by Highest Astronomical Tides and, above that, areas only inundated by rare events. Each of these zones supported different vegetation communities and different opportunities for animal and human activity.

The earliest settlement in the Mesolithic at Goldcliff occurs during a marine regression when reedswamp developed. The high ecological productivity of this successional stage has been emphasised by Welinder (1978) and by Mellars and Dark (1998) and would have made this ecotonal situation particularly attractive. However, the Mesolithic human (Aldhouse-Green *et al* 1992) and animal (Allen 1997a) footprint evidence also show that the saltmarsh conditions, which pollen evidence shows were associated with the human footprints, also attracted game and hunters.

The Neolithic and earlier Bronze Age is a period for which we have only unstratified artefacts which imply a low level of utilisation during the main period of raised bog formation. This contrasts with more abundant evidence from the wetland and its margins on the English side of the Estuary, including Neolithic trackways in the Somerset Levels (Coles and Coles 1986). In the Welsh Levels activity increased dramatically during the middle and late Bronze Age from *c* 1500 Cal BC. The occupation sites are all in a similar stratigraphic context. They are within the peat, but at a time when its surface was subject to increasing episodic marine inundation. This is seen from the stratigraphic evidence at Redwick, Collister Pill, Chapeltump, Rumney-3 and Cold Harbour-1a, and is confirmed by a wide range of palaeoenvironmental evidence at Goldcliff, including pollen, plant macrofossils, beetles, mites and diatoms (Chapters 13–15). Why should activity be so concentrated at a time when conditions were getting wetter and, one might imagine, less suitable for settlement? Various possibilities suggest themselves. It could be argued that proximity to the sea was a key factor for communication and fishing. It could also be argued that increasing marine influence caused vegetation changes to the bog surface and created a mosaic of much greater botanical diversity particularly suitable for animal grazing. A third factor is that the natural incision of drainage channels into the peat, which, as noted above (Chapter 17.6), might reflect higher sea level and/or increased storminess, would have led to a drying out of the raised bog surface, and may thus have created a more favourable context for settlement. In the Assendelver Polders and the Midden-Delfland area of the Netherlands, the earliest habitation took place *c* 600 BC on a peat surface which had become drier, not because of a regression, but because during a transgression a drainage network became established, creating for a time a drier surface and, thus, favouring settlement (Louwe Kooijmans 1985, van Rijn personal communication). Each of the three factors specified may have contributed to the concentration of activity at this interface but the last two, suitability for grazing and temporarily drier conditions on a seasonally desiccated bog, are the most strongly supported by the Goldcliff palaeoenvironmental evidence.

Although the Severn Estuary evidence does indicate that human activity tends to occur in the early stages of transgressions, we should not on this basis over-emphasise the extent to which specific environmental conditions determined patterns of human activity. It is notable that Goldcliff structures were made in the contrasting environments of fen woodland, reedswamp, and raised bog, and several trackways communicated between different environment types.

Figure 17.3 shows that a number of the dates for structures are later than the latest date for the peats on which those structures are located. We should, thus, entertain the possibility that certain structures were associated, not with the peat, but with the initial stages of succeeding minerogenic sedimentation. If so, they have either been planed off by erosion at the level of the peat, or their timbers have not been preserved where contained in sediments of the minerogenic phase. It is necessary to identify this possibility, although the evidence we have does not support the proposition. It is evident that the peat surfaces dated have, in some cases, been truncated. Where artefact scatters, or horizontal trackway, or flooring surfaces survive, they do so within the upper part of the peat. One notable exception is Trackway 1130 which is just above a thin reed peat. The conclusion, therefore, is that occupation was mainly associated with the peat, but at a time when its surface was beginning to be subject to marine influence.

We have not identified occupation horizons on the fully developed saltmarsh, although there are strong indications that such existed. Palaeochannels in the Magor Pill area contain later Iron Age sherds (Whittle 1989, Allen forthcoming b, Allen and Rippon 1997), which are best explained in terms of material washed in from closely adjacent occupation sites of

the minerogenic phases, since the sherds are later than any known peats in that area. Occupations associated with the minerogenic phase are not likely to preserve wood structures and will, therefore, be much less visible archaeologically. The overall impression, therefore, is of an environment which continued to be exploited during the later Iron Age, although perhaps at a decreased level of intensity.

17.8 People as agents of environmental change

Burning has been noted at Goldcliff during the Mesolithic 5200–5500 Cal BC (Fig 4.13), and we have noted parallel evidence from other coastal sites in the Bristol Channel and from upland sites more widely. At Goldcliff the resolution of the palynological evidence in this basal horizon does not help to clarify whether this was deliberate environmental manipulation, or the product of long continued campfires for which there was evidence in the excavated area. This is an issue which could be addressed by analysis of the peat at *c* −3.8m OD which is contemporary with initial Mesolithic occupation and would help to establish the extent of Mesolithic vegetation disturbance at this time. There is also charcoal from the base of the peat which overlies the Mesolithic site, representing a later, perhaps localised, burning *c* 4700 Cal BC (GrN-24143). The Pit 15 pollen diagram shows herbs, possibly indicating clearance, from before the elm decline and this is also seen at Vurlong Reen at the dryland edge (Walker *et al* 1998). Smith and Morgan's (1989) Goldcliff East pollen diagram and that from Pit 15 show evidence for clearance following the elm decline of *c* 3800 Cal BC. Other burning episodes are represented later: in the Neolithic at Hill Farm pond at the base of the peat *c* 3000 Cal BC (SWAN-133); during the Bronze Age at Hill Farm Trench 2, *c* 2100 Cal BC (CAR-1505), which is exactly contemporary with the *Tilia* decline and agriculture in Smith and Morgan's pollen diagram at Goldcliff East (CAR-646); during the Bronze Age *c* 1800 BP (CAR-645), when there is evidence for renewed farming in Smith and Morgan's pollen diagram and in the Bronze Age at Hill Farm Pond, peat top, *c* 1260 Cal BC (SWAN-104). Thus, the combined evidence of palynology and charcoal shows that the island was subject to periodic clearances during the Neolithic and Bronze Age.

It was during the earlier Bronze Age that the increasing clearance of the dryland surrounding the levels took place, as we know from the Barland's Farm and Vurlong Reen pollen diagrams (Walker *et al* 1998). Thus, on the dryland a cleared cultural landscape appears to have been established by the middle–later Bronze Age. The Caldicot sequence supports this because here at the wetland edge the surroundings were mainly open throughout the Bronze Age (Nayling and Caseldine 1997). At Goldcliff peat of Iron Age date did not survive in the intertidal area close to the former island. Such a peat may be represented inland of the seawall in Transect C (Fig 3.6) but was not subject to pollen analysis. Consequently, we do not have a very clear picture of what was happening on the island during the most concentrated period of wetland activity, although it is thought likely that the island was largely cleared by the end of the Bronze Age.

Given the distinct charcoal layers at the edges of the island, it is particularly noteworthy that there was an almost total lack of charcoal, even tiny fragments, in wetland contexts away from the island at Goldcliff. The only exceptions were some pieces of charred wood from the boat plank structure and one piece from the Building 6 palaeochannel, which could postdate the building. It is difficult to avoid the conclusion that people did not light fires and have hearths at Goldcliff, at least not in the vicinity of the structures we have examined. Was the use of fire restricted to other areas? Was it a practical measure to avoid setting fire to a bog surface which, seasonally at least, could have been highly combustible? Was there no necessity for the use of fire; or taboos against its use in this context? If, as the evidence hints, some of the buildings were used for joint animal and human occupancy, heat generated by the animals may have meant there was no need of hearths for heating purposes, particularly since occupation may have been during warmer parts of the year. Absence of fire at Goldcliff remains puzzling since its use is attested by charcoal and fire-cracked stones at all the Bronze Age occupation sites, and at Rumney there are probable hearth sites.

The earlier dates for human activity on the former Goldcliff Island and its fringes compared with the surrounding wetland and, in particular, contrasts in the evidence for burning, highlight the value of complementing wetland sequences by targeted investigation at the dryland/wetland interface. This is a difficult zone to work in because dessication compresses and reduces the quality of the palaeoenvironmental record and, in the specific case of Hill Farm Trench 2, disturbance by post-medieval pond digging has truncated the record.

The marked concentration of human activity and cattle trample on the surface of the raised bog means that we should consider the possibility that their effects contributed to the demise of the bog, leading perhaps to vegetation change, the development of bare patches, and promotion of gullying. We have no direct evidence in support of this premise. It is, however, probable that increasing levels of anthropogenic activity, grazing, and later drainage and seawall construction contributed to the lack of any peat formation during regression phases in Romano-British and later times. Other factors will also have contributed such as increased sediment supply and a more rapid rate of sea level rise.

None of the evidence presented points unequivocally to deliberate manipulation of the wetland environment in prehistory. People seem to have used situations opportunistically, when conditions were suitable for settlement or activity. We have found no evidence for deliberate drainage in prehistory; the slight hummocks on which buildings were situated were of natural origin, likewise, so far as we have been able to establish, surrounding palaeochannels. The main evidence of alteration of the environment during the Bronze Age and Iron Age was the creation of trackways which, at least in some cases, maintained communications across areas which were getting wetter. We could, therefore, see them as a deliberate attempt to overcome the effects of environmental change.

Evidence for opportunistic prehistoric use is in complete contrast to the succeeding Romano-British landscape (Rippon 1996a and 1997) where we have evidence for widespread drainage, the probable creation of seawalls, making a landscape suitable for a range of agricultural purposes, as well as activities such as metalworking (Fulford et al 1994). In this way Romano-British communities insulated the wetland behind the seawall from the effects of all but the most severe inundations. Paradoxically, this made themselves and their successors far more vulnerable to the effects of rare events, of which the most well documented is the flood of AD 1606 (Boon 1980).

17.9 Dating and duration

Dating

Dendrochronological evidence from Goldcliff has been discussed in Chapter 11 and radiocarbon dates in the concluding sections on the Mesolithic site (Chapter 4, Fig 4.13), the Buildings (Chapter 9, Fig 9.1), and the Trackways (Chapter 10, Fig 10.21). The foregoing figures show the ranges of calibrated dates with dendrochronological dates marked where available. These demonstrate that most of the Goldcliff buildings and trackways have similar date ranges between 400 and 100 Cal BC. Where we have dendrochronological dates, these are all in the period between 454 and 271 calendar years BC. Building 7 is earlier, and Building 8 and Trackway 1330 at Goldcliff West indicate that activity continued into the late Iron Age, or even perhaps the early Romano-British period.

The calibrated ranges of the other dated structures from the intertidal estuary are shown in Figure 17.8. Although in a similar stratigraphic context to the Goldcliff buildings on top of middle Wentlooge peat, the other structures have calibrated ranges 500 years, or more, earlier. The four Redwick structures have similar ranges within the period 1510–930 Cal BC with the main probability of Buildings 2, 4, and 5 between 1000 and 1300 Cal BC. The calibrated range of Building 1 indicates it may be older, with most of the probability lying in the period 1200–1450 Cal BC. The Goldcliff and Redwick calibrated ranges between them show that the tradition of rectangular

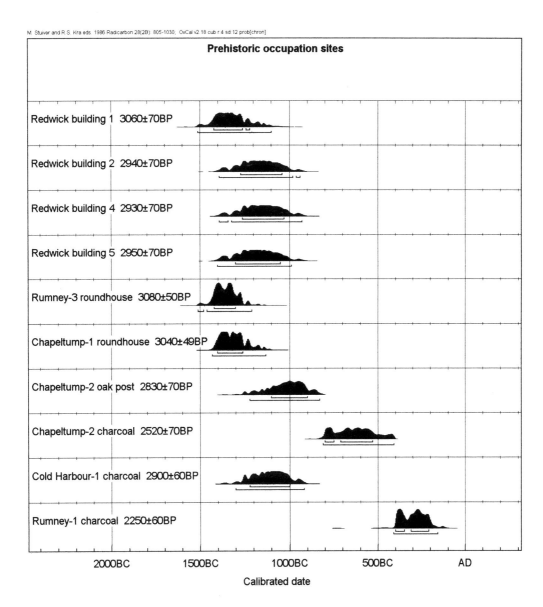

M. Stuiver and R.S. Kra eds. 1986 Radiocarbon 28(2B): 805-1030; OxCal v2.18 cub r:4 sd:12 prob[chron]

Prehistoric occupation sites

Redwick building 1 3060±70BP

Redwick building 2 2940±70BP

Redwick building 4 2930±70BP

Redwick building 5 2950±70BP

Rumney-3 roundhouse 3080±50BP

Chapeltump-1 roundhouse 3040±49BP

Chapeltump-2 oak post 2830±70BP

Chapeltump-2 charcoal 2520±70BP

Cold Harbour-1 charcoal 2900±60BP

Rumney-1 charcoal 2250±60BP

2000BC   1500BC   1000BC   500BC   AD

Calibrated date

Figure 17.8 Calibrated radiocarbon dates of prehistoric settlements in the Severn Estuary, for comparison with the Goldcliff dates shown in Figure 9.1. Based on the calibration curve of Stuiver, Long and Kra 1993 and the OxCal programme (v2.18)

buildings in the estuary had a duration of some 1500 years between *c* 1400 Cal BC and 220 Cal AD, although its range after *c* 100 Cal BC rests only on the single date from Goldcliff West, Building 8.

As regards the roundhouses, the calibrated range of Rumney-3 is 1460–1210 Cal BC and Chapeltump-1, 1320–920 Cal BC. An earlier date for Chapeltump-1 of 1550–1260 Cal BC (CAR-992) is not shown on Figure 17.8. The Rumney-3 and Chapeltump dates are very close to the range of Redwick dates and leave little doubt that the round and rectangular building traditions were in contemporary use in the period between 1400 and 1000 Cal BC.

Goldcliff trackways, like the buildings, are mostly between 400 and 100 Cal BC, with Trackway 1330 being a century or two younger and Trackways 9050 and 9060 probably a century or two older. Apart from Goldcliff, two other trackways have been dated (Fig 10.21): Collister Pill-2, which has its main probability between *c* 1200 and 1400 Cal BC and the Upton Hurdle Track, which is between 400 and 800 Cal BC, ie earlier than all but the two earliest Goldcliff tracks. The Upton trackway is between 200 and 500 years later than the nearby Chapeltump roundhouse and it shows continuing human activity in that area following the marine transgression which inundated the peat on which the roundhouse sat and laid down the clay in which the track was contained.

The radiocarbon dates from this intertidal research may be compared with the series of dates from the Caldicot palaeochannel which were presented using the same graphics (Nayling and Caseldine 1997, figs 7–8). The earliest structural wood from Caldicot is *c* 2000 Cal BC, some 500 calendar years earlier than the earliest structures on intertidal peats. This period (2000–1500 Cal BC) is filled by eight dates on worked wood of Caldicot Phase III. There are wood structures at Caldicot which are contemporary with the Redwick, Chapeltump, and

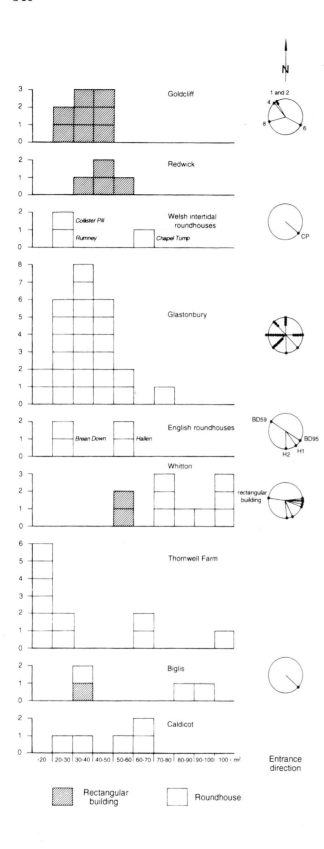

Rectangular building

Roundhouse

Figure 17.9 Diagram showing the dimensions and entrance orientations of round and rectangular buildings in wetland and dryland contexts in and around the Severn Estuary. For sources see text

Rumney-3 Bronze Age sites. Caldicot dendrochronological dates are concentrated in the period in the 990s BC, slightly younger than the main concentration of Bronze Age intertidal sites. Activity continued at Caldicot during the interval between the Bronze Age intertidal activity and *c* 400 Cal BC, which is around the time when the main activity at Goldcliff started.

Duration of activity

The Caldicot site, a palaeochannel on the wetland edge, less than 100m from dryland on either side, is notable in the longevity of its archaeological sequence *c* 2000–400 Cal BC. Similarly long-lived, from *c* 2500–800 Cal BC was the wetland edge settlement at Brean Down (Bell 1990). The more remote sites considered here, out on the peat, tell a different story; activity is mainly concentrated in two briefer periods, between *c* 1400 and 1000 Cal BC and *c* 400–100 Cal BC. The limited material cultural evidence from the intertidal sites speaks perhaps of short-lived activity and we will consider below the possibility of seasonal use. Even so, there are indications of time depth in the use of specific sites. We have noted that the area of Goldcliff Buildings 1 and 2 showed evidence of multiple phases of activity (Chapter 7). The alder curves for these buildings suggested activity extending perhaps over *c* 17 years, but uncertainties about the growth patterns of this species, mean we should not press that evidence too far (Section 12.4). The more complex Goldcliff Trackways 1108 and 1103 showed signs of repair and modification. Other Goldcliff buildings, notably 6, seem to have had a shorter life. Overall, however, the dating evidence demonstrates that when we observe archaeology on an area of peatshelf it is not necessarily all of one very transitory phase and, in some cases as at Goldcliff West, it may reflect activity over a longer period than our initial impressions might suggest.

17.10 Buildings round and rectangular

The rectangular buildings present in the middle Bronze Age at Redwick and in the Iron Age at Goldcliff contrast with the almost ubiquitous roundhouses found in both periods elsewhere in Britain. The dating evidence clearly shows that in the Bronze Age both round and rectangular forms were used in the wetland. This poses a question as to whether the two structural forms were used for similar purposes? This will be addressed by comparing wetland and dryland structures around the estuary (Fig 17.9). Sites discussed in previous chapters are compared with peatland sites at Rumney (Allen 1996b) and Chapeltump (Whittle 1989), both middle Bronze Age; Glastonbury, later Iron Age (Coles and Minnitt 1995); a site on the clay levels at Hallen, middle–late

Iron Age (Barnes 1993); the wetland edge middle-Bronze Age site at Brean Down (Bell 1990). Comparisons are also made with dryland sites of Bronze Age–Romano-British date at Thornwell Farm, Chepstow (Hughes 1996), and late-Iron Age and early Romano-British sites at Whitton (Jarrett and Wrathell 1981), Biglis (Parkhouse 1988), and Caldicot (Vyner and Allen 1988).

The floor area of the rectangular buildings at Goldcliff is in the range 20–47m² and at Redwick 34–52m². The roundhouses at Collister Pill and Chapel Tump are at either end of that size range. The Rumney roundhouse (Allen 1996b) is likely to be a minimum floor area, because only one ring of a probable double-ring structure survived. There is overlap between the floor areas of round and rectangular structures, suggesting that both fulfilled spatial requirements of a similar order of magnitude. It is notable that the floor areas of the Welsh Severn Estuary wetland structures are comparable with that of the roundhouses at Glastonbury, which are so different in terms of their rich material culture assemblages and the presence of hearths in nearly all roundhouses. The Chapeltump roundhouse stands out as a particularly large example, bigger than all but one at Glastonbury. The two Hallen Iron Age examples and a Bronze Age example at Thornwell Farm are also large. The view has prevailed that larger buildings had some special status or communal function. It is probably not, however, valid to assume that the smaller structures, below perhaps 30m², were ancillary buildings of a non-domestic type. A rich artefact assemblage from small roundhouses at Brean Down suggests otherwise and it is notable that the wetland roundhouses at Collister Pill and Chapeltump, though at the opposite ends of the size range, have comparably impoverished material culture assemblages. At Whitton two rectangular structures, which lack hearths and evidence for domestic activity, are the closest local parallels for the Redwick and Goldcliff buildings (Chapter 9), as is a fragmentary late-Iron Age or early Romano-British example at Biglis. The roundhouses dating to the very end of the Iron Age and the 1st century AD at Whitton, and two of the Biglis examples, have floor areas larger than almost all the other examples.

Parker-Pearson (1996) and Hill (1996, fig 8.8) have observed that from the middle Bronze Age in Britain the standard roundhouse had an entrance facing east, or southeast, an orientation they regard as having possible cosmological significance relating to the rising of the sun. Of the structures in our area with definable entrances, some fit this pattern: Hallen; Biglis; Collister Pill; Brean Down Structure 97; Goldcliff Building 6; a few at Glastonbury and, interestingly, every one of the later circular structures at Whitton. At Goldcliff, three structures face northwest. At Glastonbury three quarters of the structures do not conform to the stated norm, their predominant direction being west and southwest. Thus, although entrance orientation marks Goldcliff

as abnormal for domestic structures, so too is Glastonbury, where domestic activity is not in doubt. We can conclude that in the study area the stated norm is not as ubiquitous as the literature implies. Even so, there are distinct patterns of entrance orientation within and between sites. Structures which are clearly dryland and/or permanent show a greater tendency to follow the norm than those in the wetland.

There is no clear contrast in size between round and rectangular structures, or between wetland and dryland structures, or between those which are rich in artefacts and those which, like the estuary examples, have limited artefact assemblages suggestive of transitory activity. There is a tendency for the later Whitton and Biglis structures to be larger. These somewhat surprising conclusions suggest that functional considerations are unlikely to have been the main determinant of building size or form. There is a tendency for building size, shape, and entrance orientation to be similar within sites, suggesting that these traits may have formed part of the identity of specific communities.

Evidence is reviewed in the next section suggesting that the rectangular buildings may, in some cases, have provided byre accommodation at one end and human accommodation at the other. They could, therefore, represent a scaled down version of the longhouses which characterised Welsh farms in the medieval period, with a byre. The estuary evidence could, therefore, point to previously unsuspected pre-Roman origins for the longhouse and some aspects of the agricultural way of life with which it was associated.

17.11 Structure function and estuarine activities

The roundhouses have pottery, bones, charcoal, and burnt stone. They seem likely to have been the focus of at least temporary domestic activity. Redwick has all except pottery. Goldcliff is odd in the lack of charcoal and burnt stone and just one pottery sherd. This may cause us to question whether domestic activities took place in the Goldcliff structures; perhaps they were just byres and storage buildings and people lived elsewhere. There is, however, a scatter of animal bones round the entrances to Buildings 1 and 2 which are suggestive of discard from a domestic structure. The floors of the three structures, where they survived, were totally devoid of artefacts and the absence of bones in huts led Hamilakis (Chapter 15.7) to argue they had not been used as habitations. However, there is some evidence for building interiors being kept very clean: at Redwick and Collister Pill the artefacts are all outside the structures, and at Brean Down (Bell 1990) the floor areas were much cleaner of artefacts than the area outside. There is, therefore, a suggestion of spotless interiors and outside middens which opens up the possibility of social convention governing artefact disposal.

Children and Nash (1996, 95) have suggested that the plan of the Goldcliff buildings may have had a metaphorical significance, the metaphor they suggest, using ethnographic analogy, being the functioning of the human body. The interpretation they put forward is not founded on the particulars of the archaeological record as excavated, which does not support their suggestions regarding the use of specific parts of the building. However, their more general proposition that the distribution of artefacts and components of the building is as likely to reflect non-material social considerations as specific functional patterns is a valid one and it is possible that the absence of artefacts within structures may be partly explained in this way.

One of the most problematic aspects of this project was establishing whether the Goldcliff buildings had originally housed animals, as the evidence of possible stalls in Building 1 implied. Beetles, plant macrofossils, phosphates, and micromorphology produced uncertain results. However the mites show that without doubt Building 1 contained excrement and the beetle evidence strongly suggests that the reeds were byre flooring. Sheep are unimportant (8% of bones, compared with cattle 58%) and the presence of cattle lice shows that the buildings housed cattle. The entrance to Goldcliff Building 1 is very narrow at 0.6m, so calves seem the most likely occupants of the stalls. They may have been kept inside because the wetland landscape, with its palaeochannels, was a hazardous environment for young animals. Furthermore, calves probably needed to be kept away from their mothers in order to manage the milk supply for human consumption. Early medieval Irish sources (Kelly 1997) imply that it was traditional practice to keep the calf nearby at the time of milking, an activity we may envisage going on just outside the buildings, as reconstructed in Figure 17.7.

Mite evidence for excrement and cattle lice was most abundant in the upper floor levels suggesting the possibility that the byre evidence reflects a secondary use of Building 1. That could be supported by other evidence. Flooring timbers predated the subdivisions which were differently constructed of oak from the rest of the buildings and led to the deposition of a distinct area of oak woodchips outside the entrance. Reeds immediately overlying the floor continued across the line of the subdivisions, which might be later. A change of use might help to explain why some sources of evidence, such as the micromorphology, produced questionable evidence of byre activities which were so clearly attested by the mites and lice. The idea of secondary use is attractive but, given the small number of mite samples, we cannot push it too far.

Human fleas and cattle lice in the Goldcliff Building 6 palaeochannel suggests both people and cattle may have been accommodated. Burning of the peat at one end of Redwick-4 suggests the possibility of a

hearth at one end, and there are hints of stalls at the other, so shared domestic and byre accommodation does seem possible.

17.12 Seasonality

None of the settlement sites investigated has produced the quantity of artefacts or concentration of activity which we would normally associate with permanent year round settlement. There is also evidence of flooding during the life of sites. It, thus, seems probable that prehistoric use of the wetland was adapted to the very pronounced natural rhythms in tidal levels which occur on a range of timescales. These include the twice daily tidal changes and the c 14 day interval spring tide levels, which as Figure 17.10a shows, reach levels significantly higher on either side of the spring and autumn equinox. That factor, combined with reduced freshwater flooding during the summer months, would mean that a larger area of the wetland would have been accessible to grazing animals during the periods of richest spring and summer plant growth. The hypothesis of seasonally related activity may be tested and developed by comparison with the available biological evidence, largely from Goldcliff. Some of that evidence points to activity at particular times of year, although different sources tend to have variable degrees of seasonal precision. The two periods for which we have biological evidence of seasonality at Goldcliff are associated with contrasting sets of conditions; in the Mesolithic we are dealing with an essentially dryland site on the island edge surrounded by a vast expanse of wetland; in the Iron Age with activity on the wetland itself.

Mesolithic c 5750–5200 Cal BC

The limited range of tools in the Goldcliff Mesolithic assemblage argues against sedentism. If activity was episodic then when did it occur? Eels are present and they begin their migration in December–January and peak elver catches occur at the time of equinoctial tides in April–May. In the Severn adult eels are caught through the year but reduced numbers in winter when they are less active (Severn Tidal Power Group 1989, R Evans, Environment Agency personal communication). Evidence of the growth sizes of both eels and smelt point to winter, rather than summer, activity (Fig 17.10b).

We have no salmon bones from the Mesolithic (or Iron Age) sites. The various possible reasons for the absence of this evidence include: (i) the avoidance of salmon; (ii) their rarity during the times of year when the site was occupied; (iii) the limited extent of excavation and particularly sieving; (iv) the semi-calcified bones of salmon do not preserve well in archaeological contexts. In view of the possibility that preservation factors are the explanation, we cannot ignore salmon as a possible resource. A

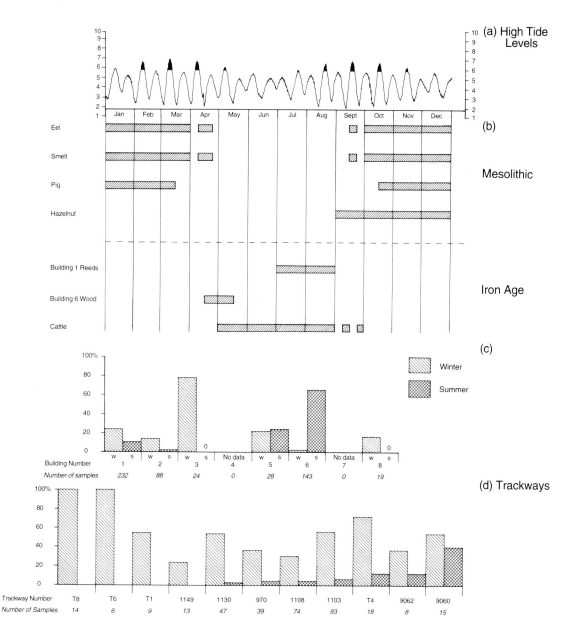

Figure 17.10 Seasonality evidence: (a) predicted high tide levels on OD scale based on Burnham-on-Sea predictions for 1989 from Institute of Oceanographic Sciences data (after Bell 1990, fig 160), (b) seasonality evidence from the Mesolithic and Iron Age periods, (c and d) Iron Age tree rings, percentage of wood cut in winter and summer, (c) Buildings 1–8, (d) Trackways (data in c and d from CD 12.35). Drawing by S J Allen

fishery has existed at Goldcliff since the medieval period and continues on a commercial basis today. Historically it has specialised in salmon (Green, C 1992). Some salmon can be caught throughout most of the year but the abundance of the resource is strongly related to season. The major salmon runs in the Estuary are from January to the end of October. January–May is particularly characterised by the return of large spring salmon (up to 50lb (22.6kg)), many of which have spent 3 years at sea (Gough *et al* 1992, Evans personal communication). On the basis of present day occurrence, it seems that fish resources as a whole would have been most abundant from about April–October. However, the seasonality evidence points to activity during the winter. The

limited precision of the growth size evidence probably does not rule out activity at the very end of winter or beginning of spring when large salmon and eels would have been available.

There is no reason to suppose that fish was the main resource in the Mesolithic. Red deer and pig are well represented, and otter, roe deer, wolf, and bird were also exploited. The animal footprint evidence (Allen 1997a) highlights the abundance of deer at this time. Unfortunately, the deer bones available do not help with the question of seasonality, but pig dentition does support the evidence of fish size in indicating winter activity (Fig 17.10b). The single charred hazelnut, for what it is worth, suggests likewise. In some respects it might be supposed that the winter was not such a suitable time for deer. Higher tides and greater flooding would have reduced the areas of grazing available and plant growth would not have been as productive as in spring and summer. Even so, the wetland might still have been attractive to animals because browse was scarce on dryland. Tides and flooding would not have affected the suitability of the island edge itself for human settlement but it would have had a significant effect on communication routes. Patterns of animal movement disrupted by flooding episodes could be the key to the question. Whatever the total biomass of herbivores in the wetland, during winter flooding those animals would have congregated in restricted higher areas, including Goldcliff Island, making them much easier to hunt.

It may be instructive to compare Goldcliff with other evidence of seasonality in the British Mesolithic. The site provides a measure of support for Jacobi's (1980) hypothesis that Mesolithic activity in Wales and the Southwest may have been concentrated on the coast and lowland in the winter, moving to the uplands in summer. Biological evidence for seasonality on a limited number of other sites points to contrasting and more complex patterns in some areas. Star Carr, a lowland lake-edge site, relied to a significant extent on the resources of reedswamp, in common with Goldcliff. Here a wide range of data sets has recently provided strong evidence of occupation in the period March–July (Mellars and Dark 1998), contrary to the earlier hypothesis of winter occupation (Clark 1954, 1972). There is seasonality evidence from two Scottish sites which have some similarity to the Goldcliff case, both in the Mesolithic were small coastal islands. Morton has seasonality evidence from molluscan growth patterns (Deith 1983) and Oronsay has evidence from otoliths, seals, and other sources (Mellars 1987). Both seem to have been visited at a range of times of year, reminding us of the possibility of more complex patterns of human usage than implied by the winter/summer dichotomy which is the limit of our seasonal resolution in the Goldcliff case.

Iron Age c 400–200 BC

During the Iron Age temporary, perhaps seasonal, activity is indicated by evidence of flooding between activity episodes and there is biological evidence of activity during summer (Fig 17.10b). The presence of neonatal and juvenile cattle suggests activity between May and August–September. Reeds for the floor of Building 1 were cut in July–August. Most of the wood for Building 6 was cut in late April or early May 273 BC, with wood for repairs being cut in the same months in 271 BC. These are the most clearly defined pieces of seasonality evidence, and they point to activity during the period of reduced flooding and tidal extremes between mid-April and mid-August

(Fig 17.10a) when grazing for herbivores would have been richest and most extensive.

However, summer may not have been the only time of year when activity took place. Morgan's tree-ring evidence (Fig 17.10c, d) shows that of the rectangular buildings only 5 and 6 have a greater proportion of summer-cut wood; summer-cut wood is less than that cut in winter in Buildings 1 and 2, and in Buildings 3 and 8 all wood was winter cut. Of the trackways, winter-cut wood predominates in every case and Building 4 contain no summer-cut wood. It is notable that three trackways (1108, 970, and 1103) which Brunning plausibly argues were made from woodworking debris of other projects, perhaps rectangular buildings, all show a greater amount of winter-cut wood.

Since eleven out of seventeen buildings and trackways contain wood cut in both summer *and* winter, it is reasonable to infer that a proportion of wood cut in one season was stockpiled for use in building, or repair, during another season. This makes it difficult to know what degree of emphasis to attach to the time of cutting. The tree-ring data certainly establishes the possibility that buildings were constructed at various times of year. It indicates, in particular, that trackway construction may have been more of a winter activity. This seems plausible, given that trackways would have been most needed under wet conditions. None of the trackways was substantial enough to have been used by cattle and the least substantial would not have survived trample for long. Some of the trackways might, therefore, relate to other forms of activity at different times of year, perhaps fishing, fowling, and boat communication in winter.

If the argument is accepted that activity was mainly concentrated during the spring and summer, then it may point to a pattern of locally transhumant land use analogous to the traditional Welsh practice of *hafod* (the summer dwelling, also sometimes called *meifod*, May-house) and *hendref* (the established dwelling or old farm). That historically attested system relates to exploitation of seasonally-rich pastures in the extensive Welsh uplands (Smith 1975, Webley 1976). However, in prehistory, before the reclamation of the coastal wetlands, they would have offered a parallel, seasonally available resource which, this evidence suggests, may have been exploited in a similar way. Seasonal exploitation of wetland contexts, probably connected with grazing during the Iron Age, is attested beyond Wales at Meare in Somerset (Coles 1987, 251) and in the Thames Valley flood plain at Farmoor (Lambrick and Robinson 1979, 134).

Summer grazing is well documented in the Severn Estuary, even into historic times, when permanent settlement had long been established on at least the drier areas of the Levels (Rippon 1997). Place-names show this: the name Somerset itself and the names of tracks and pastures in the Goldcliff and Redwick areas also incorporate the element summer (Rippon 1996a). Even more specific as to the timing of exploitation is a place name in Redwick incorporating the element Easter, which falls between 22 March and 25 April.

It may not be unduly imaginative to suppose something similar happened in prehistory. At the beginning of May, when the wood for Building 6 had been cut, the migration to the summer dairy pastures took place. The start of open pasturing and the beginning of summer was marked in Ireland by the festival of Beltaine on 1 May (Green, M 1992). Interestingly, in view of the cattle bone evidence, an Irish legal commentary employs the phrase *lulgachus Beltaine* (May calving) (Kelly 1997 and personal communication). The 9th century AD Irish literature (Green, M 1992) links *Beltaine* to purification and the driving of animals between ritual fires. This prompts speculation as to whether there could be any relationship with the puzzling absence of evidence for fire on the Goldcliff site. The dangers of importing models from later periods, and from Irish evidence to British contexts, are all too obvious from the history of Celtic scholarship. Nonetheless such speculations, however wild, may not be without value if they suggest models which can be specifically tested by future programmes of research, using independent indicators of seasonality such as tree-rings.

Other periods

For the other periods of activity represented in the Welsh Estuary as a whole, we have at present no direct biological evidence as to the seasons of activity. It is likely that the middle-Bronze Age round and rectangular structures were, in common with Goldcliff, associated with cattle grazing and occupied in spring and summer. The possibility should also, however, be acknowledged that different stages in transgressive and regressive cycles may have seen different durations and forms of seasonal use. Transgressive episodes might, therefore, be reflected in a change from permanent to seasonal use, as has been suggested towards the end of the life of the Glastonbury site (Coles and Minnitt 1995). Neumann made the interesting suggestion in Chapter 16 that a lack of evidence for the use of fire at Goldcliff, in contrast to the Bronze Age structures might, likewise, suggest a change from permanent to seasonal use. However, the very limited material culture assemblage in both periods seems more likely to be explained in terms of seasonal use. That leaves open the possibility of greater Bronze Age activity during times of the year when fires were needed.

17.13 Fishing in the Neolithic to Iron Age

We only have fish bones in the Mesolithic, not from any of the later sites including Goldcliff. In some respects this may not seem surprising because evidence of fishing is quite limited on Neolithic–Iron Age coastal sites in mainland Britain. At Brean Down, on the edge of the Severn, the collection of fish bones was small despite an extensive sieving programme (Levitan 1990). Stable isotope evidence (Chapter 5) points in a similar direction: <5% of dietary protein came from marine resources in the one Neolithic human from Alexandra Docks and the two Bronze Age humans from Goldcliff. The late Iron Age or Romano-British human from the Orb Works had 10–15% of marine protein and the medieval individual from Redwick 40–50%, in line with other evidence of greater fish consumption in the medieval period.

It would, however, be unwise and premature to conclude that fishing was little practised in the Neolithic–Iron Age. The intertidal survey identified many wooden structures in palaeochannels, some at least of these appear to be fishing structures. Those at Peterstone have been dated to the late Neolithic or Bronze Age, that at Cold Harbour Pill-2 to the late Bronze Age or early Iron Age. Probable fishing structures are also present in the palaeochannel at Caldicot during the Bronze Age, and fish bones were present (Nayling and Caseldine 1997). There is similar evidence of structures which are thought to have been used for fishing in these periods at Wotton Quarr on the Isle of Wight (Tomalin *et al* forthcoming) and the Hullbridge survey in Essex (Wilkinson and Murphy 1995). We must conclude, therefore, that evidence from different sources is somewhat contradictory as to the extent of fishing in these periods and this is a topic in need of focused research.

17.14 Comparisons with other wetlands

The emerging picture of prehistoric activity in the Welsh Severn Estuary can be compared with other work on coastal wetlands. Geographically the Somerset Levels represents a continuation of the English Severn Estuary environment and the broad outlines of its environmental sequence are closely similar (Smith and Morgan 1989). However, the pattern of human activity is strikingly different. During the Neolithic and early Bronze Age the low levels of activity recorded here contrast with the many trackways from Somerset. The evidence for building on the Welsh Levels from *c* 1500 Cal BC occurs some 1200 years earlier than the first evidence of settlement on the Somerset Levels at Glastonbury and Meare from about 300 Cal BC. It is notable that the earlier use occurs in that part of the wetland subject to greater marine influence and, thus, presumably more hazardous for settlement. That serves to highlight the attractiveness of the resources offered by proximity to marine influence.

Contrasting types of archaeological evidence in the Somerset Levels and the Welsh Severn Estuary reflect different histories of activity. These may relate partly to topographic contrasts with closely adjacent bedrock rises and ridges in the Somerset Levels. Another factor may be that different facets of the wetland have been investigated in each area: the inland bog in Somerset revealed by peat cutting, in contrast to a transect along the coast revealed by erosion.

Comparison with intertidal archaeological work in Essex (Wilkinson and Murphy 1995) also suggests contrasts. Here occupation is confined to the pre-inundation surface, dryland sites of the Mesolithic and Neolithic, which were overwhelmed by sea level rise and are, thus, comparable with the Mesolithic situation at Goldcliff. The waterlogged intertidal archaeology of Essex is mainly associated with minerogenic sediments, not with the peats as it is in the Severn. The Essex activity is, furthermore, of a specialised character: trackways, fishing, and landing places, but not settlements. It is, therefore, more comparable with the activity we have in the Severn associated with palaeochannels at the time of the upper Wentlooge transgression. There is, however, the site of Blackwater-28, with vertical posts and artefact scatter dated 960–1039 Cal AD (Wilkinson and Murphy 1995, 205), which may represent a domestic structure on the saltmarsh surface, though later than any Severn Estuary structures. The Wootton Quarr survey on the Isle of Wight (Tomalin et al forthcoming) has also produced much evidence of prehistoric trackways and possible fishing structures. Perhaps the area most comparable with the Severn in terms of the scale of the estuarine wetland and its intertidal archaeology is the Shannon in the west of Ireland, where O'Sullivan (1996, 64) has found oval huts on an intertidal peat shelf dating between 1678 and 1521 Cal BC. These he interprets in terms of seasonal cattle husbandry in the estuarine pastures.

The diversity implied by recent intertidal and wetland archaeological surveys must, in part, reflect regional diversity. This is something which prehistorians are often seeking to identify but which often proves illusive, or ambiguous. The ambiguity is accentuated in this case because in each coastal wetland we are dealing with a fairly narrow exposed corridor across much more extensive wetlands. Contrasts in the extent of sedimentation and erosion in different geographical areas mean that the transect available to any one generation of intertidal archaeologists is likely to reflect different facets of the original wetland ecosystem and human activity in each study area. The implication of this is that if we wish to understand the full range of prehistoric activity in coastal wetlands, it will be necessary for future studies to select very carefully a full range of sedimentary and environmental contexts.

17.15 Wetland/dryland interaction

In considering dryland/wetland relationships a significant unknown is Goldcliff Island. We have no evidence of activity here during the Iron Age but, as John Allen has shown (Chapter 2), it was much bigger in prehistory. Before erosion it might have contained a permanent settlement. It is possible that the lack of hearths and the paucity of domestic evidence on the wetland is explained by the fact that the buildings were byres where people tended the animals but perhaps did not live, except perhaps at key times of calving, etc. Economical as this explanation is, it is not wholly supported by the evidence. The main concentration of activity during this period was away from, rather than near, the island, and the trackway evidence (Chapter 10) suggests that communications were more focused on the open water and channels than on the island.

If the wetland was being used seasonally, then what of its relationship to the higher ground to the north? The pollen evidence (Walker et al 1998) points to relatively local and temporary clearance in the Neolithic when dryland activity is attested by some megalithic tombs and a scatter of flint axes (Savory 1980a, figs 5.2 and 5.4). The dry ground was increasingly cleared during the Bronze Age and seems to have become a largely agricultural landscape during this period. North of the levels there are some cairns and barrows and a scattered pattern of isolated bronze and other artefactual finds (Lillie 1991, figs 3 and 14). Settlement evidence is limited. Overlooking the levels at Thornwell Farm, Chepstow there is a roundhouse dated to c 8th century BC (Hughes 1996). Of particular relevance is the probable settlement hypothesised beside the Caldicot palaeochannel where activity starts in the early Bronze Age c 2000 Cal BC (Nayling and Caseldine 1997). Parts of Phases VI and VII at Caldicot are contemporary with the middle-Bronze Age intertidal rectangular and roundhouse sites and it is perfectly possible that Caldicot was the parent settlement for one of these sites; the nearest are the roundhouse sites at Collister Pill-1 (4.5km) and Chapeltump-1 (5.3km). The palaeochannel record at Caldicot suggests that site ended early in the Iron Age. On the English side of the estuary Brean Down was another Bronze Age settlement on the very edge of the wetland with a density and range of artefactual evidence that suggests year round occupation.

In the Iron Age the settlement pattern seems to have shifted away from the lowland fringes of the levels towards the hillforts and enclosures which overlook the levels from the surrounding hills (Ordnance Survey 1967). Four large hillforts in particular dominate the levels and are within 10km of Goldcliff: Tredegar, not dated (Whittle, E 1992, 46); Llanmelin, dated by Nash-Williams (1933) from the 3rd to 1st century BC; Lodgewood (undated Whittle, E 1992, 45); and Sudbrook, dated by Nash-Williams (1939) from the 2nd century BC to the Roman period. Given what we have said about seasonal pastoralism, it is interesting that both Llanmelin and Tredegar have appended enclosures of a type which is often associated with pastoralism. Another site at Wilcrick 7.7km north of Goldcliff, has been classified as a multivallate hillfort of 3.5 acres (1.4ha) (Savory 1950, Ward 1920, Ordnance Survey 1967) and is shown quite convincingly as such on the larger scale Ordnance Survey Maps (eg 1:25,000, Sheet 48/58, 1979). However, a field visit reveals a deep hollow-way to the summit of the hill, and traces of possible banks but not of a form or magnitude which is convincing as a hillfort. The character of that site, which lies on the edge of the levels overlooking both Redwick and Goldcliff, requires survey. Unenclosed Iron Age settlements also existed; the recently excavated site at Thornwell Farm, Chepstow is an example where there seems to have been some activity throughout the Iron Age (Hughes 1996). Other excavated unenclosed settlements at Biglis and Caldicot (Robinson et al 1988) were not established until the late Iron Age after the main activity on the levels.

As regards the overall pattern of dryland and wetland relationships, the evidence suggests something comparable with the concave landscape concept represented by Coles and Minnitt (1995, fig 8.1) for the Somerset Levels, each landscape facet contributing particular resources available at different times within the seasonal cycle. In the Bronze Age, judging by Caldicot, settlements may have been located at the wetland edge but, by the Iron Age, the main settlements were almost certainly the hill-top forts and hill-slope enclosures, some perhaps of Bronze Age origin. Such sites seem highly likely to be the parent settlements of seasonal cattle herders at Goldcliff.

Perhaps the hypothesised herds-people only took a limited range of material culture down to the summer pastures. Most of what we find is organic, with pottery occurring on the edge of the levels at Caldicot and on the intertidal roundhouse sites, but not, so far, at Redwick, and only one sherd at Goldcliff, which, since it comes from the palaeochannel, could be later than the occupation.

We should also consider the possibility that the rectangular buildings were constructed by communities which were largely aceramic. This may appear an illogical solution, given the evidence for the use of pottery during the Bronze Age in the intertidal roundhouse sites, and the evidence for its use in the later Iron Age from palaeochannels at Magor. It is, however, a possibility which needs serious consideration because there is good evidence from the dryland for Iron Age communities in the area which were largely, or wholly, aceramic. This is true of parts of central Wales and the Marches (Cunliffe 1991, 100), for instance Coed y Bwnydd, 22km to the north (Babbidge 1977). Manning (1981) notes the aceramic nature of Iron Age sites in South Wales, although interestingly the sites of Llanmelin and Sudbrook on the edge of the Levels and Twyn-y-Gaer (40km north, Probert 1976) have been productive of pottery. We have the possibility, therefore, of some communities which used pottery, mainly perhaps to the east, and others to the west and north which did not. In the levels, the indications are of

communities in the early and middle Iron Age which were largely aceramic living in a landscape which during the middle and late Bronze Age had been occupied by ceramic-using communities. That does open up the possibility of an intrusive aceramic group which built rectangular structures and became established in the middle Bronze Age; if so, the evidence suggest coexistence with contemporary roundhouse-using ceramic communities. On the subject of different social groups, Brunning makes the interesting observation that there are different styles of woodworking represented in Goldcliff Building 6 compared with Buildings 1–4, even within the rectangular structural tradition. In the Somerset Levels, Coles (1987, 249) has suggested similar seasonal coexistence of groups of different origins which came together to exploit seasonal grazing and engage in social interaction. However, in that case the hypothesis was developed to explain the rich material culture, including craft and productive activities, which are so conspicuously absent on the Welsh Severn Estuary sites. That being so, we must also consider other possibilities. Perhaps the wetland sites with rectangular structures were associated with a particular set of activities which did not involve pottery, either because it was not practically necessary, or because there were specific social conventions against its use in those contexts.

The animal bones demonstrate an emphasis on cattle husbandry, and the presence of neonatal and young animals suggests that dairying was important. Wooden vessels, such as represented by the Goldcliff bucket stave, have traditionally been used in dairying. The only other Severn Estuary site with a high proportion of cattle is Brean Down, where the numbers of sheep and cattle are roughly equal during the main Bronze Age occupation phases (Levitan 1990). At the levels edge site at Caldicot, sheep and goat significantly outnumber cattle (McCormick 1997). At Glastonbury, there are 88% sheep and only 5% cattle among the animal bones that survive (Coles and Minnitt 1995, 194). These contrasting ratios indicate that cattle husbandry was particularly associated with the estuary edge salt-marsh at Goldcliff and Brean Down and that sites on the more inland bogs and margins of the levels at Caldicot and Glastonbury supported larger herds of sheep.

Wider contacts are highlighted by the important evidence of Bronze Age sewn boats at Goldcliff and Caldicot, and by the recent persuasive argument for the existence of a major trade route in the Bronze Age and Iron Age linking the Wiltshire Avon and the Severn (Sherratt 1996). However, the very modest artefact assemblages from the intertidal sites contain little to encourage the belief that the intertidal sites participated directly in wider trade. This contrasts with hints of such trade in the prehistoric artefact assemblages from Wootton Quarr on the Isle of Wight (Tomalin et al forthcoming) where casual loss and breakage during unloading points to substantial later trade in the

Romano-British and medieval periods. In the much more extensive wetlands of the Severn it seems that such privileges may have been jealously guarded by high status sites at the dryland edge: at Caldicot there is exotic metalwork (Nayling and Caseldine 1997) and at Brean Down late-Bronze Age gold bracelets with evidence of salt extraction, which would have provided the currency of trade (Bell 1990). The range of goods from hillforts suggests that in the early and middle Iron Age these took over as the focal points of trade and exchange, although in the late Iron Age, after the main period of the intertidal sites, the settlements at Glastonbury and Meare fulfilled a similar role on the English side.

We may suppose that in the Severn goods were loaded and landed, not out on the wetland, but where river channels came much closer to high status sites. It may not be stretching imagination too far to infer from this, together with the limited evidence or material culture, that those engaged in seasonal cattle husbandry and dairying out on the wetland were a poor underclass, a group apart from those responsible for the articulation of trade centred on elite settlements. Such distinctions might have reflected economic, social, or ethnic factors. A distinct identity maintained perhaps by a largely organic material culture, a lack of ceramics, and the making of rectangular structures unlike most of those on dryland.

17.16 Weaknesses with the project, gaps in our knowledge, and future research agendas

In the self reflexive spirit with which we ended the Introduction (Chapter 1), it is appropriate to identify aspects to which we wish we had given greater attention and areas of particular uncertainty, in the hope that these will act as a stimulus to future work.

(i) The Goldcliff Mesolithic site is of great importance because of the association of lithics, fauna, and environmental evidence, including rare evidence of seasonality. We did not locate waterlogged horizons contemporary with the occupation to the west of the island. The Mesolithic site did not get the full attention and resources it deserved because there was always so much other archaeological evidence in urgent need of recording. The entire resources available to the project could easily have been allocated doing full justice to the Mesolithic site alone.

(ii) Our dating strategy has inevitably focused on the Mesolithic, later Bronze Age, and Iron Age horizons where the archaeological evidence is concentrated. For other parts of the sequence the chronology is less secure, limiting the precision with which we can link environmental

changes to those in other areas, and limiting the contribution of our work to sea level change studies which would have required a more specifically targeted set of dates around the island fringe.

(iii) The sieving programme should have been much more extensive at the Mesolithic site, and in the areas outside Iron Age Buildings 1, 2, and 3, where some excavation of sediments contemporary with activity took place.

(iv) Because sieving was not more extensive we remain uncertain whether this, or the nature of Mesolithic activities on the site is the explanation for the paucity of microliths and microdebitage.

(v) For the same reason there is real uncertainty about the extent to which fishing was practised in the Bronze and Iron Ages. No fish bones were found at Iron Age Goldcliff, yet we have many wooden structures in palaeochannels elsewhere in the estuary which are likely to be fish traps. Major sieving programmes should be carried out in any occupation areas investigated in future, and the fishing structures of probable prehistoric date require detailed investigation.

(vi) Insufficient attention was given to the detailed recording and analysis of the animal footprints around rectangular structures. These are a potentially rich source of information about the animal populations, age structure, size and even habitual patterns of movement. Now that Allen's (1997a) detailed study of animal footprints in the estuary as a whole is available there is a solid foundation for further work on those specifically associated with occupation sites and the archaeological issues which they raise.

(vii) If the dendrochronological programme could have been expanded, this is likely to have dramatically enhanced our chronological precision and understanding of the extent to which the structures reflect patterns of seasonal use. If dates could have been obtained for submerged forest contexts, the chronology of environmental change could also have been made more precise. A significant dendrochronological programme represents an important part of any future work on estuarine sites with suitable timbers.

(viii) Work on the wood was carried out part-time by specialists working in five different places. Originally a single database was set up but resources were not available to maintain and update this as the post-excavation programme progressed, with the result that it has not been possible to integrate each of the wood studies to the extent we originally intended.

(ix) The contrast, in terms of spatial scale, detail of recording, and resolution, between the rapid intertidal survey of c 25km and the more detailed work in 3km at Goldcliff needs to be appreciated. The Goldcliff experience has shown that the complexity of sites cannot be judged adequately from eroded surface exposures alone. Our statements about the broader survey area are necessarily more tentative and our dating less secure. The dates we have obtained from the survey area relate to specific archaeological structures. We have not carried out any environmental analysis relating to sites from the intertidal survey. This was a necessary strategic decision because our priority throughout had to be completion of the Goldcliff post-excavation programme.

(x) This project has fallen into the inevitable trap confronting many wetland projects; the emphasis has been on the wetland to the exclusion of a wider landscape with which it was articulated, although we have suggested possible relationship in the conclusions. Given the large numbers of intertidal sites undergoing active destruction, it is always going to be difficult to divert very limited resources towards facets of the landscape which are less threatened but are of equal importance in achieving a full understanding of past communities.

17.17 The main achievements of the project

Despite the foregoing, the project has significantly advanced our understanding and appreciation of coastal wetland archaeology, as we hope is evident from the volume as a whole. The following identifies some particular points.

(i) A detailed programme of augering, excavation, and dating has begun to elucidate the full stratigraphic complexity of the middle Wentlooge formation, and tentatively to identify environmental changes which may be of local significance and those which may correlate with more widespread secular sea level or climate driven changes, or events.

(ii) The Mesolithic site is representative of a class of intertidal site with charcoal, lithics, and bone which is found below several submerged forests in the West Country and Pembrokeshire. Goldcliff has highlighted the potential of these sites and indicated they may represent seasonal activity, in the case of Goldcliff probably in winter.

(iv) Bronze Age deposition of human skulls in an estuarine context occurred, complementing evidence from river valleys. It is further suggested, in the Severn Estuary, that islands may have had a special significance and there are hints that this may have been persistent from Bronze Age to Romano-British times, notwithstanding the dramatic environmental changes which took place over this timespan.

(v) The discovery of Bronze Age boat planks is a valuable addition to a growing body of evidence for sophisticated seacraft which are better represented in Britain before the Iron Age than anywhere else in Europe. This is an important aspect of the maritime heritage of Wales and England and highlights the importance of continued vigilance in the intertidal zone.

(vi) Classes of Bronze Age and Iron Age site have been recognised which represent an entirely new dimension to Welsh archaeology: the rectangular buildings, the wide range of trackway types, and the various structures associated with palaeochannels.

(vii) Cattle husbandry seems to have been the main activity carried out on the wetland in the Bronze and Iron Ages and was probably concentrated in the summer months, with an emphasis on dairying. Some buildings housed cattle. Trackways show that the landscape was also used, perhaps in other ways, during the winter.

(viii) The potential of dendrochronology in an intertidal context has been demonstrated and, with the associated tree-ring work, has made a major contribution, not just to issues of chronology but wider questions of seasonal usage and patterns of wider landscape exploitation.

(ix) Trackways have helped to identify specific patterns of movement which clarify how the landscape was being used, highlighting the importance of the sea, and enabling us tentatively to predict the location of activity areas which are still buried.

(x) Work on the insects, pollen, plant macrofossils, and other environmental evidence has highlighted the long neglected potential for palaeoenvironmental research in intertidal peats. Multiple pollen diagrams have enabled the development of a spatially detailed picture of prehistoric environmental change, which is generally highly consistent as between different sources of palaeoenvironmental evidence.

(xi) It has been demonstrated that human activity is concentrated during the early stages of transgressive episodes in the middle Bronze Age and Iron Age.

(xii) The project has developed a methodology for the rapid recording of intertidal archaeological sites and a map and databases on the CD which we hope will provide a foundation to be enhanced by future work. This should help with the evaluation of the archaeology in those many parts of the Severn Estuary intertidal area which are threatened with development proposals ranging from seawall upgrading to a southern motorway bypass for Newport and the massive scale proposals for a new airport covering the entire intertidal area between Goldcliff and Magor Pill which, if it ever came into being, would sweep away most of the archaeological resource discussed here. Now, thanks to the discoveries of Upton documented here, and others elsewhere, we can appreciate the richness and potential of the intertidal zone and wider coastal heritage (Fulford *et al* 1997). We hope that this means that the growing number of development proposals affecting the coast will be increasingly critically examined by planners and the public alike in the context of the needs of heritage and nature conservation and sustainable development.

Appendix I

Maps 1–26

**The intertidal survey area of the Welsh Severn Estuary
arranged from Rumney (1) in the west to Sudbrook (26) in the east**

(Drawings by H Neumann and B Taylor)

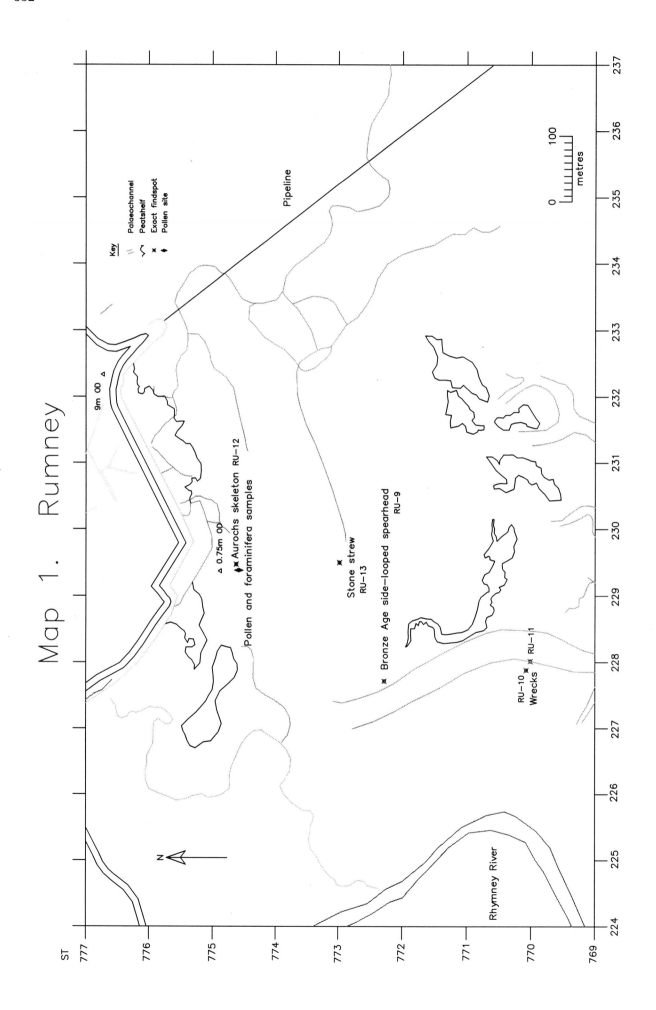

Map 1. Rumney

Map 2. Rumney

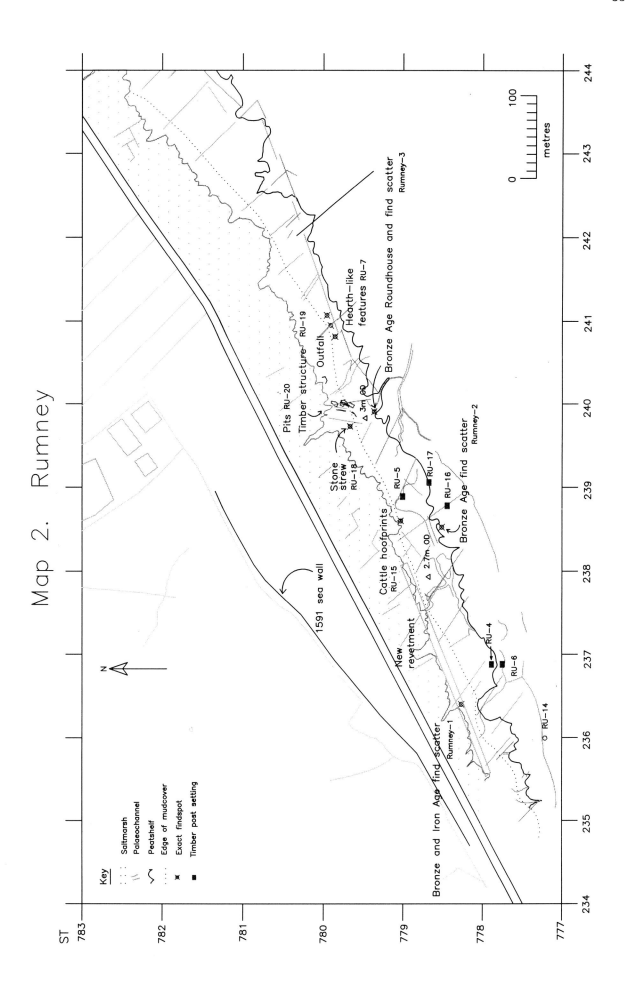

Key

::	Saltmarsh
::	Palaeochannel
$\smallsmile$	Peatshelf
	Edge of mudcover
⊗	Exact findspot
■	Timber post setting

Bronze and Iron Age find scatter
Rumney–1

1591 sea wall

New revetment

Cattle hoofprints
RU–15

△ 2.7m. OD

RU–5

RU–17

RU–16

Bronze Age find scatter
Rumney–2

RU–4

RU–6

RU–14

Stone strew
RU–18

Pits RU–20

Timber structure RU–19

Outfall

△ 3m. OD

Hearth-like features RU–7

Bronze Age Roundhouse and find scatter
Rumney–3

N

0 100
metres

ST
783
782
781
780
779
778
777

234 235 236 237 238 239 240 241 242 243 244

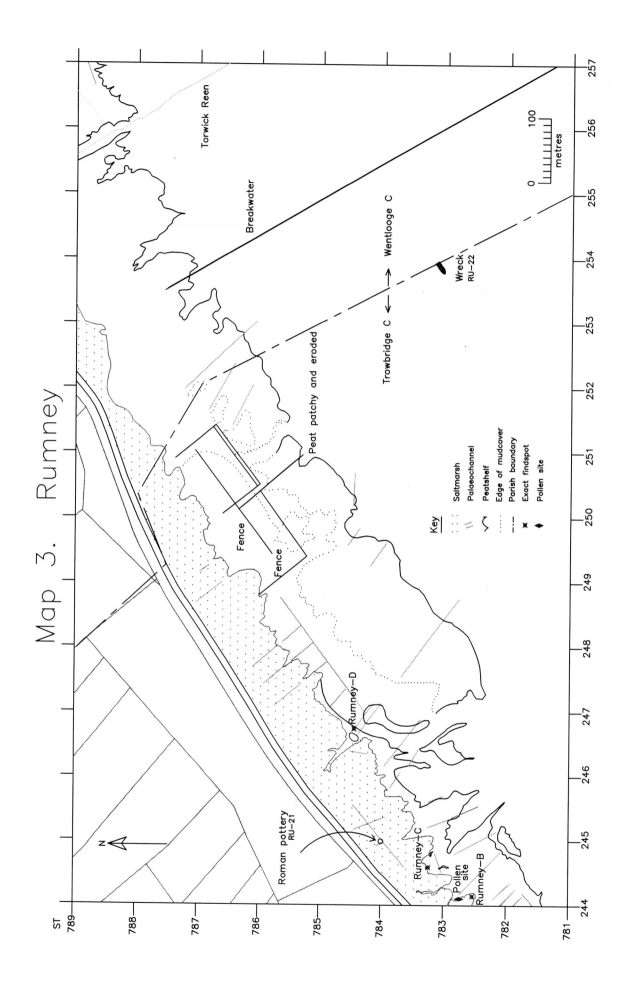

Map 3. Rumney

Torwick Reen

Breakwater

Wentlooge C

Trowbridge C

Wreck
RU-22

Peat patchy and eroded

Fence

Fence

Key

Saltmarsh
Palaeochannel
Peatshelf
Edge of mudcover
Parish boundary
Exact findspot
Pollen site

Roman pottery
RU-21

N

Rumney-D

Rumney-C

Pollen
site

Rumney-B

0   100
metres

ST

789
788
787
786
785
784
783
782
781

244 245 246 247 248 249 250 251 252 253 254 255 256 257

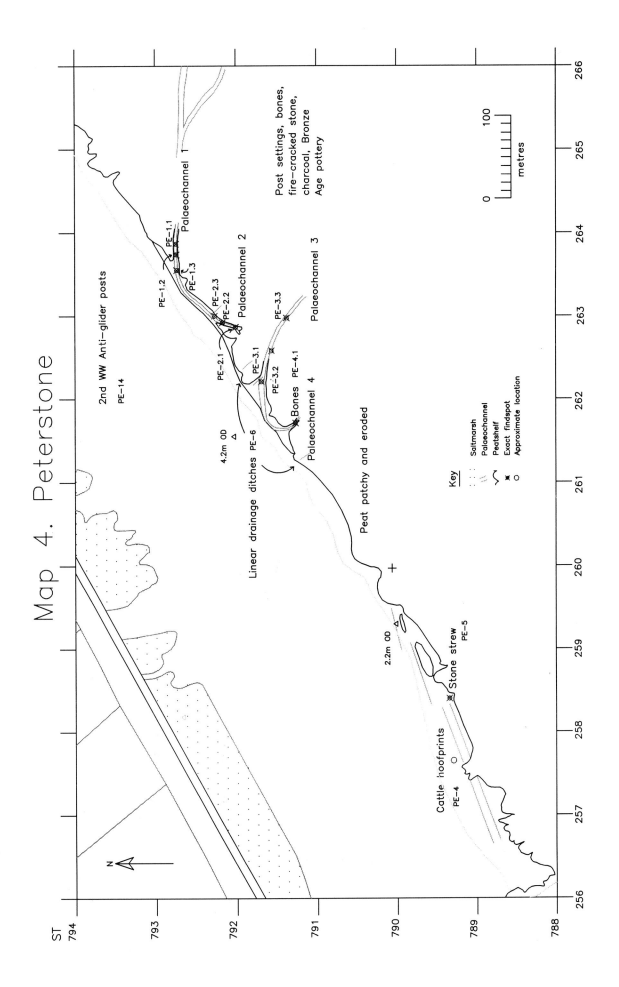

Map 4. Peterstone

2nd WW Anti-glider posts

PE-14

PE-1.1
Palaeochannel 1

PE-1.2
PE-1.3

PE-2.3
PE-2.2
Palaeochannel 2

PE-3.3
Palaeochannel 3

PE-2.1

PE-3.1

4.2m OD

PE-3.2   PE-4.1

Bones
Palaeochannel 4

Linear drainage ditches PE-6

Peat patchy and eroded

2.2m OD

Stone strew
PE-5

Cattle hoofprints
PE-4

Post settings, bones,
fire-cracked stone,
charcoal, Bronze
Age pottery

0   100

metres

Key

Saltmarsh
Palaeochannel
Peatshelf
Exact findspot
Approximate location

N

ST
794

793

792

791

790

789

788

256   257   258   259   260   261   262   263   264   265   266

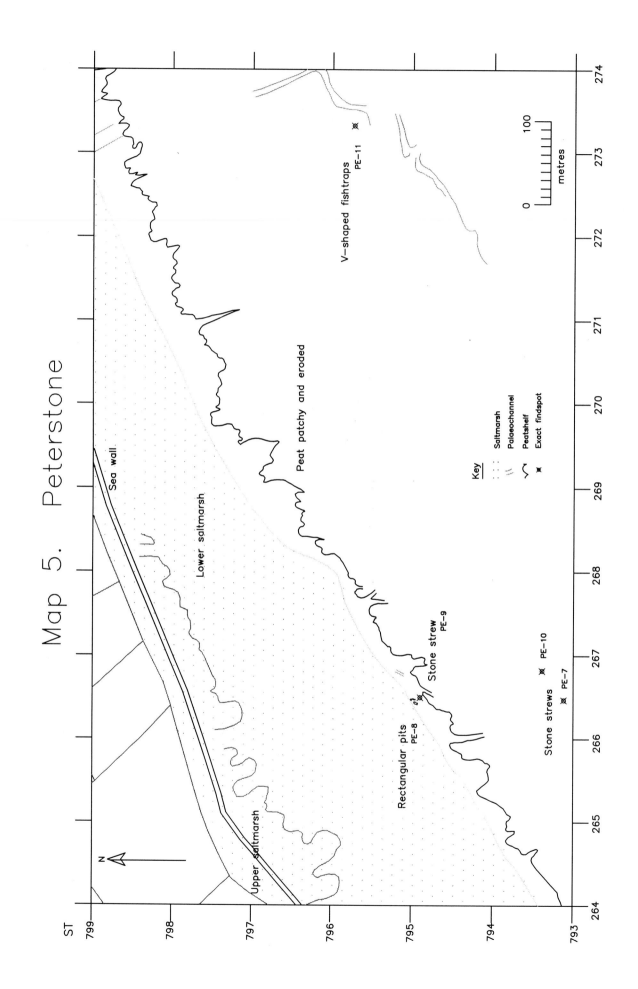

Map 5. Peterstone

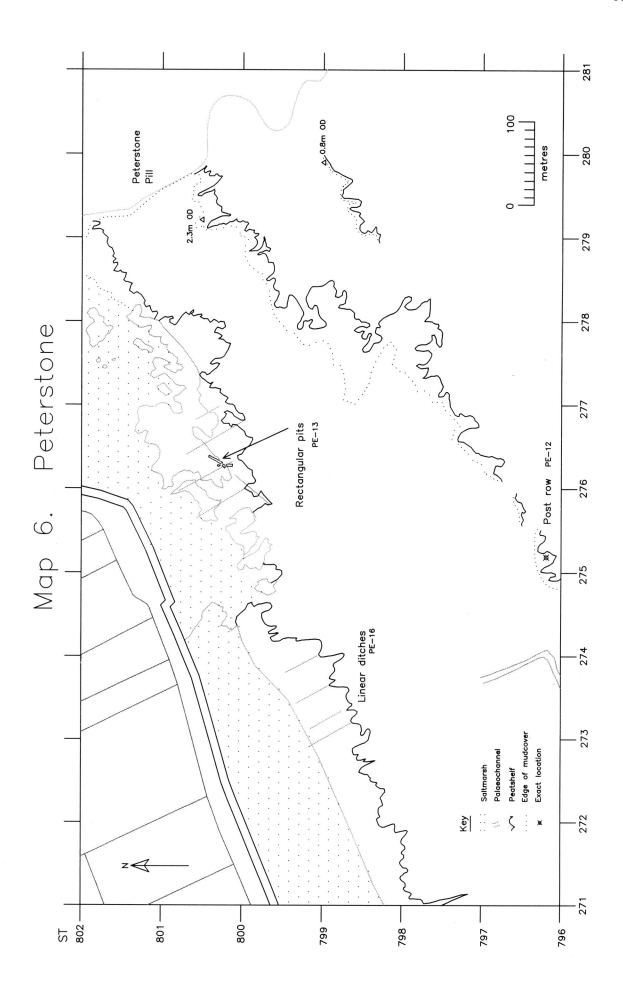

Map 6. Peterstone

Peterstone
Pill

2.3m OD

0.8m OD

Rectangular pits
PE-13

Post row PE-12

Linear ditches
PE-16

Key
Saltmarsh
Palaeochannel
Peatshelf
Edge of mudcover
Exact location

0   100

metres

N

ST

802
801
800
799
798
797
796

271 272 273 274 275 276 277 278 279 280 281

358

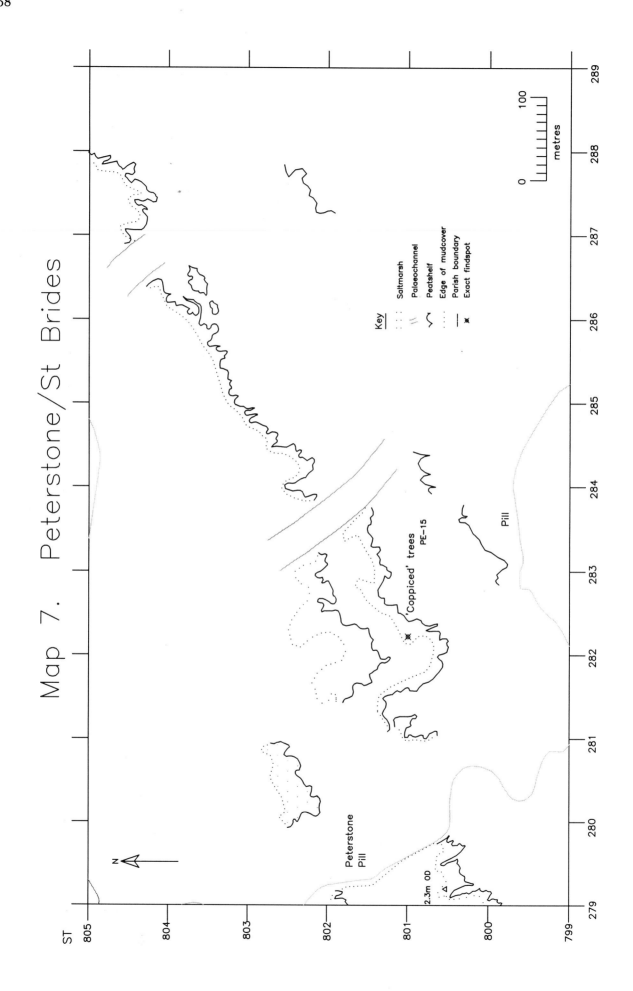

Map 7. Peterstone/St Brides

Key

Saltmarsh

Palaeochannel

Peatshelf

Edge of mudcover

Parish boundary

Exact findspot

N

Peterstone Pill

'Coppiced' trees

PE-15

Pill

2.3m OD

0   100

metres

ST

805

804

803

802

801

800

799

279   280   281   282   283   284   285   286   287   288   289

359

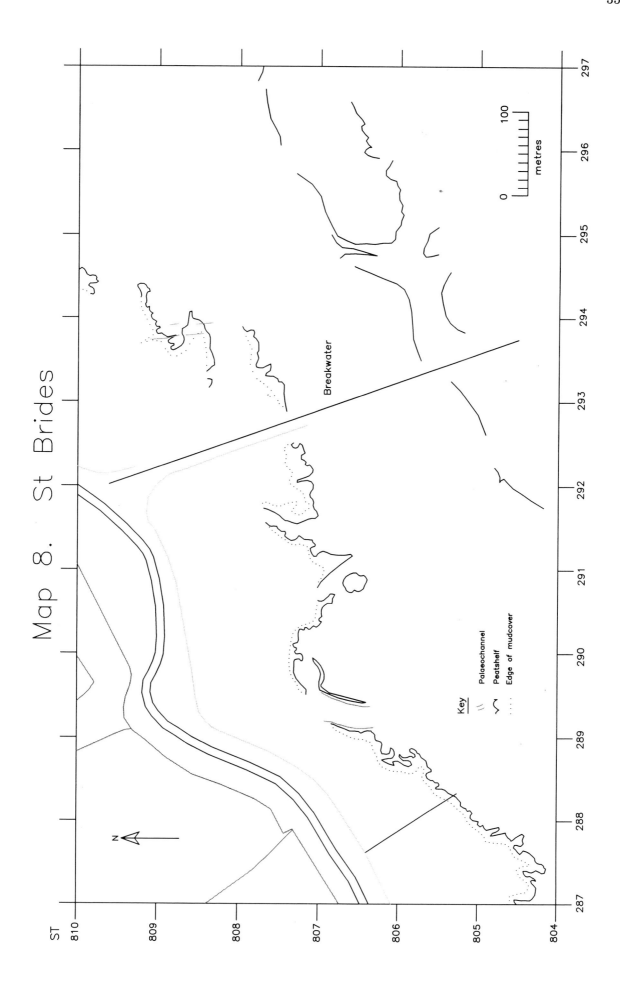

Map 8. St Brides

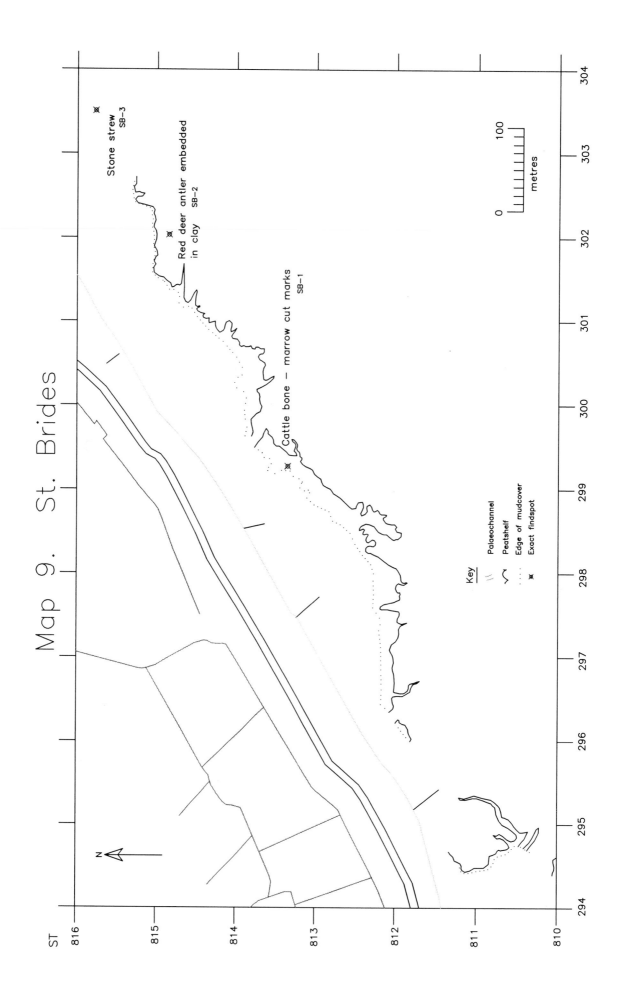

Map 9. St. Brides

Stone strew
SB-3

Red deer antler embedded
in clay   SB-2

Cattle bone – marrow cut marks
SB-1

Key
Palaeochannel
Peatshelf
Edge of mudcover
Exact findspot

0   100
metres

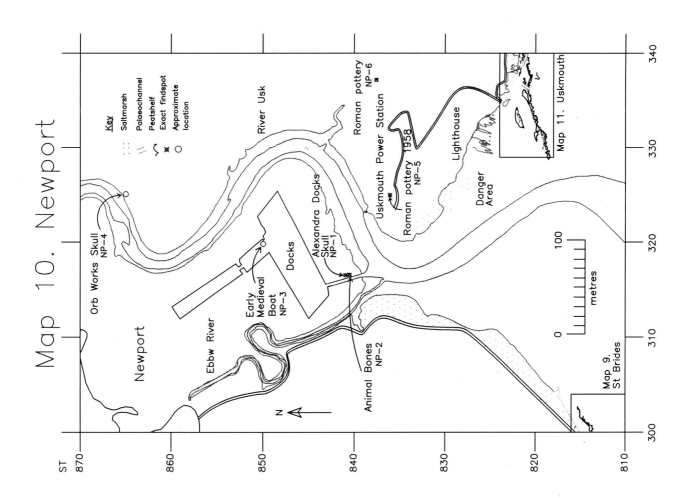

Map 10. Newport

Newport

Orb Works Skull
NP-4

Ebbw River

River Usk

Early
Medieval
Boat
NP-3

Docks

Alexandra Docks
Skull
NP-1

Animal Bones
NP-2

N

Key

Saltmarsh
Palaeochannel
Peatshelf
Exact findspot
Approximate
location

Roman pottery
NP-6

Uskmouth Power Station

Roman pottery 1958
NP-5

Lighthouse

Danger
Area

Map 11. Uskmouth

0   100

metres

Map 9.
St Brides

ST

870

860

850

840

830

820

810

300   310   320   330   340

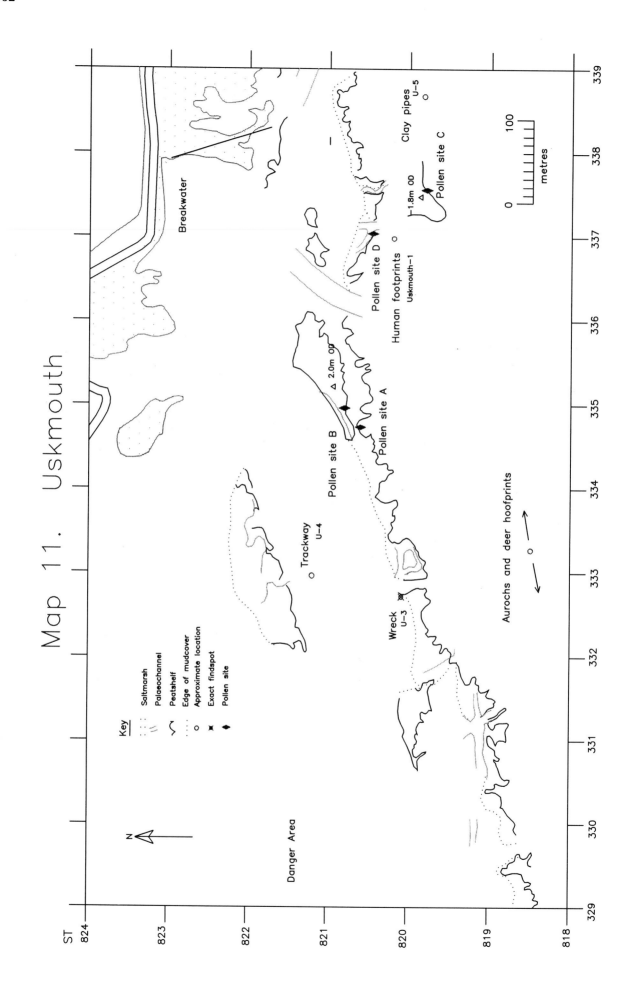

Map 11. Uskmouth

Key

Saltmarsh

Palaeochannel

Peatshelf

Edge of mudcover

Approximate location

Exact findspot

Pollen site

Danger Area

Breakwater

Pollen site B

Trackway
U–4

Wreck
U–3

Pollen site A

△ 2.0m OD

Pollen site D

Human footprints
Uskmouth–1

Clay pipes
U–5

–1.8m OD
△
Pollen site C

Aurochs and deer hoofprints

0   100
metres

N

ST
824

823

822

821

820

819

818

329   330   331   332   333   334   335   336   337   338   339

Map 12. Uskmouth/Goldcliff

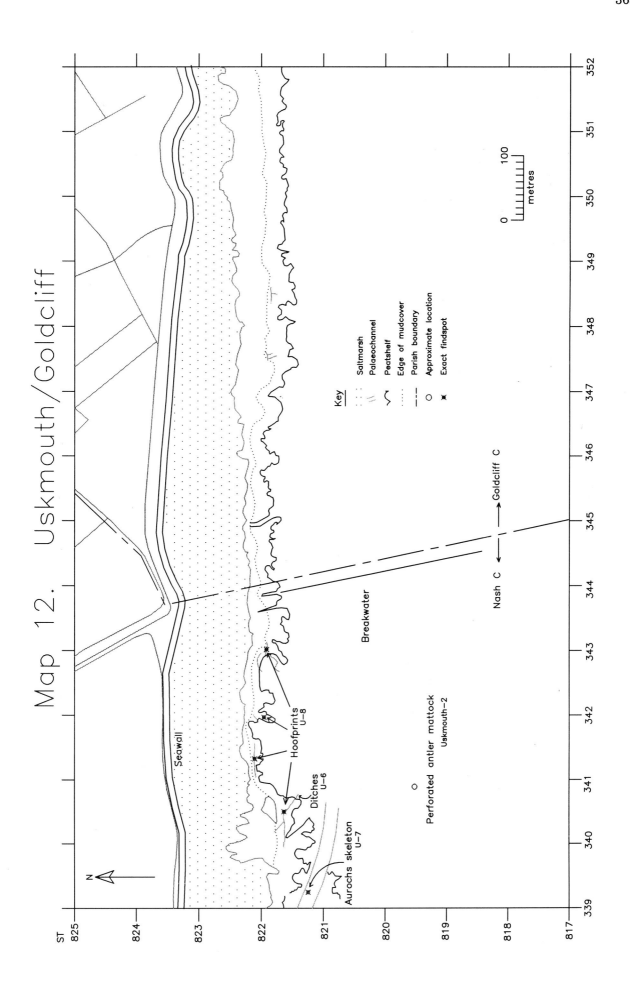

Seawall

Hoofprints
U–8

Ditches
U–6

Aurochs skeleton
U–7

Breakwater

Perforated antler mattock
Uskmouth–2

Nash C ←——→ Goldcliff C

Key

	Saltmarsh
	Palaeochannel
	Peatshelf
	Edge of mudcover
	Parish boundary
○	Approximate location
✳	Exact findspot

0   100
metres

N

364

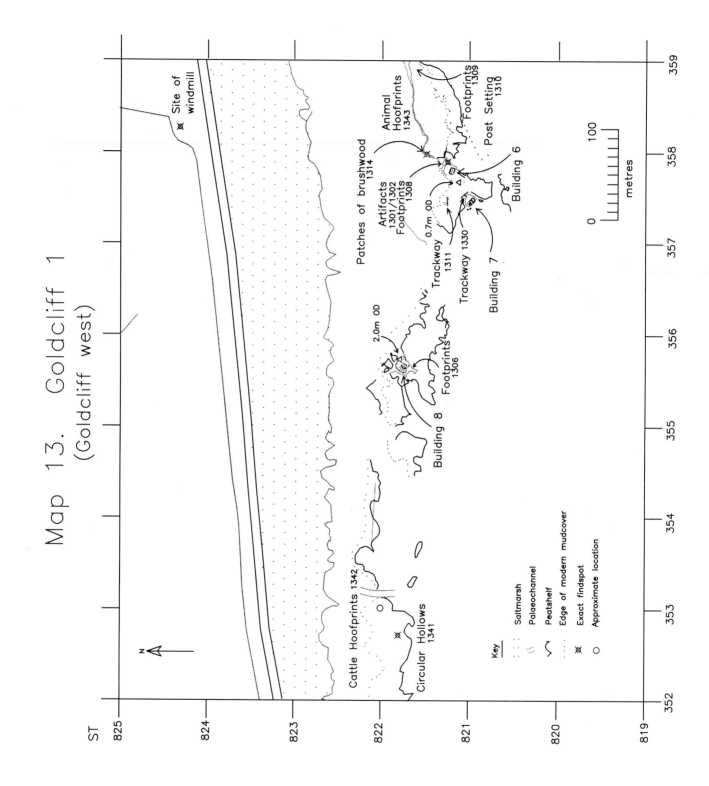

Map 13. Goldcliff 1
(Goldcliff west)

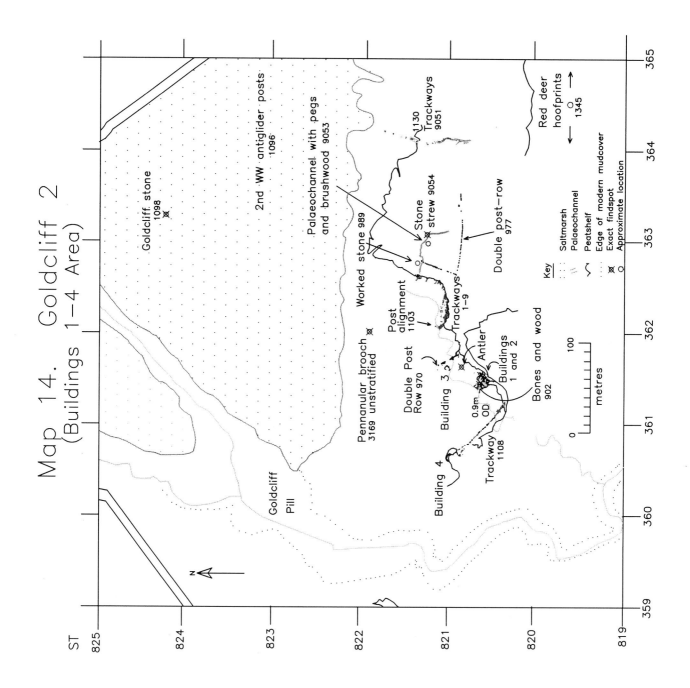

Map 14. Goldcliff 2
(Buildings 1-4 Area)

Goldcliff stone
1098

2nd WW antiglider posts
1096

Palaeochannel with pegs
and brushwood 9053

Worked stone 989

Pennanular brooch
3169 unstratified

Post
alignment
1103

Double Post
Row 970

Building 3

Building 4

Trackway
1108

Trackways
1-9

Antler

Buildings
1 and 2

0.9m
OD

Bones and wood
902

Goldcliff
Pill

1130

Stone
strew 9054

Trackways
9051

Double post-row
977

Red deer
hoofprints
1345

Key

Saltmarsh

Palaeochannel

Peatshelf

Edge of modern mudcover

Exact findspot

Approximate location

metres

0   100

ST

825

824

823

822

821

820

819

359   360   361   362   363   364   365

N

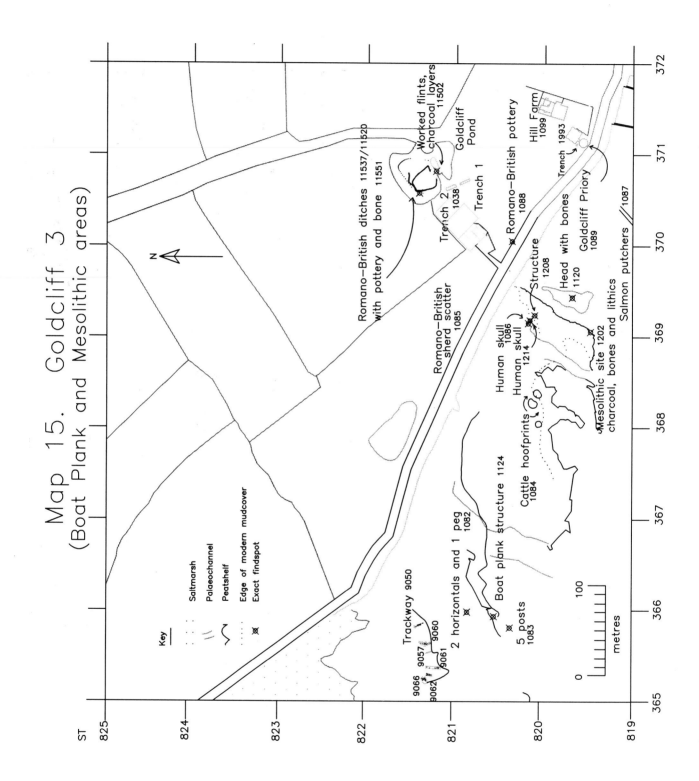

Map 15. Goldcliff 3
(Boat Plank and Mesolithic areas)

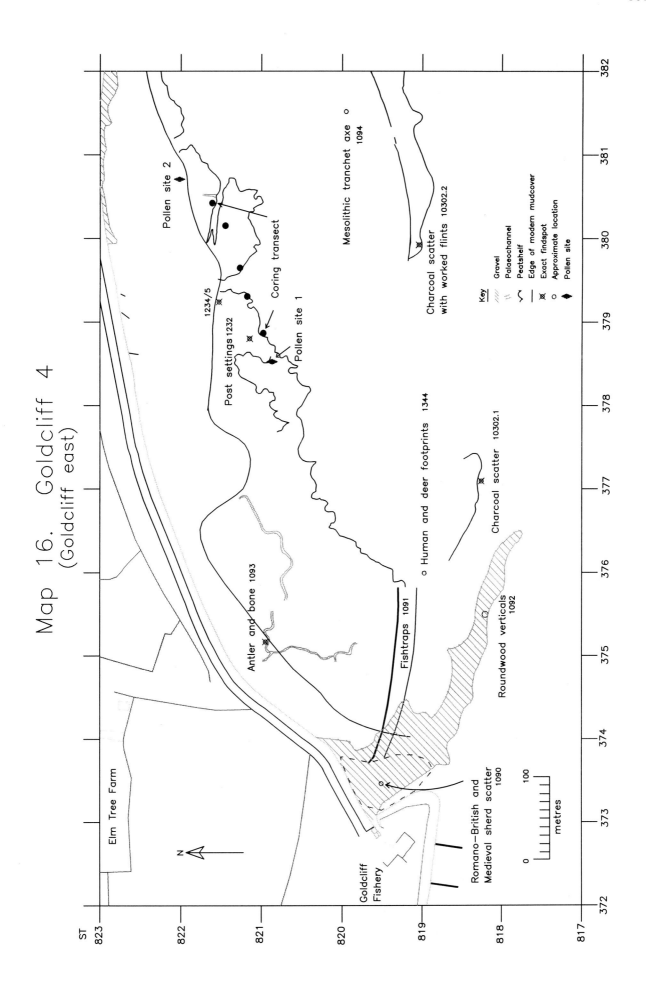

Map 16. Goldcliff 4
(Goldcliff east)

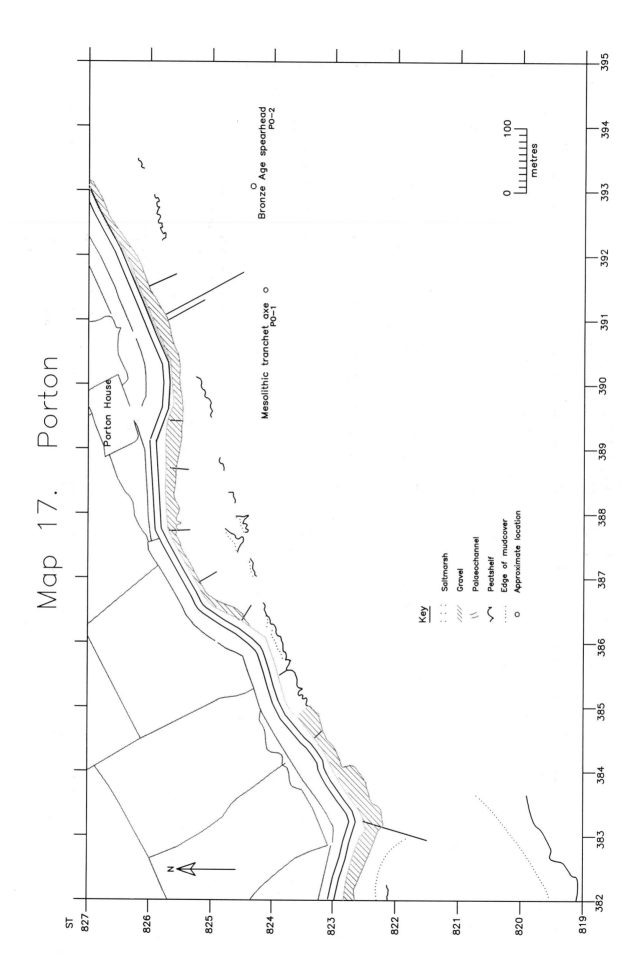

Map 17. Porton

Porton House

Bronze Age spearhead
PO-2

Mesolithic tranchet axe
PO-1

Key

Saltmarsh
Gravel
Palaeochannel
Peatshelf
Edge of mudcover
Approximate location

N

0   100
metres

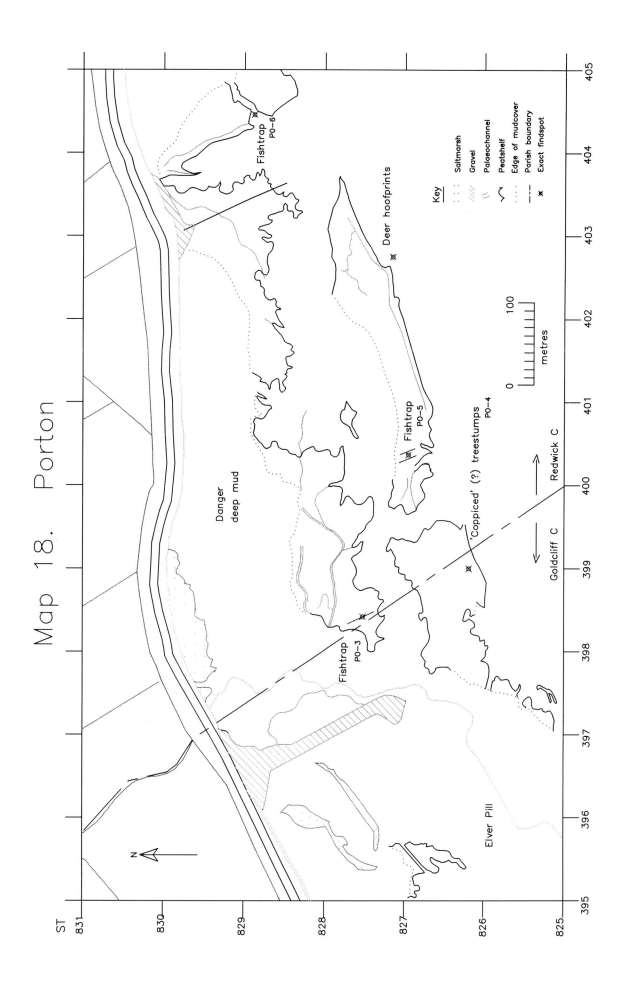

Map 18. Porton

Key

Saltmarsh
Gravel
Palaeochannel
Peatshelf
Edge of mudcover
Parish boundary
Exact findspot

Fishtrap PO-6

Deer hoofprints

Danger deep mud

Fishtrap PO-5

'Coppiced' (?) treestumps PO-4

Goldcliff C   Redwick C

Fishtrap PO-3

Elver Pill

ST

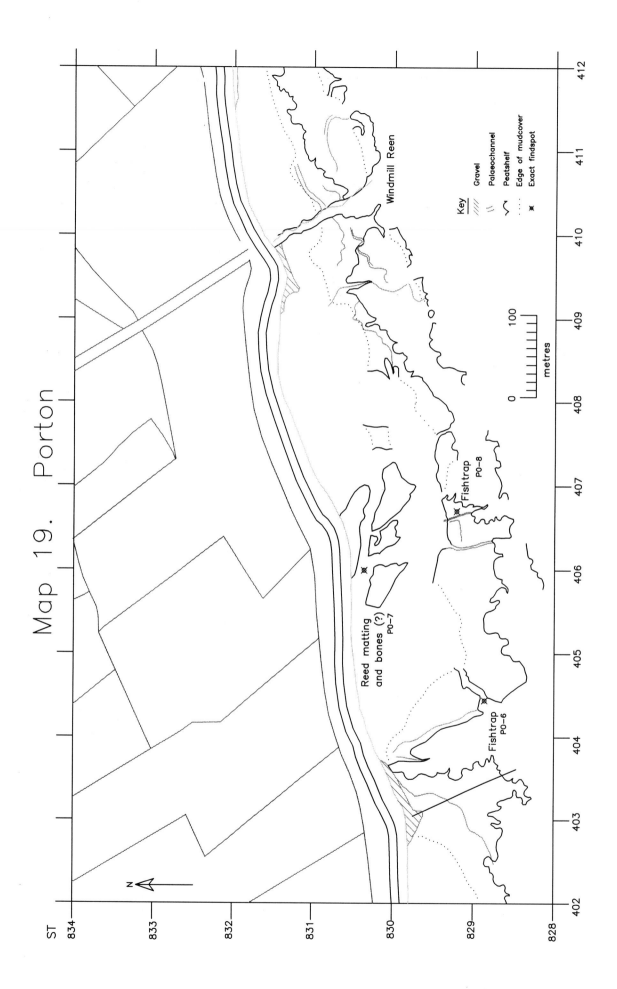

Map 19. Porton

Windmill Reen

Fishtrap
PO-8

Reed matting
and bones (?)
PO-7

Fishtrap
PO-6

Key

/// Gravel

Palaeochannel

Peatshelf

Edge of mudcover

Exact findspot

0   100
metres

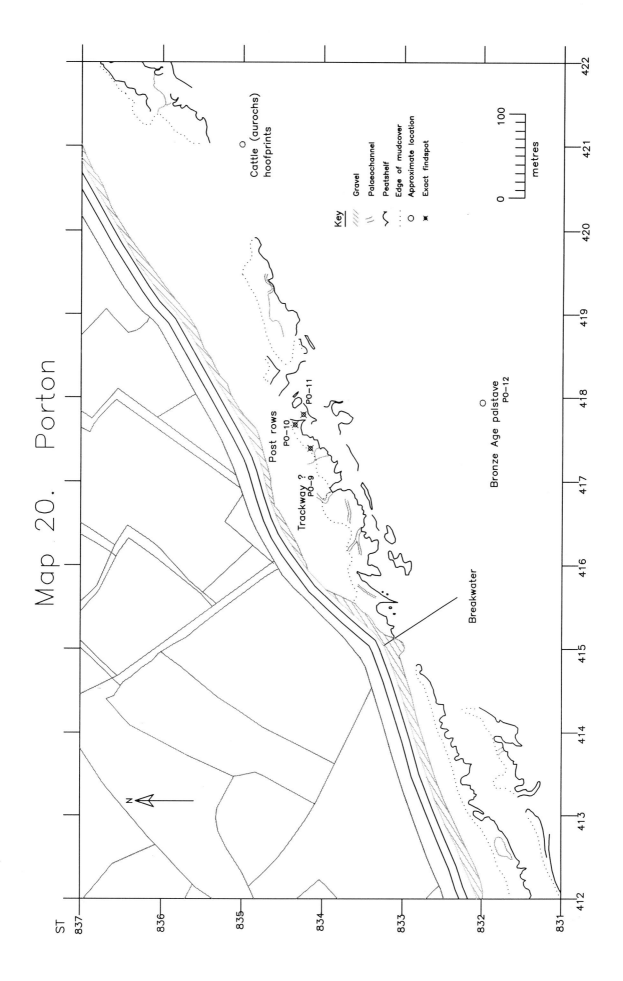

Map 20. Porton

Cattle (aurochs) hoofprints

Post rows
PO-10
PO-11

Trackway ?
PO-9

Breakwater

Bronze Age palstave
PO-12

Key

Gravel
Palaeochannel
Peatshelf
Edge of mudcover
Approximate location
Exact findspot

0   100
metres

Map 21. Redwick/Cold Harbour

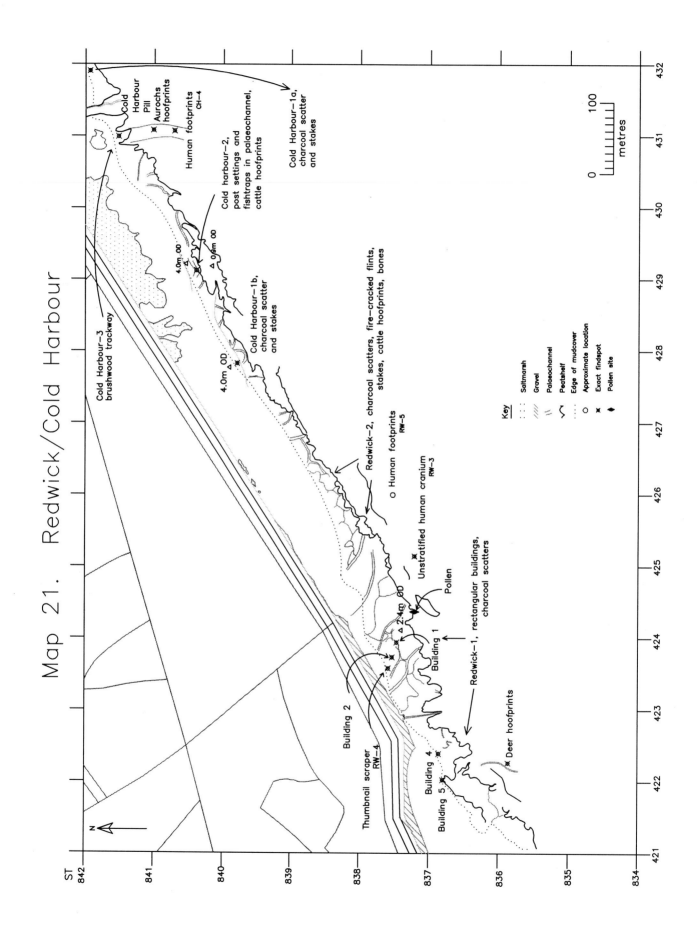

Cold Harbour-3 brushwood trackway

Cold Harbour Pill

Aurochs hoofprints CH-4

Human footprints

Cold harbour-2, post settings and fishtraps in palaeochannel, cattle hoofprints

Cold Harbour-1a, charcoal scatter and stakes

4.0m OD

△ 0.9m OD

Cold Harbour-1b, charcoal scatter and stakes

4.0m OD

Redwick-2, charcoal scatters, fire-cracked flints, stakes, cattle hoofprints, bones RW-5

O Human footprints

Unstratified human cranium RW-3

Pollen

△ 2.4m OD

Thumbnail scraper RW-4

Building 2

Building 1

Redwick-1, rectangular buildings, charcoal scatters

Building 4

Building 5

Deer hoofprints

N

Key

	Saltmarsh
	Gravel
	Palaeochannel
	Peatshelf
	Edge of mudcover
O	Approximate location
✳	Exact findspot
◆	Pollen site

0   100

metres

ST 842
841
840
839
838
837
836
835
834

421 422 423 424 425 426 427 428 429 430 431 432

373

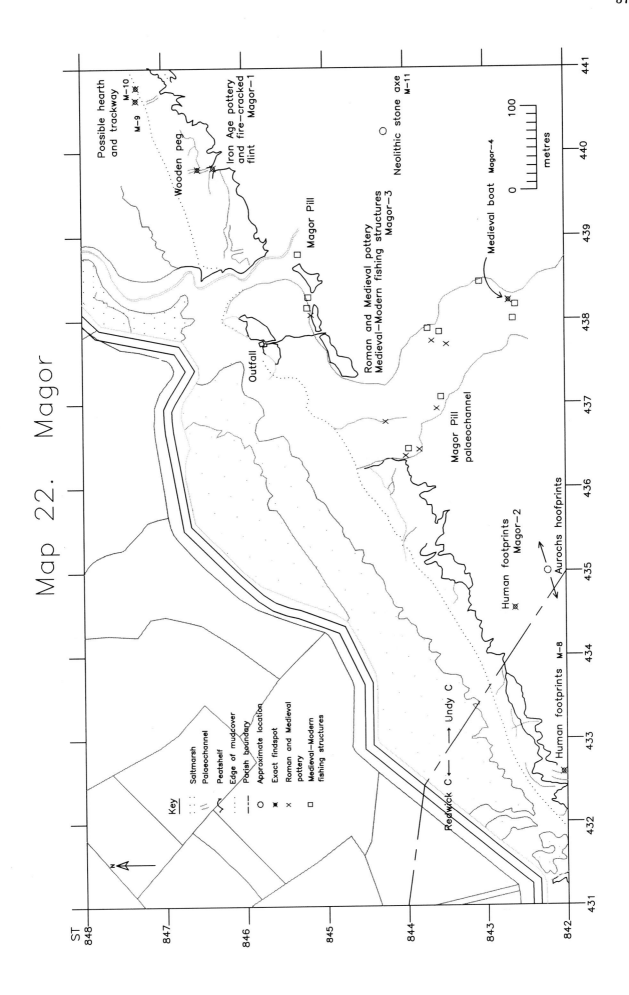

Map 22. Magor

Map 23.   Chapeltump

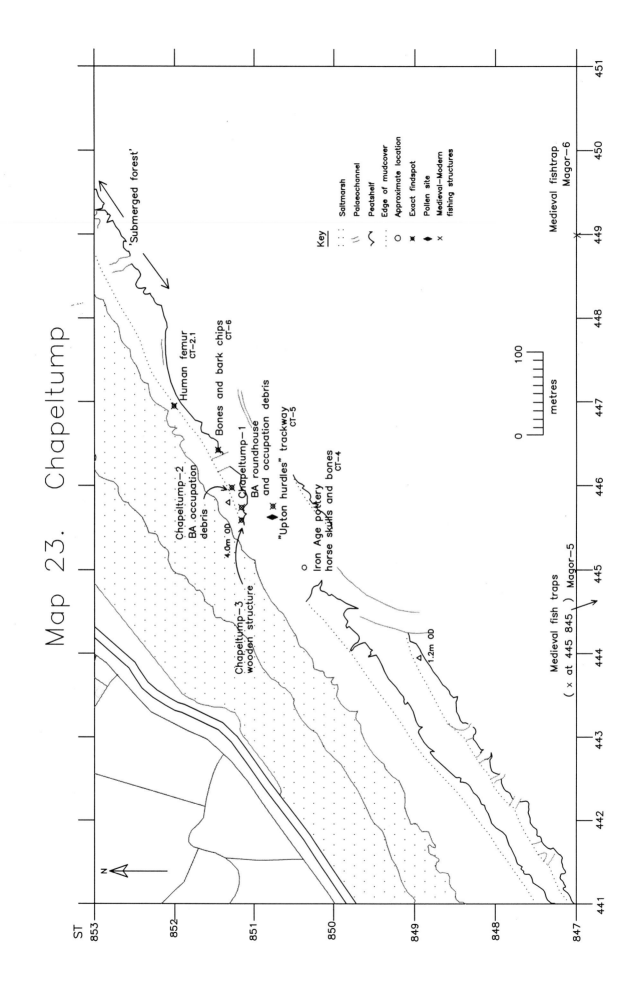

'Submerged forest'

Human femur
CT-2.1

Bones and bark chips
CT-6

Chapeltump-2
BA occupation
debris

Chapeltump-1
BA roundhouse
and occupation debris

"Upton hurdles" trackway
CT-5

4.0m OD

Chapeltump-3
wooden structure

Iron Age pottery
horse skulls and bones
CT-4

1.2m OD

Medieval fish traps
(x at 445 845) Magor-5

Medieval fishtrap
Magor-6

Key

Saltmarsh

Palaeochannel

Peatshelf

Edge of mudcover

○ Approximate location

✳ Exact findspot

◆ Pollen site

✕ Medieval–Modern
    fishing structures

0   100
|_|_|_|_|_|_|_|_____|
        metres

N

ST 853
852
851
850
849
848
847

441 442 443 444 445 446 447 448 449 450 451

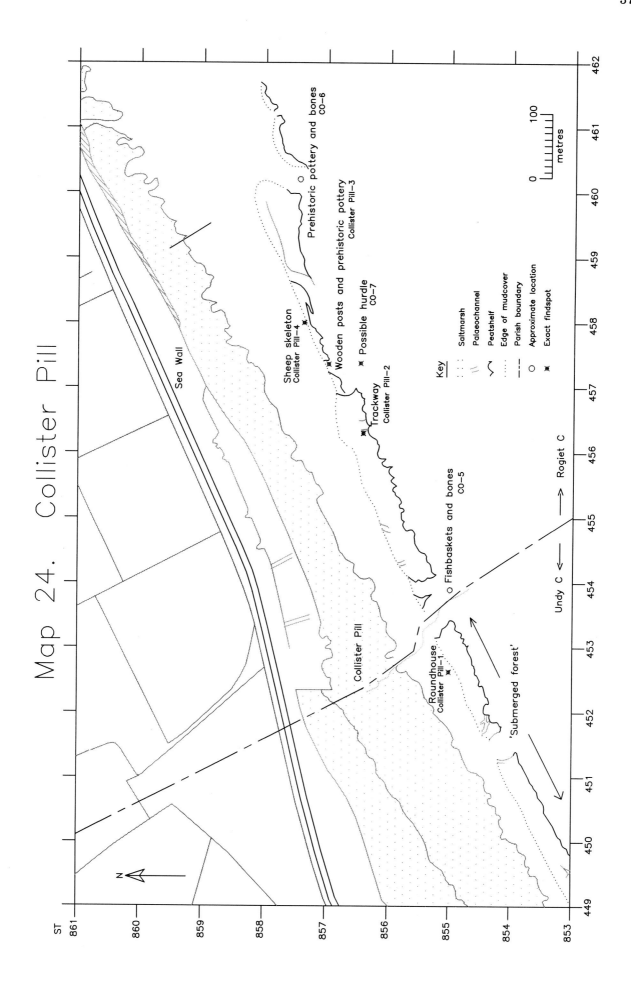

Map 24. Collister Pill

Map 25. Collister/Sudbrook

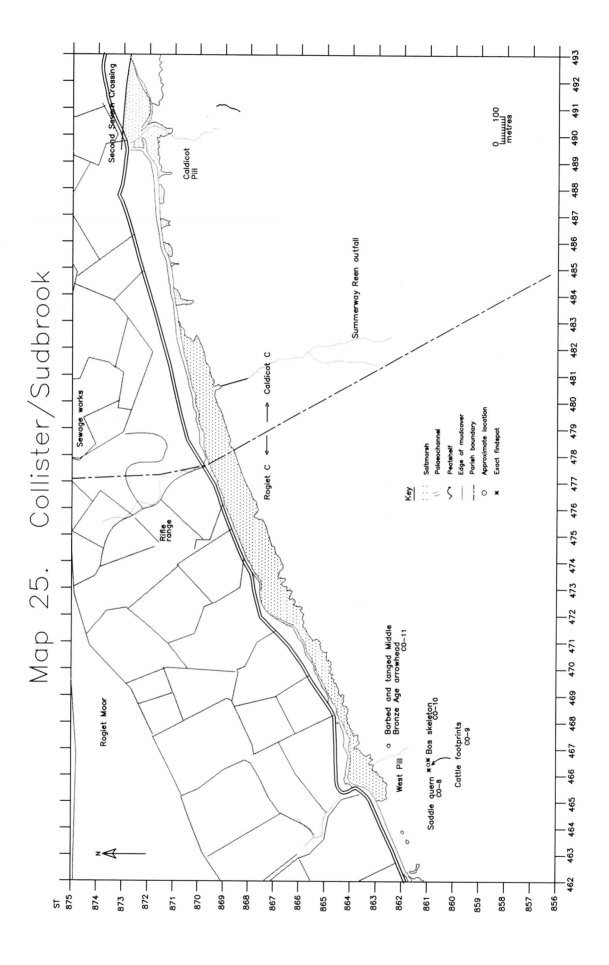

Second Severn Crossing

Caldicot Pill

Summerway Reen outfall

Caldicot C

Rogiet C

Sewage works

Rifle range

Rogiet Moor

West Pill

Saddle quern CO-8

Bos skeleton CO-10

Barbed and tanged Middle Bronze Age arrowhead CO-11

Cattle footprints CO-9

N

ST

Key

Saltmarsh

Palaeochannel

Peatshelf

Edge of mudcover

Parish boundary

o Approximate location

✱ Exact findspot

0 100
metres

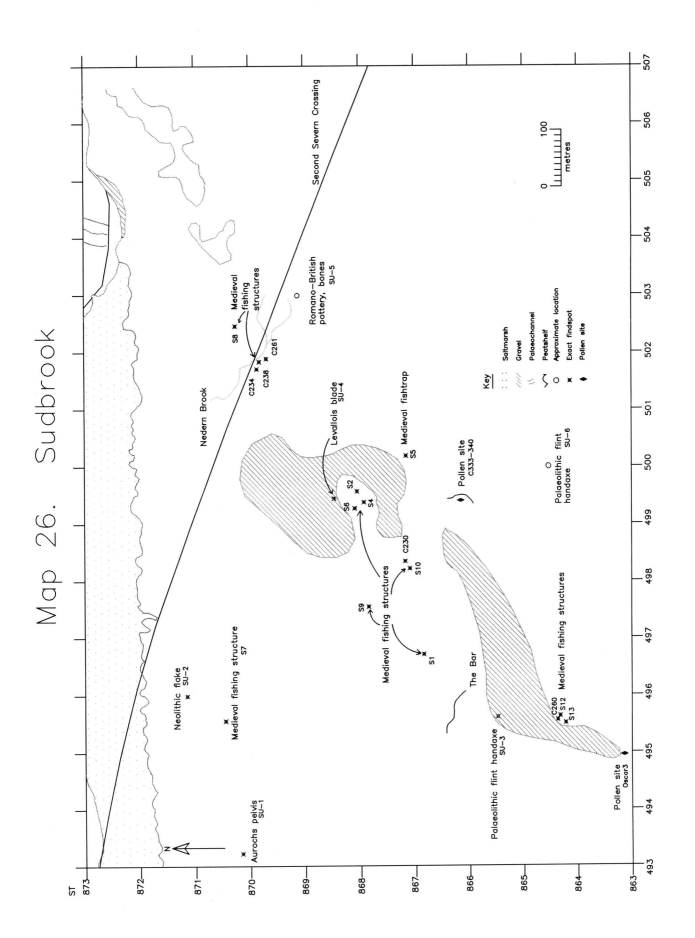

Map 26. Sudbrook

Appendix II

Radiocarbon dates for Goldcliff

For a list of radiocarbon dates from sites other than Goldcliff see CD 16.1

Radio-carbon date BP	Lab code	Cal yrs BC	Figure no	Location	Context	Material	Wood/ artefact no
1930 ± 50	Car-1503	50BC–220AD	Fig 3.4, 8.18, 9.1, 17.3	Building 8, post, NE corner	1305	*Acer campestre*	Wood 3564
1990 ± 60	SWAN-106	170BC–130AD	Fig 8.14, 10.21	Trackway 1330	1330	*Corylus / Alnus*	Wood 10130
2100 ± 60	Car-1346	360BC–20AD	Fig 7.3, 9.1	Building 1, wattle, west wall	901	*Alnus* 7–8 rings	Wood 919
2120 ± 90	GU-2912	390BC–30AD	Fig 7.3, 9.1	Building 1, post, north wall	901	*Alnus* 25 rings	Wood 127
2140 ± 60	Car-1435	380–40	Fig 7.16, 7.18, 9.1, 17.3	Building 4, post, north wall	1121	*Fraxinus excelsior*	Wood 3487
2140 ± 60	Car-1436	380–40	Fig 10.1, 10.21	Trackway 1108, diagonal support	1108	*Ulmus*	Wood 3463
2140 ± 60	SWAN-105	380–40	Fig 10.19, 10.21	Trackway 1311, west slot	1311	*Corylus*	Wood 10132
2150 ± 70	SWAN-26	390–40	Fig 3.4, 9.1	Building 6, split stake, SW corner	1300	*Quercus*	Wood 7025
2160 ± 40	GrN-24145	370–100	Fig 7.16, 13.9	Monolith 1718, Building 4, 0–2cm		Peat	Sample 1718
2160 ± 60	Car-1440	390–70	Fig 10.9, 10.21	Post row 1103, peg	1103	*Salix*	Wood 3333
2160 ± 70	Car-1348	390–50	Fig 7.3, 9.1, 17.3	Building 2, ?rebuilt wall	903	*Alnus* 14 rings	Wood 236
2190 ± 60	Car-1439	390–110	Fig 10.6, 10.21	Double post row 970, post	970	*Acer campestre*	Wood 3483
2200 ± 50	Car-1504	390–120	Fig 3.4, 10.14, 10.21	Trackway 1130, horizontal	1130	*Betula*	Wood 3796
2200 ± 70	Car-1437	400–100	Fig 7.14, 7.16, 9.1, 17.3	Building 3, post, north wall	981	*Betula*	Wood 3414
2220 ± 60	Car-1352	400–120	Fig 7.3, 7.10, 9.1	Building 2, post, east wall	903	*Alnus* 40 rings	Wood 234
2260 ± 50	GrN-24141	400–200	Fig 8.10, 13.20, 17.3	Monolith 10128, Building 6 palaeochannel, 19–20cm		Peat	Sample 10128
2260 ± 60	Car-1349	410–160	Fig 10.11, 10.21	Trackway 1, peg	971	*Alnus* 23 rings	Wood 953
2270 ± 50	GrN-24153	410–200	Fig 7.3, 17.3	Building 5, stake	946	*Frangula alnus*	Wood 707
2270 ± 70	Car-1351	520–110	Fig 7.11, 9.1, 13.13, 17.3	Monolith 1221. Surface of fen peat, 8–12 cm below Building 2	903	Woodpeat	Sample 1249
2290 ± 60	Car-1350	550–150	Trackway 3 shown on Fig 10.8, 10.21	Trackway 3 , post	972	*Alnus* 5–6 rings	Wood 954
2300 ± 70	Car-1347	800–150	Fig 7.3, 9.1	Building 1, reed matting, NW corner	901	*Phragmites* peat	Sample 1174
2320 ± 70	SWAN- 30	800–150	Fig 10.18, 10.21	Post row 9060, peg, east side	9060	*Alnus*	Wood 7494
2330 ± 70	SWAN-138	800–200	Fig 10.12, 13.18	Monolith 1716. Reed peat below Trackway 8	976	*Phragmites* peat	Sample 1716

Radio-carbon date BP	Lab code	Cal yrs BC	Figure no	Location	Context	Material	Wood/artefact no
2350 ± 60	SWAN- 29	800–200	Fig 3.4, 10.17, 10.21	Trackway 9050, from Trench 30 below blue clay	9050	Wood	Wood 7433
2350 ± 70	SWAN-137	800–200	Fig 10.12, 13.18	Monolith 1716. Reed peat overlying Trackway 8	976	*Phragmites* peat	Sample 1716
2360 ± 70	SWAN-136	800–200	Fig 7.11, 13.13, 17.3	Monolith 1221. Base of wood peat below Building 2	903	Wood peat	Sample 1221
2380 ± 70	SWAN- 27	800–250	Fig 8.14, 9.1, 17.3	Building 7, W axial post	1307	*Fraxinus*	Wood 7183
2460 ± 35	GrN-24140	770–410	Fig 8.10, 13.20	Monolith 10128, Building 6 palaeochannel, 10.5–11.5 cm		Peat	Sample 10128
2460 ± 70	SWAN-135	780–400	Fig 7.11, 13.13, 17.3	Monolith 1221. Top of wood peat below Building 2	908	Wood and *Phragmites* peat	Sample 1221
2580 ± 35	OxA-7659	830–550	17.3. Location on Fig 4.2, marked skull 31.10.90	Human cranial fragments	1086	*Homo sapiens* bone	Newport Museum 497
2580 ± 70	Car-1438	910–410	Fig 7.11, 13.13, 17.3	Monolith 1221. Surface of raised bog at Building 2	912	*Sphagnum/* Cal peat	Sample 1250
2600 ± 70	SWAN-102	920–510	Fig 3.3, 4.2, 17.3	Structure 1208	1208	*Salix/ Populus*	Wood 7605
2685 ± 45	OxA-6461	920–800	Fig 17.3; see also Chapter 5, section 7	Unstratified. Newport Museum collection, found 1990	-	Mandible of adult canid (dog/wolf)	-
2720 ± 70	Car-1434	1040–790	Fig 3.4, 6.3	Boat plank structure, horizontal, cut roundwood	1124	*Alnus glutinosa*	Wood 3443
2760 ± 70	SWAN- 31	1100–800	Fig 3.4	Raised bog peat within building 6 (Pit 79), surface truncated, 0.83–0.84m OD	1300	Peat	Sample 10107
3000 ± 40	GrN-24146	1400–1110	Fig 7.16, 13.9	Monolith 1718, Building 4,16–18cm		Peat	Sample 1718
3095 ± 40	OxA-7744	1450–1260	Fig 5.3, 17.3	Pit 15, 1.5–1.6m OD	1222	*H. sapiens* cranium	1214
3130 ± 70	Car- 644	1610–1210	Fig 17.3; Smith & Morgan 1989, fig 3	Site 1, uppermost peat		Peat	
3180 ± 70	SWAN-104	1640–1300	Fig 3.6, 3.7, 13.5, 17.3	Monolith 11600. Hill Farm Pond. Charcoal layer in pond, top of peat	11502.2	*Alnus* charcoal	charcoal 11603
3360 ± 40	GrN-24147	1750–1520	Fig 7.16, 13.9	Monolith 1718, Building 4, 26–27cm		Peat	Sample 1718
3440 ± 70	Car- 645	1950–1530	Fig 17.3; Smith & Morgan 1989, fig 3	Site 1, 17 cm		Peat	
3500 ± 30	GrN-24148	1910–1740	Fig 7.16, 13.9	Monolith 1718, Building 4, 38–39 cm		Peat	Sample 1718
3640 ± 60	Car-1499	2200–1880	Fig 3.3, 5.3, 13.4, 17.3	Monolith 2099. Pit 15, top of raised bog. Evidence of eroded hiatus at top	1222	Peat	Sample 2117
3670 ± 60	Car-1505	2280–1890	Fig 3.6, 17.3	Hill Farm, Trench 2, below marine clay	1038	Charcoal	Sample 1321

Radio-carbon date BP	Lab code	Cal yrs BC	Figure no	Location	Context	Material	Wood/artefact no
3670 ± 70	Car- 646	2290–1880	Fig 17.3; Smith & Morgan 1989, fig 3	Site 1, 30 cm		Peat	
3680 ± 70	SWAN-134	2290–1880	Fig 7.11, 13.13, 17.3	Monolith 1221. 26 cm below surface of raised bog peat below Building 2. Dates *Tilia* decline	912	*Sphagnum*/ Cal peat	Sample 1221
3780 ± 70	SWAN-232	2460–2030	Fig 5.3, 13.4	Monolith 2099. Pit 15, raised bog peat, 19–21 cm	1222	*Sphagnum*/ Cal peat	Sample 2099
3780 ± 70	Car- 647	2460–2030	Smith & Morgan 1989, fig 3	Site 1, 33 cm		Peat	
4050 ± 70	Car- 648	2880–2460	Smith & Morgan 1989, fig 3	Site 1, 43 cm		Peat	
4230 ± 35	GrN-24142	2920–2660	Fig 3.7, 13.5	Hill Farm Pond, Monolith 11600, 21–23 cm		Peat	Sample 11600
4305 ± 35	OxA-7782	3040–2880	Fig 5.3, 13.6, 13.7	Pit 15, raised bog peat above human cranium	1222	*Sphagnum*/ Cal peat	Sample 2142/3
4320 ± 80	SWAN-133	3350–2650	Fig 3.6, 3.7, 13.5, 17.2, 17.3	Monolith 11600. Base of wood peat, Hill Farm pond, c 4m OD	11502.3	Wood peat	Sample 11600
4350 ± 35	OxA-7783	3090–2910	Fig 5.3, 13.6, 13.7	Pit 15, raised bog peat below human cranium	1222	*Sphagnum*/ Cal peat	Sample 2144/5
4390 ± 80	Car- 773	3340–2890	Smith & Morgan 1989, fig 5	Site 2, 7 cm		Peat	
4440 ± 45	GrN-24144	3340–2920	Fig 5.3, 13.4	Monolith 2099, Pit 15, 49–51cm	1222	Peat	Sample 2099
4440 ± 80	Car- 649	3340–2930	Smith & Morgan 1989, fig 3	Site 1, 60 cm		Peat	
4520 ± 80	SWAN-233	3500–2900	Fig 5.3, 13.4, 17.3	Monolith 2099. Pit 15, raised bog peat, ?heather, 61–63cm	1222	*Sphagnum*/ Cal peat	Sample 2100
4660 ± 80	Car- 650	3650–3100	Smith & Morgan 1989, fig 3	Site 1, 77 cm		Peat	
4720 ± 80	Car- 653	3700–3340	Smith & Morgan 1989, fig 3	Site 1, 98 cm		Peat	
4740 ± 80	Car- 651	3700–3350	Fig 17.3; Smith & Morgan 1989, fig 3	Site 1, 88 cm		Peat	
4900 ± 60	Car-1500	3910–3520	Fig 3.3, 5.3, 13.4, 17.3	Monolith 2099. Pit 15, base of raised bog peat	1222	*Sphagnum* peat	Sample 2118
4980 ± 80	Car- 774	3980–3630	Smith & Morgan 1989, fig 5	Site 2, 26 cm		Peat	
5020 ± 80	Car- 652	4000–3680	Fig 17.3; Smith & Morgan 1989, fig 3	Site 1, 95 cm		Peat	
5090 ± 80	Car- 654	4250–3700	Smith & Morgan 1989, fig 3	Site 1, 101 cm		Peat	
5180 ± 80	Car- 775	4240–3780	Smith & Morgan 1989, fig 5	Site 2, 32 cm		Peat	
5190 ± 80	SWAN- 32	4240–3780	Fig 3.4, 17.3	Base of peat below Building 6, 0.335–0.345m OD	1300	*Phragmites* peat	Sample 10110
5190 ± 80	SWAN-234	4240–3780	Fig 5.3, 13.4, 17.3	Monolith 2099. Pit 15, fen peat, 101–103cm	1222	Peat	Sample 2101
5360 ± 80	Car- 656	4360–4000	Fig 17.3; Smith & Morgan 1989, fig 3	Site 1, 122 cm		Peat	
5415 ± 75	OxA-6682	4460–4040	Fig 4.4, 4.5	Mesolithic site	1202	*Corylus avellana* nut	4208

Radio-carbon date BP	Lab code	Cal yrs BC	Figure no	Location	Context	Material	Wood/artefact no
5440 ± 80	Car- 655	4460–4040	Smith & Morgan 1989, fig 3	Site 1, 115 cm		Peat	
5480 ± 80	Car- 776	4510–4040	Smith & Morgan 1989, fig 5	Site 2, 45 cm		Peat	
5530 ± 90	Car- 657	4700–4150	Fig 17.3; Smith & Morgan 1989, fig 3	Site 1, 138 cm		Peat	
5660 ± 80	SWAN-235	4720–4350	Fig 5.3, 13.4	Monolith 2099. Pit 15, fen peat, 121–123cm	1222	Peat	Sample 2101
5660 ± 80	Car- 778	4720–4350	Smith & Morgan 1989, fig 5	Site 2, 53 cm		Peat	
5720 ± 80	SWAN-236	4770–4360	Fig 5.3, 13.4	Monolith 2099. Pit 15, base of fen peat, 141–143cm	1222	Peat	Sample 2101
5820 ± 50	GrN-24143	4790–4540	Fig 3.3, 4.4, 4.13, 13.3, 17.2, 17.3	Monolith 1722, Mesolithic site, 15–17cm		Peat	Sample 1722
5850 ± 80	Car- 658	4890–4570	Smith & Morgan 1989, fig 3	Site 1, 160cm		Peat	
5920 ± 80	Car-1501	5060–4660	Fig 3.3, 4.13, 5.3, 13.4, 17.2	Monolith 2099. Pit 15, base of fenwood peat, c 0.58 m OD	1222	Peat	Sample 2119
5950 ± 80	Car- 659	4950–4720	Fig 17.3; Smith & Morgan 1989, fig 3	Site 1, 165cm		Peat	
6420 ± 80	SWAN- 28	5440–5280	Fig 4.4, 4.5, 4.13	Mesolithic site, Trench 50	1202	Charcoal	Sample 10557
6430 ± 80	GU-2759	5440–5280	Fig 4.13	Mesolithic site: Newport Museum	1202	Charcoal	
6480 ± 70	Car-1502	5490–5330	Fig 4.13, 17.3; Appendix 1, Map 16	GF East, charcoal below peat, 3.9m OD	10302.2	Charcoal	Sample 2093
6760 ± 80	OxA-6683	5750–5450	Fig 4.4, 4.5, 4.13, 17.3	Mesolithic site, 1202	1202	*C. elephas* cut bone	8534
6770 ± 70	Beta-60761	5740–5490	Fig 2.1, 4.13, 17.3	GF East, in peat at −3.7m OD from thin basal peat		*Quercus*	

Bibliography

Acott, T G, Cruise, G M and Macphail, R I, 1997 Soil micromorphology and high resolution images, in S Shoba, M Gerasimova and R Miedema R (eds) *Soil micromorphology: diversity, diagnostics and dynamics.* Moscow–Wageningen: International Soil Science Society, 372–8

Adam, P, 1990 *Saltmarsh ecology.* Cambridge University Press

Alcock, L, 1972 *By South Cadbury is that Camelot: excavations at Cadbury Castle 1966–70.* Thames and Hudson

Albarella, U, 1997 *The Iron Age animal bone excavated in 1991 from Outang Road, Market Deeping MAD 91, Lincolnshire.* English Heritage Ancient Monuments Laboratory Report, 5/97

Aldhouse-Green, S H R, 1993 Lithic finds from Sudbrook, in S Godbold and R C Turner *Second Severn Crossing. Archaeological response. Phase 1 The intertidal zone in Wales.* Cadw, 45

Aldhouse-Green, S H R and Houseley, R A, 1993 The Uskmouth mattock: a radiocarbon date *Archaeol Cambrensis,* 117, 340

Aldhouse-Green, S H R, Whittle, A W R, Allen, J R L, Caseldine, A E, Culver, S J, Day, H, Lundquist, J and Upton, D, 1992 Prehistoric human footprints from the Severn Estuary at Uskmouth and Magor Pill, Gwent, Wales *Archaeol Cambrensis* 1992, 141, 14–55

Allen, J R L, 1987a Late Flandrian shoreline oscillations in the Severn Estuary: the Rumney Formation and its typesite *Phil Trans Roy Soc London,* B315, 157–74

Allen, J R L, 1987b Dimlington Stadial late Devensian ice-wedge casts and involutions in the Severn Estuary, southwest Britain *Geol J,* 22, 109–18

Allen, JRL, 1990a The formation of coastal peat marshes under an upward tendency of relative sea-level *J Geol Soc London,* 147, 743–5

Allen, J R L, 1990b The Severn Estuary in southwest Britain: its retreat under marine transgression, and fine-sediment regime *Sed Geol,* 66, 13–28

Allen, J R L, 1992a Trees and their response to wind: mid Flandrian strong winds, Severn Estuary and inner Bristol Channel, southwest Britain *Phil Trans Roy Soc,* B338, 335–64

Allen, J R L, 1992b Tidally influenced marshes in the Severn Estuary, southwest Britain, in J R L Allen and K E Pye (eds) *Saltmarshes: morphodynamics, conservation and*

engineering significance. Cambridge University Press

Allen, J R L, 1995 Salt-marsh growth and fluctuating sea level: implications of a simulation model for coastal stratigraphy and peat-based sea-level curves *Sed Geol,* 100, 21–45

Allen, J R L, 1996a Three later Bronze Age occupations at Rumney Great Wharf on the Wentlooge Level, Gwent *Archaeol Severn Estuary* 1995, 6, 9–12

Allen, J R L, 1996b Three final Bronze Age occupations at Rumney Great Wharf on the Wentlooge Level, Gwent *Stud Celtica,* 30, 1–16

Allen, J R L, 1996c Shoreline movement and vertical textural patterns in salt marshes deposits: implications of a simple model for flow and sedimentation over tidal marshes *Proc Geol Ass,* 107, 15–23

Allen, J R L, 1997a Subfossil mammalian tracks (Flandrian) in the Severn Estuary, S.W. Britain: mechanics of formation, preservation and distribution *Phil Trans Roy Soc London,* B352, 481–518

Allen, J R L, 1997b The seabank on the Wentlooge Level, Gwent: date of set-back from documentary and pottery evidence *Archaeol Severn Estuary* 1996, 7, 67–84

Allen, J R L, 1997c A conceptual model for the archaeology of the English coastal zone, in M Fulford, T Champion and A Long (eds) *England's coastal heritage.* English Heritage Archaeological Report, 15, 50–5

Allen, J R L, 1997d A scatter of Neolithic–Bronze Age flintwork from the intertidal zone at Hills Flats, South Gloucestershire *Trans Bristol Gloucester Archaeol Soc,* 115, 265–76

Allen, J R L, 1997e Simulation models of salt-marsh morphodynamics: some implications for high-intertidal sediment couplets related to sea-level change *Sed Geol,* 113, 211–223

Allen, J R L, forthcoming a A medieval timber setting and subrectangular diggings in Late Flandrian estuarine sediments, Rumney Great Wharf *Archaeol Cambrensis*

Allen, J R L, forthcoming b Late Iron Age and earliest Roman calcite-tempered ware from sites in the Severn Estuary Levels: character and distribution *Stud Celtica*

Allen, J R L, forthcoming c 1999, Geological impacts on coastal wetland landscapes: some general effects of sediment autocompaction in the Holocene of northwest Europe *Holocene,* 9, 1–12

Allen, J R L and Fulford, M G, 1987a The Wentlooge Level: a Romano-British saltmarsh reclamation in southeast Wales *Britannia,* **17,** 91–117

Allen, J R L and Fulford, M, 1987b Romano-British settlement and industry on the wetlands of the Severn Estuary *Antiq J,* **67,** 237–89

Allen, J R L and Fulford, M G, 1992 Romano-British and later geoarchaeology at Oldbury Flats: reclamation and settlement on the changeable coast of the Severn Estuary, southwest Britain *Archaeol J,* **149,** 82–123

Allen, J R L and Fulford, M G, 1996 Late Flandrian coastal changes and tidal palaeochannel development at Hills Flats, Severn Estuary (SW Britain) *J Geol Soc London,* **153,** 151–62

Allen, J R L and Rae, J E, 1987 Late-Flandrian shoreline oscillations in the Severn Estuary *Phil Trans Roy Soc London,* **B315,** 185–230

Allen, J R L and Rippon, S J, 1995 Magor Pill, Gwent: the geoarchaeology of a late Flandrian tidal palaeochannel *Archaeol Severn Estuary,* 1994, 41–50

Allen, J R L Rippon, S J, 1997 Iron Age to early Modern activity and palaeochannels at Magor Pill, Gwent: an exercise in lowland coastal-zone geoarchaeology *Antiq J,* **77,** 127–70

Altschuler, Z S, Schnepfe, M M, Silber, C C and Simon, F O, 1983 Sulphur diagenesis in Everglades peat and origin of pyrite in coal *Science,* **221,** 221–7

Andersen, S H and Malmros, C, 1984 'Madskorpe' pa Erteboller fra Tybrind Vig *Aarboger for nordisk Oldkyndighed og Historie,* 1984, 78–95

Andersen, S Th, 1970 The relative pollen productivity and pollen representation of North European trees and correction factors for tree pollen spectra *Danmarks Geologiske Undersoglese,* **96**(2), 1–99

Andersen, S Th, 1973 The differential pollen productivity of trees and its significance for interpretation of a pollen diagram from a forested region, in H J B Birks and R G West (eds) *Quaternary Plant Ecology.* Oxford: Blackwell, 109–12

Anderson, J G C, 1968 The concealed rock surface and overlying deposits of the Severn Valley from Upton to Neath *Proc S Wales Inst Eng,* **83,** 27–47

Anderson, J G C, 1974 The buried rock floors and rock basins, and overlying deposits, of the South Wales valleys from Wye to Neath *Proc S Wales Inst Eng,* **88,** 11–25

Andrews, J T , Bowen, D Q and Kidson, C, 1979 Amino acid ratios and the correlation of raised beach deposits in southwest England and Wales *Nature,* **281,** 556–8

Andrews, J T , Gilbertson, D D and Hawkins, A B, 1984 The Pleistocene succession of the Severn Estuary: a revised model based upon amino acid recemization studies *J Geol Soc London,* **141,** 967–74

ApSimon, A M and Donovan, D T, 1956 Marine Pleistocene deposits in the Vale of Gordano, Somerset *Proc Univ Bristol Spel'ol Soc,* **7,** 130–136

ApSimon, A M, Donovan, D T and Taylor, H, 1961 The stratigraphy and archaeology of the late-glacial and post-glacial deposits at Brean Down, Somerset *Proc Univ Bristol Spel'ol Soc,* **9,** 67–136

Ashbee, P, Bell, M and Proudfoot, E, 1989 *Wilsford Shaft: excavations 1960–62.* English Heritage

Audouze, F and Büchsenschütz, O, 1991 *Towns, villages and countryside of Celtic Europe.* Batsford

Avery, B W, 1990 *Soils of the British Isles.* Wallingford: CAB International

Avery, B W and Bascomb, C L (eds) 1974 *Soil Survey laboratory methods.* Soil Survey Tech Monogr, **6**

Babbidge, A, 1977 Reconnaissance excavations at Coed y Bwnydd *Monmouthshire Antiq,* **3,** 159–78

Bahn, P, 1992 *Collins dictionary of archaeology.* Harper Collins

Bailey, G N,1978 Shell middens as indicators of postglacial economies: a territorial perspective, in P A Mellars (ed) *The early postglacial settlement of Northern Europe.* Duckworth, 37–64

Baillie, M G L, 1982 *Tree-ring dating and archaeology.* Croom Helm

Baillie, M G L, 1995 *A slice through time: dendrochronology and precision dating.* Batsford

Baillie, M G L and Pilcher, J R, 1973 A simple crossdating program for tree-ring research *Tree-Ring Bull,* **33,** 7–14

Bakker, J P, 1985 The impact of grazing on plant communities, plant populations and soil conditions on salt marshes *Vegetatio,* **62,** 391–8

Bakker, J P, 1989 Nature management by grazing and cutting on the ecological significance of grazing and cutting regimes applied to restore former species-rich grassland communities in The Netherlands *Geobotany,* **14,** Dordrecht: Kluwer

Bakker, J P, Dijkstra, M and Russchen, P T, 1985 Dispersal, germination and early establishment of halophytes and glycophytes on a grazed and abandoned salt-marsh gradient *New Phytol,* **101,** 291–308

Balaam, N D, Bell, M G, David, A E U, Levitan, B, Macphail, R I, Robinson, M and Scaife, R G, 1987 Prehistoric and Romano-British sites at Westward Ho! Devon: archaeology and palaeoeconomy and environment in south-west England 1983 and 1984, in N D Balaam, B Levitan and V Straker, 1987 *Studies in palaeoeconomy and environment in southwest*

England. Oxford: Oxbow BAR Brit Ser, **181**, 163–264

Balfour-Browne, F, 1940 *British water beetles,* **1,** Ray Society

Ball, D F, 1964 Loss-on-ignition as an estimate of organic matter and organic carbon in non-calcareous soils *J Soil Sci,* **15**, 84–92

Balogh, J and Mahunka, S, 1983 *The soil mites of the world: Vol 1 Primitive oribatids of the Palearctic region*. Budapest: Akadémiai Kiadó

Barnes, I, 1993 *Second Severn Crossing: English approaches. An interim statement on the 1992/93 fieldwork*. SELRC Annu Rep, 1993, 5–29

Barnett, C, 1961 A find of Roman pottery at Uskmouth *Monmouthshire Antiquary,* **1,** 12–13, 117–20

Barrett, J, Bradley, R and Green, M, 1991 *Landscape, monuments and society*. Cambridge University Press

Barrett, J C, Freeman, P W and Woodward, A, forthcoming *Cadbury Castle, Somerset: the later prehistoric and Romano-British archaeology*. English Heritage Archaeol Rep

Barrie, J V, 1980a Heavy mineral distribution in bottom sediments of the Bristol Channel, UK *Estuarine Coastal Mar Sci,* **11**, 369–81

Barrie, J V, 1980b Mineralogy of non cohesive sedimentary deposits, in M B Collins (ed) *Industrial embayments and their environmental problems*. Oxford: Pergamon, 249–57

Barrie, J V, 1981 Hydrodynamic factors controlling the distribution of heavy minerals Bristol Channel *Estuarine Coastal Shelf Sci* **12**, 609–19

Bartholin, T S, 1987 Oak and willow—active and passive periods at Alvastra pile dwelling, in *Theoretical approaches to artefacts, settlements and society*. Oxford: Oxbow, BAR, **S366**, 123–132

Barton, R N E, 1992 *Hengistbury Head, Dorset. Vol 2 The late upper Palaeolithic and early Mesolithic sites*. Oxford Committee for Archaeology Monogr, **34**

Barton, R N E and Bergman, C A, 1982 Hunters at Hengistbury: some evidence from experimental archaeology *World Archaeol,* **14**, 2, 237–48

Barton, R N E , Berridge, P J, Walker, M J C and Bevins, R E, 1995 Persistent places in the Mesolithic landscape: an example from the Black Mountain uplands of South Wales *Proc Prehist Soc,* **61**, 81–116

Bass, W M, 1987 *Human osteology* 3rd edn, Columbia: Missouri Archaeol Soc

Battarbee, R W, 1986 Diatom analysis, in B E Berglund (ed) *Handbook of Holocene palaeoecology and palaeohydrology*. Chichester: Wiley, 527–70

Beedham, G E 1972 *Identification of the British mollusca*. Amersham: Hilton

Behre, K-E, 1981 The interpretation of anthropogenic indicators in pollen diagrams *Pollen et Spores,* **23**, 225–45

Beijerinck, W, 1947 *Zadenatlas der Nederlandsche Flora*. Wageningen: Veenman

Bell, M, 1981 Valley sediments and environmental change, in M Jones and G W Dimbleby (eds) *The environment of man: the Iron Age to the Anglo-Saxon period*. Oxford: BAR, **87** 75–91

Bell, M G, 1983 Valley sediments as evidence of prehistoric land-use on the South Downs *Proc Prehist Soc,* **49**, 119–50

Bell, M G, 1990 *Brean Down excavations 1983–1987*. English Heritage

Bell, M G, 1992 *Field survey and excavation at Goldcliff 1992*. SELRC Ann Rep, 1992, 15–29

Bell, M G, 1993 Field survey and excavation at Goldcliff, Gwent 1993 *Archaeol Severn Estuary,* 1993, 81–101

Bell, M G, 1995 Field survey and excavation at Goldcliff, Gwent 1994 *Archaeol Severn Estuary,* **5** 1994, 115–44, 157–65

Bell, M G, 1996 Coastal change and wetland heritage at Goldcliff, Gwent *Monmouthshire Antiq,* Vol **XII**, 8–14

Bell, M G, 1997 Environmental archaeology in the coastal zone, in M Fulford, T Champion and A Long *England's coastal heritage*. English Heritage, 56–73

Bell, M G and Neumann, H S, 1997 Prehistoric intertidal archaeology and environments in the Severn Estuary, Wales *World Archaeol,* **29**(1), 95–113

Bell, M G, Caseldine, A E, Crowther, J, Lawler, M, Parkhouse, J and Walker, M J, 1990 *Archaeology of the Second Severn Crossing: assessment and recommendations for Gwent*. Swansea: Glamorgan–Gwent Archaeol Trust

Benecke, N, 1987 Studies on early dog remains from Northern Europe *J Archaeol Sci,* **14**, 31–49

Bennett, K D, 1994 *Annotated catalogue of pollen and pteridophyte spore types of the British Isles*. Department of Plant Sciences, University of Cambridge

Bennett, K D and Birks, H J B, 1990 Postglacial history of alder *Alnus glutinosa* [L] Gaertn. in the British Isles *J Quat Sci,* **5**, 123–33

Bennett, K D, Whittington, G, and Edwards, K J, 1994 Recent plant nomenclatural changes and pollen morphology in the British Isles *Quat Newsl,* **73**, 1–6

Bennett, P, 1992 The discovery and lifting of a middle Bronze Age boat at Dover *Past,* **14**, 1–2

Berggren, G, 1969 *Atlas of seeds and small fruits of Northwest-European plant species with morphological descriptions. Part 2. Cyperaceae.* Stockholm

Berggren, G, 1981 *Atlas of seeds and small fruits of Northwest-European plant species with morphological descriptions. Part 3 Salicaceae–Crudiferae*. Arlow

Berridge, P J and Roberts, A J, 1986 The Mesolithic period in Cornwall *Cornish Archaeol*, **25**, 7–34

Berry, A Q, Gale, F, Daniels, J L and Allmark, B, 1996 *Fenn's and Whixall Mosses*. Mold: Clwyd County Council

Bertsch, K, 1941 *Früchte und Samen. Handbücher der praktischen Vorgeschichtsforschung* **I**. Stuttgart: Ferdinand Enke

Bethell, P and Máté, I, 1989 The use of phosphate analysis in archaeology: a critique, in J Henderson (ed) *Scientific analysis in archaeology*. Oxford: University Committee for Archaeology Monogr, **19**, 1–29

Binford, L R, 1981 *Bones: ancient men and modern myths*. New York and London: Academic Press

Birks, H J B, 1973 *The past and present vegetation of the Isle of Skye: a palaeoecological study*. Cambridge University Press

Blackford, J J, 1990 Palaeoenvironmental analysis, in J Parkhouse and S J Parry *Rumney alternative feeding grounds: an archaeological assessment*. Glamorgan–Gwent Archaeol Trust, 56–74

Blanchette, R A and Hoffmann, P, 1993 Degradation processes in waterlogged archaeological wood, in P Hoffmann, T Daley and T Grant (eds) *Proc of the 5th ICOM Group on Wet Organic Archaeological Materials*. Portland

Boëda, E, 1993 Le débitage discoïde et le débitage Levallois recurrent centripète *Bull Soc Préhist Française*, **90**: 6, 392–404

Bohmers, A, 1956 Statistics and graphs in the study of flint assemblages. III. A preliminary report on the statistical analysis of the Mesolithic in North-western Europe *Palaeohistoria*, **5**, 28–38

Boon, G C, 1961 Letter quoted in Barnett 1961, 13

Boon, G C, 1967 Roman pottery from Magor *Monmouthshire Antiq*, **2**(3), 121–6

Boon, G C, 1975 Rumney Great Wharf *Archaeol Wales*, **15**, 48–9

Boon, G C, 1980 Caerleon and the Gwent Levels in Early Historic times, in F H Thompson *Archaeology and coastal change*. Society of Antiquaries, 24–36

Boschian, G, 1997 Sedimentology and soil micromorphology of the late Pleistocene and early Holocene deposits of Grotta del'Edera Trieste Karst, NE Italy *Geoarchaeology*, **12**, 227–49

Bouma, J, Fox, C A and Miedema, R, 1990 Micromorphology of hydromorphic soils: application for soil genesis and land evaluation, in *Soil micromorphology: a basic and applied science*. Amsterdam: Elsevier, 257–78

Bowen, D Q, 1994 Late Cenozoic Wales and south-west England *Proc Ussher Soc*, **8**, 209–13

Bowen, D Q, Sykes, G A, Reeves, A, Miller, G H, Andrews, J T, Brew, J S and Hare, P E, 1985 Amino-acid geochronology of raised beaches in southwest Britain *Quat Sci Rev*, **4**, 279–318

Bowman, S, 1990 *Radiocarbon dating*. British Museum

Boyd-Dawkins, W, 1870 On the discovery of flint and chert under a submerged forest in West Somerset *J Ethnogr Soc London*, **2**, 141–5

Boyden, C R and Little, C, 1973 Faunal distributions in soft sediments of the Severn Estuary *Estuarine Coastal Mar Sci*, **1**, 203–23

Boyden, C R, Crothers, J H, Little, C and Mettam, C, 1977 The intertidal invertebrate fauna of the Severn Estuary *Fld Stud*, **4**, 477–554

Bradley, R, 1990 *The passage of arms*. Cambridge University Press

Bradley, R, 1998 Ruined buildings, ruined stones: enclosures, tombs and natural places of south-west England *World Archaeol*, **30**, 13–22

Bradley, R and Gordon, K, 1988 Human skulls from the River Thames, their dating and significance *Antiquity*, **62**, 503–9

Brain, C K, 1967 Hottentot food remains and their bearing on the interpretation of fossil bone assemblages *Sci Pap Namib Res Station*, **32**, 1–11

Brennan, D, 1995 Romano-British pottery, in M Bell Field survey and excavation at Goldcliff, Gwent, 1994 *Archaeol Severn Estuary*, **5**, 1994, 139–41

Brett, J, 1996 Archaeology and the construction of the Royal Edward Dock, Avonmouth, 1902–1908 *Archaeol Severn Estuary*, **7**, 115–20

Breuil, H, 1932 Le feu et l'industrie de pierre et d'os dans le gisement du 'Sinanthropus', Chou-kou-tien *L'Anthropologie*, **42**, 1–17

Briggs, D J, Gilbertson, D D and Hawkins, A B, 1991 The raised beach and sub-beach deposits at Swallow Cliff, Middle Hope *Proc Bristol Nat Soc*, **51**, 63–71

Brinkkemper, O, 1991 Wetland farming in the area to the south of the Meuse Estuary during the Iron Age and Roman period. An environmental and palaeo-economic reconstruction *Analecta Praehistorica Leidensia*, **24**

Britnell, W J and Savory, H N, 1984 *Gwernvale and Penywyrlod: two Neolithic long cairns in the Black Mountains of Brecknock*. Cambrian Archaeol Ass Monogr, **2**

Brochier, J E, 1983 Bergeries et feux néolithiques dans le Midi de la France, caractérisation et incidence sur le raisonnement sédimontologique *Band*, **33/34**, 181–93

Bronk Ramsey, C, 1994 *Oxcal v2.0: a radiocarbon calibration and analysis program*. Oxford Radiocarbon Accelerator Unit

Bronk Ramsey, C, 1995 Radiocarbon calibration and analysis of stratigraphy *Radiocarbon*, **36**, 425–30

Brown, A G, 1987 Holocene flood plain sedimentation and channel response of the lower River Severn, UK *Zeitschrift für Geomorphologie*, **31**, 293–310

Brown, D M and Baillie, M G L, 1992 *Construction and dating of a 5000 year English bog oak tree-ring chronology* Tree Rings and Environment LUNDQUA Rep, **34**, 72–5

Brown, D M, Munro, M A R, Baillie, M G L and Pilcher, J R, 1986 Dendrochronology—the absolute Irish standard *Radiocarbon*, **28**(2A), 279–83

Brunning, R, 1995 Joinery and structural carpentry, in J Coles and S Minnitt *Industrious and fairly civilised: the Glastonbury Lake Village*. Taunton, 117–20

Brunning, R, 1998 Two Bronze Age wooden structures in the Somerset Moors *Archaeol Severn Estuary*, **8**, 5–8

Brunning, R and O'Sullivan, A, 1997 Wood species selection and woodworking techniques, in N Nayling and A Caseldine *Excavations at Caldicot, Gwent: Bronze Age palaeochannels in the Lower Nedern valley*. York: CBA Res Rep, **108**, 163–86

Brush, G S, 1989 Rates and patterns of estuarine sediment accumulation *Limnol Oceanogr*, **34**, 1235–46

Brush, G S, and Brush, L M, 1994 Transport and deposition of pollen in an estuary: signature of the landscape, in A Traverse (ed) *Sedimentation of organic particles*. Cambridge University Press, 33–46

Buckland, P C, 1979 *Thorne Moors: A palaeoentomological study of a Bronze Age site*. Department of Geography, Univ Birmingham Occ Publ, **8**

Buckland, P C and Dinnin, M H, 1993 Holocene woodlands: the fossil insect evidence, in K J Kirby and C M Drake (eds) Dead wood matters: the ecology and conservation of saproxylic invertebrates in Britain *English Nature Sci*, **7**, 6–20

Buckland, P C, Sadler, J P and Smith, D, 1993 An insect's eye-view of the Norse farm, in C E Batey, J Jesch and C D Morris (eds) *The Viking Age in Caithness, Orkney and the North Atlantic*. Edinburgh University Press, 518–28

Bull, G and Payne, S 1982 Tooth eruption and epiphysial fusion in pigs and wild boar, in B Wilson, C Grigson and S Payne (eds) *Ageing and sexing animal bones from archaeological sites*. BAR **109**, 55–71

Bulleid, A and Gray H St G 1911 *The Glastonbury Lake Village Vol 1*. Glastonbury: privately printed

Bulleid, A and Gray H St G 1917 *The Glastonbury Lake Village Vol 2*. Glastonbury: privately printed

Bulleid, A and Jackson, J W, 1937 The Burtle Beds of Somerset *Proc Somerset Archaeol Natur Hist Soc*, **83**, 171–195

Bulleid, A and Jackson, J W, 1941 Further notes on the Burtle Sand Beds of Somerset *Proc Somerset Archaeol Natur Hist Soc*, **87**, 111–116

Bullock, J A, 1992 Host plants of British beetles: A list of recorded associations *Amateur Entomol*, **11a**

Bullock, P, Fedoroff, N, Jongerius, A, Stoops, G J and Tursina, T, 1985 *Handbook for soil thin section description*. Wolverhampton: Waine Research

Burbridge, R, 1998 Study of environmental changes in the Severn Estuary during the Holocene, unpubl MRes dissertation, Univ Reading

Burgess, C B, 1974 The Bronze Age, in C Renfrew (ed) *British prehistory*. Duckworth, 163–232

Cameron, N G, 1997 The diatom evidence, in N Nayling and A Caseldine 1997, 117–128

Cameron, N G and Dobinson, S J, 1998 Diatom analysis of sediments and caulking material, in N Nayling *The Magor Pill medieval wreck*. York: CBA Res Rep, **115**, 38–40

Canfield, D E and Raiswell, R, 1991 Pyrite formation and fossil preservation, in P A Allison and D E G Briggs (eds) *Taphonomy: releasing the data locked in the fossil record*. Plenum Poree, 337–87

Canti, M G, 1997 An investigation into microscopic calcareous spherulites from herbivore dungs *J Archaeol Sci*, **24**, 219–31

Canti, M G, in press 1999 The production and preservation of faecal spherulites: animals, environment and taphonomy *J Archaeol Sci*, **26**, 251–258

Cappers, R J T, 1993 Seed dispersal by water: a contribution to the interpretation of seed assemblages *Veg Hist Archaeobot*, **2**, 173–86

Cartmill, M, 1993 *A view to a death in the morning: hunting and nature through history*. Cambridge, MA: Harvard University Press

Caseldine, A, 1984 Palaeobotanical investigations at the Sweet Track *Somerset Levels Pap*, **10**, 65–78

Caseldine, A, 1990 *Environmental Archaeology in Wales*. Department of Archaeology, Lampeter Univ

Caseldine, A, 1992 The palaeobotanical evidence, in Aldhouse-Green *et al* 1992, 21–28

Caseldine, A and Barrow, K, 1997 The palaeobotanical evidence, in N Nayling and A Caseldine *Excavations at Caldicot, Gwent: Bronze Age palaeochannels in the Lower Nedern Valley*. CBA Res Rep, **108**

Caseldine, A E and Barrow, C J, 1998 The plant macrofossil evidence from Pen-y-fan and Corn Du, in A Gibson, Survey, excavations and palaeoenvironmental investigations on Pen-y-Fan and Corn Du, Brecon Beacons, Powys, 1990–92 *Stud Celtica*, **31**, 30–45

Chambers, F M (ed) 1993 *Climatic change and human impact on the landscape*. Chapman and Hall

Chambers, F M and Elliott, L, 1989 Spread and expansion of *Alnus* Mill in the British Isles: timing, agencies and possible vectors *J Biogeogr,* **16**, 541–50

Chapman, V J, 1960 *Salt marshes and salt deserts of the world.* Leonard Hill

Children, G and Nash, G, 1996 *A guide to prehistoric sites in Monmouthshire.* Woonton Almeley: Logaston

Chisholm, B, Erle Nelson, D and Schwarz, H P, 1982 Stable isotope ratios as a measure of marine versus terrestrial protein in ancient diets *Science,* **216**, 1131–2

Chisholm, B, Erle Nelson, D and Schwarz, H P, 1983 Marine and terrestrial protein in prehistoric diets on the British Columbia Coast *Curr Anthropol,* **24**(3), 396–8

Clapham, A R, Tutin, T G and Moore, D M, 1987 *Flora of the British Isles.* Cambridge University Press

Clark, J G D, 1934 The classification of a microlithic culture: the Tardenoisian of Horsham *Archaeol J,* **90**, 52–77

Clark, J G D, 1954 *Excavations at Star Carr.* Cambridge University Press

Clark, J G D, 1972 *Star Carr: a case study in bioarchaeology.* Reading, MA: Addison-Wesley

Clarke, R O S, 1973 *Coleoptera heteroceridae: handbooks for the identification of British insects.* V. part 2 c, Roy Entomol Soc London

Cleve-Euler, A, 1951–55 *Die Diatomeen von Schweden und Finland. Kungliga Svenska Vetenskaps Handlingar* Ser 4, **2**(1), 3–163; **4**(1), 3–158; **4**(5) 3–255; **5**(4) 3–231; **3**(3) 3–153, Stockholm. Reprint in *Bibl Phycol,* **5**, 1968

Coard, R and Dennell, R W, 1995 Taphonomy of some articulated skeletal remains: transport potential in an artificial environment *J Archaeol Sci,* **22**, 441–8

Cohen, A and Serjeantson, D, 1996 *A manual for the identification of bird bones from archaeological sites.* Archetype Publications

Coles, B and Coles, J, 1986 *Sweet Track to Glastonbury.* Thames and Hudson

Coles, B and Coles, J, 1989 *People of the wetlands.* Thames and Hudson

Coles, J, 1973 *Archaeology by experiment.* Hutchinson

Coles, J, 1980 The Abbot's Way *Somerset Levels Pap,* **6**, 46–49

Coles, J, 1987 *Meare Village East.* Exeter: Somerset Levels Project

Coles, J, 1990 *Waterlogged wood. Guidelines on the recording, sampling, conservation and curation of waterlogged wood.* English Heritage

Coles, J and Minnitt, S, 1995 *Industrious and fairly civilised.* Exeter: Somerset Levels Project

Coles, J and Orme, B, 1976 The Abbot's Way *Somerset Levels Pap,* **2**, 7–20

Coles, J and Orme, B, 1978 Multiple trackways from Tinney's Ground *Somerset Levels Pap,* **4**, 47–81

Coles, J and Orme, B, 1985 Prehistoric woodworking from the Somerset Levels 2 *Somerset Levels Pap,* 11, 7–24

Coles, J, Hibbert, F A and Orme, B J, 1973 Prehistoric roads and tracks in Somerset, 3 The Sweet Track *Proc Prehist Soc,* **39**, 256–93

Coles, J, Orme, B and Rouillard, S, 1985 Prehistoric woodworking from the Somerset Levels 3: Roundwood *Somerset Levels Pap,* **11**, 25–50

Collingwood, R G and Wright, R P, 1965 *The Roman inscriptions of Britain Vol 1: inscriptions on stone.* Oxford University Press

Coope G R, 1981 Report on the Coleoptera from an eleventh-century House at Christ Church Place Dublin, in H Bekker-Nielson, P Foote and O Olson, (eds) *Proc 8ᵗʰ Viking Congress* (1977). Odense University Press, 51–6

Coope, G R and Osborne, P J, 1968 Report on the Coleopterous fauna of the Roman Well at Barnsley Park, Gloucestershire *Trans Bristol Gloucestershire Archaeol Soc,* **86**, 84–7

Courty, M A, Goldberg, P and Macphail, R I, 1989 *Soils and micromorphology in archaeology.* Cambridge University Press

Cowley, L F, 1961 A Neolithic skull and animal bones found at Newport *Monmouthshire Antiq,* **1**(1),10–11

Crone, B A, 1988 Dendrochronology and the study of crannogs, Unpubl PhD thesis, Univ Sheffield

Crouch, D and Thomas, G, 1985 Three Goldcliff charters *National Library of Wales J,* **24**(2) 153–63

Crowther, J, 1997 Soil phosphate surveys: critical approaches to sampling, analysis and interpretation *Archaeol Prospect,* **4**, 93–102

Crowther, J and Barker, P, 1995 Magnetic susceptibility: distinguishing anthropogenic effects from the natural *Archaeol Prospect,* **2**, 207–15

Crowther, J, Macphail, R I and Cruise, G M, 1996 Short-term post-burial change in a humic rendzina, Overton Down Experimental Earthwork, England *Geoarchaeology,* **11**, 95–117

Culver, S J and Lundquist, J, 1992 The Foraminifera, in S H R Aldhouse-Green, A W R Whittle, J R L Allen, A E Caseldine, S J Culver, M H Day, J Lundquist and D Upton, Prehistoric human footprints from the Severn Estuary at Uskmouth and Magor Pill, Gwent, Wales *Archaeol Cambrensis,* **141**, 29–33

Cunliffe, B W, 1984 *Danebury, An Iron Age hillfort in Hampshire. Vol 2 The excavations 1969–78: the finds.* CBA Res Rep, **52**

Cunliffe, B W, 1991 *Iron Age communities in Britain* (3rd edn). Routledge

Cunliffe, B W, 1993 *Danebury.* Batsford

Cunliffe, B W, 1995 *Danebury, An Iron Age hillfort in Hampshire. Vol 6 A hillfort community in perspective.* CBA Res Rep, **102**

Darbyshire, G, 1995 Pre-Roman Iron Age tools for working metal and wood in Southern Britain Unpubl PhD thesis, Univ Wales, Cardiff

David, A, 1990 Some aspects of the human presence in west Wales during the Mesolithic, in C Bonsall *The Mesolithic in Europe.* Edinburgh: John Donald, 241–53

Davies, P and Williams, A T, 1991 Sediment supply from solid geology cliffs into the intertidal zone of the Severn Estuary/inner Bristol Channel, in M Elliott and J-P Ducrotoy (eds) *Estuaries and coasts: spatial and temporal intercomparisons.* Fredensborg: Olsen and Olsen, 17–34

Davis, S, 1987 *The archaeology of animals.* Batsford

Dawson, A, 1995 *Newport: west of the river.* Stroud: Chalford Pub Co

Degerbol, M, 1961 On a find of a pre-Boreal domestic dog *Canis familiaris* L. from Star Carr, Yorkshire, with remarks on other Mesolithic dogs *Proc Prehist Soc,* 27, 35–55

Deith, M R, 1983 Molluscan calendars: the use of growth line analysis to establish seasonality of shellfish collection at the Mesolithic site of Morton, Fife *J Archaeol Sci,* 10, 423–440

DeNiro, M J, 1985, Post-mortem preservation and alteration of in vivo bone collagen isotope ratios in relation to palaeodietary reconstruction *Nature,* 317, 806–9

DeNiro, M J and Epstein, S, 1978, Influence of diet on the distribution of carbon isotopes in animals *Geochimica et Cosmochimica Acta,* 42, 495–506

DeNiro, M J and Epstein, S, 1981, Influence of diet on the distribution of nitrogen isotopes in animals *Geochimica et Cosmochimica Acta,* 45, 341–51

Dent, D L and Pons, L J, 1995 A world perspective on acid sulphate soils *Geoderma,* 67, 263–76

Denys, L, 1992 *A check list of the diatoms in the Holocene deposits of the Western Belgian coastal plain with a survey of their apparent ecological requirements: I. Introduction, ecological code and complete list.* Ghent Service Géologique de Belgique Profess Pap, 246, 41

Dick, W A and Tabatabai, M A, 1977 An alkaline oxidation method for the determination of total phosphorus in soils *J Soil Sci Soc Amer* 41, 511–14

Dickson, C A, 1988 Distinguishing cereal from wild grass pollen: some limitations *Circaea,* 5, 67–71

Dictionary of Welsh Biography 1940, Honorable Society of Cymmrodorion

Dingwall, L and Ferris, I M, 1993 *Archaeological investigations in 1992 on the Gwent approaches to the Second Severn Crossing; a post-excavation assessment.* Birmingham Univ Fld Archaeol Unit

Dixon, P, 1994 *Crickley Hill: Vol 1 The hillfort defences.* Southampton: Crickley Hill Trust

Duchaufour, P, 1982 *Pedology.* George Allen and Unwin

Duffy, E A J, 1953 Coleoptera: Scolytidae and Platypodidae, *Handbooks for the identification of British Insects,* Vol 15, Roy Entomol Soc London

Earwood, C, 1993 *Domestic wooden artifacts.* University of Exeter Press

Edlin, H L, 1970 *Trees, woods and man.* Collins

Edmonds, E A and Williams, B J, 1985 *Geology of the country around Taunton and the Quantock Hills.* Memoirs of the Geological Survey of Great Britain, HMSO

Edwards, K E, 1979 Palynological and temporal inference in the context of prehistory, with special reference to the evidence from lake and peat deposits *J Archaeol Sci,* 6, 255–70

Edwards, K E, 1982 Man, space and the woodland edge: speculations on the detection and interpretation of human impact in pollen profiles, in M Bell and S Limbrey (eds) *Archaeological aspects of woodland ecology.* Oxford: BAR Int Ser, 146, 5–22

Edwards, K E, 1989 The cereal pollen record and early agriculture, in A Milles, D Williams and C Gardner *The beginnings of agriculture.* Oxford: BAR Int Ser, 496, 113–35

Edwards, K E, 1993 Models of mid-Holocene forest farming for north-west Europe, in F M Chambers (ed) *Climate change and human impact on the landscape.* Chapman and Hall, 133–45

Edwards, K J and Hirons, K R, 1984 Cereal pollen grains in pre-elm decline deposits: implications for the earliest agriculture in Britain and Ireland *J Archaeol Sci,* 11, 71–80

Edwards, N, 1997 *Landscape and settlement in medieval Wales.* Oxford: Oxbow Monograph

Elling, W, 1966 Untersuchungen über das Jahrringverhalten der Schwarzerle *Flora,* 156, 155–201

Ellison, A and Drewett, P, 1971 Pits and post-holes in the British early Iron Age: some alternative explanations *Proc Prehist Soc,* 37, 183–94

Enghoff, I B, 1983 Size distribution of cod *Gadus morhua* L. and whiting *Merlangus merlangus* L. Pieces, Gadidae from a Mesolithic settlement at Vedbaek, North Zealand, Denmark *Vidensk Meddr Dansk Naturh Foren,* 144, 83–7

Enghoff, I B, 1986 Freshwater fishing from a sea-coast settlement—the Ertebolle locus classicus revisited *J Danish Archaeol,* 5, 62–76

English Heritage, 1996 *Waterlogged wood. Guidelines on the recording, sampling, conservation and curation of waterlogged wood.* English Heritage

Evans, C and Knight, M 1996 An Ouse-side longhouse—Barleycroft Farm, Cambridgeshire *Past,* 23, 1–2

Ferris, I and Dingwall, L, 1992 *Archaeological investigations in 1992 on the Gwent approaches to the Second Severn Crossing.* Lampeter: SELRC Annu Rep, 1992, 39–43

Field, M H, 1992 A study of plant macrofossil taphonomy in lakes and rivers and its application for interpreting some middle Pleistocene assemblages, unpubl PhD thesis, Coll St Paul and St Mary, Cheltenham

Fischer, J W, 1995 Bone surface modifications in zooarchaeology *J Archaeol Method Theory,* **2**(1), 7–68

Fitter, A, 1987 *Collins new generation guide to the wild flowers of Britain and Northern Europe.* Collins

Friday, L E, 1988 A key to the adults of the British water beetles *Fld Stud,* **7**

Fulford, M G, Allen, J R L and Rippon, S J, 1994 The settlement and drainage of the Wentlooge Level, Gwent: excavation and survey at Rumney Great Wharf 1992 *Britannia,* **25**, 175–211

Fulford, M, Champion, T and Long, A, 1997 *England's coastal heritage,* English Heritage

GGAT, 1994 *Archaeological monitoring of preliminary site investigation at Gwent Euro Park, Llandevenny.* Swansea: Glamorgan–Gwent Archaeol Trust

Gifford-Gonzalez, D P, Damrosch, D B, Damrosch, D R, Pryor, J and Thunen, R L, 1985 The third dimension in site structure: an experiment in trampling and vertical dispersal *Amer Antiq,* **50**, 803–18

Gilbertson, D D and Hawkins, A B, 1977 The Quaternary deposits at Swallow Cliff, Middlehope, County of Avon *Proc Geol Ass,* **88**, 255–66

Gilbertson, D D and Hawkins, A B, 1978 The Pleistocene succession at Kenn, Somerset *Bull Geol Srvy GB,* **66**, 1–41

Gilbertson, D D and Hawkins, A B, 1983 Periglacial slope deposits and frost structures along the southern margin of the Severn Estuary *Proc Univ Bristol Spel'ol Soc,* **16**, 175–84

Gimingham, C H, 1953 Contributions to the maritime ecology of St. Cyrus, Kincardineshire. III. The salt-marsh *Trans Bot Soc Edinburgh,* **36**, 137–64

Gimingham, C H, 1964 Maritime and sub-maritime communities, in J H Burnett (ed) *The vegetation of Scotland.* Edinburgh: Oliver and Boyd, 66–142

Giraldus Cambrensis trans 1908 *The itinerary through Wales: descriptions of Wales*

Girling, M A, 1976 Fossil Coleoptera from the Somerset Levels: the Abbot's Way *Somerset Levels Pap,* **2**, 28–36

Girling, M A, 1977 Fossil insect assemblages from Rowland's Track *Somerset Levels Pap,* **3**, 51–60

Girling, M A, 1980 The fossil insect assemblage from the Baker Site *Somerset Levels Pap,* **6**, 36–42

Girling, M A, 1982 The effects of the Meare Heath flooding episodes on the Coleopteran succession *Somerset Levels Pap,* **8**, 46–50

Girling, M A, 1984 Investigations of a second insect assemblage from the Sweet Track *Somerset Levels Pap,* **10**, 78–91

Girling, M A, 1985 An 'old-forest' beetle fauna from a Neolithic and Bronze Age peat deposit at Stileway *Somerset Levels Pap,* **11**, 80–3

Godbold, S and Turner, R C, 1993 *Second Severn Crossing. Archaeological response. Phase 1—The intertidal zone in Wales.* Cardiff: Cadw

Godbold, S and Turner, R C, 1994 Medieval fishtraps in the Severn Estuary *Med Archaeol,* **38**, 19–54

Godwin, H, 1938 The origin of roddens *Geogr J,* **91**, 241–50

Godwin, H, 1943 Coastal peat beds of the British Isles and North Sea *J Ecol,* **31**, 199–247

Godwin, H, 1960 Prehistoric wooden trackways of the Somerset Levels: their construction, age and relation to climatic change *Proc Prehist Soc,* **26**, 1–36

Godwin, H, 1978 *Fenland: its ancient past and uncertain future.* Cambridge University Press

Godwin, H, 1981 *The archives of the peat bogs.* Cambridge University Press

Gough, P J, Winstone, A J and Hilder, P G, 1992 *A review of factors affecting the abundance and catch of spring salmon from the River Wye and elsewhere, and proposals for stock maintenance and enhancement.* Cardiff: National Rivers Authority

Graham, R, 1929 Four alien priories in Monmouthshire *J Brit Archaeol Ass,* **35**, 102–21

Grant, A, 1984a Animal husbandry in Wessex and the Thames valley, in B Cunliffe and D Miles (eds) *Aspects of the Iron Age in central southern Britain.* Oxford Univ Comm Archaeol, 102–19

Grant, A, 1984b Survival or sacrifice? A critical appraisal of animal burials in Britain in the Iron Age, in C Grigson and J Clutton-Brock (eds) *Animals and archaeology.* Oxford: BAR, **S227**, 221–7

Grant, A, 1991 Economic or symbolic? Animals and ritual behaviour, in P Garwood, D Jennings, R Skeates and J Toms (eds) *Sacred and profane: Proc Conf on archaeology, ritual and religion, Oxford, 1989.* Oxford Univ Comm Archaeol, 109–14

Grant, A, Rushe, C and Serjeantson, D, 1991 Animal husbandry, in B W Cunliffe and C Poole *Danebury, an Iron Age hillfort in Hampshire. Vol 5 The excavations 1979–88: the finds.* CBA, 447–87

Gray, H St G and Bulleid, A, 1953 *The Meare Lake Village* privately printed, Taunton Castle

Green, C, 1992 *The Severn Fisheries.* Lampeter SELRC Annu Rep, 1992, 69–76

Green, G W and Welch, F B A, 1965 *Geology of the country around Wells and Cheddar.* Memoirs of the Geological Survey of Great Britain, HMSO

Green, M, 1992 *Dictionary of Celtic myth and legend,* Thames and Hudson

Green, M, 1993 A carved stone head from Steep Holm *Britannia* **24**, 241–2

Green, S, 1989 Some recent archaeological and faunal discoveries from the Severn Estuary Levels *Bull Board Celtic Stud,* **36**, 187–99

Greenhill, B and Morrison, J, 1995 *The archaeology of boats and ships: an introduction.* Conway Maritime Press

Greenly, E, 1922 An aeolian Pleistocene deposit at Clevedon *Geol Mag,* **59**, 365–76, 414–21

Gregory, K J, 1983 *Background to palaeohydrology.* Wiley

Gregory, K J, Lewin, J and Thornes, J B, 1987 *Palaeohydrology in practice,* Wiley

Grimes, W F and Close-Brookes, J, 1993 The excavation of Caesar's Camp, Heathrow, Harmondsworth, Middlesex 1944 *Proc Prehist Soc,* **59**, 303–60

Grimm, E C, 1991 *TILIA and TILIAGRAPH.* Springfield: Illinois State Museum

Groenman-van Wateringe, W, 1993 The effects of grazing on the pollen production of grasses *Veg Hist Archaeobot,* **2**, 157–62

Guilbert, G, 1981 Double-ring roundhouses, probable and possible in prehistoric Britain *Proc Prehist Soc,* **47**, 299–317

Hall, A R and Kenward H K, 1990 *Environmental evidence from the Colonia.* The Archaeology of York, **14**(6). CBA

Hall, A R, Kenward H K, Williams D and Greig, J R A, 1983 *Environment and living conditions at two Anglo-Scandinavian sites.* The Archaeology of York, **14**(4). CBA

Hall, D and Coles, J, 1994 *Fenland Survey,* English Heritage

Hamilakis, Y, 1998 The anthropology of food and drink consumption and the Aegean archaeology, in W Coulson and S Vaughan (eds) *Aspects of palaeodiet in the Aegean.* Oxford: Oxbow

Hamilakis, Y, In prep, *The sacred geography of hunting: wild animals in farming societies*

Hamond, F W, 1983 Phosphate analysis of archaeological sediments, in T Reeves-Smyth and F W Hamond (eds) *Landscape and archaeology in Ireland.* Oxford: BAR, **116**, 47–80

Hansen, M, 1987 *The Hydrophiloidea Coleoptera of Fennoscandia and Denmark.* Fauna Entomologica Scandinavica, **18** Leiden and Copenhagen: Scandinavian Science Press

Harde, K W, 1984 *A field guide in colour to beetles.* Octopus

Harris, C, 1987 Solifluction and related periglacial deposits in England and Wales, in J Boardman (ed) *Periglacial processes and landforms in Britain and Ireland.* Cambridge University Press, 209–23,

Harris, C, 1989 Some possible Devensian ice-wedge casts in Mercia Mudstone near Cardiff, South Wales *Quat Newsl,* **58**, 11–13

Harsema, O H, 1982 Structural reconstruction of Iron Age houses in the Northern Netherlands, in P J Drury (ed) *Structural reconstruction. Approaches to the interpretation of the excavated remains of buildings.* Oxford: BAR Brit Ser, **110**, 199–222

Haslett, S K, 1997 An Ipswichian foraminiferal assemblage from the Gwent Levels Severn Estuary, UK *J Micropalaeontol,* **16**, 136

Haslett, S K, Davies, P, Curr, R H F, Davies, C F C, Kennington, K, King, C P and Margetts, A J, 1998a Evaluating Late Holocene relative sea-level change in the Somerset Levels, southwest Britain *Holocene,* **14**, 115–130

Haslett, S K, Davies, P and Strawbridge, F, 1998b Reconstructing Holocene sea-level change in the Severn Estuary and Somerset Levels: the Foraminifera connection *Archaeol Severn Estuary,* **8**, 24–48

Hawkins, A B, 1971 The late Weichselian and Flandrian transgressions of south-west Britain *Quaternaria,* **14**, 115–30

Hawkins, A B, 1973 Sea-level changes around south-west England, in D J Blackman (ed) *Marine archaeology.* Butterworth, 67–87

Hawkins, A B and Kellaway, G A, 1973 'Burtle Clay' of Somerset *Nature,* **243**, 216–17

Haynes, G, 1983 A guide for differentiating mammalian carnivore taxa responsible for gnaw damage to herbivore limb bones *Palaeobiology,* **9**(2), 173–82

Hendey, N I, 1964 *An introductory account of the smaller algae of British coastal waters. Part V. Bacillariophyceae Diatoms.* Ministry of Agriculture Fisheries and Food, Ser 4, HMSO

Hewlett, R and Birnie, J, 1996 Holocene environmental change in the Inner Severn Estuary, UK: an example of the response of estuarine sedimentation to relative sealevel change *Holocene,* **6**(1), 49–61

Hey, R W, 1991 The Pleistocene gravels in the lower Wye Valley *Geol J,* **26**, 123–36

Heyworth, A and Kidson, C, 1982 Sea-level changes in southwest England and Wales *Proc Geol Ass,* **93**(1), 91–111

Hill, J D, 1995 *Ritual and rubbish in the Iron Age of Wessex: a study in the formation of a specific archaeological record.* Oxford: Tempus Reparatum, BAR, **242**

Hill, J D, 1996 Hill-forts and the Iron Age of Wessex, in T C Champion and J R Collis *The Iron Age in Britain and Ireland: recent trends.* Sheffield: Collis, 95–116

Hillam, J, 1985a *Fiskerton: Tree-ring analysis of an Iron Age structure.* English Heritage Ancient Monuments Laboratory Report, **4692**

Hillam, J, 1985b Dendrochronology of the North Ferriby boats, in S McGrail and E Kentley (eds) *Sewn plank boats*. Oxford: Oxbow, BAR Int Ser, **276**, 145–62

Hillam, J, 1987 The tree-ring dating, in M Millet and S McGrail, The archaeology of the Hasholme logboat *Archaeol J*, **144**, 79–84

Hillam, J, 1992 *Dendrochronology in England: the dating of a wooden causeway from Lincolnshire and a logboat from Humberside*. Proc 13th Colloq AFEAF, Guerat 1989, 137–41

Hillam, J, 1993 *Tree-ring dating of oak timbers from Site C, Skinner's Wood, Somerset*. English Heritage Ancient Monuments Laboratory Report, **86/93**

Hillam, J, 1997 Dendrochronology, in N Nayling and A Caseldine, 1997 *Excavations at Caldicot, Gwent: Bronze Age palaeochannels in the Lower Nedern valley*. York: CBA Research Report, **108**, 187–93

Hillam, J, forthcoming a 1999 *Guidelines for dendrochronology*. English Heritage

Hillam, J, forthcoming b *Tree-ring analysis of oak timbers from the excavations at Goldcliff, Gwent*. English Heritage Ancient Monuments Laboratory Report

Hillam, J, Morgan, R A and Tyers, I, 1987 Sapwood estimates and the dating of short ring sequences, in R G W Ward *Applications of tree-ring studies: current research in dendrochronology and related areas*. Oxford: Oxbow, BAR Int Ser, **333**, 165–85

Hillson, S, 1986 *Teeth* Cambridge University Press

Hodder, I, 1989 Writing archaeological site reports in context *Antiquity*, **62**, 268–74

Hodder, I, 1997 Always momentary, fluid and flexible: towards a reflexive excavation methodology *Antiquity*, **71**, 691–700

Hodder, I, 1999 *The archaeological process: an introduction*. Oxford: Blackwell

Hollstein, E, 1980 *Mitteleuropïsche Eichenchronologie*. Mainz: von Zabern

Hopkins, J S, 1950 Differential flotation and deposition of coniferous and deciduous tree pollen *Ecology* **31**, 633–41

Horn, W and Born, E, 1977 *The plan of St Gall. Vol 2*. Los Angeles: UCLA Press

Housley, R A, 1988 The environmental context of Glastonbury Lake Village *Somerset Levels Proc*, **14**, 63–82

Howard, A J, Garton, D, Hillam, J. Pearce, M and Smith, D N, in press, Middle to late Holocene environmental change in the Middle and Lower Trent Valley, in A G Brown and T Quine (eds) *Fluvial processes and environmental change*. Chichester: Wiley, 165–178

Hudson, R, 1977 Roman coins from the Severn Estuary at Portskewett *Monmouthshire Antiq*, **3**, 179–91

Hughes, G, 1996 *The excavation of a late Prehistoric and Romano-British settlement at Thornwell Farm, Chepstow, Gwent, 1992*. Oxford: BAR, **244**

Huiskes, A H L, Koutstaal, B P, Herman, P M J, Beeftink, W G, Markusse, M M and De Munck, W, 1995, Seed dispersal of halophytes in tidal salt marshes *J Ecol*, **83**, 559–67

Hume, L, 1992 *Oldbury-on-Severn silt lagoon*. Bristol: Avon Archaeol Unit

Hunt, C O and Clark, G, 1983 The palaeontology of the Burtle Beds at Middlezoy, Somerset *Proc Somerset Archaeol Nat Hist Soc*, **127**, 129–130

Hunt, C O, Gilbertson, D D and Thew, N, 1984 Molluscan and amino acid racemization studies of the Chadbrick Gravels of the Cary Valley, Somerset *Proc Ussher Soc*, **6**,129–133

Hustedt, F, 1930–66 Die Kieselalgen Deutschlands, Österreichs und der Schweiz unter Berücksichtigung der übrigen Länder Europas sowie der angrenzenden Meeresgebiete in, L Rabenhorsts *Kryptogamen-Flora von Deutschland, Österreich und der Schweiz* 7, Parts 1–3. Leipzig

Hustedt, F, 1953 Die Systematik der Diatomen in ihren Beziehungen zur Geologie und Ökologie nebst einer Revision des Halobien-systems *Sv Bot Tidskr*, **47**, 509–519

Hustedt, F, 1957 Die Diatomenflora des Fluss-systems der Weser im Gebiet der Hansestadt Bremen *Ab naturw Ver Bremen*, **34**, 181–440

Hutchinson, G, 1984 A plank fragment from a boat find from the River Usk at Newport *Int J Nautical Archaeol*, **13**, 27–32

Hyde, H A, 1936 On a peat bed at East Moors, Cardiff *Trans Cardiff Natur Soc*, **69**, 38–48

Hyman, P and Parsons, M S, 1992 *A review of the scarce and threatened Coleoptera of Great Britain. Part 1*. UK Nature Conservation, **3**, Peterborough: UK Joint Nature Conservation Committee

Hyman, P and Parsons, M S, 1994 *A review of the scarce and threatened Coleoptera of Great Britain. Part 2*. UK Nature Conservation, **12**, Peterborough: UK Joint Nature Conservation Committee

Inizan, M-L, Roche, H and Tixier, J, 1992 *Technology of knapped stone. Volume 3*. Meudon: CREP

Jacobi, R M, 1976 Britain inside and outside Mesolithic Europe *Proc Prehist Soc*, **42**, 67–84

Jacobi, R M, 1979 Early Flandrian hunters in the South-west, in V Maxfield (ed) Prehistoric Dartmoor in its context *Proc Devon Archaeol Soc*, **13**, 48–93

Jacobi, R M, 1980 The early Holocene settlement of Wales, in J A Taylor (ed) *Culture and environment in Prehistoric Wales*. Oxford: BAR Brit Ser, **76**, 131–206

Jacobi, R M, 1984 The Mesolithic of northern East Anglia and contemporary territories, in C Barringer (ed) *Aspects of East Anglian Prehistory*. Norwich: Geo Books, 43–76

Jacobi, R M and Tebbutt, C F, 1981 A late Mesolithic rock-shelter site at High Hurstwood, Sussex *Sussex Archaeol Collect,* **119** 1981, 1–36

Jacobson, G L and Bradshaw, R H W, 1981 The selection of sites for palaeovegetational studies *Quat Res,* **16**, 80–96

Jarrett, M G and Wrathmell, S, 1981 *An Iron Age and Roman farmstead in South Glamorgan.* Cardiff

Jenkins, J G 1974 *Nets and coracles.* Newton Abbott: David and Charles

Jennings, S, Orford, J D, Canti, M, Devoy, R J N and Straker, V, 1998 The role of relative sea-level rise and changing sediment supply on Holocene gravel barrier development: the example of Porlock, Somerset, UK *Holocene,* **8**(2), 165–81

Jessop, L, 1986 Dung beetles and chafers. Coleoptera: Scarabaeoidea. *Handbooks for the identification of British Insects, V part 11,* Royal Entomological Society

Jonsson, L, 1986 *Fish bones in late Mesolithic human graves at Skateholm, Scania, South Sweden.* Oxford: BAR Int Ser, **294**, 62–79

Jonsson, L, 1988 The vertebrate faunal remains from the late Atlantic settlement Skateholm in Scania, South Sweden, in L Larsson *The Skateholm project I: man and environment.* Stockholm: Almqvist and Wiksell

Juggins, S, 1993 *TRAN version 1.7. A utility programme for format conversion and simple editing of palaeoecological and ecological data.* Newcastle upon Tyne: University, Department of Geography

Kaland, P E, 1986 The origin and management of Norwegian coastal heaths as reflected by pollen analysis, in K-E Behre (ed) *Anthropogenic indicators in pollen diagrams.* Rotterdam: Balkema, 19–36

Karg, W, 1971 *Die freilebenden Gamasina, Raubmilben. Acari, Milben. Unterordnung Anactinochaeta Parasitiformes* Die Tierwelt Deutschlands, **59,** Jena: VEB Gustav Fischer Verlag

Karg, W, 1989 *Uropodina Kramer, Schildkrötenmilben. Acari Acarina, Milben. Unterordnung Parasitiformes Anactinochaeta* Die Tierwelt Deutschlands, **67,** Jena: VEB Gustav Fischer Verlag

Keith, A, 1911 *Report on human and other remains from the Alexandra Dock extension, Newport.* Newport Free Library and Museum Committee

Keith, A, 1925 *The antiquity of Man.* William and Northgate

Kellaway, G A and Welch, F B A, 1993 *Geology of the Bristol District.* Memoirs Geological Survey Great Britain, HMSO

Kelly, F, 1997 *Early Irish farming.* Dublin: Institute of Irish Studies

Kenward, H K, 1978 *The analysis of archaeological insect assemblages: a new approach.*

Archaeology of York, **19**(1). CBA for York Archaeol Trust

Kenward, H K, 1982 Insect communities and death assemblages, past and present, in A R Hall and H K Kenward (eds) *Environmental archaeology in the urban context.* CBA Res Rep, **43**, 71–8

Kenward, H K, 1997 Synanthropic decomposer insects and the size, remoteness and longevity of archaeological occupation sites: applying concepts from biogeography to past 'islands' of human occupation *Quat Proc,* **5**, 135–52

Kenward, H K and Allison, E P 1994 A preliminary view of the insect assemblages from the early Christian rath site at Deer Park Farms, Northern Ireland, in J Rackham (ed) *Environment and economy in Anglo-Saxon England.* CBA Res Rep, **89**, 89–103

Kenward, H K and Allison, E P, 1995 Rural origins of the urban insect fauna, in A R Hall and H K Kenward (eds) *Urban–rural connexions: perspectives from environmental archaeology.* Oxford: Oxbow, Monogr **47**

Kenward, H K and Hall, A R, 1995 *Biological evidence from Anglo-Scandinavian deposits at 16–22 Coppergate.* The Archaeology of York, **14**(7). CBA

Kenward, H K and Hall, A R, 1997 Enhancing bioarchaeological interpretation using indicator groups: stable manure as a paradigm *J Archaeol Sci,* **24**, 663–73

Kenward, H K, Hall, A R and Jones, A K G, 1980 A tested set of techniques for the extraction of plant and animal macro-fossils from waterlogged archaeological deposits *Sci Archaeol,* **22**, 3–15

Kidson, C, 1970 The Burtle Beds of Somerset *Proc Ussher Soc,* **2**, 189–91

Kidson, C, 1971 The Quaternary history of the coasts of south west England, with special reference to the Bristol Channel coasts, in K J Gregory and W L D Ravenhill (eds) *Exeter essays in Geography.* Univ Exeter Press, 1–22

Kidson, C, Beck, R B and Gilbertson, D D, 1981 The Burtle Beds of Somerset: temporary sections at Penzoy Farm, near Bridgwater *Proc Geol Ass,* **92**, 39–45

Kidson, C, Gilbertson, D D, Haynes, J R, Heyworth, A, Hughes, C E and Whatley, R C, 1978 Interglacial marine deposits of the Somerset Levels, southwest England *Boreas,* **7**, 215–28

Kidson, C and Heyworth, A, 1973 The Flandrian sea-level rise in the Bristol Channel, *Proc Ussher Soc,* **2**, 565–84

Kissock, J, 1997 'God made nature and men made towns': post-Conquest and pre-Conquest villages in Pembrokeshire, in N Edwards (ed) *Landscape and settlement in medieval Wales.* Oxford: Oxbow Monograph, 123–37

Kloet, G S and Hincks W D, 1977 A check list of British insects: Coleoptera and Strepsiptera,

Handbooks for the identification of British insects, **11**(3). Royal Entomological Society

Knight, JK, 1961 The Goldcliff stone—a reconsideration *Monmouthshire Antiq* **4**(2), 34–36

Knight, J 1998 Origin and significance of calcareous concretions within glacial outwash in the Tempo Valley, north-central Ireland, *Boreas* **27**, 81–7

Koch, K, 1992 *Die Käfer Mitteleuropas,* Krefeld: Ökologie Band 3

Kooi, P B, 1974 De orkaan van 13 November 1972 en het ontstaan van 'Hoefijzervormige' Grandsporen *Helinium,* **14**, 57–65

Koutstaal, B P, Markusse, M M, and De Munck, W, 1987 Aspects of seed dispersal by tidal movements, in A H L Huiskes, C W P M Blom and J Rozema (eds) *Vegetation between land and sea.* Dordrecht: Junk, 226–33

Lambrick, G and Robinson, M, 1979 *Iron Age and Roman riverside settlements at Farmoor, Oxon.* CBA Res Report, **32**

Lawrence, M J and Brown, R W 1967 *Mammals of Britain: their tracks, trails and signs.* Blandford

Leach, A L, 1918 Flint-working sites on the submerged land and submerged forest bordering the Pembrokeshire coast *Proc Geol Ass,* **292**, 46–67

Lennon, R H, 1996, Dietary reconstruction by means of stable isotope analysis of bone, in D Hall (ed) The Fenland Project 11: The Wissey Embayment: evidence for pre-Iron Age occupation *E Anglian Archaeol,* **78**, 169–71

Lepiksaar, J, 1981 Osteologia: I Pisces, Univ Goteborg, unpubl mss

Levine, M, 1986 The vertebrate fauna from Meare East 1982 *Somerset Levels Pap,* **12**, 61–71

Levitan, B, 1982 *Excavation at West Hill, Uley 1979: The sieving and sampling programme.* Bristol: Western Archaeol Trust Occ Pap, **10**

Levitan, B, 1990 The vertebrate remains, in M Bell, 1990 *Brean Down Excavations 1983–1987.* English Heritage, 220–241

Levitan, B and Locker, A, 1987 The vertebrate remains, in N D Balaam, B Levitan and V Straker (eds) *Studies in palaeoeconomy and environment in South west England.* Oxford: BAR Brit Ser, **181**

Lewis, J, Wiltshire, P E J and Macphail, R I, 1992 A Late Devensian/Early Flandrian site at Three Ways Wharf, Uxbridge: environmental implications, in S Needham and M G Macklin (eds) *Alluvial archaeology in Britain.* Oxford: Oxbow Monogr, **27**, 235–248

Lewis, M P, 1992 The prehistory of coastal south-west Wales, unpubl PhD thesis, Univ Wales, St David's University College, Lampeter

Lillie, M, 1991 The Bronze Age in Gwent, unpubl BSc thesis Dept Archaeology, Univ Sheffield

Lindroth, C H, 1974 Coleoptera: Carabidae. *Handbooks for the identification of British insects* 4(2) Royal Entomological Society

Lindroth, C H, 1985 The Carabidae Coleoptera of Fennoscandia and Denmark *Fauna Entomologica Scandinavica,* **15**(1)

Lindroth, C H, 1986 The Carabidae Coleoptera of Fennoscandia and Denmark *Fauna Entomologica Scandinavica,* **15**(2)

Locke, S, 1971 The post-glacial deposits of the Caldicot Level and some associated archaeological discoveries *Monmouthshire Antiq,* **3**(1), 1–17

Locock, M, 1997, Hill Farm, Goldcliff: a field evaluation on the proposed Gwent Levels Nature reserve, 1996 *Archaeol Severn Estuary,* **7**, 59–66

Locock, M, 1998a A prehistoric trackway at Cold Harbour Pill, unpubl rep for Cadw

Locock, M, 1998b Severn Levels survey 1987–88 GGAT 21. A summary of the results. Swansea: unpubl GGAT Rep 98/007

Locock, M, 1998c Coastal archaeology survey River Rhymney, Cardiff to River Wye, Monmouthshire GGAT 50. Swansea: unpubl GGAT Rep 98/010

Locock, M, 1998d Hill Farm, Goldcliff *Archaeol Severn Estuary,* **8,** Exeter: SELRC

Long, A J and Roberts, D H, 1997, Sea-level change, in M Fulford, T Champion and A Long *England's coastal heritage.* English Heritage, 25–49

Looijen, R C, and Bakker, J P, 1987 Utilization of different salt-marsh plant communities by cattle and geese, in A H L Huiskes, C W P M Blom and J Rozema (eds) *Vegetation between land and sea.* Dordrecht: Junk, 52–64

Louwe Kooijmanns, L P, 1985 *Sporen in het land.* Amsterdam: Meulenhoff Informatiaf

Louwe Kooijmanns, L P, 1993 Wetland exploration and upland relations of prehistoric communities in The Netherlands *E Anglian Archaeol,* **50**, 71–116

Lowe, V P W, 1967 Teeth as indicators of age with special reference to red deer *Cervus elaphus* of known age from Rhum *J Zool London,* **152**, 137–53

Lucht, W H, 1987 *Die Käfer Mitteleuropas.* Krefeld: Katalog

Lyman Lee, R, 1994 *Vertebrate Taphonomy.* Cambridge University Press

McCormick, F, 1992 Early faunal evidence for dairying *Oxford J Archaeol,* **11**, 201–9

McCormick, F, 1997 The animal bones, in N Nayling and A Caseldine *Excavations at Caldicot, Gwent: Bronze Age palaeochannels in the Lower Nedern Valley.* York: CBA, 218–241

McGrail, S, 1981 (ed), *The Brigg 'raft' and her prehistoric environment.* Oxford: Oxbow, BAR Brit Ser, **89**

McGrail, S, 1985 Brigg 'raft'—reconstruction problems, in S McGrail and E Kentley (eds) *Sewn plank boats.* Oxford: Oxbow BAR Int Ser, **276**, 165–194

McGrail, S, 1996 The Bronze Age in northwest Europe, in R Gardiner (ed) *The earliest ships: the evolution of boats into ships*. London: Conway Maritime Press

McGrail, S, 1997 The boat fragments, in N Nayling and A Caseldine *Excavations at Caldicot, Gwent: Bronze Age palaeochannels in the Lower Nedern valley*. York: CBA Research Report, **108**, 210–17

Mackintosh, D, 1868 On the mode and extent of encroachment of the sea on some parts of the shores of the Bristol Channel *Quarterly J Geol Soc London*, **24**, 278–283

McMillan, N F, 1968 *British shells*. Warne

Macphail, R I, 1994 Soil micromorphology investigations in archaeology, with special reference to drowned coastal sites in Essex, in H F Cook and D T Favis-Mortlock (eds) *SEESOIL*. University of Oxford, 13–28

Macphail, R I and Cruise, G M, in press The soil micromorphologist as team player: a multianalytical approach to the study of European microstratigraphy, in P Goldberg, V Holliday and R Ferring (eds) *Earth science and archaeology*. New York: Plenum

Macphail, R I and Goldberg, P, 1990 The micromorphology of tree subsoil hollows: their significance to soil science and archaeology, in *Soil micromorphology: a basic and applied science*. Amsterdam: Elsevier, 425–30

Macphail, R I, and Goldberg, P, 1995 Recent advances in micromorphological interpretations of soils and sediments from archaeological sites, in A J Barham and R I Macphail (eds) *Archaeological sediments and soils: analysis, interpretation and management*. Institute of Archaeology, University College London, 1–24e

Maltby, M, 1982 The variability of faunal samples and their effects on ageing data, in B Wilson, C Grigson and S Payne (eds) *Ageing and sexing animal bones from archaeological sites*. Oxford: BAR, **109**, 81–90

Maltby, M, 1987 *The animal bones from the excavations at Owslesbury, Hants. An Iron Age and Early Romano-British settlement*. English Heritage, AML Report 6/87

Maltby, M, 1996 The exploitation of animals in the Iron Age: the archaeozoological evidence, in T C Champion and J R Collis (eds) *The Iron Age in Britain and Ireland: recent trends*. Sheffield: Collis, 17–27

Manning, W, 1981 *Report on the excavations at Usk 1965–1976: the Fortress excavations 1968–1971*. Cardiff: University of Wales Press

Marvell, A E, 1987 Severn Levels survey GGAT 21 *Glamorgan–Gwent Archaeol Trust Half Yearly Review November 1987*, 14–5

Marvell, A E, 1988a Gwent Levels survey *Glamorgan–Gwent Archaeol Trust Annu Rev November 1987–88*, 6–7

Marvell, A E, 1988b Survey on the Severn Levels GGAT 21 *Glamorgan–Gwent Archaeol Trust Half Yearly Rev Oct 1988*, 34–5

Matthews, W , French, C A I, Lawrence, T and Cutler, D F, 1996 Multiple surface: the micromorphology, in I Hodder (ed) *On the surface; Çatal Hüyük excavations 1993–1995*. Cambridge: British Institute of Archaeology at Ankara

Meddens F M, 1996 Sites from the Thames Estuary wetlands, England and their Bronze Age use *Antiquity*, **70**, 325–34

Mellars, P, 1976 Fire, ecology, animal populations and man: a study of some ecological relationships in prehistory *Proc Prehist Soc*, **42**, 15–45

Mellars, P, 1987 *Excavations on Oronsay*. Edinburgh University Press

Mellars, P and Dark, P, 1998 (ed) *Star Carr in context*. Cambridge: MacDonald Inst Archaeol Res

Miedema, R, Jongmans, A G and Slager, S, 1974 Micromorphological observations on pyrite and its oxidation products in four Holocene soils in The Netherlands, in G K Rutherford (ed) *Soil microscopy*. Ontario: Limestone Press, 772–94

Moore, P D, 1973 The influence of prehistoric cultures upon the initiation and spread of blanket bog in upland Wales *Nature*, **241**, 350–3

Moore, P D, 1975 Origin of blanket mires *Nature*, **256**, 267–9

Moore, PD, 1978 Studies in the vegetational history of mid-Wales, V: stratigraphy and pollen analysis of Llyn Mire in the Wye Valley *New Phytol*, **80**, 281–302

Moore, P D, 1993 The origin of blanket mires, revisited, in F M Chambers (ed) *Climate change and human impact on the landscape*. Chapman and Hall, 217–25

Moore, P D, Webb, J A and Collinson, M E, 1991 *Pollen analysis* (2nd edn). Oxford: Blackwell Scientific

Moran, N C and O'Connor, T P, 1994 Age attribution in domestic sheep by skeletal and dental maturation: a pilot study of available sources *Int J Osteoarchaeol*, **4**, 267–85

Morgan, O, 1882 *Goldcliff and the ancient Roman inscribed stone together with other papers*. Newport: Monmouthshire Caerleon Antiq Ass

Morgan, O, 1878 The ancient Danish vessel found near the mouth of the River Usk *Archaeol J*, **35**, 403–5

Morgan, R A, 1980 Tree-ring studies in the Somerset Levels: the Abbot's Way *Somerset Levels Pap*, **6**, 50–1

Morgan, RA, 1988 *Tree-ring studies of wood used in Neolithic and Bronze Age trackways from the Somerset Levels*. Oxford: Oxbow, BAR, **184**

Morris, E L, 1987 Later Prehist pottery from Ham Hill, *Proc Somerset Archaeol and Nat Hist Soc*, **131**, 27–47

Munro, M A R, 1984 An improved algorithm for crossdating tree-ring series *Tree-Ring Bull,* **44,** 17–27

Murphy, C 1986 *Thin section preparation of soils and sediments.* Berkhampstead: AB Academic

Muus, B J and Dahlstrom, P, 1964 *Collins guide to the sea fishes of Britain and north-western Europe.* Collins

Mytum, H, 1986 The reconstruction of an Iron Age roundhouse at Castell Henllys, Dyfed *Bull Board Celtic Stud,* **33,** 283–290

Nash-Williams, V E, 1933 An early Iron Age hill-fort at Llanmelin near Caerwent, Mons *Archaeol Cambrensis,* **88,** 237

Nash-Williams, V E, 1939 An early Iron Age coastal camp at Sudbrook near the Severn Tunnel, Monmouthshire *Archaeol Cambrensis,* **94,** 42–79

Nash-Williams, V E, 1951 New Roman site at Redwick near Magor, Monmouthshire *Bull Board Celtic Stud,* **14**(3), 254–5

Nayling, N, 1998 *The Magor Pill medieval wreck.* York: CBA Res Rep, **115**

Nayling, N and Caseldine, A, 1997 *Excavations at Caldicot, Gwent: Bronze Age palaeochannels in the Lower Nedern Valley.* York: CBA Res Rep, **108**

Nayling, N, Maynard, D and McGrail, S, 1994 Barlands Farm, Magor, Gwent: a Romano-British boat find *Antiquity,* **68,** 596–603

Neumann, H S and Bell, M G, 1997 Intertidal survey in the Welsh Severn Estuary *Archaeol Severn Estuary 1996,* **7,** 3–20

Neve, J, 1992 An interim report on the dendrochronology of Flag Fen and Fengate *Antiquity,* **66,** 470–5

Newcomer, M H and Sieveking, G de G, 1980 Experimental flake scatter patterns: a new interpretative technique *J Fld Archaeol,* **7,** 345–52

Nilsson, A N and Holmen, M, 1995 The aquatic Adephaga Coleoptera of Fennoscandia and Denmark: II Dytiscidae *Fauna Entomologica Scandinavica,* **32**

North, F J, 1955 *The evolution of the Bristol Channel.* Cardiff: National Museum of Wales

O'Sullivan, A, 1996 *Later Bronze Age inter-tidal discoveries on North Munster estuaries: interim reports* Discovery Programme Reports **4**: Project results and reports 1994, Dublin: Royal Irish Academy, 63–72

O'Sullivan, A, 1997 Neolithic, Bronze Age and Iron Age woodworking techniques, in B Raftery *Trackway excavations in the Mountdillon Bogs, Co. Longford, 1985–1991.* Dublin: Crannog, Irish Archaeol Wetland Unit, **3,** 291–342

Ordnance Survey, 1967 *Map of Southern Britain in the Iron Age.* Southampton: Ordnance Survey

Orme, B, 1982 The use of radiocarbon dates from the Somerset Levels *Somerset Levels Pap,* **8,** 9–25

Orme, B J and Coles, J M, 1983 Prehistoric woodworking from the Somerset Levels: 1 timber *Somerset Levels Pap,* **9,** 9–43

Osborne, P J, 1972 Insect Faunas of Late Devensian and Flandrian Age from Church Stretton, Shropshire *Phil Trans Roy Soc London,* **B263,** 327–67

Palmer, L S, 1934 Some Pleistocene breccias near the Severn Estuary *Proc Geol Ass,* **45,** 145–61

Palmer, S, 1977 *Mesolithic cultures of Britain.* Poole: Dolphin

Parfitt, K, 1993 Dover boat *Current Archaeol,* **133,** 4–8.

Parfitt, K and Fenwick, V, 1993 The rescue of Dover's Bronze Age boat, in J M Coles, V Fenwick and G Hutchinson (eds) *A spirit of enquiry: Essays for Ted Wright.* Exeter: WARP Occ Pap, **7**

Parker-Pearson, M, 1996 Food, fertility and front doors in the first millennium BC, in T C Champion and J R Collis *The Iron Age in Britain and Ireland: recent trends.* Sheffield: Collis, 117–132

Parkhouse, J, 1988 Excavations at Biglis, South Glamorgan, in D M Robinson (ed) *Biglis, Caldicot and Llandough.* Oxford: BAR, **188,** 1–64

Parkhouse, J, 1991a Goldcliff. SELRC Annu Rep, 1990, 11–14

Parkhouse, J, 1991b Second Severn Crossing: archaeological evaluation of the Welsh side. SELRC Annu Rep, 1990, 14–16

Parkhouse, J, 1991c Goldcliff *Archaeol Wales,* **31,** 18–19

Parkhouse, J and Parry, S, 1988 Survey on the Severn Levels *Archaeol Wales,* **28,** 43–4

Parkhouse, J and Parry, S, 1990 Rumney alternative bird feeding grounds: an archaeological assessment, unpubl GGAT report

Parry, S, 1987 Gwent Levels survey *Archaeol Wales,* **27,** 41–2

Parry, S J and McGrail, S, 1991 Prehistoric plank boat fragment and a hard from Caldicot Castle Lake, Gwent, Wales *Int J Naut Archaeol,* **20,** 321–4.

Payne, S, 1972 Partial recovery and sample bias: the results of some sieving experiments, in E S Higgs (ed) *Papers in economic prehistory.* Cambridge University Press, 49–64

Peacock, D P S, 1969 A contribution to the study of Glastonbury Ware from south-western Britain *Antiq J,* **49,** 41–61

Pearce, E J, 1957 *Coleoptera: Pselaphidae, Handbooks for the identification of British insects,* **4**(9), Royal Entomological Society

Peate, I C, 1940 *The Welsh house.* Honorable Society of Cymmrodorion

Pedersen, L, 1995 7000 years of fishing: stationary fishing structures in the Mesolithic and afterwards, in A Fischer (ed) *Man and the sea in the Mesolithic.* Oxford: Oxbow, 75–85

396

Peglar, S M, 1993 The mid-Holocene *Ulmus* decline at Diss Mere, Norfolk, UK: a year-by-year pollen stratigraphy from annual laminations *Holocene,* **3**, 1–13

Peterson, R T, Mountfort, G, and Hollom, P A D, 1993 *Collins field guide: birds of Britain and Europe.* Harper Collins

Pitts, M W and Jacobi, R M, 1979 Some aspects of change in flaked stone industries of the Mesolithic and Neolithic in southern Britain *J Archaeol Sci,* **6**, 163–77

Price, M D R, and Moore, P D, 1984 Pollen dispersion in the hills of Wales: a pollen shed hypothesis *Pollen et Spores,* **26**, 127–36

Probert, L A, 1976 Twyn-y-Gaer hillfort, Gwent: an interim assessment, in G C Boon and J M Lewis (eds) *Welsh Antiquity.* Cardiff: National Museum of Wales, 105–20

Proctor, M C F, 1980 Vegetation and environment in the Exe Estuary, in G T Boalch (ed) *Essays on the Exe Estuary.* Exeter: Devonshire Ass, 117–34

Proudfoot, V B, 1976 The analysis and interpretation of soil phosphorus in archaeological contexts, in D A Davidson and M L Shackley (eds) *Geoarchaeology.* Duckworth, 93–113

Pryor, F, 1991 *Flag Fen prehistoric fenland centre.* English Heritage

Rackham, O, 1980 *Ancient woodland.* Bungay: Chaucer Press

Raftery, B, 1990 *Trackways through time.* Dublin: Headline

Raftery, B, 1996 *Trackway excavations in the Mountdillon Bogs, Co Longford 1985–1991.* Dublin, University College: Dept Archaeol

Ranwell, D S, 1974 The salt marsh to tidal woodland transition *Hydrobiol Bull Amsterdam,* **8**, 139–51

Reid, C, 1913 *Submerged Forests.* Cambridge University Press

Reynolds, P J, 1979 *Iron Age farm the Butser experiment.* British Museum

Reynolds, S H, 1906 On the erosion of the shores of the Severn Estuary, *Proc Bristol Natur Soc,* **4**(1), 204–8

Richards, M P, 1998 Palaeodietary studies of European human populations using bone stable isotopes, unpubl DPhil thesis, Univ Oxford

Richardson, L, 1905 The Rhaetic rocks of Monmouthshire, *Quarterly J Geol Soc,* **61**, 374–84

Rieck, F, 1994 The Iron Age boats from Hjortspring and Nydam, in C Westerdahl *Crossroads in ancient shipbuilding.* Exeter: Oxbow Monogr, **40**, 45–54

Rippon, S, 1993 Wetland reclamation and landscape evolution around the Severn Estuary, unpubl PhD thesis, Univ Reading

Rippon, S, 1996a *The Gwent Levels: the evolution of a wetland landscape.* York: CBA Res Rep, **105**

Rippon, S, 1996b Roman and medieval settlement on the north Somerset Levels: survey and excavation at Branwell and Puxton 1996 *Archaeol Severn Estuary,* **7**, 39–52

Rippon, S, 1997 *The Severn Estuary: landscape evolution and wetland reclamation.* Leicester University Press

Risdon, T, 1811 *The chorographical description or survey of Devon*

Roberts, A, 1996 Evidence for late Pleistocene and early Holocene activity and environmental change from the Torbryan Valley, South Devon, in D J Charman, R M Newnham and D G Croot (eds) *Devon and East Cornwall Field Guide.* Quaternary Research Association, 168–204

Robinson, D M (ed), 1988 *Biglis, Caldicot and Llandough.* Oxford: BAR, **188**

Robinson, M A, 1981 Appendix 1: the use of ecological groupings of Coleoptera for comparing sites, in M Jones and G Dimbleby *The environment of man: the Iron Age to the Anglo-Saxon period.* Oxford: BAR Brit Ser, **87**, 279–86

Robinson, M A, 1983 Arable/pastoral ratios from insects? in M Jones *Integrating the subsistence economy.* Oxford: BAR Int Ser, **181**, 19–53

Robinson, M A, 1991 The Neolithic and late Bronze Age insect assemblages, in S Needham *Excavation and salvage at Runnymede Bridge, 1978: the late Bronze Age waterfront site.* British Museum, 277–325

Robinson, M A, 1992 The Coleoptera from Flag Fen *Antiquity,* **66**, 467–9

Robinson, M A, 1993, in T G Allen and M A Robinson *The prehistoric landscape and Iron Age enclosed settlement at Mingies Ditch. Hardwick-with-Yelford, Oxon: Thames Valley landscapes: the Windrush Valley Vol 2.* Oxford Archaeol Unit

Rodwell, J S, 1991a *British plant communities. Vol 1 Woodlands and scrub.* Cambridge University Press

Rodwell, J S, 1991b *British plant Communities. Vol 2 Mires and heath.* Cambridge University Press

Rodwell, J S, 1995 *British plant communities. Vol 4 Aquatic, swamp and tall herb fen communities.* Cambridge University Press

Roe, F, 1995 Stone, in J Coles and S Minnitt, 1995 *Industrious and fairly civilised.* Exeter: Somerset Levels Project, 160–1

Rogers, E H, 1946 The raised beach, submerged forest and kitchen midden of Westward Ho! and the submerged stone row of Yelland *Proc Devon Archaeol Explor Soc,* **3**(3), 109–35

Rowley-Conwy, P, 1993 Season and reason: the case for a regional interpretation of Mesolithic settlement patterns, in G L Peterkin, H M Bricker and P M Mellars (eds) *Hunting and animal exploitation in the later Palaeolithic and Mesolithic of Eurasia* Archaeol Pap Amer Anthropol Ass, **4**, 179–88

Ryder, M L, 1970 The rural economy of prehistoric Denmark *Span,* **132**

Sands, R, 1997 *Prehistoric woodworking: the analysis of Bronze and Iron Age toolmarks.* Institute of Archaeology

Saville, A, 1990 The flint and chert artifacts in M Bell *Brean Down excavations 1983–1987* English Heritage Archaeol Rep, **15**, 152–7

Savory, H N, 1950 List of hillforts and other earthworks in Wales *Archaeol Cambrensis,* **13**, 321–8

Savory, H N, 1954 Barbed and tanged arrow-heads from Glamorgan and Monmouthshire *Bull Board Celtic Stud,* **16**(1), 50

Savory, H N, 1980a The Neolithic in Wales, in J A Taylor (ed) *Culture and environment in prehistoric Wales.* Oxford: BAR Brit Ser, **76**, 207–32

Savory, H N, 1980b *Guide catalogue of the Bronze Age collections.* Cardiff: National Museum of Wales

Scaife, R G, 1987 Pollen analysis, in N Balaam, M Bell, A David, B Levitan, R Macphail, M Robinson and R Scaife, Prehistoric and Romano-British sites at Westward Ho!, Devon: archaeological and palaeoenvironmental surveys 1983 and 1984, in N D Balaam, B Levitan and V Straker *Studies in palaeoeconomy and environment in south west England.* BAR Brit Ser, **181**, 223–32

Scaife, R G, 1993 The palynological investigations of the peats and sediments, in S Godbold and R Turner *Second Severn Crossing, archaeological response: Phase 1, the intertidal zone in Wales.* Cardiff: Cadw, 51–9

Scaife, R G, 1995 Pollen analysis and radiocarbon dating of the intertidal peats at Caldicot Pill *Archaeol Severn Estuary, 1994,* 67–80

Scaife, R G and Burrin, P J, 1992 Archaeological inferences from alluvial sediments: some findings from southern England, in S Needham and M G Macklin (eds) *Alluvial archaeology in Britain.* Oxbow Monogr, **27**, 75–91

Scaife, R G and Long, A, 1995 Evidence for Holocene sea-level changes at Caldicot Pill *Archaeol Severn Estuary, 1994,* 81–6

Schelvis, J, 1990. The reconstruction of local environments on the basis of remains of oribatid mites Acari; Oribatida *J Archaeol Sci,* **17**, 559–71

Schelvis, J, 1992a Mites and archaeozoology. General methods; applications to Dutch sites, unpubl PhD thesis, Univ Groningen

Schelvis, J, 1992b The identification of archaeological dung deposits on the basis of remains of predatory mites Acari; Gamasida *J Archaeol Sci,* **19**, 677–82

Schlichtherle, H, 1990 *Siedlungsarchäologie im älpenvorland.* Stuttgart: Kommissionsverlag

Schmid, E, 1972 *Atlas of animal bones.* Amsterdam: Elsevier

Schoch, W H, Pawlik, B and Schweingruber, F H, 1988 *Botanical macro-remains.* Berne and Stuttgart: Paul Haupt

Schoeninger, M J and DeNiro, M J, 1984 Nitrogen and carbon isotopic composition of bone collagen from marine and terrestrial animals *Geochimica et Cosmochimica Acta,* **48**, 625–39

Schoeninger, M J, DeNiro, M J and Tauber, H, 1983 Stable nitrogen isotope ratios of bone collagen reflect marine and terrestrial components of prehistoric human diet *Science,* **220**,1381–3

Schulting, R J, 1998 Slighting the sea: The Mesolithic–Neolithic transition in Northwest Europe, unpubl PhD thesis, Dept Archaeology, Univ Reading

Scollar, I, Tabbagh, A, Hesse, A and Herzog, I, 1990 *Archaeological prospecting and remote sensing.* Cambridge University Press

Sealy, J C and van der Merwe, N J, 1985, Isotope assessment of Holocene human diets in the Southwest Cape, South Africa *Nature,* **315**, 138–40

SELRC, 1990–1998 *Severn Estuary Levels Research Committee Annual Reports.* From 1993 published annually, as *Archaeology of the Severn Estuary* 1993–1997; 1990–1995 Lampeter: SELRC; 1996–1998, Exeter: SELRC

Serjeantson, D, Wales, S and Evans, J, 1994 Fish in later prehistoric Britain, in *Archaeo-ichthyological studies: Papers presented at the 6th meeting of the ICAZ fish Remains working group.* Neumünster: Wachholz Verlag, 332–9

Severn Tidal Power Group, 1989, *Severn Barrage project, detailed report Vol 4 Ecological studies, landscape and nature conservation,* Department of Energy

Shackley, S E, 1981 The intertidal soft sediments and their macrofauna in the greater Swansea Bay area Worm's Head to Nash Point, South Wales *Estuarine Coastal Shelf Sci,* **12**, 535–48

Sherratt, A, 1996 Why Wessex? The Avon route and river transport in later British prehistory *Oxford J Archaeol,* **15**, 211–34

Shipman, P, 1981 *Life history of a fossil.* Cambridge, MA: Harvard University

Shirt, D B (ed), 1987 *British Red Data Books. 2. Insects.* Peterborough: Nature Conservancy Council

Shotton, F W, 1978 Archaeological inferences from the study of alluvium in the lower Severn–Avon valleys, in S Limbrey and J G Evans (eds) *The effect of man in the landscape: the lowland zone.* CBA Res Rep, **21**, 27–31

Siepel, H, in prep *De Westeuropese Mosmijten Acari; Oribatida*

Silver, I A, 1969 The ageing of domestic animals, in D Brothwell and E S Higgs (eds) *Science in archaeology.* Thames and Hudson, 283–302

398

Simmons, I G, 1996 *The environmental impact of later Mesolithic cultures.* Edinburgh University Press

Smith, A G and Cloutman, E W, 1988 Reconstruction of Holocene vegetation history in three dimensions at Waun-Fignen-Felen: an upland site in South Wales *Phil Trans Royal Soc London,* **B322**, 159–219

Smith, A G and Morgan, S, 1989 A succession to ombrotrophic bog in the Gwent Levels and its demise: a Welsh parallel to the peats of the Somerset Levels *New Phytol* **112**, 145–67

Smith, D N, 1996a Thatch, turves and floor deposits: a survey of Coleoptera in materials from abandoned Hebridean blackhouses and the implications for their visibility in the archaeological record *J Archaeol Sci,* **23**, 161–74

Smith, D N, 1996b Hebridean blackhouses and a speculative history of the 'culture favoured' Coleoptera of the Hebrides, in D Gilbertson, M Kent and J Grattan *The Outer Hebrides; the last 14,000 years.* Sheffield : Sheffield Academic Press, Environmental and Archaeol Res Campaign in the Hebrides **2**, 207–17

Smith, D N, Osborne, P J and Barrett, J, 1997 Preliminary palaeoentomological research at the Iron Age site at Goldcliff, Gwent, 1991–1993 *Quat Proc,* **5**

Smith, P, 1975 *Houses of the Welsh countryside.* HMSO

Spencer, B, 1983 Limestone-tempered pottery from South Wales in the late Iron Age and early Roman period *Bull Board Celtic Stud,* **30**, 405–19

Squirrell, H C and Downing, R A , 1969, *Geology of the South Wales Coalfield. Part I. The country around Newport, Mon.* (3rd edn). Memoirs of the Geological Survey of Great Britain, HMSO

Stace, C, 1991 *New flora of the British Isles.* Cambridge University Press

Stanford, S C, 1974 *Croft Ambrey.* Hereford: Adams

Stead, I M, 1984 Some notes on imported metalwork in Iron Age Britain, in S MacReady and F H Thompson *Cross-Channel trade between Gaul and Britain in the pre-Roman Iron Age.* Society of Antiquaries, 43–66

Steers, J A, 1946 *The coastline of England and Wales.* Cambridge University Press

Strenzke, K, 1952 Untersuchungen über die Tiergemeinschaften des Bodens: Die Oribatiden und ihre Synusien in den Böden Norddeutschlands *Zoologica,* **104**, 1–173

Stuart, A, 1924 The petrology of the dune sands of South Wales *Proc Geol Ass,* **35**, 316–31

Stuart, A J, 1982 *Pleistocene vertebrates in the British Isles.* Longman

Stuiver, M and Becker, B, 1993 High-precision decadel calibration of the radiocarbon time scale AD 1950–600 BC *Radiocarbon,* **35**, 35–65

Stuiver, M, and Kra, R S (eds), 1986 Calibration issue: Proc 12th Int Radiocarbon Conf *Radiocarbon,* **28**, 805–1030

Switsur, V R and Jacobi, R M, 1975 Radiocarbon dates for the Pennine Mesolithic *Nature,* **256**, 32–24

Tauber, H, 1965 Differential pollen dispersion and the interpretation of pollen diagrams *Danmarks Geologiske Undersogelse* Ser 2, **89**, 1–69

Tauber, H, 1967 Investigation of the mode of pollen transfer in forested areas *Rev Palaeobot Palynol,* **3**, 277–87

Taylor, J A (ed), 1980 *Culture and environment in prehistoric Wales.* Oxford: BAR Brit Ser, **76**

Tebble, N, 1966 *British bivalve seashells.* British Museum

Therkorn, L L, 1987 The structures, mechanics and some aspects of inhabitant behaviour, in R W Brandt, W Groenman-van Waateringe and S E van der Leeuw *Assendelver Papers 1.* Amsterdam

Therkorn, L L, Brandt, R W, Pals, J P and Taylor, M, 1984 An early Iron Age farmstead: Site Q of the Assendelver Polders project *Proc Prehist Soc,* **50**, 351–75

Thesiger, W, 1964 *The Marsh Arabs. Collins*

Thompson, R T, 1958 *Coleoptera: Phalacridae. Handbooks for the identification of British insects* 5(5b), Royal Entomological Society

Tite, M S, 1972 The influence of geology on the magnetic susceptiblity of soils on archaeological sites *Archaeometry,* **14**, 229–36

Tite, M S and Mullins, C, 1971 Enhancement of magnetic susceptibility of soils on archaeological sites *Archaeometry,* **13**, 209–19

Tixier, J, 1963 Typologie de L'epipaléolithique du Maghreb, *Mémoires du Centre de Recherches anthropologiques, préhistoriques et ethnographiques,* **2,** Paris: AMG

Tomalin, D, Loader, R and Scaife, R forthcoming *Coastal archaeology in a dynamic environment: a Solent case study.* English Heritage Archaeol Rep

Tooley, M J, 1978 *Sea level changes in northern England during the Flandrian stage.* Oxford: Clarendon Press

Tooley, M J, 1985 Climate, sea-level and coastal changes, in M J Tooley and G M Sheail (eds) *The climatic scene.* Allen and Unwin, 206–34

Tottenham, C E, 1954 Coleoptera Staphylinidae. Section (a) Piestinae to Euaesthetinae. *Handbooks for the Identification of British Insects,* **4**(8a), Royal Entomological Society of London

Trett, R, 1988a Chapeltump II, Interim Report site A7, unpubl report, Newport Museum

Trett, R, 1988b Site A6: Upton Trackway, unpubl report, Newport Museum

Trett, R and Parry, S, 1986 Newport Museum, Gwent *Archaeol Wales,* **26**, 6–7

Trolle-Lassen, T, 1987 Human exploitation of fur animals in Mesolithic Denmark—a case study *Archaeozool*, **1**(2), 85–102

Trolle-Lassen, T, 1990 Butchering of red deer *Cervus elaphus* L.—A case study from the late Mesolithic settlement of Tybrind Vig, Denmark *J Danish Archaeol*, **9**, 7–37

Trudgill, K M, 1974 A hydrological model for the development of peat typography, Godney Moor, Somerset, unpubl MSc dissertation, Univ Bristol

Turner, J, 1962 The *Tilia* decline: an anthropogenic interpretation *New Phytol*, **61**, 328–41

Turner, R C and Scaife, R G, 1995 *Bog bodies: new discoveries and new perspectives*. London: British Museum

Tyers, I G, 1997 *Dendro for Windows program guide*. ARCUS Report, **340**

Vandenberghe, J, 1988 Cryoturbations, in M J Clark (ed) *Advances in periglacial geomorphology*. Chichester: Wiley, 179–98

van de Plassche, O, 1982 Sea level change and water level movements in The Netherlands during the Holocene *Mededelingen Rijksgeologische Dienst*, 36–41

van der Noort, R and Davies, P, 1993 *Wetland heritage*. English Heritage

van der Noort, R and Ellis, S (eds), 1998 *Wetland heritage of the Ankholme and Lower Trent valleys*. Hull: Humber Wetlands Project

van der Werff, A and Huls, H, 1957–1974 *Diatomeenflora van Nederland* (10 vols). The Hague. De Hoef

Varley, W J, 1968 Barmston and the Holderness crannogs *E Riding Archaeol*, **1**, 11–26

Varley, G C and Gradwell, G R, 1962 The effect of partial defoliation by caterpillars on the timber production of oak trees in England, *Proc 11th Internationaler Kongress für Entomologie Wien 1960*, 211–14

Vogel, J C and van der Merwe, N J,1977 Isotopic evidence for early maize cultivation in New York State, *Amer Antiq*, **42**, 238–42

von den Driesch, A, 1976 A guide to the measurement of animal bones from archaeological sites. *Peabody Museum Bull*, **1**, Cambridge, MA: Harvard University

von Woelfle, E, 1967 *Vergleichend morphologische Untersuchungen an Einzelknochen des postcranialen Skelettes in Mitteleuropa vorkommender Enten, Halbgänse und Säger* Inaugural-dissertation zur Erlangüng der tiermedizinischen Doktorwürde der Tierärztlichen Fakultät der Ludwig-Maximilians-Universität München

Voorhies, M R 1969 *Taphonomy and population dynamics of an early Pliocene vertebrate fauna, Knox County, Nebraska*. University of Wyoming Contributions to Geology, Special Paper, **1**, 1–69

Vyner, B E and Allen, D W H, 1988, A Romano-British settlement at Caldicot, Gwent, in D M Robinson (ed) *Biglis, Caldicot and Llandough*. Oxford: BAR, **188**, 65–122

Walker, D, 1970 Direction and rate in some British post glacial hydroseres, in D Walker and R G West *Studies in the vegetational history of the British Isles*. Cambridge University Press, 117–139

Walker, M J C, 1982 Early and mid-Flandrian environmental history of the Brecon Beacons, S Wales *New Phytol*, **91**, 147–65

Walker, M J C, 1994 Paludification and pollen representation; the influence of wetland size on *Tilia* representation in pollen diagrams *Holocene*, **4**, 430–4

Walker, M J C and James, J H, 1993 A radiocarbon dated pollen record from Vurlong Reen, near Caldicot, South Wales *Archaeol Severn Estuary*, 1993, 65–70

Walker, M J C, Bell, M, Caseldine, A E, Cameron, N G, Hunter, K L, James, J H, Johnson, S and Smith, D N, 1998 Palaeoecological investigations of middle and late Flandrian buried peats on the Caldicot Levels, Severn Estuary, Wales *Proc Geol Ass*, **109**, 51–78

Waller, M, 1994 The Fenland project. No. 9: Flandrian environmental change in Fenland. Cambridge *E Anglian Archaeol*, **70**

Ward, J, 1920 *Guide to Cardiff*. British Association

Warren, M S and Key, R S, 1991 Woodlands past and present and potential for insects, in N M Collins and J A Thomas *The conservation of insects and their habitats*, 155–212

Warren, S H, Piggott, S, Clark, J G D, Burkitt, M C, Godwin, H and Godwin, M E, 1936 Archaeology of the submerged land-surface of the Essex coast *Proc Prehist Soc*, **2**, 178–210

Waterbolk, H T, 1995 Patterns of the peasant landscape *Proc Prehist Soc*, **61**, 1–36.

Waters, R A and Lawrence, D J D, 1987 *Geology of the South Wales Coalfield. Part 3 The country around Cardiff* (3rd edn). Memoirs of the Geological Survey of Great Britain, HMSO

Watson, J P N, 1978 The interpretation of epiphyseal fusion data, in D R Brothwell, K D Thomas and J Clutton-Brock (eds) *Research problems in Zooarchaeology*. Institute of Archaeology, Occ Pub, **3**, 97–102

Watson, J P N, 1979 The estimation of the relative frequencies of mammalian species: Khirokitia 1972 *J Archaeol Sci*, **6**, 127–37

Webley, D, 1976 How the west was won: prehistoric land-use in the Southern Marches, in G C Boon and J M Lewis (ed) *Welsh antiquity*. Cardiff: National Museum of Wales, 19–36

Welch, F B A and Trotter, F M, 1961 *Geology of the country around Monmouth and Chepstow*. Memoirs of the Geological Survey of Great Britain, HMSO

Welinder, S, 1978 The concept of 'ecology' in Mesolithic research, in P Mellars (ed) *The early postglacial settlement of northern Europe: an ecological perspective.* Duckworth, 11–26

Wells, C, Huckerby, E, and Hall, V, 1997 Mid- and late-Holocene vegetation history and tephra studies at Fenton Cottage, Lancashire, UK *Veg Hist Archaeobot,* **6**, 153–66

Wheeler, A, 1968 *The fishes of the British Isles and North-west Europe.* Macmillan

Wheeler, A, 1978 Why there were no fish remains at Star Carr? *J Archaeol Sci,* **5**, 85–9

Wheeler, R E M, 1925 *Prehistoric and Roman Wales,* Oxford: Clarendon Press

Whitaker, A and Green, G W, 1983 *Geology of the country around Weston-super-mare.* Memoirs of the Geological Survey of Great Britain, HMSO

Whitehouse, N J, 1997 Insect faunas associated with *Pinus sylvestris* L. from the mid-Holocene of the Humberhead Levels, Yorkshire, UK *Quat Proc,* **5**, 292–303

Whittle, A W R and Green, S, 1988 The archaeological potential of the Severn Estuary: an initial assessment for STPG, unpubl SELRC report

Whittle, A W R, 1989 Two later Bronze Age occupations and an Iron Age channel on the Gwent foreshore, *Bull Board Celtic Stud,* **36**, 200–23

Whittle, E, 1992 *A guide to ancient and historic Wales: Glamorgan and Gwent.* HMSO

Wilkinson, D M, Clapham, A J and Clare, T, 1997 The ground flora of the British wildwood *Quat Newsl,* 1997, 15–20

Wilkinson, T J and Murphy, P L, 1995 *The archaeology of the Essex Coast: Vol 1 The Hullbridge Survey.* Essex County Council

Williams, A T and Davies, P, 1987, Rates and mechanisms of coastal cliff erosion in Lower Lias rocks, in N C Kraus (ed) *Coastal sediments '87.* New York: American Soc Civil Engineers, 1855–71

Williams, A T and Davies, P, 1989 A coastal hard rock sediment budget for the inner Bristol Channel, in S Y Y Wang (ed) *Sediment transport modelling.* New York: American Soc of Civil Engineers, 474–9

Williams, D H, 1964 Goldcliff Priory *Monmouthshire Antiq,* **3**, 37–54

Williams, D J, 1968 The buried channel and superficial deposits of the lower Usk and their correlation with similar features in the lower Severn *Proc Geol Ass,* **79**, 325–48

Wills, L J, 1938 The Pleistocene development of the Severn from Bridgnorth to the sea *Quarterly J Geol Soc,* **94**, 161–242

Wilson, B, 1992 Considerations for the identification of ritual deposits of animal bones in Iron Age pits *Int J Osteoarchaeol,* **2**, 341–9

Wilson, B, 1993 Reports on the bone and oyster shell, in T G Allen and M A Robinson *The prehistoric landscape and Iron Age enclosed Settlement at Mingies Ditch, Hardwick-with-Yelford, Oxon.* Oxford Univ Comm Archaeol, 123–34

Wilson, B, Hamilton, J, Bramwell, D and Armitage, P, 1978 The animal bones, in M Parrington *The excavation of an Iron Age settlement, Bronze Age ring-ditches and Roman features at Ashville Trading Exchange, Abingdon Oxfordshire 1974–76.* Oxfordshire Archaeol Unit and CBA, 110–39

Woodman, P and Anderson, E, 1990 The Irish later Mesolithic, a partial picture? in P M Vermeersch and P Van Peer (eds) *Contributions to the Mesolithic in Europe.* Leuven University Press, 377–88

Woodman, P and O'Brien, M, 1993 Excavations at Ferriter's Cove, Co Kerry: an interim statement, in E S Twohig and M Ronayne *Past perceptions.* Cork University Press

Woodward, A, 1990 The Bronze Age pottery, in M Bell *Brean Down excavations 1983–82.* English Heritage Archaeol Rep, **15**, 121–145

Woodward, A, 1992 *Shrines and sacrifice.* Batsford

Woodward, A, 1996 The pottery, in G Hughes *The excavation of a late prehistoric and Romano-British settlement at Thornwell Farm, Chepstow, Gwent 1992.* Oxford: BAR, **244**, 36–45

Woodward, A, forthcoming The Bronze Age pottery from Chapeltump II, unpubl report

Wright, E V, 1990 *The Ferriby boats: seacraft of the Bronze Age.* Routledge

Wright, V P, 1992 Problems in detecting environmental change in pre-Quaternary palaeosols, in H F Cook and R A Kemp (eds) *SEESOIL* 5–12, University of Brighton

Wuttke, M, 1992 Conservation–dissolution–transformation. On the behaviour of biogenic materials during fossilisations, in S Schaal and W Ziegler (eds) *Messel: an insight into the history of life and of the Earth.* Oxford: Clarendon Press, 265–75

Wymer, J (ed), 1977 *Gazetteer of Mesolithic sites in England and Wales.* CBA Res Rep, **20**

Wymer, J and Harding, P, 1997 *The Southern Rivers Project.* Salisbury Trust Wessex Archaeol

Yates, M, 1995 Coastal archaeology *Heritage in Wales,* **3**, 9–11